Mixanthrôpoi

Animal-human hybrid
deities in Greek religion

Correspondance et information

Revue *Kernos*, Université de Liège, 7, place du 20-Août, 4000 Liège (Belgique)
E-mail : kernos@ulg.ac.be
http://www.kernos.ulg.ac.be

Cover: South Italian bronze statuette of Acheloos; early fifth century BC. (Private collection). Drawing by R. Aston.

ISBN: 978-2-9600717-8-8
ISSN: 0776-3824
D/2011/0480/26

KERNOS

Supplément 25

Mixanthrôpoi

Animal-human hybrid deities in Greek religion

Emma ASTON

Centre International d'Étude de la Religion Grecque Antique
Liège, 2011

Preface

This book began as a doctoral thesis, written at the University of Exeter between 2003 and 2007. When I started to work upon the topic of animal-hybrid gods, I was attracted by their peculiarity and their apparent rarity; like Jane Harrison, I relished the strange and the (as I then saw it) marginal. Gradually, however, as my research progressed, it became apparent that this might be a mistaken perception. Divine mixanthropes came to seem more and more pervasive in ancient literature and cult. I began to realise that, so far from occupying an obscure corner of the ancient religious experience, they crop up both frequently and significantly across the Greek world; also, that they raise implications far wider than the minutiae of their worship. This book is an attempt to give them the attention they deserve.

My interest in divine mixanthropes was not depleted by the realisation that they are more than isolated oddities; rather the reverse. However, writing the book would not have been possible but for the help and advice of a number of people, whose contributions it is a pleasure to acknowledge. Warmest thanks go to my Ph.D. supervisor Daniel Ogden for all his help and support, not only during my doctoral work but since then as well. The comments of my Ph.D. examiners Robert Parker and Tim Whitmarsh were invaluable in setting the piece on the road to eventual publication. Generous assistance with the preparation of images was provided by Tony Garrett, and by my colleague Amy Smith who also contributed photographs of some of the objects in Reading University's Ure Museum of Classical Archaeology (a repository of first-rate mixanthropes and much else besides). The process of publication has been considerably smoothed by the professional efficiency of my editor Vinciane Pirenne-Delforge.

Special thanks go to my parents: to my father for clear-headed comments on a succession of drafts over the years; to my mother for her work on the illustrations; to both for all their unflagging support.

Table of contents

Section One: Cults and composition of mixanthropic deities

Section two: Movement, absence and loss

Section three: Mixanthropy and representation

Introduction

1. Beyond the 'Animal god'

The Greeks did not have animal gods, and there is no real proof that they ever did. Fully theriomorphic deities are rare to the point almost of non-existence. But a significant number of Greek deities were imagined and depicted as partly animal in form – as anatomical combinations of human and non-human. These deities, and this mode of representation, are the subject of this book, which turns the spotlight on a group of beings who, despite being quietly pervasive in the religion, myths and representation of antiquity, have not previously been given scholarly attention in their own right.

The concept of the 'animal god' (god as animal, animal as god) has long since become a scholarly cul-de-sac, an interesting ingredient in late-nineteenth and earlier-twentieth-century historiography, in which such figures as Cook and Harrison[1] and a host of other, lesser exponents[2] posited theriomorphism as a dominant feature of the earliest religious systems, and constructed theories around ideas such as totemism.[3] Despite finding a few surprisingly late adherents,[4] the animal god approach cannot *per se* be taken further, relying as it does on an unacceptable level of retrospective conjecture and certain basic teleological fallacies. And yet the iconographic connection between gods and animals is a fruitful field, and gods whose representation combines animal and anthropomorph in hybrid anatomy provide a new and under-exploited way in which the topic may be encouraged to progress. It is hoped that the current

---

[1] Cook (1894); Harrison (1908), esp. 257-60, (1912), esp. 445-53; such theories will be discussed further in Chapter 5. Early scholarship on this topic is by no means uniform, however; for example, the work of de Visser is marked by a striking caution and reluctance to posit a single overarching theory as an explanation of all manifestations of the animal in Greek religion; instead he argues cogently for the perils of conjecture and the necessity of recognising the diversity of circumstances from case to case (de Visser [1903], esp. 13-16). However, he does not shrink from adopting an evolutionary schema whereby nature-worship gives way ineluctably to divine anthropomorphism.

[2] See e.g. Raglan (1935).

[3] An especially influential exposition of totemism was Smith in his *Lectures on the Religion of the Semites* (1894).

[4] E.g. Gregoire, Goossens and Mathieu (1950); Lévêque (1961).

study goes some way towards offering such encouragement and displaying its value.

The study of hybrids in art and in myth has not languished as animal gods have; early interest[5] is matched by a continuous and – of late – increasingly exciting attention resulting in some very valuable publications.[6] And yet hybrids as gods, specifically as recipients of worship, have not found a secure and extensive place in this field, despite their substantial and important implications. It is time to close the gap between myth, art and cult, to examine hybridism specifically as a form of cultic iconography, and to reflect on the position of deities so represented within the dizzying range of ancient Greek religious experience.

The extent and the nature of the convergence between these three interlocking elements, myth, art and cult, differs from deity to deity. Some of the figures examined in this study, such as Pan and Cheiron and the Sirens, are famous beyond the study of ancient religion because of their prominence in myth and art; none the less, their worship, their rôle as cult-receiving deities, is a side of them which urgently lacks detailed study. Others, such as Demeter Melaina, are not widely known, but certainly deserve to be, because they represent significant local variations of divine personalities we regard as canonical. This book's most important task, however, is to place all these deities together, to look at them together, to assess their interrelation and the patterns which links them. That said, this very act of combination is not without its difficulties, and requires careful definition.

2. Terminology, categorization and unity

The Greeks did not have a single noun in widespread use to denote a being of mixed animal and human anatomical form. This fact is certainly significant. It is also surprising, as animal-human hybrids throng Greek myth and folktale. Often, of course, animal-human composites are described using one of the several common Greek words for 'monster', 'prodigy' or 'unnatural being', the most common being *teras* and *pelôr/pelôron*; the significance of this will be examined below, but it remains the case that none of the 'monster words' is precise enough for the purposes of this study.

---

[5] Much of it focused on the depiction of centaurs, on which see Colvin (1880), Baur (1912) and Buschor (1934). On other mythical hybrids in art: Brommer (1937) on satyrs; Shepard (1940) on fish-tailed beings.

[6] Perhaps especially the catalogue and collection of essays published following Princeton University Art Museum's exhibition 'The Centaur's Smile: The Human Animal in Early Greek Art': Padgett ed. (2003). The huge scope of this publication allows for a valuable new overview of Mischwesen and their significance.

Adjectives indicating 'half human, half animal' are to be found in ancient texts in relation to these beings: *diphuês* is the most common, meaning 'of dual nature or form';[7] others are *hêmibrotos* ('half man')[8] and *mixothêr*/*mixothêros* ('part/mixed beast', that is, 'beast mixed with man').[9] For an often-used noun, however, one looks in vain.

This book, then, for its own practical purposes adapts a rather rare Greek word which, unlike the adjectives above, lends itself well to conversion. *Mixanthrôpos*, which can function as either adjective or substantive, occurs in the work of two authors, Libanius and Themistius, who, interestingly, are close to each other both in place in time: both are thought to have been working in Constantinople around the middle of the fourth century AD. Libanius uses the word in the context of praise of Constantine; speaking of the latter's upbringing, he tells us that it was not wild like that of Achilles *chez* the centaur Cheiron: 'μήτοι νομίσῃ τις ἀκούσεσθαι Πηλίου κορυφὰς καὶ κενταύρου σῶμα διφυὲς καὶ τροφέα μιξάνθρωπον.'[10] In Themistius' narrative, the subject is once more centaur-related, though in this case another famous story is chosen, the assault on Kaineus by the centaurs, who are described as 'μιξάνθρωποι ἢ μιξόθηροι',[11] an interesting use of two alternative expressions for the same concept, one approaching it from the human end, so to speak, the other from the animal.

Themistius and Libanius are a world away, in time and space, from the material on which this book focuses, and their term is not chosen because it has any intrinsic connection with that material. It has, however, other points to recommend it. First it is relatively specific, carrying within itself the sense of a combination of human and non-human parts; in antiquity this is its only sense. Second, it is very easy to render into convincing English forms (this is its main advantage over *mixothêr*), and for the purposes of this work it provides both a pair of nouns and an adjective, on the extremely useful model of 'misanthrope', 'misanthropy' and 'misanthropic', which they closely resemble: 'mixanthrope', 'mixanthropy' and 'mixanthropic'. To clarify, then: 'mixanthrope' is used to denote a composite form containing both human and non-human parts;

---

[7] *Diphuês* does not in itself carry to automatic association with animal-human combination; it can, depending on context, also mean 'of dual race' (Egyptian and Greek in Diod. 1.28), or even 'of dual gender' (in the *Suda, s.v.*). The fact that it places the stress on general duality and combination rather the specific constituents of animal and human is significant.

[8] Opp. *Kyneg.* 2.7., of a centaur. Fascinatingly, *hêmianthrôpos* means 'eunuch' – the other form of half-man.

[9] *Mixothêros* is an adjective (see e.g. Themist. *Or.* 23.284a); *mixothêr* is substantive but tends to occur in apposition to nouns, as in Eur. *Ion* 1161 (*phôtes mixothêres*).

[10] Lib. *Or.* 59.30.

[11] Themist. *Or.* 23.284b. The gods who protect and cherish philosophy have made him invulnerable to assault, like Kaineus.

'mixanthropy' the phenomenon of such forms, their use and representation; and 'mixanthropic', consisting of or pertaining to such forms.[12]

Coining these words is actually necessary because of a lack in English, not in Greek. The Greeks did at least have a rather confused assortment of terms denoting the animal-human combination; we have none that really works with the precision needed in this study. Most often used is the word 'hybrid' (both noun and adjective), but to this may be made two objections. First, in other – for example scientific – disciplines, 'hybrid' indicates a being of mixed parentage rather than mixed form. Issues of parentage and procreation are going to be of interest, but are not always in the equation, so to speak. Secondly, 'hybrid' contains no specific suggestion of the combination of human with non-human which is the prime focus of this study. The Chimaira, for instance, could be called a hybrid because of its various animal parts, and yet is excluded from the present work because of the lack of a human component. This objection can be raised against other common terms also, such as the German word *Mischwesen* ('mixed being'), and the vaguer 'composite'. The only remaining possibility is a cumbersome phrase such as 'animal/human composite', hardly efficient. Mixanthrope and its forms repair this lack. However, the most well-chosen neologism cannot remove the fact that the Greeks did not at any stage develop a consistent and universal term for these entities – a fact which certainly needs some examination.

The variety, inconsistency and flexibility of the Greek terminology as described above is not coincidental or meaningless. It is symptomatic of certain features of Greek mythography generally: mythical accounts featuring mixanthropes tend, being story-driven, to focus on individual mixanthropes within their individual contexts; in any case, Greek mythology generally lends itself to variation much more than to unity – regional variation, variation of genre, variation of narrator, variation of theme. These general points, however, cannot conceal the particular truth about mixanthropes: that the Greeks rarely discussed them as a class,[13] and never worshipped mixanthropic gods as a class.

It must be observed that a single, common term does not by itself indicate simple and unquestionable unity. Take the example of heroes: united linguistically by the word *hērōs*, this group of beings none the less displays enough internal variety to make their study together methodologically challenging,

---

[12] Occasionally one finds the terms therianthrope, therianthropic etc. used of animal/human hybrids in anthropological works; see for example Aldhouse-Green (2005), esp. 60-69 *passim*. These words, however, lack a precedent in ancient usage and are therefore considered less desirable for use in the current study than mixanthrope and its cognates.

[13] The exception to this is the persistent grouping, in art and myth, of mixanthropic figures around the god Dionysos, and the Dionysiac element, which will be discussed passim throughout this book, is perhaps the single most consistent linking feature of mixanthropic deities. However, to study them all from this angle, or to expect them all to conform to its themes and aspects, would grossly oversimplify the richness of divine mixanthropy across the board.

though not excessively so. Heroes in epic and heroes in cult; heroes in northern Greece and heroes in the Peloponnese; heroes who dwell underground and heroes who have ascended to Olympos; the single category contains a great number of distinctions which have to be acknowledged and incorporated by any scholarly treatment of 'the hero'. The same can be said of nymphs, another cult-receiving class: the Greeks used the term *numphê* with great frequency in both literary and cultic contexts, and yet in the opening pages of her study of Greek nymphs Larson freely admits that the category of nymphs faces scholars with a 'taxonomic dilemma'.[14] One term there may be, but it is a flexible one: *numphê* can mean 'bride', both mortal and divine; it can mean virgin or newly-wed; as Larson says, the only unifying feature is that the word 'points to [a person's] status as a sexual being.'[15] Having a single and consistent Greek word, then, is not the end of the story.

It is, however, meaningful; and we cannot elide the nymph-situation with the mixanthrope-situation. The nymphs are consistently referred to in ancient texts in a collective sense, and however we read their interrelationship, they undoubtedly had one in the ancient mind. Especially striking is the frequency with which the nymphs appear as a group in votive inscriptions: plainly their identity as individuals was often unimportant compared with their identity as a group or class, with a shared divine function. This collective perception is completely absent for mixanthropes and, within them, for mixanthropic deities.

So if the Greeks did not think of them together, or worship them together, why should this book study them together? First, it must be established at once that it is not the intention here to argue for functional unity in ancient thought or practice among mixanthropes generally, or mixanthropic deities specifically. Rather, the underlying rationale is that it is valuable and worthwhile to study them collectively – but *not as a collective* – for several reasons.

What mixanthropes have in common is their mixanthropy. This is a study not so much of a class as of a mode of divine representation. Why were certain deities depicted using this very striking and particular form? Do the deities thus imagined and depicted have anything *else* in common, beside their physical form? How does this form relate to divine personality and function? Such are the questions which this book addresses. The figures included are all subject to one further criterion of selection, beside their mixanthropy: they all received some form of cult, and were involved in the ritual lives of communities as well as in their mythology.

The mixanthropy of cult-receiving entities is in fact a highly specific phenomenon, and cannot be treated meaningfully without some acknowledgment

---

[14] Larson (2001), 3. Ch. 1 (pp. 3-60) is in fact entitled 'What Is a Nymph?'. The question is answered by looking at a wide *variety* of different manifestations depending on context. This does not preclude a powerful and coherent study.

[15] Larson (2001), 3.

and examination of its context. Three preliminary matters will be discussed in this introduction: first, Greek attitudes towards the non-human animal and its relationship with man; second, mixanthropy in different ancient cultures; and third, homing in on the Greek world, mixanthropy generally in Greek culture and the attitudes which attended it. The focus of these last two parts will be on mixanthropes generally; only after this broad scrutiny has been performed can the question be asked of how mixanthropic *deities* specifically operate within the associations and the symbolic rôle of mixanthropy in Greek thought.

3. Greeks and the non-human animal

The topic of the position of animals within Greek society and thought has in fact been treated to a good deal of effective scholarly attention, and has received recent interest also. Particularly worth mentioning are the following. As a wide-ranging survey, Keller's *Die antike Tierwelt* (1909-13) remains useful as a work of reference despite its age, providing extensive collation and discussion of material on a species-by-species basis. Moving up to the present, two collections of conference proceedings[16] have pushed the topic in new directions, and reflect the continued exploration of the demarcation of human identity in antiquity and the use of the animal for this symbolic purpose. In the 1960s, Lévi-Strauss recognised that, across cultures including that of the ancient Greeks, animals were 'good to think with',[17] and scholars continue to make valuable observations on the varied nature of this symbolic valency.[18] It is interesting to note that both sets of conference proceedings mentioned above include mixanthropy prominently as a key expression of human and animal interrelation, which it undoubtedly is.

More specifically, Gilhus has written on changing connections between animals and gods;[19] and there have been numerous studies of individual animal species and their symbolic significance. Pastoralism and animal husbandry have been examined as social and economic practices and as practices charged with ideological value.[20] Finally, scholars such as Lloyd, Sorabji and Newmeyer have

---

[16] Cassin, Labarrière and Dherbey edd. (1997) and Alexandridis, Wild and Winkler-Horaçek edd. (2008).

[17] Lévi-Strauss (1969), 162; see the discussion of the phrase by Lloyd (1983), 8.

[18] See e.g. Borgeaud (1984), discussing the cross-cultural involvement of animals in systems of categorisation which allow man to make sense of the world. The two chief (interrelated) strands identified by Borgeaud are the division of animals into edible and inedible (according to taboo rather than pure gastronomics) and their categorisation according to whether they are wild or tame.

[19] Gilhus (2006). For an earlier and briefer treatment of ancient attitudes towards animals, see Lonsdale (1979).

[20] See Howe (2008), esp. 1-26, for an excellent recent survey of the various past theories concerning the rôle of animal production in the economy and society of ancient Greece.

examined ancient philosophical discussions of animals and their relations with humanity.[21] So the present brief discussion of the topic benefits from a wide basis of existing work; moreover, its aim is simply to summarise the key themes in order to inform the treatment of mixanthropy as the graphic combination of animal and human parts.

The most important aspect of ancient attitudes to bring to the fore is the fact that animals are always, implicitly or explicitly, evaluated *according to their impact on, and relation to, humanity.* The Greeks may have lacked a word which unambiguously designated the non-human animal,[22] but there is no doubt that they operated on a strongly 'us and them' basis. On the most pragmatic level, animals could either be useful to man, or damaging to his concerns.[23] Even texts whose purpose is a detailed analysis of the lives and composition of animals will always bring the matter round to comparison and connection with humanity, in one way or another. A perfect example of this is Aristotle.[24] It has long been recognised that Aristotle's work on animals contains two strands. On the one hand, in treatises such as *On the Generation of Animals* and *On the Locomotion of Animals* he is a dedicated and thorough natural historian, obviously working from detailed direct research and interested in animal species for their own sakes, as a scientist. Moreover, the effect of his interest in classification and taxonomy of the animal kingdom[25] is to make man appear just as one of a great variety of different types and species.[26] The bipolar approach, therefore, despite an underlying tendency to assess animal characteristics by comparing

---

[21] See Lloyd (1983), 7-57; Sorabji (1993 and 1997); Newmyer (2006).

[22] At first sight, the Greek word *zôion* seems to correspond closely to our own word 'animal', but it is not an exact match: whereas 'animal' carries the automatic assumption, if not qualified, that the animal in question is a non-human one, *zôion* seems to be vaguer, and more prone to apply to the human animal as well. There are several examples of this flexibility. For *zôion* meaning simply 'that which has a share in life': Plat. *Tim.* 77b. As the basic antithesis of *phyta*: Plat. *Phd.* 70d, 110e. In art, the word can mean a figure, not necessarily of an animal. The alternative Greek terms, *thêr* and *thêrion*, denote specifically a wild rather than domesticated animal, reflecting the emphasis placed on the relationship between animals and man, and whether or not species are integrated in the human community.

[23] That the usefulness of domestic animals was not just purely practical but also related to values and status is forcefully set out in Howe (2008).

[24] Lloyd (1983) has shown that in many ways Aristotle was still operating within the framework of traditional thought concerning animals, and that he responded to and in some ways accorded with the 'prevailing ideology' of his times. It is indeed important not to view his zoological works as entirely new or peculiar in their perspective.

[25] For some interesting remarks about the formidable methodological challenges of classification, see *de Partibus Animalium* 642-3.

[26] In fact, Aristotle inveighs against a snobbish or disgusted response to certain lowly or unlovely species of animal by arguing that they are amply worthy of study because they are perfectly adapted to fulfil their own lives and purposes. See *de Partibus* 645a. This idea of anatomy perfectly suited to need is also to be found in *de Generatione Animalium* 717a.

them with human ones,[27] does not dominate in these zoological works; animals are not a single opposing mass, but nuanced, differentiated.

However, as soon as the matter of intelligence is touched on, and especially in ethical and political works such as the *Nicomachean Ethics* and the *Politics*, the author's outlook is quite different. No longer is the animal world a rich continuum with man occupying his little space within the taxonomy; suddenly the 'them and us' mentality is fully in evidence.[28] It is in Aristotle that we find the fullest and most influential exposition of a theory which pervaded Greek philosophical thought on the subject, that between man and animals lies an insuperable barrier: men possess *nous* and *logos*, the capacity for rational thought, and animals do not.[29] This is not the only quality which makes humans special: speech, hands, upright posture, closeness to the gods: all these are pushed to the fore by individual authors. But the fact that animals are incapable of rational thought and enquiry, the fact that their minds are limited to instinctive properties such as *aisthêsis* (perception), remains at the heart of the discourse of difference. As Renehan says, our own modern Western society is its inheritor.[30]

The philosophical debate about what made man man and animals animals continued after Aristotle, finding strong expression among the Stoics,[31] and also occasional challenges from such as Plutarch who argued that animals should not be relegated to the inferior level of existence typically ascribed to them.[32] However, more interestingly for our purposes perhaps is the fact that

---

[27] There are some intriguing variations on this approach; for example, at *de Partibus* 687a-b he refutes the notion that humans are physically inferior to animals.

[28] On the relationship between these two divergent attitudes in Aristotle's work, see Sorabji (1993), 13-14, and (1997), 358-9. He argues that Aristotle's 'gradualism' is abruptly abandoned as soon as reason and intellect are the topic. See also Renehan (1981), 252-3; Gilhus (2006), 38-9. Lloyd (1983, 25-6), points out that 'man is allotted a special place in Aristotle's account of the animal kingdom', but that, in the zoological works, this does not amount to a sharp and consistent distinction between humans and animals.

[29] On the expression of this theory in Aristotle and other authors, see Sorabji (1993), *passim*, Gilhus (2006), 37-63; Renehan (1981), esp. 239-45. Sorabji makes the point that in this regard Aristotle is pivotal, marking and precipitating a 'crisis' in thought about mind and morality. In particular, he argues that the denial of reason to animals necessitates an (at times laborious) expansion of the idea of perception, which is attributed to animals in lieu of *logos*. This expansion, according to Sorabji, requires and provokes a perilous series of intellectual gymnastics by Aristotle and his successors, chiefly the Stoics. See esp. pp. 7-29.

[30] Renehan (1981), 243-4.

[31] In particular, the Stoics stressed the idea that animals were meant to be useful to, and exploited by, man; the most notorious expression of this view is Chrysippos' assertion that, yes, the pig has a soul, but the function of that soul is simply as a kind of salt to keep the animal's meat fresh for consumption. (This remark is reported by Cicero, *de Nat. Deor.* 2.64. Cf. the theories of Epiktetos as recounted in Arrian, *Discourses of Epiktetos* 1.6.18-20.)

[32] For example, in his *Gryllos*, Plutarch has one of Circe's victims, temporarily returned to human form in order to communicate his views, argue for the great superiority of the pig to man. Some of the dialogue is distinctly humorous (see e.g. 6 for the porcine pleasure of lounging in mud with a full stomach), but there are serious points also: Plutarch uses the figure of Gryllos to

Aristotle and his fellow philosophers were reflecting an abiding pattern of Greek thought: that description of and ideas about animals are governed by their relation to humanity. Renehan traces back to Hesiod[33] the idea that animals count as a single class when seen in contrast with man: men exist on one side of the fence, animals on the other. The precise composition of the fence (possession of *dike*, possession of *logos*, possession of opposable thumbs, and so on) may change, but its presence does not. This is widely so in myth and folklore, which constantly rub animals and humans up against each other in various ways to produce sparks of meaning. In myth, the three motifs which are most often employed to address the animal/human relationship are combat, bestiality and metamorphosis. Particularly rich sources of material on these matters are the *Metamorphoses* of Antoninus Liberalis and the *Bibliotheke* of Apollodoros, though indeed a large number of ancient authors include some mention in their works.

Combat pits the human hero against the violent beast, and thus can be used to express their essential differences. A particularly striking use of this motif is the myth of Phylios,[34] who is compelled by his young lover Kyknos to kill a lion with his bare hands. Phylios eats heartily and drinks much wine, then regurgitates the contents of his stomach before the beast, which devours the resulting matter. The wine, the product of viticulture, does not affect the human, but it stupefies the lion. We are reminded of the inability of bestial monsters such as Polyphemos and the centaurs to handle strong wine; humans can retain their self-control with wine inside them, animals and monsters cannot. Once the lion is thoroughly doped in this way, Phylios is able to stuff up its mouth with his clothing and thus kill it. Clothing is another quintessentially human thing, used to the animal's disadvantage. Phylios thus defeats the lion using aspects of his humanity. In this myth, the man-animal difference is played out in particularly concentrated form; but a great number of stories of hero-beast combat serve a similar function.

From war to love: the second motif which features frequently in myths of animal/human interaction is that of bestiality, of transgressive coupling between human and animal.[35] Whereas for man to fight wild beast is depicted generally as a heroic necessity, bestiality breaks all the rules and tends to receive corresponding punishment. In addition, it is itself often used as divine retribution. Perhaps the most famous example is Pasiphaë,[36] whose passion for

---

assert that animals have such qualities as *sôphrosunê* and courage, and that even if the intelligence of animals is different from the *logos* and the *phronêsis* of humans, it should not be regarded as inferior. See also the author's *On the Cleverness of Animals*.

[33] Renehan (1981), 255-6; see e.g. Hesiod, *W&D* 276-9.

[34] Ant. Lib. *Met.* 12.

[35] On this topic, see Robson (1997).

[36] Diod. 4.77.1-4.

the miraculous bull on Crete was inflicted by Poseidon as punishment for Minos' earlier failure to sacrifice the bull to him. The result of the transgressive union is the mixanthropic monster the Minotaur, which has to be confined within the Labyrinth and which feeds on human flesh. In some ways similar, and a little richer in detail, is the Thracian myth of Polyphonte,[37] who rejects Aphrodite, and instead goes into the mountains as a devotee of Artemis. As punishment, Aphrodite makes her fall in love with, and couple with, a bear. Artemis sees the act and, disgusted, turns all the wild beasts against Polyphonte, who is consequently forced to flee to her father's house, where she gives birth to monstrous (though *not* mixanthropic[38]) offspring, who dishonour the gods and eat human flesh. An interesting extra element is added by this story: Polyphonte is punished twice, and in the first instance the animal/human boundary is broken down, while in the second it is made unnaturally intense. Unnatural love gives way to unnatural hatred. Both stages play with the human-animal divide.

Metamorphosis is another mythological way of exploring the divide by a motif of its transgression. Like bestiality, it is very often inflicted on humans by gods as retribution, though just as often, humans choose it as a means of escape from some (often sexual) threat. The instances in myth are overwhelmingly numerous, thanks in part to the interest in the subject of such authors as Antoninus Liberalis and Ovid (to name only two whose work survives). The cases and the trends involved in their retelling are exhaustively collated and discussed by Forbes Irving and Buxton,[39] and discussions of its significance in the discourse of human identity are to be found in Gilhus[40] and Bynum.[41] Metamorphosis in relation to mixanthropic deities will play an important part in later discussion. Here it is important simply to note its great rôle in delineating the animal/human relationship in myth. There is no doubt that this relationship is behind both the creation and the recreation, over centuries, of a considerable bulk of the myths known to us. Scholarship, particularly that beneath the Structuralist umbrella, has long recognised it as one of the chief themes in Greek self-expression.

So there is no doubt that mixanthropy, divine or otherwise, exists against an extensive backdrop of themes concerning the divide between humans and animals. Like metamorphosis and bestiality, mixanthropy is important because it elides divisions and brings the two states, human and non-human, into an

---

[37] Ant. Lib. *Met.* 21.

[38] Though, interestingly, one of the offspring is called Agrios ('Wild'), which is also the name of one of the centaurs on the François Vase; see Padgett (2003), 15-16 and fig. 10.

[39] Forbes Irving (1990); Buxton (2009).

[40] Gilhus (2006), 78-86.

[41] Bynum (2001): she performs a broad and comparative study of the theme of metamorphosis in both ancient and medieval material. For the former, see esp. 166-170.

unusual and perilous proximity. Without doubt, mixanthropes are good to think with. They are useful tools for self-expression and the exploration of identity. But what of mixanthropic *deities*? However, before they can be approached, further contextualisation of Greek mixanthropy generally is required.

4. Mixanthropy across ancient cultures: Egypt and the Near East

There are few ancient religions which do not have some cases of divine mixanthropy. Horned gods, for example, are remarkably universal, occurring among the Celts of Britain and Gaul, in Cyprus, Phoenicia and Libya, to name but a few places. However, this study does not attempt a grand world-wide sweep; and it must be asked how and why other cultures may inform our understanding of Greek mixanthropy. From this point of view, Egypt and the Near East (especially Mesopotamia, on which I shall concentrate) have special contributions to make. We know there to have been substantial contact between them and Greece from an early date, but that in itself is not significant, since the lines of cultural influence are not as clear as to be consistently useful: a few individual mixanthropes seem to derive aspects of their physical form from these non-Greek cultures, but what we cannot tell is the extent to which characterisation, function and associations travelled along with basic anatomy. So little can be achieved by trying to establish basic influence on Greek mixanthropy from Egypt and the Near East. Rather, the two regions are valuable as comparanda, as models of how mixanthropy may function within a religious system. Egypt serves as a model of contrast; the Near East seems to offer some fruitful analogies.

Whereas their Greek counterparts tend to be relatively unknown, Egyptian mixanthropic deities have a kind of iconic status in the modern imagination. They represent all that is otherworldly and bizarre in a society which has lent its imagery (in distorted form) to the genre of science fiction and fantasy. In ancient reality, too, mixanthropic gods plainly occupied centre stage in Egyptian sacred imagery. The Egyptian mixanthrope *par excellence* is zoocephalic, a humanoid body and limbs crowned with the head of an animal with which the deity in question was associated, though there were also rarer examples of gods manifest in wholly animal form, such as the Apis bull or the ram of Mendes. Moreover, whereas mixanthropy in Greek religion tended to be the preserve of particular deities whom it distinguished from the anthropomorphic norm, few Egyptian deities were without the possibility of mixanthropic depiction; for most it was conventional.

Given the obvious importance of mixanthropy in Egyptian religious imagery, can it tell us anything about what mixanthropy 'means', and can this be applied to Greek culture? Well, as has been said, it is immediately clear that difference is more in evidence than similarity; but contrast can in itself be revealing.

It has been observed by scholars of the region that, for the Egyptians, the world around them could be read and decoded, and the world of the divine was no exception. This has been connected with the use and the magical potency of hieroglyphics: nature and the gods were thought to present mankind with symbols which were a form of communication and which the learned might train themselves to read. The Universe consisted of a copious vocabulary of signs, natural hieroglyphs, there for the reading for those who possessed the required expertise. Knowledge was power; secrets were there to be unlocked. It is against this backdrop that animal-headed gods should be viewed, and indeed the rarer theriomorphic ones. Animal form, or, more usually, an animal head, were symbols the gods could use when manifesting themselves to mortals; and they were symbols mortals could use when depicting the gods in certain manifestations.

So, symbols of *what*? Though consistency should not be stressed to the exclusion of all regional and temporal variety, Egyptian culture had a palette of associations between certain animal species and certain qualities which the gods (and for that matter mortals) could display. Cows were associated with maternal tenderness, lions with wildness, the jackal with tombs and the afterlife, and so on. On these associations gods could draw for their manifestations; on them too mortal artists could draw to depict not just the perceived appearance of gods but also their inner nature, their dominant functions and characteristics. It has long been recognised that the zoocephalic form was not simply how the Egyptians perceived their gods to look, but rather a way of designating in pictogram form all the ingredients of the divinity.[42] This is reflected in the fact that the same god could adopt different animal attributes, depending on the aspect required for display and emphasis at any given time.[43] The anthropomorphic body and limbs in representations of zoocephalic gods tend to have a rather generic quality, and there is no doubt that the greatest expressional intensity resides in the head.

As Hornung observes, however, even this well-developed system of signs could not give a mortal a complete picture and understanding of a god's nature. It was part of the power of gods that their full nature was cloaked in mystery which could only ever be partially penetrated. The limitation of physical depiction, and the existence of unknowable godhead beyond depiction, beyond the humanly discernible, is one of the most striking features of Egyptian religion; however, this topic must wait for the final chapter of this book in

---

[42] On this matter the work of Hornung remains paramount: see esp. Hornung (1982; orig. publ. 1971), 100-142.

[43] Buxton (2009), 180.

which there is a full discussion of the relationship between representation and imagined form.

Here it is sufficient to remark that mixanthropy in Egypt was part of a highly developed semiotic system, but was also 'kept in its place' by the acknowledgment that outward signs did not equate precisely to inner truth. It is in the recognition of this developed system, however, that we discern the greatest contrast with the Greek material. In Egypt it depended on extensive religious writings and a priestly caste, both of which allowed for theological and philosophical thought of a highly developed nature, as well as a sense of basic coherence and orthodoxy. This in turn allows us to comment on the 'meaning' of mixanthropy across the board in Egyptian religion.

We find little like this on the Greek side. There were of course no truly canonical or canonising religious texts to forge unified principles in this matter; the picture is far more fragmented, and we see instead a folk religion built up from generations of habitual cult practice and the repetition of folklore. Priests there were, but rather than being the keepers of cherished and secret religious truths these functioned largely to officiate at rituals and ensure their continuation *kata ta patria*.[44] The upshot for the present study is that it is impossible to make any immediate and straightforward remarks about what mixanthropy means. A brief summary of its significance such as has been provided for the Egyptian material is impossible for the Greek because of its extreme variety; also because it is governed by subtle and implicit patterns which must be drawn out and revealed by lengthy study and comparison of individual instances. As for animal symbolism, there are some persistent associations at work, and these will be discussed where relevant, but to decontextualise these and present them as universally applicable within Greek culture as a whole is quite impossible. So, the case of Egypt tells us what, on the Greek side, we do not have. The Near East by contrast presents us with a tantalising set of similarities whose value is less purely theoretical.

Mesopotamian culture, like Egypt, provides a profusion of mixanthropic imagery[45] in all forms of artistic visual media from near-ubiquitous cylinder seals to the great stone reliefs of the neo-Assyrian societies of Nimrud and Nineveh. Anatomical variety is considerable among the demons of the region: animal-headed humans, human-headed animals, winged figures, horned figures,

---

[44] The frequency of this expression in sacred laws reflects the emphasis on the continuity of ritual according to custom. See e.g. *IG* I² 76, an Eleusinian cultic decree of the later fifth century: the phrase occurs four times within this single text, on lines 4, 11, 25-6 and 34.

[45] Useful descriptions of the various recurring mixanthropic personalities of the Near East are to be found in Westenholz ed. (2004), 20-42, and Black and Green (1992) – see esp. pp. 64-5 for their excellent illustrative compilation. This diagram gives a good impression of how many demons can be accorded Mesopotamian names, because they have been identified through textual evidence of one sort of another; a large number can only be known by their modern 'nicknames', e.g. snake-dragon and bull-man.

and other arrangements and combinations besides. Certain characters arise repeatedly in consistent form (such as the bull-man and the goat-man), but this material does reveal how much sheer flexibility there is within the basic idea of the animal/human hybrid. Moreover, true mixanthropy is part of a wider palette of animal/human boundary transgressions. Sometimes, for example, an animal is given quasi-human appearance simply through upright posture; sometimes again the animal parts seem to be functioning as costumes or accessories, as is the case with some of the horned beings,[46] and with the fish-*Apkallu* who wear their fish-skins like a sort of cloak.

As with Egypt, the *richesse* of these images, plainly absolutely central to the art of the region, shows up the relative obscurity and marginality of Greek mixanthropes. However, it presents its own difficulty of interpretations. As has been recognised by scholars of Mesopotamian art, the sticking point in our understanding is the uncertain relationship between text and image, an uncertainty always present in ancient societies but especially troublesome in this region where imagery abounds and clearly related texts are in distinctly short supply. The scenes in which mixanthropic figures appear rarely accord with the literary narratives we do possess,[47] and the result is that in most cases we are dealing with anonymous and mysterious personalities engaged in scenes and activities which we do not fully understand.[48]

There are two major exceptions to this rule, both of which are significant for the purposes of this study: first, the idea of the demon as protective agent; second, that of the demon as defeated adversary. Both these motifs straddle the text/image divide, allowing for more extensive and fruitful interpretation than would otherwise be the case. Both also highlight features of Greek mixanthropy which will come up repeatedly in the present study.

The ancient Mesopotamians clearly had one frequent and urgent use of their imagined demons: to ward off ills such as disease and robbery. A significant number of texts and artefacts can be included within this apotropaic type.[49] For example, we have amulets designed to keep at bay the malign powers of Lamashtu, snatcher of children; these amulets show Lamashtu's semi-bestial form, and also depict the various beings who may be harnessed for aid against

---

[46] For an example of 'non-integral' horns, see Porada (1995), 31, fig. 9: a figure of the goat-man, dating from c. 3000 BC, whose horns, and indeed ears, are worn on a kind of helmet. The horned helmet motif has Celtic and Cypriot counterparts. In Mesopotamian imagery, an especially elaborate and stylised multi-horned hat is thought to have designated divinity: see Black and Green (1992), 93-8.

[47] The glyptic images in question tend to be ritual and cultic in theme; however, we have to acknowledge the fact that in some cases a mythological scene may be depicted without identification as such being possible.

[48] On this difficult relationship between text and image, see Wiggermann (1992), x-xii and 148-9.

[49] For a helpful general discussion see Westenholz (2004), 15-16.

him: shown are ranks of helpful demons (safety from numbers), including the wind-demon Pazuzu and the fish-*Apkallu*, or sages, with their scaly carapaces. Our understanding of the amulets, however, largely derives from texts which have been discovered instructing on the warding off of Lamashtu.

If we look more closely at another example, the rôle of mixanthropic and theriomorphic demons is illustrated further. The text called *shêp lemutti ina bît amêli parâsu* ('To block the entry of the enemy into someone's house') instructs the reader on the creation of apotropaic figurines.[50] The substance out of which the effigies are to be made (including cornel-wood and tamarisk) is dictated, as are their colours, forms and attributes. Some are to have wings; some are to have bird faces; some are to have fish-scales.[51] Effigies are to be made of characters who seem wholly animal (Viper, Bison, the catalogue of dogs at lines 191-205 who have names such as 'Who makes the evil ones go out'), and of others named from animals with qualities specified (Furious-snake, Mad-lions), and, last but not least, of composite creatures, including Scorpion-man, Fish-man, Lion-man and Carp-goat. These characters are known from the material record as well: just such apotropaic figurines have been discovered (we know that they were typically placed at or near building entrances, as guardians), and personalities such as the Scorpion-man may be recognised on cylinder-seals as well.

It is clear that the demons of the Near East are not objectively bad. They are frightening and uncanny, but these very properties give them their practical value to beleaguered mortals in search of assistance against malign forces. Malign forces are also conceived as demons;[52] so it is a matter of suborning malleable demons to one's aid using magic ritual, to ward off those who are mankind's implacable foes. Crucially, a large part of the effectiveness of effigies and amulets derived from their (laborious and symbolically charged) creation. Porada argues that the very forging of such an image, in Near Eastern thought, was a potent magical act, and that carved and modelled forms had their own inherent power.[53] Monsters, of course, because they do not occur in nature, are 'extra created' and have an especially strong relationship with the act of manufacture, and this may in part account for their particular prominence among the apotropaic ranks.

This emphasis on harnessing the destructive potential of demons surely connects with the second significant aspect to be discussed: their characterisa-

---

[50] The text has been pieced together from different manuscripts, and translated and discussed, by Wiggermann (1992). All line references given here are to those in his text.

[51] Lines 170-82.

[52] For example, in the second-millenium text known as the *Description of Gods*, we find demonic abstractions: for example, Niziqtu ('Grief') is depicted as winged and with bull-horned cap. See Wiggermann in Porada (1995), 83-4.

[53] Porada (1995), 24-6.

tion as defeated and subordinate. It has been observed that in several cases this characterisation appears to be a secondary development rather than an original feature; however, it comes to dominate. It has various manifestations. Demons can be subordinate adjuncts of deities, symbolically connected with their nature and functions. In some cases, also, they fall prey to the conquering might of heroes, especially Ninurta and Marduk, the latter of whose deeds are described in the epic *Enûma Elish*. This text was probably the product largely of the later second millennium BC, during the reign of Nebuchadnezzar, and one of its aims seems to have been the reinforcement of Marduk's rôle as ruler of the Universe, and the corresponding designation of the sea-goddess Tiâmat as his Adversary.[54] The malign demons become her offspring and her cohorts, and when they are defeated by Marduk they are turned into his trophies, emblems of his victory over the monstrous hordes. Another demon-slayer with an even earlier pedigree is the Sumerian Ninurta, whose exploits are recounted in epic works such as *Lugale*, in which the defeat of demons is significantly combined with acts of civilisation and organisation.[55]

The depiction of monsters as defeated foes reflects a wider Near Eastern tendency to depict demons as subsidiary. Working chiefly with Anatolian imagery, Mellink examines the appearance of demons, very often mixanthropic, in the rôle of offering-bearers and other cult servants, especially associated with libation. This figure he identifies as prevalent also in Minoan art: the so-called 'Minoan Genius' tends to serve a (probable) deity in this manner.[56] Mesopotamian texts allot demons to certain deities as their subordinate adjuncts.[57] The pattern, in Near Eastern material, of placing the demon in a servile position, if not a defeated one, is highly comparable to their ritual use: harnessed and channelled, using ritual, to ensure that their energies are employed to the benefit of the practitioner concerned.

That this finds strong echoes in Greek attitudes towards mixanthropes and other monsters is beyond doubt. Christopher Faraone argues, entirely convincingly, for the existence of a pervasive set of ancient ideas concerning the power of objects and representations to avert evil; among these 'phylacteries', theriomorphic, mixanthropic and monstrous forms have an unsurpassed rôle. Malignity is widely expressed through animal and animal-hybrid imagery. This is undoubtedly the strongest link between the mixanthropes of Greece and

---

[54] For the date and context of the poem's composition, see Wasilewska (2000), 49-51. As she points out, the poem was almost certainly recited during the New Year festival at Babylon, where Marduk had his most important cult centre. However, it is a strong possibility that elements of the poem, if not the whole thing, originate at an earlier date, for example to the reign of Hammurabi (1848-1806 BC); see Dalley (1909), 229-30.

[55] For discussion of the various mythological rôles of Ninurta, see Annus (2002), 109-86.

[56] See Mellink (1987).

[57] See Westenholz (2004), 14.

the Near East, and it reveals the value of acknowledging cultural contexts beyond the Greek world in its narrower sense. Whether, to quote Faraone, the use of demonic figures for apotropaic purposes constitutes 'a cultural substratum shared by all eastern Mediterranean civilizations'[58] it is hard to say. But it is certainly worth identifying common ground.

However, a comprehensive study of all eastern Mediterranean civilisations and their mixanthropes is not the aim of this book. The next stage of this Introduction turns to examine Greek attitudes towards mixanthropy generally, as the last contextualising preliminary necessary to understanding the special significance of mixanthropic gods.

5. Mixanthropy in Greek culture

The way in which Greek mixanthropy comes most forcefully to the attention of the viewer is through visual means. Put simply, Greek artists delighted in monsters. The pervasiveness of this imagery can leave us in no doubt that it would have shaped and informed the perceptions in which mixanthropic gods participated, to a massive extent. This book is not intended as an art-historical survey (such studies have been made, some of them recent and many of them excellent); but to ignore widespread mixanthropic imagery when it would have been so much part of the man-made landscape of daily life in ancient Greece, and thus implicitly at least so formative, would be thoroughly mistaken. This part of the Introduction, therefore, begins with visual material, before proceeding to the mythical narratives which are the second most copious 'vehicle' for the mixanthrope in Greek culture.

5.1. A world of decoration

There is no clear line of separation, in Greek art, between narrative and decorative scenes. Arrangements of forms which might at first glance seem to function purely as patterns, without 'plot', can in fact often be shown to be full of meaningful interaction. Even a single figure may tell a simple story. Moreover, to be purely decorative, were that even possible, does not equate to a lack of meaning.[59] Meaning may also be latent, or even lost. Mystery attends the identity and the significance of numberless ornamental mixanthropes, such as the beautiful golden bee-women shown in fig. 1. Are they Melissai, bee-

---

[58] Faraone (1992), 26. He identifies strong Eastern influence on Greece as the other, rather simpler, possible explanation of the similarities; he rightly notes, however, the inadvisability of assuming that Eastern talismans necessarily originated earlier than their Greek equivalents, and the importance always of noting divergence between Eastern and Greek traditions (on which see esp. pp. 28-9).

[59] This argument is made forcefully by Winkler-Horaçek (2008, 507) in the context of the Korinthian animal-friezes discussed further below.

nymphs? Do they relate to Artemis? Or are they simply visual whimsies, products of ingenious artistic imagination? In most cases we shall never know.

Fig. 1

Despite the inadvisability of equating 'decorative' with 'meaningless', it is true that a large part of the visual impact of the mixanthropic form in early Greek art is made in media which have a dominant decorative function, and this use of mixanthropy to engage the eye using the aesthetic of the fabulous, so to speak, is significant. Many of the decorative mixanthropes in early Greek art owe much to the intense Eastern influence in the seventh century. Osborne notes the heightened interest in the fabulous witnessed by this century, and speaks of a 'fantastic invasion';[60] among the unnatural anatomies, mixanthropes are by a long way the most numerous participants in this invasion-force. Once taken into the Greek repertoire, Eastern forms rapidly become charged with associations and meaning drawn from their host culture.

As Osborne also notes, this influx marks a shift from the previous century's general preoccupation with animals found in nature, including domestic animals such as formed a part of daily life.[61] That noted, however, one of the most interesting and significant features of the decorative mixanthrope in this early period and beyond is its inclusion within a bestiary flexible enough to contain, side by side, real domestic animals (though admittedly these are relatively rare), real wild animals, and impossible forms such as the mixanthrope and other hybrids. Indeed, several of its denizens straddle the real/imagined divide, showing a fluid continuum of reality which it is essential to examine as the context of mixanthropy in the realm of ornament. This is best seen at work in the animal-frieze pots of the Korinthian workshops, a type of pottery which has its inception at the end of the eighth century and reaches its zenith around 600 BC. Though emerging from a single polis, Korinthian pottery had a massive range of exportation and exerted considerable artistic influence on the

---

[60] Osborne (1998), 43.

[61] *ibid.*, 43-7.

Greek world.[62] At the same time, it clearly reveals Eastern influence, and its own adaptation of Eastern conventions.

Fig. 2

Though the fabulous animal frieze is the *sine qua non* of Korinthian pottery, its use was widespread, as can be seen in fig. 2, a vessel which, though simple in design, shows the range of the popular bestiary at work. The Sirens in the decoration, a popular choice of mixanthrope in this medium, are juxtaposed with birds and panthers, the panthers tending to present their faces frontally, another characteristic of their species on these pots.[63] As Winkler-Horaçek remarks, panthers (and other artistically popular beasts such as lions) are half-way between real and imagined: they are not impossible, and did indeed exist, but would not have been part of the average Greek's daily life, and would certainly have participated in the aura of the wild, the unfamiliar and the exotic such as mixanthropes and other hybrids inhabited. Thirdly, in the example given, we see wild goats, bulls and long-necked birds. The goats are long-horned and by no means quotidian, but the bulls and birds have nothing unusual about them, and these forms would not have presented an especially

---

[62] Winkler-Horaçek (2008), 504-5.

[63] It is interesting that, as Osborne notes, the Orientalizing period sees a coincidence between the heightened popularity of exotic beings and a heightened emphasis on the face and head, an emphasis apparent in representations of humans, animals and gods. See Osborne (1998), 47-8.

exotic spectacle to the ancient viewer. So what is remarkable is the way in which mixanthropy is part of a sliding scale of peculiarity. It occupies one extreme end, but is not visibly differentiated from the rest of the scale: the very regularity of the frieze arrangement brings all its creatures into visual harmony, reduces difference, stresses continuity. As Winkler-Horaçek puts it, 'Die Monster sind eingebunden in einer Welt der Tiere, in der Realität und Fiktion verschwimmen.'[64]

This, in his argument, has two implications. First, it ties the creatures on the pots in with a wider pattern in Greek literary descriptions of wild and imagined places whereby places and beings are ordered into three interlocking zones: the real, the speculative and the mythological. On the Korinthian pots as in Herodotos and other authors, the three zones blur but retain some mutual distinction. The second concerns another effect of the extreme regularity of arrangement of forms on the pots: for Winkler-Horaçek, this represents the taming and the ordering of animal life, a theme given impetus by the development of the polis.[65] This theme of control will be revisited when we examine the rôle of the mixanthrope in myths.

The seventh century may have started the ball rolling, but the mixanthropic form continues to appear alongside animals and other forms of hybrid in Greek decorative arts with a remarkable persistence, adorning all material media from tiny carved gems and pieces of jewellery to monumental sculpture both relief and free-standing. Increasingly, however, it also manifests itself within narratives which place it firmly within the mythological zone.

5.2. The retinue of Dionysos

It has already been remarked that, though on the one hand mixanthropic forms are ubiquitous in Greek art, one notable cluster is discernible: this cluster is around the figure of the god Dionysos. It is a literal cluster as well as a metaphorical one: mixanthropic creatures are part of the retinue depicted as thronging around the god, tending his cult and conducting his revels. Scenes showing the god and his followers are particularly prevalent on painted Attic pottery, and arise in the early sixth century,[66] in the age of black figure, after

---

[64] Winkler-Horaçek (2008), 508.

[65] *ibid.*, 516-9.

[66] To be precise, Dionysos' first appearances are on the famous dinos painted by Sophilos, and on the François Vase painted by Kleitias, both dating from roughly 580 BC (London 1971.11-1.1 and Florence 4209 respectively). On both vessels he is shown without his *thiasos* when attending the wedding of Peleus and Thetis; however, the François Vase also shows him participating in the Return of Hephaistos, and in this context he does have companions: mixanthropes (on whom see n. 67 below) and women. On these two pots, see Carpenter (1986), 1-12 and pll. 1- 3. On the rôle of satyrs in the retinue of Hephaistos, see Hedreen (1992), 13-30.

which they enjoy a lasting popularity, though the presentation of the theme undergoes some changes and developments.

In accordance with Greek art across the board, in these scenes mixanthropy is juxtaposed with other types of anatomical form: human (the god himself is almost undeviatingly anthropomorphic, as are his female followers) and animal (panthers become Dionysiac creatures, for example, and the mule is a regular member of the *thiasos*). Mixanthropes, however, are especially present, and it is interesting to note that in this context other forms of hybrid, animal/animal combinations such as the Chimaira, are not in the mix. There is clearly something about beings who amalgamate human and non-human that makes them especially suited to the Bacchic environment.

The Dionysiac mixanthrope *par excellence* is the satyr.[67] Generally horse-tailed and sometimes also horse-hoofed, and with snubbed, animal-type features, the satyr has long been recognised by scholars as an expression of the world outside social normality, a being who does not live by human rules and who obeys only the commands of the Wine God and the promptings of its own animalistic nature. Satyrs do what humans cannot (and get away with it), and yet their human components ensure that they are not simply animals behaving as animals ought. Their incorporation of both human and non-human parts allows them to maintain the piquancy of transgression without infringing the values of actual human society.[68]

Satyrs may be the mixanthropic core of the thiasos, but it is interesting to note the magnetic attraction which it has for mixanthropy, drawing several different beings, including some of the deities studied in this book, into Dionysos' orbit.[69] Pan is a case in point; so is the river-god Acheloos. It is clear from immediate inspection that the *thiasos* in art is a very suitable milieu for mixanthropes, divine and otherwise, allowing them to deploy their phantasy-qualities in a company where wildness and illusion are rife. Dionysos as a god in myth both causes and presides over a magical distortion of nature's laws as well as those of society: he can turn men into beasts, as in the case of the Tyrrhe-

---

[67] That said, the earliest manifestations of the mixanthropic companions of Dionysos, ithyphallic, horse-legged and -tailed personalities, are labelled as 'Silenoi' by Kleitias on the François Vase (see above, n. 66). Carpenter (1986, 76-9) argues that from the fifth century we are right to call Dionysos' 'pet' mixanthropes satyrs; by contrast, Hedreen (1992, 1-2, 9) prefers to use the term 'silens' throughout, on the basis of its use on the François Vase. The two types of being cannot, however, be satisfactorily disentangled, since they were always close enough to be almost interchangeable, and in the present study 'satyr' is used.

[68] On this valuable quality of the satyr, see esp. Lissarrague 1990 and 1993; see also Padgett (2003), 27-8.

[69] Interestingly, the satyrs themselves seem to be drawn into proximity with the god, having previously enjoyed independent representation; at least, they occur on vases without Dionysos slightly earlier than they do with him. For a discussion of the 'pre-Dionysian' examples, see Carpenter (1986), 80-81; Padgett (2003), 30-32.

nian pirates who attempt his capture and become dolphins for their pains;[70] and he can, like the wine he partly represents, break down men's perceptions of what is actual and what is imagined. In Euripides' *Bacchai*, Pentheus famously sees two suns, a double Thebes, and Dionysos himself as bull-like and horned.[71] In other texts Dionysos also has shape-shifting properties himself (see Chapter 2). For Dionysos to be at the centre of a varied throng of impossible forms is consistent with his wider artistic and literary portrayal.

The *thiasos* is perhaps the heartland of a noteworthy development in mixanthropic imagery in the later Classical, Hellenistic and indeed also Roman periods: its increasing tendency to be playful, charming and picturesque. Von Blanckenhagen has noted that various monsters, mixanthropes among them, gradually lose their most threatening visual characteristics and become more winsome and appealing, frequently naughty but rarely seriously frightening.[72] It is this adaptability which allows mixanthropy and fabulous beings in general to maintain an astonishingly long-lived popularity in art, a popularity which in fact never truly ended, finding late expression, for example, in medieval church carving, and entering our modern sculptural canon through neo-Classical motifs. Returning to antiquity, it is very interesting to note the types of mixanthrope which are especially popular in post-Classical art. Those associated with Dionysos, satyrs and silens and Pans, are a perennial favourite of artists in all media, and the Dionysiac sphere branches out into a new dimension, or rather a new element, to provide the increasingly repeated scene of the marine *thiasos*, as it is called, in which Tritons (half-man, half-fish) frolic with hippocamps and Nereids in a frothy wave-borne revel.[73] Like its terrestrial counterpart, the marine *thiasos* allows the artist to play with a parade of figures, like a frieze, but one full of movement and interaction, as Nereids perch on Tritons' coiling tails, and hippocamps are harnessed.[74]

---

[70] See *Hom. Hymn* 7.6-53.

[71] Eur. *Bacch.* 918-22.

[72] Von Blackenhagen (1998).

[73] Lattimore's 1976 study of the marine *thiasos* is still useful; slightly more recent discussion is provided by Barringer (1995), 141-51. Lattimore observes that the novelty of the marine *thiasos* lies in the assemblage of figures who had existed previously, but separately. For example, the chief mixanthrope of the group, the Triton, is a fourth-century addition to the collective (whose fundamental components are Nereids). The fourth century BC is also the rough time at which the marine *thiasos* is taken up into monumental sculpture. This is not to say that Nereids and Tritons had not previously associated: Nereids on vases sometimes watch the battle between Herakles and Triton. (The pluralisation of mixanthropes is a theme which will be touched on at a later stage of this study.) On the relationship between the collective and its pre-existing individual members, see Lattimore (1976), 28-30.

[74] It would be unwise to regard the marine *thiasos* as purely decorative froth, without meaning. Barringer in her work generally argues that Nereids have the rôle of intermediaries between the worlds of living and dead, and she discusses the probability that the popularity of the marine *thiasos* on sarcophagi during the Roman period relates to this eschatological aspect. See Barringer (1995), 142-7. She debates the interesting question of whether this dimension derives from the

So, throughout antiquity, the people of the Greek world (and the Roman) would have lived with a visual backdrop in which the decorative mixanthrope bulked large, though seldom in isolation but rather in a varied spectrum of anthropomorphic and fabulous forms. Decorative mixanthropes could be static shapes — satyr-face antefixes on temple roofs, for example — or they could be 'living' forms in scenes full of movement and drama. Often, of course, art depicted them as part of a myth known also from the textual material, and the mythological contribution of mixanthropes was no less than their artistic one. The next part of this Introduction will examine mixanthropes in myth, beginning with a general discussion of the idea of the monster, a category in which mixanthropes undoubtedly operated, but which requires definition.

5.3. Myth and the monster: the combat motif

Many mythological stories attach specifically to mixanthropic deities, and these will be examined in due course. However, it is necessary to view these against a wider pattern whereby mixanthropic beings appear in myth as destructive and unhelpful entities, designated as monsters. That certain deities should be visually so similar to a large number of malign mythical figures is very striking, and this subsection will examine these figures and their literary representation. However, first some remarks on definitions are necessary.

Two Greek words and their cognates are regularly used of the beings here to be discussed, and these show up the typical characterisation of Greek monsters. The first is *teras*. This indicates something contrary to nature, and especially something ominous, a portent. The ultimate *teras* is the unnatural birth, which the Greeks regarded not just as unfortunate but also an indication of divine wrath and future contingent suffering. In this regard *teras* is directly comparable with Latin *monstrum*, the word which gives us 'monster' and whose primary meaning is that of something revealed or shown. Malformed or inhuman infants and prodigies of all kinds have a communicatory and revelatory function and can be read as signs, usually signs of imminent ills. The word *teras*, however, comes to be applied widely to unnatural creatures of all kinds, including the mythological entities here discussed.

The second term is *pelôr* (or *pelôron*). This indicates *bulk*, and reflects the second key property of the monster in Greek culture: a certain quality of excess. This does not have to be merely in size, but can also be in number, for example the three heads of Kerberos or the hundred hands of the Hundred-

---

Dionysiac properties of the marine *thiasos* or from its original mythical association with the Achilles-Thetis relationship and therefore the theme of heroic immortalisation. She regards both as influential, but places rather more weight on the latter.

handed Ones.[75] However, a superfluity of body-parts is always accompanied by extreme bulk also. The crux of this quality is that monsters exceed nature. Thus *pelôr* and *teras* link up because they both indicate the unnatural, things which deviate from the regularly occurring norm.

The unnatural anatomical combinations of the mixanthrope accord with this theme perfectly, but it is important to note that mixanthropes are only one type of monster, though they are certainly the dominant type. The two monster-words can be used also of huge and terrible beasts and of beings with unnatural but not mixanthropic anatomies.[76] The designation of mixanthropes by the words *teras* and *pelôr* has the effect not of setting them apart but of including them in a certain varied group, which one might term the 'canon of the monstrous'. Interestingly, mixanthropes can also be described using the words *thêr* and *thêrion*, which mean simply 'wild beast' and thus ignore the human element entirely. The words can be used of monstrous animals[77] and of mixanthropes[78] seemingly interchangeably. One is reminded of the frieze-arrangements on the Korinthian pots discussed above, and of the artists' disinclination to distinguish different types of creature within the fabulous ranks. Human parts are not enough by themselves to lift mixanthropes out of the canon of the monstrous and into a wholly different semiotic register.

The rôles of monsters in Greek myth may be summarised as consisting of a perennial foe-status. This is often manifested as an enmity to man, which has two aspects: direct combat with human characters in myth, especially a hero or heroes; and a more general destructive impact on the works of man. Of course the two aspects are often combined. A mixanthropic example is the Sirens. They plague shipping, and hinder man's efforts to navigate safely the inherently perilous sea; they are defeated, according to several mythological accounts, by Odysseus' failure to yield to their song. A non-mixanthropic example is the Erymanthian Boar, who is a pest to humanity because he destroys crops, and who is dealt with by Herakles in one of his twelve labours. Herakles is, of course, the foremost monster-slayer in Greek mythology, and the ranks of his victims gives us a representative *tranche* of the canon of the monstrous, comprising mixanthropes such as the centaurs, non-mixanthropic physical 'freaks' such as Geryon, and numerous monstrous animals.

---

[75] Occasionally, a monster has an unnaturally *low* number of a particular body-part; examples are the Cyclopes with their single eyes, and the eye-sharing Graiai. Physical excess, however, is far more common.

[76] An example of a mythical beast called a *teras*: a giant serpent at Hom. *Il.* 12.209. *Pelôr* is used of a gigantic dolphin in *Hom. Hymn* 3.401.

[77] Nemean Lion as *thêr*: Eur. *HF* 153; the Erymanthian Boar: Soph. *Trach.* 1097; Kerberos: Soph. *OC* 1659.

[78] Of centaurs: Soph. *Trach.* 556-8; of satyrs: Eur. *Cyc.* 624.

Monsters are foes, and they are almost always defeated. In this they are strongly reminiscent of the beings defeated by Ninurta and Marduk in Near Eastern mythology. There is, however, an important difference: whereas, as has been noted above, the defeat motif may be seen as a secondary development in the Near Eastern material, it would be unwise to posit a similar evolution on the Greek side. The foe-status of Greek monsters, and the general inevitability of their defeat, appear to go back as early as we have literature allowing us to analyse their rôle. In fact, one of the most extensive and significant treatments of the subjugation of monsters occurs in Hesiod's poetry, probably seventh century in date, and therefore (it should be noted) roughly contemporary with the heightened artistic interest in monstrous forms and in Eastern imports. While we find individual hero/monster combats in almost all mythographical texts (for example, a great slice of Apollodoros' *Bibliotheke* is given over to Herakles' conquests[79]), Hesiod's *Theogony* is unique in the way it meshes such tales together into a great cosmic *aition* in which monsters make a significant contribution.

In the *Theogony*, Hesiod does not present monsters as a perfectly distinct category of beings; rather, they are incorporated within the *mélange* of divine, elemental and fantastical beings who play their parts within the creation and development of the kosmos. Moreover, though the word *pelôron* occurs frequently to designate them, Hesiodic monsters are not uniform: some are mixanthropic, but others display alternative types of unnatural or excessive form. However, although integrated and various, they do appear strongly at key junctures, and some overarching patterns may be discerned in their characterisation.

The greatest concentration of monsters in the narrative occurs at lines 270-336, in which the poet describes the offspring of Phorkys and Keto, who are themselves siblings born of Pontos (Sea) and Gaie (Earth). The children of Phorkys and Keto all have some aspect of the monstrous about them: they include the Graiai, born grey-haired, the Gorgons (including Medusa, who is the mother of Pegasos) and the anguipede Echidna. Echidna produces a second generation of such beings when she couples with Typhaon: the hounds Orthos and Kerberos and the Lernaian Hydra; and, from her own son Orthos, the Theban Sphinx and the Nemean lion. The genealogical spate of monsters derived from sea-beings Phorkys and Keto is part of the early and elemental phases of the *Theogony*.

Gaie gives birth to Phorkys and Keto, but she is also a direct producer of monstrous young. Her offspring with Ouranos (Heaven) are various, not uniformly monstrous like those of Phorkys and Keto, but they do include the Kyklopes and the Hekatoncheires[80] and – later in the text and privileged by

---

[79] Apollod. *Bibl.* 2.5.1-12. See Scarpi (1998).
[80] Lines 139-56.

isolation from the main catalogue of her children with Ouranos – the super-monster Typhoios, whose father is Tartaros and whose many physical peculiarities are treated with an unusually lavish detail.[81] Typhoios is essentially mixanthropic: to a human frame are added a hundred snake-heads springing from the shoulders, and his voices are inhuman, incorporating those of bull, lion, dog and serpent in a grim polyphony. These animal-human combinations are juxtaposed with excessive might and fire flashing from eyes and snake-heads. In the complexity of Hesiod's description, simple mixanthropy (human plus one animal species) is rejected in favour of a multiplicity of monstrous features.

For all their physical variety, Hesiod's monsters have certain important things in common. They are all potentially if not actually dangerous, and they all have to be dealt with, most frequently by direct defeat. Zeus' frantic battle with Typhoios which leads to the monster being vanquished and hurled into Tartaros[82] is the most intense example of the motif, but there are others, and Zeus is not the only protagonist; his son Herakles takes up the baton, so to speak, and frees mankind from several of Keto's scions, the Lernaian Hydra and the Nemean lion among them.[83] Divine father and hero son work hand in glove in this regard, though Perseus and Bellerophon also have rôles to play, killing Medusa and the Chimaira respectively.[84]

Two fates await monsters defeated in this way: death is one, but another is some form of confinement, such as that of Typhoios in Tartaros. Revealing is the case of the Hekatoncheires, Obriareus, Kottos and Gyes, who are confined in bonds under the earth by their father Kronos; however, Zeus releases them from their captivity and they fight for him in the war against the Titans.[85] This reflects the way in which the dangerous might of Hesiodic monsters may be harnessed and exploited, especially to the benefit of Zeus' régime (though they are also aimed against him: Typhoios is produced as a direct and deliberate threat to his rule).[86] Not all monsters have to be defeated; a few are both dread and useful from the start, such as Echidna who, for all that she is an *omêstês* and *lugrê*,[87] has a guardian rôle – albeit ill-defined – in her subterranean cavern, granted her by the gods.[88] Another monster, Kerberos, is the guard of Hades' gates, and thus a preserver of boundaries, despite (anatomically) challenging

---

[81] Lines 820-35.

[82] Lines 836-68.

[83] Lines 313-18; 326-32.

[84] Lines 280-81 and 319-25.

[85] Lines 617-663.

[86] Typhoios is unusual in that he retains some pestilential qualities (being the source of destructive winds), but even he no longer challenges Zeus' authority.

[87] Lines 300 and 304.

[88] Line 303.

them himself; this reminds one of the 'fighting fire with fire' principle identified by Faraone as central to the power of monstrous images in Greek culture,[89] a principle also at work among the Near Eastern protective demons discussed above. Like the Near Eastern demons, figures like Kerberos become subordinate to the will of the presiding gods, and help to ward off the chaos they inherently represent. So some monsters are useful, others are made so; those that cannot be so are slain or imprisoned.

It is vital to note that the formation of these motifs corresponds to the particular purposes and preoccupations of the *Theogony* and its poet. The *Theogony* is about the process whereby Zeus establishes and enforces his rule over the world of the immortals, and in this process monsters have their rôle to play, though it is not a rôle which should be viewed in isolation. Monsters such as Typhoios are among the enemies which his régime faces; and monsters such as the Kyklopes and the Hekatoncheires are among those beings who are incorporated into it usefully and made to serve its ends.[90] It is impossible to divorce the motif of defeated and subordinated monsters in Hesiod from these specific themes and mechanisms of the poem, and for that matter from the poet's perception of his own contribution; for in describing the arrival of Zeus onto the divine stage, and his imposition of order and control, Hesiod is depicting a process in some ways parallel to his own task as author. His work orders the complicated and tangled ranks of the divine, their genealogies and interrelationships. It forges a taxonomy of beings,[91] rather as Aristotle later forges a taxonomy of the animal world. Likewise, Zeus instils order in a cosmos previously dominated by the chaotic entities of the preceding generations, monsters among them, with their complex and species-defying anatomies and their unnatural procreation.[92] Chaotic forces are not all removed, but they are all somehow made safe.

And yet despite this unique and complex structure is it justifiable and indeed necessary to draw attention to the *Theogony*'s correspondence with other narratives of monster-defeat in Greek myth. Early and influential, the work would certainly have helped to shape the way such episodes were imagined and

---

[89] See Faraone (1992), 36-53.

[90] The usefulness of the Kyklopes to Zeus: lines 139-46.

[91] Clay (1993), 106.

[92] Clay points out the importance in this narrative of endogamy and a kind of *concentration* of elemental principles which is a cosmic recipe for monsters, though it should be noted that not all products of such unions are physically aberrant: monstrous form is just one visual expression of the kind of defiance of natural law which prevails before Zeus establishes his rule. See Clay (1993), 107-8. The rôle of marine beings, Pontos, Keto and Phorkys, cannot but remind us of sea-goddess Tiâmat's monster-producing rôle in Mesopotamian mythology. However, the Greek examples carry their own associations particular to their host culture, in particular reflecting the ambivalent attitudes towards the sea which will be discussed later in the context of the goddess Thetis.

described, acting also as a major point of influx for Near Eastern mythology into Greek thought.[93] At the same time one can also speculate that both it and other works were drawing upon common background stores of folkloric material. In any case, we find in the *Theogony* themes which emerge regularly in ancient literature: that monsters are dangerous, that they must be defeated and either killed or safely harnessed or confined.

Greek literature after Homer and Hesiod continues to characterise monsters in this way. In addition, these are strong prevailing themes in the visual record too, and a large proportion of non-divine (and sometimes also divine) mixanthropes are shown fighting against a hero or other human protagonist. This pitting of human against monster plainly accomplishes something which monster-on-monster combat does not, for the latter is almost unseen in Greek art. On the other hand, the unequal battle of the man and the animal, mixanthrope or other *teras*, a battle which the viewer knew the man would win, has a lasting popularity throughout ancient art. Its manifestations are countless, but an instructive glimpse of the matter may be gained by examining the case of the centaur.

Fig. 3

Centaurs are not always shown fighting men. There are anonymous stand-alone examples, especially in the earlier material; one of these is shown in fig. 3. Good centaurs Cheiron and Pholos are shown on vases pursuing peaceful activities. Even when peaceful, centaurs often register their potential aggression, for example by the carrying of pine branches, their favourite weapons. However, in a large proportion of cases they are depicted fighting, either in single combat, or engaged in the group turmoil of a centauromachy (the prevalence of combat with centaurs is reflected in the modern development of a special term). There are two main centauromachy stories: in one, the Lapiths of Thessaly fight the disruptive local centaurs at the wedding of their chieftain, Peirithoös; in the other, Herakles, between Labours, battles centaurs in the

---

[93] Walcot (1966).

Peloponnese when they crash his quiet dinner *à deux* with Pholos. Within the first is a sub-story, in which the Lapith Kaineus, made invulnerable by Poseidon, is battered into the earth by branch-wielding centaurs; this scene is especially popular on painted potter, and many vases show Kaineus' beleaguered top half disappearing into the lower edge of the field.[94]

The Kaineus episode does not have the same prominence, however, in the monumental sculpture from which the battle of the Lapiths and the centaurs is probably best known today. The popularity of the centauromachy in massive building decoration reflects a corresponding surge in its use on pottery, but this begins much earlier: the first full treatment is on the François vase, in around 570 BC, and this seems to establish its popularity. In the fifth century, the motif spreads from the domestic and relatively private medium of painted pottery, and from the sort of sympotic ware on which the mixanthropic retinue of Dionysos was found, onto a far grander and more public stage. This development shows that mixanthropes could be symbolically important in the civic sphere, a context which guaranteed a wide and varied audience and therefore suggests mass appeal. Not everyone could afford a pot by Sophilos or the Amasis Painter, but everyone living in Classical Athens could afford to stroll past the Parthenon and look up at the towering relief-carvings which decorated it. It would be simplistic to assume, however, that everyone had the same response to the sculptures, and single meanings are of course impossible, but scholars have been right to wonder what social features of the time contributed to, and chimed with, the repeated use of the centauromachy on public buildings.

Monsters on temples are known from earlier times; an example is the great Medusa-figure on the pediment of the temple of Artemis at Corcyra, dating from the early sixth century BC. This image contains a certain element of narrative: Medusa was flanked by her children Pegasos and Chrysaor, in a conflation of two chief phases of her story, pre- and post-decapitation by Perseus.[95] However, her stark visual simplicity and relative isolation, which make her seem as much a symbol (apotropaic?) as a living form, are very different from the multiple forms of the fifth-century centaurs and their Lapith antagonists, the complexities of their combat, the challenges of movement and anatomy this offered. In addition, the special popularity of the centauromachy on fifth-century temples is noteworthy, and is partly attributable to the particular symbolic potency of the man/animal combination which Medusa does not truly provide.[96]

---

[94] The earliest known example is on the François Vase, for which see Padgett (2003), 14-17. Later vase-paintings of the same episode are to be found in Padgett ed. (2003), nos. 27 and 28.

[95] See Osborne (1998), 72-5.

[96] In a sense Medusa is mixanthropic: her anatomy comprises a beast-like face and peripheral snakes, and her offspring, one human and one animal, reflect her mating with Poseidon in horse form. She is highly significant when compared with Demeter Melaina, whose mixanthropy is discussed at length in the ensuing chapters. However, unlike that of the centaurs, her anatomy

The first monumental centauromachy which we know of and can reconstruct from substantial archaeological fragments was on the west pediment of the temple of Zeus at Olympia, dating from around 460 BC.[97] A supremely (and sternly) serene Apollo fills the apex; on either side of him, narrowing into the corners, centaurs struggle to abduct women and Lapiths battle them to prevent it. Later, in the 430s, we find two Athenian uses of the same scene: on the south metopes of the Parthenon, and on the west frieze of the Hephaistieion. In addition to these large-scale depictions, we know from ancient authors that it was used also in smaller but still significant decoration on two statues by Pheidias: on the shield of that of Athene Promachos, and on the sandals of that of Athene Parthenos.[98] This sheer concentration of its usage asserts its importance. Finally, it turns up once more, in Arkadia in the Peloponnese, where a centauromachy occupies one of the decorative friezes inside the temple of Apollo Epikourios at Bassai. According to Pausanias, there was a connection between the Parthenon and the Bassai temple which might have has something to do with the appearance of similar imagery on both (though in other ways the temples are wildly different): both structures were designed by the architect Iktinos.[99]

The Bassai temple and the Parthenon have two important things in common: their centauromachies appear in close proximity to representations of other, analogous combats. In the case of Bassai, this is an Amazonomachy; the Parthenon sculptures are more varied, and include several mythological scenes, but the metopes hold a gigantomachy and Amazonomachy. So in both cases the centaurs are just one kind of dangerous foe to be overcome by warriors who adhere more closely to the Greek identity and values of the ancient viewer. If this last sentence sounds cagey, there is a reason for that: the extreme inadvisability of certain easy assumptions about the images generally. In particular, it does violence to the subtlety of the myths in question to assume a simple 'us versus them' message in which the (male citizen) viewer identifies almost inextricably with the men battling giants, Amazons, and centaurs. A detailed criticism of this assumption is beyond the scope of the present discussion; but in fact, it is the centaurs particularly who reveal and illustrate the impossibility of single meanings. This appears first through the inherent aspects of the myth and secondly through certain features of its sculptural treatment. It also leads us

---

does not present the viewer with a clear conjunction of animal and human half: rather, she is a tangle, a confusion, of the two elements, and all the more dangerous for that.

[97] That said, the mid-sixth-century temple of Athene at Assos in the Troad bore a relief showing another centaur-combat: Herakles single-handedly routing the centaurs while the benign centaur Pholos looked on concernedly. (Boston MFA 84.67; see Padgett (2003), 22. Herakles' conflict with the centaurs also enjoyed some popularity among vase-painters, but did not become widespread in Classical temple sculpture as the Lapith centauromachy did.

[98] See Paus. 1.28.2 and Pliny, *NH* 36.18 respectively.

[99] Paus. 8.30.4 and 8.41.7-9.

to modify the stark idea that a mixanthropic monster's foe-status is absolute and simple, and this is an important modification to make at this early stage, since a particular intensity of ambivalence will also be shown to surround the divine mixanthropes who form the chief focus of this book.

There has been much discussion of a remarkable feature of the Parthenon centauromachy: the variety with which the centaurs are depicted. Several have the face which tends to characterise so many mixanthropes (including satyrs, Silenoi, Pan): snubbed nose, wrinkled brow, tangled hair, undoubtedly the antithesis of the regular, straight-nosed male ideal. Others, however, do not follow this type. Their faces are grave, dignified, straight-nosed, framed by neat hair and beards. It is quite possible that the different types may have been carved by different craftsmen, but the inclusion of both – by no means accidental in such a meticulously executed structure – is significant. It prevents the viewer from regarding the centaurs simply as bestial, chaotic, and the exact opposite to their human antagonists.

Neither Olympia nor Bassai contains this special facial variety; but the complexity of the centaur/human combat does find expression elsewhere. For example, their inclusion in the long list of beings tackled by Herakles is important here. Herakles' rôle as scourge of monsters in Hesiod has been noted above; but in art the striking thing about his depiction is the extent to which he resembles his monstrous enemies, reflecting their bestial characteristics back at them. The effect of Herakles' lion-skin, which he is never without, is to make him seem half animal himself, a lion-hybrid fighting horse-hybrids, rather than a perfect expression of human physiology and identity. One is strongly reminded of Faraone's 'fighting fire with fire' motif; also of Near Eastern apotropaic monsters. Herakles' monster-killing efficacy depends on him having an element of the monstrous himself.

This is not, of course, the case with the Lapith crew on the three temples. On the Parthenon, however, the blurring of the divide works the other way around: the humans do not gain bestiality, but the centaurs gain humanity. It has been pointed out that this has the effect of making them worthier foes, and indeed, they are. Padgett has rightly asserted that the horse could stand for that species' aristocratic credentials, so nothing in their composition itself debars them from nobility, though nor does it make it inevitable: the satyrs, also horse hybrids, always carry with them an air of farce which does not often accompany the 'brave and haughty centaurs'.[100] The potential of the centaur for nobility is also partly reflected, however, in the existence of two good and wise centaurs, Pholos and (especially so) Cheiron, about whom much will be said in this study. Of the satyrs, an individual (Silenos) does emerge from the throng, with prophetic qualities and with some of the dignity of older age; but Silenos, unlike

---

[100] Padgett (2003), 36.

Cheiron, can never quite lose the buffoonish character of his fellow satyrs. And satyrs are not man's foes in the way centaurs are: intrinsically they oppose his values and his civilisation, but they do not stand against him in heroic struggles.

So mixanthropes, like all monsters, vary, and their characterisation is extremely versatile; but although foe-status typifies them as a class, we cannot take that as an indication of simple opposition: the centaurs show us that.

5.4. Mixanthropic *thaumata* exhibited

The figures of myth did sometimes intrude into real life, breaking down the already blurred boundaries between (to return for a moment to Winkler-Horaček's terms) the zones of the real, the speculative and the mythological. On the whole people in antiquity did not see centaurs, for example, and could choose to believe in them or to be sceptical about their existence; but there were rare situations in which personal experience could be arranged. Occasionally, mixanthropes and their fellow *terata* were on display.

For example, Hadrian kept a preserved centaur in one of his store-houses. We know this because his freedman Phlegon, who would have been in a position to make a personal inspection of the object, describes it in his *Book of Marvels*. The description is an intriguing one. Captured on its native mountain in Arabia, the centaur was then sent to Egypt, but transplantation did not suit it, and it died, and its embalmed body (the Egyptian location was convenient for the mechanics of preservation!) was sent to Rome to be exhibited in the palace. Phlegon describes it as fierce-faced, hairy-armed, rather smaller than one might expect, and dark from the embalming. And he remarks, 'anyone who is sceptical can examine it for himself.'[101] Thus a creature from the realm of marvels finds itself in bustling Rome, functioning as a corroboration of myth and legend.

One might think that this preserved centaur depends a great deal on its political and social context: that, whatever it actually was (an ape's torso grafted to a headless pony?) it serves an expression of a time when imperial might controlled the wild lands that in earlier centuries were the stuff of fable, lands whose most exotic denizens could now be brought to the Emperor like any other imported produce. But in fact, although there is something particularly mournful about Hadrian's centaur, exhibited mixanthropes turn up in other situations, times and places too. Pausanias, for example, reports that in the temple of Dionysos at Tanagra, Boiotia, there was a stuffed headless Triton – 'the saddest Triton of them all,' as Vermeule calls it,[102] remarking on the pathos that surrounds these displaced monsters. The Tanagra Triton was defeated as well as decapitated – by Dionysos, in whose temple it had a trophy function,

---

[101] Phlegon of Tralles, *peri Thaumatôn* 35.

[102] Vermeule (1979), 188. See also Paus. 9.20.4-21.1; Schachter, vol. 1 (1981), 183-5; Mayor (2000), 228-33.

clearly. Pausanias of course wrote in the same era as Phlegon; but there are earlier examples of monstrous relics kept and displayed, some of which will be discussed further in Chapter 5. There is a long-standing link between mixan-thropes and ancient paradoxography[103] and interest in marvels, *thaumata*; once again mixanthropes are part of the canon of the strange.[104] And it is worth noting that, in addition to their artistic and literary prominence, 'real' specimens were occasionally on view. We can and should treat mixanthropes as symbolic entities and cultural products, but many people, at many times in antiquity, would simply have believed in them.

Mixanthropes generally were part of the canon of the strange, and the Greeks did not set them apart very strongly from other monsters such as enormous animals and animal/animal hybrids. They were 'good to think with' in a special way, but this did not place them in artistic or literary isolation, and they cannot be viewed in isolation. However, mixanthropic *deities* are different. Whole animals were almost never worshipped by the Greeks; nor were species-combinations with no human part. Of all the monsters, mixanthropes are lifted out of the canon by cult. Something about the mixanthropic form made it potentially – though not automatically – suited to worship. We cannot fully understand mixanthropic deities without examining the canon of the mon-strous, but we are right in recognising the unique property of the form when divinity is concerned. The nature of the monstrous in ancient thought has received considerable scholarly attention in recent decades,[105] laying valuable foundations for the current study, but what has not yet been fully examined is the use of the mixanthropic form, so strongly associated with monsters, as a way of depicting the divine recipients of cult.

6. Explicit comment on mixanthropic deities

This book is largely concerned with the (usually) implicit symbolic quality of the mixanthropic god, and with the underlying connections between its form, its cult, and its mythological representation. However, we do sometimes hear direct comment on divine mixanthropy by Greek – and Roman – authors, and it is necessary to acknowledge such direct remarks.

---

[103] On this genre, see Hansen (1996), 1-22.

[104] Relics were not always out-and-out monsters, but they did always have an unnatural quality, as in the excessive size of the skeletons thought to be heroes'. An example is the enormous shoulder-blade of Pelops kept at Olympia (though not in existence at the time of Pausanias' visit): Paus. 5.13.4-6. The *peri Thaumatōn* of Phlegon of Tralles contains three 'giant bones' stories (11-14).

[105] E.g. Farkas, Harper and Harrison edd. (1987); Atherton ed. (1998); Gilmore (2003). Somewhat related has been the interest in the ancient discourse of deformity and unnatural births: see e.g. Ogden (1997), Garland (1995). This topic has some earlier exponents, however, chief among them Delcourt (1938).

Mixanthropy does not, interestingly, form a substantial philosophical discourse in its own right, despite its apparent potential as a tool for thought and exploration. It receives sporadic and isolated comments from philosophers. Aristotle in his zoological work is interested in the birth of *terata*, who have animal features, and whose production he attributes to a failure of the sperm of the male to control and shape the material contributed by the female.[106] However, Aristotle explicitly denies the existence of mixanthropes and other fabulous beings as creatures in their own right rather than accidental and singular aberrations of human birth, and on this basis of course excludes them from his taxonomy, a taxonomy based firmly on what he was able to observe. And indeed otherwise, in the Classical period especially, there is a dearth of explicit comment, and in particular a disinclination to remark on mixanthropic *gods*. This picture changes somewhat in the post-Classical period, and it seems that the greatest motivating factor is a growing reaction to mixanthropy in Egyptian religion. Greek attitudes towards animals in Egyptian religion have been the study of two very effective surveys, the extremely full discussion by Smelik and Hemelrijk (1984), and the recent re-evaluation of the material by Pfeiffer (2008). The current exposition merely presents the salient trends relevant to the topic in hand.

It must be said at the outset that Greeks reacted to a cocktail of related aspects of Egyptian religion, of which mixanthropic representation of gods was only one: the sacrosanctity of animals, their worship, their place in Egyptian society more generally: within this assortment divine mixanthropy is just one component, not always precisely distinguished. The fact that part-animal representations of gods do not receive an especially intense response is to be noted. The Greeks who commented on Egypt were in fact typically more exercised about the Egyptian custom of paying cult honours to actual animals than they were about the iconographic habit of mixanthropy. The unworthiness of animals for cult underpins most Greek discussions, and as scholars have remarked betrays a fundamental dissimilarity in the ways the two cultures perceived animals.[107] As has been said, zoolatry and the depiction of gods as theriomorphic were, in contrast with divine mixanthropy, almost unheard of in Greek culture.

Egyptian zoolatry appears first among extant texts in Herodotos, where it receives a largely sympathetic, if sometimes inaccurate, treatment, being discussed piecemeal rather than systematically.[108] Herodotos' interest in Egypt generally is one of broad-minded ethnographic enthusiasm, which sets him at sharp variance

---

[106] See *de Generatione Animalium* 769b; Lloyd (1983), 54.

[107] See e.g. Smelik and Hemelrijk (1984), 1858-62: the Egyptians regarded animals as being closer to the divine than humans. This is a reversal of the Greek picture of man as positioned between animals (the basest stratum) and gods (the apex) in the *scala naturae*.

[108] Smelik and Hemelrijk (1984), 1879-81; Pfeiffer (2008), 375-6; Gilhus (2006), 97.

from most Greek descriptions of the region's religion: these derive from a later period (chiefly first to second centuries AD, though some fourth-century comic fragments are also relevant[109]) and are distinctly hostile or else seem to be predicated on an assumption of hostility in the audience. However, even in Herodotos' work we see early manifestations of one consistent later trend: the desire to provide logical explanations for the peculiarity of animal worship and its cognates. A Herodotean example occurs in the case of Zeus Ammon, and attempts to rationalise the unusual iconographic form of the Egyptian Zeus, with his ram's horns (as well as the Egyptian Thebans' abstention from sheep sacrifice). The story is told that Herakles demanded to see Zeus in person, and Zeus disguised himself for the encounter by donning the fleece of a ram and holding a ram's severed head before his face.[110]

This explanatory vein is found with far more intensity (even urgency) in the later works of Diodoros and Plutarch, both of whom are extremely interested in Egyptian religion: Diodoros opens his universal history with a substantial section of Egyptian material, and Plutarch devoted a treatise, the *de Iside et Osiride*, to the region's religious beliefs and customs. Both were concerned more with the worship of animals than that of animal-headed gods, but the latter do receive some significant mention.

Diodoros' chief strand of rationalization rests on the argument that the Egyptian worship of animals derives from their recognition of the latter's *usefulness*. This constitutes a form of acceptable reciprocity, and a virtue in the author's mind; as he remarks: 'In general, they say, the Egyptians surpass all other peoples in showing gratitude for every benefaction.'[111] Thus a commendably anthropocentric and utilitarian sentiment is placed at the heart of zoolatry,[112] in which divine mixanthropy may also participate:

> The dog is useful both for the hunt and for man's protection, and this is why they represent the god whom they call Anubis with a dog's head, showing in this way that he was the bodyguard of Isis and Osiris.[113]

It is interesting to note that the singling out of Anubis' canine[114] mixanthropy (he was actually jackal-headed) accords with the relative frequency with which

---

[109] On these, see Smelik and Hemelrijk (1984), 1881-2; Pfeiffer (2008), 377-80.

[110] Hdt. 2.42.

[111] Diod. 1.90.2.

[112] It has been noted above that Greek assessments of the value of animals rested on the extent to which they benefited and assisted mankind; thus this form of explanation in Diodoros and Plutarch would have accorded exactly with audience attitudes. Of course, Plutarch's appreciation of animals went far beyond the utilitarian, but this is not strongly in evidence in the *de Iside*.

[113] Diod. 1.87.2: τὸν δὲ κύνα πρός τε τὰς θήρας εἶναι χρήσιμον καὶ πρὸς τὴν φυλακήν· διόπερ τὸν θεὸν τὸν παρ' αὐτοῖς καλούμενον Ἄνουβιν παρεισάγουσι κυνὸς ἔχοντα κεφαλήν, ἐμφαίνοντες ὅτι σωματοφύλαξ ἦν τῶν περὶ τὸν Ὄσιριν καὶ τὴν Ἴσιν.

that particular deity is explicitly described as mixanthropic. When Vergil wishes to paint Cleopatra's forces at Actium in the most grotesque colours possible, for example, he uses Anubis to represent the divine powers on the Ptolemaic queen's side, and the barking of the god is the *sine qua non* of his peculiarity and – by extension – that of Egypt.[115] For some reason, Anubis more than any other deity of Egypt brings mixanthropy to the fore in the ancient imagination.

Plutarch shares with Diodoros the explanatory drive, based once again on the usefulness of certain animals and their past and ongoing services to man, but also focusing on the more sophisticated ideas of symbolism, allegory and veiled meaning which the well-informed may interpret.[116] Once again Anubis and mixanthropy go hand in hand. The most common sacred animals in Egypt are, says Plutarch, 'the ibis, the hawk, the *kunokephalos*, and the Apis himself, as well as the Mendes, for thus they call the goat in Mendes.'[117] In this list we have the gamut of zoolatric types described in Greek sources: real and naturally occurring animals held sacred wherever they occur (ibises and hawks), special sacred individuals like the Apis-bull, which represent the incarnation of divinity in a single animal body; and the 'dog-headed one', who can surely only be Anubis, rather curiously listed as just another type of animal, though we would surely perceive an animal-headed god as of quite another order. It is hard to explain the Anubis-mixanthropy connection, except to remark that dog-headed forms have a wider currency in Greek thought[118] which could have allowed Anubis' mixanthropy to gain a purchase in their imagination which other Egyptian mixanthropes never gained. In any case, it is important to note that the extreme prevalence of mixanthropy among Egyptian divine representations is not seized on wholesale by Greek authors as a vehicle or criticism or as a special peculiarity to be explained. Rather, Anubis receives special treatment, which persists in Roman treatments also.[119]

So, ancient authors such as those examined here are generally concerned to describe and explain the worship of animals; divine mixanthropy, however, is

---

[114] The fact that the god was actually depicted as part jackal rather than part domestic dog does not tend to be recognised by the Greek sources.

[115] *Aeneid* 8.698-700: ranged against the anthropomorphic Roman gods at the battle are 'omnigenum ... deum monstra et latrator Anubis.' Smelik and Hemelrijk (1984, 1854-5) remark on the frequent use of the barking motif in descriptions of Anubis, citing passages in Ovid, Propertius, Lucian, Prudentius, Epiphanius and Avienus. The word *monstra* is vague, but must refer to non-anthropomorphic divine forms.

[116] On this aspect, see Gilhus (2006), 97-9.

[117] Plut. *de Iside* 73.

[118] For example, the *kunokephaloi* were regarded as a tribe of real if strange dog-headed people living in a distant location. (See Romm [1992], 77-81.)

[119] See for example Juvenal *Sat.* 6.532-4. Here as in Lucian (see below) the special incongruity of the combination of animal head and human *clothing* seems to lend the figure extra piquancy as an expression of the foreign grotesque.

touched on, most often in relation to Anubis. Despite this, in none of these texts are connections drawn with Greek divine mixanthropy, and this fact is surprising. Surely Egyptian mixanthropic gods would remind Greek authors of their own. Local Greek treatments of certain animal species as sacred are described by Plutarch[120] as analogous to Egyptian zoolatry, but the analogy is not extended to mixanthropy.

This sharp separation between Greek and Egyptian mixanthropy breaks down somewhat in the work of Lucian,[121] and in particular in his humorous dialogue *The Council of the Gods*. This text stages a debate in heaven about the dangerous influx of new deities, or persons claiming to be deities, and the attack on these immigrants is led by Momos ('reproach'). A wide range of questionable divinities is assailed: deified heroes, Eastern characters such as Attis and Sabazios, divine personifications; and among these an unsurprising inclusion:

> Momos: But I should just like to ask that Egyptian there – the dog-faced gentleman in the linen suit – who *he* is, and whether he proposes to establish his divinity by barking? And will the piebald bull yonder, from Memphis, explain what use he has for a temple, an oracle, or a priest? As for the ibises and monkeys and goats and worse absurdities that are bundled in upon us, goodness knows how, from Egypt, I am ashamed to speak of them; nor do I understand how you, gentlemen, can endure to see such creatures enjoying a prestige equal to or greater than your own. And you yourself, sir, must surely find ram's horns a great inconvenience?
>
> Zeus: Certainly, it is disgraceful the way these Egyptians go on. At the same time, Momos, there is an occult significance in most of these things; and it ill becomes you, who are not of the initiated, to ridicule them.
>
> Momos: Oh, come now: a God is one thing, and a person with a dog's head is another; I need no initiation to tell me that.[122]

So Anubis the arch-mixanthrope and his notorious barking appear once more in typical vein, along with the Apis-bull and numerous sacred species.[123]

---

[120] See *de Iside* 74: Lemnians honouring larks, Thessalians storks, and so on – again, based on utility.

[121] For detailed discussion of Lucian's attitudes towards non-Greek gods, see Spickermann (2009).

[122] Lucian, *Conc. Deor.* 10-11: Μῶμος· σὺ δέ, ὦ κυνοπρόσωπε καὶ σινδόσιν ἐσταλμένε Αἰγύπτιε, τίς εἶ, ὦ βέλτιστε, ἢ πῶς ἀξιοῖς θεὸς εἶναι ὑλακτῶν; τί δὲ βουλόμενος καὶ ὁ ποικίλος οὗτος ταῦρος ὁ Μεμφίτης προσκυνεῖται καὶ χρᾷ καὶ προφήτας ἔχει; αἰσχύνομαι γὰρ ἴβιδας καὶ πιθήκους εἰπεῖν καὶ τράγους καὶ ἄλλα πολλῷ γελοιότερα οὐκ οἶδ' ὅπως ἐξ Αἰγύπτου παραβυσθέντα ἐς τὸν οὐρανόν, ἃ ὑμεῖς, ὦ θεοί, πῶς ἀνέχεσθε ὁρῶντες ἐπ' ἴσης ἢ καὶ μᾶλλον ὑμῶν προσκυνούμενα; ἢ σύ, ὦ Ζεῦ, πῶς φέρεις ἐπειδὰν κριοῦ κέρατα φύσωσί σοι; – Ζευς· αἰσχρὰ ὡς ἀληθῶς ταῦτα φὴς τὰ περὶ τῶν Αἰγυπτίων· ὅμως δ' οὖν, ὦ Μῶμε, τὰ πολλὰ αὐτῶν αἰνίγματά ἐστιν, καὶ οὐ πάνυ χρὴ καταγελᾶν ἀμύητον ὄντα. – Μῶμος· πάνυ γοῦν μυστηρίων, ὦ Ζεῦ, δεῖ ἡμῖν, ὡς εἰδέναι θεοὺς μὲν τοὺς θεούς, κυνοκεφάλους δὲ τοὺς κυνοκεφάλους.

[123] On Lucian's characterisation of Egyptian zoolatry as entirely ludicrous, see Spickermann (2009), 248-52. He makes the important observation that Lucian reverses the Herodotean schema

Rather more unusual (though logical in the context) is the reference to the ram-horned Egyptian Zeus. Zeus' response to the attack is also significant: his references to 'occult significance' and to initiation recall the tenor of Plutarch's *de Iside*, with its emphasis on animal symbolism and on initiation and the acquisition of secret knowledge about the meaning of divine forms. Rubbish, says Momos (and Lucian?[124]): no secret knowledge is required to know that Anubis is bogus. This seems a deliberate tilt at Plutarch's mysticism.

Lucian does not reserve all his parodic ammunition for the gods of Egypt, however. Momos blames Dionysos for the arrival among the gods of a great horde of his satellites, whose mixanthropy is a defining characteristic:

> You all observe, I believe, that he is effeminate and womanish in form, half-crazed, breathing fumes of unmixed wine from early in the day. But he has also foisted a whole clan on us – appears at the head of the dancing train and makes gods of Pan and Silenos and the satyrs, rustic characters and goat-herds, most of them, frisky fellows with outlandish forms. One of them, Pan, has horns and looks like a goat from the waist down, and with that long beard he sports he is little different from a goat; another, Silenos, is a bald old man with a flat nose and generally rides a donkey – and he's a Lydian. The satyrs have pointed ears, and they too are bald, and have horns like those that sprout on new-born kids, and they are Phrygian. The whole lot of them have tails. So you see what kind of gods he's making for us, this fine fellow? And then we're amazed when humans despise us because they see that their gods are so ludicrous and monstrous![125]

He does not distinguish between those who were actually accorded cult in antiquity (chiefly Pan) and those who were not (such as the satyrs). For his Momos they are just a shabby amalgam who bring the Greek pantheon into disrepute. Their mixanthropy is not the only thing he has against them, but it is expressive of their general unworthiness of godhead. A feature of particular interest, however, is the emphasis Lucian places on the non-Greek origins of the Dionysiac cluster here railed against; clearly the rhetorical link between

---

whereby the gods of Greece derive from Egypt; for Lucian, Greece is – and must be – the source of the religious system, and the Egyptians then twist the gods they have adopted into bizarre and laughable forms.

[124] We should almost certainly take this as an authorial opinion; as Spickermann (2009, 246-8) demonstrates, Lucian deliberately opposes himself to the characterisation of Egyptian religion (especially its priests) by Plutarch and others as a repository of mystic, secret wisdom.

[125] Lucian, *Conc. Deor.* 4-5: πάντες γάρ, οἶμαι, ὁρᾶτε ὡς θῆλυς καὶ γυναικεῖος τὴν φύσιν, ἡμιμανής, ἀκράτου ἔωθεν ἀποπνέων· ὁ δὲ καὶ ὅλην φατρίαν ἐσεποίησεν ἡμῖν καὶ τὸν χορὸν ἐπαγόμενος πάρεστι καὶ θεοὺς ἀπέφηνε τὸν Πᾶνα καὶ τὸν Σιληνὸν καὶ Σατύρους, ἀγροίκους τινὰς καὶ αἰπόλους τοὺς πολλούς, σκιρτητικοὺς ἀνθρώπους καὶ τὰς μορφὰς ἀλλοκότους· ὧν ὁ μὲν κέρατα ἔχων καὶ ὅσον ἐξ ἡμισείας ἐς τὸ κάτω αἰγὶ ἐοικὼς καὶ γένειον βαθὺ καθειμένος ὀλίγον τράγου διαφέρων ἐστίν, ὁ δὲ φαλακρὸς γέρων, σιμὸς τὴν ῥῖνα, ἐπὶ ὄνου τὰ πολλὰ ὀχούμενος, Λυδὸς οὗτος, οἱ δὲ Σάτυροι ὀξεῖς τὰ ὦτα, καὶ αὐτοὶ φαλακροί, κεράσται, οἷα τοῖς ἄρτι γεννηθεῖσιν ἐρίφοις τὰ κέρατα ὑποφύεται, Φρύγες τινὲς ὄντες· ἔχουσι δὲ καὶ οὐρὰς ἅπαντες. ὁρᾶτε οἵους ἡμῖν θεοὺς ποιεῖ ὁ γεννάδας; εἶτα θαυμάζομεν εἰ καταφρονοῦσιν ἡμῶν οἱ ἄνθρωποι ὁρῶντες οὕτω γελοίους θεοὺς καὶ τεραστίους;.

ludicrous deities and non-Greek culture is being maintained. In my opinion, Branham is wrong to see this as a Lucianic invention. For Branham, Lucian is making foreign 'one of the most inalienably Greek of gods' (Dionysos), and this fact reveals that his overall purpose is an ironic one, showing up the absurdity of trying imposing social stratification on the jumble of the traditional pantheon. Of course, we now know that Dionysos' inclusion within this pantheon is as old as that of any other deity, but for the Greeks Dionysos was indeed frequently perceived as something of an incomer.[126] By choosing to emphasise this strand of his character, Lucian is not overturning tradition but rather exploiting it for his own purposes, and his condemnation of the alien origins of Dionysos and his company may, I believe, be taken as sincere.

Before the advent of early Christian responses to Greek pagan religion, Lucian's text provides our most direct comment on Greek mixanthropy, and it stands in isolation, to be viewed against the backdrop of a general lack of comment. Greek attitudes towards mixanthropic gods are subtler and more disparate than one might expect: they emerge when one performs a closer and more detailed scrutiny of individual instances; and they emerge above all on the level of the implicit and the symbolic. These dimensions are the subject of this book.

7. Aims and structure of the book

This book does not claim to present an absolutely complete treatment of all aspects of mixanthropy within Greek religion; so vast is the topic that this would necessitate a work of several volumes. Section One does, however, acknowledge the huge range and variety of the mixanthropic deities known to us from the evidence. Deities and groups of deities are treated in turn, with discussion of their physical depiction and of the forms of cult tendance they received; this is intended to provide an overview of the personalities, forms and religious sites which form the basis of later sections, and to establish some preliminary trends in representation and worship. In Section Two, the chief focus of the book is revealed. Here it will be argued that the way in which mixanthropic deities were imagined and presented, their nature as deities and the patterns and purposes of their worship, were massively dominated by a number of interlocking themes. These themes are:

– **Expulsion** – A number of mixanthropic deities and/or their cult images were perceived as having suffered expulsion from their place of worship

---

[126] Greek myth does not make Dionysos an out-and-out foreigner (after all, he is the son of Zeus and Semele in most accounts), but there is a frequent motif of his arrival from the east as an adult, for example in Euripides' *Bacchai*.

or their sphere of divine influence. In the most extreme cases, expulsion results in the death of the deity.

– **Withdrawal** – Other deities precipitate their own removal by withdrawing from their cult site or sphere of divine influence. This is active rather than passive, but is similar to the expulsion-schema in that it tends to be brought about by another, often human, agency.

– **Movement, absence and loss** – It will be shown that both the expulsion- and withdrawal-schemata are part of these overarching themes.

Although focusing on certain themes is bound to involve a certain amount of selection, the dominance of motifs of absence and loss will emerge as the material is examined. The aim is to argue that a great deal of the cult practice and the mythology surrounding mixanthropic deities may better be understood by viewing it in the light of the above themes. Moreover, in Section Three it will be shown that absence and loss are not superficial attributes but rather relate to, and to some extent result from, the single most important aspect of a mixanthrope's nature: its *connection with metamorphosis*. Chapter 7 examines the evidence for this connection, and its implications for mixanthropes as gods. Chapters 8 and 9 continue to explore the implications of visual representation for our understanding of mixanthropic deities, and Chapter 10 broadens the discussion in order to contextualise the foregoing observations within wider themes and patterns of divine representation in ancient thought.

It is inevitable that in a study of this kind, a range of different types of evidence and material will be used. Vital in this book are the following. Most important are details of cult practice and of ritual; these are perforce gleaned from a wide variety of sources. The same is true of myths, the second vital type. Sometimes a myth may be seen to relate closely to worship, but this is not always the case, and mythological narratives therefore have both value and hazards which need to be taken into account along the way. Finally there is visual imagery and iconography. This book is not primarily a study of material culture. Although its topic concerns a class of deities defined by their physical form, our perception of that form rests just as heavily on textual as on material sources; the aim is to negotiate a productive *rapport* between the two. This is not always easy, but it is essential. A Greek's mental image of a deity *would* have been a composite creation, made up of stories he had heard, images he had seen, and rites in which he had participated. It is the complexity of this ancient viewpoint which this book aims to express.

8. A brief note on ancient sources used

By its nature, this study is obliged to make reference to a wide range of ancient texts, many of them late in date; this cannot be avoided. A significant proportion, however, of the sources repeatedly employed derive from roughly the same period: the first to second centuries AD. Second Sophistic authors, as they may loosely be called, are of course later then the time here studied. But there is one shared feature of their work which perhaps militates against this. They are consistently interested in the Classical Greek past, and may be seen to include in their work much material from this earlier time. This feature of Pausanias' narrative is discussed in some detail in Chapter 4. It is shared also by Apollodoros,[127] Hyginus and Antoninus Liberalis, who are so frequently cited in this study as to require a brief discussion at this preliminary stage. What these three have in common is that their works are collations, rather than creations,[128] often of considerably older myths.[129] They are antiquarians. Their collections are dangerous in that they can give a false impression of orthodoxy, of a canonical Greek mythology; but for the purposes of this study they are undeniably useful.

Unless otherwise stated, all translations given throughout the book are my own.

---

[127] It would be more correct (though it is not generally the practice, and will not be the practice here) to refer to the author of the 'Library of Greek Mythology' as ps.-Apollodoros, as since the late nineteenth century it has been widely accepted that the mythographer was not, as had previously been thought, the same person as the Alexandrian scholar Apollodoros of Athens, who worked in the second century BC. The mythographer commonly designated by that name appears rather to have lived in the second century AD, though it is probable that his work incorporates elements of that of his earlier namesake.

[128] A great deal of scholarship surrounds the work of Apollodoros especially, who is also the author most frequently cited in this study. The *Bibliotheke* has long been recognised to be a digest, a collation of numerous known and unknown sources, grouped schematically but without great imagination. It is valuable in that it makes use of earlier material. It is dangerous in that it gives the myths a misleading impression of coherence, of stability, of occupying a fixed canon; this has been extremely influential in modern approaches (see Dowden [1992], 18-21). Our reliance on it for the myths, however, is great and inevitable. The scholarship on Apollodoros, especially on the fraught issue of his identity and on the manuscript tradition, has been thoroughly assessed by Huys (1997; updated and augmented in 2004).

[129] On Apollodoros' selection of both Classical and Hellenistic sources, see Huys (1997), 347. Hellenistic sources have been identified as providing most of the material in the *Metamorphoses* of Antoninus Liberalis, and the *Fabulae* and *Astronomia* of Hyginus; Nikandros and Boios appear especially well-represented, and are also thought to have been used by Ovid in his *Metamorphoses*. For a thorough and detailed discussion of Antoninus Liberalis and Hyginus, and their sources, see Forbes Irving (1990), 19-37.

Section One:
Cults and composition of mixanthropic deities

Chapter I

Deities of the sea and rivers

Water-related mixanthropic deities reveal especially strong similarities in their iconography and divine natures. For the Greeks, Thetis, Proteus and Eurynome shared as their home the imagined realm of the sea's depths; Glaukos and the Sirens were associated also with the sea's margins, its junction with the land; and Acheloos, though a river-god, seems to have had a broader elemental connection with water and a strong link with Okeanos. For us, it is also clear that these deities express consistent themes related to the water they inhabit and to its symbolic significance in the ancient imagination. These themes will be discussed in the ensuing chapters; here, in chapters 1 to 3, the background of cult and form will be established. For each deity, the evidence for cult will be discussed first, followed by examination of the patterns and significance of composition.

1. Marine mixanthropes: Proteus, Thetis, Eurynome, the Sirens and Glaukos

Proteus is so similar to his fellow sea-gods Nereus and the Halios Gerôn that one suspects that the ancients did not always clearly distinguish, though individual names and personalities are almost always of narrative importance.[1] However, Proteus is the only one whose cult is in any way satisfactorily

---

[1] This type, however, certainly has something of a generic quality; it is that of the Halios Gerôn, of which all fish-tailed sea divinities may be seen as versions. On the Halios Gerôn and his relationship with individually named sea-gods, see Shepard (1940), 10-16. In a sense, Proteus presents the same issue as Acheloos: he is named, but there are numerous anonymous figures discernible in the ancient material on whom we are essentially unable to comment because of lack of evidence. An example is the mysterious merman on coins of Cyzicus (*BMC* Mysia pl. IV, no. 8) and of Itanos in Crete (*BMC* Crete and the Aegean Islands pl. XIII, no. 30). Like local river-gods, these figures were clearly of some importance to individual communities, but their significance is impossible to reconstruct. As with Acheloos, therefore, the decision has been made to focus on the named individual. Necessary as this is on a practical level, however, the observations made in Chapter 9 will suggest that to focus entirely on mixanthropes for whom we have a distinct individual identity is to ignore an important element of the collective which pervades their character.

documented and he is therefore the main focus here; where we do have details of other cults, they are highly comparable with his in nature, and will be brought in to supplement and reinforce.[2]

Proteus is connected chiefly with two locations: the island of Karpathos, and Egypt. As regards the former,[3] we have no direct evidence of cult, and literary treatments describe him as a marine pastoralist, herdsman of seals.[4] However, the very close connection of Karpathos with Rhodes might encourage a conjectural similarity between Proteus in this region and the Rhodian Telchines, shape-changing sea daimones and mythical metallurgists. They are of the same stamp as the Kabeiroi, who on Lemnos were considered smiths, and since Proteus is occasionally designated the grandfather of the Kabeiroi[5] it seems plausible to consider his Karpathian manifestation as part of a range of shape-changing island divinities. However, as with the Telchines, all traces of worship in this Aegean sphere are sadly lost.

The connection of Proteus with Egypt appears in Homer.[6] Herodotos repeats the story that Helen never went to Troy but instead spent the duration of the war in Egypt with Proteus, its just ruler.[7] Euripides elaborates on this theme in the *Helen*, in which Proteus has died; his tomb is the chief piece of stage furniture and Helen's place of sanctuary when she is menaced by the good king's bad son, Theoklymenos. Overall, Proteus is depicted as an ideal ruler, relegated to the past. According to Herodotos, the dead Proteus had a sacred temenos at Memphis; it is interesting to observe this report of *Totenkult*, but its reality remains impossible to substantiate. In any case, Proteus was clearly regarded as one of the powerful dead.

When Pharos, the lighthouse at the harbour-mouth of Alexandria, was built in the third century BC, Proteus came to be associated with this navigational aid. Poseidippos of Pella, for example, a Hellenistic poet, wrote of Proteus being involved in the creation of the towers, and referred to him as a *sôtêr* of the sea; the text is somewhat uncertain, but this rôle would tally with other

---

[2] It is impossible to provide evidence, or much enthusiasm, for Shepard's claim (1940, 92), that the Halios Gerôn type of which Proteus is one version was the forerunner of Poseidon as dominant sea-deity and was ousted by him (at some undefinable stage). This is typical of the assumption, discussed and challenged in Chapter 5, that mixanthropic deities are earlier than their anthropomorphic counterparts.

[3] Proteus living in the Karpathian sea: Verg. *Georg.* 4.387; as Karpathian: Ovid, *Met.* 11.249; Stat. *Ach.* 1.134.

[4] For example, Vergil says that he tends Neptune's 'immania…|armenta et turpis…phocas.' Vergil in the *Georgics* adapts the figure of Proteus to be in many ways a marine version of the monstrous herdsman Polyphemos; however, this analogy has its roots in Homer, and the fourth book of the *Odyssey* in which Proteus appears as the shepherd of the deep.

[5] The Kabeiroi were the offspring of his daughter Kabeiro, according to Pherekydes cited in Strabo 10.3.21.

[6] *Od.* 4.349 ff.

[7] Hdt. 2.112-9.

instances in which sea-gods safeguard shipping. For example, the Halios Gerôn, who was worshipped on the Bosphoros, had a shrine on high ground; in myth, he showed the Argonauts their route and guided them through the narrows.[8] The presence of an actual heroön of Proteus at Pharos is not unlikely, but the chief source is the *Alexander Romance* of Ps.-Kallisthenes,[9] hardly reliable evidence. As with the Sepias cult of Thetis, we may be dealing not with built structures but with an area of general association and sacrosanctity which is enough to allow for a god's divine assistance within a certain place.

We have no secure evidence for an actual oracle of Proteus, but his oracular powers are strongly represented in literature. Menelaos in Homer, and Aristaios in Vergil, force him to deliver prophetic information. This function is part of a more general characterisation as wise and knowledgeable. According to Homer, he knows all the depths of the sea.[10] Later authors describe him as *sophos*,[11] *phronimos*,[12] *polyboulos*.[13] His wisdom is a theme which is increasingly expanded, developed and put to new purposes; in the Orphic Hymn, for example (whose date is uncertain but probably either later Hellenistic or early Imperial), it has a cosmic dimension and is connected with his shape-changing abilities: his mind is as many-faceted and as complex as his form, and this equips him to control and manipulate the principles of life.

Shape-changing – that is, the rapid assumption of a succession of different physical forms – is the dominant feature of Proteus' depiction in our textual sources, especially in the later ones. His representation in visual media presents the same difficulties as that of other sea-gods, because it follows a type applied to a number of beings, and identification is not always easy, but it can be seen that he sometimes shares the form of Triton and Nereus, that of a bearded man with the coiling fish-tail instead of legs.[14] The fish element is an uncomplicated reflection of his marine domain. By contrast, mixanthropy is strikingly under-represented in literature, in which shape-changing receives more attention. In

---

[8] Dion. Byz. *de Nav.* 49. He also received cult at Gytheion, here called simply Gerôn: Paus. 3.21.9.

[9] 1.32.2.

[10] Hom. *Od.* 4.385-6. Proteus' wisdom, prophetic and general, is strongly reminiscent of the depiction of Cheiron. Cheiron's wisdom and prudence are stressed to an unusual degree; moreover, it often takes an oracular form. See e.g. Eur. *Iph. Aul.* 1062-75: here Cheiron, described as a *mantis*, prophesies the birth of Achilles to Peleus and Thetis. Both are conceived as old, and age and wisdom are concomitant.

[11] Julian, *Ep.* 187; schol. Verg. *Georg.* 4.406.

[12] Schol. Hom. *Od.* 4.456.

[13] Orph. Hymn. 25.4.

[14] The earliest such figure is the merman who wrestles a human on a bronze plaque from Olympia (see Shepard, 1940, 10, fig. 10). Shepard regards the Halios Gerôn as the fore-runner of all branches of the merman-type (Nereus, Proteus, Triton, Okeanos), and remarks: 'He was probably a pre-Hellenic sea-divinity, worshipped rather generally throughout Greece' (p. 10). As usual with such claims, evidence is not forthcoming.

the earliest treatment, Homer's account of Menelaos' consultation of the sea-god,[15] Proteus' form (that is, the form he possesses when he is not undergoing shape-changing) is left unspecified; I suppose we assume it to be humanoid. In later authors, the emphasis is very firmly on his shape-changing. So although mixanthropy is a significant ingredient in the way in which the ancients imagined Proteus, it is not the only one. Flexibility of representation is in fact a common feature of mixanthropic deities and will be discussed further in the course of this book.

Thetis appears to have received cult in various locations in the ancient Greek world. As Graf notes, she was worshiped in Ionia,[16] though largely as an adjunct to her famous son Achilles, with whose cult in the Euxine she was also connected.[17] She had cults in Sparta,[18] at Leuktra[19] and near Gytheion.[20] About these, however, we know next to nothing. Thessaly by contrast provides us with a fusion of cult and myth, though the former is far from well documented. Literary sources tell us that there was a Thetideion near Pharsalos,[21] and it is possible that a cult of Thetis was active within the city of Pharsalos itself, though the evidence for this is problematic.[22] There was also an area of the Thessalian coast which was sacred to Thetis – the promontory of Sepias, where in myth her encounter with Peleus and her shape-changing take place.[23] At this site the nature of the cult is hard to establish. We are told by Herodotos[24] of an

---

[15] Hom. *Od.* 4.382-570.

[16] Graf (1985), 351-3.

[17] This is attested by epigraphic evidence, though this tends to be from the Roman period: see e.g. Hirst (1903), 47, for a dedication Ἀχιλλεῖ Ποντάρχῃ καὶ Θέτιδι. The worship of Achilles himself is undoubtedly manifested earlier in this particular region. The major literary source for the connection of Thetis with Achilles in cult around the Hellespontine region and the Black Sea is Philostratus' *Heroikos* (53.10) in which Thetis is invoked in prayer as part of *Thessalian* rituals in honour of Achilles in the Troad. For further discussion of the implications of this text for our understanding of Thetis' character, see Slatkin (1986); Aston (2009).

[18] Paus. 3.14.4.

[19] Paus. 3.26.7.

[20] Paus. 3.22.2.

[21] Polybios 18.20.6; Pherekydes *FGrHist* 3 F 1; Strabo 9.5.6; Eur. *Andr.* 16-20; Plut. *Pel.* 31-32.

[22] *SEG* XLV (1995) 637 might provide epigraphic evidence of a considerable civic cult, if one accepts the reading of Arvanitopoulos (1911); however, Decourt (1995) reinterprets the inscription in question, whose text is badly damaged, to the exclusion of Thetis' name, and his conclusions are hard to disagree with; perfect certainty either way is not possible without further evidence. It is, however, undeniable that the region of Phthia in which Pharsalos was located was associated with Thetis-worship by numerous ancient authors; in addition to the mentions of a Thetideion, see Ovid, *Met.* 11.359.

[23] See Larson (2007), 69-70, for Thetis' Sepias worship as part of a range of Greek sea-related deities and cults, largely designed to protect mariners and their concerns.

[24] Hdt. 7.191.2: 'The storm lasted for three days. Finally the Magi brought it to an end on the fourth day by making sacrifices and by singing spells to the wind, and also by sacrificing to Thetis and the Nereids – though perhaps the storm abated rather of its own accord.'

instance of worship, but it occurs in highly specialised circumstances and cannot be taken to reflect consistent practice in the area. When the Persian forces are stranded by the weather on a potentially hostile stretch of coast, their Magi perform a number of acts of devotion to achieve succour, of which offering to Thetis and the sea-nymphs is listed last. Clearly, they were casting round for any power which might be expected to help them, and Thetis seemed one of the possible candidates. The reason Herodotos gives for her selection is interesting:

> They sacrificed to Thetis because they had learned from the Ionians the story of how she was carried off from this region by Peleus, and that the whole promontory of Sepias was sacred to her and to the other Nereids.[25]

So the Persians are aware of and able to exploit an existing phenomenon: the sacrosanctity of the Sepias promontory to Thetis and her Nereid companions. Sadly for us, their informants are given as 'the Ionians'; we are not treated to a direct view of Thessalian belief. Still, given her strong cult presence in and around Pharsalos, it would seem likely that Thetis would have continued to be associated with the setting of a vital episode in her mythological career.

Attempts have been made to narrow down the Thetis-connection of Sepias, and to prove that the area hosted a specific cult – rather than the more general sacrosanctity suggested by Herodotos' account – by unearthing material remains; but they have not met with success.[26] That Thetis did have a *temenos* on the Sepias promontory is suggested by a single source[27] which may well be correct; but to be concerned only with built remains gives a lopsided view. The Sepias area was clearly *sacred territory*; that is in itself significant.

So what kind of deity was Thessalian Thetis? Her rôle as nurse and parent seems to be dominant in myths. She is protectress and nurse of Hephaistos[28] and Dionysos;[29] in both episodes, she takes in what has been rejected, damaged, hounded. Even more famous is her maternal relationship with Achilles, which establishes her as a figure of paramount importance in epic and beyond. But does

---

[25] τῇ δὲ Θέτι ἔθυον πυθόμενοι παρὰ τῶν Ἰώνων τὸν λόγον ὡς ἐκ τοῦ χώρου τούτου ἁρπασθείη ὑπὸ Πηλέος, εἴη τε ἅπασα ἡ ἀκτὴ ἡ Σηπιὰς ἐκείνης τε καὶ τῶν ἀλλέων Νηρηΐδων.

[26] Wace and Droop excavated at Theotokou, 'the traditional site of Sepias', where they found, beneath a modern chapel, Doric architectural fragments but no inscriptions or substantial temple remains. They concluded, dramatically, that Sepias itself cannot have been in the Theotokou area but must, instead, have been 'near the foot of Mount Pelion at Cape Porí.' A position near the foot of Pelion would bring Thetis' sacred territory, whatever worship took place there, into even closer proximity to the cave of Cheiron. However, it is likely that in making this conclusion, based on a lack of material remains, Wace and Droop were over-prioritising buildings and other material remains as evidence of cult. See Wace and Droop (1906-7), esp. 311.

[27] Schol. Lyk. *Al.* 175.

[28] Hom. *Il.* 18.369; *Hom. Hym.* 3.319; Apollod. *Bibl.* 1.19.

[29] Hom. *Il.* 6.135.

this mythological theme mean we should view her as a kourotrophic deity, in addition to one with (as Herodotos suggests) the power to aid sailors in peril?

We do not have enough information about her cult sites in Thessaly itself to answer this question with regard to them. However, Philostratus describes a ritual performed annually by the Thessalians in which she features in a significant capacity. In the *Heroikos*, he describes a yearly *theoria* by the Thessalians to the tomb of Achilles in the Troad. Two sacrifices are made to the hero: the first consists of a black bull killed at night 'as to one who is dead', the other, of a white bull killed 'as to a god'. During the ritual, the participants also invoke Thetis in the following hymn:

> Dark Thetis, Pelian Thetis,
> you who bore the great son Achilles:
> Troy gained a share of him
> To the extent that his mortal nature held sway,
> But to the extent that the child derives from your mortal lineage,
> The Pontus possesses him.
> Come to this lofty hill
> In quest of the burnt offerings with Achilles.
> Come without tears, come with Thessaly:
> Dark Thetis, Pelian Thetis.[30]

Thetis is invited to share in the offerings made to her son, and is described as the source of Achilles' divine portion, in a ritual which consistently emphasises the dichotomy between Achilles as mortal hero and Achilles as god. Also highlighted is her Thessalian identity; in the foreign – and indeed hostile, as it here appears – land of the Troad, she is Pelian; she is to 'come with Thessaly'.[31] Elsewhere in the *Heroikos*, Thetis has a slightly different rôle, as a kind of maternal enforcer; when the Thessalians let the rites to Achilles lapse, the angry hero employs his mother to wreak vengeance. He punishes the Thessalians by blighting their crops, by inflicting them with 'some misfortune from the sea', a marine-borne pestilence also referred to as 'something from Thetis.' Thetis' maternal rôle clearly has a punitive aspect in this particular text.

The details of the ritual are impossible to substantiate as historical in the absence of any evidence besides Philostratus, but the framework on which they

---

[30] Philostr. *Her.* 53.10: Θέτι κυανέα, Θέτι Πηλεία, | τὸν μέγαν ἃ τέκες υἱὸν Ἀχιλλέα, τοῦ | θνατὰ μὲν ὅσον φύσις ἤνεγκε, | Τροία λάχε· σᾶς δ' ὅσον ἀθανάτου | γενεᾶς πάις ἔσπασε, Πόντος ἔχει. | βαῖνε πρὸς αἰπὺν τόνδε κολωνὸν | μετ' Ἀχιλλέως ἔμπυρα, | βαῖν' ἀδάκρυτος μετὰ Θεσσαλίας, | Θέτι κυανέα, Θέτι Πηλεία. For this text I use the translation of Maclean and Aitken (1977, 78).

[31] Compare the fact that the Thessalians are described as bringing with them from Thessaly all the materials for the sacrifice that they will need, so as to require nothing from the land in which they finally make land. Overall, their activities in the Troad come across as cautious and furtive, like those of warriors conducting a night raid on an enemy outpost.

rest is accurate: Achilles as worshipped in Ionia[32] and the Euxine;[33] he was worshipped in conjunction with Thetis; Thessaly and Ionia did have strong cultural links, at least from the Hellenistic period onwards.[34] It is possible that details such as the words of the hymn are Philostratus' creation. But if they are they are perfectly in keeping with the depiction of Thetis' maternal rôle in other literary material,[35] and there is no evidence that her cult persona deviated significantly from this characterisation.

The *Heroikos* text has placed a very different complexion on the Thessalian cult of Thetis. It has lifted it from the local to the pan-Hellenic, and from the parochial to the epic. It was certainly a cult influenced by the Achilles/Thetis relationship in epic; this fact has been amply discussed by such as Slatkin,[36] with very interesting results, some of which will be brought in at a later stage of the book. How exactly epic influences rubbed shoulders with native Thessalian customs we cannot be entirely sure. What is certain is that the *Heroikos* provides a particularly substantial set of evidence for the wide-ranging importance of Thetis as cult recipient, probably over a very long period of time.

Moving from cult to composition, it must be said that no record of a cult image survives from the Thessalian sites of worship. In other regions we know of images, but have very little information apart from this. She had an *agalma* at Migorion, near Gytheion;[37] and at Sparta her *xoanon* was kept out of sight; it was forbidden to see it.[38] As to the form of this intriguing hidden *xoanon*, we are condemned to ignorance; none the less, some points of comparison allow for some speculation. A similar prohibition was placed on the Arkadian statue of Eurynome; and Eurynome was closely connected with Thetis. Thetis and Eurynome are almost elided in the *Iliad* as recipients of the wounded Hephaistos,[39] and Pausanias picks up this point when describing Eurynome's Arkadian shrine.[40] The Arkadian Eurynome's *nefas* image was a mixanthropic one;

---

[32] At Sigeion near the Hellespont: Hdt. 5.94; see also Strabo 13.1.32. In the *Iliad*, though of course the cult of Achilles is not explicitly mentioned, there is a description of his tomb as a beacon helping foundering sailors at sea: see 19.374-80.

[33] See Hedreen (1991), 313-330; Hommel (1980); Hirst (1902), 245-67, esp. 247-51; *id.* (1903), 24-53, esp. 45-8. The various locations excavated in this region have thrown up some fascinating material, including some intriguing pottery disks (possibly gaming-counters) inscribed with various abbreviations of Achilles' name; worship can be seen to have begun in the sixth century BC and to have continued for many centuries.

[34] For epigraphic evidence of this link, see Helly (2006).

[35] See Slatkin (1986): Thetis' chief maternal attributes are grief and anger. See also Aston (2009).

[36] Slatkin (1986).

[37] Paus. 3.22.2.

[38] Paus. 3.14.4.

[39] Hom. *Il.* 18.394-405.

[40] Paus. 8.41.5: the Phigalians treat Eurynome as a surname of Artemis and some also believe the Homeric identification of Eurynome with Thetis. This view he himself vigorously rebuts, with the words: Ἀρτέμιδι δὲ οὐκ ἔστιν ὅπως ἂν μετά γε τοῦ εἰκότος λόγου μετείη τοιούτου σχήματος.'

describing it, Pausanias remarks: 'If she is a daughter of Ocean, and lives with Thetis in the depths of the sea, the fish may be regarded as a kind of emblem of her.'[41] If an Oceanid could have a mixanthropic image, could not a Nereid? It seems not implausible that behind the religious strictures of Thetis' Spartan cult lay just such an image. But this is impossible to confirm.

Fig. 4

In non-cultic visual material the physical conception of Thetis is at the same time like that of Proteus, and vitally different. She is valuable in that she illustrates the flexibility of the sea-god form. In the cases of Proteus and Acheloos, depiction in literary sources is dominated by metamorphosis and shape-changing, while visual depiction in art involves mixanthropy. In Thetis we find an interesting variation of this trend. Like her fellow water-deities, she is in myth a shape-changer, and no mention of mixanthropy is ever made. Unlike them, however, she is not given to mixanthropic depiction in art, either; but hybridism of a sort does feature. The typical artistic method of showing her transformations in the clutches of Peleus is to show her with her animal forms protruding from her (completely anthropomorphic) body, and assailing her assailant; there is a clear unwillingness to compromise the humanity of her anatomy in any profound way.[42] However, two artists at least clearly felt that this approach did not convey the idea of transformation between states as clearly as they wished. Therefore they opted for a highly unusual compromise: one of the animals attached to the struggling Thetis is a hybrid composite of two species, a lion and a fish. An example is given at fig. 4. This is a very striking artistic expedient: the hybridism which is so consistently employed to express transformation is manifested not in the goddess herself but in her immediate surroundings, as an appendage; and it is not a mixanthropic hybridism but an animal/animal combination.

---

[41] Paus. 8.41.6.

[42] A famous example is the depiction in the tondo of an Attic red figure kylix of c. 500 BC signed by Peithinos, showing the pair wrestling, and Peleus attacked by snakes and a lion which have seemingly emanated from Thetis. (Berlin, Staatl. Mus. F 2279; *LIMC s.v.* 'Thetis', cat. no. 13. See Woodford (2003), 166-7, on this use of 'subsidiary figures' to show Thetis' transformations, a mode which also seems to have been employed on the Chest of Kypselos, which according to Pausanias (5.18.5) depicted her with a snake emerging from her body and threatening Peleus.

Thetis' shape-changing is not limited to the adoption of animal forms. She becomes a snake, and a panther or lion; but elements are also included, fire and water. However, in the ancient material certain forms are undeniably prioritised. In the first place, visual imagery deals almost wholly with the animal forms; only literature is seriously interested in the elemental ones. Second, and more specifically, particular emphasis seems to have been placed on the adoption of key animal forms; in other words, Thetis is given not only to shape-changing as a means of evading sexual assault, but also to metamorphosis, the temporary adoption of single animal forms. An example is the (admittedly rare and late) story that she killed Helen while in seal-form;[43] this shows a general ability to metamorphose into a marine creature, independent of her encounter with Peleus and the use of shape-changing for evasion.

More widely attested in this way is her transformation into a cuttlefish.[44] Here, the cuttlefish form is the chief, if not the only one; she is in this form when she mates with Peleus. Once again, we seem to be dealing with a tradition somewhat separate from that in which Peleus attempts to grasp her while she adopts a series of forms.[45] It is also particularly important to her religious persona via the name of the Sepias promontory, which was sacred to her and which in myth was also the setting of her metamorphosis.[46] It seems likely that the motif of transformation into cuttlefish form always lurked behind the more popular story of the multiple metamorphoses. However, it would be unwise to suggest that the story of rapid shape-changing was a more superficial element; it is a key feature of various water-related deities, and as we shall see later forms one of the chief facets of their personality.

There are ways, however, in which the cuttlefish in particular may be seen as an important part of Thetis' persona. Its evasive qualities go beyond those of the other animal forms and the fire and water; these are fierce, painful, hard to grasp, but the cuttlefish is specially designed for evasion in its ability to eject black ink. Borgeaud connects both the evasiveness and the ink with Thetis' persona as a 'sombre déesse des profondeurs marines,'[47] a persona which he regards as indissoluble from her Thessalian cult.

Further layers of significance in the cuttlefish are brought to light in Matron's *Attikon Deipnon*, a fourth-century BC text which consists of a parodic description of a banquet including several fish dishes.[48] One of these is the cuttlefish, which

---

[43] Ptolem. Heph. in Photius *Bibl.* 149b.1ff.

[44] Eur. fr 1093 Nauck; schol. Ap. Rhod. *Arg.* 1.582; schol. Eur. *Andr.* 1266; schol Lyk. *Al.* 175-8.

[45] Forbes Irving (1990), 182.

[46] The scholiast on Ap. Rhod. *Arg.* 1.582 suggests that the place took its name from Thetis' *sepia*-metamorphosis.

[47] Borgeaud (1995), 23.

[48] Quoted by Athenaios, *Deipn.* 134d-137c.

Matro describes as 'the daughter of Nereus, silver-footed, the fair-tressed σηπίη, dread goddess with the voice of a mortal.'[49] So Thetis and the sepia are presented as one and the same, supporting the theory of their very close association, though of course it is partly for humorous effect. The description continues on line 35 of the text: 'ἡ μόνη ἰχθὺς ἐοῦσα τὸ λευκὸν καὶ μέλαν οἶδε'. There is an uncertainty in the text, and Degani argues[50] that this should be translated 'who *alone of all fish* [my italics] knows the difference between white and black.'[51] This is not incontestable, but is certainly suggestive. Why should Thetis have a special insight into white and black? Degani demonstrates that the passage as a whole deals consistently with the whiteness and/or shininess of fish as (humorously) analogous to the elegant whiteness of women; so all fish have that quality. The sepia, however, is different. It is unusually[52] white on the outside, but filled inside with black ink. It is unique in containing this contrast, this disparity. Borgeaud is right to point to the importance of darkness in the composition of the *sepia*-Thetis; but just as important is the stark discrepancy between outer and inner. To some extent, the *sepia*-Thetis is a perfect embodiment of her marine element. She is flexible and fluid, like the sea.[53] She has its darkness, but also its disparity between the shining surface and the murky depths.[54]

Like Demeter Melaina, Eurynome is a unique phenomenon in cult, worshipped at a single known site (though unlike Demeter Melaina her mythological persona is widespread). The site in question is in Arkadia, near Phigalia and

---

[49] Trans. Degani (1995), 417.

[50] Degani (1995), 425.

[51] See Degani (1995), 426, n. 9 on the textual uncertainty and his conjecture. As the text stands in the form given above, the participle *eousa* could have either a causal or a concessive sense ('because she is a fish' or 'despite being a fish'. The latter would in fact yield quite a similar sense to that Degani wants to argue for: fish don't know the difference between white and black, but Thetis, though a fish, does, because of her special *sepia*-qualities. The causal option would invalidate any distinction between the cuttlefish and the rest of the fish, and given the ancient awareness of the peculiarities of the *sepia*, its composition and habits, this does seem unsatisfactory.

[52] The extreme whiteness of cuttlefish is recognised by ancient authors, and connected with the pale complexions of women: see e.g. Aristoph. *Ekkl.* 126. Here a woman in a false beard is compared with a cuttlefish similarly disguised, and the scholiast explains this with the words λευκαὶ γὰρ αἱ σηπίαι. See Detienne and Vernant (1978), 160-61 and 174 n. 139.

[53] For the sea as untrustworthy, see Pittakos fr. 10 5.10 DK.

[54] Indeed, literary treatments sometimes make her appearance reminiscent of her marine home. For example, in Homer, her veil is described as *kuaneos*, a colour-word very often applied to the sea (*Il.* 24.94); and when she emerges from the marine depths to comfort Achilles in Book 1 of the *Iliad*, she 'comes forth from the grey sea like a mist' (l. 359), clearly echoing its colour once more. On the disparity between the sea's shining surface and its murky, *kêtos*-ridden depths (a disparity which Thetis' character could be thought to echo), see Vermeule (1979), 179: 'The sea is the more dangerous because you cannot look far below the surface, however much light plays across the top; it is as dark as the underworld below…'. Fascinatingly, Semonides uses the sea as an image to describe a *beautiful but deceitful woman*, raising just the quality of deceptive feminine beauty that Thetis has (as does Pandora).

Demeter Melaina's sacred cave; it is situated at the junction of the rivers Lymax and Neda. Typically, our only information comes from the narrative of Pausanias,[55] and as usual this requires a cautious approach. In this instance, however, in contrast with that of Demeter Melaina, there is no reason not to accept the basic features of his description.[56] He tells us that Eurynome was here represented by a *xoanon* in the form of a woman with a fish's tail in lieu of legs (a mermaid, essentially), bound with gold chains, which he himself was not able to see but which was described to him at the scene.

Eurynome was identified both as a form of Artemis and as one of the Nereids; now it is impossible to decide which identification is more accurate, and both had currency in ancient thought. Of course, the mermaid form of the goddess suggests sea-deity affinities especially strongly, and it is not surprising that Pausanias finds the marine association more comprehensible than the Artemis one, saying in rationalising vein that if Eurynome is an Oceanid closely related to Thetis,[57] the fish might be 'a kind of emblem' of her marine nature.[58] However, Artemis and the Oceanids are not entirely unconnected;[59] in fact, a variety of literary sources speak of Artemis as having a retinue of Oceanids, rather as Thetis is depicted in some texts as a leader of the Nereids.[60] The two identifications, Artemis and Oceanid, are not mutually exclusive, though their relationship is mysterious.

No non-cultic representation shows Eurynome in mixanthropic form.[61] This is a situation similar to that of Thetis, whose shape-changing is a vital feature of myth but is generally excluded from her artistic form in favour of idealised female beauty.[62] It is not surprising that Eurynome also should receive only anthropomorphic treatment by vase-painters and other craftsmen. However, the mermaid form of her Arkadian image finds plenty of corroborative parallels if we regard her Oceanid connections as paramount and see her as a female equivalent, visually, of the Halios Gerôn type. The gender discrepancy on this matter is interesting, however. Male sea-gods appear to be able to sustain mixanthropic

---

[55] Paus. 8.41.4-6.

[56] Whereas with regard to Demeter Melaina Pausanias' narrative is clearly composed largely of interlocking myths, his description of Eurynome's shrine is brief and factual.

[57] Thetis was a Nereid rather than an Oceanid; but there does not appear to have been significant difference between the two groups.

[58] Paus. 8.41.6.

[59] A possible connection between Eurynome's form and Artemis is provided by a fish-tailed female depicted on a relief from the sanctuary of Artemis Orthia: see Bevan (1986), 193, no. 58.

[60] Artemis with a retinue of Oceanids: Kallim. *Hymn.* 3.12, 40; Nonn. *Dion.* 16.127. Thetis with a band of Nereids: Hom. *Il.* 18.37-67.

[61] It is also remarkable that, as Shepard observes (1940, 23), Eurynome is the only Greek female deity represented as a mermaid.

[62] The mermaid form is in fact extremely rare among females in Greek art: see Shepard (1940), 24.

form without becoming wholly monstrous and hideous. Sometimes, the fish-tailed form is used to depict an opponent of Herakles, and thus by definition a monster; but not always. A neck-amphora by the Berlin Painter, for example (fig. 5), depicts an unnamed merman in such a way that he appears strikingly august and stately: he is decorously robed, and carries a long sceptre in one hand (in the other, the typical dolphin).[63] But this kind of 'honourable mixanthropy' does not seem possible for female sea-deities and nymphs.[64] When a female is consistently portrayed with a fish-tail, the resulting creature is monstrous and fraught with negative associations: for example, Echidna,[65] companion of Typhoios, or Skylla, whose fish tail is also combined, of course, with dogs' heads sprouting from her groin.[66] For an example of Skylla alone, see fig. 6.[67]

Fig. 5

For all the paucity of mixanthropic iconography, Eurynome in myth is surrounded by motifs of mixanthropy, even though they are not her own. She is the daughter of Okeanos, who is himself often represented with a fish-tail in place of legs (see for example fig. 7, the *dinos* painted by Sophilos in the early sixth century, in which Okeanos, named, has this form). Her husband is Ophion, a Titan, whose form is not explicitly described as mixanthropic but whose name is clearly (and unsurprisingly) snake-related. Fish-tails and snakes are often juxtaposed in Greek mythological representation; Okeanos on the Sophilos *dinos*, for example, is fish-tailed but clutches a snake. Eurynome and Ophion in some (mainly post-Classical) sources have an interesting cosmic rôle: they are named as former rulers of the world from Mount Olympos, who suffered banishment by Rhea and Kronos and are driven into the sea.[68] Eurynome is

---

[63] See Padgett ed. (2003), 346-8, cat. no. 97.

[64] Whereas the male Triton is a frequent member of marine *thiasoi* in art, the female equivalents are non-mixanthropic: Nereids holding fish or riding sea-monsters.

[65] Hesiod characterises Echidna as monstrous and frightening: *Theog.* 295-305.

[66] On the copious representations of Skylla in Etruscan art, see Boosen (1986), 5-63.

[67] This is a common representation in vase-paintings: see e.g. *LIMC s.v.* 'Skylla', cat. no. 6: a fourth-century Campanian pyxis showing Skylla swimming among fish (Agrigente, Mus. Reg. C 948). Such harmless and non-aggressive settings are interestingly typical of depictions of Skylla, who usually appears as one of a flock of marine beings, fabulous or otherwise.

[68] Ap. Rhod. *Arg.* 1.503; Lyk. *Al.* 1191; Nonn. *Dion.* 2.563.

therefore, according to these sources, among the mixanthropes who belong to a past cosmic order and now exist in exile.

Fig. 6

So in one sense it is hardly surprising to find Eurynome in mermaid form: her background in myth is full of mixanthropy and marine associations. However, both the marine and the cosmic aspects of her personality seem very far removed from our Phigalian cult in its isolated, land-locked position. It will later be argued that one can only really begin to 'read' Phigalian Eurynome's mixanthropy by looking at it in combination with her depiction as a bound goddess. Fish tail and restraining chains combine in the figure of a goddess constantly restrained from escape. The elusiveness which the fish tail expresses seems more important, in the Phigalian context, than any direct reference to the sea.

In general terms, a bound statue indicates a desire to curb the destructive powers of a deity and (the two tend to be simultaneous), to conserve and maintain its beneficial ones.[69] The idea of Eurynome's image as an especially potent one – either for good or for ill – perhaps ties in with the heavy restrictions placed upon its being seen. Her shrine was inaccessible to an extreme. First, as Pausanias reports, it was physically difficult to reach because of the rough terrain; second, it was only open for public worship one day a year. The cult activity was clearly highly ordered, kept within strict bounds, like the *xoanon* itself. The invisibility of the cult image is extremely significant and will be discussed further in a later chapter.

---

[69] On bound statues generally, see Faraone (1992), 74-81; for a collection of the ancient evidence and the main strands of modern interpretation, see Icard-Gianolio in *ThesCRA* vol. II, *s.v.* 'Statues enchaînées', 468-71.

Fig. 7

The mixanthropy of the Sirens is, by contrast with the shape-changing Thetis and the obscure and hidden Eurynome, a consistent and clear feature across their representation in both texts and art.[70] It is not without questions, and these will be discussed after a description of the Sirens' cult. When looking at their worship, we face the situation that while their literary and mythological rôle is of great antiquity (beginning of course with their famous confrontation with Odysseus), the sources for their cult are all late. They are, in (probable) chronological order, pseudo-Aristotle, Lykophron (plus a scholion on his work which cites Timaios, the third-century BC Sicilian historian), and Strabo. The earliest mention is therefore probably fourth century; the most extended treatment, that of Lykophron, Hellenistic. We must acknowledge the strong possibility, if not probability, that the cult was shaped, or even created, by the influence of the literary persona of the Sirens. This does not make it insignificant or uninteresting; it is simply a likelihood to bear in mind. It is still valid to try to establish the features of the cult and its relationship with the character of the Sirens in myth.

There is a strong consistency among the sources. Locations given are all within the Western Greek world, Sicily and South Italy. Our earliest and our latest source agree on the Sorrento peninsula.[71] By far the most detailed account of cult is given by Lykophron, whose description is worth quoting in full. The context is Kassandra's prophecy that Odysseus will kill the Sirens. In the following passage she describes what will happen to the Sirens after their deaths:

> Her [Parthenope], cast up on the shore, will the tower of Phaleron
> Receive, and Glanis, moistening the earth with its streams.

---

[70] Though in literature the emphasis is on their wings; see e.g. Eur. *Hel.* 167.

[71] Ps.-Aristotle, *Mir.* 103; Strabo 1.2.12.

Here, having built a tomb for the maiden, the inhabitants
Will honour Parthenope, the bird-formed goddess,
Annually with libations and with sacrifices of oxen.
And Leukosia, cast onto the jutting strand of Enipeus, will long haunt
The rock that bears her name, where boisterous Is
And the neighbouring Laris pour out their waters.
And Ligeia will come ashore at Terina,
Spitting out the surf, and her will sailors
Bury on the saffron-coloured shore,
Near to the eddies of Okinaros.
Bull-horned Ares will wash her tomb with his streams,
Cleansing the foundation of the bird-like one.
And there one day the commander of the whole fleet of Attica,
In honour of the eldest goddess of the sisters [Parthenope],
Will furnish a torch-race for sailors
In accordance with an oracle; this race the people of the Neapolitans will
One day make greater...[72]

The cultic features of his own time which the author is here presumably describing (in aetiological vein) are various. There are three main strands which are significant (and which will receive further discussion in a later section). The first is the association of Sirens with topographical features: the rock named for Leukosia reminds us of Strabo's description of the rocks called Seirenoussai.[73] The second is the repeated juxtaposition of Siren-sites with rivers and indeed river gods. Is and Laris seem at least partly personified through the words *labros* and *geitōn*, and Ares is clearly conceived of as a mixanthropic deity with the bull's horns typical of river god iconography.[74] All three Sirens come ashore, and receive some form of cult, in the vicinity of these rivers; this is surely not coincidental, especially given their relationship with Acheloos, river god *par excellence*.[75] It suggests a cultic, as well as a mythological, connection between the goddesses of the shore and the gods of the rivers; this will be discussed further

---

[72] Lyk. *Al.* 717-736: τὴν μὲν Φαλήρου τύρσις ἐκβεβρασμένην | Γλάνις τε ῥείθροις δέξεται τέγγων χθόνα. | οὗ σῆμα δωμήσαντες ἔγχωροι κόρης | λοιβαῖσι καὶ θύσθλοισι Παρθενόπην βοῶν | ἔτεια κυδανοῦσιν οἰωνὸν θεάν. | ἀκτὴν δὲ τὴν προὔχουσαν εἰς Ἐνιπέως | Λευκωσία ῥιφεῖσα τὴν ἐπώνυμον | πέτραν ὀχήσει δαρόν, ἔνθα λάβρος Ἴς | γείτων θ' ὁ Λᾶρις ἐξερεύγονται ποτά. | Λίγεια δ' εἰς Τέριναν ἐκναυσθλώσεται | κλύδωνα χελλύσσουσα, τὴν δὲ ναυβάται | κρόκαισι ταρχύσουσιν ἐν παρακτίαις, | Ὠκινάρου δίναισιν ἀγχιτέρμονα. | λούσει δὲ σῆμα βουκέρως νασμοῖς Ἄρης | ὀρνιθόπαιδος ἴσμα φοιβάζων ποτοῖς. | πρώτη δὲ καὶ ποτ' αὖθι συγγόνων θεᾷ | κραίνων ἁπάσης Μόψοπος ναυαρχίας | πλωτῆρσι λαμπαδοῦχον ἐντυεῖ δρόμον | χρησμοῖς πιθήσας, ὅν ποτ' αὐξήσει λεώς | Νεαπολιτῶν... On the life and times of Lykophron, see Fusillo, Hurst and Paduano (1991), 17-27; pp. 27-37 for the nature of the poem, its themes, etc.

[73] 1.2.12 and 5.4.8.

[74] I have been unable to discover a single other reference to Ares the river-god, who is clearly quite separate from the war-god.

[75] For the Sirens as daughters of Acheloos, see Lucian *de Salt.* 50, Hyg. *Fab.* 141, Ap. Rhod. *Arg.* 4.893-6.

below. The third important feature is the *aition* of tomb-cult. Worship stems from death and burial; the centre of worship tends to be a *sêma*[76] or a *mnêma*[77]; compare the tomb of Proteus. The status of several mixanthropes as dead and departed is highly significant and will be discussed in a later section.

From the slightly tangled picture of Siren-worship in the South Italy and Sicily region, the figure of Parthenope emerges with especial force; there is no doubt that she was singled out for particular ritual attention. Most often reported is her cult in Neapolis, and the institution by the Athenian nauarch Diotimos, in 439/8 BC, of a torch-race in her honour, thenceforth performed annually by the local inhabitants. This is mentioned by Lykophron and Strabo; but the scholiast on Strabo (ad loc.) traces it back to the early-Hellenistic author Timaios. This ritual, the torch-race, has perhaps some funerary connotations,[78] but these are certainly not exclusive; Pan, for example, was honoured in Athens with an annual torch-race after his epiphany to Philippides, in a context without overt death-associations.[79]

Fig. 8   Fig. 9

In their physical composition, Sirens are human-faced birds, sometimes with human arms, sometimes without; an example with arms is given at fig. 8.[80] The earliest Greek Sirens (that is, the earliest cases of the form conventionally associated with Sirens) can be either male, as in fig. 9,[81] or female, but quickly their female nature becomes the orthodoxy, and they are never male in myth.

---

[76] Lyk. *Al.* 719 (tomb of Parthenope) and 730 (that of Ligeia).

[77] Strabo 1.2.12. In this context, the word *mnêma* – monument or memorial – seems funerary. Worth noting is Strabo's use of the word *hieron* – not a tomb-related monument – when describing the sanctuary of the Sirens on the Sorrento peninsula.

[78] Parisinou (2000), 60-72, explores the connection of the torch with death and the afterlife in a largely religious and mythological sphere.

[79] Hdt. 6.105.

[80] See Tsiafakis (2003), 75.

[81] Padgett ed. (2003), 287-9, cat. no 75. See also Tsiafakis (2003), 74-5.

What must be asked for the purposes of this study is what the mixanthropic element of the Sirens contributes to their character as expressed in both material and textual sources. But before we can do that, some questions regarding their nature must be addressed.

Fig. 10

The Sirens have two alternative genealogies in Greek literature, which have a bearing on their nature. The chief disagreement concerns the identity of their mother:[82] one tradition makes her Chthôn,[83] the other a Muse (either Melpomene or Terpsichore).[84] The former is represented in our earlier sources;[85] the latter is post-Classical, and feels very much like a mythographical elaboration on the theme of the Sirens' musical abilities. The earlier tradition on the other hand places the Sirens firmly in the ranks of Hesiod's Children of Earth, including such monsters as Typhon and the Giants; however, the Sirens do not actually feature in the *Theogony*. We can only assume that, by making them the children of Earth, authors are attempting to fit them into that primordial company. The divergence between the two traditions is mirrored also in the way in which more and more emphasis comes to be placed, in literary accounts, on the Sirens as producers of sweet and fatal song, to the exclusion of other elements. (One recalls for example

---

[82] Their father is widely said to be Acheloos: see e.g. Hyg. *Fab.* 141; Ap. Rhod. *Arg.* 4.893-6. On the variants in their parentage, see Bettini and Spina (2007), 39-54.

[83] e.g. Eur. *Hel.* 168; Ovid, *Met.* 5.552.

[84] Melpomene: Apollod. *Ep.* 7.18. Terpsichore: schol. Lyk. *Al.* 653, 671, 712. Unspecified Muse: Lyk. *Al.* 713.

[85] As is the claim that they were offspring of Phorkys, the sea-divinity, an elemental force closer in nature to Chthôn than to the Muses (see Soph. fr. 777 Nauck). This is an unsurprising connection: Phorkys was parent to a number of monstrous and fabulous beings: see Hes. *Theog.* 270-336.

Pausanias' remark that 'even in the present day men compare to a Siren whatever is charming in both poetry and prose.'[86])

Fig. 11

Their appearance in material representation contains another dichotomy. It is in the sixth century that they become widespread (though it can be traced back as early as the eighth century),[87] and their use takes two basic forms. The earliest Sirens are decorative, without narrative context and clearly owing much to Oriental influence. As time goes by, artists (especially vase-painters), place this borrowed form within a Greek mythological story, most often in depictions of the legend of Odysseus.[88] There has been some debate about the sequence of these two types, the decorative and the narrative.[89] However, fascinatingly, there is considerable overlap between the associations of the non-Greek decorative siren and the mythological beings to which the siren form comes to be applied. Their association with death in particular links their decorative function, which is often funerary (a famous example is given at fig. 11), with their mythological rôle. In the latter, the death association takes two forms. On the one hand, they are sometimes depicted as living in the under-

---

86 Paus. 1.21.1.

87 See Tsiafakis (2003), 74.

88 The most famous example is fig. 10 (above, p. 71), an Attic red figure stamnos of c. 490 BC, showing Odysseus tied to the mast of his ship while on the crags to either side perch two Sirens; a third plunges from her rock, presumably dying because her blandishments have been resisted. See Tsiafakis (2003), 77.

89 For a valuable, concise discussion of some important stages in modern thought on the subject, see Pollard (1965), 141-144.

world;[90] and they are death-bringers, with their fatal song. But on the other hand, their own deaths are never far from sight. If their song fails to prove fatal, this failure is fatal for the singer; once resisted, the Siren dies.[91] As we have seen, their cult is based on tombs. It is not unknown for a mixanthrope's main characteristic, be it good or bad, to be turned against him or her in this way. Acheloos' emblematic horn is wrenched off; Cheiron the healer dies of an incurable wound. An irony, bitter or gratifying, underlies many mixanthropic defeats. But in the case of the Sirens, it seems in part to be the product of a special predominance of death-imagery in their characterisation. This appears to owe something to non-Greek models, such as Egyptian *Ba*-birds (an example is given at fig. 12),[92] though the precise contribution of such beings remains elusive.

The other major theme, connected with that of death, is that of song. Some scholars have argued that the Sirens were conceived of as negative counterparts of the Muses,[93] though Pollard challenges this inverse equivalency.[94] In either case, the Sirens can undeniably represent the destructive power of music and song; this is clearly the image we draw from their rôle in the *Odyssey*.[95] There is, however, another element to their musicality that is worth exploring. On an early red figure vase, a Siren plays the pipes in the retinue of Dionysos, among the more usual satyrs. Pollard conjectures that this Siren is 'personifying … possibly

[90] E.g. in Plat. *Kra.* 403d; Euripides (*Hel.* 168-78) and Apollonios (*Arg.* 4.896-7) make them companions of Persephone. One version of their metamorphosis makes it self inflicted, as they become half-birds the better to search for Persephone after her abduction: see Ovid, *Met.* 5.552-62. Interestingly, Ovid adds the detail that their faces are kept human so that their beautiful singing might continue (ll. 560-62).

[91] See Lyk. *Al.* 712; Hyg. *Fab.* 141; for discussion of this and other traditions in the ancient material, see Bettini and Spina (2007), 87-93. One might compare the story of their suicide with the effect on the Sphinx of a correct answer to her riddle.

[92] Both *Ba*-birds and Sirens appear often in funerary contexts, and both are associated with death and the afterlife, though in very different capacities. The *Ba* in Egyptian thought is the soul of a dead person, which is able to detach itself from the body; it is this essential mobility which appears to have dictated its frequent depiction in bird-form. For examples and discussions, see Taylor (2001), 20-23 and figs. 8-10. For the connections between *Ba*-birds and Greek Sirens, see Vermeule (1979), 74-7; on p. 75 she remarks, 'There is little doubt that the Egyptian *ba*-soul was the model for the Greek soul-bird and for its mythological offshoots the Siren and the Harpy, both of whom had intense and often sustaining relations with the dead.' See also Tsiafakis (2003), 75.

[93] See e.g. Buschor (1944), who emphasises the Sirens' underworld rôle; also, Wilamowitz, vol. 1 (1932), 268-9. Vernant (1991), 104, vividly describes the death-bringing element which distinguishes the Sirens from the Muses: 'The Sirens are the opposite of the Muses. Their song has the same charm as that of the daughters of Memory; they too bestow a knowledge that cannot be forgotten. But whoever succumbs to the attraction of their beauty, the seduction of their voices, the temptation of the knowledge they hold in their custody, does not enter that region to live forever in the splendor of eternal renown. Instead, he reaches a shore whitened with bones and the debris of rotting human flesh.'

[94] Pollard (1952), esp. 60.

[95] See Vermeule (1979), 200-205: a lyrical description of the potent mixture of beauty and death which characterised the Sirens and their song in Greek thought.

the kind of music that could only be heard by adepts in a state of ecstasy.'[96] One cannot, from one vase, extrapolate a significant connection between Sirens and Dionysiac revelry or altered consciousness; but this instance shows that the conception of the Sirens' music was not so overwhelmingly negative that it could not, occasionally, be incorporated into the *thiasos*, with all its associations of fertility and bliss.

Fig. 12

So we return to the essential question: how much of the Sirens' characterisation is fuelled by or reflected in their animal elements and their mixanthropy? A study of birds in myths reveals two strands. On the one hand, they are often associated with suffering, loss and death; on the other, they can at times themselves be destructive and death-bringing.

Mythological bird-metamorphosis revolves with particular emphasis around the idea of evasion and departure, facilitated by flight. Clearly birds' wings made them uniquely able to embody swift, sometimes unexpected movement, especially escape. On the one hand, this is a practical ability; but Forbes Irving shows that it makes them expressions of a number of themes concerning movement from a domestic to a wild setting.[97] Bird-metamorphosis is undergone often by young women fleeing their homes following some form of transgressive and/or traumatic event, usually sexual in nature. The location in which the human-turned-bird finds herself is remote and lonely.[98] Even more prevalently, bird metamorphosis is associated with grief and death; miraculous birds attend dead heroes in a state of perpetual remembrance and lamentation;[99] and characters sometimes become birds in a response to unbearable sadness.[100] These twin themes of departure and grief seem particularly strongly associated with bird metamorphoses, and this cannot but have

---

[96] Pollard (1965), 141.

[97] Forbes Irving (1990), 96-127.

[98] A good example is the case of the Minyades, who are driven mad as punishment for denying Dionysos and then are turned into night-birds which avoid daylight and haunt the wilderness. See Ant. Lib. *Met.* 10; Aelian, *VH* 3.42.

[99] E.g. the birds of Memnon, though all sources are late: the earliest is Ovid, *Met.* 13.600 ff.

[100] E.g. the sisters of Meleagros, transformed into partridges and continuing to mourn him in this state. Pliny tells us that Sophokles used the myth: see *NH* 37.40.

implications for bird-mixanthropy, especially as in the case of the Sirens there is explicit overlap: in one account, they transform into birds to search, grief-stricken, for the raped Persephone, and their mixanthropy results from this transformation.[101]

Birds are not always victims, however; they can also be symbols of aggression, either against other birds (as in much hawk-imagery), or even against humans in mythological contexts. The most famous example is the Stymphalian birds which are said to have haunted Lake Stymphalos in Arkadia until Herakles either killed them or drove them off.[102] Not only are these birds man-eating, but they are also described as damaging crops and agricultural production.[103] Borgeaud has argued convincingly that the crop-destroying properties of the birds is part of a wider myth-structure surrounding Stymphalos, to do with the human struggle to preserve agricultural production in the face of various hostile natural forces; the birds are associated with the destructive flood-waters to which the locality was indeed prone, and both birds and floods were associated with Artemis, the presiding deity of the lake.[104] Stymphalos also provides another case of bird-mixanthropy. Pausanias tells us that the temple of Artemis Stymphalia was decorated not only with images of the Stymphalian Birds, but also with bird-legged women, bird-mixanthropes very like Sirens.[105] There is no doubt that worship of Artemis in this location was aimed primarily at ensuring her support against the destructive natural forces of the area. The inclusion of the savage birds within her temple shows that they are within her domain and her control and that she is able to restrain their power. So why also the mixanthropes? A mixanthropic form depicts a juxtaposition of animal and human which raises a question constantly being posed in Arkadian mythology: which element is in control – human or animal? The Stymphalian bird-women show that human and animal meet in a tenuous and shrouded divide.

So it is possible for birds to represent either passive suffering, grief and loss, or active aggression causing suffering to others. In the Sirens' case, the dichotomy is at work, since they are both pathetic and alarming. However, it has another,

---

[101] Ovid, *Met.* 5.552-62.

[102] The fullest account of the story is given by Pausanias as part of his description of the area of Stymphalos: 8.22.4.

[103] See e.g. Diod. 3.30, which highlights their damaging effect on agriculture. In this, they may be compared with the Harpies, again bird-woman mixanthropes, whose activities were in some sense parallel: they prevented Phineus from eating by devouring and befouling any food set before him, and thus acted on a single individual rather like the Stymphalian Birds acted on a whole region and community. See Apollod. *Bibl.* 1.9.21.

[104] Borgeaud (1988), 18-19.

[105] This type of physical composition is different from the typical Archaic and Classical Greek Siren, in which the human component is limited to the face, and sometimes the arms. It is, however, shared by a relatively late (fourth century, Hellenistic and Roman) form of Siren, especially used in the decoration on sarcophagi, in which the figure is human to the waist and avian below. Examples are *LIMC s.v.* 'Seirenes' cat nos. 88 and 109.

related aspect as well, for they combine allure with savagery, the beauty of their voices and their human parts combined with the murderous quality embodied, to a large extent, in their avian parts. It is interesting to compare this ambiguity with the far simpler characterisation of the Harpies. Whereas the Sirens are never relegated wholesale to the realm of the monstrous, but retain elements of attraction and pathos, the Harpies are wholly bad. Their snatching and spoiling of Phineus' food are faintly reminiscent of the crop-spoiling activities of the Stymphalian birds. However, unlike the Stymphalian birds, the Harpies are mixanthropic. They are never depicted sympathetically, and they are never accorded cult. The contrast between the Harpies and the Sirens, both bird-mixanthropes yet so divergent in character, makes an important point: that though it is possible to isolate the associations and significance of a form of mixanthropy, it is not a constant. Whereas the Sirens are allowed to harness the duality of bird-imagery, its positive and negative aspects, the Harpies display only the destructive side.

The sea-god Glaukos is a character with a wide and rather vague distribution, made harder to pin down by his equation with the Halios Gerôn, that most generic figure of the sea. At the same time, there is one site at least in which he certainly received cult: Anthedon, in Boiotia. This location is not surprising: as Schachter points out, this area of Boiotia was 'a favourite area for fabulous figures, the most famous being Glaukos, Orion and the Triton.'[106] Our chief source for his worship here is Pausanias,[107] who tells us that its focus was a place called the *Glaukou pedêma* – 'Glaukos' Leap'. Pausanias tells us nothing of Glaukos' famous jump, but other sources repair this omission, though not with complete consistency. The common pattern is that Glaukos is a mortal, a fisherman, who discovers, in some form, the secret of immortality, whereupon he jumps into the sea and becomes a *thalattios daimôn*. Usually, the source of immortality is a magic herb;[108] in one account it is a spring.[109]

In addition to his discovery of the secret of immortality, Glaukos as deity is chiefly associated with prophecy. Pausanias tells us that on entering the sea he became a mantic god, especially in the eyes of seafarers.[110] This was clearly his main function at Anthedon. The theme of prophecy is widely used in literary sources and brings him into very close conjunction with Proteus, another marine mixanthrope. In Euripides' *Orestes*, for example, he appears to Menelaos and tells

---

[106] Schachter vol. 1 (1986), 228.

[107] 9.22.7.

[108] Although he says nothing explicitly about Glaukos' leap into the sea, Pausanias does tell of his discovery and consumption of the magic herb, after which he becomes a δαίμων ἐν θαλάσσῃ. This story is expanded by Ovid, *Met.* 13.920-48.

[109] Schol. Plat. *Resp.* 611d.

[110] Paus. 9.22.7.

him of his brother Agamemnon's death; this must surely recall Menelaos' encounter with Proteus in book four of the *Odyssey*. In this passage of the play, Glaukos is called ἀψευδὴς θεός, προφήτης and ὁ ναυτίλοισι μάντις,[111] this last clearly reinforcing his special connection with sailors. Athenaios recounts a tradition in which Apollo himself is taught prophecy by Glaukos;[112] this clearly paints him as a mythical forerunner and a primordial exponent of a *techne*, just as Cheiron was thought to have been the origin of the healing art. Glaukos was also, according to one writer,[113] regarded as the ancestor of the people of Anthedon. He is therefore a mythological founder-figure of considerable local significance, and this is surely connected with his abiding association with the seafaring way of life.

So as a deity of the sea Glaukos presents us with no great surprises: like Proteus, he is an oracular sea-god whose cult, also, was shore-based and connected with the marine realm. Like many mixanthropic gods, he was regarded as of extreme antiquity and ancestral status. His discovery and use of a miraculous herb is also perhaps faintly reminiscent of Cheiron, who in his healing capacity made use of magic herbs which grew on Pelion.[114] In Glaukos' case, however, we have no evidence for a healing function in his cult; it appears only as a mythological element.

For Glaukos, as for Thetis, we have no extant cult image; we are therefore reliant, when trying to determine how he was imagined physically, on literary descriptions and visual depictions unconnected with his quite limited worship. When, in ancient literature, his shape is described at all, it is mixanthropic and follows the pattern of Proteus and the Halios Gerôn: human above the waist but with a fish tail in place of legs.[115] Material sources are not unproblematic owing to issues of identification. A number of coins, most of them fourth century BC and most from Crete, bear a fish-tailed figure which may be Glaukos;[116] but since his form is shared by a number of other marine deities it is impossible to be certain. At the same time, the very prevalence of the merman type makes it extremely hard to believe that Glaukos was *not* imagined in this form, both in the context of his cult and more widely.

---

[111] Lines 360, 364 and 363 respectively.

[112] Athen. *Deipn.* 7.296f.

[113] Herakl. Kret. 1.24.

[114] See e.g. Nik. *Ther.* 500 ff.: Cheiron discovers a herb on Pelion which cures snakebites.

[115] See e.g. Ovid, *Met.* 13.959-62.

[116] See *LIMC s.v.* 'Glaukos I', cat. nos. 7-9.

2. Acheloos and other river gods

So far the aquatic associations of the deities discussed have been marine, but a large number of mixanthropic deities in Greek cult were gods of rivers.[117] There are several iconographic elements which they share with sea-deities, chiefly the importance of shape-changing and metamorphosis which might be thought a natural corollary to the fluidity of all water, whether salt or fresh. They have, on the other hand, some aspects of mixanthropy peculiar to themselves.

Just as with sea-deities we have observed the presence of a strong *type* which tends to obscure, and sometimes even override, so with river-gods it is sometimes difficult to identify and name individual gods; sometimes 'That is a river-god' is as far as the evidence will take one. To generalise (and for once the consistency of the imagery allows for generalisation) there are two main river-god types, used in countless local instances. The first is an anthropomorphic form, usually youthful and beardless, with taurine horns – hardly mixanthropic at all. The second has a far more obvious animal element: it combines a bull's body with a human head and face (and sometimes neck). The two types are in a sense opposites of each other: one is a humanoid with a touch of the animal about the head; the other is a bull, bulky and four-square, with a human head attached. Copious numbers of both types are to be found, especially, in South Italy and Sicily, where river-god worship was plainly important; and they also appear widely, in various contexts and media, throughout the Greek world in the Classical and Hellenistic periods.

Rich as this cache of imagery is, it is very often anonymous, and the problems of identification which surround it are considerable. Most often, one is unsure as to whether an image represents a specific local deity or one of more pan-Hellenic scope, such as Acheloos, whose worship was extremely pervasive and may occasionally have displaced a local river-god from cult and representation. We have, on the whole, little material evidence for their cults. Literary sources stress their importance in rites of passage, especially in the lives of young men,[118] and this association with private concerns appears to be uppermost, though occasionally we find them occupying some form of civic rôle. The great exception to the general dearth of material evidence is coinage, on which they are overwhelmingly popular, especially in Sicily and South

---

[117] General treatments of the nature, cults and iconography of river-gods – in addition to the entries in *RE* and Roscher – may be found in Brewster and Gais. Brewster (1997) gives a lyrical description of ancient texts and modern landscape: the result is not entirely scholarly but is well worth reading for the sense of atmosphere it creates. Gais (1978) focuses chiefly on a particular type, but at pp. 356-60 in particular gives a useful summary and discussion of iconographical trends.

[118] For a collection of the literary sources on this, see *RE s.v.* 'Flussgötter', esp. coll. 1495-6. The discussion by Larson (2007, 64-6) is valuable in that it contextualises river-gods in the wider pattern of nature deities and their worship.

Italy.[119] The problem with coinage is that it does not necessarily indicate cult in the full sense. For this reason, it has been decided to concentrate on Acheloos in this book, mentioning other river-gods where relevant along the way.[120]

In terms of location and distribution of worship, Acheloos presents us with an interesting dichotomy. On the one hand, as a deity he seems unusually localised: he is the god of the river Acheloos which runs between Akarnania and Aitolia in northern Greece.[121] At the same time, some of the earliest representations of Acheloos on his own (not involved in combat with Herakles, for example) come from outside 'Greece proper', and far away from Akarnania: from Asia Minor and from the western Greek world, south Italy and Sicily. Only rather later do we find widespread worship in Greece. And we do seem to be dealing with two (partially) separate strands of development: his mixan-thropic image, entering Greek culture from the East,[122] and his river-based cult spreading outward from Akarnania. How the two processes really relate is extremely uncertain. At some stage, the Eastern *Mannstier* type (see below) meets and merges with a native Greek river-god; by the time of most of our material and evidence, the two are almost unvaryingly fused in cult imagery.

In the western Greek world of Sicily and South Italy, Acheloos is just one of a number of local river-gods, many of whom continue to receive attention in their own right despite his success as a ubiquitous personality.[123] In Greece itself, the situation is a little different. Though there are problems with reading evidence on this point, it seems that here he dominates more definitely; he has far fewer local variants to contend with. His enthusiastic adoption into Attic

---

[119] The sheer scale of this manifestation may be grasped by scrutinising their entry in Head's index (1911), which spans two pages (955-6) and reflects the immense abundance of local variants, whose iconography is strikingly consistent. For detailed discussion of this, see Jenkins (1976), 26-30 and Rutter (2001), passim.

[120] Despite the relative abundance of material concerning his cult and his representation, Acheloos has been accorded relatively little attention from scholars. The monograph by Isler (1970) treats chiefly the trends and developments in his representation. The images discussed often come from religious contexts, but their full implications for our understanding of his cult are not explored (this is not the real aim of the work). Nowhere does Acheloos' cult receive undivided attention, instead receiving tangential mention as part of larger subjects, or localised treatment with regard to individual sites or artefacts. The most thorough treatments are in reference books, particularly in the *RE*. It is hoped that the current study will do something to flesh out our picture of Acheloos' worship, and particularly how it compares with other mixanthropic cults.

[121] There were other, far less famous rivers of the same name in Arkadia, Achaia, Lydia, Mykonos and the Troad; these, however, were not associated with the god Acheloos.

[122] On early Eastern Acheloos-images, see Isler (1970), 76-82.

[123] Sometimes it is hard to tell whether Acheloos or a local river god is depicted in the art or coinage of a region, given the similarity of iconography and Acheloos' pervasive quality; for an example of this difficulty see Isler (1970), 81-2: discussion of coins of Paphos showing a Mannstier called 'Bokaros', which Isler takes to be a local title of Acheloos; this remains, however, controver-sial.

and central Greek cult causes a profusion of imagery. The use of his image changes, also, as will be described.

Among other river-gods, Acheloos is represented, in Ionia and the Greek west, on countless coins,[124] gems and other artefacts. We know, too, that in certain sites he was accorded full cult. At Metapontum he had games in his honour; coins, which may have served as prizes, bear the words ΑΧΕΛΟΙΟ ΑΕΘΛΟΝ (though, interestingly, on these Acheloos is shown as mainly human rather than as a man-faced bull).[125] It is from Greece itself, however, that the most substantial evidence of worship derives.

In north-western Greece as at Metapontum, Acheloos was associated with athletic contests; a festival of games was part of his Akarnanian cult.[126] It is possible that Acheloos' most famous mythical exploit, wrestling with Herakles, contributed to this association (though of course he was not the victor!). In any case, he appears to have been a deity of considerable importance in Akarnania, his image dominating the local coinage at times when the region was trying to assert its individual identity and character. In the Hellenistic Period, for example, the Akarnanian League produced staters with an unusual Acheloos-type, youthful and beardless heads in profile with horns and taurine necks.[127] Acheloos was clearly a figure sufficiently closely associated with the region to lend himself to programmatic exploitation in this way.

Further north, at Dodona, Acheloos seems to have had a part to play in the oracular cult of Zeus Naios. Ephoros, transmitted by Macrobius, tells us that 'In practically all of them [i.e. oracular responses] the god is accustomed to command to sacrifice to Acheloos.'[128] This statement leaves much uncertain. Was Acheloos the only god included in this injunction? Was the consulter meant to sacrifice to him there in Dodona, or back in his native region; or did it involve a special pilgrimage south to Akarnania? The presence of a shrine to Acheloos in Dodona suggests the former and backs up Ephoros' statement. But at the same time, given that Dodona and Akarnania were both within the northern Greek massif, Acheloos' cult in the latter would surely have gained in prominence thanks to the endorsement of the oracle.[129]

---

[124] By contrast, within Greece itself, only Akarnania and Aitolia make use of Acheloos' image on coinage.

[125] See Head (1911), 76; Rutter (2001), 132 and plate 27, no. 1491 (a very clear photograph).

[126] Schol. Hom. *Il.* 24.616.

[127] See e.g. Imhoof-Blumer (1878), 175, no. 22; also Isler (1970), cat. no. 96.

[128] Ephoros, *FGrHist* 70 F 20 (Macr. *Sat.* 5.18.6).

[129] Parke (1967, 153) believes that the god's response amounted to the *propagation* of the Acheloos-cult, and accounted in part for his widespread worship. This is plausible for the Greek mainland; less so perhaps for other regional centres of Acheloos-worship, such as south Italy, which seem to have followed a path quite different from the mainland in this respect.

Important cult sites of Acheloos in central Greece were in Megara, Oropos and Attica. The first of these was the oldest, said to have been set up by Theagenes, the local tyrant in the seventh century; our one source of information on this is Pausanias, who mentions only an altar.[130] The Oropos worship is similarly scanty, and again is only attested by Pausanias, who tells us that Acheloos was one of many deities depicted on the altar of the Amphiareion; before one consulted Amphiaraos, one sacrificed to all the deities named on the altar. In his particular panel on the altar, Acheloos is depicted alongside the nymphs and Pan, and the river Kephis(s)os.[131] This company is typical of a huge proportion of Acheloos' worship, throughout Greece; it is an arrangement that finds most frequent expression in Attic sites, which will now be discussed.

Acheloos-worship in Attica was chiefly located in caves, and its main span of time was from the fifth to the third century BC. Never do we find Acheloos worshipped alone. The nymphs are his most constant cult-companions; but various finds show a range of possibilities. Acheloos appears repeatedly as one of a group of cave-dwelling deities whose numbers are flexible but whose characteristics are dominated by the themes of birth and plenty. He has this group function in common with Cheiron, significantly, who in a Thessalian sacred cave shares worship with the nymphs and Pan, among others (see below). In the case of Acheloos, these group appearances are in contrast with his depiction in Eastern and west-Greek artefacts, in which he tends to be alone. Attic usage especially slots him into an existing canon of rustic deities.

The most expressive example of an Attic relief in which Acheloos is represented as one of a group in this way is the dedication of Xenokrateia (see fig. 13). The shrine in which the dedication was made was at Echelidai, near the river Kephisos. Two dedications have been found, one by a certain Kephisodotos to the nymphs and Hermes, the other that of Xenokrateia, a mother, made apparently in gratitude for some less than certain divine favour.[132] This latter is addressed to 'Kephisos and the *sumbômoi theoi*', who are represented on the carved picture that accompanies the text. Not all the deities shown can be securely identified, but Acheloos can. On the stele is also a list, naming the gods: Hestia, Kephisos (reminding us of the Oropos monument), Apollo

---

[130] Paus. 1.41.2. Interestingly, Theagenes' institution of the cult coincides with his re-direction of the flow of the local river, the Rhys: a placatory gesture to the god of the waters? The problem with this instance is the highly mythologized nature of Theagenes; see Nagy and Figueira edd. (1985), 143-5.

[131] Paus. 1.34.3-5. See Schachter (1986), vol. I, 1. The notion of a preliminary sacrifice to Acheloos (albeit to others as well) is faintly reminiscent of the Dodona injunction and Acheloos' rôle there. Perhaps even more pertinent to this point, however, is the remark made in Grenfell & Hunt Oxyrrh. Pap. vol 2. 221 col. 9: πολλοὺς πρὸ Δήμητρος θύειν Ἀχελώῳ ὅτι πάντων ποταμῶν ὄνομα ὁ Ἀχελῷος καὶ ἐξ ὕδατος καρπός. This seems to be another interesting case of Acheloos receiving a preliminary sacrifice before that of a major deity.

[132] On this, Parker (2005), 430.

Pythios, Leto, Artemis Lochia and Eileithyia (these last two goddesses of childbirth), Acheloos, Kallirhoë, Geraistan Nymphs of Birth, Rhapso.[133]

Fig. 13

Not only is Acheloos in company, but that company is largely familiar from other instances of his worship, and has a clear overall character: kourotrophy. Parker in a recent discussion remarks that the plurality of these deities and their function were not unconnected: 'The tendency of the Greeks to appeal to a plurality of gods, to recruit a team, appears in this area of life perhaps more clearly than in any other.'[134] When enlisting aid for the survival and growth of children (or crops or animals), the Greeks generally tried to cover all the bases, so to speak. Within the 'team', each constituent deity had his or her particular credentials, and Acheloos is no exception. Of his inclusion in this case, and the inclusion of Kallirhoë and Kephisos, Parker says: 'Rivers and springs, this sanctuary reminds us, are almost as important *kourotrophoi* as is earth.'[135]

So Acheloos, along with his fellow river-god Kephisos and his daughter, the spring Kallirhoë, is a very suitable inclusion in the divine group, in this as at other sites. It is impossible to say what individual aspects of Acheloos are obscured by his incorporation into the generic collective. It would be desirable to know more about the Akarnanian cult and its regional character, and about his precise function at Dodona. Without further evidence, however, this is not possible.

I turn now from cult to composition. In our one explicit description of his form in a literary retelling of myth, the emphasis is on his shape-changing, though

---

[133] The inscription from the site which lists the deities is *IG* II² 4547 & 4548; see Isler (1970), 35-6 and cat. no. 30.

[134] Parker (2005), 430.

[135] Parker (2005), 430. The fertility-aspect of Acheloos will be discussed further when we come to examine his anatomy and its significance.

mixanthropy is also present. Sophokles in the *Trachiniai* (lines 9-14) describes Acheloos' attempt to win the hand of Deianeira by wrestling with Herakles, her other suitor. He transforms into, successively, a bull, a snake, and finally a bull-faced man like the Minotaur. Taurine mixanthropy appears as one of various assumed shapes. As will later be argued in more detail, there is no doubt that here mixanthropy is an interloper into an existing motif of animal shape-changing, a spin-off from patterns of visual representation which are the artistic corollary to a literary emphasis on transformation.

The visual depictions of Acheloos are almost undeviatingly mixanthropic. His non-cultic representations, particularly on painted vases, reveal a multiplicity of possible forms, as artists follow their own aims or respond to the requirements of the context they portray. He can be a man-faced bull, as in figs. 14-16 (this is overwhelmingly the most common form); less frequent types depict him as a man-faced bull with arms, a taurine centaur, and, in one unique and striking instance, a

Fig. 14

Triton, human as far as the base of the pectoral muscles, beneath which an intricately scaled fish tail undulates away to the viewer's right instead of human legs and feet.[136] Overall, he tends to be drawn into individual canons of depiction; when he is shown as a centaur, for example, he adopts some of their mannerisms, such as throwing stones. The Triton-Acheloos is clearly making use of another established form, that of the marine deity.[137] It is, however, the man-faced bull which is most successful in the long run. This form's success may well owe much its dominance in cult representation. The cult images generally are far more uniform than those not explicitly connected with cult, and far less responsive to short-term artistic trends.[138]

---

[136] Red figure Attic stamnos by Oltos; c. 520 BC. Herakles fights Acheloios. (London BM 1839,0214.70; *LIMC s.v.* 'Acheloos', cat. no. 245). For these experimental and relatively unpopular modes of representing Acheloos, see Isler (1970), 13-17.

[137] As Isler (1970, 16) points out, the artist, Oltos, has felt the need to label Acheloos, as if to say, 'Das ist Acheloos, nicht Triton, wie du bestimmt meinst!' The stamnos in question is number 84 in Isler's catalogue.

[138] On this relative conservatism, see Isler in *LIMC s.v.* 'Acheloos', p. 30.

Fig. 15

Less common than the man-faced bull in the reliefs, but also noteworthy, is the type which depicts Acheloos merely as a mask, a detached face with taurine ears and horns, positioned on a cult table within the scene or on the wall of the cave shown in the relief, as in fig. 17.[139] This mask phenomenon is highly significant when compared with other trends in Greek mixanthropy, and its relation to Acheloos will be discussed further in Chapter 8.

Acheloos' mixanthropy is dominated by the bull, though other species do appear occasionally. On a mid-sixth-century gem from Falerii a fish occupies the field beside him.[140] The Oltos Acheloos is fish-tailed. Fish imagery is of course quite in keeping with the water association of Acheloos, but the bull is far more in evidence throughout, and at the same time is less obviously connected with water. I shall first say more about Acheloos' water-associations (for they are not as simple as they seem), then about their connection with the bull.

Acheloos' water-associations seem at first sight simple because, on one level at least, he is the divine personification of a particular river, in a particular place. The river Acheloos rises in the Pindos mountains, and further south forms the

---

[139] Even in cases where the body is shown, the face is very frequently of a pronounced quality, often full frontal; striking in this regard are a number of votive reliefs from Lokri in Magna Graecia which show Acheloos standing with body in profile but face turned full to the viewer, and a row of nymphs' heads above. (An example is *LIMC s.v.* 'Acheloos', cat. no. 206; Reggio Calabria Mus. Naz. 118; early fourth century in date.)

[140] *LIMC s.v.* 'Acheloos', cat. no. 221; Berlin Staatl. Mus. F 136.

border between Akarnania and Aitolia.[141] Other rivers in Greece share its name, but there is no disputing the fact that the god Acheloos originates in this region and landscape; as we have seen, his cult continued to have firm connections with that area. It is not hard to imagine that, as in the case of Pan, a cult that was at first local, highly place-specific, later spread and achieved popularity all over the Greek world, perhaps sometimes supplanting existing river-gods and their worship.

Fig. 16

This is a plausible model for the basic shape of events; but it is not the whole truth. Behind, beside or beneath Acheloos' persona as Akarnanian/Aitolian river-god appears to have been, in our earliest sources, a much wider water-related identity, not restricted to an individual river. In the first place, sources, many early, give Acheloos a place among water-divinities whose scope is universal: his father is usually given as Okeanos;[142] he is the oldest of the rivers,[143] and kingly,[144] and is father to many water-related nymphs,[145] and to the Sirens.[146] From the texts available, it is impossible to gain access to a time when Acheloos was purely a local figure. But there is more: D'Alessio has argued that a disputed line in the *Iliad* (21.195) provides potential evidence that at one stage Acheloos was considered to be the origin and 'overseer' of all the waters of the world, a

---

[141] Brewster (1997), 9-14.

[142] Hes. *Theog.* 337-40.

[143] Macr. *Sat.* 5.18.10.

[144] Hom. *Il.* 21.195.

[145] E.g. Kallirhoe (Apollod. *Bibl.* 3.7.5), and Dirke (Eur. *Bacch.* 519-20). See Larson (2001), 4, 6, 148.

[146] Apollod. *Bibl.* 1.3.4

function then shifted to Okeanos.[147] The cosmic function of Acheloos is strongly connected with some Eastern mythological figures.[148] Both the form and the character of Acheloos seem to owe much to Eastern models. However the adoption of the Eastern model, with all its associations, into Greek usage,[149] was probably only possible because of an existing association between bulls and water-deities.

Fig. 17

[147] If this line is excised as being a later interpolation, then Acheloos, not Okeanos, is given that universal function. D'Alessio cites various other texts to support the existence of this alternative and earlier version which gives Acheloos primacy. But he also suggests that, in some accounts at least, 'Acheloos … was a figure in functional competition with Ocean', rather than simply being superseded by him (D'Alessio [2004], 33). In any case, the implications of this argument take us even further away from where we started, with a river in a northern backwater; they take us back, also, into comparison with Eastern motifs and parallels. It appears that we are dealing with a fusion between a cosmic figure, substantially derived from Eastern sources, and a local Greek river-god; the latter seems to have been overlaid with the former, creating a complex and wide-ranging entity whose water-associations encompass all rivers and also, in some traditions, the sea. For Acheloos as linguistically synonymous with water, see Macrob. *Sat.* 5.18.4-11.

[148] D'Alessio remarks (2004, 26) that it is 'difficult … to trace any functional relationship between the Greek water-god and his oriental model.' He does go on, however, to explore some of the overlapping motifs between Acheloos and some prominent near-Eastern mixanthropes, who are also water-associated. The prominence of the Mannstier type, especially – in cult imagery – the more Eastern variety with the human neck, sets Acheloos apart from other river-gods, as has been said; the imposition of the Eastern form on a Greek figure surely reflects the vestigial strands of Eastern mythology caught up in his persona.

[149] For the Eastern origins both of the form and of some mythological aspects of Acheloos, see D'Alessio (2004), 26-7.

This association is articulated both by the river-gods and by Poseidon, the latter being also the most consistent focus for the connection between water and horses.[150] (In fact, bulls and horses receive very similar mythological treatment in this regard.) Supernatural horses often feature alongside springs, rivers and the sea in myths[151] (though the figure of Poseidon tends to be discernible in the background of the story, suggesting that he

Fig. 18

remains pivotal to the relationship). Some mythological episodes appear to show bulls and water similarly linked, but they are few. Bulls sometimes emerge from the sea. In the myth of Hippolytos, for example, as told in Euripides' play, the young man's death is brought about when his chariot-horses are panicked by a monstrous bull which comes out of the sea; the beast is sent by Poseidon, but none the less the bull-water relationship is strong. Likewise, when a bull emerges from the sea to abduct Europe, that bull is Zeus in disguise; but it is significant that this particular animal form is chosen to effect a sea-passage.[152] We can see that the connection between Acheloos' bull parts and his watery domain is part of a much wider pattern of association. However, this connection does not appear always to have been so self-evident that it did not require explanation; Strabo, for example, offers a rationalising account in which

---

[150] Reflected most directly in his title Hippios, and in horse-related rituals in his worship. The Thessalians hold an *equestre certamen* in his honour (Serv. *Verg. Georg.* 1.12). The same author (loc. cit.) also tells us that the Illyrians annually throw a horse into the sea for Poseidon; and from Pausanias we hear that the Argives would throw bridled horses into Dine, a spring of fresh water welling up in the sea, as part of his cult – Paus. 8.7.2. For a possible instance of horse-masked ritual in his honour in Arkadia, see Mylonopoulos (2003), 118.

[151] For example, Pegasos was thought to have created various springs by striking the ground with his hoof: see e.g. Paus. 9.31.3; 2.31.9. Hippocamps are also frequent participants in marine *thiasoi* depicted in art. In addition, it is interesting that occasionally a river-god, or at least a river-haunting mythological figure, can be conceived in centaur rather than taurine form. Examples are Nessos and Euenos; however, neither of these figures received worship, instead being consigned purely to the 'monster' category. There must be a relationship between the lack of worship and the different form, but in which direction it would function one cannot say: did the centaur form preclude cult honours (after all, centaurs are almost never worshipped), or did a monstrous, non-cultic rôle lead to them being depicted as centaurs rather than in the form used for cult-receiving river-gods? It is impossible to answer this question; but there is an undeniable link between their rôle in myth and the choice of form for their depiction.

[152] Apollod. *Bibl.* 3.1.1.

Acheloos' bull form derives from the bull-like roaring of the waters of the river Acheloos, whose windings were called 'horns', thus adding another element of explanation.[153] Perhaps by Strabo's time the traditional bull-water connection had lost its force.

Does the bull have any other associations which should be taken into account as potentially important to the character of Acheloos? Forbes Irving points to a connection between bull-form and fertility, which is undoubtedly an important strand of significance.[154] Fertility is one of the haziest and most misused concepts in Greek religion; here, however, in the case of Acheloos, we are fortunate enough to find an explicit connection. Acheloos is one of two possessors and sources, in myth, of the famous and ubiquitous *cornucopia*, the horn of plenty whose rôle as a detached emblem of fertility ranges from featuring in Hellenistic coin propaganda to being the accessory of the goddess Tyche/Fortuna. One version of its origins makes it the horn of Amaltheia, who is either a nymph or a goat.[155] The other attributes it to Acheloos.[156] The context for the latter account is almost always Acheloos' combat with Herakles. Though they fight ostensibly for the hand of Deianeira, the cornucopia is in fact just as dominant a theme in the story, if not more so: Herakles breaks it off, gaining a prize no less great than his bride.[157] In visual depictions, Herakles is frequently shown grasping the horn; on one (fig. 18), the horn is shown already detached and lying on the floor, though Herakles and Acheloos still fight (presumably a case of synoptic composition).

This myth puts Acheloos in the rôle of monstrous adversary; but there is no doubt that the cornucopia is also an important element in his cult persona. Horns are an indispensable feature of his iconographic representation;[158] moreover, sometimes the cornucopia is shown in the same cult relief as Acheloos, in highly significant contexts. The most striking example is a relief from Ilissos from the second half of the third century BC, which shows the

---

[153] Strabo 10.2.19.

[154] Forbes Irving (1990), 43: 'With both Dionysos and the river-gods bull form seems connected with metaphors of fertility, as it was with the Mesopotamian bulls.'

[155] Sources differ; the horn, however, is always – when species is specified – a cow's/bull's. See e.g. Pherekydes, *FGrHist* 3 F 42.

[156] See e.g. Ovid, *Met.* 9.87-8. A significant number of sources find a way of combining the two origins; see e.g. Strabo 10.2.19. In Hyginus (*Fab.* 182) Amaltheia is Acheloos' sister and hands over the horn to him; Apollodoros (*Bibl.* 2.7.5) tells that Acheloos, having been robbed of his horn by Herakles, offered the hero the cornucopia, the horn of Amaltheia, instead (the trade being accepted).

[157] See e.g. Apollod. *Bibl.* 2.7.5.

[158] The importance of the horn to river-gods generally is reflected in the name Bokaros, 'Bull-horned', used of river-gods in, for example, Paphos and Salamis. See Isler (1970), 81-2. It is also significant that while the representation of river-gods is variable, with most having a mainly human form, in contrast with the Mannstier Acheloos, the horn is indispensable, always present, and the key to identification.

dead coming before Persephone and Hades in the underworld.[159] Acheloos is present in mask-form (in fact, Hades sits on the mask); Persephone holds the cornucopia. Here we have departed from the mythological expression of the relationship which sees the cornucopia as something wrested from the god to his detriment. Acheloos and the cornucopia co-exist within a scene packed with significance. In this underworld setting, both aspects of the chthonic – death and fertility – are expressed, and Acheloos is associated with both.[160] His fertility aspect tends to be to the fore, reflected in his frequent juxtaposition with Dionysos, the nymphs and Hermes in pastoral mode. But echoes of his death-associations are occasionally felt; for example, he is the father of the Sirens, who live in the underworld,[161] are companions of Persephone,[162] and feature prominently on grave monuments from the fourth century onwards.[163]

So, diversity and similarity co-exist in mixanthropic deities of water. On the one hand, there is variety of species: bull-parts for river-gods, fish tails for sea deities, and for both the startling welter of different forms taken on during shape-changing. On the other hand, shape-changing and metamorphosis are constant ingredients. They reflect the fact that, in myth, humans are almost always attempting to grasp these beings (whether in lust or anger or the desire for information), and their victims are using all their slipperiness, all their transformative power, to elude them. How this relationship reflects on the quality of aquatic mixanthropes *as deities*, as recipients of cult, will be examined in a later section.

---

[159] *LIMC s.v.* 'Acheloos', cat. no. 204; Isler (1970), 38-9 and cat. no. 35; Athens NM 1778.

[160] Isler (1970), 39.

[161] Plat. *Kra.* 403d.

[162] Eur. *Hel.* 168-78.

[163] Tsiafakis (2003), 77-78.

Chapter II
Terrestrial mixanthropes

1. Horse mixanthropes: Cheiron and Demeter Melaina

The juxtaposition of these two personalities is intended chiefly to demonstrate a cardinal truth about divine mixanthropy: that a single animal species cannot be considered to have an absolute and permanent symbolic meaning. A horse element (the example treated here) can carry completely different associations and significance, depending on context. We cannot use mixanthropic deities to build up a vocabulary of animal symbols in ancient thought.

There are various small traces of Cheiron-worship in the Greek world. For example, a boundary-marker discovered bearing the word ΧΙΡΩΝΟΣ, a genitive, suggests a temenos at Poseidonia, in S. Italy.[1] Little can be done with such scraps, beyond noting that they corroborate the status of Cheiron as a cult-receiving deity. However, somewhat more substantial evidence comes from Thessaly, where there are two attested sites of worship. In a cave near Pharsalos in Phthia,[2] on a spur of Mount Othrys, was found a long fourth-century inscription (still in situ but now rendered largely illegible by lichen)[3] recording the favours granted by various deities to a person called Pantalkes who, roughly a century before, set up a dedication to the nymphs.[4] Cheiron is included in the fourth-century text, which is long and metrical, alongside numerous others: the nymphs, Pan, Hermes, Apollo, Heracles and his companions (whoever they are), Cheiron, Asklepios and Hygieia. Cheiron, the inscription tells us, gave Pantalkes wisdom and musical ability, in line with his mythological qualities. This inscription is an interesting variation on the divine collective which so often features in cave-cult: some familiar faces are there (Pan, Hermes, the nymphs), but in addition some less typical ones, including

---

[1] For a somewhat over-imaginative reconstruction of Cheiron's religious significance in this region, see Picard (1951); see also Guarducci (1948).

[2] For the cave and its contents, see Giannopoulos (1912) and (1919); Levi (1923).

[3] On the inscription, see Comparetti (1921-2); Decourt (1995), 90-94, no. 73.

[4] On Pantalkes and other real-life nympholepts, see Larson (2001), 13-20; for nympholepsy as a mythological motif, *ibid.* 66-71. See also Ustinova (2009), 61-4.

Cheiron himself; besides, there is an unusual level of differentiation, by which each deity is described as having contributed his or her special property to the fortunate Pantalkes. This is more nuanced than the groupings discussed with regard to Acheloos in which the divine functions of the several deities seem substantially the same. However, although Cheiron is distinguished, he is not prioritised above the other recipients of worship in the cave.

A second site in Thessaly is at once more promising and more problematic. The Hellenistic geographer Herakleides[5] describes the following site and ritual on the summit of Mount Pelion:

> On the peaks of the mountain's top there is the cave called the Cheironion and a hieron of Zeus Aktaios,[6] to which, at the rising of the Dog Star, at the time of greatest heat, the most distinguished of the citizens and those in the prime of life ascend, having been chosen in the presence of the priest, wrapped in thick new fleeces. So great is the cold on the mountain.[7]

The Greek archaeologist Arvanitopoulos, whose work in the early years of the twentieth century added so greatly to our knowledge of Thessalian material remains, partially excavated a site on the Pliassidi peak of Pelion which may be identifiable as the one described by Herakleides.[8] It does not, however, yield much further insight into the relevant ritual practices; in addition to a cave were found the remains of two small buildings which Arvanitopoulos interpreted as shrines, one of Cheiron and one of Zeus Akraios. However, this is tendentious, especially the notion that Cheiron would have had a built shrine in addition to his sacred cave.

The Cheironion mentioned in the text above must have been equated with the mythological cave-home of Cheiron on Mount Pelion. The word Cheironion may itself suggest worship, as does Thetideion, though this is not certain. The ritual described by Herakleides has as its chief recipient Zeus Akraios,[9] whose cult was of great regional significance, but Buxton is surely right to argue that

---

[5] The text in question was originally attributed to Dikaiarchos, and appears under his name in *FHistGr* 2 F 60. For the attribution to Herakleides: Pfister (1951).

[6] This spelling of the title is generally thought to be a mistake of Herakleides: inscriptions from the area (e.g. *IG* IX² 1103, 1105, 1008, 1009.54, 1110, 1128) support the variant *Akraios*.

[7] Herakleides 2.8: Ἐπ' ἄκρας δὲ τῆς τοῦ ὄρους κορυφῆς σπήλαιόν ἐστι τὸ καλούμενον Χειρώνιον καὶ Διὸς Ἀκταίου ἱερόν ἐφ' ὃ κατὰ κυνὸς ἀνατολὴν κατὰ τὸ ἀκμαιότατον καῦμα ἀναβαίνουσι τῶν πολιτῶν οἱ ἐπιφανέστατοι καὶ ταῖς ἡλικίαις ἀκμάζοντες, ἐπιλεχθέντες ἐπὶ τοῦ ἱερέως, ἐνεζωσμένοι κώδια τρίποκα καινά. τοιοῦτον συμβαίνει ἐπὶ τοῦ ὄρους τὸ ψῦχος εἶναι.

[8] See Arvanitopoulos (1911); Philippson (1944), 147; Chourmouziades (1982), 98. Unfortunately, the site excavated by Arvanitopoulos is not now possible to locate; during my visit to Thessaly in November 2009 the Commander of the Pliassidi Air Force base very generously facilitated some exploration in the area, but no ancient remains were found.

[9] There has been a determination in the older scholarship to edge Cheiron into greater prominence within the rite; for example F. Stählin (1924, 43), believed (on the basis of no evidence) that Zeus was a relative newcomer into the partnership.

Cheiron's cave, steeped in mythological significance, would have contributed to the function of the ritual as part of the symbolic 'furniture' of the site.[10] So what kind of ritual was it, and how might the Cheironion have fitted into its performance?

The main question is whether we can relate it to Cheiron's mythological rôle as a nurse and educator of heroes. In myth, the centaur rears and tutors an impressive number of child heroes, feeding them strengthening foods and equipping them with aristocratic skills such as hunting and music. His care of Achilles is especially popular among vase-painters; an example can be seen at fig. 19. Can we see the Pelion ritual as forming a cultic counterpart to this rôle, demonstrating that Cheiron had a kourotrophic function as a deity, overseeing the development and the transitions of the young?

This possibility presents difficulties. First, it elides the rôle of Zeus, to whom the ritual is chiefly directed. Second, the men taking part in the ritual cannot be seen as historical counterparts of the young heroes whom Cheiron assisted to adulthood. They are described by Herakleides as *akmazontes*, that is, at the *akmê* of their strength: young, certainly, but already in adulthood, not just about to enter it. This is not a male, Thessalian equivalent of 'playing the bear' at Brauron. Like

Fig. 19

some rites of passage, the ritual does appear to involve a temporary stepping into the wild, through the donning of fleeces, primitive clothing associated with herders and huntsmen, and as Buxton points out, Cheiron's cave would have assisted in this symbolic process, since caves, like fleeces, represent the realm of 'Outside and Before', in contrast with the sphere of human civilisation. However, the element of adolescent transition cannot be extrapolated from the scanty evidence. It is worth noting, however, that Cheiron (spelled Chiron) appears as one of several deities in a seventh-century BC dedicatory inscription[11] found near the temple of Apollo Karneios on Thera, in the vicinity of which was also a

---

[10] Buxton (1994), 93-4.

[11] *IG* XII.3, 360. See Vogel (1978), 218.

sacred cave which was apparently used in ephebic rites.[12] This provides a slight suggestion that Cheiron's mythical rôle as nurse and educator found ritual expression, but it is far from substantial, and far from Pelion.

That Thessalian Cheiron had a kourotrophic aspect as a deity is not really to be doubted. It is made clear by the juxtaposition of Cheiron with the nymphs in the Pharsalos cave inscription. This connection may be seen as referring to the nurturing function of both, dominant in myth. For example, Pindar makes the hero Jason say that he was nursed in infancy by Cheiron, his mother Philyra and his wife Chariklo, both nymphs, and by his nymph daughters, the kourai hagnai.[13] However, vague kourotrophy is one thing, overseeing ritual transitions is another.

Cheiron's divine function which, in Thessaly, seems most unambiguously attested is healing. Plutarch relates that the Magnetes brought offerings to Cheiron as a healer.[14] Earlier, Herakleides tells us that a dynasty of physicians living at the foot of Mount Pelion, who practiced their craft strictly free of charge, traced their line back to the centaur himself, though no worship is actually mentioned.[15] In his healing capacity, Cheiron was strongly associated with the natural forces of his mountain home. Cheiron, Pelion and the mountain's native healing herbs form an inseparable triad in the works of many ancient authors. This is reflected especially strongly in a fragment of the Hellenistic author Nikandros' *Theriaka*, which gives the following medicinal instruction:

> Choose first the medicinal root of Cheiron,
> Which carries the name of the centaur, Kronos' son; Cheiron once
> Discovered and took note of it on a snowy ridge of Pelion.
> It is encircled by waving leaves like sweet marjoram,
> And its flowers are golden in appearance. Its root, at the
> Surface and not deep, resides in the grove of Pelethronios.[16]

Cheiron, then, is the mythical discoverer of a major natural resource, and a form of culture-hero. This plainly accords with his healing persona among the Magnesians. He gives his name to the plant called 'Cheironeion', whose properties are described by Theophrastos: it is used to cure the bites of snakes,

---

[12] Philippson (1944), 150-55. She posits a process whereby the cult travelled from Pelion in Thessaly to the Peloponnese, and from there to Thera; it retained, she argues, its Thessalian character, including the cave-association and the kourotrophic element. The evidence adduced is somewhat questionable. (For example, Apollodoros' account of Cheiron's expulsion from Pelion to Malea – *Bibl.* 2.5.4. – is taken as referring, mythologically, to the first leg of the journey.) The theory is not, however, *per se* implausible.

[13] Pind. *Pyth.* 4.102-3.

[14] Plut. *Quaest Conv.* 3.1.

[15] Herakleides 2.12.

[16] Nikandros, *Theriaka* 500-505: πρώτην μὲν Χείρωνος ἐπαλθέα ῥίζαν ἑλέσθαι, | Κενταύρου Κρονίδαο φερώνυμον, ἥν ποτε Χείρων | Πηλίου ἐν νιφόεντα κιχὼν ἐφράσσατο δειρῇ. | τῆς μὲν ἀμαρακόεσσα χυτῇ περιδέδρομε χαίτη, | ἄνθεα δὲ χρύσεια φαείνεται· ἡ δ' ὑπὲρ αἴης | ῥίζα καὶ οὐ βυθόωσα Πελεθρόνιον νάπος ἴσχει.

spiders and other venomous creatures.[17] So Cheiron in a sense embodies the healing properties of Mount Pelion itself, in the form of its native herbs. More generally, literary sources stress almost without exception his kindness, justness and goodwill towards humanity. In this regard, literary characterisation and divine function are in accord.

How – if at all – do these benign characteristics connect with Cheiron's physical form? It is meaningless to make vague assertions about the fertility-associations of the horse. Cheiron's equine element has no absolute and intrinsic meaning. However, it does operate within a set of piquant contrasts in Greek thought, and these are illuminating. In fact, Cheiron's centaur form cannot be understood at all without an examination of his relationship to the other centaurs, a relationship which mythological episodes often bring to the fore. However, this, in turn, cannot be understood without taking into account the two sides to the horse in Greek thought.

Horses had their place within the reality of Greek life; but they did not have the domestic ubiquity of the ox, or the pastoral ubiquity of the goat. Rather, they belonged to certain spheres – war, hunting – and to certain groups, chiefly the richer classes. They were not generally used for haulage; and mules and asses would have been more widely used as saddle-animals among the poorer elements of Greek societies.[18] None the less, they had their place within the canon of domestic animals as equipment for human activity. Their rôle in myth, however, often goes against this fact. A significant number of stories, some well-known, some less so, show the horse as an aggressive, destructive and terrifying creature – to all intents and purposes a *thêr* – a wild beast – rather than a docile honorary member of the human community.

The best-known examples of horses in this rôle are the horses of Diomedes, which probably owe their fame, both ancient and modern, to their inclusion in the myth-complex of the labours of Herakles. Diomedes is a Thracian king, who feeds his guests to his murderous horses in drastic transgression of the laws of guest-friendship. Herakles defeats him, and pays him in kind, causing him to be devoured by his own horses.[19] The myth has an interesting finishing touch: released by King Eurystheus (to whom Herakles has presented them), the horses wander on Mount Olympos and are themselves there eaten by wild beasts: clearly, for all their savagery, they are no match for the *thêres* of the

---

[17] Theophrast. *Peri Phytôn* IX.11.1-7. It is clear from the description of the plant (golden flowers) that it is the same species as described in the Nicander passage.

[18] As Hodkinson (1988, 64) puts it, 'The horse was the useless animal *par excellence* in an era before the invention of harness enabled it to be used for traction.' Its value was largely as an indicator of wealth and status. On cattle used for draught rather than horses, see Jameson (1988), 94-6.

[19] Diod. 4.15; Hyg. *Fab.* 250. The animals also consume Abderos, Herakles' servant, who has been set to guard them: Strabo 7, fr. 47.

mountain.[20] Sometimes the horses are explicitly mares, sometimes stallions. There exist a number of variations of this theme of the man-eating horses who eventually turn against their owner: the very strength of this theme in myth reflects the tense symbolic potency of the horse.[21]

A perennial theme in the accounts is the horse's ambiguous and perilous quality. It is an animal which is meant to serve its owner, even though in some cases the use to which it is put is unnatural in itself: devouring of guests, abnegation of intercourse, failure to maintain pastoral land, a transgressive sacrifice. However, the horse turns on its owner, and the transgression involved in its use rebounds on the human perpetrator. The horse may be the instrument of a wider punishment; but there is still huge significance in the repeated choice of this particular animal to take this rôle. The domesticity of the horse is not, in myth, to be relied on.

Just as there are two sides to the character of the horse, so there are two kinds of centaur, the mixanthrope in which the horse-form is most famously and consistently incorporated. Both myth and representation are used to make and keep a very definite divide between, on the one hand, 'the centaurs' as a group, sometimes named but more often an anonymous rabble (called here, for convenience of expression, the group-centaurs), and on the other the virtuous individuals, Pholos and − far more prominently − Cheiron.[22] Cheiron's parentage sets him apart from the group-centaurs: he is the son of Kronos and the nymph Philyra, who are caught by Rhea *in flagrante* and are transformed by Kronos into horses.[23] Whereas his parentage is not far removed from the god-nymph combination typical of heroes (on the face of it at least, before the metamorphosis element is taken into account), the way in which the group-centaurs come into being recalls much more strongly the 'recipes' for monsters to be found in myth. They are the products of an unnatural, a transgressive union. Ixion, legendary king of Thessaly, attempts to rape Hera but is thwarted by Zeus, who substitutes for his wife an *eidôlon* made of cloud; from the unwitting coupling of Ixion with this cloud comes Kentauros, the progenitor of the race.[24] So the difference between the origin of Cheiron and of the group-centaurs is striking, though it should be noted that in the former case too, transgression and boundary-crossing are involved, in the forms of adultery and metamorphosis. Key to the latter,

---

[20] Aelian *HA* 15.25; Apollod. *Bibl.* 2.5.8. Domestic animals released into the wild do not always become hapless victims. Those of Geryon's cattle which giver Herakles the slip become *thêres* in the mountains of Thrace: see Apollod. *Bibl.* 2.5.10.

[21] For some pertinent myths, see Ant. Lib. *Met.* 7 and 20.

[22] On the ancient characterisation of centaurs, and on the symbolic distinction between the group-centaurs and Cheiron and Pholos, see Kirk (1971), 152-62.

[23] Ancient descriptions of the event in Pind. *Nem.* 3.74-5, *Pyth.* 4.181-4; *Pyth.* 3.83-95; Servius *Verg. Georg.*. 3.93; Ap. Rhod. *Arg.* 2.1232-42 (this last unusually gives the location of mating as on the Black Sea); Hyg. *Fab.* 138. See Gantz (1993), 43 and Guillaume-Coirier (1995), esp. 114-120.

[24] See Pind. *Pyth.* 2.42-8; Diod. 4.69-70; Hyg. *Fab.* 62.

though, is the motif of the futile mating, which does not achieve its (violent) aim; this motif as recipe for monsters has a parallel in the birth of Erichthonios, created when Hephaistos fails to rape Athene and his sperm lands on, and fertilises, the earth.[25]

So the group-centaurs are monsters; Cheiron seems more the hero-with-a-difference.[26] He might also be thought to embody the positive aspects of the horse, just as the group-centaurs typically display that species' mythical potential for violence against humans. In fact, as was said in the Introduction, all centaurs may be accorded aspects of nobility. However, whereas the group-centaurs display them only occasionally and unreliably, Cheiron is undeviatingly good, never sharing in their ambiguity.[27] His prime mythological rôle as nurse and educator of heroes places him at the heart of an enduring pattern of obsolete Homeric aristocracy just as powerful, as an idea, in democratic Athens as in Thessaly.

Occasionally, Cheiron is directly pitted against the group-centaurs in myth. An example occurs in the account by Apollodoros, who describes an attempt against the life of Peleus by his enemy Akastos. Peleus is marooned on Mount Pelion by Akastos who hides his sword, and is thus at the mercy of the group-centaurs who attack him while he is sleeping. Cheiron, however, comes to his aid, and finds his sword for him so that he is able to defend himself, and so escape to safety.[28]

This distinction between Cheiron and the group-centaurs is also expressed in artistic representation. Vase-paintings – mostly Attic, of course – are especially important for this observation because the consistent popularity in this medium of both group and individual centaurs allows for comparison and for isolation of patterns and trends; but these trends are not limited to painted pottery.[29] Put simply, whereas the group-centaurs have a whole horse's body joined to the torso, arms and head of a man, Cheiron's composition has a far more dominant human element, a man's body, clothed and entire, to which the trunk and hindquarters are rather awkwardly attached.[30] Whereas the group-

---

[25] Apollod. *Bibl.* 3.14.6. A parallel of sorts is the birth of Typhon to Hera, which is accomplished without the usual intercourse. In anger at Zeus, Hera decides to bear a child without his assistance, but the result is, inevitably given the circumstances of conception, a monster: see *Hom. Hymn* 3.331-55; Fontenrose (1959), 13-14.

[26] It should be noted that one unusual and isolated variant on the myths elides the difference between Cheiron and the group-centaurs: Lucan (6.386-7) makes Cheiron a child of Ixion and Nephele and a brother of Peirithoös.

[27] Jeanmaire's (1949) discussion of the character of Cheiron in ancient poetry is still of great value despite its age.

[28] Apollod. *Bibl.* 3.13.3.

[29] See e.g. Gantz (1993), 145 on the patterns at work in the representations of centaurs in the metopes of Heraion I at Foce de Sele.

[30] An example of this composition is his depiction on the François Vase.

centaurs are almost always shown in violent movement and in conflict with heroes, Cheiron is most often shown poised and solemn, usually receiving or caring for the infant hero Achilles.

In Cheiron's composition the human element is the more powerful, whereas that of the group-centaurs is dominated by the horse. But there is another significance of their divergent forms which is perhaps even more telling. Cheiron preserves an older type of centaur-representation which is lost from his rowdy colleagues.[31] Naturally, the centaur-type with whole human body does not yield abruptly to the new; there is considerable overlap. But from the end of the seventh century BC, the new type with equine forelegs becomes more frequent, and gradually becomes the standard, in Attic vase-painting at least.[32] In the same medium, Cheiron keeps the human-forelegs type.[33]

So although the horse does have certain recognisable associations in Greek thought, in Cheiron's case it is significant not by and in itself, but in combination with the human part which dominates it. A different composition of human and horse is to be found in another case of equine mixanthropy in Greek cult: the figure of Demeter Melaina, 'Black Demeter', worshipped in Arkadia in the Peloponnese.

The geographical specificity that we found in the cult of Cheiron is even more striking in that of Demeter Melaina. We are here dealing with an extreme example of the phenomenon of the local form of a deity who also has a pan-

---

[31] For examples of the early type of centaur with human front legs, see Padgett (2003), figs. 4-8

[32] Gantz (1993), 145; Mylonas Shear (2002), 151; Padgett (2003), 14.

[33] Why does Cheiron not move with the times? Is it simply to keep the dominant humanity, or is there another reason behind his conservatism? The animal element of Cheiron is not generally played down in our sources; true, in Homer, he is named whereas the group-centaurs are called *phêres*; but Pindar calls him *phêr theios*. This question cannot be answered for certain, but there is a parallel example which suggests a very interesting possibility. In the representations of the river-god Acheloos (as has been described above) we find the preservation of an early type at the same time as the development and increasing popularity of a new version. The older type shows the god as a bull with a human neck and head; the new one attaches a human face to a taurine neck. The new, more popular image renders the mixanthrope more plausible as a 'living' creature, less stilted and stylised. But the stiffer image continues and, in the case of Acheloos, what ensures its survival is its rôle in the imagery of Acheloos' *cult*. Cult representation is far more conservative than 'secular' forms such as painted pottery; there is an almost superstitious unwillingness to depart from a sanctified norm. Can this example inform us as to Cheiron's representation? There are important divergences. First, though Cheiron received cult in Thessaly, no cult icons or images have been found. None is mentioned in literary sources; instead, his cave on Mount Pelion is his most important tangible monument. Thus we cannot claim for certain that the existence of a *Kultbild* of some sort affected his non-cultic depictions. And yet there are two objections to complete scepticism on this matter. The first is that we cannot know absolutely that no cult image of Cheiron ever existed; perhaps it was a wooden *xoanon* and was lost before our literary sources were operating. Secondly, and more importantly, it might very well be that the mere knowledge that Cheiron was a god, a recipient of cult, militated against changes to his representation. A third factor may well have been the fact that Cheiron was persistently regarded both as old himself and as a denizen of an earlier, Archaic age (for which see below).

Hellenic dimension. Hugely pervasive as the figure of Demeter is in Greek religion, the goddess under the *epiklesis* Melaina appears only at a single site, and in this form is radically different from the widespread Eleusinian persona of Demeter.[34]

Demeter Melaina was worshipped in a sacred cave on the Arkadian Mount Elaion, in the territory of Phigalia.[35] Not far away was Thelpousa, at which was worshipped Demeter Erinys, 'Fury', a near-identical form of the goddess whose name reflects the importance of anger and vengeance to both forms.[36] As Jost has shown,[37] both Phigalia and Thelpousa were located within the mountainous, largely uncultivated zone, and this location is far from coincidental. Neither Demeter Melaina nor Demeter Erinys is the goddess of straightforward agrarian abundance, as the myths, described below, make clear.

The cave of Demeter Melaina has never, alas, been found. Frazer thought he had discovered it in the course of his travels in the area; but it is almost certain that he was mistaken.[38] The absence of any archaeological data mean that we rely solely on our literary informant for the site: the relevant section of Pausanias' *Periegesis* (provided in full in the Appendix). This is a problematic state of affairs; Pausanias was by no means a straightforward eye-witness, to the extent that a later section of this book must be given over to his ideas and their possible impact on our perceptions. At this stage, however, we are justified in making what use we can of his account, dealing with specific issues as they arise.

While recounting his visit to the sacred cave of Demeter Melaina, Pausanias describes a startling cult image:

> [The Phigalians say] the image was made by them in this way. It was seated on a rock, and resembled a woman in everything but the head. It had the head and hair of a horse, and images of serpents and other wild animals grew from its head. It wore a tunic reaching to the feet. On one hand was a dolphin, on the other a bird, a dove. As for why they made the effigy like this, that is clear to any intelligent man who is learned in traditions.[39]

---

[34] Despite the infiltration of the Eleusinian form into Arkadia itself: see Paus. 8.25.2-3 for a sanctuary of Eleusinian Demeter in Thelpousa, the location of the radically un-Eleusinian Demeter Erinys. The more pan-Hellenic form did not cause the local one to be obscured or removed.

[35] For a discussion of landscape, settlement and sacred space in Arkadia, see Jost (1999).

[36] In fact, as Burkert has shown, various strands of mythology connect not only Phigalia and Thelpousa, but also the Boiotian sanctuary at the spring of Tilphoussa, near Haliartos: see Burkert (1979), 123-9.

[37] The relationship between cult-type and topography is one of the consistent foci of Jost's work, and one of its most important contributions to the understanding of Arkadian religion. See esp. Jost (1985), 82-3; (1994), 221-3; (1999), 208-9.

[38] Frazer (1898), 406-7. Autopsy is important to his discussion. (p. 407: 'I visited the cave 2nd May 1890, and have described it from personal observation.') See also Voyatzis (1999), 149.

[39] Paus. 8.42.4 (for the Greek text, see the Appendix below).

Fig. 20

Only rather later in the section does he reveal the important fact that at the time of his visit the *xoanon* was not actually in existence. It had in fact been succeeded by two replacement images: a bronze *agalma* crafted by the sculptor Onatas of Aegina, and the image which we may perhaps assume was in place when the author visited and made an offering, though of this he makes absolutely no mention.[40] Most scholars have had no difficulty in taking on trust the existence of the *xoanon* in exactly the form described by the Periegete, and in adopting it as an important early instance of such mixanthropic representations.[41] But in fact the description of the successive statue has far more of the mythological about it than the historical. The mare-headed *xoanon* has a mythological *aition*; its loss is accompanied by a story of Demeter's anger which forms a doublet with that of her earlier anger following her rape by Poseidon; the ways in which the *xoanon* and Onatas' statue disappear have a strong element of

---

[40] It seems fairly feasible to assume the existence of a cult image at the time of Pausanias' visit; the total lack of any representation of the goddess on the site would surely have occasioned explicit comment. This conjecture cannot, however, support anything approaching certainty, especially since other mixanthropes in this study offer no evidence of a cult image (for example, Cheiron, the Sirens and Kekrops). In the case of Demeter Melaina, it is interesting to entertain the possibility of an element of aniconism in Pausanias' day; but the matter cannot be settled one way or the other without further evidence.

[41] Unsurprisingly, the scholars who treat the *xoanon* without caution are those seeking traces of animal-gods; an example is Lévêque (1961), 102; he quotes in full the relevant passage of Pausanias without identifying any problematic qualities. Farnell is rare among scholars who have treated this passage in that he urges caution, and he rightly draws attention to the fact that, in any case, 'Some of the Phigalians were uncertain whether [the *xoanon*] had ever belonged to them.'. See Farnell, vol. 3 (1907), 51.

the mysterious; all in all, as Bruit has demonstrated,[42] there is much more to the whole narrative than religious history. Pausanias' account by itself is not enough to prove that the mixanthropic statue ever existed.

That said, it is not implausible that Demeter Melaina should be represented in mare-headed form. Horse-imagery was plainly important in the cults at Phigalia and Thelpousa, not just in mythology but in coin imagery also.[43] Coins do not display mixanthropy, but a striking parallel is provided by Medusa, who has many points of similarity with Demeter Melaina.[44] For example, both

Fig. 21

produce equine offspring after mating with Poseidon in horse form (Medusa's horse-child is Pegasos, Demeter's is Areion). For Medusa we have no evidence of worship, so we are not dealing with cult imagery in her case; but on a small but noticeable number of vases, she is given mixanthropic, half-equine form. Most famously, she appears as a centaur on a Boiotian relief-pithos (fig. 20).[45] But there seems to be an anatomical alternative. On an Archaic Rhodian kylix, the Gorgons are shown pursuing Perseus.[46] To one side is Medusa, who is distinguished from her fellow Gorgons by having the head of a horse instead of the usual hideous gorgoneion-face which they possess (see fig. 21). It does not seem that the vase showing the mare's-head Medusa was intending to depict her after decapitation, with Pegasos protruding from the wound; we must therefore assume that they were treating Medusa as a mixanthrope, and as one very similar to the *xoanon* of Demeter Melaina. Clearly the mare's-head type never became in any way canonical; but its appearance might encourage tentative belief in the mare-headed *xoanon* at Phigalia. And in any case the mixanthropic image is of great importance as an *idea* in Phigalian legend, regardless of its questionable reality.

It is easy to imagine the sacred cave of Demeter as a remote and sequestered site, of limited religious importance, but this seems not to have been the case. In fact, it was connected with other locations in Arkadia in a significant configura-

---

[42] Bruit (1986).

[43] Coins of Thelpousa depicting Demeter and a horse, inscribed with the name Erion (a form of Areion), see Head (1911), 382.

[44] Jost (1985), 304-7. See also Dietrich (1962), 130-134.

[45] Cf. a depiction of a gorgon-centaur fighting a lion on a sixth-century amethyst scarab from Byblos: *LIMC s.v.* 'Gorgo, Gorgones', cat. no. 285; London BM WA 103307.

[46] See Smith (1884), 239-40 and pl. XLIII; Gantz (1993), 144; Frontisi-Ducroux (2003), 210.

tion. The closest link existed between Phigalia and Thelpousa, as has been said. Both Phigalia and Thelpousa generated cult myths which told of Poseidon raping Demeter while both were in equine form; they differ on the resulting offspring, with the Thelpousans claiming that they were the miraculous horse Areion and a daughter whose name might not be spoken,[47] and the Phigalians that it was Despoina. It seems almost certain that the unnameable daughter is in fact the same personage as Despoina. Despoina is a cult title of the goddess in question; her real name is *nefas* to the uninitiated, as Pausanias tells us at 8.37.9. So in fact the real divergence between the two stories is the figure of Areion.[48] It may at first seem peculiar that the mare-headed Demeter of Phigalia was firmly dissociated by the Phigalians from an equine offspring. However, a very plausible explanation is that in Phigalian myth Areion was displaced by Despoina because of the latter's increasingly overwhelming importance, an importance which derived chiefly from the relationship between Phigalia and the sanctuary at Lykosoura, discussed below.[49]

In myth, there are also significant resonances between the cult of Demeter Melaina and that of Zeus Lykaios on Mount Lykaion. First both are associated with cannibalism. At Phigalia cannibalism is divine punishment for a human failure to maintain – among other forms of tendance – appropriate sacrifices; on Lykaion, the cannibal, Lykaon, is himself the one who trespasses against the gods, not by failing to sacrifice, but by sacrificing transgressively.[50] Second, both cults have the motif of animal metamorphosis in their surrounding mythology, though of very different kinds.[51] It has been argued that both reflect persistent Arkadian

---

[47] Paus. 8.25.7.

[48] For Areion (under the alternative name Erion) on the coins of Thelpousa – a reflection of his importance there – see Jost (1985), 64, and pl. 11, no. 2.

[49] Jost claims that Demeter Erinys at Thelpousa would have been depicted mixanthropically before Eleusinian influence eradicated this form (Jost 1985, 302); however, this is an unprovable supposition.

[50] In ancient myth, Lykaon kills and serves up a human infant. In Pausanias' version this occurs as a sacrifice to Zeus (8.3.2), but the commoner setting is a banquet at which Zeus is present (see e.g. Apollod. *Bibl.* 3.8.1; Ovid, *Met.* 1.199-243; Hyg. *Fab.* 176). The two variants are closely linked, however; feast and sacrifice are elided in Greek culinary and religious practice, and both versions of the story strongly echo Hesiod's description of Prometheus' deceptive sacrifice to Zeus at Mekone (Hes. *Theog.* 521-616), in which the sacrifice takes place during a banquet shared by gods and men.

[51] In several accounts, Lykaon is punished for his child murder by being turned into a wolf, though in another variant he is blasted by Zeus' thunderbolt. See Paus. 8.1.3; Hes. fr. 163 MW; Apollod. *Bibl.* 3.8.1; Lyk. *Al.* 480-81 with schol.; Ovid, *Met.* 1.198-239. For discussion of the episode, see Burkert (1983), 84-93, which examines the connection between the myth and the Arkadian lycanthropy-ritual which was claimed to have existed in reality; a similar conjunction of myth and ritual is attempted by Buxton (1987), 67-74. Bynum (2005), 166-70, gives a treatment based largely on the Ovidian version but still interesting from a wider perspective. The fullest discussion of the myth remains Piccaluga (1968). For a discussion of the myth's place in Pausanias' work and its themes, see Pirenne-Delforge (2008a), 67-72.

(rather than local) religious concerns: with transgressive eating, a slide back into savagery, and the thin line between human and animal.[52] But the discernible implications of this for cult are limited. They do not suggest a connection on the level of ritual and practice between Lykaion and Phigalia.

Such a relationship does, however, seem to have been in place between Phigalia and another site, Lykosoura, a place of particular religious significance on a pan-Arkadian level.[53] Lykosoura was dominated in religious terms by the figure of Despoina, Demeter's daughter according to Phigalian (though not Thelpou-san) legend. Numerous aspects of ordinance[54] and iconography recall the central elements of the Phigalian cult. Of the latter, the most famous example must be the various animal-headed human forms found in the material remains from the sanctuary of Despoina. These mixanthropic images are generally described as referring in some way to Demeter Melaina's mixanthropic cult statue at Phigalia, though the correspondence is not exact; relatively few of the Lykosouran figures are *mare*-headed, and their relationship to Demeter remains troublingly vague. Detailed discussion of this issue must wait till a later section (see below, Chapter 6). Here the most important point to note is that the Phigalian cave was not a cult site in total isolation, unique and untouched. Demeter Melaina's remote cave, then, had in fact a part to play within some of Arkadia's most visible and prominent cult activity.[55]

Her horse-form mating and her horse-headed image set Demeter Melaina apart, as has been said, from the manifestations of the goddess in other regions of Greece. What significance, however, does the horse have in this instance?

We have seen in relation to Cheiron that, generally speaking, horses can have two potential strands of significance. They can be emblems of aristocratic status, with an associated military and hunting-related cachet. They can also, however (and this form dominates mythology) be aggressive, destructive, and with a taste for human flesh. It will be argued that Demeter Melaina encapsu-

---

[52] See Bruit (1986), esp. 95; Borgeaud (1988), 34-44 (on Lykaion).

[53] For example, it was because of its famous Despoina-sanctuary that Lykosoura was allowed to keep the status of city after the synoecism of Megalopolis: see Paus. 8.28.6 and Jost (1994), 226.

[54] Especially suggestive is the text of a sacred law from Lykosoura (IG V², 514), which details certain requirements and prohibitions on visitors to the shrine of Despoina. Some of these seem to echo features of the Phigalian site: female visitors are forbidden to wear black, and the type of sacrifice demanded also, in the words of Jost, 'rappelle le rite de Phigalie' (Jost 1985, 330). On the sacred law, see Loukas and Loukas (1994), which focuses on the date (probably third century BC) and the historical context; for an early discussion of its significance, Leonardos (1896). For a recent analysis of the inscription and its links with the known rituals and beliefs of the site, see Jost (2008), 94-102. Cf. also SEG XXXVI 376 (no. 8 in Lupu [2005]): a second-century BC addition to the sacred ordinances of Lykosoura: the text is badly damaged and yields little information, but appears to concern 'cathartic requirements' (Lupu [2005], 216).

[55] For the interconnected cults of Phigalia, Lykosoura, Lykaion and Megalopolis, see Jost (1994).

lates many important aspects of the negative side of the horse, but that in her case these are discernibly shaped by the local conditions of belief and folklore.

Phigalia was at the centre of an interlocking series of myths concerned with the progress of human society from savagery to civilisation, a progress which is articulated in the myths through food-symbolism. The details of this articulation have been examined very thoroughly and to great effect by Bruit (1986). Bruit, however, concentrates in her article on the practice of the bloodless sacrifice to Demeter, and does not really look at the position of the horse element within the resulting schema. In the Phigalian myths, the foodstuff which chiefly represents the primitive state is the acorn, which the earliest Arkadians are said to have lived on; this is a food which occurs naturally, and is not the product of human agricultural activity.[56] Then they learn to cultivate the land, and to produce grain; this breakthrough stands for their development into a civilised society. However, in Arkadian myth as a whole, there is an alternative primitive food to the harmless acorn: human flesh. Lykaon, the son of Pelasgos brings this alternative into the frame in the opening section of Pausanias' Book 8 when he sacrifices a human child to Zeus Lykaios;[57] as we shall see, it also features instrumentally in the Phigalian narrative. So we have two main possibilities for primitive fare, two opposing ways of representing and viewing the primitive stage of human development.[58]

The opposing expressions of the primitive life via food are of course not limited to Arkadian myth. Perhaps the most famous example of their juxtaposition is the figure of Polyphemos the Cyclops in Homer's *Odyssey*.[59] Polyphemos is a herdsman, and his day-to-day diet is a harmless, dairy-based one.[60] But given

---

[56] At the start of Book 8 (8.1.5) we are told by Pausanias that in fact the acorn-eating phase was not the first: before this, men ate leaves and roots, which were sometimes poisonous. The proto-king Pelasgos introduced them to the relatively nutritious acorn, and also to the construction of huts and the wearing of fleeces. In other words, he takes them out of the condition of undifferentiated animals, and places them on the first, and most primitive, step of human development.

[57] Paus. 8.1.3.

[58] There is also a third, which pervades Arkadian mythology particularly: that is the life, and the food, of the hunter and herdsman, both of which rôles are represented in the figure of Pan. Perhaps this third way stands somewhere between the other two, for it involves the consumption of flesh, but avoids the extreme of flesh-consumption, cannibalism. If we follow the central argument of Burkert's *Homo Necans*, we may perhaps see that even the consumption of non-human flesh has its share of the guilt of murder; but in any case, the life of the hunter and herdsman is presented as another acceptable face of the primitive life. It does not play such an explicit rôle in the Phigalian narrative, for that is dominated by the antithesis between acorns and human flesh. But it pervades both the idea and the reality of Arkadia just as Pan pervades its mountains and caves.

[59] 9.215 ff. For the significance of food in connection with a primitive *modus vivendi*, see Kirk (1971), 162-8. He argues for the special intensity of the nature/culture theme in this myth, saying that 'various aspects of nature and culture are being manipulated into proximity for the purposes of evaluation' (p. 168).

[60] Indeed, he does not even eat the sheep he herds, and his care of them is verging on the tender.

the chance, he naturally and automatically turns cannibal, with an extra layer of transgression as he is eating those to whom he should offer ritual hospitality. Polyphemos brings together two food-options which the Phigalian narrative is essentially trying to keep apart, as will be explained.[61]

So how does Demeter Melaina fit into this theme as it is expressed in Phigalian myth? *Not* (and this is the most striking point) as the embodiment of grain and agriculture, the 'finished' phase of the human process. This despite the fact that we are told explicitly that the discovery of agriculture was facilitated by her. Rather, she embodies both of the two chief manifestations of the primitive, the pre-grain phase.

In the first place, the bloodless sacrifices offered to her by long custom consist of the harmless primitive foods: various fruits and goods (grapes, honey, raw wool),[62] from which grain is notably absent. But according to the myths, if these rites are neglected (as they were following the destruction of the mare-headed *xoanon*),[63] primitive food-type number two comes into play. Demeter Melaina's punishment for the lapse of the cult on that occasion was to cause *akarpia* – a lack of food, famine – but moreover, this was a famine that had a particularly extreme possible outcome: a resort to cannibalism and child-eating. The vital section is the text of the oracle given by the Pythia to the Phigalians when they send to Delphi for a cure for their suffering.

> Azanian Arkadians, acorn-eaters, who live
> in Phigalia, the cave in which hid Deio horse-bearer,
> you have come to learn a cure for painful famine,
> who alone have twice been nomads, who alone have been eaters of wild fruits
> > once more.
> Deio made you cease from pasturing, Deio made you pasture
> again, after being binders of corn and eaters of cake,
> because she was deprived of the prize given by former men, and ancient ho-
> > nours.
> And she will quickly make you eaters of each other, and eaters of children,
> if you do not assuage her anger with public libations,
> and adorn the recess of her cave with divine honours.[64]

Demeter (here called Deio) led man from the stage of herding, from being *agriodaitai,* to the cultivation of grain; but if not accorded the proper offerings, she

---

[61] Just as there are various possible versions of primitive food in ancient thought (acorns; leaves and roots; cheese; human flesh), so there are different types of primitive sacrifice. There is the vegetarian variety described by Plato (*Leg.* 782c) in a passage which is strikingly reminiscent of the offerings to Demeter Melaina, including as it does fruits of the earth and honey, free from both meat and the products of agriculture. In opposition to this is the transgressive sacrifice of Lykaon, the killing and eating of a human child.

[62] Paus. 8.42.11.

[63] Paus. 8.42.5-6.

[64] Paus. 8.42.6 (for the Greek text, see the Appendix below).

has the corresponding power, not just to undo that stage, but to push them into the unacceptable form of primitive life, cannibalism (especially the ultimate taboo, eating their own children). This is the outcome represented by the mythical figure of Lykaon, just as the harmless life of herding and acorn-eating is embodied by Pelasgos. And Demeter is the deity who can undo the process of civilisation completely.[65] If not placated by the food of harmless savagery, her punishment is to inflict savagery of the worst kind. Of course, the sacrifices to Demeter Melaina are also – as well as being grainless – bloodless, avoiding flesh-consumption altogether. We see from the myth of Lykaon, perhaps, that in Arkadian myth especially, any sacrifice, even when the victim is ostensibly animal, has the potential to turn out to be human. The Phigalian rite bypasses this possibility entirely.

So, Demeter Melaina is a kind of inverted Demeter, one whose chief potential rôle seems to be to blight crops rather than safeguarding them. Her shrine is in the wild, uncultivated land; she is, in the words of Bruit, a 'force sauvage de la terre.'[66] But what of the horse in her myths and in her cult image? How – if at all – does that animal fit in with her persona as described?

Various aspects of the associations borne by the horse in Greek myth have been outlined already with regard to Cheiron, and surface, I believe, with regard to Black Demeter also. The first, perhaps the most fundamental, is the ambiguity of the horse's mythical relationship with, and position within, human culture and civilisation. The horse is a domesticated, vegetarian quadruped that works on man's behalf; but this side of its nature can vanish in a flash, to be replaced with the qualities of a *thêr*, a wild beast. The horse can never be relied upon, in myth, to play its part consistently in the wider picture of man's taming influence on nature.[67] Therefore it is highly appropriate that Demeter Melaina, who represents above all the fragility of human civilisation, its potential for instant reversal,[68] should have the horse as the chief component in her representation.

Moreover, as we have seen, when a horse in myth does depart from its domestic aspect, it feasts on human flesh; that is the unwavering outcome. Once again, we may see the connection with Demeter. The horse goes to the extreme of savagery, its worst, most destructive aspect; it is with this very contingency that Demeter threatens her worshippers. The connection grows stronger when we note also that very often in myth a horse turning man-eater is the instrument of

---

[65] Jost (1992 b, 56) relates this in part to Demeter's mountain location and affinity with the mountain zone, and sees her nature as a reflection of 'la précarité de la civilisation dans les montagnes.'

[66] Bruit (1986), 85.

[67] Scheffer (1994) argues for a more specific association between horse-related deities and uncontrolled sexuality; but this may be seen as part of a wider theme of uncontrolled nature. There is no doubt, however, that horses had a particular association in Greek thought with female sexuality. See Scheffer (1994), esp. 129-33.

[68] See Borgeaud (1988), 16-17.

divine vengeance for a religious – *particularly sacrificial* – transgression on the part of the humans involved. We might think, for example, of the myth of the sons of Klinis, and their taboo ass-sacrifice to Apollo.[69] More generally, the aggression of horses is vengeful: Glaukos refuses to let his mares breed, thus breaking a rule of nature and enraging Aphrodite; Anthos tries to drive his father's horses out of their meadow, enraging them.[70] Arkadian Demeter too is characterised by vengeful anger, both in a specific and a general way. The specific sense relates to religious failure, the lapsing of her cult; but themes of anger and revenge suffuse her myths more widely. She is angry at Hades for the rape of her daughter; angry at Poseidon for her own sexual misuse; angry at her worshippers for their neglect. Anger and the potential for subsequent punishment appear to dominate her persona. The horse is a fitting ingredient of the expression of this motif.

This theme of anger and vengeance is shared equally between the two Demeters of the region, Melaina and Erinys. In fact, the latter raises a special point of interest with her name, which seems to be the most explicit reference we have to the central importance of the theme to her persona: after all, the pluralized Erinyes are the embodiment of the drive to exact punishment for a transgression. The motif may be reflected in the title of Melaina as well as that of Erinys. Pausanias tells us (8.42.4) that the Phigalians explained the name by reference to the myth that Demeter put on black clothing when angry at the snatching of Persephone and at her own rape. So, black is an indication of anger; and this is very reminiscent of another cult in Arkadia, that of the Eumenides, near Megalopolis. The Eumenides are the same as the Erinyes, and the cult in question is connected with a unique variant of the well-known myth of Orestes and his madness, a variant which introduces the idea of colour. When the Eumenides are pursuing Orestes in their vengeful fury, they appear to him black; after he has expiated his crime by biting off his own finger, they change to white. There follows in Pausanias' account a revealing statement:[71]

> So he made an offering (*enêgisen*) to the black goddesses to avert their wrath, and sacrificed (*ethuse*) to the white ones.

The verbs used here to designate the two sacrifices, *enagizein* and *thuein*, are significant, in a way which no English translation can capture. *Enagizein* is especially conspicuous in this context. Although in ancient texts across the board it does not have a wholly consistent meaning,[72] in Pausanias, as Pirenne-Delforge has shown, it almost always refers to sacrifices made to dead heroes (though its use is by no means simple and without variation), and, what is more, occurs in

---

[69] See Ant. Lib. *Met.* 20.

[70] *ibid.* 7.

[71] Paus. 8.34.3: καὶ οὕτω ταῖς μὲν ἐνήγισεν ἀποτρέπων τὸ μήνιμα αὐτῶν, ταῖς δὲ ἔθυσε ταῖς λευκαῖς.

[72] For full analysis of the use of such terminology in ancient texts, see Ekroth (2002).

many instances where the contrast between heroes and gods is being explored.[73] Therefore its use with regard to divinities like the Eumenides is striking. What it would appear to emphasise is their link with death and the underworld,[74] a link reinforced by the proximity to the shrine of the 'tomb of the finger' (supposedly the final resting-place of Orestes' severed digit).[75] *Enagizein* also carries with it a sense of the deflection of a baneful and destructive power.[76]

Given the bundle of associations that Demeter and the Eumenides have in common (anger at a transgression; the need for ritual placation, the name Erinys; the importance of colour; the underworld connections), we are surely justified in regarding Black Demeter as a goddess in angry, vengeful mode.[77] Offerings to her are rites of aversion, though they are very different in nature from the typical form of the *enagismos* (a holocaust). Demeter Melaina requires constant appeasement; but the means of doing so have to tally with the food-symbolism at work in the mythology discussed above.

So the horse-element of Demeter and her blackness combine to express her quality of anger and the potential hazards if suitable ritual placation is not maintained.[78] We are left with the question of how the associations of the horse in her case fit in with those of Poseidon Hippios, which appear to be substantially different. For Poseidon Hippios, the horse-element is closely connected with the fertility-aspect of his nature, especially in association with water. As is usual in Greek religion, the fertility aspect has its underworld associations also.[79] It would be perverse to argue that Demeter had no share in this quality.[80] But whereas her horse-representation is underpinned by the motif of vengeful anger, in Poseidon's case this feature is completely absent.

---

[73] Pirenne-Delforge (2008a), 187-241; see esp. 229-234 for the sacrifice by Orestes.

[74] *Pace* Scheffer (1994), 128-9.

[75] Paus. 8.34.2.

[76] Pirenne-Delforge (2008a), 233.

[77] There is a connection between anger/grief and blackness in the characterisation of Thetis, too, as Slatkin (1986) has shown, demonstrating that in fact Thetis and Demeter are linked in ancient texts by their assumption of dark clothing to indicate anger. It is interesting to recall that, as noted above, Thetis in the *Heroikos* of Philostratus also deals out, like Demeter Melaina, vengeance for the human neglect of cult rites (in that case, those of Achilles).

[78] In the myths surrounding the cults at Phigalia and Thelpousa, metamorphosis into horse form is used by the goddess to escape Poseidon's amorous attentions: that is, it is manifested rather earlier in the narrative sequence than the goddess's anger. However, on this point we are justified in supposing that the myth has an explanatory function. The motif of evasion dominates Greek stories of metamorphosis; and though Forbes Irving (1990, 38-50) is right to deplore the tendency to search 'behind' and 'beneath' the stories themselves for traces of lost animal-gods, in the cults of Phigalia and Thelpousa we have enough complementary evidence to see the horse association as reaching beyond the single mythical episode of Demeter's attempts to avoid rape. We may assume that the goddess's horse-element, deeply lodged in her divine character and functions, was at some stage made to tally with the well-established motif of evasion.

[79] For the chthonic aspect of Poseidon Hippios, see Detienne and Werth (1971), 167-8.

[80] Though Scheffer (1994, 128-9) argues that it is less important than has often been claimed.

Thus the horse's significance in the case of Demeter Melaina is completely at odds with Cheiron, horse-bodied but man-headed, who, with his involvement in *paideia* and his concern for the welfare of humans, works to preserve human civilisation in the face of various aggressors, including his own fellow-centaurs. We learn from this that an animal ingredient does not by itself confer one simple and immutable significance. Rather, its import depends on the way in which it is anatomically disposed, and on regional religious and mythological context. The horse does have some consistent traits in ancient thought, but they are distinctly ambiguous, and how they are reflected in the character of the deity concerned is intensely, and fascinatingly, variable.

2. From Arkadia to Attica: Pan

Pan's is a cult whose diffusion, from the Classical period on, is so wide as to render a full survey of sites and practices impossible here. That said, two chief foci emerge from the wider picture: Arkadia and Attica. Arkadia is highly significant as being the place where Pan's worship began, and Attica was the region which later adopted it most enthusiastically, and adapted it most revealingly.

That said, one could at this point be accused of taking on and perpetuating a vicious dichotomy. There is no doubt that, as Borgeaud has shown, Athens and Arkadia were involved in a complex dialogue of identity and self-exploration, driven at first mainly by Athens but, from the fourth century at least, engaged in actively by the Arkadians also in their bid for increased cultural self-definition.[81] Athens used Arkadia as a model for various concepts: her own past, the primitive, the Other, and so on; this model was then taken up by the Arkadians and applied to themselves. So by concentrating on these two areas, to the exclusion of countless other regions and their local Pan-cults, are we not simply perpetuating a dualistic fiction generated in antiquity and dominant ever since? Athens and non-Athens – this is in many ways a pernicious schema which must be challenged by a recognition of local diversity across Greece, for which (given that textual sources are almost always themselves the products of that schema) archaeological evidence is especially valuable.

In most cases, this would be an unassailable truth. In the case of Pan, however, local diversity is hard to find for the simple reason that Pan cults throughout Greece follow very closely the Attic pattern in terms of imagery and practice. It might plausibly be said that, as Athens was the first region to take Pan out of Arkadia, so she mediated Pan's arrival on the wider Greek scene. Many other Greek states, at least outside the Peloponnese, received the god not directly from

---

[81] On the 'reinstitutionalization' of Pan in Arkadia after – and massively fuelled by – his diffusion elsewhere, see Borgeaud (1988), 52.

his Arkadian homeland but from Athens.[82] Naturally, local adaptations of the Athenian way occurred.[83] But the Pan they took on cannot be understood as an unmediated Arkadian phenomenon. For this reason, the focus on Arkadia as place of origin, and Attica, as the region in which the vital latter stage of development took place, appears inevitable and justified.

When we look at the differences between his Arkadian and his Attic worship, Pan's case starts to chime very strongly with others, particularly those of Acheloos and Cheiron. We shall summarize the worship in each region before analysing their divergences.

The obscurity of evidence surrounding Pan's cult in Arkadia is to a huge extent dispelled by Jost's treatment, which brings out particularly strongly, as ever, the vital relationship between a cult and its topography. Pan was accorded, on the whole, small shrines in mountainous areas,[84] though occasionally he is to be found in an urban setting, as in Peraitheis[85] and Megalopolis.[86] His cult generally links him with the same types of landscape as do his myths – the 'paysage panique' as Jost calls it.[87] Though Herbig's picture[88] of his worshippers as all simple shepherds has now been questioned,[89] there is no doubt that on the whole he received small private offerings and presided over the concerns of the herdsman and hunter.

---

[82] See Larson (2001), 97, on the rôle of Athens in disseminating the cult of Pan through Attica and then in other regions of Greece.

[83] For an example one might look at a case already discussed, the deities – among them Cheiron – included in the long verse inscription in the cave near Pharsalos in Thessaly. Here Pan keeps exactly the type of company we find in Attic sites, including the nymphs and Hermes. Local associations cause the addition of unusual elements, most notably Cheiron, to what is otherwise an orthodox selection familiar from many Attic reliefs.

[84] Jost (1985), 458-9.

[85] Paus. 8.36.7; Jost (1985), 200, 458-9

[86] Paus. 8.30.2-3; Jost (1985), 221-2, 458-9.

[87] ibid. 458.

[88] Herbig (1949), 15. This notion also pervades Lamb (1926), who says of the *kriophoros*-type effigies found in Pan's shrine on Lykaion, 'Evidently the figures are dedicated by pious Arcadians in their own likeness' (p. 134).

[89] See e.g. Hübinger (1992, 203-6; 1993, 25-6) on the finds from Lykaion and what sort of people may have dedicated them – *not* all simple shepherds. He makes the very important point that many of the votives found were too costly to have been dedicated by poor shepherds and hunters (Hübinger [1993], 29). He paints a slightly more complex picture than Jost (1985, 13, 467-8) who focuses on the *kriophoros* figures from the sanctuary in particular and sees them simply as generic self-portraits of the individuals who dedicated them. Parker (2005, 167) sums the matter up when he says that 'the familiar notion that certain 'country' gods such as Pan were honoured only by countrymen, and countrymen honoured none but them, appears to be part of the pastoral dream.' This is particularly true of Athens, which Parker is discussing, in which Pan held a decidedly civic status. (See Parker [1996], 166-7.)

However, there are sites which deviate from or go beyond this rôle, and the most striking is that on Mount Lykaion.[90] The sanctuary of Zeus on Lykaion was an exceptionally important religious site in Arkadia, and wielded a pan-Arkadian scope and sway; it was the location, for example, of games – the Lykaia[91] – which brought in competitors from the whole region. Its significance to Arkadian identity from the fourth century on[92] is demonstrated by the use of Lykaian iconography on Arkadian federal coinage,[93] and by the inclusion of Lykaian religious elements in the programmatic new centre of Megalopolis, created by synoecism in around 370/69 BC.[94] This was therefore no unimportant zone for Pan to appear in, and by no means the haunt only of a small number of local peasants. The sanctuary of Pan has not been found, but Pausanias tells us[95] that it was sited by the race-track used in the games (a prominent location) and had around it a grove of trees. In addition to the bare fact that they shared a cult location, there are other indications that Pan and Zeus Lykaios were in a dynamic religious relationship of which their worshippers were fully conscious. On the coinage cited above, they appear together, each on one side of the same coin. In Megalopolis, which to a large extent mirrored the religious arrangement on Lykaion,[96] an image of Pan stood within the *abaton* of Zeus Lykaios.[97]

There is also evidence that suggests that Pan had an oracular function on Lykaion. It is true that this evidence is by no means unproblematic. The sole source for a *manteion* of Pan on Lykaion is a scholion on Theokritos,[98] though as Jost remarks, other texts make more general connections between Pan and prophecy and the link is indisputable.[99] In his description of Lykosoura, when describing an effigy of Pan, Pausanias states: 'It is said that at a yet earlier time, this god too gave oracles, and that the Nymph Erato became his prophetess, she who married Arkas the son of Kallisto.'[100] With these words, which appear to apply not only to Lykosoura but more generally, Pausanias consigns any

---

[90] Initial excavation reports: Kourouniotis (1902), (1903) and (1904).

[91] Paus. 8.38.5. Pausanias says that in his day these games were no longer celebrated there, a statement which may be read in various ways; but their importance in the Classical period, especially the fourth century, is certain. See Jost (1985), 185.

[92] Jost (1985), 183-5,267-8; *id.* (1994), 226.

[93] For a clear example, see Jost (1985), pl. 63, no. 4.

[94] The precise date of the synoecism is uncertain. For the event and its context of growing Arkadian self-assertion, see Rhodes (2006), 217-8. For the religious manifestations of the event, see Jost (1985), 184-5 and (1992), 224-38.

[95] Paus. 8.38.5.

[96] On Megalopolitan doublets, see e.g. Jost (1994), 227.

[97] Paus. 8.30.2. Also at Tegea: Paus. 8.53.11.

[98] Schol. Theok. 1.5.123c.

[99] Jost (1985), 474-5.

[100] Paus. 8.37.11: λέγεται δὲ ὡς τὰ ἔτι παλαιότερα καὶ μαντεύοιτο οὗτος ὁ θεός, προφῆτιν δὲ Ἐρατὼ νύμφην αὐτῷ γενέσθαι ταύτην ἣ Ἀρκάδι τῷ Καλλιστοῦς συνῴκησε.

actual oracular function to the realm of myth and the distant past. It is therefore hard to assess at what stage prophecy was a significant part of Pan's cultic function on Lykaion.

More generally, Pan's position in Arkadian religion seems to share with that of Cheiron in Thessaly a certain power to keep at bay the malign natural forces of the landscape. For example, Servius says that Pan's *epiklesis* was Lyceus because he keeps wolves – *lykoi* – away from the flocks.[101] This has all the hallmarks of a bogus etymology, but it does echo some of the most potent names in Arkadian mythology, names which draw on the intense symbolic valency of the wolf. In this context, wolves are not merely real-life threats to young lambs. As has been said, Lykaon, with his wolf-metamorphosis, represents the transgressive past, a past into which humanity always risks lapsing; the cult site of Mount Lykaion, on which Pan had his shrine, was in essence a monument to this terrible possibility. Moreover, it is Pan who, in Phigalian myth, leads Demeter Melaina out of the condition of angry seclusion which has the potential, by crippling agriculture, to push man back into primitive savagery. There appears, therefore, to have been a loose bundle of religious ideas concerned with 'keeping the wolf from the door' – or sheep! – and Pan seems to have been a helpful figure in this regard. This is not dissimilar from Thessalian mythology which pits Cheiron against the destructive group-centaurs in the glens of Pelion. Both cases illustrate the apotropaic usefulness of the man-friendly monster.

It was this deity, so firmly woven into the fabric of Arkadian mythology, who during the Persian Wars, in famous circumstances, made the jump to Attica and Athens. Philippides' encounter with Pan appears really to have marked the inception of his Attic worship.[102] The cult site which followed directly from the epiphany was a cave on the north-west skirt of the acropolis, right in the heart of the city. Here Pan was honoured with torch races, which clearly echo the scenario of his initial manifestation.[103] It is possible that the torches also echo those connected in art with the return of Persephone and the restoration of natural abundance, a restoration over which Pan and Panes more than once preside.[104]

---

[101] Serv. *Verg. Geor.* 1.5.17. For discussion of the passage, see Jost (1985), 474-5; Larson (2007), 63.

[102] For this encounter, see Hdt. 6.105. See Parker (1996), 163-5 for the introduction and dissemination of the cult in Attica following Philippides' revelation.

[103] See Borgeaud (1988), 134-5. Borgeaud argues convincingly that Pan's key character in Athens was as a peaceful, unwarlike entity, the antithesis to war (135-8) rather than as a martial ally. Parker (2005, 477) remains doubtful that the races in his honour simply mirrored that of Philippides, and expresses uncertainty about their exact meaning.

[104] For the torch, its rôle in the Persephone myth and its fertility-associations more generally, see Parisinou (2000), 81-99; plates 14, 15, 16 and 40 are of especially interest in this matter. In her study, Pan is connected with torches only via his participation in the torch-lit *pannuchides* of Cybele (pp. 160-61); but note the torch-racing Silenoi in plate 2; the Dionysiac context may be another important connection. To return to the theme of Persephone, two Panes attend her

If so, this would certainly not be out of place with the wider picture of Pan's typical character in Attic cult, outside the urban centre of Athens.[105] The form which that cult usually takes is near-identical with that of Acheloos in Attica. A number of deities are worshipped on a single site, normally a cave; they are often depicted together, and named, in a votive relief. Their number includes the nymphs most frequently,[106] Pan also very often, with Hermes, Acheloos and Dionysos sometimes present, and a number of other less frequent instances such as Herakles. Sometimes a connection is also made with the goddesses of Eleusis, and the fertility rôle of Pan, like that of the nymphs, is explicitly expressed.[107] In addition, Pan is often linked with Cybele, the Mother of the Gods, and takes a place in her retinue, but this is as much a Boiotian as an Athenian allegiance, and goes back at least as far as Pindar.[108]

Overall, Pan appears as one of a company, and as a component within a number of canonical groupings: Eleusinian, Dionysiac, korybantic. This is not a pattern unknown in Arkadia, but it is very different from the duality (albeit unequal) of Pan and Zeus on Lykaion. We might compare the difference between Cheiron in his cave on Pelion, and in his cave near Pharsalos: in the former his function and character are perhaps more mysterious, but he emerges as an important half of a divine double-act; in the Pharsalos cave, a later arrangement, he has joined a rustic collective. It is this collective persona that Attic Pan tends most often to have.

Several scholars have noted the key difference between Pan before and after the diffusion of his cult: the importance of the cave. In Arkadia Pan is almost never worshipped in a sacred cave, yet as soon as his cult moves beyond his homeland this becomes the setting *par excellence*.[109] Borgeaud's famous thesis is surely right: that by placing Pan in a cave, other Greeks, Athenians especially, were placing him in a small segment of the Arkadian landscape with which he

---

return in fig. 26 (p. 118); see below for discussion. We have already noted Pan's rôle in bringing back Kore's mother Demeter from her destructive sojourn in the Phigalian cave.

[105] Examined in great detail by Borgeaud (1988); the present section is merely a summary of some vital aspects.

[106] The nymphs already had cult in Attica before the arrival of Pan, but Parker (1996, 163-5) argues that the prominence of cave-locations is a fifth-century phenomenon. Larson (2001, 97) is less certain on this point, and contends that some caves may have been sacred to the nymphs before this time. The question is relevant because it affects whether we see Pan being grafted onto an existing pattern of worship (as Larson believes) or whether his arrival was in itself influential, perhaps bringing the cave to greater prominence. The latter would not be implausible given the strong thematic connection between mixanthropes and caves (see below).

[107] Documents illustrating this are assembled and discussed by Borgeaud (1988), 140-43, where he also ties in Pan's Arkadian relationship with Demeter. Pan's fertility function is therefore both general and highly specific.

[108] In fr. 96.2 Snell, he calls Pan the 'dog of the Great Mother'.

[109] Parker (1996, 165) remarks that 'the new cult was not a simple re-creation in Attica of what had been practised in Arkadia hitherto.'

was so closely associated;[110] he was thus always surrounded by his *imagined* Arkadian identity.[111] However, this does not do justice to another, wider truth: the consistent and significant relationship between caves and mixanthropes. This relationship might at first appear to be the result merely of the cave's character as rustic locale; after all, mixanthropic deities tend to be gods of the countryside. But, as I shall argue more fully later, there is more to it than that.

Fig. 22

On the face of it seems superfluous to describe Pan's physical form. Of all the mixanthropic deities included in this study, he is the one whose image was and is the most widespread, the most familiar, and the most influential in shaping both the ancient and the modern perception of mixanthropy. The long-lasting appeal of his representation is reflected in the tendency of the scholarship on the subject to take an extremely wide temporal range, encompassing at least Greek and Roman material if not Renaissance and modern as well.[112] It is not, however, without controversy.

---

[110] For discussion of all that Pan *meant* to the Athenians, wildness and animality, see Parker (1996), 167-8.

[111] Borgeaud (1988), esp. 50-52. The function of the cave on the acropolis is particularly interesting; as Parker (2005, 52) remarks, it allowed the Athenians to 'square the circle, both granting their honoured new divine guest a place near the heart of things, and also respecting that strange wildness which made him unsuitable to occupy a normal temple.' This 'strange wildness', and the rarity of temple-occupation, is common to all mixanthropes. See further Loraux (2000), 39-46.

[112] For example, Herbig's monograph covers almost the whole swathe of antiquity; for treatment of later material up to and including the modern age, see Boardman (1997) and Merivale (1969). Both offer very interesting discussion of the modern reception and use of the Pan-image, which shed a retrospective light on the ancient sources but are outside the scope of this study. Pan's form and nature have been extensively discussed, and Borgeaud's 1988 work on the subject in particular took the subject forward by a great leap in terms of sophistication of thought. The current discussion will not try to encompass the huge wealth of material or ideas; instead, the focus will be on Pan's mixanthropy, its significance and its development in the period under review. As ever, I shall be attempting to establish the contribution of the animal component and its relation, both physical and thematic, to the human part.

Fig. 23   Fig. 24

Chief among the uncertainties is the question as to when we find our first identifiable Pan-images. Both Herbig and Boardman[113] tentatively include in their collations of Pan-images a number of very early figures which are essentially goats standing on their hind legs. (Jost, interestingly, does not; her catalogue starts with Classical period objects.) The first example of this form (dated as it is to somewhere in the seventh or sixth century BC) is fig. 22, the small bronze group of four animal figures standing in a circle with hands joined, from Methydrion in Arkadia.[114] A small number of other early objects follow this type: the upright goat-man, or sometimes a group of such beings. Herbig suggests that we may see these as fore-runners of the being later designated Pan, but this is fraught with uncertainty: the Methydrion group demonstrates the difficulty even of identifying species with any accuracy. That said, a small number of Attic black figure vases of the early fifth century do provide examples of a Pan-form which may support the pedigree of such objects of the Methydrion group: in these, the god is shown essentially as a goat on his hind legs. (See figs. 23-24.)

In any case, the Classical period, as Herbig notes,[115] sees the dramatic arrival of the first recognisable and identifiable mixanthropic Pans, and also with the clear partitioning of animal and human body-parts. The change from upright animal to mixanthrope is extremely important. As Herbig remarks (p. 51), the former type is 'Nie Bock plus Mann, der halb Gott halb Tier, sondern immer göttlicher Bock oder bockhäfter Gott.' By contrast, the Pan of the Classical period, of vase-painting first and foremost, belongs anatomically to the same basic class of creatures as other early Mischwesen and particularly the satyrs whose physical composition resembles his own fairly closely.[116] There is no

---

[113] In *LIMC s.v.* 'Pan'.

[114] Fig. 29; *LIMC s.v.* 'Pan', cat. no. 1; see Herbig (1949), 51-3; Brommer (1949-50), 6-7.

[115] Herbig (1949), esp. 53-7.

[116] For a typical Classical Pan, see fig. 30.

doubt that he becomes part of the artist's popular mixanthropic palette. That means the *Athenian* artist first and foremost. This raises another fundamental difficulty attendant on Pan's representation: the impossibility of giving it any secure anchor in Arkadia, the region which was undoubtedly the starting-place of his cult. The earliest known site of his worship in Arkadia, on Lykaion, has yielded no mixanthropic Pan-images.[117] Only after Pan becomes popular as a character in art *outside* Arkadia (chiefly in Attic vase-painting) does his image also start appearing regularly *inside* Arkadia. We must certainly resign ourselves to the probability that the iconic mixanthropy so universally associated with the god is not an entirely accurate reflection of early Arkadian belief. That said, it swiftly attained iconic status within Arkadian cult and iconography; Athens can be said to have given Arkadia back her own god.

Pan's mixanthropic form, once it has emerged, dominates completely, though it continues to develop. One major development is the increasing popularity of young, attractive Pans who are, necessarily, more anthropomorphic, especially about the face.[118] Cult images of Pan are generally less given to innovation than 'secular' ones, however, and a strongly consistent mixanthropic type was established, with goat or goatish head,

Fig. 25

usually a goat's legs and feet, human arms and body, and very often holding a musical instrument or the *lagobolon*. This type is repeatedly employed across a large number of locations, in sculpture in the round (for example fig. 25)[119] and in relief.[120]

So what does the god's goat-element contribute to his character? In the most nebulous sense, the animal – like the bull and even perhaps the horse –

---

[117] Hübinger (1992).

[118] An example of the 'young and pretty' type is *LIMC s.v.* 'Pan', cat. no. 36: an Apulian red figure krater of the fourth century (Vatican AA 2 18255), which shows Pan human-faced but for animal ears and horns, a composition very familiar from the river-gods of that type.

[119] Numerous other examples come from Arkadia. Examples are given by Jost (1985), 464-6. Several of these have an explicitly cultic origin, being votives from known sanctuaries of the god. An example is a small fifth-century bronze which bears the words Κέος ἀνέθηκε and which shows Pan with bearded human face, horns and animal hooves (Mariemont Mus. G 57).

[120] This latter medium tends to consist of the same nymph-reliefs in which Acheloos (see above) figured so persistently.

has associations with fertility and sexual energy, both animal and human.[121] In Pan's case, however, these associations are given a more concrete form in his firm connection both with herdsmen and with their animal charges. His name, though its etymology is not unquestioned, would definitely have 'spoken' of the pastoral life and its concerns.[122] Pan embodies both the human and the animal side of a particular way of life, that of animal-herding. Older scholarship has seen this embodiment as emerging from within the pastoral society itself; rather later views see it as a personification imposed on both Pan and Arkadia from outside.[123] But whichever line one takes, there is no doubt that Pan's goat element is inextricably linked with his character of patron god of shepherds and guardian of their concerns.

The company that Pan keeps in Classical and post-Classical art reflects his fertility associations. He is worshipped and depicted alongside the nymphs, Hermes, Dionysos and Acheloos, especially in Attic votive reliefs which we have already examined with regard to the river-god. In other words, he joins an existing iconographic and cultic canon, in which his strange dual form and his goat elements are by no means incongruous. They are simply incorporated into an expanding collective of rustic curiosities. For our ancient sources are not unaware of the disturbing and grotesque aspects of Pan's mixanthropy and animal parts. This is very much to the fore, for example, in the *Homeric Hymn to Pan* (lines 35-47), which makes much of the shocked reaction to the birth of the 'monster'[124]: the nurse runs from him in fear,[125] though his strangeness delights the gods on Olympos.[126] This fear-inspiring quality of Pan's mixanthropy is not explicitly connected in ancient sources with his ability to inspire the panic which bears his name, but one might suppose them to be related. At any rate,

---

[121] Herbig (1949), esp. 33-4.

[122] The conventional, pastoral etymology is discussed by Larson (2007, 63) as being the most resonant and significant in antiquity. A number of possible etymologies are explored in Borgeaud (1988), 185-7 (appendix). A radically divergent view is presented by Brown (1977), who argues that the name's starting-point is the Mycenaean form *Opaon*, meaning, in his words, 'the Companion par excellence' (see p. 59); this form is preserved in Cypriot cult, while Arkadia is the source of the truncated form Pan. Impossible as it is to verify, this certainly seems another possible strand in the god's remote past. On the whole, it seems to me that pastoral associations would be more likely to be discerned by Pan's worshippers in the historical period.

[123] An example of the earlier, simpler view is that of Herbig (1949, esp. 15-18), who imagines Pan created by Arkadian pastoralists in their own image, as a reflection of their own concerns. cf. also Immerwahr (1891), 203-4; Lamb (1926). Borgeaud developed the more complex later argument that sees Pan and his character as largely the creation of Athenian thought, and part of their discourse on the primitive, the rustic, the pastoral, all of which both Pan and his native Arkadia represent in a symbolic function largely irrespective of the realities of Arkadian life.

[124] His monstrous quality is expressed in the phrase τερατωπὸν ἰδέσθαι, 'like a *teras* to behold'.

[125] *Hom. Hymn* 19.38-9. One might compare the terror of the nurses of Erichthonios when they see his half-snake form (or, in other sources, the snakes in his cradle): see below, p. 126.

[126] *Hom. Hymn* 19.45-7.

alongside the positive associations of Pan's goat parts (fertility, playfulness) there existed an underlying awareness of their potential to disturb and disquiet.

Fig. 26

The composition of Pan's mixanthropy reveals some interesting trends which are reminiscent of other instances already discussed. When they mention his mixanthropy at all, literary sources tend to focus on his horns, face and hooves, the same parts in which animality resides in his material depictions.[127] This is also reflected to some extent in the material evidence; though his feet may be human depending on time and context, horns are always present even when all other theriomorphic components are not. The importance of and emphasis on animal horns and feet is to be discerned also in the case of the horned Dionysos, discussed below, even though there the animal species is different. The significance of feet is hard to pin down, but horns are important for a number of reasons. They are the non-human feature *par excellence*, and by themselves are enough to render a being mixanthropic. They suggest power, aggression, and sometimes fertility. They are laden with possible echoes, all of which may have been present in the case of Pan. His mixanthropy is neither chaotic nor random; it belongs to a type which is occupied also by the horned Dionysos and by his mixanthropic followers, the Silenoi and satyrs.

---

[127] For example, the second line of the *Homeric Hymn to Pan* calls him *aigipodes* and *dikeros*, goat-footed and two-horned. The same two words in the same order are repeated on l. 37. In Aristoph. *Fr.* 230 he is called *kerobatas*; this appears to mean horn-footed, that is, with feet made of (the substance) horn, but which also surely serves to recall both the vital anatomical parts. Later references abound; see e.g. Nonn. *Dion.* 27.290 (feet) and *Orphic Hymn* 10, l. 5 (both horns and feet).

The final aspect which is repeatedly alluded to is the animal face of the god, a feature sometimes shared again by Dionysos. This can be made a subject of derision, as in Lucian, where Pan's nose is one of a list of grotesque features;[128] sometimes in art, too, there is the possibility that an artist is making use of its humorous or grotesque potential, as in the red-figure vase which depicts a pair of Panes reacting to the return of Persephone, with open animal mouths and staring eyes which it is hard not to view as comic, in conjunction with their wild leaping (fig. 26).[129] But the grotesque or comic quality is not usually brought out. The animal shaping of the face varies in extent, but is a highly significant aspect of mixanthropy, having considerable implications for identity. In terms of human ritual, including theatre, masking the face, more than any other form of costume, is the quintessential way of effecting a transformation into another being, even across gender or species.[130]

Dominant though the goat is in his character and physical form, Pan illustrates the possibility for mixanthropy to involve a multiplicity of species. First, Pan is enmeshed in a complex web of animal/god and animal/human relationships in Arkadian myth. According to one variant,[131] his mother is Kallisto, which makes him the half-brother of Arkas, with two effects: first, to tie him into the foundation-mythology of Arkadia and place him at the start of its history, and second, to involve him indirectly in the famous story of Kallisto's transgression and bear-metamorphosis, and the birth of an offspring called Arkas – 'Bear'. His association with Mount Lykaion links him with Lykaon's wolf-transformation, and the rumoured ritual reality of cannibalism and werewolfism.[132] Finally, he is involved in Demeter's horse-metamorphosis, or rather its aftermath, coaxing her out of her anger.[133] All these stories attempt to negotiate the states of human and non-human, or of divinity and beast, using

---

[128] Luc. *Dial. Deor.* 22.1: How can you be my son, asks Hermes of Pan, 'κέρατα ἔχων καὶ ῥῖνα τοιαύτην καὶ πώγωνα λάσιον καὶ σκέλη δίχηλα καὶ τραγικὰ καὶ οὐρὰν ὑπὲρ τὰς πυγάς;'

[129] See Boardman (1997), 32-3. On the motif of the *anodos* of Persephone in vase-paintings, see Bérard (1974); examples of the participation of satyrs and Panes may be seen in his pll. 11-13, demonstrating the frequency of the theme. See also Brommer (1949-50), 22-7.

[130] One could argue, though without the possibility of proof, that the fact that Pan's face is so frequently animal corroborates the supposition that he started out as wholly animal, since it has such a profound effect on identity. Certainly, to refer again to the case of Dionysos, that god also can be treated as wholly bull as well as bull-faced or -horned. By contrast, mixanthropes whose wholly animal portions do not include the face (such as centaurs and Acheloos) are never referred to in this way, simply as a holy animal without mention of a human part. This is not an observation on which one should place too much weight; the number of cases on each side is too small to give reliable statistics. But I believe that Pan's goat identity is rendered far stronger by his caprine facial features.

[131] Epimenides fr. 16 DK.

[132] For scholarship on the topic of cannibalism on Lykaion, both mythical and ritual, see above, n. 51.

[133] Paus. 8.42.3. The emphasis in this passage is on Pan's rôle as a denizen of the mountain realm: he is hunting and roaming from mountain to mountain when he finds Demeter.

episodes in which those states are dangerously transgressed or combined; and in every major instance, Pan is there on the fringes.

In addition to these various animal-metamorphosis associations, Pan's own animal element is occasionally flexible. An example is his mysterious connection with the fish. This crystallises in the person of Aigipan, who is sometimes but not always treated as a separate entity from Pan; however, there is no doubt that the two have common roots. In our (rather late) sources, Aigipan turns himself into a goat-fish hybrid to escape the murderous attack of Typhon; it is in this form that he is catasterised as Capricorn.[134] All actual hybridism and metamorphosis involving fish elements is restricted to Aigipan, but faint echoes are also discernible in Pan, through two *epikleseis*: Haliplanktos ('Sea-roaming') and Aktios ('Of the shore').[135] These are marine rather than specifically fish-connected but connect significantly with the Aigipan material. They also seem as odd in the depths of Arkadia as the fish-tail of Eurynome, with which it is interesting to compare them. No explanation suggests itself, though ancient authors were not always so fatalistic and subjected the matter to rationalistic scrutiny.[136] It is simply advisable to recognise that, with Pan as with so many divine mixanthropes, a dominant animal species in his composition co-exists with more shadowy alternatives which never achieve the same prominence.

3. Mixanthropy at the heart of Athens: Kekrops

As we have seen in the previous sub-chapter, it is a mistake to think of mixanthropes as occupying only an extra-urban cult-setting, and of being always divorced in location and function from the zone of civic life. A mixanthropic deity whose position on the Athenian acropolis is obviously significant for the understanding of his character is Kekrops, whose mixanthropic form was that of a man with the coiling body and tail of a snake from the waist down. Kekrops was considered an early king of Attica, normally the first, although ancient

---

[134] Hyg. *Fab.* 206; Hyg. *Astr.* 2.28; Opp, *Hal.* 3.15; Luc. *de Sacr.* 14.

[135] For the title Haliplanktos, see Soph. *Ai.* 695; for Aktios, see Theok. *Id.* 5.14. Of course, we have to ask whether these are in fact divine titles at all, or just poetic adjectives; the literary sources which contain them do not allow for an assumption of religious significance. That *haliplanktos* is an epiclesis seems, however, probable when we take into account the Suda entry (*s.v.* 'Haliplanktos') which says that Pan was called Haliplanktos because he hunted Typhon with nets; this has the feel of an *aition* to explain a rather mysterious cult title; but we know nothing about where and in what circumstances the title may have been used. *Aktios* is similarly mysterious. Apollo was titled Aktios, but this is almost always in connection with the site of Aktion, in Akarnania, and the epiclesis seems to have been a reference to the place-name; see Strabo 7.7.6, 10.2.1-7; Paus. 8.8.12. The Theokritos passage in which Pan is called Aktios sadly offers no evidence of cult practice; it merely testifies to some form of marine element in Pan's nature.

[136] Hyginus for example (*Astr.* 2.28) derives Aigipan's fish element from the fact that he hurled sea-shells instead of stones at the Titans.

authors differ somewhat about chronology and succession.[137] He is so closely bound up with Erichthonios and Erechtheus (who are themselves thoroughly intertwined[138]) that at times it seems perverse to separate them. However, he is selected for this study for two reasons: first, only Kekrops is consistently mixanthropic, and second, only for Kekrops do we have definite mention of worship. However, it should be recognised that in many ways he formed a close-knit group with Erichthonios and Erechtheus, especially on the level of mythology.[139]

The worship of Kekrops is an almost exclusively Attic phenomenon; the only other concrete mention is of a cult in Haliartos.[140] The two chief branches of his cult were within the city of Athens itself: on the acropolis, and, as *eponymos*, in the agora. The latter is the less certain, resting almost entirely on a mention of a single dedication in the fourth century.[141] It shows the use of a mythical figure to spearhead an aspect of political identity and loyalty, and reflects a particularly Athenian institution.

The cult on the acropolis is more varied and in some respects more interesting for the current study. It is another case of mixanthropic Totenkult, based on a supposed tomb; it has been suggested that the basis was a Mycenaean grave which came to be venerated as that of a dead hero. In any case, Kekrops undoubtedly belongs to the canon of heroes whose worship was an augmented form of regular grave-offerings, a canon widely associated with snakes, though not of course exclusively. The shrine of Kekrops on the acropolis clearly belongs to a type of hero tomb of civic importance discernible throughout Greece; the most closely analogous Athenian example is perhaps the tomb of Theseus. According to Plutarch, the remains of Theseus, brought back to Athens by Kimon, were established in a tomb near the gymnasium, another

---

[137] He is described as the first king of Attica by Apollodoros (*Bibl.* 3.14.1), and this is also strongly implied in Thuc. 2.15.1. For a divergent opinion, see Paus. 1.2.6.

[138] See Kearns (1989), 110.

[139] It should also be noted that the daughters of Kekrops, Aglauros, Pandrosos and Herse, were themselves of religious importance in Athens in conjunction with the figure of Kourotrophos: see Parker (2005), 216, 433-4; Shapiro (1995). They are non-mixanthropic and therefore do not merit inclusion in the main discussion, but it is interesting to bear this kourotrophic function in mind: could it be analogous to the same rôle played by the *kourai hagnai*, the daughters of mixanthropic Cheiron?

[140] Paus. 9.33.1. The Kekrops Pausanias mentions is perhaps a rather different figure from the one worshipped on the Athenian acropolis. This latter figure comes later in the mythical succession of Attic kings, being the successor of Erechtheus; but as Kearns rightly says (1989, 110), this distinction is in fact 'a somewhat desperate atthidographic hypothesis' designed to give chronological order to a morass of mythological variants, and the two Kekropes are in fact 'branches' of the same basic entity.

[141] See Kearns (1989), 160. Gourmelen (2004) argues strongly that Kekrops' rôle as *eponymos* constituted cult: see pp. 295-309. There is no doubt that, whether or not we believe that in this rôle he received the mechanics of worship, Kekrops was an important figure within the conception and organisation of the tribes.

central and vital city location, where the hero's cult is said to have had broad appeal.[142] Though the akropolitan location had its own political and religious resonances, there is no detaching it from the workings of the Athenian polis.

If Kekrops' tomb earns him at least partial inclusion within a certain type of cult-receiving hero, there is another dimension of his Attic worship which may connect more closely with his mixanthropy: in Euripides' *Ion* (l. 1400) we hear of a sacred cave, also on the acropolis. Was this a true cult site, or was Kekrops' name simply applied to a topographical feature? We cannot say, for the evidence of offerings, dedications and so on is lacking; but we may draw a comparison with the periakropolitan cave of Pan, which placed the god at once in the civic heartland and inside a microcosm of his imagined native environment. A significant number of mixanthropic deities appear as residents of caves, both in myth and in cult, and it is not surprising that Kekrops should be one of them.

So in some important ways Kekrops builds on patterns which recur among mixanthropic cult-recipients, and his contribution in this regard is valuable. However, these should not encourage us to ignore the locally specific manifestations of these patterns, and the particular symbolic rôles they place within a particular community. So often this relationship between mixanthrope and community is made obscure by lack of evidence, but the relative abundance of material from Athens allows Kekrops' symbolic function in Athenian myth to emerge. Most strongly represented in the ancient literature is his link with the all-important theme of autochthony.

The Athenians claimed to have been born from their very land, thereby pinning their projected identity on the idea of the entirely indigenous – or at least they did so in certain times and contexts. As Hall has noted, such claims gained prevalence in the fifth century, after the Persian invasions had reduced the appeal of Ionian origins (though the two traditions were to some degree reconciled).[143] In this situation, the Athenians were distinguishing themselves from other Greek communities whose origins were 'barbarian'; they were also choosing not to stake a claim within the wider Greek genealogy but rather to strike out on their own as uniquely uncontaminated products of their native land.[144]

Kekrops provides an embodiment of these claims through his own autochthony; he himself is literally *gêgenês*,[145] even though mythology does not dwell on his birth from the earth as it does in the case of Erichthonios, and in this regard

---

[142] Plut. *Thes.* 36.1-2.

[143] See also Rosivach (1987) and Parker (1987, 193-207) for further analysis of the political application of the autochthony theme in Athens; Loraux (2000) for a recent discussion of Athenian autochthony claims, esp. 29-31 on Erichthonios, Kekrops and the Kekropidai.

[144] Hall (1997), 51-6.

[145] See e.g. Hyg. *Fab.* 48; Ant. Lib. *Met.* 6.

he is the ultimate native.[146] He also, however, has a rôle to play in another episode which expresses the theme: the birth of Erichthonios. Erichthonios is *gêgenês* through special circumstances: the earth is fertilised by the seed of Hephaistos which he lets fall in his attempt to rape Athene. Kekrops presides at the birth, and his daughters, Aglauros, Pandrosos and Herse, undertake the care of the child.[147] He, as one being who emerged from the earth, helps to facilitate the emergence of another. As *autochthôn*, Kekrops encapsulates the mythical past of the Athenians, and it is interesting in this regard to compare him with the case of Pan, discussed above. The incorporation of Pan into the periakropolitan fringe allows for a reflection of another past, someone else's, that of the imaginary Arkadia, wild and primitive; Kekrops, on the other hand, ruler, civiliser, culture-hero, is an embodiment of self, not other.[148]

Although it is constantly inadvisable to attach unchanging symbolic characteristics to an animal species in ancient thought, one can suggest some points of connection between the snake element of Kekrops and his character as *gêgenês* and *autochthôn*. We have occasional references in ancient literature to snakes being earth-born and residing in the earth,[149] and this quality is plainly relevant to Kekrops; as Parker observes, 'Having emerged from the earth he still in part resembled the creature that slips to and from between the upper and lower worlds.'[150] In addition, the Greek pantheon provides numerous cult-heroes whose snake-associations coexist with an association with underground residence, figures such as Asklepios and Trophonios.[151] Plainly a persistent theme is at work.[152] Yet again, however, more is revealed by the peculiarities of the individual case, and what is peculiar about Kekrops here is his mixanthropy, a highly specialised manifestation of snake imagery. Gods associated with, and represented as, snakes, form the largest and most coherent body of animal-related

---

[146] Fascinatingly, a less strongly attested variant tradition makes Kekrops Egyptian (see Philochoros, *FGrHist* 328 F 93; Diod. 1.28; schol. Ar. *Plout.* 773; *Suda s.v.* 'Kekrops'); Fourgous (1993, 233-46) argues convincingly that this represents an ancient critique of the Athenian construction of ideal Greek identity through autochthony. The curious dichotomy between the Athenian and the Egyptian Kekrops will be remarked on further in chapter 5.

[147] Apollod. *Bibl.* 3.14.6.

[148] As Loraux (2000, 41-2) notes, there is in fact an implicit underlying analogy between Pan and the Athenians since both are autochthones; she accepts, however, the impossibility of knowing for certain whether this ever really overrode the 'otherness' of Pan.

[149] For example, in Hdt. 1.78.3, snakes featuring in an omen are interpreted as representing native inhabitants because the snake is a *gês paida*, a child of the earth. Writers of natural history give a scientific slant to this folkloric association by remarking on the tendency of snakes to reside in underground burrows: see e.g. Arist. *HA* 8 c 15. There is a striking convergence of the mythological and the biologically actual in this regard.

[150] Parker (1987), 193.

[151] See Ustinova (2002).

[152] On the connection between Kekrops' mixanthropy and his autochthony, see Fourgous (1993), 331-2.

deities in ancient Greek culture. Indeed, the snake appears to be an especially popular animal for divine representation. However, within this group, *mixanthropy is very rare*. Only Kekrops is consistently portrayed as mixanthropic. To give his form context, however, something must be said about non-mixanthropic snake imagery and its relative abundance.

Fig. 27

Snake-related gods, separately and collectively, have received the extensive scholarly attention that their clear importance merits (another reason not to undertake a full discussion here).[153] Two main sub-groups are discernible, the first composed of heroes, associated with underground chambers and with healing and prophecy, the second of various forms of Zeus, especially Zeus Meilichios, Philios and Ktesios. The latter are almost invariably depicted, in cult reliefs, in wholly snake form.[154] A large proportion of these images derive from Piraeus, where snake-Zeus worship was concentrated.[155] The snake element of the heroes is rather differently expressed. Snakes appear more often as attendants and attributes than as the form of the divinity itself; their rôle is often that of an instrument of healing, a divine emissary which carries out the

---

[153] The fullest treatment of them as a group is that of Mitropoulou (1977), who collates and catalogues the material evidence for snake-iconography of a number of cult figures, though with limited discussion.

[154] An example is a fourth-century votive relief from Mounychia, probably dedicated to Zeus Philios, showing the god in snake-form (Athens NM 1434); for a drawing see Garland (1987), 136. Sometimes the serpent-gods dwarf human worshippers: for an example, see Mitropoulou (1977), 112, fig. 48a (stele dedicated to and depicting Zeus Philios as a gigantic snake with two small humans). For this type, and for the type consisting of a lone coiled serpent, see Mitropoulou (1977), 112-121.

[155] See Garland (2001), 135-7.

deity's miraculous work.[156] The exception to this trend is the use of the snake as a temporary epiphanic form, especially by Asklepios. This is more in keeping with the representation of the snake Zeus; after all, when the latter is shown as a snake appearing before mortals, we have no way of knowing whether that form was considered permanent or simply adopted as a medium for communication.[157] For Asklepios, the snake form is sometimes the one in which he travels and in which he appears in a new cult site. It is the medium of choice for movement and revelation.[158]

It is highly significant that in the midst of all this rich snake imagery, mixanthropy hardly features. Is mixanthropy avoided as in some way unsuitable? In any form, mixanthropy is the preserve of the monstrous; even 'respectable' figures like Cheiron have a strong element of the monstrous, and one can imagine a reluctance to depict a god of Zeus' stature in that way. However, in the case of snake-mixanthropy, more specific objections existed. It is most commonly used in the depiction of the *enemies* of the gods, for example Typhon and (in some instances) the Giants,[159] and for a number of lesser mythical villains such as Delphyne and Echidna. So its unpopularity in the iconography of most deities is not surprising. And yet it was consistently used for Kekrops – why? Why was snake-mixanthropy, the juxtaposition of snake and human parts, particularly appropriate and important to that deity in that context?

First a word on the representation of Kekrops. This follows a pattern clear from many other mixanthropes: painted pottery favours a mixanthropic form, a bearded man with, in lieu of legs, a coiled serpent tail. The human upper half is almost always carefully and decorously clothed, the overall air one of solemnity and composure.[160] This form appears to have been well-established by the fifth

---

[156] See e.g. Aristoph. *Plout.* 730ff.; also the early-fourth-century marble relief from the Amphiaraon at Oropos (Athens NM 3369; *LIMC s.v.* 'Amphiaraos', cat. no. 63), which shows both Amphiaraos and his sacred snake ministering to sick people. On this sanctuary, see Schachter, vol. 1 (1981), 19-25.

[157] Divine metamorphosis into animal form often seems to be used as a means of achieving close communication with mortals, and Zeus in myth employs this method especially frequently to perform seductions.

[158] See e.g. Paus. 2.10.3: Asklepios turns up in Sikyon in the forms of a gigantic serpent in a chariot drawn by mules. For a similar snake-form arrival in Rome, see Ovid, *Met.* 15. 620-744. Alexander of Abonouteichos takes advantage of this trend when he chooses to introduce his fake Asklepios to the public in the form of a snake, here one which was first 'discovered' inside a miraculous egg (see Lucian, *Alex.* 14-15), though in this case the 'deity' remains a snake.

[159] The most famous instance of anguipede Giants is surely their depiction on the Hellenistic Great Altar at Pergamon, on which see Radt (1999), 168-80; Queyrel (2005). It should be said that in this case the Giants have *two* snakes below the waist, rather than the single snake-tail of Kekrops' type.

[160] This is very clear seen on an Attic red figure cup of c. 440 BC attributed to the Kodros Painter showing a snake-tailed Kekrops watching placidly as Athene takes the new-born Erichthonios into her arms (*LIMC s.v.* 'Kekrops', cat. no. 7; Berlin Staatl. Mus. F 2537). Very similar physical form may be seen in fig. 27 (above, p. 124).

century BC, when it reached its peak of popularity.[161] On the other hand, sculptural forms prefer wholly human anatomy.[162] This means that the cult artefacts that we have (largely reliefs, not numerous) are less inclined to depict Kekrops as a mixanthrope than is the less explicitly cultic medium of ceramic. Does this suggest that his serpent element was relatively unimportant in cult? Gourmelen suggests otherwise.[163] He demonstrates effectively that the conception of Kekrops as a composite being with an animal part was absolutely central to his rôle, in Athenian thought, as cult-receiving hero, mythical figure and legendary early king. The fact that sculpture seems reticent about portraying his mixanthropy is interesting, but clearly does not eliminate the importance of the mixanthropic element which vase-painters repeatedly portray.[164]

The context in vase paintings is often connected to the birth of Erichthonios.[165] Unlike Kekrops, Erichthonios as an adult is most often depicted as wholly human, in myth and art, though with snakes in the offing; at the same time, however, the snake aspects in his case are treated as far more alarming than those of Kekrops. The daughters of Kekrops open the chest which contains the infant, and receive a hideous snake-related revelation: the child in half-snake form,[166] or with a snake coiled around it.[167] They are then driven mad,[168] or else are destroyed by the snake that accompanies the child.[169] Erichthonios is rendered 'respectable' through his association with Athene and Kekrops, and he succeeds the latter as king of Attica; but it is significant that his animal elements carry associations of terror and shock, whereas those of Kekrops do not.

As so often with mixanthropic deities, we can remark on a species' associations in Greek thought, but what really characterises individuals is the dynamic

---

[161] As Fourgous notes (1993, 232-3), literary references to the part-serpentine form of Kekrops go back to the fifth century also: see e.g. Ar. *Wasps* 438; Eur. *Ion* 1158-65.

[162] e.g. *LIMC s.v.* 'Kekrops', cat. no. 37: a relief showing Kekrops and Athene from 410/9 BC (Louvre MA 831). In fact, as in most of the anthropomorphic cases, some doubt attends the identification of the relevant figure as Kekrops: for discussion of this, see Gourmelen (2004), esp. 304-6.

[163] Gourmelen (2004).

[164] This point is also made by Kearns, who remarks that 'despite a few fully human representations, everyone knew how the hero should look'. Kearns (1989), 111.

[165] On the manifestations of this episode in Attic vase-painting and their political significance, see Shapiro (1998).

[166] Hyg. *Fab.* 166. A faint suggestion of wholly-snake form is perhaps to be found in Philostratus (*Vit. Ap.* 7.24) in which Apollonios jokes that Athene once bore a *drakôn* for the Athenians; this appears to contain a punning reference to the famous Athenian law-giver Drakon as well as to Erichthonios.

[167] Apollod. *Bibl.* 3.14.6; Ovid, *Met.* 2.558-61.

[168] Pausanias (1.18.2) says that it was the sight of Erichthonios that drove them mad, but does not specify exactly which aspect of the child wrought this effect: perhaps his mixanthropy? Compare the reaction of the nurse to the birth of Pan: *Hom. Hymn* 19.38-9.

[169] Both traditions are recorded by Apollodoros (loc. cit.).

juxtaposition of animal and human. As a being with a double form and a double nature, Kekrops is ideally suited to his rôle as mediator between states: between wild and civilised, male and female, and so on.[170] It is this mediating rôle which emerges most strongly from ancient literary descriptions of his character and deeds. Kekrops was said to have invented monogamous marriage,[171] an invention considered to have contributed to Athens' escape from savagery over which Kekrops presided; he also united the tribes in a single community[172] and invented funeral rites.[173] His characterisation is that of a culture-hero who assists his community through important boundaries of development and civilisation. In Kekrops' case, the potentially dangerous power of the snake is harnessed, yoked to a controlling human component, and directed entirely for the good of his native Attica.[174]

4. Dionysos: a god on the borders

The god Dionysos in his infinite flexibility challenges the definitions and the parameters within which scholarship attempts to function. His inclusion within this book is debatable. On the one hand, there is much to connect him to other deities discussed; like Proteus and Thetis, he is a shape-changer; his occasional mixanthropy exists within this varied palette of forms. However, in cases of attested cult the animal element of the god tends to be manifested not through mixanthropy but rather through full theriomorphism, rare, as already noted, in Greek religion. His mixanthropy, on the other hand, is a feature chiefly of literary accounts, and late ones at that. Whether or not he should be considered a mixanthropic god at all is frankly open to question. However, failing to include him creates an artificial distinction between 'true' or 'proper' mixanthropes and those who fall short of certain criteria. As in the case of Thetis, Dionysos, though divergent from the main trend, provides an invaluable model of variety without which the concept of mixanthropy and its meaning would seem unnaturally and unhelpfully rigid.

There is one suggestion of a mixanthropic Dionysos receiving cult in that form. This is a Macedonian ritual, in honour of Dionysos Laphystios (the name echoes Zeus Laphystios). Lykophron mentions, briefly and cryptically, the

---

[170] Fourgous (1993), 234-6; Gourmelen (2004), esp. 97-112.

[171] Schol. Aristoph. *Plout*. 773.

[172] Philochoros, *FGrHist* 328 F 94.

[173] Cic. *Leg*. 2.63.

[174] Of course, the snake carries several positive associations as well, with fertility, knowledge, and the provision of special protection to those it favours: on this last, see Kearns (1989), 111, which compares the example of the Elean Sosipolis, and makes the point that the protecting snake uses its power to terrify to the advantage of its chosen human community. She aptly describes this as 'a belligerent protectiveness'.

Λαφυστίας κερασφόρους γυναῖκας, about which the scholiast Tzetzes explains that they are the female participants in a rite, in honour of a bull-headed Dionysos, which involved the wearing of horned masks (presumably in a dance or procession).[175] In this cult Dionysos appears to have functioned as mixanthrope rather than as theriomorph, but the evidence of Tzetzes is, in isolation, extremely unsatisfactory.

Dionysos' theriomorphic cult manifestation receives two disparate mentions. First, Plutarch records a ritual (whose date is essentially unknown)[176] in which the women of Elis call upon Dionysos to come to them βοέῳ ποδὶ θύων, 'rushing with ox-foot', and address him as ἄξιε ταῦρε, 'worthy bull'.[177] Among various tentative explanations,[178] Plutarch suggests that, since the bull's foot is less destructive than his horn, this formula is asking the god to be mild and propitious. It is easy to dismiss this peculiar explanation out of hand. However, it is not insignificant that, for Plutarch, this Dionysos is one whose presence could be a violent, destructive one. This sense is conveyed in the participle θύων. Indeed, accounts of the taurine Dionysos are often characterised by depictions of his turbulence, violence, menace, ability to inspire terror. This is contained in, but by no means restricted to, texts which appear to be dealing with the so-called 'Orphic' Dionysos, sometimes called Zagreus, who was the son of Zeus and Persephone.[179]

Moreover, there is an explicit connection between the frightening aspect of Dionysos and his animal form(s), expressed via the motif of his shape-changing. The adoption of a series of animal forms is always intended to alarm and deter, even when it is used evasively and the user is at a distinct disadvantage. Antoninus Liberalis[180] records the myth in which Dionysos terrifies and maddens the

---

[175] Lyk. Al. 1237 and schol. ad loc.

[176] Pausanias (6.26.1) gives considerable information concerning the important cult of Dionysos at Elis, and in particular a festival called the Thyia, but it is by no means certain that the hymn recounted by Plutarch is to be connected with this context. Exhaustive discussion may be found in Schlesier (2002).

[177] Plut. Quaest. Gr. 36. On the hymn, see Daraki (1985); Schlesier (2002). Further difficulty is added to an already cryptic source by considerable uncertainty over the text; for example, an alternative reading of thuôn is duôn ('plunging', 'descending'), which would convey a rather different set of associations. The reading thuôn is technically problematic (Schlesier 2002, 161-22 ns. 5 and 7), but the explanations of the alternative (that it refers to a sacred cave of Dionysos at Elis into which the god was being invited to plunge) feels awkward and finds no secure corroboration in archaeology or in ancient literature. The matter must perforce remain uncertain; the reading of 'with bull-foot' is not, however, in doubt.

[178] The level of authorial uncertainty in this section is indeed high, as Schlesier (2002, 163) notes ruefully.

[179] The nature, and indeed the very existence of coherent Orphic ideas are a notorious source of controversy. Here it is not necessary to become involved in the debate, since no claim is made that the mixanthropic Dionysos was a product of any one religious system or affiliation. On the relationship between Orpheus and Dionysos, see Guthrie (1952), 107-33; Linforth (1941), 307-64.

[180] Ant. Lib. Met. 10.

daughters of Minyas using animal metamorphoses, the first of which is a bull. Shape-changing is similarly (but defensively rather than aggressively) used by Dionysos when he is threatened by the murderous Titans in Nonnos' account;[181] to escape their clutches, he adopts several forms in succession, most of them ferocious animals. Among these forms, however, that of the bull is clearly distinguished. It is the final shape assumed; and it is the shape the god is in when he is finally slain and dismembered.

With regard to this last point, the bull seems often to have a dual association with, on the one hand, active destruction, and, on the other, passive suffering and death. This leads us to our next rite, apparently practiced on Tenedos, and described by Aelian:

> The people of Tenedos keep a cow in calf for Dionysos Anthroporraistos (Man-Slayer), and as soon as it has calved they tend to it as though it were a woman in child-bed. The new born calf they dress in buskins and then sacrifice. But the man who dealt it the blow with the axe is pelted with stones by the people and flees until he reaches the sea.[182]

This rite brings out the juxtaposition of violence and vulnerability. Dionysos is embodied, to some extent at least (this is the effect of the buskins), in a calf,[183] which is then killed in guilt-laden circumstances.[184] But this particular form of Dionysos is called Anthroporraistos, 'Man-slayer'. That is not the title of a simple victim. The bull-Dionysos can mete out violence as well as suffering it, it would seem, and this duality appears to be focused on the emblem of the bull as both fierce animal and sacrificial victim.[185] This duality underpins the

---

[181] Nonn. *Dion.* 6.179-205. On the special rôle of metamorphosis within the *Dionysiaka*, see Buxton (2009), 143-53.

[182] Aelian, *HA* 12.34: Τενέδιοι δὲ τῷ ἀνθρωπορραίστῃ Διονύσῳ τρέφουσι κύουσαν βοῦν, τεκοῦσαν δὲ ἄρα αὐτὴν οἷα δήπου λεχὼ θεραπεύουσιν. τὸ δὲ ἀρτιγενὲς βρέφος καταθύουσιν ὑποδήσαντες κοθόρνους. ὅ γε μὴν πατάξας αὐτὸ τῷ πελέκει λίθοις βάλλεται δημοσίᾳ, καὶ ἔστε ἐπὶ τὴν θάλατταν φεύγει.

[183] For an Argive ritual in which Dionysos is addressed as Bougenês, 'Cow-born', see Plut. *de Isid. et Osir.* 35. On this detail he is, however, citing one Sokrates, probably a third-century BC Argive historian (see *RE s.v.* 'Sokrates'); if this identification is correct, it would make the source for this passage relatively early and potentially very well-informed.

[184] The equation of Dionysos with the sacrificial victim is famously strong. As Daraki (1985, 65) remarks, 'Le 'sacrifice dionysiaque par excellence' est une mise à mort du dieu.' See also Seaford (2006), 84-6. Obbink (1993) is more sceptical: he casts doubt on the idea that the Greeks explicitly equated Dionysos with the sacrificial animal, and makes the point – admittedly important – that the myths of the Titans' killing of Zagreus does not reflect the pattern of sacrificial ritual in Dionysos' cult. The Tenedian ritual, he observes, is a very isolated instance. (Obbink [1993], 67-75.)

[185] This matter is treated in a fascinating discussion by Daraki (1985, 45-71), in which she questions the relationship between the rite of *ômophagia* (the rending and eating of raw flesh), and the associations which Dionysos also had with the world of vegetation and with vegetarian offerings. In the former, she argues (68-71), his devotees mimic the animal savagery of the god. Dionysos is slain and slayer (see pp. 62-3), aggressor and victim. Interestingly, Dionysos appears

Greek attitude to bulls more widely, and mythological settings sometimes place the two possibilities in at least potential opposition. An example is the myth of the bull of Poseidon which emerges from the sea onto the shore of Crete. The proper rôle of the bull is as a sacrificial victim; when that rôle is denied (by Minos keeping the bull to add to his own herds), the animal becomes a destructive force, engendering a monster – the Minotaur – and finding a narrative counterpart in the second bull sent by Poseidon, which kills Hippolytos between Athens and Troizen. Though this example is far removed from the case of Dionysos, one might argue that it illustrates the underlying purpose of the killing of the Dionysos-calf: to remove, by a sanctified method, an entity potentially destructive to the community.[186]

Dionysos' theriomorphic form is less anomalous within Greek tradition than it may seem, for it is distinctly epiphanic and thus related to shape-changing, the adoption of temporary animal forms. The calf in the Tenedian ritual is only a temporary sacrificial stand-in. The Elean pleas to him to come 'with ox-foot' are, as Jaccottet notes, equivalent to the cry of the god's followers in Euripides' play: φάνηθι ταῦρος (line 1018) – not 'come, bull' but 'come as a bull'. Throughout the *Bacchai*, the bull form is treated as guise rather than identity. This sense is reinforced if one looks at the whole sentence, lines 1018-9: Dionysos is implored to come as a bull, *or* as a serpent, *or* as a lion, and the words *idein* and *horasthai* – though not applied to the bull form, but only to the other two – make explicit the sense of epiphanic guise. The variety of species also connects with his shape-changing tendency.[187]

Theriomorphism and shape-changing: what of mixanthropy? We have no explicit references to mixanthropic cult statues; these seem to be wholly theriomorphic, although the terms used by the ancient authors tend to be ambiguous. Athenaios records a cult statue at Cyzicus, on the Propontis, which was *tauromorphos*;[188] Plutarch says that many of the Greeks make *tauromorphos* statues of the god.[189] *Tauromorphos* looks like a designation of full theriomorphism, but it is too vague for certainty. It is probable that Dionysos was shown as

---

to have received occasional human sacrifices, though these are not associated with his mixanthropic form: see Hughes (1991), 111-15.

[186] Interestingly, another of Dionysos' bull-related cult titles is 'Bull-eater'. The *Suda* entry (*s.v.* 'taurophagon') explains this by reference to the sacrifice of an ox to Dionysos, but also mentions the custom of *ōmophagia*, the eating of raw flesh. Cryptic though this is, it suggests that the sacrifice explanation is not enough, and that we are dealing with further divine violence, this time directed at the very animal in which the god is sometimes incarnate. The violence of maenads, the followers of Dionysos, against animals, seems to be reflected in this aspect of the god himself; or is it the other way round? Do the destructive tendencies of the maenads reflect the destructive potential of the deity they serve?

[187] Cf. lines 920-22: when Pentheus sees Dionysos as a bull, this is simultaneously delusional and truthful. See Jaccottet, vol. 1 (2003), 103.

[188] *Deipn.* 11.476.

[189] *de Isid. et Osir.* 35.

bull-horned on coinage of south Italy, but there are problems of identification; the images could show river gods, prevalent in that region.[190] Horns are inconveniently transferrable. The same uncertainty attends a small number of sculpted male heads with horns, which could be Dionysos, river gods, or Diadochoi.[191]

Mentions of Dionysos' mixanthropy in literature are more substantial but are late; they are also from texts which cannot really be regarded as typical. The chief examples are the Orphic Hymns to Dionysos,[192] and the sections of Nonnos' *Dionysiaka*[193] which appear to contain similar themes; though the dates of the Hymns are both uncertain and (probably) various,[194] it is almost certain that they predate Nonnos and may have been among his influences.[195] The Orphic Hymns and Nonnos contain several elements not found outside the Orphic tradition, such as the birth of Dionysos to Zeus and Persephone, and his murder by the Titans;[196] however, they also incorporate ingredients familiar to us from (for example) Euripides' *Bacchai* – the rôle of Semele is one of these – and should not be regarded as a wholly separate cultural, religious or literary phenomenon.[197] Attempts to make them the product of specific and separate groups have tended eventually to founder.[198] The concentration of mixanthropic motifs in the Orphic

---

[190] *LIMC s.v.* 'Dionysos', cat. no. 156 seems the only certain instance, a third-century coin thought to be of the Brettioi, showing a nude, bearded and horned Dionysos. Numerous other items in the catalogue may or may not depict the god.

[191] *LIMC s.v.* 'Dionysos', cat. nos. 157-9.

[192] For the text of the hymns, see Quandt (1962); the most recent edition, however, is that of Ricciardelli (2000). On their date, nature and context, see Guthrie (1952), 257-61; Linforth (1973), 179-89; West (1983), 28-9. For a recent detailed discussion of their form and content, see Rudhardt (2008); see also Morand (2001).

[193] This is a fifth-century AD text, which immediately necessitates some caution in the present study, although there is no doubt that the work makes use of many long-standing elements of Greek mythology. On date and context, see Vian (1976), XV-XVIII; Lindsay (1965), 359-65.

[194] Rudhardt (2008), 171-2.

[195] For discussion of similarities between the texts, see Morand (2001), 83-6.

[196] *Orphic Hymn to D.* 30, line 6, calls him the son of Persephone. In Nonnos, this Dionysos is also called Zagreus; he is killed by the Titans, after which Zeus replaces him with a second Dionysos, this one the son of Semele. See Nonn. *Dion.* 5.562 ff. and 6.155 ff. (The murder of Dionysos/Zagreus ties in with another feature prevalent in these sources: the close identification of Dionysos with the bull killed in sacrifice, discussed above). On the death and rebirth of Dionysos in Orphic literature, and its wider significance within Greek thought, see West (1983), 140-75.

[197] On the relationship in the Hymns between material particular to them and material known from elsewhere, see Rudhardt (2008), 266-74, discussing especially the dual maternity of Dionysos (Semele and Persephone).

[198] For example, echoes do appear to exist between the Hymns (especially their choices of deity and their language) and inscriptions and other artefacts found in Pergamon, and it may be that the religious climate of Asia Minor at various periods had a relatively high concentration of the names and principles associated with the Orphic literature; but this does not allow for a definite claim that an Orphic community dwelling in Pergamon was the sole source of the Hymns and used them consistently in its ritual (*pace* Guthrie [1952, 258-61], who argues strongly for a Pergamene centre of cult).

material is interesting, but cannot really support theories about the distinct theologies of specific groups of worshippers. So when the god is worshipped as a bull in Elis or as bull-formed in Cyzicus, the echoes with the mixanthropy in Orphic texts are interesting, but not indicative of any measurable convergence or influence. The overall impression one receives is that mixanthropy, theriomorphism and animal metamorphosis are pervasive themes in the depiction of Dionysos across the board, but that the story of his dismemberment by the Titans – a highly specific manifestation – gives them especial concentration and intensity.

Even when mixanthropy is not explicitly defined, however, it is notable that particular emphasis is placed on certain animal parts. Very often, texts link bull form to specific parts of the body. These tend to be the head/face,[199] horns[200] and feet.[201] These are the key 'points' of the body on which mixanthropy is often focused. They are particularly clearly seen in the case of Pan, whose extremities are – generally speaking – animal, and, crucially, remain so even when his torso becomes more human and more attractive. Certain parts of the body are critical in registering animality, and their distribution is not random. The head is clearly vital; it contains expression, thought and speech; if it is animal rather than human, this has profound implications for identity. And almost no mixanthrope has human feet. Put briefly, the animal parts brought out with regard to Dionysos are those which appear repeatedly in the trends of mixanthropic representation; this potentially brings the god into the animal-human discourse of which mixanthropy is a working part. However, Dionysos must be acknowledged as a borderline case, not unsuitable for such a perennial boundary-crosser as he is.

---

[199] For example, in *Orph. Hymn* 45, line 1, Dionysos is called *taurometôpe*.

[200] This is the most common element, and appears in early sources: see Eur. *Bacch.* 100, 921; Soph. fr. 874 Nauck; also Nonn. *Dion.* 6.165, 9.14.

[201] As in the Elean hymn cited in Plutarch's 36th *Greek Question*. Another example occurs at Soph. *Ant.* 1143.

Chapter III

Winged and horned gods

So far the deities discussed in this section have been represented with what might be termed 'integral mixanthropy' – that is, their animal elements replace parts of the anthropomorphic anatomy, or at least substantially alter it. Other deities, however, are superficially mixanthropic: animal parts are added on to a complete anthropomorphic form in a way which augments but does not substantially compromise it. The superficial mixanthropic elements which occur repeatedly in Greek religion are wings and horns. Of course, these have been touched on already, because the Sirens are winged, and Pan is horned (and Dionysos can be also). However, the Sirens, Pan and Dionysos also have integral mixanthropy. This chapter focuses rather on deities for whom wings or horns are the full extent of their attested mixanthropy.

If mixanthropy is defined in the strictest sense as the replacement of some anthropomorphic parts with their theriomorphic equivalents, winged and horned gods do not really belong in the canon. However, they still involve anatomical fusions of the two states, and as will be seen the characters of winged and horned gods register contributions from their non-human elements; for this reason, their inclusion is merited. Moreover, as will be seen in Chapter 8, there is a strong relationship in ancient depictions between integral mixanthropy and the imagery of costumes and accessories. Horns especially will reappear in this later discussion, and it will be argued that the extent to which they are organically connected to a deity may be varied significantly in representation, suggesting an ancient interest in the integral/superficial dichotomy which should discourage a too rigid definition of the mixanthropic type. Wings are, by contrast with horns, always organically connected where present at all, but their presence is extremely variable in the depiction of mythical beings; their inclusion is often a matter of artistic choice rather than fixed convention. For example, Eos is typically shown winged, but sometimes she is wingless but in a chariot drawn by winged horses. Wings facilitate her airborne activity, but it does not always have to be she who wears them; they can be transferred to her equipment, her immediate surroundings. This flexibility in the application of mixanthropic features is an important trend in the iconography of mixanthropic deities.

Wings are widely applied to mythical forms in ancient art. Winged cult-receiving deities, by contrast, are rather rare, and what we find are sporadic instances of worship dwarfed by a far more substantial body of material in which mythological activities and artistic popularity are of far more importance than ritual tendance. A good example of this is Boreas, the god of the north wind, whose winged form, usually carrying off Oreithyia, emblazons many vases. Boreas was also accorded cult in a few locations, but these instances are represented by ancient authors as responses to special aid rendered by the god to a community (usually against their enemies) and are certainly secondary in development to mythological career.[1] Most winged personalities are best considered as non-cult-receiving *daimones*. This is not, however, to say that ritual observance is not significant when and where it occurs.

The few winged beings that receive cult participate in two main themes discernible among the class of winged beings generally: on the one hand, flight, on the other, attack. The most famous case of the former – indeed the most famous winged deity by any measurement – is Nike. Nike is generally a rather generic character, in line with her personification of a contingency: a longed-for contingency, victory. This generic quality is reflected in the fact that she is a frequent decorative element in statuary and architecture, often in the plural (two or more Nikai);[2] also frequently Nikai function as votive dedications.[3] However, a singular Nike does emerge occasionally as a cult figure. In Athens this is the case; there she is very closely related to, but not indistinguishable from, Athene, who has Nike among her *epikleseis*.[4]

The famous Nike Apteron, the wingless wooden *xoanon* of the goddess which stood on the Athenian acropolis, is compared by Pausanias with the fettered Enyalios of Sparta.[5] Just as, says the Periegete, the fetters of Enyalios prevent the war-god deserting his human dependants, so her lack of wings will stop Nike leaving the Athenians. It is not surprising to find wings presented in this way, as expressing the potential for flight, for escape, for departure. Like Enyalios, Nike represents a commodity (military success) which the community is desperate to maintain.[6]

---

[1] The most famous example of this kind is the foundation of the sanctuary of Boreas beside the river Ilissos, in response to the god's aid against the Persians: see Hdt. 7.189.1-3.

[2] The most famous decorative instance is surely the Hellenistic Nike of Samothrace. For a plural example, see Paus. 2.11.8: Nikai adorn the temple of Asklepios at Titane, Argos.

[3] See e.g. Paus. 3.17.4: Lysander dedicated two Nikai in the temple of Athene at Sparta.

[4] Parker (2005), 298-9; Osborne (1998), 183-7.

[5] Paus. 3.15.7; cf. 5.26.6, 1.22.4.

[6] Steiner (2001, 243-5) also connects the wings of Nike with the elusiveness of the object of erotic desire, an interesting parallel discourse given the ancient equation between military and sexual activity. Isler-Kerényi (1969, 34-6) makes the related point that she can embody victory in all types of competitive endeavour, not just military; erotic competition may be included.

The explicit wings = escape equation, however, is rather rare among winged gods; more often the attribute signals the potential for active aggression. The characterisation of this aggression reveals a striking divergence between cult-receiving and non-cult-receiving entities. Among the former, the aggression usually has a punitive function, this being (to choose the most famous example) the speciality of the Erinyes (also called the Eumenides or Semnai Theai), who were quite widely wor-

Fig. 28

shipped in the Greek world, at Athens and elsewhere.[7] It has already been noted that Arkadian Demeters Erinys and Melaina are similar to the Erinyes in character (vengeful anger); there is also iconographic convergence. Demeter Melaina was apparently depicted with snakes emerging from her hair, a stock feature of Erinyes as shown on vase-paintings, along with wings. Interestingly, literary depictions make more of the snakes than of the wings;[8] perhaps art relies more heavily than text on showing the wings to convey speed of attack. Across the board, the Erinyes' wings are one of a number of non-human elements which combine for frightening effect. The juxtaposition of wings and hair-snakes is also of course reminiscent of Demeter Melaina's/Erinys' other close relation, Medusa. What the Erinyes do not have is any noticeable association with the horse.

Aggression among non-cult-receiving winged beings tends by contrast to be acquisitive and (especially among female characters) erotic. The full range of the theme of erotic acquisition is displayed by Eos, the winged goddess of the dawn.[9] On vases Eos is most often shown either pursuing or abducting a youth, named in accordance with myth (Orion, Kephalos, Tithonos and others) or anonymous. (See fig. 28.) Her rôle as lover and snatcher of handsome young

---

[7] On their worship in Athens, see Paus. 1.28.6; on their cult at Titane near Sikyon, see Paus. 2.11.4.

[8] E.g. Aisch. *Choe.* 1048-9: Orestes cries out in horror at the Erinyes' approach, and says that they are like Gorgons. This passage also mentions another regular feature: dark garments, indicative of vengeful anger among female divinities and reminiscent of Demeter Melaina.

[9] Ovid (*Met.* 13.486-8) appears to be suggesting some very slight worship of Eos by making the goddess declare that her temples are few, but the narrative context makes this inadequate evidence of cult without other sources.

mortals is strongly represented in literature[10] as well as art. But this motif is more than just erotic rapacity. As the myths of Tithonos and of the death of Memnon show, Eos is also someone who takes men away from, and beyond, death.[11]

Though not herself a recipient of cult, Eos belongs to a group of beings which includes both winged women and bird-mixanthropes; thus avian identity is plainly in the picture. It has been shown that the Sirens, like their Egyptian *Ba*-bird cousins, are conductresses of the souls of the dead, and this funerary function connects them with Eos and her mortality-transcending powers.[12] Wings facilitate flight, wind-swift pursuit, the sweeping up and off of desired young men; but bird identity is in the mixture too, caught up somehow in the theme of death and the afterlife. This places the Sirens within a broader context in which they are highly unusual in their receipt of cult. It also reinforces the need to look beyond integral avian mixanthropy and to perceive the full palette of visual forms in which it operated. The exclusion of winged deities would render this perception impossible.

Horns too have some symbolic qualities which we may sometimes see contributing to the characters of their divine wearers; it has been argued, for example, that they can indicate both power[13] and fertility.[14] At the same time, in Greek culture they evoke even more explicitly than wings the non-human animal, and they almost always designate a particular species and its significance.

The phenomenon of the horned god appears to exist, in a sense, beyond individual names, characters and cults; this is reflected in the number of figures whose name actually means 'horned' or a variant of that.[15] Horned gods are also unusually widespread between cultures, as is revealed for example by the material collected by Bober in her lengthy article on the iconography of the Celtic horned

---

[10] On the love of Eos for Orion: Hom. *Od.* 5.118 ff.; for Kephalos: Apollod. *Bibl.* 3.14.3; for Tithonos: *Hom. Hymn* 5. 218-238.

[11] Indeed, Eos represents a cluster of death-transcendence: not only does she obtain perpetual life - though not youth - for Tithonos (see e.g. *Hom. Hymn* 5.218-36), but their son Memnon is also eventually conveyed by her to Leuke, the White Isle, the final destination of certain privileged heroes and an antithesis to the murky impotence of Hades. This was the dénouement of the lost epic the *Aithiopis*, preserved in Prokl. *Chrest.* 11.

[12] Vermeule recognised the close association of erotic pursuit with death in the Greek imagination: see Vermeule (1979), 145-78.

[13] On bull-horns as indicating royal power, see Rice (1998), 116.

[14] See for example Athenassopoulou (2003), 79-84. Deyts makes the very interesting point concerning the ancient Gaulish material that a bull may be represented as an '*über*-bull' by giving it three horns; thus the properties of the horn (fertility and power) may be harnessed and augmented. (Deyts [1992], 30.)

[15] For example, the rather obscure figure Bokaros (bull-horned'): see *RE s.v.* 'Bokaros'; Cernunnos also has this meaning (see Bober 1951, 14), and Karneios, a title of Apollo, clearly derives from the same root.

god Cernunnos.[16] The material record abounds in anonymous horned figures, such as the ram-headed terracottas of Lykosoura, or the various horned figures from Cyprus.[17] These representations, however, cannot reliably be identified, and tell us next to nothing about particular named divinities or their cults. It has therefore been decided to focus discussion here on Apollo Karneios and Zeus Ammon, the only instances of Greek horned gods for whom some evidence is available concerning iconography and divine function. This evidence is simply not available in many other cases. For example, Cook makes an ingenious attempt to link several forms of Zeus (especially Zeus Sabazios, Laphystios, Akraios/Aktaios, Meilichios and Ktesios) with the ram, and uses this to argue for the erstwhile existence of a ram-god.[18] However, it is indisputably true that only Zeus Ammon is actually and unambiguously depicted with ram parts. He is therefore the only form of Zeus included in this discussion.

In addition to their horns, Apollo Karneios and Zeus Ammon had a historical connection. Apollo Karneios was a Peloponnesian deity, Zeus Ammon a Libyan one, but they were connected by a process of colonisation linking Sparta, Thera and Cyrene.[19]

Apollo Karneios' worship is largely but not exclusively centred on the Peloponnese; we have evidence, for example, for worship in Kos, Knidos, Argos, Messenia and Sikyon.[20] He was, however, of by far the most importance as a deity in Lakonia, and particularly Sparta. Although his mixanthropy is of the superficial type, the myths about his identity and origins tie him in with a number of animal, and horn, associations. The fullest treatment is to be found in Pausanias' third book, though other sources appear largely to accord with the substance of his account.[21] Pausanias tells us about a figure whom he simply calls Karneios, with the title Oiketas ('Of the House'), who was worshipped in Sparta before the return of the Herakleidai, and whose cult was based in the house of a seer called Krios ('Ram'). To the cult of *Apollo* Karneios Pausanias gives a slightly different pedigree. Its inception, he says, followed the murder of an Akarnanian seer called Karnos, for which Apollo punished the Dorians. The purpose of Apollo's cult is thus 'to propitiate the Akarnanian seer', giving the figure of Karnos such prominence in the narrative that it is little wonder that some have, in the past, posited that he originally enjoyed a separate identity as a (nature) deity

---

[16] Bober (1951). On Cernunnos and his Celtic associates, see also Green (1992), 311-19; Deyts (1992), 26-48.

[17] For the Cypriot artefacts involved, see C. Vermeule (1979); on their Arkadian counterparts, Perdrizet (1899), and Chapter 6 below.

[18] Cook, vol. 1 (1914), 420-2 and 428-30.

[19] Malkin (1994), 143.

[20] For a collection of the evidence for these sites, see RE *s.v.* 'Karneios', col. 961.

[21] The full range of sources on this matter is collected by Malkin (1994), 149-50.

in his own right, which was then usurped by Apollo.[22] Whether or not one gives any credence to this notion, there is no doubt that by the time all our sources were writing, Apollo was thoroughly embedded in the complex of ram-related figures in the myths. How the various entities – Apollo Karneios, Karneios, Karnos, Krios – related to each other exactly one cannot say. Some familiar motifs are discernible in the tangle, however, most notably the combination of animal features with prophecy found also in the cases of Pan, Cheiron, Proteus and others.

If Apollo Karneios comes from a complex background of animal associations, however, this is in contrast with his rôle as a god of manifest civic importance in Lakonia, who gave his name to both a month and a festival.[23] Is his animal element of any importance at all to this very public dimension of the god? Malkin argues interestingly that it is, seeing Apollo Karneios' ram element as continuing to play a rôle in his characterisation as a deity. He is the 'lead ram' of the herd, of the community, a rôle pertaining both to a past life of nomadic pastoralism, and – importantly for Malkin's thesis – to his political rôle as spearhead of colonisation.[24] It is interesting to compare and contrast this use of his ram element by the community with the depiction of Pan's goat persona in and outside Arkadia. They are in some ways similar, with both embodying at the same time an animal and the way of human life associated with its care; both also are associated with a *past* way of life and with the community's own social history. But Pan's character is typically presented in a much more light-hearted way, for all his importance to Arkadian self-representation.

Despite the prevalence of animal motifs in his surrounding mythology, Apollo Karneios' own mixanthropy is an understated affair.[25] A horned Apollo Karneios does appear on coins, but from outside his Peloponnesian heartland, mainly from Kyrene.[26] From Lakonia itself we have an emblem of horns carved on a dedicatory relief,[27] and a ram-headed herm which may well have been meant to represent Apollo Karneios.[28] Also significant is the fact that we find

---

[22] For such theories and for a stringent rebuttal, see Farnell, vol. 5 (1909), 259-61.

[23] See Thuc. 5.54; schol. Theok. *Id.* 5.83.

[24] Malkin (1994), 149-57.

[25] It would certainly be inadvisable to follow Keller, vol. 1 (1909), 320 in branding Apollo Karneios as the later development of a straightforwardly theriomorphic ram-god; the subtle nature of the god's animal elements should not be dismissed as the result of religious evolution, for which there is no real proof.

[26] The coin type of the beardless Apollo Karneios first appears on the coins of Cyrene in the early fourth century, and continues through the Hellenistic period. For early examples, see *BMC* Cyrenaica li, 100a-c, pl. XII, nos. 12,13,15.

[27] Malkin (1994), 153.

[28] See Cook, vol. 1 (1925), 352. The herm, if it is Apollo Karneios, is an exception to the trend in that it is ram-headed, not merely ram-horned; it is the only instance of such a composition connected with Apollo Karneios and does not detract from the overwhelming impression that his animal element was focused in the horns to the general exclusion of other components.

an 'Apollo Kereatas' ('Horned') worshipped beside the river Karnion, at the meeting-point of Messenia, Lakonia and Arkadia.[29]

We should not let the prominence of Pythian Apollo blind us to the existence of other, more rustic forms of the god, especially in the Peloponnese. Mixanthropy is rare, but many of the god's Peloponnesian cult titles reveal his pastoral connections. For example, in some parts of Arkadia he shares with Pan the epiklesis 'Nomios',[30] a title with particularly interesting associations, not only *via* Pan but also as revealed in a passage of Clement of Alexandria.[31] The author lists five different Apollos, of which the fourth is called Nomios by the Arkadians; he is the son of Silenos, and thus very much caught up in the world of rustic mixanthropy though not himself described as mixanthropic. Other titles which recall the same milieu are Tragios and Poimnios, attested (albeit in late sources) for his worship on Naxos.[32]

Apollo Karneios' identity as a horned god in Greece is to a large extent subtly and indirectly expressed, but for all that is undeniable. And what emerges is the paramount importance of the horns, such that on the carved inscription they can act alone as emblem of the god. Both titles, Karneios and Kereatas, echo the horn motif,[33] as does the river's name, Karnion; Pausanias' alternative etymology[34] involving cornel-trees is clearly a late invention.

Zeus Ammon takes us into territory far removed from these pastoral gods of southern Greece, despite the fact that he shares the element of the ram's horns. He was an important god of Kyrene, being by far the most frequently depicted deity on the coins of the region (with Apollo Karneios in second place).[35] In his case those horns have a very different cultural pedigree, though it is likely that the existence of horned gods within Greece itself facilitated his popularity as in import. His worship in Greece was widespread and enthusiastic up until the fourth century BC,[36] and strangely marked, for us, by the celebrity of the poet Pindar, who dedicated a statue in his temple in Boiotian Thebes;[37] other shrines were located, for example, in Gytheion,[38] Sparta,[39] Athens and

---

[29] Paus. 8.34.5. See Jost (1985), 482: 'Apollon serait un dieu 'cornu', protecteur des troupeaux.'

[30] Jost (1985), 481-2.

[31] Clem. Alex. *Pr.* 2.28.3.

[32] See Macr. *Sat.* 1.17.45, Steph. Byz. *s.v.* 'Tragia'; the latter says that Tragia ἔστι [καὶ] πόλις ἐν Νάξῳ, ἐν ᾗ Τράγιος Ἀπόλλων τιμᾶται'. See also Farnell, vol. 4 (1906-9), 360-61.

[33] For the names Karneios and Kereatas, and their etymological links to *keras* and *kara* see Chantraine *s.v.* 'κάρνος' and 'Κερεάτας'.

[34] Paus. 3.13.5.

[35] Zeus Ammon also appears especially early on coins of Cyrene, in the late sixth century; see e.g. *BMC* Cyrenaica xxiii, 12 a-c, pl. III, nos. 1-3; *LIMC s.v.* 'Ammon', cat. no. 99.

[36] For the introduction of the cult into Greece, see Parke (1967), 202-7. He also speculates as to when exactly Greeks became aware of the existence of Ammon's oracle at Siwah: see pp. 200-202.

[37] Pind. *Pyth.* 4.14-16; 9.51-3; see Parke (1967), 207-8.

[38] Paus. 3.21.8.

Piraeus.[39] As with Apollo Karneios, popularity is greatest in the Peloponnese, but is not limited to it.[40]

However, one striking feature of Zeus Ammon's cult is the continued importance, concurrent with the establishment of local shrines in Greece, of his Libyan oracle at the Siwah oasis as a place to which people would travel huge distances and which they would take pains to consult, sometimes on matters of great moment.[42] The earliest known instance of a consultation is that of Kroisos of Lydia,[43] and the visits continued, up to and beyond the most famous, that of Alexander the Great in 331.[44] Throughout this section we repeatedly find mixanthropy and prophecy going hand in hand; but only Zeus Ammon prosecutes the combination so successfully and in such a public and official context.

Unlike that of Apollo Karneios, the mixanthropy of Zeus Ammon is clear and persistent. It receives several literary mentions,[45] and we have no shortage of images. The horns are his persistent identifying feature, but other patterns are discernible: he tends to be bearded, is often shown enthroned;[46] he can also be shown simply as a mask.[47]

As with Apollo Karneios, in visual representation his mixanthropy is almost always limited to the horns, which in the case of Zeus Ammon is especially interesting because it may indicate that an original non-Greek model was adapted to lessen the animal element (the Egyptian Amun, for example, is ram-*headed*),[48] an intriguing possibility but one which rests on the vexed issue of the origin of the god's form.[49] This adaptation may be because horns do not really compro-

---

[39] Paus. 3.18.3.

[40] For the evidence concerning these two locations, see Garland (2001), 134.

[41] Pausanias (3.18.3) tells us that the Spartans were especially keen on consulting his Siwah oracle; see Parke (1967), 210-11.

[42] On Greek connections with Siwah, see Classen (1959), who deals both with Greeks visiting the oracle, and with the introduction of the cult of Ammon into Greece. The worship of Ammon in Athens, as revealed in epigraphic sources, is discussed by Woodward (1962).

[43] Hdt. 1.46.

[44] See Parke (1967, 196-200) for the site of Siwah and the manner of consultation.

[45] See e.g. Hdt. 2.42, 4.81; Diod. 3.73.1-2.

[46] e.g. *LIMC s.v.* 'Ammon', cat. no. 12c: an Archaic representation from Meniko in Cyprus (Nikosia Cyprus Mus.); see Karageorghis (1977), 35-6 and 45 pl. A. It is worth noting that a significant proportion of the depictions of the horned Zeus Ammon come from Cyprus, a place with a high concentration of horned gods.

[47] e.g. *LIMC s.v.* 'Ammon', cat. no. 88: small bronze attachment, fifth century, probably from Dodona (Louvre 4235); see Parke (1967), 59, 208.

[48] Parke (1967), 194.

[49] I shall not enter into the debate as to the origin of his form, particularly the as yet unsolved question of whether Egyptian Amun was the sole, or most important, source. The Greeks certainly equated the two; see e.g. Hdt. 2.42, discussed further below, in which the historian suggests that the name Ammon and its cognates derived from the association between Zeus and

mise the anthropomorphism of the Greek Zeus; and yet the mythological accounts – most of them post-Classical – concerning Zeus Ammon tend to adopt an explanatory tone. This suggests that even horns could not go without comment; and the manner in which authors attempt to excuse them is highly revealing.

The narratives tend to be euhemeristic; in a number of cases, Zeus Ammon is presented as a Libyan king. For Silius Italicus, for example, he was a mortal ruler accustomed to wearing horns on his helmet; after his deification, these external accessories became integral elements of iconography.[50] Another consistent feature is the involvement of Dionysos in some way. It could well be argued that Dionysos is included in the stories simply because he was already thought of as having spent time campaigning in the East, as was Herakles, who also crops up in one variant.[51] But an account by Diodoros[52] suggests that there is further significance in the Dionysos/Zeus Ammon connection. His version tells how Dionysos' parents were Zeus Ammon (once more a king of Libya) and a girl named Amaltheia; Zeus Ammon hides his illegitimate offspring on the banks of the river Triton.[53] Amaltheia is here presented as a normal human, but we cannot but connect the name with the divine goat who in one myth nursed Pan, and whose horn was the cornucopia. Add to this the presence of a river Triton, and we find we have one of the small tangles or clusters of mixanthropy with which Greek myth abounds, as usual a cross-species affair. More specifically, it is a story full of goat, ram and horn motifs, and this suggests that the inclusion of Dionysos may have owed something to *his* identity as a horned god, a form which in one account at least he took while prosecuting his Eastern campaign.[54]

Another frequent *topos* in this series of accounts has Dionysos, himself this time the Libyan ruler, saved from death by thirst in the desert by the appearance of a miraculous ram who leads him to water. Dionysos sets up a shrine to Zeus and gives the god ram's horns as a tribute to the saviour-animal.[55] This touches on a crucial element of Zeus Ammon's character – his connection with

---

Egyptian Amun. On this association, see Dunand and Zivie-Coche (2002), 241-7. Lipinski (1986, 307-8) firmly states that the god of Siwah was purely Egyptian in origin, refuting a suggestion that he may have contained elements of a native Libyan ram-god, but the matter is still unsettled.

[50] Sil. 1.415.

[51] Serv. Verg. *Aen.* 4.196.

[52] 3.68-74.

[53] One might note here that occasionally Zeus Ammon himself was represented in a rather Tritonesque form, with a long serpentine tail; see Kavvadias (1893), though in this piece more emphasis is placed on Zeus Ammon's snake-associations than on any marine element which the link with Triton might suggest. See however *LIMC s.v.* 'Ammon', cat. nos. 50, 51, 53 – instances where the god's form is juxtaposed with marine imagery.

[54] Luc. *Bacch.* 2.

[55] Serv. Verg. *Aen.* 4.196; Hyg. *Fab.* 133, *Astr.* 2.20; Ampel. *Lib. Memor.* 2.1.

water in a largely waterless landscape. As god of the oasis, this is not surprising. But there may be more here than a response to particular local circumstances; some form of dialogue with existing Greek religious ideas may have been at work. In Greece, Zeus was frequently worshipped as a weather-related deity with a special power over rain, and ability to supply it if properly treated;[56] this fact may have been partly responsible for the original association of the non-Greek Ammon with Zeus, out of all available Greek deities. But there are perhaps faint echoes of Acheloos, also. He is a god of streams and rivers, and his horn is central to that persona. More generally, horns of all kinds have fertility significance, and this is surely so with Zeus Ammon. The cluster formed by Zeus Ammon, Dionysos (with his horns- and fertility-associations) and the water-name Triton combine with the fact that the dominant theme of many of the myths describing both the origin of Zeus Ammon's horns and the foundation of his Siwah shrine are chiefly about the finding and securing of a vital natural resource.

A separate type of ancient explanation of Zeus Ammon's horns is to be found first appearing rather earlier, and this one centres round the theme of evasion, disguise and metamorphosis. Herodotos tells how Zeus, not wanting to be seen by Herakles, covers himself in the pelt of a ram, after which, in commemoration, the Egyptians depict Zeus with a ram's head, a form taken on by the people of Ammonia (Siwah).[57] In later versions, disguise becomes metamorphosis, with Zeus, along with the other gods, this time escaping from Typhon, and turning himself into a ram for the purpose.[58] This story, almost always in association with Egypt, has various other forms in which the ram-elements of Zeus are not included;[59] our 'branch' was clearly developed to fit Zeus Ammon's particular form and the necessity of explaining it. These myths, then, make mixanthropy the 'souvenir' of an episode of disguise or transformation, in a way which is reminiscent of the Arkadian myth of the mating of Demeter Melaina in mare form, which is then – according to the cult *aition* – commemorated by her mixanthropic statue. This myth is an early one, so this pattern, of deriving mixanthropy from one brief event in the deity's career, has a long pedigree. There is no mistaking its effect: to designate the animal element, whatever it is, as a symbolic attachment rather than an inherent and original part of the god's identity. That said, in the case of Zeus Ammon, reference to his horns is made in literature with a frequency which reveals their deep importance.[60] Less easy to determine is the possible significance of the

---

[56] See Cook, vol. 2 (1914), 1-4.

[57] Hdt. 2.42.

[58] Ovid, *Met.* 5.319 ff.; Lact. *Narr. Fab. Or.* 5.5.

[59] E.g. Plut. *de Isid. et Osir.* 72.

[60] Though it must be said that the authors who use the horns as the prime way of designating the deity – with such epithets as 'horn-wearing' and 'ram-horned' – tend to be late, e.g. Nonn.

species, the ram. It chimes with Peloponnesian figures, such as Apollo Karneios and the pastoral Hermes,[61] and reminds us that a vital relationship existed in antiquity between Dorian Lakonia and Kyrene; but in terms of origins it probably owes most to whatever non-Greek influences were at work in the early stages of the cult.

Dion. 3.232; Arnob. 6.12; Macr. *Sat.* 1.21.19; Ovid, *Met.* 4.670-71. It is possible that the focus on the horns increased over time.

[61] For Hermes in his pastoral Arkadian form, closely associated with the ram, see Jost (1985), 446-7.

Section One: Conclusion

1. Cult

Diverse as is the material collated above, it is possible to discern some features notable for their manifestation in a number of instances. These will be summarised. Many will also be returned to in more depth in subsequent chapters, and their contribution to the wider thematic picture examined.

First, mixanthropic deities show a strong tendency towards worship in extra-urban settings. They had a place within the cultic environment described by Larson in her recent article on nature deities in Greek religion.[1] Like the nymphs, deities such as Pan and Acheloos belonged, in both literary imagination and religious reality, to the god-haunted countryside with its sacred mountain-tops, caves and springs. This was an essential feature of their character as recipients of cult. The prevalence of extra-urban sites is not, however, the whole story. Mixanthropes were not absent from the urban sphere. Attic religion especially placed key mixanthropes, most notably Pan and Kekrops, at the heart of the city; Pan had a sacred cave on the acropolis, and at the same time numerous cave-sites in rural Attica. The two aspects of his worship are important in combination.

Within the duality of urban and extra-urban, the cave is of crucial importance. Wherever a cave was located (in Athenian thought at least, and no doubt more widely) it stood for the land beyond the city and its environs, for the uncultivated zone of shepherd and hunter. It is no accident that several mixanthropes were brought within the cave-setting and its symbolic preserve. That is not to say that they did not have long-standing cave associations (Cheiron for one did), but this association is hugely reinforced in the cults of Pan and Acheloos, especially within Attica. Neither Pan nor Acheloos was worshipped in a cave in their earliest cult sites (in Arkadia and Akarnania respectively), and yet the cave-setting came to dominate the worship of both across Greece. This happened because the cave was symbolically suitable for the mixanthrope in a way that the built temple was not; we find almost no evidence of mixanthropic gods worshipped within significant man-made structures.

The prevalence of caves has the function of simultaneously connecting mix-anthropic gods with the realm of animals, and at the same time of setting them apart. In the Greek imagination (and to a certain extent in geological reality) caves

---

[1] Larson (2007). She rightly notes (p. 56) that the idea of a clear category of 'nature deities' (and even more, the implied existence of deities who had nothing to do with nature) is a modern one not exactly mirrored in ancient thought. The deities she deals with, however, which include Pan and river-gods, are distinguished because they 'personified special features in the landscape or phenomena.' This characteristic, combined with the prevalence of extra-urban cult sites, is typical of a significant number of mixanthropes.

were placed within the untamed and mountainous territory associated with wild animals. Wild animals in myth use mountains as places of refuge and of aggressive power. However, they are almost never described as living in caves. Why is this?

In Greek thought, caves are proto-houses. They are an earlier stage of the human *modus vivendi* as defined, in large part, by some form of roofed dwelling-place. This is reflected in beliefs that early humans lived in caves,[2] and also in the fact that, in myth, primitive *Urmensch* figures such as the Kyklopes and the group-centaurs consistently live in them. The Cyclops Polyphemos lives in a cave in a parody of domestic order, but just as his home is naturally occurring, so he himself lives without agriculture, the crucial symbol of man's manipulation of the natural world.[3] The centaur Pholos receives Herakles into his cave as if it were an *oikos* like any other, but while his guest feasts on roasted meat he prefers his raw.[4] In these cases, caves allow for an inversion of human norms, in which the setting – a house that is not a house, a dwelling that was not built by man – plays an important rôle. The beings that live in caves, likewise, are not completely inhuman (wild animals), but are often combinations of beast and man, beings that combine elements of civilisation with elements of wildness. Given this character in myth it is not surprising to find that the actual worship of mixanthropes in caves is similarly prevalent.

So mixanthropes were increasingly included in the divine groupings of the rural sphere. Another – not unrelated – group in which they had an important rôle is that of Dionysos. Dionysos himself sometimes had mixanthropic features, though not with any iconographic consistency; more importantly, perhaps, he appears to have collected mixanthropic figures about him. A retinue of satyrs is a feature of his iconography as far back as may be seen; but his ties with other mixanthropic deities grow stronger from the Classical period onwards. This is especially so of Pan and Acheloos. Once again, as with the extra-urban and specifically cave-based locations, it is a matter of a natural affinity enhancing an existing feature of mixanthropic deities, rather than a case of outright innovation. Divine collectives grow in prevalence, and yet even in the earliest material it is rare to find mixanthropes worshipped singly; rather, we find several significant pairings, such as Zeus and Cheiron on Pelion, Zeus and Pan on Lykaion, and Zeus and Acheloos at Dodona. In the last two of these three situations there is also a mantic element, shared by the two deities.

These are not the only manifestations of a not infrequent, yet highly variable, connection between mixanthropes and prophecy. These may be divided into two (sometimes overlapping) types: an oracular function in ritual, as seen in the cases

---

[2] Buxton (1994), 90, 104-5.

[3] Hom. *Od.* 9.116-35.

[4] Apollod. *Bibl.* 2.5.4.

of Pan and Acheloos, and an element of the mantic in general character, as typified by Cheiron and Proteus.

The oracular contexts of Lykaion and Dodona in which Pan and Acheloos respectively participated are of course highly specific; this should not, however, obscure a wider ritual trend in the case of Pan at least. As Ustinova has recently shown, Pan's rôle as an oracular deity was widespread in sacred caves, but operated chiefly in collaboration, so to speak, with the nymphs. This should not surprise us, given the constant concurrence of Pan and the nymphs in cave cults, already noted, but there is more to it than juxtaposition, as Ustinova demonstrates: prophecy in these sites is often associated in ancient texts with the *mania* which results from possession by Pan or by the nymphs.[5] However, despite this strong convergence through the themes of inspiration and possession, the two groups cannot simply be elided; the prophetic powers of the nymphs extend beyond those of Pan and in many contexts are independent of him. Likewise, Pan's rôle on Lykaion gives him a dimension particular to him. Despite this important distinction it may be said that prophecy is a common shared feature of the 'divine collective' which so often operated within the sacred cave environment, in which Pan was a significant player.

Turning to mantic properties for which no actual ritual dimension is attested, we may recall that Cheiron is referred to as a *mantis*,[6] this being one aspect of the ancient emphasis on his wisdom. This wisdom finds a very particular manifestation in the case of sea-gods; though Thetis generally receives erotic approaches, Proteus is caught and held by heroes[7] who seek information and insight such as only he can give.

Prophetic properties, with or without a ritual aspect, cannot be seen as distinguishing mixanthropic gods from non-mixanthropic gods, since it is by no means a universal quality of the canon, nor is it limited to deities with mixanthropic representation. What it does on the whole do is distinguish divine from non-divine mixanthropes. The mantic wisdom of Cheiron is not shared by the brute rabble of the group-centaurs; that of Pan is not shared by the satyrs or the Silenoi.[8] It is not the case that all half-animal beings are by their very nature imbued with a special knowledge. The distinction between wise mixanthropes and their less lofty counterparts will be revisited in Chapter 5, where it will be shown that age is an important symbolic component of mixanthropic wisdom.

The final strong pattern is an association with death in various forms. Kekrops, Proteus and the Sirens received a form of tomb-cult, and so fall within the broader category of dead heroes in Greek religion. Acheloos, Dionysos, the

---

[5] See Ustinova (2009), 55-67.

[6] Eur. *Iph. Aul.* 1064.

[7] Most famously by Menelaos: Hom. *Od.* 4.385-6.

[8] Though Silenos is an exception to this rule, at least in later sources (see Ael. *VH*, 3.18).

Sirens and the centaurs (and by extension probably Cheiron) had distinct underworld connections. Demeter Melaina has often been described as a chthonic power, and though this is a rather loose and unsatisfactory designation her underworld links are undeniable. (It must be noted, however, that this is common to Demeter in general and not specifically related to her mare-headed form, though this does not negate the undoubted rapport between mare-associations and underworld-associations.) The significance of the themes of death and burial will be dealt with in depth below.

Of the deities studied in this book, Demeter Melaina is unusual in that she is a mixanthropic version of a deity with, in other contexts, an Olympian dimension. On the whole, however, it is helpful to regard mixanthropic deities as having less in common with the Olympian gods and goddesses than with the heroes, heroines and nymphs accorded cult throughout the Greek world. Heroes in particular share with many mixanthropes a mantic function, a tendency towards tomb-cult, and a stronger connection with particular sites than with the pan-Hellenic dimension. Heroes, heroines and nymphs give us a good broad model for viewing the cults of mixanthropes. Mixanthropes of course have their own peculiar identity, expressed in their distinctive peculiar form; the exploration of this identity is the purpose of Section Two.

2. Composition

Composition presents us with, if anything, a rather less coherent picture. Patterns are not absent. There are strong types at work in mixanthropy. One of these is the arrangement of an animal – or chiefly animal – head on a largely human body: this is the type of Pan and of several river-gods. In this type, the concentration of animality is on the head and face, but other extremities, such as feet and legs, tend also to be affected. As a rough reversal of this is the second chief type in which an animal body is paired with a largely human face, and sometimes shoulders and torso. This type includes Proteus, the Sirens, Cheiron, Kekrops and Acheloos in his most common form, and demonstrably owes more than the first to non-Greek artistic models. It is also rather more strongly associ-ated with non-divine monsters and with the negative character they possess.

These generalities, however, should not blind us to the aspects of mixan-thropic composition which display diversity. Important to note is the lack of any sense of consistent hierarchy between human and animal parts, deriving from or related to anatomy. One would think, surely, that the face would be the greatest signifier, and that a largely human face would indicate a largely human identity, and an animal face likewise. This does not appear to be so to any reliable extent. Cheiron, human-faced, has many civilised and quasi-human qualities; but the same cannot be said of the group-centaurs. They arguably have more in common with the satyrs, whose personality theirs closely resembles.[9] True, Cheiron tends to have a larger portion of human anatomy than the group centaurs, and this no doubt reflects his more civilised persona, but the fact that they share a basic compositional type is clearly no guarantee of shared character. Likewise, Pan's animal face may be thought to reflect his conspicuously bestial nature; but can we really say the same of Demeter Melaina? No one rule seems to govern the whole matter of identity across the board.

A similar picture is seen in the matter of animal species. As has been said, it is not possible to determine a single 'meaning' which will apply to a particular type of animal component regardless of place and time. This is unsurprising, given the acknowledged regional variety of Greek religious thought and practice. At the same time, it has been shown that animal elements, though varied in their symbolic force, are not disposed chaotically or at random. It is possible, by taking mixanthropes on a case-by-case basis, to make some observations as to the significance of animal species, when interpreted within the overall context of a cult, its mythology and its iconography.

Even regional variety should perhaps not be overstated. As will be revealed in Section Two, mixanthropic deities are bound together by strong interconnecting themes. It seems that mixanthropy itself is extremely important and distinctive; the precise nature of that mixanthropy, however, does not always respond to exhaustive rationalising analysis. What defines the class is the very fact of animal/human combination. The significance of this overarching condition over-rides, I would argue, the significance of details regarding species or arrangement.

---

[9] On the strong ties between centaurs and satyrs, see Hedreen (1992), 73. He notes, however, that when the centaurs and the satyrs are compared and contrasted by ancient authors, this tends to be favourable to the centaurs; Plato, for example, refers to centaurs as fierce, to satyrs as weak and cunning. (Plat. *Plt.* 291a-b.)

Section Two:

Movement, absence and loss

Introduction

In the Introduction to this book, it was shown that the characterisation of non-divine mixanthropes in Greek myths followed certain flexible but meaningful patterns. In particular, it was shown that mixanthropic monsters are almost without exception the adversary of humans (and sometimes of gods); and that in this position of foe they are doomed to suffer defeat and removal, sometimes even death. It was remarked that this motif of defeat and supersession is not limited to Greek culture, but also dominates the rôle of monsters in the myths of the Near East. The foe-status and removal of mixanthropes is a strikingly pervasive motif.

Are mixanthropic gods entirely immune to this characterisation? Do they occupy an entirely different position in ancient thought? Clearly not; not only does their physical depiction connect them with it, but several of them, such as the Sirens, are explicitly described as monstrous adversaries of man, defied and defeated. But a closer examination of the ancient material reveals that the discourse of the defeated monster finds a subtle counterpart in the depiction of mixanthropic deities, a complex adaptation of motifs which makes itself felt both in myths and rituals. Section Two lays out the dominant themes at work, and the way in which divinity and monstrosity accomplish a consistent implicit dialogue.

By far the most prominent motif in the ancient material is that of expulsion (and the closely associated motif of withdrawal). This is therefore the subject of the ensuing Chapter 4. It will be shown that mixanthropic deities are consistently depicted as being expelled, or as being caused to withdraw, from their cult site and/or their sphere of influence. In ancient thought, there are two chief ways in which the theme of expulsion or withdrawal is delineated. Both of them are spatial. Sometimes it is a matter of movement within a landscape fraught with symbolic significance, a landscape of imaginary topography dominated by certain physical features. At other time the focus is narrower: the physical setting of a cult, and the movement of a mixanthropic image within that setting. In both types, however, we find the same motif: the mixanthropic deity is made absent from its position of power or influence, and this absence is attended by a high degree of anxiety and regret.

Chapter IV

Expulsion, withdrawal and absence in the myths and cults of mixanthropic deities

1. The deity within the landscape

Mixanthropic deities are represented as highly prone to movement within an imagined landscape, a landscape conceived in terms of spatial zones and boundaries which may be passed between and crossed. It is typical of Greek myth that certain topographical features are used in a highly symbolic manner to reflect on both human and divine existence.

1.1. The mountain cave: Phigalian Demeter

The association of caves with themes of movement has been recognised with regard to their function in myth as portals, especially portals between the world of the living and the world of the dead.[1] Indeed, this rôle is to be found in ritual and practice as well as in myth, for caves were sometimes the sites of Nekyomanteia,[2] and were connected in cult with figures specialising in *katabaseis* and overworld-underworld transit, such as Herakles and Hermes.[3] This sub-chapter, however, explores the very particular rôle played by caves in the myths and cults of divine mixanthropes, arguing that that rôle was to give focus and a reference-point in the theme of the expulsion or withdrawal of mixanthropes.

The myth-cult combination here discussed has already been touched on: the account of the arrival of Demeter in the cave on Mount Elaion, in the territory of

---

[1] Hence their importance as places of birth. Typhon was born in a cave (Pind. *Pyth.* 1.16-17), as were Dionysos, in one local legend (Paus. 3.24.4), and the Cretan Zeus (Apollod. *Bibl.* 1.1.6).

[2] Particularly dramatic examples are the nekyomanteia at Herakleia Pontika and at Tainaron: for discussion with diagrams, see Ogden (2001), 29-34.

[3] Nekyomanteia and Herakles frequently overlap, as the former were often thought of as places where the hero emerged from the underworld, Kerberos in tow; this is the case at both Herakleia Pontika (a name which echoes Herakles) and Tainaron. On the former, see e.g. Xen. *Anab.* 6.2.2; Diod. 14.31.3. On Herakles at Tainaron: Soph. *Herakles at Tainaron* frr. 205-13 Nauck; Apollod. *Bibl.* 2.5.12.

Phigalia, where her worship was conducted. The details of that myth are recounted by Pausanias who claims to have obtained the account from local informants.[4] Demeter is angry both at her own enforced mating with Poseidon and at the abduction of Persephone by Hades. She puts on black clothes and withdraws into the cave 'for a long time' (ἐπὶ χρόνον … πολὺν[5]). Akarpia afflicts mankind. Demeter is eventually discovered by Pan and persuaded to leave the cave and undertake her normal functions once more.

This myth is presented by Pausanias as an *aition* of the cult's inception, and various aspects of it have an aetiological flavour: the black clothes donned by the goddess, for example, are given as an explanation of her title, Melaina.[6] And indeed, the myth as a whole can be seen as attempting to answer certain potentially troublesome questions about the cult. It is possible that as the Eleusinian Demeter-persona gained a purchase in Greek culture, the cave-cult of Phigalia began to seem anomalous: why should the goddess of the corn and of cultivated land be worshipped in a mountain grotto, in the realm of the herdsman and the hunter, away from the fields which were thought to be her preserve? Not only does the myth of her withdrawal answer this question, it also reassures the listener that her spell in the mountain zone was a temporary one, for it tells of the relief of her departure from the cave and resumption of her normal powers.[7]

This anxiety about a Demeter so far from her 'natural environment' may well have driven the creation of the myth, and yet it does not entirely explain (or reduce in wider significance) the form that the myth takes. Its key elements take on a greater weight when we see, reading on in Pausanias' account, that several of them are repeated strikingly in a second myth of withdrawal, at a later stage in the narrative of the cult's history. This second withdrawal follows the destruction of the original *xoanon* by fire and the subsequent lapse of Demeter's cult (discussed at length in Chapter 2); once more the goddess withholds her powers of fertility from mankind, leaving them suffering the resulting *akarpia*. It is interesting that this second story is hard to regard as an *aition*. There is no aspect of the cult that it really seems designed to explain. So an initial myth with strong aetiological patterns is built on by a second story that picks up the crucial motif of withdrawal as being particularly important and worthy of narration.[8]

---

[4] Paus. 8.42.1-3.

[5] 8.42.2.

[6] Pausanias tells us that she was named 'Black' because of this black clothing: 8.42.4.

[7] Borgeaud (1988, 48) comments on the cave's importance, in the Phigalian context and elsewhere, as a point from which a return is facilitated.

[8] Both the strong parallelism of the two episodes of withdrawal and their significant divergence have been explored by Bruit (1986), who points out (77-8) that whereas the first takes place in the divine sphere, being caused by an affair between deities and being resolved, also, without reference to humanity, in the second, human failure and negligence are responsible for Demeter's angry withdrawal. Bruit goes on (79 ff.) to analyse the rôle of the myth within the themes which she is discussing, namely the risk, should the Phigalia cult be discontinued, that the

To examine the significance of the cave in the two halves of the doublet, a diagram is helpful. Under 'Anger 1' are the essential features of the first, purely mythical, story, that of Demeter's angry withdrawal into the cave. Under 'Anger 2' are the essential features of the second, her anger at the destruction of the *xoanon* and the lapse of her cult.

ANGER 1	ANGER 2
Demeter <u>present</u> in cave	Demeter's *xoanon* <u>absent</u> from the cave
Her powers <u>absent</u> from the agricultural sphere	Her powers <u>absent</u> from the agricultural sphere
Demeter has to be <u>brought out of the cave</u>, and kept out of it	Her image has to be <u>brought back into the cave</u>, and kept in it

In both stories, the cave is a means of articulating the implications for mankind of the withdrawal of Demeter's powers. In the first, this is caused by her presence in the cave; in the second, by her absence from it.

It is, after all, the cave that gives the withdrawal-myths of Phigalian Demeter their individual character.[9] For a deity to take offence at some human misdemeanour – negligence, hybris, the transgression of a natural law – is indeed a contingency that peppers our ancient sources. And for a fertility deity, the most obvious way in which offence might be registered is through the withholding of the crucial influence on weather, earth and crops. The cave, as so often in Greek myth and ritual, lends a special physical dimension to a process of withdrawal. The above diagram encapsulates its ambiguity. Her cult ensured her divine favour by maintaining her presence – the presence of her image – in the cave. And yet, in myth the cult is inaugurated to celebrate her *leaving* the cave and becoming present once more in the world of agriculture. This is a highly significant twist on the familiar myth-element in which the miraculous epiphanic arrival of a deity in a specific location inaugurates a cult by conferring on the site the special status of having witnessed a divine presence. The Phigalia cult was enacted in the one place where Demeter herself – to the relief of all – was not. It was a monument to absence. And yet, at the same time, the presence of her image in the cave was clearly of the most deadly importance.[10]

---

process of civilisation might be reversed and mankind return to a state of cannibalism. Her arguments are extremely cogent, and have the very great value of demonstrating the ties binding the Phigalia episode with other sections of the Arkadia narrative.

[9] After all, most accounts of Demeter's anger after the rape of Persephone focus on the motif of her wandering. This is almost antithetical to the Phigalian consequence: instead of going abroad in the wide world, she confines herself to a small space.

[10] The reason for this inversion has a great deal to do with the fact that in Demeter Melaina's cult, the *containment and confinement* of her image within the cave are central: these themes will be

1.2. The cave as junction of departure: Thessalian Cheiron

As in the case of Demeter, the cave was a crucial factor in both the cult and the myths of Cheiron. Indeed, his cave is far more central to his career and personality than Demeter's, for whereas, as has been said, hers represented a state of temporary residence, his was a permanent home and an unchanging element of the 'furniture' of his existence in myth, though it receives little attention from vase-painters, despite their general interest in various Cheiron-related themes.[11] Cheiron was by nature a cave-dweller; this is quite different from the case of Demeter, in which cave-dwelling is aberrant, a symptom of disorder and inversion. Furthermore, in Cheiron's case, the cave becomes a focus of the irreversible loss of the deity by mankind, a contingency accompanied by regret and anxiety.

In an article,[12] I have argued that the character of Cheiron's cave in myth is illuminated by its difference from a closely related phenomenon: the underground chamber of certain dead heroes such as Trophonios, Amphiaraos and Asklepios. Underground chambers such as were thought to be inhabited by such heroes[13] act, in effect, as containers, guaranteeing the heroes' presence at cult sites where they may be consulted (for prophecy or healing). This is reflected in the language of personal visitation: people at Lebadeia 'went down to' Trophonios, for example, and there is a general sense of personal immediacy key to these heroes' efficacy in dealing with humanity's most pressing and personal concerns. Their containment in part derives from their manner of death, which tends to 'bury' them under the earth and to exercise a fixative function. If we look at Cheiron, however, we find two chief points of contrast: first, the centaur himself is described as anything but present and available; second, his cave – and to some extent caves generally – have very different symbolic implications from those of the underground chamber.

Pindar in his third *Pythian* says the following:

> I wish that Cheiron son of Philyra
> (if it is right for me to give tongue
> to a common prayer)
> were alive, who is departed,
> the wide-ruling son of Kronos Ouranidas, and that
> he ruled in the glades of Pelion, he, the wild beast

---

studied more closely later in the chapter. The current discussion focuses on absence and presence.

[11] Most popular are scenes where the infant Achilles is brought to Cheiron for instruction; loving detail is accorded the centaur's accoutrements of branch and dead game, but the mouth of the cave tends not to be depicted. This is unsurprising in light of the fact that the depiction of landscape with its challenging perspectives was something that entered the vase-painting canon rather after Cheiron had lost his great popularity as a subject.

[12] Aston (2006).

[13] For such underground heroes, see Ustinova (2002) and (2009), 89-109.

with a heart friendly to man; as he was when once he reared
our worker of sound limbs and relief from pain, Asklepios,
the hero, healer of every kind of illness.[14]

This expression of regret owes much to the context of the poem: nostalgia for lost innocence, expressions of concern for the patron, Hieron of Syracuse. However, it also raises, with particular intensity, themes which are found across many works and authors: the depiction of Cheiron as dead and gone, and the depiction of his cave as a place no longer inhabited.

The fullest accounts of the death of Cheiron are provided by Apollodoros and Ovid, but the event certainly predates them, receiving mention in Sophokles' *Trachiniai*.[15] In the account of Apollodoros, the context is significant: Cheiron's death occurs in the midst of the labours of Herakles and that hero's victorious struggles against a series of monsters and wild animals in the Peloponnese.[16] Herakles is entertained on Mount Pholoë by the native centaur Pholos, who is hospitable and non-violent;[17] as soon as the wine is opened, however (at Herakles' insistence), the other centaurs of the area arrive on the scene. They reduce the quiet dinner-party to confusion, and Herakles chases them with flaming brands and arrows to Malea. Here they find Cheiron, in exile from Magnesia after the expulsion of the centaurs by the Lapiths, and cluster round him in their panic. An arrow shot by Herakles passes through the arm of one of them and accidentally lodges in Cheiron's knee. Anguished, Herakles tries to heal the wound he has caused, but without success, and Cheiron withdraws to his Malean cave in great pain.[18] So severe is his discomfort that he wants to die; this is accomplished when Herakles arranges the transfer of his unwanted immortality to a new owner, Prometheus.[19] Ovid is less concerned with misguided aggression on the part of Herakles: in his version, Cheiron brings about his own death when, visited by Herakles in Thessaly, he drops one of the hero's poisoned arrows on his own foot and wounds himself incurably.[20]

For Apollodoros, Cheiron once dead is entirely removed from the picture. Ovid, by contrast, ends his version with Cheiron becoming a famous constellation in the heavens.[21] Unlike Apollodoros, he thus makes death result in a more

---

[14] Pind. *Pyth.* 3.1-7: ἤθελον Χίρωνά κε Φιλυρίδαν, | εἰ χρεὼν τοῦθ' ἁμετέρας ἀπὸ γλώσσας | κοινὸν εὔξασθαι ἔπος, | ζώειν τὸν ἀποιχόμενον, | Οὐρανίδα γόνον εὐρυμέδοντα Κρόνου, βάσ- | σαισί τ' ἄρχειν Παλίου φῆρ' ἀγρότερον | νόον ἔχοντ' ἀνδρῶν φίλον· οἷος ἐὼν θρέψεν ποτὲ | τέκτονα νωδυνίας ἄμερον γυι- | αρκέος Ἀσκλαπιόν, | ἥροα παντοδαπᾶν ἀλκτῆρα νούσων.

[15] Soph. *Trach.* 714-15.

[16] Apollod. *Bibl.* 2.5.4.

[17] On the character of Pholos, see Kirk (1971), 158-61; Padgett (2003), 20-21.

[18] Χειρώνεια ἔλκη: see Eustath. *Il.* 463.33-4.

[19] Apollod. *Bibl.* 2.5.4 and 2.5.11.

[20] Ovid, *Fast.* 5.397-414. In Diodoros' account this is more or less what happens to Pholos: 4.12.8.

[21] This version may be traced back to the third-century BC Eratosthenes: *Katast.* 40; cf. Hyg. *Astr.* 2.38.

exalted state; in this, he has much in common with the depiction of the story on the Chest of Kypselos, as described by Pausanias.[22] But in both versions the result is that Cheiron is rendered permanently absent from his Pelion cave. He is made distant, remote, unlike the underground hero whose miraculous death causes, as has been said, a state of heightened presence in a single fixed location, and a state of special accessibility for humans. His death is presented as a tragic error, and a real loss to mankind.

The link between caves and departure is one which surfaces in other contexts too within Greek mythology. A perfect illustration of this double quality is to be found in Apollodorus' account of Herakles' assault on the Nemean lion. Pursued by the hero, the lion quite naturally runs to take refuge in a cave. Caves are somewhere to hide.[23] This cave, however, has a special feature:

> The lion fled into a cave with two entrances, and Herakles, blocking up one, went in against the beast through the other.[24]

In other words, if Herakles had not taken special measures, the lion could have exited through one aperture as he was entering through the other. The cave allows for departure as well as – at the same time as – arrival. The cave itself does not allow Herakles to trap his lion until he has modified its design.[25]

The double-mouthed cave is not unique to this instance. Another example is the cave of the nymphs described in Homer's *Odyssey*.[26] This cave also has two openings which are distinguished from each other by function: through one the nymphs come in and out, while the other is for humans. Once again, movement is regulated: mortals and divinities are kept apart, but the cave also allows them to communicate.[27] It is a junction between two states of being; and this rôle recalls the fact that caves were thought to be portals to the underworld. Through a cave, movement between the realms of living and dead can be effected.[28] Overall,

---

[22] Paus. 5.19.9, in which Cheiron is thus described: ἀπηλαγμένος ἤδη παρὰ ἀνθρώπων καὶ ἠξιωμένος εἶναι σύνοικος θεοῖς.

[23] Although they do not tend to function as permanent homes for wild animals; see below.

[24] Apollod. *Bibl.* 2.5.1: συμφυγόντος δὲ εἰς ἀμφίστομον σπήλαιον αὐτοῦ τὴν ἑτέραν ἐνῳκοδόμησεν εἴσοδον διὰ δὲ τῆς ἑτέρας ἐπεισῆλθε τῷ θηρίῳ.

[25] Diodoros (4.11.3-4) provides an interesting variation: instead of a cave with two mouths, the lion's lair is a cleft running right through a mountain called 'Tretos' ('pierced'). The effect is the same, however: the cleft allows passage right through, and Herakles has to stop up one end.

[26] 13.103-12.

[27] Compare Quintus Smyrnaeus' description of the Nekyomanteion at Heracleia Pontica (6.469-91). In this, there is one path for gods and another for mortals. And the two paths are differently orientated: one goes up and the other goes down; one faces north and the other south. Thus they suggest movement both on the vertical and the lateral plane, up and down and along.

[28] Ogden also points out (2001, 252) that a cave can itself represent the realm of the dead, not merely an entrance; 251-253 for discussion of the spatial complexities of the connections between living and dead. But a downward movement is usually required to reach the underworld, and if so, the underground chamber or the cave facilitates this.

whereas the underground chamber is a container that holds a being in place, the cave acts, or can act, as a meeting of the ways. *It does not guarantee presence.* It facilitates movement, both physical and in terms of states of being. It can cause absence just as easily as presence. All caves can have this quality, of which the double opening is just the most graphic expression.

1.3. The cave as cult-site

In the case of Demeter Melaina, the cave represents the dangerous potential for absence. It was a (natural) monument to her mythical absence from the non-cave world of agriculture, a reminder of the perpetual risk of driving the goddess and her gifts away. The cave-cult was one largely based on anxiety on a number of levels – anxiety about forfeiting the fertility of the fields, but also anxiety about slipping back into the savage condition which prefigured the grain-culture of which Demeter was patron (Bruit's thesis). The cave itself stood for the pre-civilised state[29] which was always there in the background, threatening commu-nity-regression. One might say that there was a tense paradox at the heart of the cult: Demeter had both to be kept out of the cave (out of the uncultivated realm) and in it (in the cult space where her worship could be safely continued).

A very different condition prevails in the case of Cheiron. The Pelion cave which was the site of his worship was also the site of his mythical expulsion, an expulsion from which he never returns, falling prey first to wounding and then to death. In other words, Cheiron on Pelion has actually completed the process of removal which in the case of Demeter remains a permanent threat. His presence has been lost to man, not through negligence but through Herakles' open aggression, albeit aggression aimed not at him but at his kin. In expelling the savage centaurs, Herakles accidentally expelled the one of their number who had 'a mind friendly to man'.

Gaifman, in her important treatment of Greek aniconic cult images, discusses what she terms 'empty space aniconism'.[30] This is the practice whereby a deity is represented not by an image but by a deliberate and crafted vacancy, a building or sometimes a throne. In a sense, Cheiron's cave is a case of empty space aniconism. Neither ancient texts nor modern archaeology suggest that it contained a cult image. Like a carved stone seat it represents where the god *might be*. And yet, there is a crucial difference: a lack of potential. Cheiron, we know, is not in his cave, nor will he be; his departure is a permanent one. Whereas an aniconic empty space of the sort discussed by Gaifman derives its religious potency from the evocation of presence – either potential or invisible – Cheiron's cave derives

---

[29] For the cave as first dwelling and thus as emblem of the primitive state, see for example Buxton (1994), 105 ff. 'Caves … are before. Until Prometheus brought culture, mankind lived 'in sunless recesses of caves'.' (105.)

[30] See Gaifman (2005), 170-95.

its poignancy from the impossibility of that. His name, past deeds, and erstwhile presence infuse Pelion, but their effect is an elegiac one. There is a plangent contrast between the *aphthiton*[31] cave and its dying inhabitant.

1.4. The sea: Thetis

There is a strong and persistent connection between the sea and the group of beings whose defining characteristic is shape-changing: that is, those who take on a series of (mainly animal) forms in quick succession. Scholars have observed that the extreme fluctuations of state to which these shape-changers are given accords with the persona of the sea: restless, in perpetual movement, taking no fixed form.[32] There is a great deal of truth in this cliché. However, what the ensuing section attempts to show is that what the sea expresses in the cults and the myths of the shape-changers has a great deal in common with the patterns we have already observed surrounding mountain caves in the cases of other divine mixanthropes. It remains of undoubted interest that the sea should be the topographical feature most often found in connection with the shape-changers, and the special qualities of this element will be explored at the same time as comparison is drawn with our existing observations.

For all the poverty of our evidence for her Thessalian cult, its mechanics and indeed its precise location, Thetis offers a uniquely revealing juxtaposition of cultic and mythic phenomena related to the subject of spatial and geographical relationships. As was described in the first chapter of this book, her cult had two chief locations of which we are aware. The coast of Sepias was a zone whose strong identification with Thetis made her the goddess to which stranded mariners might turn to in prayer,[33] for all that we still cannot say what monuments may have marked out this sacrosanctity. Then there was the Thetideion in the territory of Pharsalos, mentioned by Euripides,[34] Phereky-des,[35] Strabo[36] and Plutarch,[37] and perhaps a shrine of the goddess also in Pharsalos itself. Thetis features on coins mostly in the south part of Thessaly.[38] Overall, though, we seem to see two main zones of worship: that on the shore, extending over a stretch of coastline, and that inland, near and maybe also in a major city.

---

[31] This is the word used of it in Pind. *Isth.* 8.45.

[32] For such theories and a refutation of the idea that shape-changing derives simply from the Greeks' observation of the ever-changing nature of the sea, see Forbes Irving (1990), 173-4.

[33] Hdt. 7.191.

[34] Eur. *Andr.* 16-20.

[35] *FGrHist* 3 F 1.

[36] Strabo 9.5.6.

[37] Plut. *Pel.* 31-32.

[38] For examples and discussion, see Moustaka (1983), 28-9.

Is it mere coincidence that the myths surrounding Thetis also occupy two main geographical spaces, corresponding closely to her two zones of worship? Unfortunately, as with Cheiron, we have not in this case the luxury we enjoy in Phigalia: the clear trace of a myth which developed in conjunction with the cult, to which it responded. Our Thetis-myths come to us from sources far removed from her Thessalian homeland, and any connection between them and the cults must have an element of speculation. None the less, our understanding of the cult sites can be enhanced by comparing them with the main stages in the myths.

The fame of Thetis which has endured to the present day rests largely on her association with Peleus. His amorous advances occasion her violent series of metamorphoses upon the shore,[39] and it would seem that the Sepias coastline received its name from the chief of her forms, the cuttlefish.[40] Peleus is successful in subduing the sea-nymph, and after an on-the-spot coupling by the sea the pair go to the cave of Cheiron where they are married.[41] Thetis bears Peleus seven children. Last of the seven is Achilles, and it is after Peleus interrupts her attempt to make Achilles immortal by dipping him in magic fire that Thetis forsakes his hearth and the care of her children and returns to the sea whence she came.

Thetis' myths, then, occupy two main positions, that on the shore (scene of her shape-changing, submission, mating) and that inland (scene of her marriage and subsequent life with Peleus). Likewise, her cult had both a shore aspect and an inland aspect, the Sepias and Pharsalos areas respectively.[42] Sadly, lack of evidence precludes any suggestion that these two sites were connected by ritual, that people would have travelled between the two, conscious of their interconnection.[43] However, one is justified in examining what, in the myths, the two locations signify, and whether this significance can be applied to the two locations of her cult.

At the heart of the story is Peleus' struggle to acquire Thetis as wife, and his subsequent failure to retain her. On the sea-shore, Thetis is half in one element, half in another, and her shape-changing surely reflects this ambiguity.[44] Likewise, her eventual submission and adoption of a single – human – form is closely followed by her departure from the liminal territory of the shore. Her geographi-

---

[39] Our earliest source is Pind. *Nem.* 4.62-3.

[40] See the discussion of her composition in Section One for the importance of her cuttlefish form and its connection with her character.

[41] Apollod. *Bibl.* 3.13.5.

[42] That the Thetideion near Pharsalos was connected in thought with the married life of Peleus and Thetis is suggested by Eur. *Andr.* 19-20, in which Andromache, speaking the prologue, says that the Thessalians call the site Thetideion in honour of Thetis' *numpheumata* – marriage.

[43] In other words, we do not have for Thetis what we have for Cheiron on Pelion: evidence for a ritual journey from the settlement to the rural shrine. It is interesting to speculate that the rituals of the Pharsalians included movement to two 'outside' zones: the mountain cave of Cheiron, and the shore of Thetis.

[44] As well as the ambiguity of her beauty; see Chapter 1.

cal movement is also accompanied by a progression between states: from that of the virgin, ambiguous and untamed, to that of the married woman and the mother.

Many studies have been conducted into the way in which physical space complemented and reflected the stages of human life as perceived in Greek culture, and therefore the rôle that spatial enactments played in rituals of development, rites of passage. In a way, the rituals of space and movement which were performed within real human lives in Greek society were designed to express the change which their subjects were undergoing and to do so in a shared and formalised setting.[45] Thetis undergoes movement in a similar fashion – away from youth and virginity, into maturity, marriage and mother-hood. Her spatial journey from the sea to the inland settlement mirrors this. The sea has a number of thematic connections, in Greek thought, with the state of the unmarried maiden. Nereids are frequently regarded as *parthenoi*, as nymphs tends to be.[46] Like the *parthenos*, the sea is untamed and unharvested,[47] and unpredictable. The marine *thiasos*, in which Nereids are staple ingredients, is strongly associated with life-transitions, whether into adulthood or into death.[48]

But for Thetis, a spatial change is no guarantee of permanent development. She retains an element of changefulness and instability, properties which shape the dénouement of her career, her abandonment of husband and children and her return to the sea.[49] For Thetis, unlike human participants in a rite of passage, change remains an integral part of her persona, and is not neutralised

---

[45] See e.g. Cole (1998), 27-43, on the importance of marginal sites (and movement to and from such sites) to the transition-rituals of girls connected with the worship of Artemis. A comparable male example is the Cretan custom whereby boys on the verge of becoming warriors have a spell in the countryside with their *erastai*: see Dillon (2002), 220. The most famous example of spatial liminality being associated in modern scholarship with human rites of passage is surely the argument of Vidal-Naquet's *The Black Hunter* (1986); see, however, Polinskaya (2003) for important modifications to his view: she makes the point that in reality the frontiers of a *polis* were not necessarily wild and uninhabited. However, the mythological and ritual significance of spatial movement remains undeniable.

[46] Larson (2001, 100-12) makes the important point that nymphs were not thought of always as virgin girls, but rather were strongly associated both with that prenuptial state and with the transition to that of the mature and married woman.

[47] The sea in Homer is described as being *atrugetos* (see e.g. *Il.* 1.316; *Od.* 2.370). The scholion on *Od.* 2.370 gives the translation 'unharvested', from the verb *trugao*, but this sense is not incontestable. See *LSJ s.v.* ἀτρύγετος. Chantraine *s.v.* ἀτρύγετος discusses the controversy without coming to a firm conclusion about the relative merits of the two main possibilities; 'unharvested', however, has something of the upper hand and is certainly very likely.

[48] Barringer (1995), 141-51.

[49] The impermanence of Thetis' stay on land is emphasised in the sources by references to her unhappiness and humiliation at being married to a mortal: see e.g. Hom. *Il.* 18.433-4. Euripides (*Andr.* 18-19) adds an intriguing element: while she is living with Peleus, Thetis is χωρὶς ἀνθρώπων ... φεύγουσ' ὅμιλον ('apart from men and shunning their gathering'). So it appears that, even once tamed and wed, she is unwilling to be fully integrated into human concourse. On Thetis as ambiguous mother, see Aston (2009).

by the movement – however symbolic – away from the sea and into the home of Peleus. She cannot be fixed for ever in the domestic and the tamed sphere. Like mermaids in Celtic legends, she will inevitably make the journey in reverse, back into the changeful element from which she emerged. Although she retains maternal ties to Achilles, she is none the less able to be re-integrated into the Nereid band, that most un-domestic setting. Even the Sepias promontory loses her to the sea.

The existence of cult sites in the two zones – inland and on the shore – may be read as a continued religious expression of this quality and of the two poles between which the goddess's movement took place. It may also be conjectured that the impermanence of Thetis in the household of Peleus was matched by an aspect of her persona as a deity in Pharsalian cult; but this argument will be postponed until the discussion of evasive mixanthropic statues. Here it must just be noted that both cult-sites known to have contained her worship, that inland and that on the shore, are associated with her absence.

To return, *in fine*, to the theme of expulsion/withdrawal and how it relates to Thetis, we may see that she bears some similarity with Demeter Melaina. Human action causes her to withdraw from involvement in the human sphere. As with Demeter and with Cheiron, both her cult sites are sites of absence, and points of departure.

1.5. Coastal jumping-off points: Glaukos and associates

Strongly analogous is the site of the worship of Glaukos at Anthedon, in Boiotia, on a spot called the *Glaukou pedêma* or Glaukos' Leap. As was detailed in Chapter 1, Glaukos was a mortal fisherman who, after discovering a magical source of immortality, leapt into the sea and became a prophetic marine deity. His leap is associated with a dual change of state: from mortal to immortal and from anthropomorph to mixanthrope. This metamorphic combination is treated with especial vividness by Ovid,[50] whose account, though it is far later than the worship which is the chief focus of this study, does offer some interesting insights into the peculiar liminality of the littoral cult-site; he does not invent a new narrative but rather expands and explores existing mythology (see above on Glaukos' cult for the other sources).

Most significant is the rôle played by the magic grass growing at the sea's edge, mentioned also by Pausanias.[51] This plant essentially represents the uncertain territory of the shore, and allows for passage between land and sea, and also between mortality and immortality. The latter is more simple: eating the plant makes mortals immortal. The former transition is subtler. Fish who are brought up onto the land are re-vivified just by lying on the grass: they

---

[50] *Met.* 13.904-67.
[51] 9.22.7.

move over it with a swimming motion, says Ovid,[52] and then slip back into the sea, confounding the fisherman who caught them. Glaukos himself, on tasting the grass, feels an insurmountable urge to leave the land and enter the sea; his identity and allegiance are immediately re-aligned.[53]

The magic grass which lines the shore is really just a concentrated expression of the curious quality which that zone always possesses in Greek thought. Glaukos' Leap was a cult site at a place of passage, of movement between states, movement which he himself exemplifies. More than that, the site is a place of departure: movement takes place from land to sea, and is not reversed. Once again, we find a mixanthrope being worshipped on the location of his mythological disappearance, like Cheiron, like Demeter Melaina, like those who receive a form of Totenkult. It is an overwhelmingly strong pattern.

Glaukos is not the only figure of this type. Especially comparable are Melikertes and Ino, whose mythology is also dominated by a departure from the land. Ino, driven mad by Hera, leaps into the sea with her child Melikertes, and they become sea-divinities called Leukothea and Palaimon; this change of state is closely similar to that of Glaukos.[54] Leukothea and Palaimon are, like Glaukos, accorded cult honours;[55] however, they are not represented mixanthropically. The class of the sea-leapers is not, then, exclusively a mixanthropic one; mixanthropy is one of a number of ways of expressing the marine associations of such beings, and their potential to move between states.[56]

1.6. Proteus and the sea-cave

We have noted similarities between the cave and the sea as cult-sites and as mythical homes of mixanthropes. Both are loci of expulsion, withdrawal and absence; the cave loses its mixanthrope, the sea receives one who is departing. In some cases, however, there is a spatial proximity also: a cave is depicted as being on the shore: not up on the elevation of a mountain but right on the *akte* so that

---

[52] Lines 936-8: it is significant that, under the grass's influence, the fish behave on land as they would in the sea: the two realms are temporarily conflated.

[53] Lines 942-8.

[54] See Hyg. *Fab.* 2; Apollod. *Bibl.* 3.4.3.

[55] In fact, their cult was on a much grander scale than Glaukos': it is said to have been in Palaimon's honour that the Isthmian Games were established (see Paus. 1.44.8; Apollod. *Bibl.* 3.4.3; Plut. *Thes.* 25.4; Hyg. *Fab.* 2). More comparable with Glaukos' cult is their worship on the Molurian rocks in the vicinity of Megara: this was thought of as the point from which they leapt into the sea (Paus. 1.44.7-8) and is thus a cultic departure-point such as are common in the worship of mixanthropes.

[56] Melikertes illustrates another possibility, being often shown riding on a dolphin, in accordance with the legend in which a dolphin brought him ashore at the Isthmus of Korinth. See Paus. 1.44.7-8 and 2.1.2 for this myth; at 2.3.4. the Periegete describes a Korinthian effigy of Palaimon on the back of a dolphin.

waves wash into it.[57] Once again there is some geographical reality behind this idea: sea-cliffs are almost invariably pitted with fissures and chasms, and the Greeks would have observed this on their own coastline. Such a sea-cave, in myth, is the home of Proteus, the mantic god depicted often as a man with a fish-tail in place of legs. He differs from Demeter Melaina, Cheiron, Thetis and Glaukos in an unfortunate way: we do not know that the topographical feature – in his case a cave – in which he appears in myth also housed his worship, though this does not mean that one did not. We are therefore dealing solely with the significance of the sea-cave as his fabled home, not as a cult site. That said, the cult of Proteus was associated with littoral environments, and so the schism between myth and worship is not insuperable.

The myths involved present a familiar and repeated situation: Proteus must be caught by a mortal hero and forced to impart words of prophecy and special wisdom relevant to the hero's (usually difficult) circumstances. In this, Proteus is like and yet unlike Thetis: both are sought out and grasped by mortals, but for different reasons. Thetis is valuable for her beauty, sexual allure, and prospective uxorial status, Proteus for his mysterious knowledge of present and future.[58] The motif of Proteus' capture finds its earliest expression in the *Odyssey*, when Menelaos consults the reluctant mantic for advice and information on his journey home.[59] In Roman literature, this episode is adapted by Vergil in the fourth *Georgic* when Aristaios seeks the reason for the mysterious death of his bees.[60] These two distant examples, the only substantial treatments of the myth which survive, fit Proteus and his consultation into two very different canons of thought and association, as will be made clear; and Vergil subjects his model to a fascinating mixture of loyalty and re-working. The central point of this discussion, however, is one on which the two converge: the sea-cave as setting of the encounter between hero and sea-god.

The cave is an odd hinge between sea-world and mountain-world, the two most frequent realms of the shape-changer and the mixanthrope. Vergil uses the word *mons* of its setting,[61] making the connection explicit; but it is implicit in both. The cave inland is the shelter of the herdsman, and of gods associated with herdsmen, such as Pan. Likewise, the sea-cave of Proteus is a littoral counterpart to that environment, just as he is a marine version of the inland pastoralist, with his flocks of seals which, like the Cyclops with his sheep, he carefully counts and

---

[57] One brief reference gives Thetis a sea-cave as well: Eur. *Andr.* 1265-6.

[58] For example, as Vergil puts it (*Georg.* 4.392-3): 'novit namque omnia vates, | quae sint, quae fuerint, quae mox ventura trahantur.'

[59] Hom. *Od.* 4.382-480. For discussion of the episode within the wider theme of metamorphosis in the *Odyssey*, see Buxton (2009), 37-47.

[60] Verg. *Georg.* 4.387-529.

[61] Line 419.

oversees.[62] This parallelism is taken to an extreme length with the notion of Proteus retiring into his cave to escape the heat of the day, an urge surely out of place in the depths of the sea, which remain cool at all times. This idea, of the god seeking shelter from the heat in his cave, is especially emphasised by Vergil, who uses terrestrial imagery to convey the conditions – withered grass, shrinking streams[63] – in a way which is curiously out of touch with Proteus' actual environment,[64] and draws the mind back to the land-based herdsman with whom he is explicitly compared. It also reminds us strongly of Pan's habit of sleeping away the noontime, a peril to any who might unwittingly wake him.[65] Thus the cave connects Proteus (in both texts, though in Vergil's most strongly) with the major mixanthropic preserve of the herd and its overseer, and the landscape in which they operate.

All the same, why have a cave? When Thetis comes out of the sea into the arms of the lurking Peleus, no cave is mentioned and in our surviving accounts their struggle simply takes place on the sands. With Proteus, the cave's function is as a lodging-place, albeit a temporary one: it is where the god and his seal-flock come to rest at midday. It is a place of (ostensible) security, and in it the god relaxes his vigilance, and can therefore be assailed. Hiding is not enough for either Menelaos or Aristaios: the god must be asleep before an attempt can be made. For whereas Peleus, if he is not careful, runs the risk of Thetis slipping back into the sea before she can be grasped, with Proteus one is given the impression of an adversary dangerous and to be feared from the first.[66] The cave is, ironically, a place of unusual vulnerability for a being normally quite able to look after himself. We are also familiar with the widespread idea that a cave is somewhere that mortals and immortals may meet. Like (in some ways) the underground chamber of a hero such as Trophonios, it provides a junction-box between the two states. 'A god is hard for a mortal man to master', remarks Menelaos gloomily,[67] but in this setting such an event is possible. It should also be noted that Proteus, unlike for example Zeus, *is* the kind of deity whom a mortal may fight and, with strength and guile, defeat. It is his mythic rôle to have his knowledge choked out of him.

---

[62] Counting his seals: Hom. *Od.* 4.411-12, 451; Verg. *Georg.* 4.436. Compared with a shepherd: Hom. *Od.* 4.413; Verg. *Georg.* 4.433-6.

[63] These conditions are mentioned twice: lines 401-3 and 425-8.

[64] Though the actual function of the cave, as a haven for storm-tossed mariners, is also hinted at on line 421.

[65] See e.g. Theok. *Id.* 1.15-18: Pan rests at noon, after a morning's hunting, and the shepherds fear to wake him.

[66] As Vermeule notes (1979, 188), gnashing, grinding teeth are a persistent ingredient of sea-divinities, emblematic of the danger they pose to assailants. Cf. Proteus in Verg. *Georg.* 4.452, described as 'graviter frendens' when approached by Aristaios.

[67] 4. 397: ἀργαλέος γάρ τ'ἐστὶ θεὸς βροτῷ ἀνδρὶ δαμῆναι.

A cave situated between sea and land has an even more intense intermediary function. The utterly alien quality of the sea is stressed especially in the Odyssean version, as is the extent to which Menelaos is encountering beings profoundly different from himself. The seals are the most potent emblem of this fact: their briny stench is unbearable not just because it offends the nostrils, but because it is the smell of the black and mysterious deep. It takes a dose of ambrosia administered by the helpful sea-goddess Eidothea to make it tolerable. 'Who would lie down beside a beast of the sea?' asks Menelaos ruefully.[68] And yet that is exactly what his ruse requires: he must lie among the seals, draped with a flayed seal-skin as a disguise, and so be counted by Proteus along with the rest of the flock, in a way which must remind us of Odysseus' ruse for escaping the Cyclops' cave, hidden under the belly of a ram and thus passing the monster's inspection. One is reminded also of the young Thessalians' ritual approach to the cave of Cheiron, wrapped in new fleeces. In some cases, a human, approaching a mixanthrope, must himself undergo a form of animal-transformation.

Thus the sea-cave's junction-quality may be seen to work in various ways. Proteus emerges onto the land, though still briefly cloaked in his watery element; Menelaos, to tackle him, has to enter a marine state. And once again the cave is where the mixanthropic deity suffers at the hands of a mortal hero: this, as we have seen, is the case with Cheiron, and if we think in terms of her cult-image and its destruction, we might see Demeter Melaina also as conforming to this pattern of misuse. In discussing *pharmakoi*, below, it will be shown that the sea has a rôle in this motif, receiving suicides, those expelled, those harried. However, the similarities are accompanied by important differences. So far, we have been dealing mainly with victims of expulsion, sometimes resulting in death, as with, for example, Cheiron and the Sirens. But Proteus is not expelled from his sea-cave. Rather, Menelaos is concerned to keep him in it, long enough to prophecy. In this, Proteus is to be compared with Thetis, who eventually fulfils her constant potential for absence by slipping back into the sea and abandoning Peleus. Proteus' sea-cave is a place of sporadic presence in which it is imperative that the god be kept and held while consultation takes place, and his absence from it is self-inflicted. This departs from the motif of expulsion, but has much in common with that of withdrawal, its voluntary counterpart, to be found in the case of Demeter Melaina. It is when Demeter's image is not kept in her cave that trouble is inflicted on mankind. Proteus is the ultimate in slippery gods, and the cave is at best a briefly-tenanted shelter.

Generally speaking, sea-related myths and figures bring us a subtle shift in emphasis away from deliberate expulsion by human agency. Human error often triggers the disappearance of the deities in question, for example Peleus' interference in Thetis' immortalisation of her children; and the approach of a

---

[68] 4.443: τίς γάρ κ'εἰναλίῳ παρὰ κήτεϊ κοιμηθείη;

mortal will send Proteus slipping back into the brine. Little, however, is required to set off their extreme innate tendency for disappearance. They are by nature supremely evasive, and their loss is accompanied less with guilt such as we have seen in the cases of Cheiron and Demeter Melaina, more with straight-forward regret that man is not able to retain a firm hold on a power he desires to keep. That said, the sea is very heavily associated with deliberate expulsion, as will be shown in the next chapter; and this must connect, on some level, with the mixanthropes and shape-changers who dwell in it.

The above sub-chapter has shown how themes of the expulsion, withdrawal and absence of mixanthropic deities are expressed in spatial terms, *via* a series of significant topographical settings. Sometimes, however, as has been said, the focus is a narrower one: on the mixanthropic image and its position within the setting of a cult.

2. The image within the cult: Pausanias and lost statues

We have seen above that Pausanias' narrative concerning the cult of Deme-ter Melaina at Phigalia connects the goddess with angry withdrawal and with an intensely uncertain presence. This is expressed through the motif of the cave and Demeter's movement into or out of it. There is, however, another side to Pausanias' account. Running alongside the story of Demeter's anger is an extraordinary narrative of lost statues in the goddess's sacred cave. The *xoanon* and its destruction by fire have been mentioned; but this is only the first stage in a sequence of statue-loss which the Periegete recounts. It must be reiterated that he appears to be reporting local Phigalian stories on the subject.

As has already been noted (see Chapter 2), Pausanias gives a very vivid description of Demeter Melaina's *xoanon*. Only after this does he tell us that the *xoanon* was *destroyed by fire*. This is the first clear indication, apart from tense, that Pausanias himself did not actually see the image to which he has given so much attention. The narrative continues[69] with the cult falling into neglect after the destruction of the *xoanon*, and, as a consequence, Demeter growing angry at the interruption of her worship and afflicting the land with *akarpia*. Seeking advice from the oracle at Delphi, the Phigalians are told the reason for their distress and immediately renew the cult with more zeal than before and commission a new statue from the craftsman Onatas, about whom Pausanias gives us some background information. Of this second effigy we are told:[70]

> Then this man, having found a drawing or copy of the old *xoanon* – but working more, as it is said, in accordance with a vision seen in dreams – made a bronze *agalma* for the Phigalians.

---

[69] For the fire, the neglect and the oracle: 8.42.5-6.

[70] Paus. 8.42.7 (for the Greek text, see the Appendix below).

And it is not until chapter twelve, after the digression on Onatas and a description of what offerings Pausanias himself dedicated in the cave, that we are informed almost casually that *the effigy made by Onatas was no longer in existence at the time of his visit.* Not only that, but most of the locals did not even know that Onatas' statue had ever been there. Pausanias, however, apparently undertakes some detective-work and finds an old man who is able to tell him that the Onatas statue was destroyed in a fall of stones from the cave-roof. And Pausanias ends his description of the region of Phigalia with the assertion: 'And in the roof it was still clear to me too, where the stones had broken away.'[71]

The question of whether or not the *xoanon* ever actually existed was largely the topic of an earlier section. Here, I shall treat the passage not as evidence, reliable or otherwise, but as 'a coherently conceived piece of writing', to borrow the phrase used by Elsner when he urges the recognition of the complexity and depth of the *Periegesis*.[72] The narrative of Demeter Melaina's statues has as good a claim as any part of the work on the kind of attention Elsner encourages us to give it.

That said, the account of the succession of statues seems at first glance an unproblematic description of the changes in a cult site over the centuries. After all, for all the importance in Greek cult of continuance and tradition, circumstances must sometimes have necessitated alterations such as the replacement of a statue. A wooden *xoanon* can suffer burning, and a bronze *agalma* can be damaged by falling rocks.[73] And yet, if one looks more closely at a few key phases in the narrative, it becomes clear that we are dealing with a heavily mythologizing story. Two points especially lend themselves to this reading. The first is the account of how Onatas achieved inspiration for the creation of the *agalma*. The second is the way in which the destruction of that *agalma* is described.

Pausanias tells us that Onatas made his *agalma* by working from a 'drawing[74] or copy' of the *xoanon*; but *mostly* according to a vision seen in dreams, a strongly mythological motif. In other words, the form is partly dictated by the original, but more by a new source, the dream. Since it seems unwise to take this episode simply as 'fact', how are we to interpret its creation? For answer, we turn to the story of the roof-fall. As has been said, there is nothing implausible about the roof of a cave crumbling and the falling stones damaging a bronze image. But in Pausanias' account, the statue is not merely damaged. It is entirely obliterated. Pausanias' recounts what an old man on the spot said of the *agalma*'s fate: 'He

---

[71] Paus. 8.42.13.

[72] Elsner (2001), 3.

[73] For convenience, I shall refer to the first statue as the *xoanon* and to the second as the *agalma*.

[74] The word γραφή can mean a drawing or a painting. It is very hard to envisage what kind of γραφή can have been available of the *xoanon*. A μίμημα – copy or replica – of the central icon of an obscure cult in its earlier stages is not much more plausible. Already the narrative has left reality behind it.

said that it had been broken to pieces by these [rocks], and had vanished entirely.'[75] The verbs could not be more emphatic. *Katagnumi* means 'break into pieces or shatter', and *aphanizomai* 'be wiped out or disappear'. In other words, the roof-fall did not simply render the *agalma* unsightly and so necessitate its replacement; it made it cease to exist.

There is no hope of trying to reconstruct what actually happened to either of the two lost statues. But what the myths do is to describe their absolute removal. The agents of the removal are miraculous accidents. And now we may reappraise the dream of Onatas. Just as the fire and the roof-fall deal with the disappearance of statues, so the dream of Onatas deals with the replacement of a statue with one that is not true to the original. Dreams, whether or not it is explicitly stated, tend to be divinely sent in Greek culture. Onatas' dream gives him supernatural carte blanche to deviate from the pattern of the *xoanon*; yet at the same time, the lesser influence of the drawing or copy ensures that the *xoanon* is not entirely left behind. In sum, key elements in the stories appear to combine to *justify and explain* certain changes (either historical or mythological) in the cult of Demeter Melaina which were thought to need justification. And though Pausanias does not tell us exactly what is lost as *agalma* succeeds *xoanon* (nor indeed what kind of statue was in position when he visited) it seems extremely likely that the discarded element was the mixanthropy of the original, the mare's head.[76] If it had still been in existence, he would surely have mentioned it. Continuity and innovation are kept in effective juxtaposition by the motif of Onatas' inspiration. But the mixanthropic image is a thing of the past, conceived of as having been obliterated long before the memory of the oldest inhabitant and yet clearly maintaining huge symbolic importance in Phigalian folklore.

In the light of the material already discussed in this chapter, it is clearly right to regard the story of Demeter's succession of statues as part of a wider motif of mixanthropic expulsion and loss. However, the matter does not end there. In order to place the Phigalian statue-narrative within its proper context, there are two things which must be taken into account: first, its relationship with Pausanias' character as an author and as a product of the period in which he lived;[77] second, its position within a far wider *topos* of the loss of statues, which is not limited to mixanthropic images.

When we say that Pausanias was part of the cultural environment of the Second Sophistic, we are using rather tendentious and potentially misleading terms. The period commonly designated by that term covered much time (the second and third centuries AD) and many forms of creative thought, though as

---

[75] 8.42.13.

[76] For debate as to the extent to which Onatas adhered to or departed from the form of the *xoanon*, see Dörig (1977), 9. Dörig's treatment is framed in art-historical terms and does not regard the matter in a mythological light, as the current study does; it is, however, entirely inconclusive.

[77] For a useful general discussion of the author's life and times, see Pretzler (2007), 16-31.

Whitmarsh has noted, one definition of the period (out of several) restricts it essentially to the works of the Sophists who give it its name.[78] In this group Pausanias does not belong, and indeed the genre of the *Periegesis* has been subjected to question, so that it is rendered more difficult to assess his place and rôle within the writing of his age.[79] But there is no doubt that certain features, themes and preoccupations characterise a period whose defining circumstance was the operation of Greek writers and thinkers within a Roman imperial context. This context gives unity and motivation to the literature produced by Greeks at the time, as well as one set of explanations of certain trends discernible in it.

One such trend, as has long been recognised, is a nostalgic attitude towards the Greek past, before the Roman occupation, manifested in various ways, both linguistic (Atticism in rhetoric and other forms of text and public speech) and thematic (a renewed interest in Greek mythology and long-past events). There is no doubt that Pausanias shares this attitude: his narration of monuments in Greece is notable for its omission of post-Classical, especially Roman-period buildings,[80] and also for its lengthy inclusion of mythological and historical material. The recognition of these tendencies has fuelled the acknowledgment that Pausanias is by no means a simple or basic narrator, and considerable study has gone into the ways in which his narrative of landscape, both human and natural, is used to convey his ideas of Greek cultural and religious heritage. The landscape as described by Pausanias is not simply a real arrangement of hills, trees and buildings; it is, rather, a constant series of traces of the past, traces which allow Pausanias to uncover and describe some item of myth or history.[81]

This mention of 'the prodigious phenomenon that Greece once was' raises the associated theme in Pausanias' work: that of loss. The past, and the greatness of the past, are things dead and gone, but through his narrative may be at least partly recovered and assured a place in human (Greek?[82]) memory.[83] But

---

[78] Whitmarsh (2005), 4-5. On the Sophists and the characteristics of their work, see Bowie (1971), 4-10.

[79] For a summary of the controversy, see Bowie (2001), 25-7. Bowie argues that the chief models for Pausanias' work are in fact Classical historiographers, especially Herodotos; backward-looking Atticism combines with the literary traits and concerns of his own day in a complex mixture. For a nuanced discussion of the ways in which Pausanias' work does and does not accord with the literary milieu of the time, see Hutton (2005), 30-53.

[80] On this and other aspects of Pausanias' archaising tendencies, see Bowie (1971), 22-3.

[81] On this conjunction of the real and the imagined, Porter remarks: 'What Pausanias gives his readers is a fantasy of Greece, of the prodigious phenomenon that Greece once was, made credible by its physical and contemporary attestations. Empiricism here subserves a romanticizing imagination.' (Porter [2001], 68.)

[82] Habicht (1985), 26 believes that the *Periegesis* was composed with a Greek audience in mind, but the question is not without controversy; for a selection of different views (including the assertion that Pausanias spoke to philhellene Romans), see Habicht (op. cit.) 24; Bowie (2001), 28-32.

this feeling is not couched only, or even chiefly, in the terms of grandeur that one might expect – the largest Classical temples, the most famous and glorious battles, the most prominent statesmen. The *Periegesis* preserves endless details of local landscape, the detail of small towns and their monuments, and especially their cults.[84] Many extraurban religious sites are also described. It is through the minutiae of cult that the narrative of loss, and the drive for preservation and commemoration, are most strongly expressed.

Pritchett has argued convincingly that at the heart of this use of religion is the figure of the cult statue.[85] Pausanias is noticeably concerned with the preservation of cult statues, especially *xoana*,[86] and with the question of whether they have survived the long centuries between the supposed date of their creation and the time of his visit.[87] This preoccupation applies to a wide variety of cults and deities. The narrative of Demeter Melaina's statues is unusually long and intricate, but it is one of a number which are concerned with the theme of the failure to preserve and maintain ancient cult effigies.

One thing must be made clear at this point. It is certain that in the Phigalia narrative Pausanias is recounting myths which were told by the inhabitants of the region.[88] He is not the primary author of the myths. They are not the product of his Second Sophistic imagination, but of the local oral tradition at work over many generations. The influence of his own background is felt through selection and arrangement, not through invention.[89] The Demeter cult, and particularly the lengthy narrative of her statues, are plainly of special importance to Pausanias, chiefly because they tie in very strongly with his wider

---

[83] Bowie (2001), 75; see also Habicht (1985), 164.

[84] Habicht (1985), 23 remarks on 'Pausanias' predilection for the sacred as opposed to the profane.'

[85] Pritchett, vol. 1 (1998): on p. 61 he remarks: 'The work … might be subtitled περὶ ἀγαλμάτων.' On Pausanias' attitudes towards statues, and his cultural context, see Donohue (1988), 140-47.

[86] Although the connotations of the word *xoanon* are not fixed, but rather change from author to author, it is undeniable that for Pausanias the most important meaning is that of an early cult image, primitive in form and of massive religious significance. On Pausanias' use of the word *xoanon*, and its shades of meaning, see Pritchett, vol. 1 (1998), 204-93. Donohue (1988, 231) makes the point that archaic wooden statues are a consistently important *idea* in Greek thought rather than a definite stage in cult practice.

[87] Some examples of narratives concerning the preservation of, or failure to preserve, cult statues are Paus. 1.22.3 (a cult statue being replaced); 10.15.4 (a statue sustaining damage); and 5.11.10 (maintenance work on statues). On the author's anxiety about lost and damaged effigies, see Pritchett, vol. 1 (1998), 68-80; Pritchett makes the point that this anxiety is fuelled by the Roman habit of appropriating Greek artefacts, religious and others, though as he observes (80), *xoana* were too inelegant and peculiar to be very popular with such art-collectors.

[88] See Hejnic (1961), 45-63: this work explores the complicated amalgamation of local and pan-Arkadian mythology surrounding the Phigalia cult.

[89] This combination is plainly not peculiar to Pausanias. For discussion of the relationship between fact and imagination in Greek travel writing generally, see Pretzler (2007), 44-56.

concerns as an author, and contribute something of huge (implicit) mark to the *Periegesis* as a whole.[90] This is reflected in the fact that the amount of space which the site, the cult and its mythology receive in the narrative of Book Eight is disproportionately large (far larger, for example, than that allotted to Bassai, for all that the latter is, and was, a far more 'impressive' site).[91] Within the *Periegesis*, the theme of the preservation or loss of statues is vital and frequently raised; within that theme, the narrative of the Phigalian statues bulks large. But it would be wrong to read it in isolation.

The fact that Pausanias was drawing on local stories alerts us to a deeper contextual issue. Pausanias' anxiety about cult statues, their preservation and maintenance, the constant danger of their loss, has been connected with features of his time and context, and with matters of Greek religious heritage and its survival. But the vocabulary in which these concerns are couched, the vocabulary of moving and disappearing statues, was surely provided to the Periegete by far older material, much (though not all) of which intimately involves mixanthropy and mixanthropic deities.

There is a wide canon of material in ancient sources on the idea of the cult statue endowed with supernatural agency. There are stories of cult statues sweating, bleeding, shooting fire. Within this pattern, however, one motif is particularly in evidence: that of the statue which must be restrained to prevent it – and the powers it contains – leaving the community in which it resides. For example, Pausanias tells us[92] that in Sparta the image of the war-god Enyalios was bound to prevent him running away and thus removing his military assistance. The military dimension continued potent even in rather later contexts: Diodoros reports[93] that during Alexander the Great's siege of Tyre there was anxiety lest Apollo forsake the beleaguered city; the god's image was therefore chained. Numerous other cases of this type are to be found in ancient literature, not all of them military in nature. The bound Eurynome of Phigalia[94] may certainly be seen as belonging to the canon of statues requiring tethers to prevent them disappearing. In her case, the chains combine with her mermaid form to give this impression: fish-tailed beings in Greek thought, such as Proteus and Nereus, are always associated with evasion and impermanence; and Eurynome's close conjunction with Thetis, the legendary shape-changer and mistress of escape, makes it clear that she is to be thought of as dangerously

---

[90] Much has been done by Bruit (1986) to argue for the programmatic connections between the Demeter Melaina episode and the wider text.

[91] On Bassai: 8.41.7-9. Pausanias does here concede that the temple of Apollo there is exceptionally lovely, but displays little interest in the details of the building or the cult.

[92] Paus. 3.15.7; on the restraining of statues, see Pritchett, vol. 1 (1998), 329-38; Merkelbach (1971).

[93] Diod. 17.41.7-8.

[94] Paus. 8.41.4-6.

slippery and in need of restraint. Winged deities can be similarly elusive, as was observed in Chapter 3 with regard to Nike Apteron, whose physical curtailment was compared by Pausanias with the chaining of Enyalios.

Bound images will be touched on further when we turn to divine aggression. Here, however, we can see that Pausanias is not innovative in focusing his anxieties on the statue, especially the *xoanon*. In Greek thought, *xoana* are especially potent representatives of a deity's power, and the possibility of their disappearance is an alarming one.[95] That said, one very important difference lies between Pausanias and most myths of statue-binding. In the latter, statues are generally recorded as departing or threatening to depart of their own accord, in an act of deliberate withdrawal. Pausanias is far more worried about *human* agency, whether it takes the form of neglect or of active removal of cult images. For him, deities, as represented by their statues, are not the authors of their own disappearance but are helpless victims of human misuse. This is an important divergence.[96]

We can see in the above material mixanthropic images taking a share of wider zones of thought and belief, rather than occupying one exclusive to themselves. Pausanias is not concerned only with the loss of mixanthropic images (although his longest narrative of statue loss concerns a mixanthrope); bound statues are not always mixanthropic. As so often, the situation is one of overlapping and closely related discourses. Mixanthropy as a tool of icono-graphic expression shares some semantic significance with others (bound images, lost images) and draws a significant portion of its own symbolic power from the conjunction.

In sum, both mixanthropic deities and their images were considered to be especially prone to movement and absence, both within the mythological landscape and its topography, and within the physical setting of a cult. In the next sub-chapter, spatial movement is still important. But the focus is on the figure of the *pharmakos*, or scapegoat, and on what light this can shed on the motif of mixanthropic expulsion. So far in this chapter, the loss of the mixanthropic deity or its image has been presented, through the ancient material, as chiefly a contingency to be avoided, accompanied by anxiety and/or regret. There is, however, another side to the matter, revealed in the thematic relationship which existed between mixanthropy and the figure of the *pharmakos*.

---

[95] On the mobile, animated and evasive qualities of *xoana*, see Frontisi-Ducroux (1975), 100-106.

[96] Occasionally myths of statue-binding blur the divide. For example, in a story retold by Athenaios (Athen. *Deipn.* 15.672a-673d = Menodotos in *FGrHist* 541 F 1) Tyrrhenian pirates attempt to steal the *xoanon* of Samian Hera; the goddess, however, miraculously immobilises their ship, thus preventing her own departure. When the Carians recover her they bind her to ensure that she never strays again. It is uncertain here whether the threat of departure is focused more on divine or human agency.

3. The scourging of Pan: the mixanthropic deity and the *pharmakos*

The subject which follows is one of the frequent instances in Greek society where two cultural phenomena, with their surrounding layers of reaction and depiction, are loosely but meaningfully conjoined. At first glance, the figure of the *pharmakos* appears to have little to do with the mixanthropic deity – he is, after all, human, and the participant in a real-life ritual. And yet on closer inspection it becomes clear that the two entities converge on a number of significant points. First, they are characterised in strikingly similar terms. Second, their treatments (in the case of mixanthropes, both mythical and ritual) also bear similarities. These similarities will be explored, and I shall ask what they contribute to the picture of the mixanthropic god which has been emerging in this section.[97]

The *pharmakos* is a person, usually one of low birth and/or outlaw status and of ugly if not deformed appearance.[98] The ceremony in which such a person is employed is sometimes occasioned by particular circumstances, such as plague[99] or famine,[100] sometimes part of a regular ritual event.[101] In either case, the *pharmakos* is generally ritually mistreated[102] and paraded through the town before being cast out and, sometimes, stoned outside the town walls.[103] His participation often ends in his death. The precise meaning of this rite has been debated at great length, with two poles of thought: an earlier notion was that the flagellation of

---

[97] A considerable amount of distinguished scholarship has been devoted to drawing together all ancient mentions of the institution of the *pharmakos* and his use. See Bremmer (1983); Burkert (1979), 59-77 and (1985), 82-4; Parker (1983), 24-6, 257-80.

[98] As Ogden (1997, 16) puts it: 'Like the *teras*, the scapegoat was ideally a disgusting marginal.' On the marginality of scapegoats, see also Bremmer (1983), 303-5.

[99] For example, in the Greek colony of Massilia, when plague struck, a poor man was wont to offer himself as a *pharmakos*: see Serv. Verg. *Aen.* 3.57; Lact. Plac. *Comm. Stat. Theb.* 10.793; Hughes (1991), 158-60.

[100] Plutarch tells us of the ritual of the *boulimou exêlasis* in his native Chaironeia, in which a slave – low status again – was beaten with rods of the *agnus castus* and expelled with the formula 'Out with hunger and in with wealth and health'. See Plut. *Quaest. Conv.* 6.8.1; Frazer, vol. 9 (1913), 252; Hughes (1991), 163. For a comparable Athenian example of this type, see schol. Ar. *Frogs* 734 and *Knights* 1136; Hesych. *s.v.* φαρμακός.

[101] For example, as part of the Thargelia in Athens: Harpokration *Lex. s.v.* φαρμακός. On this rite, see Frazer, vol. 9 (1933), 254; Bremmer (1983), 301-2; Hughes (1991), 139, 149-55.

[102] For example, in the most famous case, that described in fragments of the sixth-century Ionian poet Hipponax: here the *pharmakos* is beaten on the penis with squills, a plant with purificatory qualities in Greek thought. See Tzetzes *Chil.* 5.745-8 = Hipponax frr. 5-10 West; Hughes (1991), 141-9. For a detailed discussion of the plants involved in the pharmakos-ritual, see Bremmer (1983), 308-13. At the same time as such cases of ritual mistreatment we also hear of instances in which the victim is first maintained in unusual luxury: this is so in the Massilian rite (see n. 99 above).

[103] For example, in the Massilian rite according to Lactantius, and in both Athenian rituals mentioned.

the *pharmakos* was designed to stimulate fertility and natural renewal and increase,[104] whereas more recent scholars place more emphasis on the driving away of ills.[105] This latter sense is made explicit especially in the sources which describe rituals to counteract particular disasters such as famine; but one can also, as Hughes points out,[106] take it as inherent in the word *pharmakos* itself, and in the closely-associated term to denote the same person and his rôle, *peripsêma*.[107] So the purgative function of the rite appears most strongly in the Greek examples, but at the same time, the connection between fertility and flagellation undeniably does exist in some of the ancient *loci*. But the motif of the driving out, and even the extermination, of an ill is clearly the one uppermost in the Greek material.

Here a connection with mixanthropes will begin to be apparent: they too are often depicted, as has been shown, as being subjected to a process of expulsion which sometimes results in death. Yet this alone is not a similarity which can be usefully built on; we need to be sure that there were active connections between the *pharmakos* and mixanthropy in Greek thought.

That such connections did exist is suggested, as I have said, by parallels of characterisation. First, the *pharmakos* is almost always associated with ugliness and deformity, and this is an area of thought within which mixanthropes are included. A human/animal hybrid was most definitely classed as a *teras*, as was made clear in the Introduction to this book; it was considered something against nature, something potentially unlucky and ominous. Mixanthropes frequently inspire terror, disgust or uneasy laughter in myth, especially when they burst suddenly upon the sight: they confound with their paradoxical and unnatural qualities. This *teras*-quality of the mixanthrope is surely key to its tendency towards expulsion and rejection.

But the *pharmakos* is sometimes also connected with animal form or nature, thus reinforcing the connection with mixanthropes yet further. Ogden points to the aggressive use of *pharmakos*-animals as a means of sending plague or a curse into an enemy camp;[108] this is an inverted version of the motif of expulsion, but carries the same significance. He cites a passage in Diodoros (2.55), in which Erythrai is captured by the use of a bull-*pharmakos*, cursed and then sent into the enemy's midst. Often inanimate effigies of animals are used in the same

---

[104] A view taken, unsurprisingly, by Frazer, vol. 9 (1933), who cites (p. 229) the driving out of the Old Mars, in Rome, signalling the end of one year and the commencement of a new one. Frazer's comparative approach does not define a precise connection between this and the Greek rites.

[105] For example, Ogden (1997), 15-23, who connects the expulsion of the scapegoat with a society's need to rid itself of a *teras*.

[106] Hughes (1991), 140.

[107] 'Offscourings'; lit. 'something wiped off' – see *LSJ s.v.* περιψάω.

[108] Ogden (1997), 20. This practice is perhaps better attested in non-Greek cultures; the famous example is the Old Testament passage from which the term 'scapegoat' is derived (on which see Bremmer [1983], 299). For a well-documented Hittite case, see Bremmer (1983), 305-6; Ogden (1997), 20-21.

way; and from these instances, a strong pattern emerges whereby an animal form was clearly considered suitable as a bringer of ill, to be driven out of one's own community and into that of a foe.[109]

So animals can be used as *pharmakoi*; but it is also sometimes the case that human *pharmakos*-figures have animal characteristics. An interesting example of this is the event narrated by the third century AD author Philostratus in his *Life of Apollonios of Tyana*,[110] which has many hallmarks of the *pharmakos*-ritual though it is clearly a fantastical and imaginative use of the motif. When a plague strikes Ephesos, the community appeals to Apollonios, who advises them to drive out a particular beggar (low and marginal status again). At first they are unwilling, but soon perceive a supernatural gleam in the beggar's eyes, and take his advice. So many stones do they cast that the beggar is entirely concealed under them; when the stones are removed, the Ephesians find no human corpse but that of an enormous dog.

The dog is especially connected with *pharmakos*-type expulsion, as the myth of Hekabe's end also demonstrates. In the *Hekabe* of Euripides, our earliest source,[111] it is prophesied that the heroine, after her savage (and inhuman – perhaps even *un*human) blinding of Polymestor, will turn into a dog *with fiery eyes* and disappear into the sea. In this variant, Hekabe has become cursed and outlawed because of her crime, and as is often the case, animal metamorphosis follows such a transgression.[112] This example strengthens the impression that the *pharmakos*-figure is associated with a loss of human status and an adoption of animal nature. This brings it very strongly into line with the mixanthrope, which is also constantly connected with metamorphosis and the loss of humanity (this will be discussed in the next section). So the *pharmakos* and the mixanthrope share some characterisation as unnatural, outlawed and sometimes inhuman.

With *pharmakoi*, as with mixanthropic deities, topography is symbolically significant. The expulsion of the *pharmakos* contains two possible phases of movement, appearing either singly or together: expulsion out of the city, and expulsion into the sea. The former is almost universal, the latter less essential and yet extremely common. For example, the Suda's entry under 'περίψημα' says that the word is used (where is not made clear) of the *pharmakos* who is thrown into the sea. Hipponax's *pharmakos* is burned, and his ashes then flung into the sea. Vermeule has argued convincingly that the sea is a zone which takes in the rejected, the discarded, the outlawed,[113] all of which are qualities of the *pharmakos*.

---

[109] Ogden (1997), 26-7; cf. Faraone (1992), 36-53.

[110] Philostr. *Vit. Ap. Ty.* 4.10. On the context and milieu of the work and its creator, see Billault (2000), 105-26.

[111] See also Nik. *Het.* fr. 62.

[112] For discussion of the particular significance of Hekabe's transformation and of the dog and its character in the context of the play, see Segal (1993), 159-69; Mossman (1995), 194-201.

[113] Vermeule (1979), 185-6.

It is therefore not surprising to find the sea appearing as the final destination of the *pharmakos* in several cases.

For Hekabe also, a plunge into the sea follows immediately on her dog-metamorphosis; and she is part of a significant group of mythological figures, *comprising both metamorphosists and mixanthropes* – who, after some transgression or misfortune, leap into the sea and disappear (see previous sub-chapter). The great majority of these cases are bird-associated,[114] and the pattern is as follows: transgression or misfortune – plunge into the sea – transformation into a sea-bird. Sometimes the person dies; sometimes their transformation saves them from drowning.[115] The most famous case in which mixanthropy is explicitly involved is that of the Sirens, though they deviate from the usual pattern somewhat, in that their metamorphosis comes much earlier in their story than their death-plunge into the sea, and does not accompany it.[116]

But surely it is a little fanciful to suggest a dynamic connection between the ritual of the *pharmakos* cast into the sea, and the mixanthrope who plunges into the sea? It could be read as a very superficial and coincidental similarity. One is encouraged, however, to believe that the two are to be understood as very strongly bound together in thought and significance, by a ritual attested for the island of Leukas.[117] This ritual contains both the leap into the sea, and, fascinatingly, traces of bird-metamorphosis which align the participant very strongly with the mythical figures described. Criminals are flung off the high cliffs with live birds tied to them, an arrangement which our source explains as a way of preventing their fall being fatal; however, given the existence of several myths combining a sea-plunge with bird-metamorphosis, we are surely justified in seeing in this rite a less pragmatic meaning. The *pharmakos*-figure is made to resemble very closely the mythical characters who lose their humanity as they leave the land and enter the sea. This loss of humanity reminds one of the Ephesian beggar as well as of Hekabe.[118]

---

[114] Though dog-metamorphosis of a sort is also present in the case of Skylla, another marine figure (transformed by Circe: Ovid, *Met*. 14.51-67; transformed by Amphitrite: schol. Lyk. *Al*. 45; Serv. Verg. *Aen*. 3.420). She is also, however, transformed into a bird, the *kiris*, and in another version into a fish: for sources and discussion, see Forbes Irving (1990), 226-8.

[115] For various examples and discussion, see Forbes Irving (1990), 123-5. Typical is the story of the Ismenides, the companions of Ino, who leap into the sea after her and, as they do so, are turned into birds by Hera. They are mentioned in an anonymous dictionary of metamorphoses (P. Mich. Inv. 1447 verso; Renner [1978], 289), and also in Ovid, *Met*. 4.551-62.

[116] See e.g. Hyg. *Fab*. 141: Demeter transforms the Sirens into half-birds to punish them for failing to save Persephone from abduction.

[117] Strabo 10.2.9.

[118] An interesting case for comparison is that of the demonic ghost which the boxer Euthymos expelled from Temesa (Paus. 6.6.7-11). Not only is the ghost called Lykas – a wolfish name – but he wears a wolfskin; he is also black and dreadful in appearance, and more animal than man (Paus. 6.6.11, describing a picture of the ghost which he apparently saw at Temesa). Euthymos

So far we have been dealing, in the mythical examples, with a tangled combination of metamorphosis and mixanthropy; and the intimate association of the two is undeniable. But if we turn to those sea-leaping figures who actually *receive cult*, the importance of mixanthropy emerges as being the visual form of a significant number of these deities. They were discussed in the previous subchapter; it will be recalled that their cults tended to be sited on their points of departure, the spots from which they were supposed to have leapt into the sea. We are, I think, justified in seeing sea-leaping mixanthropic deities as having strong connections both with their purely mythical counterparts and also, most interestingly, with the figure of the *pharmakos* who is driven or flung into the sea.

The sea is, in Greek thought, consistently a recipient of what is rejected, unwanted and expelled.[119] Perhaps the most famous example of this function occurs in the case of Hephaistos, flung into the sea immediately after birth by his mother Hera, who is disgusted by his weak and malformed (and thoroughly *pharmakos*-like[120]) appearance.[121] In the depths he is cared for by Thetis and Eurynome,[122] who also, in another, rather similar myth, take in Dionysos when he is hounded by Lykourgos.

So, to summarise, we have identified various conjoined groups. We have the *pharmakoi* – actual humans involved in rituals of expulsion and purgation. We have identified mythical figures, often metamorphosists or mixanthropes, who undergo in myth something very similar to what the *pharmakos* undergoes in ritual. The sea is the most important shared feature of these two groups. Finally, we have a number of mixanthropic deities who have in common several motifs, chiefly a leap into the sea following transgression or misfortune. Often their cult is seen as ensuing from their departure from the land; and its site is the site of that disappearance. This is highly reminiscent of a key pattern already observed in the nature of mixanthropic cults: that they were often located on the site of the mythical departure and/or death of the recipient. In the case of Parthenope, the cult site is the place where the dead Siren is washed ashore and given burial, rather than the point of her departure from the land.[123] But it is still a monument to her disappearance from the land of the living, as is perhaps the Totenkult of Proteus in Egypt.

---

chases him into the sea. Animal nature and expulsion into the sea: the combination is familiar from the cases of the Ephesian beggar and of Hekabe, and from many traits of the *pharmakos*.

[119] Vermeule (1979), 185-7. An example from many in ancient texts occurs in Euripides' *Iphigenia Among the Taurians*, in which the titular heroine decrees immersion in the sea as a means of purifying the miasmatic and unlucky Orestes; at line 1193 she explains, 'The sea washes away all the sins of men.'

[120] For Hephaistos as part of the ancient discourse on the expulsion of *terata*, see Ogden (1997), 35-7.

[121] As she herself tells us in the *Homeric Hymn to Apollo* (3), 311-18.

[122] Hom. *Il.* 18.395-9.

[123] Lyk. *Al.* 717-21.

So far the very close relationship between some mixanthropic deities and the figure and ritual of the *pharmakos* reinforce the chief contention of this section: that the theme of expulsion is central to the way in which mixanthropic deities were perceived, and central to the manner in which they were worshipped. However, there is one case in which the mixanthropic deity and the *pharmakos* seem directly conjoined.

Evidence for the case in question comes to us from the Hellenistic poet Theokritos, and from the scholiasts who commented on his work. In his seventh *Idyll*, the poet invokes the god Pan and implores him to induce an unresponsive boy to return the love of Theokritos' friend Aratos, who is suffering the pains of unrequited passion. Having made this request, Theokritos says:

> And if you do this, dear Pan, may the boys
> of Arkadia not whip you with squills across your flanks
> and shoulders whenever there is too little meat;
> but if you won't consent, all across your body with your nails
> may you scratch, biting yourself, and sleep in nettles…[124]

The whole poem has received much discussion;[125] here the crucial section is that which appears (and there is no reason to doubt it) to detail a real Arkadian rite: the flagellation of Pan's image at times of lean hunting. This meaning is elaborated by the scholiast on the passage, who also, through reference to other sources, mentions a festival at which the ritual beating took place. The relationship between a regular ceremonial occasion and an action designed to counteract specific and peculiar circumstances (poor hunting) is explained by Borgeaud, surely rightly, with the conjecture that the whipping took place at the festival only if the hunting was also poor.[126]

Two facts are immediately clear: first, that the ritual is strikingly similar to that of the *pharmakos* in some ways, and second, that in others it is strikingly different. The similarities lie in the technical details – chiefly the use of squills – and also in their purpose: to deflect a hardship which has befallen the community. Often in *pharmakos*-rituals that hardship is general shortage; here it is shortage of game, in accordance with the special preserve of Pan, who could after all hardly be expected to take responsibility for agrarian difficulties. The

---

[124] Theok. *Id.* 7.106-10: κἢν μὲν ταῦθ' ἔρδῃς, ὦ Πὰν φίλε, μή τί τυ παῖδες | Ἀρκαδικοὶ σκίλλαισιν ὑπὸ πλευράς τε καὶ ὤμους | τανίκα μαστίσδοιεν, ὅτε κρέα τυτθὰ παρείη· | εἰ δ' ἄλλως νεύσαις, κατὰ μὲν χρόα πάντ' ὀνύχεσσι | δακνόμενος κνάσαιο, καὶ ἐν κνίδαισι καθεύδοις. There follows a catalogue of threatened woes to assail the god if he does not comply with the request: cold and heat, in wild and foreign landscapes.

[125] For example, in Harrison (1908), 101; Bremmer (1983), 309.

[126] For a lengthy discussion of the ritual and its implications, see Borgeaud (1988), 68-73. The scholiast also mentions a similar rite which took place in Chios, where a cult of Pan is not otherwise known. In all likelihood this is because it escaped representation both in the literary record and the archaeological one (after all, cults of Pan did not tend to be accompanied by substantial building-works or grand civic dedications, and could leave relatively few traces).

combination of shortage as problem and beating as solution bears undeniable similarities with the use of *pharmakoi*.

Then one must acknowledge the divergences, as Borgeaud has done.[127] Vitally, Pan is not some ugly outcast or unwanted human misfit who can easily stand in for, or represent, the misfortune which the community wishes to be rid of. Almost the reverse: as patron of the hunt, his are the very powers which his worshippers wish to attract. So why are they seemingly going through motions associated with driving out, with expulsion? Does the rite perhaps have some completely different meaning, most obviously that of simply punishing the god for neglecting to apply his divine powers correctly?

Borgeaud's answer to this question is twofold. First he suggests that there *is* an element of expulsion: what is being driven out is the threat of famine.[128] Second, and more compellingly, he argues that the whipping is designed not to expel the god, to drive him out, but rather to recall him from inactivity or absence.[129] This is a very convincing suggestion, especially when laid beside the Arkadian myth of Demeter and her fatal absence, her withdrawal of her powers from mankind. The Phigalian cult was intended to prevent such a withdrawal happening again; just so, the rite of Pan's beating may well have been meant to stimulate his presence as a useful and beneficent force.

Both these lines of explanation are well-founded and surely correct; but I believe that they leave one important element in need of further appreciation. I would argue that the flagellation of Pan *was* on one level intended to expel the god, at the same time as stimulating his powers and his presence; and that we ought to give more credence to the idea of the mixanthropic god as something which ancient communities might in certain circumstances have wished to drive out. It is not random or accidental that mixanthropic deities are represented in a form associated with monsters, which in myths are banes, destroyers of humanity and its achievements, which must be defeated and driven out. Mixanthropy is used in the depiction of certain deities who have destructive and undesirable characteristics, as will now be demonstrated.

So far, we have seen the mixanthrope harming humanity predominantly through absence. The Phigalians starve when Demeter withdraws from their agrarian territory; Cheiron's death robs man of a wise and kind healer; Pan's neglect causes the game to be depleted. But the mixanthropic god is also capable of a malign and harmful presence. On one level, this is simply a branch, so to speak, of a universal quality of gods: they constantly threaten mankind with the dual perils of their neglect and their destructive, unwanted attention. But in mixanthropes we have a very much intensified and dominant form of this

---

[127] *Op. cit.* 71-2.

[128] *Op. cit.* 71.

[129] *Op. cit.* 72.

perennial theme, which often finds symbolic articulation through the conjoined modes of animality and deformity, the two defining features of the mixanthrope (modes also combined within the figure of the *pharmakos*, as described above).

The malign presence of Pan tends to be described in semi-humorous terms, in line with his persona as a grotesque but light-hearted figure;[130] but it is there none the less. He is the god of the frightening and disconcerting epiphany. His shout or the sound of his pipes[131] creates sudden, uncontrollable fear, and it emerges from a landscape which had seemed to be deserted. The panic-shout reflects the god's potential for sending madness. This potential is reflected in the moment in Euripides' *Hippolytos* when Phaidra's old nurse asks whether her mistress's distraction is due to her being *entheos* – possessed – by Pan.[132] It is also reflected in the myth of Echo, who spurns Pan's advances; in anger, the god sends madness upon the herdsmen of the area, who tear her to pieces like dogs and wolves.[133]

This double feature of Pan, terrifying presence and the ability to derange, is highly reminiscent of Dionysos. In Dionysos also it is very much involved with the god's animal aspects, and sometimes with his mixanthropy. For example, the women of Elis in their ritual hymn implore Dionysos to come 'rushing with bull-foot'. Plutarch's explanation in his thirty-sixth *Greek Question*, that they do so because the foot is less dangerous than the horn, and so the women are trying to deflect the god's full violence, is surely misguided, and yet it reflects the general truth that the destructive force of the god is very much concentrated in his horns, and in his other animal features. Perhaps the clearest manifestation of this is in the myth of the Minyades, who defy Dionysos and thus incur his wrath. The furious god changes into a bull, a lion, then a leopard. Terrified and driven mad, the women tear apart the son of one of their number, Leukippe, then run wild as Maenads.[134] Therefore with Dionysos, as with Pan, the animal form is the key to the frightening and the maddening epiphany, the malign presence.

---

[130] For Pan as balanced between 'too present' and 'too absent', see Borgeaud (1988), 122, fig. 6.2.

[131] e.g. Euseb. *Peri tês ek logiôn philosophiês* 5.5-6: Pan's shrill piping leaves some woodcutters transfixed with terror. The attempt of Harrison (1926) to detach Pan from the phenomenon of unreasoning fear, by deriving the word *paneion* not from the god but for the word for fire-signal, is not convincing.

[132] Eur. *Hipp.* 141-50: in this passage, a number of deities are listed as possibly responsible: Hekate, associated with frenzied hounds, and the Corybantes and the Mountain Mother, both of whom received orgiastic worship.

[133] Longus, *Pastorals* 3.23.

[134] Ant. Lib. *Met.* 10, which cites Nikandros and Korinna (fr. 665). The latter *could*, depending of dating, make the myth an early one: Korinna was thought in antiquity to have been contemporary with Pindar (see Paus. 9.22), but this is now held in some suspicion, and she may in fact be of Hellenistic date. The papyrus bearing her verse dates from around 200 BC. See Campbell (1967), 408-10.

Pan's unexpected and unwanted presence can also bring with it the threat of sexual violence. Like the satyrs,[135] he is associated with bestial appetites and with bestial ways of going about satisfying them. The mythical examples of his unwelcome assaults are numerous; but perhaps the most interesting, and also the most tantalising, example of this side of his nature is to be found on the famous name-vase of the Pan-painter (fig. 29).

Fig. 29

One of the two scenes on this vessel shows a young man (Borgeaud calls him a goatherd) recoiling and turning to flee as Pan – goat-faced and sexually aroused – leaps out at him from behind an ithyphallic herm. This is one visual example of the common theme of Pan's aggression as taking a sexual form.[136] There is one detail of the painting, however, which, though not often remarked by scholars, seems to me to add another stand of possible meaning to the depiction of Pan's sudden and unwanted presence. The boy holds a whip. If he is indeed a goatherd, this is a perfectly logical accessory for him to carry. However, it forms an ironic juxtaposition with Pan. Pan's own power to madden and terrify is often expressed in the symbol of the whip, as Borgeaud shows.[137] So the youth finds the power of his own implement turned against him by the divine whip-bearer *par excellence*. This irony is enhanced if we think of the ritual mentioned by Theokritos in which Pan himself was whipped by youths; here, perhaps, the god is turning the tables on one of his young devotees.

In Demeter Melaina we find perhaps the most pointed exploration of the uneasy relationship between the wanted and the unwanted divine presence. In the Arkadian myths which have been discussed, the goddess's chief weapon, when angry, is absence, withdrawal, the removal of her life-giving presence. This would seem to be the main threat with which she faces mankind. And yet there is another dimension to the Arkadian goddess, which underpins the differences between her and the manifestations of Demeter in other parts of Greece.

---

[135] On the nature of the satyrs, see e.g. Dowden (1992), 165: 'The unacceptable extremes of male sexuality are exported from men to satyrs. These licentious creatures are part animal, like centaurs, and therefore define behaviour which is beyond the human pale.' (In fact, although this last statement is true of satyrs, it is by no means the case that mixanthropes always present the antithesis to humanity; see the Conclusion to this book.)

[136] See Borgeaud (1988), 74-80.

[137] Borgeaud (1988), 123-9.

Demeter's rôle as source and guarantor of agrarian fertility is of course pan-Hellenic, and also at the centre of her influential Eleusinian persona. Part of this rôle is her ability to take that fertility away from mankind if displeased. The *Homeric Hymn to Demeter* reflects the centrality of the motif of Demeter's anger and her subsequent catastrophic withdrawal.[138] The theme of angry withdrawal is therefore by no means unique to her Arkadian form; on the contrary, it is her most universal aspect.

But her Arkadian form has a dimension, associated with this, that her others lack; and this extra dimension is encapsulated in the mare's head which Arkadian myth (if not iconographic reality) attributes to her. It has been shown above that, in essence, the mare's head has two chief layers of significance, which rest on the species and its connections in Greek thought. First, the horse (male or female) is frequently placed in symbolic opposition to agrarian fertility. This is reflected, for example, in the myth recounted by Antoninus Liberalis,[139] in which Autonoös and Hippodameia own horse-herds and let their land go uncultivated so that it produces only thistles and rushes. Such uncontrollable growth, depicted here as the symbolic corollary of the horses' presence and rôle, is the antithesis of ordered and fruitful crops.

Secondly, it is associated with the potential for active destruction. When Anthos, the son of Autonoös and Hippodameia, tries to drive the horses from their weed-choked pasture, they turn on him and begin to eat him. Horses in Greek myths can display violent, destructive aggression, especially against humans and especially manifested in devouring. This is also very much in evidence in the persona of Demeter Melaina. She does not herself devour, but she causes humans to commit the cardinal transgression of cannibalism: she transfers to them the savage behaviour of the man-eating horse, an extremely common figure in myth. She threatens them with the malign animal qualities which she herself encapsulates.[140] Her blackness, as has been shown, also expresses her potential for destructive and punitive anger, and is one of the features which connects her – along with the closely linked Demeter Erinys – with the Erinyes. It is Demeter Melaina's very strong association with the Erinyes that gives us the clearest glimpse of her potential for active aggression.

---

[138] See Mylonas (1961), 5, for the rôle of the myths of withdrawal in the cult at Eleusis.

[139] Ant. Lib. *Met.* 7.

[140] The wording of the oracle related by Pausanias at 8.42.6 stress that Demeter's threat is to remove the social advances that she herself has made possible: 'Deio made you cease from pasturing, Deio made you pasture| again, after being binders of corn and eaters of cake,| because she was deprived of the prize given by former men, and ancient honours.| And she will quickly make you eaters of each other, and eaters of children,| if you do not *assuage her anger* with public libations,| and adorn the recess of her cave with divine honours.' So Demeter can confer either civilisation or – if in her 'angry mode' – savagery. The connection between the horse and her angry and vengeful mode is reinforced in the opening lines of the oracle: 'Azanian Arkadians, acorn-eaters, who live| in Phigalia, the cave in which hid *Deio horse-bearer...*'

So the mare's head of Phigalian Demeter has two symbolic aspects. On the one hand, it represents the possibility of a loss or removal of agrarian fertility; this is the quality which the myth of Demeter's withdrawal brings to the fore. But at the same time, it represents the goddess's potential role as a destructive force. So Demeter Melaina threatens more than absence. Her most famous punishment of neglectful man may be a sudden absence; but her presence is also conceived as a terrifying and potentially malign one.

It has also been shown, in the discussion, above, of the disappearance of the mare-headed *xoanon* at Phigalia and its replacement, that the destructive animal aspect of Demeter Melaina is one which human agency might wish to dispose of. That is the import of the lengthy and anxiety-infused narrative[141] of the *accidental* destruction of two successive cult images and – as a corollary of that – the gradual dilution of the animal part of her representation. The discourse of good and bad presence or absence is rendered more piquant in the Phigalian case by a peculiar irony, contained in the statues-narrative. The cult of Demeter in the cave lapses when her *xoanon* is destroyed, and it is this lapse which angers her and causes her to withdraw her benign powers. The destruction of the *xoanon* is part of the mythical process of disposing of the undesirable animal element of the image. Therefore, it is in contriving to be rid of the *unwanted* part of the goddess that the Phigalians of myth end up losing her *wanted* part. In other words, one could imagine the myth to contain a deeply embedded moral: you cannot separate the malign and the benign sides of the deity; displacing one will risk displacing the other. If one retains the desired aspect of Demeter, one has to resign oneself to having her less pleasing aspect also.

Another potent symbol of the conflict of good and bad presence is that of the bound image.[142] The bound statue of Eurynome in Arkadia has been discussed, as a case of an evasive marine figure, iconographically restrained. But if we examine the wider discourse of bound images, and its relationship with the mixanthrope, we can see that the deity's escape is not the only contingency which binding was intended to prevent. The dual significance of binding might be thought to be reflected in the dual nature of Eurynome. Pausanias records local uncertainty as to her identity (see above in the section of her cult): some of the Phigalians say that she is a form of Artemis, others an Oceanid, akin to Thetis.[143] Now it is most likely that both identities were at least instrumental in how she was regarded. As an Oceanid like Thetis, she can clearly be considered, as has been said, as one of a number of marine figures strongly associated with evasion and evasive shape-shifting. But she is also a manifestation of Artemis, and bound Artemis-images tend to have a rather different quality: that of aggression.

---

[141] Paus. 8.42.4-11.

[142] On bound images see Icard-Gianolio in *ThesCRA* vol. II, *s.v.* 'Statues enchaînées', 468-9; Faraone (1992), 74ff.; Pritchett, vol. 1 (1998), 329-38; Merkelbach (1971).

[143] Paus. 8.41.5.

Bound statues are very often associated with warfare, as was said earlier: they are bound to prevent them going over to the enemy, and to retain instead their power for the benefit of the community which possesses the image and cult; this power can then be unleashed in times of need. But bound goddesses such as Hera and, most of all, Artemis, have a slightly less practically defined nature and function. Sometimes the symbolic force of the binding is extremely hard to discern, as in the case of the bound Aphrodite of Sparta, which baffled Pausanias,[144] and yet elsewhere trends do emerge. One of these is a certain passivity: such images are sometimes the victims of attempted robbery; but the robbers tend to receive a more or less nasty surprise when they make the attempt. In other words, a pattern familiar from some mixanthropes is also discernible here: an attempt to remove the deity from her place of cult results in her punitive anger being visited upon the perpetrators.

Sometimes this takes a relatively mild form, such as the magical immobility which afflicts the ship of the pirates who try to steal the image of Samian Hera.[145] Here the statue is in effect preventing itself from being displaced. But bound statues can be more destructive. A clear case is the Spartan myth of the statue of Artemis Orthia, and the cult which existed in her honour. Pausanias tells us[146] that Artemis Orthia was also called Lygodesma, 'Willow-bound', because it was discovered in a willow-thicket, bound upright by osiers of the same plant.[147] It was supposed to have come from the land of the Taurians, stolen thence by Orestes and Iphigeneia, and to have been the recipient of barbaric sacrifices in its native land.[148] The impact of this statue, in the myth as recounted by Pausanias, is a highly destructive one. The two young Spartans who find it in the thicket, Astrabakos and Alopekos, are driven mad by their discovery. Then, when the local people are sacrificing before the image, they begin to quarrel and many are butchered; those who are not die of disease. At this, the survivors receive an oracle telling them to stain the altar with human blood; this human sacrifice was changed by Lykourgos to the famous rite in which boys were whipped until they bled, so maintaining the terms set out in

---

[144] Paus. 3.15.11 records various ancient explanations for the statue of Aphrodite in fetters, but is not really satisfied by any of them. For discussion of the image and its symbolic relationship with the bound Enyalios of Sparta, see Pirenne-Delforge (1994), 199-211.

[145] Menodot. *FGrHist* 541 F 1 = Athen. *Deipn.* 672a-673d.

[146] Paus. 3.16.11.

[147] The appearance of the *lygos*-plant is interesting. It has a rôle also in some *pharmakos*-rituals, for example in the Chaironeian 'expulsion of hunger' (see Plut. *Quaest. Conv.* 6.8), and this may not be purely coincidental. Like the *pharmakos*, the bound statue is sometimes used to deliver a community from a pestilence or other catastrophe. For example, when their land is ravaged by the ghost of Aktaion, the people of Orchomenos are instructed by an oracle to make and chain up a statue of the hero; this restrains his destructive power (see Paus. 9.38.5). Similar advice is given to the inhabitants of Iconium, harassed by pirates. The link between the *pharmakos* and the bound image is a loose one, but interesting given the relationship of both with mixanthropy.

[148] Paus. 3.16.7.

the oracle. 'And so a love of human blood has remained in the statue, ever since the sacrifices in the Tauric land,'[149] remarks Pausanias, leaving us no doubt that the goddess – or rather, her statue, as the embodiment of her malign powers – is held responsible for the violence which attends her cult. That this is associated with her binding is reflected in the madness which falls upon Astrabakos and Alopekos when they first see her in that state. As Bremmer remarks, their madness shows that the statue was 'a dangerous one'.[150]

As has already been pointed out, madness is one of the chief ways in which mixanthropes also manifest their malign presence, as in the cases of Pan and Dionysos. It is associated with a terrible revelation or epiphany, as in the case of the daughters of Kekrops who see the child Erichthonios – either part-snake or accompanied by snakes – and run mad on the instant, throwing themselves from the acropolis.[151] The animal element of the mixanthrope is often depicted as achieving this effect; in the case of Artemis Lygodesmos and other aggressive bound goddesses, this means of expression is not used; instead, binding and concealment have a similar symbolic import. They suggest destructive forces kept precariously in check.[152] Given the containment to which Arkadian Eurynome was subjected – not only binding but also strict religious concealment – it seems plausible to suppose that she may be considered as belonging among those bound goddesses who threaten aggression as well as escape.[153]

Perhaps the most famous madness-inducers of Greek mythology, however, are the winged and snake-carrying Erinyes, who share the vengeful anger of Demeter but channel it into a different human disorder: insanity rather than cannibalism (though the two things occasionally elide, as in Orestes' biting off of his own finger in the Arkadian myth). Like Dionysos and Pan, the Erinyes are deities of swift approach (in their case, wings express this). Their presence is entirely destructive and terrible until they are placated.

It could reasonably be argued that there are several mixanthropic deities to whom this theory of malign presence does not appear to apply. It is certainly true that for some, such as Zeus Ammon and Apollo Karneios, we simply do not have sufficient evidence concerning their myths and cults to discern whether or

---

[149] Paus. 3.16.11: οὕτω τῷ ἀγάλματι ἀπὸ τῶν ἐν τῇ Ταυρικῇ θυσιῶν ἐμμεμένηκεν ἀνθρώπων αἵματι ἥδεσθαι·

[150] Bremmer (1983), 311. Faraone (1992, 137) sums the matter up neatly: 'Greek legends and rituals that concern bound or imprisoned statues repeatedly express the desire to control directly the potentially dangerous activities of powerful deities of an arbitrary and often malicious disposition.'

[151] Ovid, *Met.* 2.254; Eur. *Ion* 21ff, 265; Paus. 1.18.2; Apollod. *Bibl.* 3.14.

[152] The fettering of divine images is part of a wider motif of the control of powerful and potentially malign supernatural forces through rituals of binding: see Faraone (1992), 74-93.

[153] Faraone (1992), 136-40, building on the work of Graf on the subject (1985, 81-98), includes Eurynome in a canon of bound aggressive statues dominated by forms of Artemis and of Dionysos.

not they shared the patterns of representation that are being discussed. It is also true that there exists a group of marine figures, such as Proteus and Thetis, in whom departure and absence are the overwhelming characteristics. These shape-changers are defined by evasion; they are designed, so to speak, to absent them-selves from man. This aspect is far more in evidence than their aggressive or destructive sides although these do make themselves felt from time to time. Thetis is closely related, mythologically at least, with the bound Eurynome of Arkadia, and should perhaps be thought to share that deity's combination of evasion and aggression; also, the disturbing imagery of Thetis' *sepia*-form has been discussed in Chapter 1, and the point was made in this chapter that Proteus is a threatening as well as slippery character. But there is no doubt that the most overt threat posed by these two sea-deities is that of disappearance rather than active aggression.

And again, there are some figures in whom malignity seems entirely lacking, most notably Cheiron. Time and again, our sources stress the benevolence of the centaur-god: he is just, restrained, a friend to man.[154] The secret to Cheiron's anomalous perfection of character lies in the puzzling relationship between him and the group-centaurs, already remarked on in Chapter 2. Clearly connected through near-identical physical representation, the two are yet so completely divergent in nature and behaviour. It is certainly not accidental that the group-centaurs seem to contain so many of the malign qualities which one might expect from the mixanthrope and which are absent from Cheiron. A number of their traits are strikingly like those of Pan. They haunt the country-side, and assail wayfarers suddenly and without warning;[155] they perpetrate acts of sexual violence.[156] Their presence is generally undesirable and destructive. All the negative qualities which might have attached to Cheiron are attributed instead to his boisterous fellow-centaurs. This represents a striking way of dealing with the ambivalence which always attached to the mixanthropic god: rather than allowing benign and malign aspects to rest uneasily within a single being, Greek myth splits good and bad in separate directions. The group-centaurs, the monsters, become a vessel for all destructiveness; and Cheiron, the god, is purged of the ability to harm.

---

[154] Pindar is particularly keen to stress this characterisation, but is not alone. Just: Eur. *Iph. Aul.* 929 (*eusebestatos*); restrained: Pind. *Pyth.* 3.63 (*sôphrôn*); a friend to man: Pind. *Pyth.* 3.5. For other laudable qualities, see e.g. Hom. *Il.* 4.219; Pind. *Nem.* 3.53.

[155] For example, when they ambush Peleus: Apollod. *Bibl.* 3.13.3.

[156] In myth the accounts of their sexual assaults are far too numerous to list. An example is the attempted rape of Atalanta by Rhoikos and Hylaios: see Apollod. *Bibl.* 3.9.2; also that of Deianeira by Nessos: see Soph. *Trach.* 555-77.

4. Expulsion and burial

We have been using the term expulsion to cover a range of different ways in which, in myth, the mixanthropic deity is displaced from a position of worship and/or power. However, within this wide topos there is one particular variant which merits individual attention. In a significant number of cases, expulsion is combined with some form of burial, which has the dual rôle of hiding the mixanthrope from view and confining it in an enclosed space.

Burial and confinement are persistent ingredients of the monster-expulsion motif, especially in Hesiod's *Theogony* and later Hesiod-inspired narratives. It is applied mostly to non-divine monsters vanquished by (usually) Zeus, though the god Hephaistos is included in the pattern when he is flung from Olympos. Their defeat typically has two parts: they are cast down from a high (and therefore powerful) place; then they are imprisoned in the opposite environment, most often the depths of Tartaros, where their malevolent powers are held in check and their dreams of power ended.[157] In the cases of Hephaistos and the Kyklopes (monstrous, though not mixanthropes, it must be noted) there is also a sense that confinement allows their powers to be exploited by the controlling gods, directed for their advantage rather than their destruction. Both Hephaistos and the Kyklopes are represented, in some sources at least, as having their smithies and workshops, in which they forge items of use to the gods, in confined and underground spaces, such as under Mount Etna.[158] The motif of expulsion from high to low is a widespread one; the centaurs' flight from Pelion is the most prominent example, and Cheiron's own fate has a share in it.

These aims behind burial as confinement find a faint but striking echo in *pharmakos*-rituals. Though expulsion – the straightforward removal of something unlucky and undesirable from a community – is by far the most important element in those rites, burial makes the occasional appearance as a secondary theme. For example, in Philostratus' account of the stoning of the Ephesian beggar at Apollonios' insistence, we find a slightly surreal twist: so many stones are cast that they completely bury the victim.[159] This could be put down to the particular literary requirements of the context, but given the consistent relationship between expulsion and burial one wonders whether perhaps the stoning of

---

[157] *Theog.* 617-623; 729-735; 868.

[158] Our earliest source, Hesiod (*Theog.* 501-5), places the confinement of the Kyklopes and their work as smiths in different stages of their narrative: first they are confined by Kronos, but Zeus frees them so as to acquire their assistance. (He is still making use of their imprisonment, but they work in comparative freedom.) Likewise, in the *Iliad*, Hephaistos' workshop is in an overground building, a hall of bronze on – we assume – Olympos. Later authors team the Kyklopes up with Hephaistos, and place them in a subterranean smithy. The most elaborate treatment of this is in Vergil's *Aeneid* (8.416-38): the Kyklopes, under the direction of Vulcan, in their clanging underground chambers, work on the thunderbolt of Zeus and the aegis of Athene.

[159] Philostr. *Vit. Ap. Ty.* 4.10.

the *pharmakos* (as distinct from the action of whipping) often carried this unspoken auxiliary significance: the urge to cover and confine as well as to drive out.

Echoes of this pattern are to be found also in cases where a mixanthropic deity is concerned. First, and most basically, it has been shown that there is an overwhelming tendency for mixanthropic gods to be housed, in both myth and cult, in caves. It has also been argued that caves are on one level small extensions of the underworld realm; therefore, the need to place mixanthropes in caves may perhaps be compared with the confinement of monsters in Tartaros in the narrative of Hesiod and elsewhere. Is the cave essentially a form of burial? Does placing the mixanthropic god in a cave thus serve to confine his or her potentially malign powers? On the one hand this seems a likely undercurrent; on the other, it has been argued in the section on the cave of Cheiron that caves can be unreliable containers, especially in contrast with the underground chamber of the subterranean hero. They facilitate movement as much as they restrict it. None the less, failed or unreliable confinement could be as potent a theme in cult as confinement achieved; we have seen that attitudes towards mixanthropes constantly flirt, so to speak, with the notion of their dangerous side and the impossibility of fully controlling it.[160]

A further link between caves and burial is found in the myths surrounding the statues of Demeter Melaina, recounted by Pausanias. There, not only is the goddess's image lodged in the cave, but the second in the series, the *agalma* made by Onatas, suffers burial under stone, *pharmakos*-style, when the roof of the cave collapses.[161] The cave-function taken to extreme lengths? There is one vital difference. As we have seen, the result of the roof-fall is not so much confinement as *complete obliteration*: the statue disappears from the scene entirely, and thus makes way for its guilt-ridden replacement, either by one not influenced by the mixanthropic original, or else by no statue at all.[162] In other words, it seems that burial can, in some circumstances, result not in holding the mixanthrope in position but in displacing it entirely. As we have seen, complete displacement of mixanthropic gods is attended by huge anxiety in Greek thought.

---

[160] To return to the Philostratus story for a moment, it may be seen that, there also, burial does not restrict the victim's movement entirely, if one sees metamorphosis as a form of movement: under cover of the stones, the Ephesian beggar is able to transform into a hell-hound, and the fact that the change was concealed makes its revelation all the more uncanny.

[161] Paus. 8.42.13. One could in fact argue that the *xoanon* too – which is burned – suffers a *pharmakos*-style fate: Tzetzes' description of the *pharmakos* rite makes burning the culmination of the poor man's mistreatment (*Chil.* 23.736-8), after which his ashes are thrown into the sea. This casting of ashes into the sea is an extreme form of the more common general motif of the casting of the *pharmakos* into the sea. References to the burning of the *pharmakos* are very rare, and Bremmer (1983, 315-8) questions whether in actuality death of any sort tended to be meted out.

[162] As has been said, it is unclear from Pausanias' description whether or not Onatas' statue was replaced by another after its destruction, although it seems more likely that it was.

In addition, a more obvious form of burial is associated with certain mixanthropic deities – burial in a tomb. Proteus, the Sirens, Kekrops and Cheiron: all have cult sites which are more or less explicitly sites of death and burial (Cheiron is the odd one out in that his death is sometimes described as being followed by removal to Olympos or by catasterism[163]). Thus burial is strongly connected with absence, which has been identified as a central theme in the depiction of mixanthropes. Burial indicates in many cases a mixanthrope whose expulsion is rendered complete by his death, even though cult keeps a part of his powers in existence.

Expulsion, withdrawal and absence: conclusion

It is now possible to see how the discourse of the expelled monster is adapted in the case of mixanthropic deities. There are in fact a striking number of similarities between mixanthropic monsters and mixanthropic gods. In the first place, of course, some characters are both: the Sirens and Acheloos, for example, are both explicitly worsted by heroes. In the Sirens' case, cult was perceived to be consequent on defeat and indeed on death. They are worshipped only once reduced to the status of fallen foe. They and several other mixanthropic deities are banished from topographical positions of power, pushed into obscurity, with the result that their cult sites are full of the sense of absence, of departure, which characterises the monstrous adversary in myth.

However, mixanthropic deities are not merely cult-receiving monsters. What really sets them apart from the expulsion of monsters and its corresponding discourse can be summed up in the single word: ambivalence. It was noted in the Introduction that even monstrous foes are not presented as simple antitheses of man; however, on the whole their defeat and removal are seen as inevitable, just, right, and (especially in Hesiod's *Theogony*) part of a narrative of progress in which unacceptable beings are left behind.

The situation with mixanthropic deities is different, as this chapter has shown. In many cases we have seen that the absence of a mixanthropic deity is conceived in terms of regret, loss or anxiety about dire consequences. Moreover, whereas monsters are always the passive victims of expulsion, this is not always so among mixanthropic deities. Absence is almost always caused by human agency in some form, but deities such as Demeter Melaina actively withdraw, using their absence as a catastrophe with which to punish erring mankind.

The situation with winged beings and bird-mixanthropes is a little special. Nike and the Erinyes resolve the ambivalence by separation: Nike embodies the

---

[163] See e.g. Paus. 5.17.9: Cheiron on the chest of Kypselos, described as 'having been deemed worthy to be a *sunoikos* to the gods.' On catasterism, a late variant, see e.g. Hyg. *Astr.* 2.38; Ovid, *Fast.* 5.379-414.

good to be maintained, the Erinyes the evil to be averted. Other figures, however, combine both elements: the Sirens, like Eos, are both rapacious attackers and assistants of mankind in the great transition between life and death. Of all this rich and varied class, only the Harpies emerge as wholly monstrous. Perhaps the abiding ambiguity of most winged beings may be related to their death-associations: like death, they are swift in pursuit and feared, but contain the promise of some better condition thereafter.

In other words, mixanthropic deities can be frightening and destructive like monsters, but unlike monsters they cannot simply be disposed of without repercussions or disadvantages. Both their presence and their absence are potentially harmful. This tense dichotomy is quite different from the expulsion-motif in monster narratives. Representing a deity as a mixanthrope draws on the character of the mixanthropic monster but does not limit the deity to that character.

Chapter V

Mixanthropic deities in time and place

Introduction

This chapter explores the spatial and temporal characterisation of mixanthropic gods, and shows that the dimensions of time and place combine to connect these deities with the distant past. The relegation of mixanthropic monsters to the past and to obsolescence was noted in the Introduction. Monsters remain known through stories, but also through relics: giant bones, the stuffed Triton of Tanagra. They are potent and enduring symbols, but not (with a few peculiar exceptions[1]) part of the real life of now.[2] But in the case of mixanthropic deities, how does this discourse of past time combine with active divinity and with the receipt of cult? How can a god function as its worshippers require if it is thought to belong to time long gone?

Before discussion of this matter and its implications, there is one important preliminary to deal with. An association with the distant past is being treated as part of the discourse of mixanthropes and their tendency to absence; but might it not have an element of corresponding historical reality and, if so, should this not be included in the picture? This historical reality would be that, at some time before that which produced the bulk of our evidence, mixanthropic (and perhaps other animal-related) deities were much more common in Greek religion. Were this the case it would have to be taken into account as an underlying and probably contributing factor of the time-related themes identified here. The need to address this possibility is strengthened by the fact that past scholarship has argued for, or in some cases assumed, the existence of a process of evolution

---

[1] An intriguing rare example of reality apparently mirroring myth is to be found in Plutarch's *Life of Sulla* (27.2), in which Sulla, while at Apollonia near Dyrrhachium in north-western Greece, is presented with a satyr which has been captured while sleeping. Though depicted as historical reality, this episode has certain echoes of the mythological realm; the capture takes place near a Nymphaion, calling to mind the consistent nymph/satyr association in Greek thought, and it also bears some resemblance to the capture of the sleeping Silenos. Whatever the truth of the event, its retelling is plainly coloured by the *topoi* of longstanding folklore.

[2] As Boardman points out (2002, 127), consigning fabulous beings to the past is, in part, a way of dealing with their non-existence in real and present life.

whereby mixanthropic and theriomorphic gods were displaced from Greek religion by a change in social *mores*, leading to a relative scarcity of such types. This idea of evolutionary displacement is bound up with the once-pervasive notion of the animal god as an early phase of Greek religion, now entirely discredited. A closer inspection shows that, though not without some superficial plausibility, the idea of evolutionary displacement simply finds no convincing evidence with regard to mixanthropic deities.

1. A growing scarcity?

Were there once more mixanthropic deities than are represented in the available evidence? Are those that remain left over from a time of relative abundance? The idea that mixanthropic deities generally slipped out of usage typically rests on one or more of four hypothetical processes:

- Mixanthropic deities simply vanishing through cessation of worship.
- Hypostasis: mixanthropic deities losing their divine status, and generally entering the canon of monsters.
- Transfer: undesirable animal features are moved from a deity to a mythologically adjacent human figure.
- Anthropomorphisation: mixanthropic deities taking on increasingly human form until most or all of their animal elements are lost.

The first possibility is clearly impossible to prove, requiring argument from total absence, so scholarly attention has tended to focus on numbers 2, 3 and 4. The hypostasis and transfer theories offer the chance, very popular in earlier scholarship, of finding traces or vestiges of earlier gods in the existing evidence, and so have been quite popular. The theory of increasing anthropomorphisation is one which has been claimed to be discernible in the material and artistic evidence for a number of mixanthropes. These notions will be examined in the ensuing chapter with the aim of establishing their general value; if they can be seen as taking place, it has major implications for the current study, suggesting that we are in fact dealing with the lonely remnants of an earlier religious milieu. First the ideas at work must be described in rather more detail.

1.1. Transfer and hypostasis

Both these ideas are essentially lost causes, and in most quarters have long been consigned to the history of the subject, as being influential in their day but now thoroughly discredited.[3] This is not, largely, because unshakeable proof has

---

[3] That said, they do have one or two surprisingly recent exponents, such as Lévêque (1961, esp. 96-8) in his discussion of Arkadian religion. He posits the notion that Kallisto, with her bear-metamorphosis, is 'une hypostase de la déesse' – that is, a demoted form of the goddess-as-bear;

been found which renders their claims invalid; after all, they operate so much in the territory of speculation as to make that unlikely: this is the source of a peculiar strength, as well as their main weakness. It is, however, a significant weakness. Not a single monster can be shown beyond doubt to have once been a god; not a single mythological mortal can be proved to have taken over the animal associations of a deity. In a broader sense, however, challenges have been levelled at the way of thinking which governs these theories. Why *should* we try to reclaim a theriomorphic/mixanthropic god? Why would such a being be more interesting or illuminating to us than, for example, a deity with a wider range of animal-associations, extending into her mythological surroundings? This is a question posed by Forbes Irving[4] when he discusses the theory, among others, that behind Kallisto's bear-transformation in myth there lurks the earlier entity of the bear-goddess, whether Artemis herself or an even more obscure being.[5] There is no *need* to uncover lost and buried animal gods, whether 'disguised' as monsters or as mortals; therefore, given the dearth of convincing evidence, the aim has justly been abandoned in almost all quarters. Certainly within this study, if a being has no lasting symbolic power but has rather been allowed to slip into complete obscurity, the grounds for according that being attention are considered greatly reduced.

---

other mythical Arkadian figures also are brought into the same schema of the transfer of animal parts from goddess to companion/enemy – a classic expression of the animal displacement idea. This reading of Kallisto's identity as hypostasis of a bear-goddess is to be found rather earlier in Guthrie (1950), 104. The hypostasis notion found especial favour with regard to the cult of Artemis at Brauron (again the attempt was to uncover a lost bear-goddess): see e.g. Bachofen (1863); Farnell, vol. 2 (1896), 435. Perhaps the most extreme single case of the theory at work in scholarship, however, is Thomson's 1914 study of the *Odyssey* in which numerous characters, including Odysseus himself, are denoted 'faded gods'. This expands an argument of Fougères (1898, 240-49), that Odysseus and Penelope once formed, as gods, a doublet with Poseidon and Demeter. In almost all instances in both Thomson and Fougères, the 'original' deity is an animal-god: For Thomson, Odysseus was a wolf-god and Penelope was a waterfowl-goddess. Interestingly, perhaps because this was so drastic a use of the theory, it attracted refutation almost at once: see Shewan (1915 a and b). However, it finds a more recent echo in the work of Mactoux (1975, 221), who argues that Penelope was originally an 'antique déesse de la fertilité.' Mactoux also argues for the hypostasis of Kallisto: 'Callisto, fille de Lycaon, est une arcadienne, ancienne divinitée locale dépossédée par Artemis qui portait parfois l'épiclèse de Kallisté.' This idea of a deity, once relegated, supplying the cult title of its usurper is a fairly frequent one: see e.g. Fougères (1898), 227-8 (Hippos gives way to Poseidon Hippios); Séchan and Lévêque (1966), 14. The classic examples of the hypostasis and transfer theories are Harrison and Murray: see esp. Harrison (1912), 449 and Murray (1912), 33-4; the latter remarks confidently, 'these animals [the divinised totems central to the *ancien régime*] have all been adopted into the Olympian system. They appear regularly as the 'attributes' of various gods. ... Allowing for some isolated exceptions, the safest rule in all these cases is that the attribute is original and the god is added.'

[4] Forbes Irving (1990), 38-50.

[5] Forbes Irving (1990), 46.

1.2. Anthropomorphisation

Did mixanthropic deities become less animal and more human over time?[6] If so, this would appear to lend support to the idea that the animal parts of gods are generally undesirable and subject to a process of removal, just as, in the theory of growing scarcity, mixanthropic gods themselves are undesirable and gradually removed. In other words, what happens within one mixanthropic form may be taken as a microcosmic reflection of what happens to mixanthropes on the Greek cult scene. Moreover, if such a process is to be envisaged as having been at work at some undefined past stage, surely we should expect that it would still be going on in some form? Thus, evidence of *continued* removal of animal parts in the representation of mixanthropy would be a very important addition to the arsenal of the displacement-theorist, allowing for retrospective extrapolation of a similar process at earlier stages.

At first sight the theory of gradual anthropomorphisation seems to hold up, at least with regard to the evidence of the historical period. There are a number of well-attested cases in which the artistic representation of a mixanthrope appears to develop away from the bestial and the monstrous and towards the human and the idealised. The example most often remarked on, perhaps, is Pan, but another worth mentioning is Acheloos. The two instances show some similarities. We have already noted in Chapter 2 that Attic vase-painters discard the 'upright goat' type in favour of a version with more human parts. From the early fifth century onwards, Pans may also be young, and have attractive faces, their animal element betrayed only by unobtrusive horns (this development is discernible also in sculpture and occasionally coinage).[7] Similarly, later Classical and post-Classical imagery explores the potential for Acheloos to be young, attractive, and even vulnerable. He is sometimes shown as a human youth with small horns (or lacking a horn and bleeding after Herakles has torn it from him), a form very like those cited for Pan, and quite different from the Mannstier type more usually associated with Acheloos.[8]

---

[6] A belief in an evolution towards anthropomorphic representation underpins de Visser (1903), esp. 25-35; for discussion see Buxton (2009), 187-9, who points out that de Visser's evolutionary assumptions derive in large part from his heavy reliance on Pausanias and Clement of Alexandria.

[7] Typical examples are as follows. Vase-painting: Apulian red-figure bell krater, early fourth century, Pan stands by while Nike crowns a youth, in a theatrical context (BM F 163; *LIMC s.v.* 'Pan', cat. no. 263); sculpture: bronze statuette, late fourth century, Pan seated with *lagobolon* and goatskin (Basel, Antikenmus.; *LIMC s.v.* 'Pan', cat. no. 63); coinage: a number of coins of the Arkadian League, fourth century, showing Pan generally seated on a rock with *lagobolon* and *syrinx* – see e.g. *BMC* Peloponnesus 173, 48-49, pl. XXXII, no. 10; *LIMC s.v.* 'Pan', cat. no. 274.

[8] Pathetic young Achelooi are largely a Roman trope, appearing sometimes on mosaics: see *LIMC s.v.* 'Acheloos', cat. nos. 260 and 261a. The youthful, beardless type begins earlier, however, e.g. a mid-fourth-century red-figure krater from Lipari showing Acheloos with only very small horns in the company of Herakles, Deianeira and her father Oineus (Lipari Museo Eoliano; *LIMC s.v.* 'Acheloos', cat. no. 259a). It is very interesting to note that other river gods,

These two examples suggest that at least hypothetically, the loss by mixanthropes of their animal elements is not inconceivable. Very little (tiny horns, usually) is needed to identify a particular mixanthrope and indicate its mixanthropy, and as time goes by artists do strip the animal part down to that bare essential. However, in fact, all is not what it seems in the matter of anthropomorphisation, and a closer inspection does not reveal a straightforward progression from animal to human. Apparent trends can be deceptive and that care has to be taken to examine context and medium at all times; this done, a rather different picture emerges. Pan and Acheloos showed the *prima facie* possibility of the process, but they also reveal its problems.

The first is that while the topic under discussion is the treatment of part-animal *gods*, the evidence mustered is all of a sort not readily or straightforwardly connected with cult; in particular, there is heavy reliance on vase-paintings. Painted pottery clearly reflects religious themes and ideas, and may well in many cases have been used in ritual; and yet it has to be distinguished from cult imagery proper – that is, images of the god present in his shrine and involved directly in his worship,[9] cult images thus defined surely give a better impression of the physical conception of a deity which underpinned cult observance. So there is a methodological problem with basing a theory of religious squeamishness on a medium detached from an explicit religious context. Moreover, one can discern ways in which vase-painting especially takes a different route, when depicting mixanthropic deities, from that taken by cult images. Put simply, vase-paintings and other non-cult imagery tend to humanise, while cult images do not.

In Pan's case, once what may be regarded as the most typical Pan-form[10] is developed in the fifth century, it becomes the one used almost unvaryingly in cult imagery. It is also popular in non-cultic imagery, of course, but less unwaveringly. The tendency sometimes to humanise and to glamorise, which we remarked on, is not generally found in cult imagery. It is interesting that the Arkadian League chose a highly humanised Pan-type for their coins;[11] clearly they did not want

---

none of whom have the popularity or wide circulation enjoyed by Acheloos, tend to be far more anthropomorphic than he does in their visual representation.

[9] Not necessarily cult statues; as we have seen, we cannot generally hope for these! Cult imagery in the case of mixanthropes is composed largely of small votives in the round, and votive reliefs.

[10] Boardman's definition, in *LIMC*, of the 'standard type' is very useful, though some of the images he places outside it deviate from it only very slightly. He describes it as follows: 'The head is humanoid goat, horned, with human beard sometimes approximating to a goatee, and sometimes goat neck-warts. The nose may be snub (like a satyr's) but the whole head is more like a muzzle and the artist usually makes some attempt to deviate from the normal human or satyric type…. Horns usually spring from the centre forehead, rather than behind the ears as formerly. Ears are seldom realistically folded. The body is human with goat tail and legs. He is commonly ithyphallic, with genitals more often animal then human. Many Pans are shown small, Eros-size. Commonest attributes are the *syrinx* and *lagobolon/pedum*, dress a goatskin.' (*LIMC s.v.* 'Pan', p. 927.)

[11] An especially clear example is *LIMC s.v.* 'Pan', cat. no. 274; *BMC* Peloponnesus 173, 48-49, pl. XXXII, no. 10.

their federal ambassador to be substantially theriomorphic. These coins, however, are a very specific form of imagery in a very particular context, and context is all-important when it comes to assessing levels of mixanthropy in the representation of a god. On the whole, though some early images of Pan are strikingly therio-morphic,[12] consistent anthropomorphisation is absent from Pan's cult iconogra-phy. A similar, or even more striking situation, is found with regard to Acheloos, whose iconography in votive reliefs, most of which are from Attica and central Greece, shows such conservatism that Isler felt impelled to posit the existence of some highly influential *Urbild*.[13] The commonest types are the Mannstier form and the horned mask. The former of these in particular is notable for being about as animal as is possible while still maintaining some human features. There is no discernible attempt to replace these forms with something less animal.

Even in non-cult imagery, the humanising trend is far less clear than it might at first seem. It does not always proceed in the expected direction, for one thing. Though in the earlier fifth century there is a drive among vase-painters to human-ise Pan by giving him human legs and often a human face,[14] this is substantially reversed later in the century by the sudden popularity of goat legs and animal rather than human genitals, though the face is more often satyric than completely goatlike.[15] From this point, *both* types, the more human and the more fully mix-anthropic, continue to be used, *depending on context*. The chief influencing factor is the scene depicted on the pot, and Pan's rôle within it. This is not easy to define. Boardman is of course right to say that 'The mainly humanoid Pan remains in use … for more dignified images.'[16] But there is no clear schism by which the humanised Pan appears as calm, august, well-behaved, and so on, while his more animal counterpart is always ribald, violent, lecherous or absurd. Plenty of the latter type stand calmly, alone, sometimes smiling mysteriously,[17] while a number of humanised Pans prance and cavort exuberantly.[18] Interestingly, the Pans who attend and react to the return of Persephone are almost always thoroughly mixanthropic, suggesting perhaps that these images, informed by Pan's religious persona, follow his cult imagery.

So we can see that the choice of a more animal or a more human Pan is governed not by the artist's position on an evolutionary scale, but rather by what he is trying to express in a particular depiction. (There are no doubt other,

---

[12] See figs. 23 and 24.

[13] See Isler in *LIMC s.v.* 'Acheloos'.

[14] Herbig (1949), 55-6.

[15] As Boardman remarks: *LIMC s.v.* 'Pan', 940.

[16] *Ibid.*

[17] E.g. fig. 25.

[18] E.g. on a red figure Apulian bell-krater, dated 380-370 BC: human-legged Pan with satyric humanoid face dancing in company of maenad (Marburg Univ. 786; *LIMC s.v.* 'Pan', cat. no. 171).

less easily established, factors such as the regional market for which a pot or other object was intended, and the fashions of that place.) All in all, no clear trend of humanisation can realistically be suggested. The same is true of Acheloos. His non-cultic imagery is far more complex than that. Humanised Achelooi are a late rather than an early phenomenon, it is true. But they are slight in number compared with a long sequence of different artistic variants – Acheloos as triton,[19] Acheloos as centaur[20] – and certainly do not come to claim a position of orthodoxy. Mixanthropes on vases especially are subject to a constant process of experimentation, in which humanisation can be seen as playing a fairly minor rôle.[21]

One such experiment might be termed the 'charming mixanthrope': that is, the exploration of the potential for an ostensibly grotesque form to exercise appeal and attraction over the viewer. The clearest example of this is the gorgon Medusa, who from the fourth century BC (again, painted pottery is the main medium for these artistic adventures) becomes fairer and fairer of face until she is just a young woman with rather tangled-looking hair. This is a striking departure from the fanged and snarling horror-masks of Archaic art.[22] One might point also to the Sirens. Like Medusa, in early art they can be bearded; later, their femininity and power to attract become their most important features.

A parallel trend is the increasing tendency for Classical vase-painters to accord some pity and empathy to the monstrous foes they depict being worsted. This is often facilitated by a reduction of animal parts, a playing up of the common humanity shared by monster and attacking hero. But this reflects a particular artistic intention, rather than a general distaste for the animal component. Stern also makes the interesting point[23] that although the animal element may be lessened, the divide between animal and human parts within a monster's anatomy becomes more clearly marked. This suggests that so far from playing down their subjects' mixanthropy, vase-painters tended to want to play up the animal-human juxtaposition, the essence of the mixanthrope's unnatural quality.

---

[19] See Isler (1970), 16 (cat. no. 84), for the famous stamnos by Oltos, of which he says 'Nur das Horn und das Stierohr unterscheiden ihn von Triton.'

[20] Isler (1970), 17.

[21] Lissarrague (1993), 209-12, discussing satyrs on vases, remarks that, instead of anything as simple as a process of anthropomorphisation, what we see is a constant experimentation with the juxtaposition of human and animal in which the two components are varied and rearranged. The variability of the satyrs' animal element is a key element of their identity, he argues, and this is surely true of mixanthropic deities across the board.

[22] The development of Medusa's image was charted by Roscher (s.v. 'Gorgon'), who divided the extant material into three periods, Archaic (eighth to fifth centuries BC), middle/transitional (fifth to fourth centuries) and late/beautiful (fourth century onwards). Wilk is right to criticise this division as being overly strict and schematic, and failing to take account of the complexity of the image's usage in different contexts, places and media (Wilk [2000], 33-5). None the less, the prevalence of the attractive type definitely increases over time.

[23] Stern (1978), 13.

Such trends, however, should not be confused with the theory of mixanthropic displacement. They have *nothing to do with religious squeamishness.* The
figures concerned are not deities. Rather, what is being explored in such painted
pottery is the concept of the monstrous: its boundaries and its artistic potential
are being tested and flexed. This is a largely separate process from any which
might have seen mixanthropic gods displaced and humanised. Gods clearly are
sometimes caught up in it (Pan and the Sirens receive cult) but it is their non-
cultic imagery which is primarily affected, and it cannot be taken as evidence
for a shift in religious attitudes towards them.

Moreover, there are instances where the overt mixanthropy of a deity appears to be a later development rather than the deity's earliest and most
primitive form. Animal elements which before occupied a rather undefined and
nebulous position in the deity's iconography are made more manifest and are
given an integral place within his or her physical composition. The clearest
examples in which this appears to happen are Hekate[24] and Dionysos.

Mixanthropy lurks in the persona of some forms of Dionysos from an early
stage; that is undeniable and has been discussed in the sections on his cult and
composition. The elements of the bull's foot, horns and voice are all repeated
motifs, and follow the typical distributive patterns of mixanthropy. But,
significant as that is, it is a little different from actual mixanthropic cult images.
Throughout the span of his worship, cult images of Dionysos are almost
universally anthropomorphic; only in the later stages, from the Hellenistic
period on, do we start finding some mixanthropic (generally horned) depictions.[25] This in direct opposition to some basic assumptions about Dionysos'
mixanthropic form, an example of which is Harrison's assertion that 'Dionysos

---

[24] The François Vase gives us one early instance of Hekate represented in monstrous form,
with dog-parts (on this see Vermeule [1979], 190). This is highly isolated, however, and in other
sources she is not only entirely anthropomorphic but also free from any overtly monstrous
associations. A key example is her persona in the *Homeric Hymn to Demeter* (in which she consoles
and assists the grieving Demeter). Her rôle here seems to tie in strongly with her common
iconographic depiction as a light-bearing goddess with fertility-associations (see Parisinou [2000],
60-67 and 83-4). Vases show her in such fertility-related contexts as the departure of Triptolemos
(for example on the Niobid Painter's volute krater from the second quarter of the fifth century –
Louvre G343; *LIMC s.v.* 'Hekate', cat. no. 19). These benign aspects are far more apparent than
any connection with the dog, let alone a mixanthropic connection. Later (chiefly literary)
depictions of Hekate, by contrast, bring out the grotesque and terrifying elements of which the
dog is – or comes to be – emblematic. Perhaps the most extreme case of this later trend is Verg.
Aen. 6.255-8: on the threshold of the underworld, Hekate appears in a nightmarish baying of
dogs and a shaking of the ground. So this is one instance certainly where a deity's animal
associations, negative as they largely are, are played up rather than down in line with the
manipulation of her persona to suit changing usage. It reveals the importance of individual
circumstances over wide trends: the treatment of particular deities depends on their own
particular symbolic value and how that develops over time.

[25] See above in Chapter 2. The exception is the tauromorphic image at Cyzicus, which
though mentioned only in the relatively late work of Athenaios (*Deipn.* 11.476a) may well have
been an old artefact.

the Bull-god and Pan the Goat-god both belong to early pre-anthropomorphic days, before man had cut the ties that bound him to the other animals; one and both they were welcomed as saviours by a tired humanity.'[26] The enthusiastic later response to the animal form of gods is an interesting point; but we have no evidence in the case of Dionysos that an earlier form of the god is being joyously rediscovered. Rather, Dionysos' mixanthropy appear to be a later feature of his actual iconography, if not a complete innovation. What came before it is far more complex and, for us, revealing: a tangled array of different animal associations, different connections between god and beast of which mixanthropy is only one.

To sum up, it is of course possible that some mixanthropic deities who were once worshipped later ceased to be worshipped and left no trace of their cult. But the processes which would have brought about their disappearance cannot be identified in our material, cannot be measured or tested or checked. They are almost entirely hypothetical, based on models of religious and artistic evolution which receive little or no support from our available evidence. Moreover, even if some isolated and slight instances of increased humanisation were visible in the material, we would not be justified in using these to read backwards and posit an earlier time of relative abundance. Such problematic retrospective logic is the hallmark of the theory of mixanthropic displacement through evolution. It rests on a belief that we have at our disposal the tail end, so to speak, of a developmental process, and that from the end we can build up a reliable picture of the whole, like reconstructing a dinosaur only its hindmost vertebra as evidence to work from. This is simply not possible with the material at our disposal.

However, the model on which the theory rests persists. It continues to occupy a subtly influential position even in the scholarship of recent decades. There has been a common assumption that mixanthropic deities were early, primitive, belonging to a past and also to a largely lost era, superseded by religious developments which increasingly placed anthropomorphic conceptions of divinity centre-stage. Rarely is this theory explicitly evoked; it enters arguments by a small side-door and its workings are hard to pin down. Its persistence, however, is extremely interesting and significant, and is not accidental. I would argue that the theory owes its longevity to its astonishingly deep roots. The next chapter of this book will examine its basis in ancient thought.

---

[26] Harrison (1908), 651.

2. Time

2.1. Mixanthropes and the past

Once again, symbolic topography is a potent expression of the connection between mixanthropic gods and past time. In Section One, it was striking how frequently mixanthropic deities were found to receive worship in the setting of a mountain, or a cave, or both. The significance of this is manifold, and should not be over-simplified, but one of its aspects is a temporal one: caves and mountains are both associated with the remote past of both humanity and the gods. Buxton has argued this convincingly,[27] citing the myths in which, after a Great Flood, human life re-starts on mountains.[28] And, as he points out, mountains are also associated with the early stages of the lives of individuals: gods are born on mountains,[29] and heroes are raised on them.[30] In a sense, mountains are the setting for events which take place *before the main action* (a hero's bold deeds, a god's divine career) *begins*. Caves largely share this significance. They too house mythical births and infancies, both human and divine.[31] They too are primitive sites of habitation, being regarded as proto-dwellings in which mankind began by residing[32] and in which primitive beings continue to reside.[33] The determination to locate mixanthropic deities in caves, which certainly does not diminish over time,[34] is a reflection of the belief that they belong in essence to the past time which the cave and mountain represent.

Other details of mixanthropic worship often reflect their association with past time. We have noted in Section One a number of cases of tomb-cult, or something like it. This is present, for example, very strongly in the cults of Proteus, Kekrops and the Siren Parthenope. By the time they are worshipped, their mythical careers are perceived as being behind them, over and done. Cult, of course, allows for their powers to be maintained and harnessed, but as has been argued in the previous chapter, worship does not itself imply a very strong sense of the deity's presence, in any reliable sense, on the spot. In the case of Kekrops,

---

[27] Buxton (1994), 90, 104-5.

[28] e.g. in Plato, *Leg.* 677b-c and Apollod. *Bibl.* 1.7.2 (the latter is the famous case of Deukalion).

[29] For instance Hermes, whose birth was claimed by Mount Kyllene in Arkadia: *Hom. Hymn* 4, esp. ll. 228-30.

[30] For instance all the heroes raised by Cheiron; for an exhaustive list see *RE s.v.* 'Chiron'.

[31] The most famous divine example is that of Cretan Zeus; see e.g. Hes. *Theog.* 477-80. A mortal example is Ion in the play by Euripides of that name.

[32] Aisch. *Prom. Vinc.* 453.

[33] For example the Cyclops Polyphemos in the *Odyssey*, esp. 9.216-43. On the symbolism of his primitive life, see Kirk (1971), 162-71; Hernández (2000).

[34] In the case of Pan it may be seen as gaining ground, given that the god's earlier Arkadian worship does not tend to be cave-based, but that when it is exported to other regions it becomes almost exclusively sited in caves. See Borgeaud (1988), esp. 50-52; above, pp. 113-114.

the hero's burial places him back into the earth out of which he originally emerged.

Tomb-cult does not, of course, set mixanthropes apart from other forms of cult recipient in Greek religion; countless fully anthropomorphic heroes were worshipped at such sites, and were themselves considered as belonging to a long-distant age, their function within the community maintained through ritual. The aim of this discussion is not to argue that mixanthropic deities exercise a unique claim on tomb-cult and its associations. Rather, what gives them their particular character as a group is the way in which such relatively common features of Greek religious practice are incorporated within a particular range of semantic tools expressive of an affiliation with the past. It is the variety and configuration of such expressions that, taken in combination, as a cluster, allows an analysis of the particular position of mixanthropes within the ancient religious imagination. For tombs are not the only forms of cult site which functioned as monuments to erstwhile presence. A different and especially graphic example is provided by the the case of Glaukos, the sea-god worshipped on the cliff-top spot from which he leapt into the sea and thus vanished, the *Glaukou pedêma*. In his case, vanishing, becoming mixanthropic and attaining divinity are depicted by some ancient authors as well-nigh simultaneous; he effects a multiple departure, abandoning a location, his human form, and his mortality, in one fell swoop. This sense of absence is, as has been said, a corollary of the expulsion-motif; it also contributes to the depiction of mixanthropic deities as belonging to, and operating largely in, the mythical past.

Perhaps the most complex and interesting case of the past deity, however, is Cheiron. It has been argued that his Pelion cave is a site of absence; but his worship in the area is also infused with a more positive sense of his rôle as a fore-runner, an antecedent. It is important for his function as one of the key deities of the Pelion area that he should have this persona.

One of the capacities in which Cheiron was worshipped on Pelion was as the ancestor of a line of healers. This founder-figure rôle is important, especially when combined with Cheiron's depiction as the inventor of at least some forms of healing.[35] At least within the Pelion area, he is the creator of a *techne*. Now mythical inventors of *technai* in Greek thought come in various shapes and sizes: sometimes they are gods, sometimes heroes, sometimes mortals. That said, however, in the case of Cheiron the *combination* of the originator-rôle with the motif of banishment and death is highly reminiscent of a pattern discernible in the presentation of a number of mixanthropic figures in Greek mythology. These figures, for example the Telchines[36] and Marsyas,[37] invent or discover some *techne*

---

[35] For this aspect of his cult, see above in Chapter 2; see also Aston (2006), 357.

[36] The Telchines especially provide a useful counter-example to Cheiron in various ways. Their mixanthropy is not frequently mentioned; but they are said to have flippers or fins in place of feet (Suet. *peri Blasph.* 4, in which we are also told that some of them were wholly serpentine in

or *technai*, but subsequently suffer expulsion and/or death, usually at the hands of a god, generally as punishment for misuse of their special skills. There is a strong sense that these primordial figures associated with the birth or the early stages of a *techne* have to be disposed of and superseded, their craft appropriated. They are always locked into the remote mythical past.

Cheiron does not, of course, abuse his special skills as do the Telchines; but they do fail to avail him when he is dying from the wound caused by Herakles' arrow; it is the inherent limitation of his skill which is his undoing, not its misuse. His death is accompanied by the revelation of the flaw within his power. He is not a perfect practitioner, and the imperfection of his practice makes him non-lasting. This makes him a very suitable founder-figure: extraordinary, but finite, leaving room by his departure for others to come in after him. He stands at the start of a mythologized schema of succession which inevitably consigns him to a past age. It was in such a capacity, I suggest, that he was worshipped by the healers on Pelion: as an original, but not a lasting, power.

Likewise, his kourotrophic rôle renders him, on one level at least, inherently obsolete. He contributes chiefly to the early lives of heroes, before their main careers begin. Although in some instances he continues to be friend and ally into a hero's adulthood (the chief example being Peleus), on the whole his rôle becomes unnecessary once his charges are fully-fledged. It is the fate of teachers and – in some ways – nurses and parents to be left behind. Cheiron belongs to a generation which is almost always *earlier* in the time-structures of Greek myths.

Cheiron's case is an extreme one; his belonging to the past appears to be quite systematically expressed and is at the heart of his Thessalian cultic rôle. But it compares in many ways with other mixanthropes and mixanthropic deities, who are presented in Greek myth as dead, deposed, redundant or simply part of a long-departed age. The fact that many mixanthropic gods have this connection with past time is reflected also in their widespread depiction as old themselves. Interestingly, this is only the case with the male ones; female mixanthropic deities such as Parthenope the Siren tend to rely on an element of dangerous allure

---

form and others wholly piscine), and also, interestingly, to have been the dogs of Aktaion, changed into men (Eustath. *Il.* 771), a detail which brings them tantalisingly within the same myth-complex as Cheiron though it is the only real point of convergence. (This dual animal association is complex but not unique – cf. the caprine/piscine nature of Aigipan.) They were thought to have invented metallurgy and to have forged the sickle of Kronos – see Diod. 5.55; Strabo 14.2.7 (further discussion of this theme in Chapter 10). Thus far their skills benefited mankind, but their behaviour was sometimes destructive. Strabo (op. cit.) calls them sorcerers and says that they blighted animals and plants – the products of agriculture – with Styx-water (Ovid, *Met.* 7.365 makes them use the evil eye to achieve the same end). They converge with Cheiron in their primordial aspect – as first inhabitants of Rhodes, as associated with Kronos (Diodoros and Strabo respectively).

[37] Although Marsyas does not actually invent the *aulos* (rather he picks it up when Athene has dropped it in disgust), he is still presented as a mythical originator. See Diod. 3.59; Strabo 10.3.14; Paus. 1.24.1; Apollod. *Bibl.* 1.4.2.

which is perhaps the chief factor dictating their depiction as (fairly) young women. (It is a truism that frightening females in Greek myths are often young and nubile, in contrast with the hideous crones of our own witch-dominated folk-tradition.) But there is a significant class of male mixanthropes who were perceived as belonging to the latter years of life.[38] They are, generally, those associated with special wisdom and knowledge, especially in a prophetic sense.

Even more remarkable is the fact that old age and wisdom tend to be the preserve of *individual* mixanthropes, while their multiple counterparts are less likely to be so characterised.[39] The clearest example is Silenos compared with the Silenoi/satyrs. Silenos, who is after all often called Papposilenos, was explicitly regarded as an older version of the others.[40] Silenos the individual had the mantic qualities his younger cohort lacked. (At least, this is so in Roman sources: the fullest example is Vergil's account – *Eclogues* 6 – of his capture by Chromis and Mnasyllus, who force him to prophecy. It is possible, if not probable, that he is being drawn into the *topos* of the capture of mixanthropic seers established by Proteus in the *Odyssey*, but even if this is so, it is interesting that no hint of oracular power is ever accorded to the other Silenoi and satyrs.) Proteus, however, is certainly the literary original of this *topos*. He tends to be depicted in literary sources as of advanced age, and indeed is one manifestation of the marine archetype the Halios Gerôn, the Old Man of the Sea (in the *Odyssey*, he is himself repeatedly called Halios Gerôn[41]); later sources too pick up on the age motif. By the time such figures as this enter the narrative of a myth, they are already old; we hear nothing of their youth (though we sometimes know their parentage). Even in the remote past of the myths, they, because they are old, are products of an even remoter one.[42]

---

[38] A significant proportion of the mythical figures identified as depicted as old by Richardson (1933, 86-97 and 182-214) are mixanthropic. Her study is not without its problems, chief among which is a failure to grasp the difficulty inherent in the visual material with regard to physical signifiers, especially baldness. Rather than being a straightforward indicator of old age, baldness in Greek thought has as much to do with absurdity and grotesqueness (for which see Aristoph. *Peace* 767, 771) and even, for one author, an overly high sex-drive, which would seem especially relevant to satyrs and centaurs (Arist. *de Gen. Anim.* 5.784a 31 – 785a 6).

[39] See the still-valuable discussion in Richardson (1933), 182-214.

[40] See e.g. Paus. 1.23.5, claiming that Silenos is the name given to an old satyr. Lissarrague (1993, 215-7) argues for the importance of age-relationships and the juxtaposition of young and old among Silenos and the satyrs: the old and wise Silenos is surrounded by his younger clan, the satyrs. Hedreen (1992), 107, notes also that the age and relative wisdom of Papposilenos is registered in satyr-plays, their content and their staging.

[41] Hom. *Od.* 4.365, 384. At 395 he is called '*theios gerôn*', the divine old man; at 410 and passim throughout the episode, *gerôn*. Vergil calls him a *senex* at *Georg.* 4.403. On the use of the name Halios Gerôn, see Shepard (1940), 10-16.

[42] In later sources, Cheiron too is fitted into this picture of the old mixanthrope: see for example Stat. *Ach.* 1.106 (he is called *longaevus*) and Nonn. *Dion.* 35.61 (*gêraleos*). In earlier sources, both visual and literary, his old age is less positively emphasized, though of course he is always

It is surely not unconnected that Cheiron is an offspring of Kronos, a figure who is primordial in the extreme, according to all the ancient accounts of the origins of gods and men:[43] he is one of the Titans, who are defeated by Zeus;[44] he is the father of Zeus, and is of the generation before the Olympian gods.[45] His parents are Ouranos and Gaia; his siblings include the Kyklopes and the hundred-handed Briareos, Kottos and Gyes.[46] The Titans are also, after their defeat by Zeus, incarcerated by him in Tartaros,[47] which as we have seen was the repository for a number of monsters vanquished and banished by Zeus in the latter's rise to power. Kronos belongs to the ranks of the dispossessed, according to the Hesiodic tradition. That Cheiron is his son reinforces the impression that Cheiron too is affiliated with that lost order of beings. He does not share their fate of initial banishment; but he does succumb to the aggression of Herakles, who, as has been said, was perceived as continuing Zeus's work, purging the world of left-over monsters from the time before Olympian rule.

But Kronos' persona and the nature of his rule have another dimension. He is also the presiding figure in the mythical Golden Age, a time of abundance and goodness;[48] this seems strikingly different from his persona as transgressive[49] foe of Zeus. This is not simply a later variant, for our sources are Hesiod (from whom the tradition of his defeat derives) and Pindar.[50] In the latter's account, when the Golden Age is over, Kronos becomes the ruler of the Islands of the Blessed. His description of the place over which Kronos presides is lyrical, with both natural beauty (shining flowers) and an ethos of justice and goodness among the inhabitants. Kronos' rôle in the Islands of the Blessed makes them in a sense the continuation of the Golden Age, which has been lost to all but the heroic and the deserving.

This strange mixture of motifs (Kronos as foe defeated; Kronos as preserver of the Golden Age) reveals above all the persistent Greek ambivalence regarding the past. The past is a time of monsters, of terrible deeds, extreme savagery, to be

---

shown as bearded. More prominent, in his case, than *actual* old age is *relative* old age; Cheiron is always older than those he advises, educates and assists.

[43] A number of mixanthropes are born from the earliest figures in the Greek mythological lineage. For example, Acheloos is the son of Okeanos and Tethys (Hes. *Theog.* 340); and the Sirens are sometimes made the children of Gaia or of Phorkys (Eur. *Hel.* 168; Soph. fr. 777 Nauck).

[44] Hes. *Theog.* 664-735.

[45] Lines 453-8.

[46] Lines 147-9.

[47] Defeat of Kronos by Zeus: line 73; incarceration of all the Titans in Tartaros: lines 729-35. Kronos is certainly confined there with them: see line 851.

[48] For discussion of the positive associations of the Age of Kronos, see Versnel (1993), 92-9; Davidson (2007), 213-5.

[49] Transgressive because of his castration of his father and swallowing of his children by Rhea: see *Theog.* 176-87 and 453-67 respectively.

[50] Pind. *Ol.* 2.

disposed of and superseded. But it also contains elements whose loss and passing are explicitly regretted.[51] As has been shown in the chapter on the expulsion-motif, a very similar ambivalence surrounds many mixanthropic deities; their absence is both desired and feared. They are regarded as dangerous and potentially destructive; but at the same time their loss can be regrettable (Cheiron) or even downright catastrophic (Demeter Melaina). The similarity is not accidental. Often mixanthropes encapsulate some good element of the remote past which is perceived as being largely lost to mankind.[52]

Arkadia provides a full example of the ambivalence and complexity surrounding the association of mixanthropic deities with the past (Arkadia, that is, as reflected in myths and in the Greek imagination). The region does not become the pastoral setting *par excellence* until after Classical antiquity;[53] it does, however, feature constantly *via* her most famous son, Pan, who is omnipresent in pastoral verse, and who is depicted as haunting the landscape in which it is set – as has been said, a potentially threatening presence.[54] He is only one of a number of rustic deities presiding over the scene, however: the satyrs and Silenos are fellow-mixanthropes, and Priapos shares their associations with animal sexuality and violence.[55] Arkadia and Pan often, however, work in concert. For example, in Theokritos' first *Idyll*, Pan is summoned to Sicily from the Arkadian landscape which is taken as his permanent and usual haunt: Mounts Mainalon and Lykaion are the key place-names used to recall his homeland. So Pan is both in and of Arkadia, and at the same time may be appropriated for universal application wherever the pastoral way of life is being described.

---

[51] On the elaborate complex of ambiguities in the character of Kronos and its relationship to the ritual of the Kronia, see Versnel (1993), who also surveys other manifestations of the ancient ambivalence towards the distant past, including its embodiment in the figures of Polyphemos and Cheiron. On the latter he observes, 'Cheiron's status … as the son of Kronos, is in my opinion, based on this ambiguity: Cheiron, too, is a creature midway between human and animal. He betrays elements of the wild, bestial and uncontrolled (especially when associated with the centaurs as a group). But he possesses elements of culture and justice as well' (pp. 110-11). If this line of thought has a fault, it is that it underestimates the extent to which the character of Cheiron, for all his mixanthropy, is always delineated as the opposite of the group-centaurs'; he is allowed none of their savagery.

[52] For example, Demeter Melaina is associated both with the Golden Age foodstuffs that form her sacrifice, and with the nightmare diet of the child-eater: she represents, single-handedly, the two versions of the remote past as expressed in the imagery of foodstuffs.

[53] See Halperin (1983), 129.

[54] Pan resting at noon and reacting angrily to disturbance: Theok. *Id.* 1.16-18. For discussion of the latter-day reception of Pan and his pastoral setting, see Merivale (1969).

[55] The satyrs: see Theok. *Id.* 4.62; Priapos: 1.81-2. Pan and Priapos together creep up to ravish the sleeping Daphnis: Theok. *Inscr.* 3. Silenos is added to the company by Vergil in his *Eclogues* and is there given a striking rôle as narrator and mediator of the past, both cosmic and mythological. This is reminiscent of the rôle of Proteus, but is an innovation within the pastoral genre. See *Ecl.* 6.13-86.

The land of pastoral is both old-fashioned and utopic. It is also a setting in which man and beast are so close in nature and way of life as to be occasionally almost interchangeable. For example, when in Theokritos' fifth *Idyll* Komatas mocks Lakon by recalling their supposed sexual encounter, he creates a picture of their mating being one of many, and of the cries of his partner mingling with the bleats of the she-goats around them. The comparison suits the particular humour of the context, but other examples abound.[56] The strong association of shepherds with their charges is not limited to pastoral verse; it receives far more widespread expression in, for example, their wearing of fleeces, a type of garment linked with a time before agriculture, when hunting and herding were humanity's chief means of survival.[57] Pan as presiding mixanthrope in the imaginary rustic landscape is the physical embodiment of this closeness between animal and man: his anatomy brings together animal and human in a harmonious whole. A life in tune with animals is seen as simple, bounded only by their uncomplicated needs, concerns and patterns of behaviour.

The picture created in pastoral verse and sketched briefly here is, however, revealed as an isolated one in ancient thought if one turns one's attention to mythological material of earlier genesis. In fact, it is a product of the post-Classical literary and cultural milieu, and has very little to do with the themes discernible in the mythology generated within the regions concerned, especially Arkadia itself. If we look at Arkadian mythology we find a very different picture of the relationship between mixanthropic deities and the past; and we encounter once more the ambivalence which characterizes so much Greek thought on the subject. We also find a very different portrait of Arkadia and of the mixanthropes of the rustic scene, including Pan.

As has been observed, images of animal metamorphosis and of mixanthropy in Arkadian mythology cluster around two interrelated episodes: the crime and transformation of Lykaon,[58] and the angry withdrawal of Phigalian Demeter. Taken together, these episodes present a co-ordinated appraisal of the animal-human relationship which is as far from the sunny intimacy of pastoral as it is possible to be. Lykaon's crime is to kill a human child as a sacrifice; his punishment at the hands of Zeus is to be transformed into a wolf.[59] Demeter, angry at the neglect of her Phigalian cult after the loss of her mare-headed *xoanon*, withdraws her powers from mankind and visits them with famine and with cannibal-

---

[56] Carried to an extreme in the figure of Daphnis, pastoralist *par excellence*, who is so much in tune with the natural world that at his death, wolves, foxes and herd-animals mourn him. Theok. *Id.* 1.71-5.

[57] Buxton (1994), 94.

[58] Jost (1989, esp. 286-9) has shown, with regard to the third-century BC *Alexandra* of Lykophron, that Lykaon and lycanthropy continued to be central symbols in the perception of Arkadia by other Greeks.

[59] Paus. 8.2.3; cf. Hyg. *Fab.* 176. Apollodoros, on the other hand, has Zeus blast Lykaon and his sons with his thunderbolt: Apollod. *Bibl.* 3.8.1.

ism.[60] There are two key themes in the two episodes, and they work together. The first theme is the conception of the past and of the passage of time; the second is the animal-human relationship.

Lykaon is a primordial figure, the son of Pelasgos, the first king of Arkadia.[61] He represents the remote past, and it is an ambiguous time.[62] On the one hand, gods and mortals feast together; on the other, it is a time of taboo-breaking savagery expressed in the sacrifice of the human child. The most detailed narrative of the crime of Lykaon is that of Pausanias, whose particular contribution must again be acknowledged. Though drawing on local mythology, the author injects his own preoccupations; this is the case throughout Book Eight, which is, as has been recognized, an especially sophisticated enmeshing of geography, myth and religion,[63] but within this the episode of Lykaon reveals an unparalleled intensity of authorial intrusion into traditional stories.[64] Among the many themes at play here, Pausanias' narrative captures the duality discernible in the perception of past time, for immediately after describing Lykaon's crime he says:

> For the men of that time were guests and table-sharers of the gods because of their righteousness and piety; and honour from the gods was clearly visited on those who were good, and on the unjust likewise their anger, since at that time gods came from the ranks of men, those who even now still receive worship, like Aristaios, and Britomartis of Crete, and Herakles son of Alkmene, and Amphiaraos son of Oikles, and in addition to these Polydeukes and Kastor. So one might believe that Lykaon became a beast or Niobe, Tantalos' daughter, a stone. But in my own time, since wickedness grows hugely and spreads over all the land and all cities, no god came from the ranks of men, except inasmuch as flattering speeches are addressed to despots, and the anger of the gods against the unjust is reserved until they have departed this life.[65]

---

[60] Paus. 8.42.5-6.

[61] Paus. 8.2.1.

[62] Buxton makes a strong argument that not only is Lykaon a primordial figure but that wolves were associated in Greek thought with primitive savagery. See Buxton (1987), 60-64.

[63] Hutton (2005), 91-5.

[64] On the rôle of Arkadia in delineating Pausanias' attitude towards the Greek mythological past, see Hutton (2005), 303-311; Buxton (2009), 135-7. On the Lykaon episode and its particular position within this discourse, see most recently Pirenne-Delforge (2008a), 67-72.

[65] Paus. 8.2.4-5: οἱ γὰρ δὴ τότε ἄνθρωποι ξένοι καὶ ὁμοτράπεζοι θεοῖς ἦσαν ὑπὸ δικαιοσύνης καὶ εὐσεβείας, καὶ σφισιν ἐναργῶς ἀπήντα παρὰ τῶν θεῶν τιμή τε οὖσιν ἀγαθοῖς καὶ ἀδικήσασιν ὡσαύτως ἡ ὀργή, ἐπεί τοι καὶ θεοὶ τότε ἐγίνοντο ἐξ ἀνθρώπων, οἳ γέρα καὶ ἐς τόδε ἔτι ἔχουσιν ὡς Ἀρισταῖος καὶ Βριτόμαρτις ἡ Κρητικὴ καὶ Ἡρακλῆς ὁ Ἀλκμήνης καὶ Ἀμφιάραος ὁ Οἰκλέους, ἐπὶ δὲ αὐτοῖς Πολυδεύκης τε καὶ Κάστωρ. οὕτω πείθοιτο ἄν τις καὶ Λυκάονα θηρίον καὶ τὴν Ταντάλου Νιόβην γενέσθαι λίθον. ἐπ' ἐμοῦ δὲ - κακία γὰρ δὴ ἐπὶ πλεῖστον ηὔξετο καὶ γῆν τε ἐπενέμετο πᾶσαν καὶ πόλεις πάσας - οὔτε θεὸς ἐγίνετο οὐδεὶς ἔτι ἐξ ἀνθρώπου, πλὴν ὅσον λόγῳ καὶ κολακείᾳ πρὸς τὸ ὑπερέχον, καὶ ἀδίκοις τὸ μήνιμα τὸ ἐκ τῶν θεῶν ὀψέ τε καὶ ἀπελθοῦσιν ἐνθένδε ἀπόκειται.

The author regrets the passing of the mythical age because in it the gap between gods and men had not yet developed; the two could feast together, and, more than that, men could become gods.[66] This is enmeshed with the author's own explicit dissatisfaction with the conditions of his own day, but the essential nostalgia, for a time when men and gods lived in harmony, is an old motif. In the story of Lykaon, however, it is combined with another form of closeness: between animals and men. The closeness of gods and men encourages Pausanias to believe that a man might also become an animal; the two fragile boundaries appear to complement and resemble each other. And Lykaon's wolf-nature reveals the dark side of the past as conceived in the myth: a time of savagery and transgression, and the *theriôdes biotos*.[67] Borgeaud has shown that the myth forms a doublet of sorts with that of Kallisto's seduction by Zeus and the birth of Arkas, another founder-figure: this episode, too, takes place at a time of dangerous closeness between the three states of man, animal and god.[68] It is this closeness that facilitates both divine/human mating and animal metamorphosis in a single episode.

What renders the past actively perilous, however, is its constant potential for catastrophic repetition. The myth of Demeter's anger sees Lykaon's wolfish crime visited once more upon the Arkadians: when famine strikes, the oracle they receive threatens that they will soon begin to eat their own children: a mass breakout of the transgression of Lykaon.[69] So, to summarize, the past is associated chiefly with the negative and extreme aspects of animal behaviour, and with the tendency of humans to slip into that animality; and the past is always waiting to reclaim Arkadia if the region should fail to stave it off with the correct religious (especially) practices. This is in a way the reverse of the pastoral view of Arkadia as 'the land that time forgot': a return to the close conjunction of animal and man is not something appealing but something to be striven against: the subject not of nostalgia but of fear. Inherent in the Lykaon myth, and explicit in Pausanias' narration of it, is regret at the lost closeness of man with god, but the accompanying closeness with the animal world and its perceived character is treated as purely malign.

Pan is a component of Arkadia's foundation-myths. It has been observed above (Chapter 2) that his cult played a part within the complex religious site of

---

[66] On the importance of this state of closeness in the Lykaon-myth and more widely in Greek thought, see Buxton (1987), 72-3.

[67] For an example of the use of this phrase, see Eur. *Suppl.* 201-2. For the wolf as standing for the savage Arkadian past, see Buxton (1987), 67-8. It is very interesting also that the primitive nature of Arkadians in Greek thought can lead to them being regarded as both unusually pious and unusually impious or transgressive. Both are contained in a passage of Polybios (4.21.1-6), who remarks that the Arkadians are the most pious of all Greeks, but one Arkadian community, the Kynaithians, are the most impious.

[68] Borgeaud (1988), 23-31.

[69] Paus. 8.42.6.

Lykaion, especially the worship of Zeus Lykaios, and it might thus be argued that he is a background figure within the nexus of associations surrounding that place. He appears to have been worshipped in close conjunction with Zeus, and the cult of Zeus Lykaios, as Borgeaud argues,[70] is a constant reference to the mythical interaction between Zeus and Lykaon. But he also plays a central rôle in the Phigalian narrative, discovering Demeter in the cave after her first withdrawal, and facilitating her return to the agricultural sphere. He could therefore be seen as belonging and operating squarely in the same distant past described above: another primordial mixanthrope. However, in the case of Pan, something a little more complex is to be found with regard to time-associations.

The essential dichotomy of Pan (it would be too strong to call it a paradox, although it has some paradoxical qualities) is that he is both a primordial figure and, in some sources at least, a young god. In the human sphere he is primordial: as half-brother of Arkas, according to one version of his parentage, he is woven into the foundation-myths of Arkadia, myths which define not only the inception of the region and its inhabitants but also its continuing nature.[71] A further connection with Arkas consists of the rôle of the latter's wife Erato as Pan's prophetess.[72] When the history of Arkadia was being shaped, in the mythic dimension, Pan was an important component in close conjunction with the eponymous Arkas. Pan too lends his name to Arkadia, which is sometimes referred to as Pania. There is no doubt that he figures as an ur-inhabitant in Arkadian mythology. This is reinforced by an alternative tradition of parentage, which makes Pan the son of Hermes and a mortal woman, the daughter of Dryops. According to Lykophron, Dryops was the grandson of Lykaon and the forefather of the Arkadians. His is a less commendable career than that of Arkas; his people, the Dryopes, are associated with violence and brigandage. But it is still significant that, across different versions of his birth, Pan is consistently related to the early founding figures of Arkadian mythology. A similar observation may be made about other mixanthropic gods: for instance Cheiron, as has been noted, is thoroughly enmeshed with early Thessalian figures. But Pan's case is unique in containing such an emphasis on placing him within the mythical *origins* of Arkadia and its people. He is intimately bound up in its process and development.

Arkas is not the first Arkadian, but he does mark an important watershed in the place's mythical history. In Pausanias' account, he marks the change from Pelasgian to Arkadian, and as an accompaniment invents bread-making and cloth-weaving:[73] thus he clearly takes the region forward a step along the path of imagined civilization. Other sources delineate the break more forcefully, by

---

[70] Borgeaud (1988), 35-8.

[71] Epimenides fr. 16 DK; schol. Eur. *Rhes.* 36; Aisch. fr. 65 b-c Mette.

[72] Paus. 8.37.11.

[73] Paus. 8.4.1.

recounting how Lykaon and his sons are destroyed by Zeus' thunderbolt; there follows a world-deluge, also sent by Zeus, in which the Pelasgians and their rulers the sons of Pelasgos (among them Lykaon) are destroyed.[74] As Borgeaud says, 'The crime of Lykaon and his sons marks the end of an epoch, that of the Pelasgian "régime" and of meals shared with the gods.'[75] Arkas, however, the son of Kallisto and grandson of Lykaon, survives the flood and the purging of Lykaon's line, and founds a new succession of mythical Arkadian rulers.[76]

So Pan's relationship to the reign of Arkas is twofold. He stands at the end of one 'régime' and the beginning of another: he is both original and new. This marries, I believe, with the rather contradictory treatment of Pan's actual age. The sources on his birth as son of Hermes often make much of the fact that he is a new arrival on the divine scene; an example of this is the *Homeric Hymn to Pan*, from which come the following lines:

> And she[77] bore in the halls
> a dear son to Hermes, marvellous to look upon,
> goat-footed, two-horned, noise-loving, sweetly laughing;
> but his nurse leapt up and fled and left the child,
> for she was afraid, when she saw his face, uncouth and well-bearded.[78]

Pan is a new arrival among the gods,[79] and his youth is part of his characterisation; but he is also born miraculously ready-bearded, already in the stage of life which the beard represents, full manhood (if one can use that term of a mixanthrope!).[80] It is hard to discern how this old/new paradox of the bearded baby connects with Pan's position in Arkadian mythic history, and yet it seems a striking parallel. The agedness which tends to accompany the mixanthrope and which may be seen as an irreducible part of Pan's image (young mixanthropes are something of an artistic innovation, a deliberate departure from the tradition of representation) is perhaps combined with a recognition that Pan is part of a *nouveau régime* in Arkadia. It is also possible that one is reading too

---

[74] See Apollod. *Bibl.* 3.8.1-2; Ovid, *Met.* 1.259-312.

[75] Borgeaud (1988), 27.

[76] Apollod. *Bibl.* 3.8.2-9.1. Pausanias (8.4.1) does not mention the flood, and instead makes Arkas the successor to Nyktimos, the only son of Lykaon to survive Zeus' thunderbolt (on this see Apollod. *Bibl.* 3.8.1).

[77] The subject is the daughter of Dryops, Hermes' mortal lover.

[78] *Hom. Hym.* 19, 35-9: ... τέκε δ'ἐν μεγάροισιν | Ἑρμείῃ φίλον υἱόν, ἄφαρ τερατωπὸν ἰδέσθαι, | αἰγιπόδην, δικέρωτα, φιλόκροτον, ἡδυγέλωτα· | φεῦγε δ'ἀναΐξασα, λίπεν δ'ἄρα παῖδα τιθήνη | δεῖσε γάρ, ὡς ἴδεν ὄψιν ἀμείλιχον, ἡγένειον.

[79] This observation is found already in Herodotos (2.145), who tells us that Pan was one of the youngest gods, born after the Trojan War. How exactly this fits in with the chronology of Arkadia's early kings is uncertain.

[80] cf. Lucian, *Dial. Deor.* 22.1: Hermes describes the young Pan as 'κέρατα ἔχων καὶ ῥῖνα τοιαύτην καὶ πώγωνα λάσιον καὶ σκέλη δίχηλα καὶ τραγικὰ καὶ οὐρὰν ὑπὲρ τὰς πυγάς;'

much into the bearded-baby motif; perhaps the chief factor behind it is simply the freak-show humour of a grotesque anti-infant.

Our observations about Pan as both old and new may interestingly be compared with the observation already made in this chapter, that the great weight of ancient thought connects mixanthropic deities with past time. Pan's case is complicated by the treatment of Arkadia's past in the mythology of that region. The earliest stage is contaminated by a kind of primordial sin, exemplified by the cannibalistic feast of Lykaon; it has to be renewed, started afresh. Pan belongs to the age of renewal, post-deluge in the Apollodoros version. This is at very striking variance with the fact that many mixanthropes are not regarded as having outlasted the distant past which they inhabit. They die with their eras; they have no place in the post-heroic age. This absence from the Greek contemporary has been noted and discussed. But Pan is different. What sets him apart is an extreme tenacity, a power of endurance unique among mixanthropic gods. There is, however, one highly significant exception to this picture of endurance: the strange episode of his death.

2.2. The death of Pan

The story of Pan's death is in fact so fraught with problems that it cannot be accorded the centrality in this study that its theme might at first sight seem to merit. A dying Pan would surely combine persuasively with foregoing observations about the death of Cheiron, and the tendency of mixanthropic gods towards absence – and yet the nature of the source makes it necessary to handle the episode with the greatest caution. The chief difficulties are the isolated quality of the single source, and the very particular context in which it existed.

Put briefly, Plutarch reports the following curious story.[81] A ship sailing from Greece to Italy was becalmed near Paxos, when from the island a voice was heard hailing Thamos, the ship's pilot. The voice enjoined Thamos, when he came opposite Palodes, to announce that Great Pan was dead. This he did, and the announcement provoked a many-voiced disembodied cry of lamentation and amazement. Death and lamentation: it will immediately be apparent that this narrative could reinforce the strong ancient *topos* explored in the previous chapter, of the mixanthropic god as absent and regretted; also this chapter's observation that mixanthropic gods are often presented as of the past.

The main problem with making use of the story in this way is that Plutarch is our only source and a very particular one at that. The episode falls within a wider discussion of the obsolescence of oracles and oracular demons; mixanthropy might have a place in this, but it is not a dominant one. From this highly specific

---

[81] Plut. *de Def. Or.* 17.

context it would be unwise to create a general theory.[82] However, there are some points of the story which are worth briefly noting. The first is that it seems deliberately to cast Pan as an entity mysterious both in identity and in presence. Tiberius, following the report of the event in Rome, organizes a scholarly inquiry into who Pan is (concluding that he is the son of Penelope and Hermes).[83] This strongly suggests that even before his demise Pan is a figure of uncertainty and enigma, requiring antiquarian reconstruction. As to his uncertain presence, the disembodied voice which calls to Thamos reminds one strongly of Pan's trade-mark shout, the main expression in many sources of his unpredictable manifestations in the Greek countryside.[84] That he *can* die is interesting, as Herbig notes:[85] his immortality is not unshakeable. The episode is full of familiar themes, interesting to note though intrinsically unreliable in this form.

3. Place

I now turn to consider the significance of location to the ancient conception of the mixanthropic deity. This subject has two quite discrete aspects. Particular meaning is imparted by a location within Greece; something quite different is suggested by a non-Greek location. The two aspects will therefore be treated separately.

3.1. The Greek world

Place and location within Greece are very often of special importance in the worship of and the attitudes towards mixanthropic deities. For a start, the very

---

[82] The best treatment of the various interpretations of the story which have been advanced since antiquity is that of Borgeaud (1983). This article reflects the various uses to which the death of Pan has been put, being cast in late antiquity as the death of the last pagan god in the face of advancing Christianity (see Euseb. *Praep. Ev.* 18.13); or, in the sixteenth century, as the revelation of the death of Christ himself as 'All' ('Pan'). On this see esp. pp. 266-7. For all the problems of the narrative, it is interesting for the purposes of this study to note that, for Eusebios especially, Pan represents the pagan 'old guard', a vestige of an obsolete religious system; this is in keeping with many of the foregoing observations of this chapter, arguing that mixanthropes are especially prone to being characterised as part of an *ancien régime.*

[83] This is despite a strongly un-Greek flavour in the designation *Pan ho megistos*: see Borgeaud (1983), 256. This is a further reason for treating the source with caution in this study, as it may have as much to do with Eastern and Egyptian religious notions as with Greek cult.

[84] That the shout may be Pan's own voice is suggested by Borgeaud (1983), 257. Mannhardt argued (1877, 132-48) that the chorus of lamentation which greets Thamos' message at Palodes is voiced by the plural Panes, spirits of the countryside and daemonic attendants of the singular Pan (this is echoed by Herbig [1949], 70-71). This is largely based on comparative evidence of dubious soundness, but would suggest, if it were true, more invisible mixanthropic presences in the narrative. Perhaps more interesting for this study is the lamentation itself, recalling the regret that attends the death of Cheiron in myth (see Aston [2006]).

[85] Herbig (1949), 70-1.

peculiarity of a large number of examples makes them extremely location-specific. Of course, it could reasonably be argued that every different cult site throughout Greece had its own unique variant of a god, so that this is not a particular feature of the mixanthropes. To a certain degree this is true. But there are several cases where a deity with a well-defined pan-Hellenic persona existed in a certain location or area in a form strikingly distinguished from that pan-Hellenic persona by its mixanthropic elements, not just by a different title or accompanying rites; and, sometimes, these elements are distinctive enough to give the deity the quality of a unique local speciality, tied firmly to that place. A number of 'one-off' mixanthropes function in this way. A good example is Demeter Melaina. Even in the depths of Arkadia, the imagery of Eleusis can be seen to have penetrated,[86] and with it a wider Greek idea of Demeter and her attributes that was at variance with Demeter Melaina, her mythical metamorphosis, the legend of her mixanthropic *xoanon*, and her mountain-cave location. There was no doubt that the animal associations of this Demeter set her apart from the pan-Hellenic deity and made her primarily a Phigalian, rather than a Greek, deity. Pausanias expresses the reason for his visit to Phigalia thus: ταύτης μάλιστα ἐγὼ τῆς Δήμητρος ἕνεκα ἐς Φιγαλίαν ἀφικόμην. He has come to see *this* Demeter.[87] Mixanthropic qualities gave versions of several 'mainstream' deities just such a special, location-specific quality, such as the fish-tailed Eurynome of Arkadia and the horned Apollo Karneios of Lakonia.

In addition, several mixanthropes, in common with the nymphs and other nature deities, have an especially strong connection with the natural landscape in which their cults are located. Looked at on the general level, there is a connection between gods and particular topographical features (Pan and caves, for example), but as soon as one comes down to specific cult sites, and specific topographies, a more intimate and particular relationship emerges. In several cases, a mixanthrope confers on his natural environment elements of his own divine persona and surrounding mythology. The most striking example of this is perhaps Cheiron, whose name and nature infuse the landscape of, and around, Mount Pelion in Thessaly. Central was the cave called the Cheironion, both a cult site and a setting of myth; but the surrounding glades also were connected with the centaur via countless episodes in his mythical career. We are also told that in the vicinity grew medicinal plants named after the great healer. Cheiron's mother, the nymph Philyra ('lime-tree'), also reflects the natural environment, though in a less

---

[86] For example, there was a cult of Demeter Eleusinia at Basilis: see Paus. 8.29.5 and Jost (1985), 338-40. She also notes several cases of 'overlay', the imposition of Eleusinian imagery onto Arkadian cults of Demeter: an example is the image of Demeter Erinys at Thelpousa, shown with torch and *kiste* and 'manifestement influencé par l'imagerie éleusinienne.' (op. cit., p. 302). On the combination of Eleusinian and local ingredients in Arkadian Demeter-worship, see also Pirenne-Delforge (2008a), 312-5.

[87] Paus. 8.42.11.

Pelion-specific way. Overall, though, Cheiron's ties to the physical landscape of Magnesia are especially close, held fast in the names of cave and plants.

This closeness perhaps encouraged those past scholars who have argued that the centaurs generally (and it must be said that in the main their arguments refer to the group-centaurs) were in origin purely nature-spirits, embodiments of rushing mountain torrents, or of the forces of the winter. For all their appeal, such identifications are impossible to prove; and in any case their one-sidedness does nothing to address the complexity of the centaurs' character and rôle in myth and art. None the less, they rest upon an indisputable truth, that centaurs, Cheiron included of course, are impossible to divorce from a specific type of landscape, that of the wooded mountain. The actual location is sometimes Thessaly, sometimes Arkadia, and one can argue at length (though without hope of ultimate resolution) about which region holds primacy; but in each the mountain is the centaur's world, from which he barely strays. If forced from one mountain, the centaur will flee to another. The same goes for the cave, in Cheiron's case; expelled from his cave on Pelion, he finds a new one on Cape Malea.[88] One cannot write off this state of affairs as a mere doublet, the Pelion setting[89] unthinkingly recreated when the myth is transposed; it is important to the myth's structure that one mountain takes over from the first as the centaurs are harried, like animals, from covert to covert. And one Arkadian mountain in particular, Pholoë, has its own particular centaur, Pholos; the names suggest a long-held association. Whatever one might think about the relationship, the sequence of the parallel myth-structures of Cheiron and Pholos, there is no doubt that a mountain setting 'attracts' centaur-associations in a way which low-lying land never does.

A particular landscape/deity relationship exists in the case of river-gods, who were almost unvaryingly depicted and imagined, as has been shown, with mixanthropic features, though to differing degrees. These deities are peculiar in that they both stand for and *are* a local river. They are detachable from the waters and are depicted as forms in their own right, yet the river is not merely their dwelling-place, it is their identity as well.[90] As a result of this, an element of the local landscape has a name, mythological deeds, and often a cult, of its own. This may be read as one step further on from the state of affairs by which

---

[88] Apollod. *Bibl.* 2.5.4.

[89] Or indeed the Pholoë setting, if that is considered the original.

[90] An example of a river-god operating in its watery manifestation is Skamandros, who fights with Achilles in *Iliad* 21 (211-71). Here the river *is* a river, not a bull-horned man or other emblematic personification, and he uses his waters against Achilles to swamp and drown him. In other texts, the form of the river-god is more flexible. In Ovid's description of the river Alpheios' pursuit of Arethousa (*Met.* 5.595-642), the god first appears as a voice from the depths of the water; when Arethousa flees, however, he is able to pursue her far and wide, and to do so adopts human form (this is made explicit at lines 637-8). He reverts to water, however, as soon as the human embodiment is no longer necessary.

the Pelion cave was infused with the character and divinity of Cheiron; even from the way in which springs and groves were thought to be haunted by the nymphs.[91] Though in some cases a nymph and a spring could be thought to be almost one and the same thing, I would argue that she tended to retain a separable persona in a way which the river-god, bound to his element, did not.[92] In a way, though, both served the same purpose as instruments of local and regional self-definition, as is attested by the popularity of both local nymphs and local river-gods on coins.[93] The coins of a region must bear some motif peculiar to the place, something which will instantly announce the coin's provenance should it leave its native soil, and for this purpose the river-god is a perfect choice. He is named, unique, and reflects a visible and tangible part of the area thus advertised.

I would argue that the mixanthropic quality of the river-god helps to maintain the connection with the waters of the river he embodies, a connection which might otherwise be at risk of being weakened once the god is removed from context and – in particular – depicted in the highly allusive, minimal format of the coin's face. There are two ways in which the mixanthropic form could accomplish this. First, there appears to have been a lasting link between the waters of both river and sea and certain animals and animal characteristics, most strongly the bull whose parts most often go to make up the river god, either a bull's body, legs, ears and horns in the Mannstier form, or just ears and horns attached to an otherwise human form in the second common type. The relationship between the bull and both sea and rivers has been described in an earlier part of this book. The second way in which mixanthropy reinforces the god's connection with the river has to do more with convention than with belief. Despite the fact that, as has been said, river-gods are highly specific to their surroundings, their iconography was early established and shaped into a strong, recognisable orthodoxy. (Or perhaps it would be more correct to speak of two conjoined orthodoxies, given the parallel use of both the Mannstier and the horned human types.) In any case, certain mixanthropic forms would immediately have suggested to the viewer, almost anywhere in Greece, 'river-god'. This is not to say that the forms would not have carried other associations

---

[91] For the persistent connection between nymphs and springs and groves, see Larson (2001), 8-11 (and *passim* for specific examples).

[92] Though nymphs and their natural embodiments are sometimes very closely fused, for example in the case of hamadryads, who die when their trees are cut down. Sometimes this seems to be because tree and nymph are virtually identical, as when Erysichthon cuts down the 'oak of Deo' in Ovid (*Met.* 8.738-78): the tree bleeds and the nymph within it dies. In other examples, the tree is presented rather as the favourite haunt of hamadryads, but they are similarly dependent on it: in his account of Paraibos, cursed because his father cut a nymph's tree, Apollonios (*Arg.* 2.456-89) describes the tree as the home of the nymph, not her *alter ego*. See Larson (2001), 73-8.

[93] An example of an eponymous nymph popular in coinage is Larissa, frequently depicted on the currency of the Thessalian town of that name. See Larson (2001), 165; Head (1911), 297-9.

in the background, especially Dionysiac ones. But the mixanthropic elements of the river-gods never allowed their aquatic identity to be forgotten. The existence of strong pan-Hellenic conventions of representation[94] are interesting, when set besides the highly local quality of named, specific river-gods. It allowed for a dual process. A river-god could be employed as the special emblem of an area, while at the same time exploiting the power of a universally recognised form which would connect the individual deity with a wider class, or type, and the human community with wider Greek religious practices. This said, it is doubtful to what extent the members of a particular place would have been aware of customs and artefacts from other, far-flung areas of Greece; it is possible that the river-god representational types were spread and transmitted without an accompanying awareness of their universal and coherent quality.

The appropriation and use of the river-god motif as ambassadorial can be seen in surviving coinage all over Greece, though there are striking clusters in, for example, south Italy and Sicily.[95] There one also finds an unusual number of coins depicting the god Acheloos, whose worship had taken firm root in those regions. Yet the place to make most use of the named Acheloos-image on its currency was, unsurprisingly, Akarnania, where the river Acheloos runs and where the cult of the deity originated. In other words, although the cult of Acheloos attained a pan-Hellenic dimension and lost its purely local quality in contrast with, for example, Cheiron, it was still of course possible for one place to assert a special relationship and to use him as the unmistakeable emblem of the land. Indeed, the representations of Acheloos on Akarnanian coins greatly outnumber those of Cheiron on the coins of Magnesia or Thessaly, and this surely reflects the river-god's more prominent and central religious rôle, reinforced by his connections with Dodona.

Sometimes the relationship between mixanthropic deity and place goes beyond the immediate physical environment. Some mixanthropes can be argued to contribute significantly to the perceived nature of a whole region, as well as, at the same time, deriving from that region elements of their own personality. The clearest examples of this are to be found in Arkadia and Thessaly, which have already been mentioned in this section: now, however, the way in which they are partly characterised in ancient thought by their most prominent mixanthropes will be discussed in more detail.

It has been said that Cheiron is enmeshed in the myths of Pelion; and it is with that tract of land, indeed, that he is most strongly connected. But it is also true that his nature and deeds stand at the heart of Thessalian mythology far

---

[94] See *RE* s.v. 'Flussgötter'; Gais (1978).

[95] The examples in both these regions are far too numerous to list (Head [1911] index *s.v.* River-gods 955-6 gives a sense of their superabundance). However, an especially prominent and clear example is Gelas, the river-god of Gela in Sicily, shown both as a horned human and as a man-faced bull: see Head (1911), 140-42.

more widely. Not only does he stand behind many of the most prominent episodes; he also, fascinatingly, often acts as a connection between mythical figures and events, and in fact gives the mythology of Thessaly a coherence, an interconnection, which it would otherwise lack. On the most basic level, the childhoods of a catalogue of prominent heroes (primarily Thessalian) converge, in place if not in time, in his Pelion cave,[96] so that one may see him as a central figure holding radial cords, at the end of which other figures move in their own stories but always with a connection to Cheiron and to their own infancy. The links are not necessarily severed when childhood and education end. Perhaps the most extensive myth-amalgam surrounds the house of Peleus. As a long series of events unfolds, the centaur participates at almost every stage. He helps to save the young Peleus from a murderous human and then murderous centaurs, once more on Pelion.[97] He gives him the advice necessary for the winning and wedding of Thetis.[98] His Pelion home is the venue for the nuptials; his wedding present to Peleus is a marvellous ash-wood spear.[99] After the departure of Thetis, he undertakes the rearing and education of the young Achilles. Achilles at Troy wields the ashen spear which came to his father from the hands of the benign centaur.[100] Pelion is the centre, but the other heroic figures take Cheiron's influence outwards into Thessaly more widely.

It must be said that alongside Cheiron's presence in Thessalian lore is the presence of the other centaurs, the wild inhabitants of the mountains whose violence towards Peleus Cheiron intercedes to prevent. This episode sees Cheiron and the other centaurs as opposing forces, a not uncommon characterisation, parallel to the depiction of the Peloponnesian Pholos and his less civilised fellows. I would suggest that Cheiron and the group-centaurs together *combine* to express and reflect aspects – not simply opposing polarities – of the land in which they live in myth. Both contain elements of the horse, the animal for which Thessaly was famous in antiquity.[101] It has already been observed that the horse in Greek thought could be both a destructive animal, eating human flesh, and at the same time one with strong connections with the aristocratic

---

[96] Of the many heroes nurtured by Cheiron, some prominent Thessalian examples are Jason, Achilles and Asklepios: see respectively Pind. *Pyth.* 4.102-3; Hom. *Il.* 11.831; Pind. *Pyth.* 3.5-7, 44-6.

[97] Apollod. *Bibl.* 3.13.3.

[98] Pind. *Nem.* 4.60-65; Apollod. *Bibl.* 3.13.5.

[99] Pind. *Nem.* 3.52-8; Apollod. *Bibl.* 3.13.5.

[100] Hom. *Il.* 19.390-91.

[101] As Westlake remarks (1935, 4), 'Thessalian horses were proverbial, Thessalian cavalry the best in Greece.' Ancients made frequent remarks to this effect: see Soph. *El.* 703-6; Eur. *Andr.* 1229; Plat. *Leg.* 625d; Theok. *Id.* 18.30. The Thessalians themselves were clearly proud of their horses; horses with and without riders appear with great frequency on the coins of all parts of Thessaly, but especially those of Pherai and Pharsalos (see Head [1911], 306-8) – this may be due in part to the fact that these cities had an unusual level of contact with states outside Thessaly and therefore had an especial interest in displaying their most prestigious products.

way of life. In Thessaly, where horse-rearing and the use of cavalry flourished, that way of life perhaps retained the prominence in actuality which it had lost in more democratic states. And Cheiron, tutor of heroes and instiller of aristocratic *paideia*, may be seen as embodying the horse-aristocrat connection.[102] The group-centaurs, on the other hand, contain a far larger dose of the violence potential in the horse in Greek thought.

It is extremely interesting, however, that Cheiron and the group-centaurs are not separated more than they are; that they continue to share a mountain environment (at no stage is Cheiron brought down onto the plains, away from the wild zone). It is important that both parties should partake of the wildness of the mountain, though in different ways, and their juxtaposition is crucial. At the same time, Cheiron's cave marks him out. His location is highly focused on that one topographical feature. By contrast, the group-centaurs roam generally, and, as in the case of Peleus' adventures, have a tendency to turn up unexpectedly, bringing with them violence and confusion.

It is clear that Cheiron and the group-centaurs were recognised by the Thessalians themselves, as well as by other Greek communities, as being peculiarly Thessalian figures, for both are used on coins at certain points in the history of the land. Cheiron is depicted on the coins of Magnesia in the Hellenistic period,[103] which again reveals his particular connection with that part of Thessaly.[104] The group-centaurs (that is to say, unnamed centaurs presumed, because of context, not to be Cheiron) are also quite popular, sometimes in contexts which reflect something of their rôle as opponents to human beings.[105] To a lesser extent, centaurs appear also on Macedonian and Thracian coinage,[106] and they seem to be a feature of the northern Greek massif; but Thessaly has the greatest concentration, and Cheiron on coins is a firmly Thessalian phenomenon. Cheiron was a figure who could be used as an emblem for the region, as well as for his narrower homeland of Magnesia.

---

[102] This point is made by Padgett (2003), 4-5

[103] Moustaka (1983), Taf. 6, no. 20: this is a second-century BC example. Cheiron holding a branch decorates the reverse; on the obverse is Zeus, surely a reference to their cult association on Pelion. The inscription is ΜΑΓΝΗΤΩΝ.

[104] It is probable that an example from the first century BC also depicts Cheiron: in this case the centaur is unnamed, but is carrying a kithara, which suggests Cheiron (who taught music to his young charges) rather than one of his wild fellows. Moustaka (1983), Taf. 6, no. 188. On the reverse is a ship – the Argo: a reference to another prominent Thessalian/Magnesian myth. The inscription is again ΜΑΓΝΗΤΩΝ. To the third century AD belongs a very interesting variation: a coin of the Thessalian *koinon* seems to have appropriated Cheiron (again, the identification is suggested by a lyre), while at the same time acknowledging his more local affiliations: the inscription reads ΧΕΙΡΩΝ ΜΑΓΝΗΤΩΝ – Cheiron of the Magnesians. (Moustaka [1983], Taf. 13, no. 189.)

[105] For example, a coin from Mopsion shows a human (probably the Lapith Mopsos, revealing a specific mythical reference) fighting with a centaur. (See Moustaka [1983], 73.)

[106] In the area of Mount Pangaion, coins frequently depicted nymphs and centaurs together. See Head (1911), 194-7; Hammond and Griffith (1979), 77-91; Larson (2001), 171-2.

The relationship between Arkadia and its most famous mixanthrope, Pan, is even more complex. This complexity reflects the fact that, as Borgeaud has shown, the idea of that relationship was developed extensively both from outside Arkadia and from within the region itself. It is this level of self-presentation, combined and in dialogue with non-Arkadian thought,[107] which sets Arkadia apart from Thessaly, the land which in so many ways it resembles. There is an unmistakeable link between the drive to create a pan-Arkadian cultural identity and the various political developments of the fourth century which saw federal structures emerge in Arkadia, connecting communities where previously connections had been particularly slight. (It is interesting that, even when parallel structures were forged in Thessaly and emblematic Thessalian figures such as Cheiron were brought to the fore on coins and the like, we nevertheless do not find nearly such a coherent striving for shared identity as we do in Arkadia;[108] it seems highly likely that this had to do with a relative lack of external aggression, for whereas Arkadia was subject to almost continuous pressure and interference from Sparta, Thessaly suffered little of the kind until the Macedonian dominion in the fourth century. A clear connection can be seen between the drive for self-definition and the presence of a threat from outside.) Studies have been conducted into the ways in which Arkadian cult was used to express new-found ideas of unity following the synoecism of Mega-lopolis, with versions of various local cults being established in the new centre and rituals – such as processions – being employed to stress the religious ties between centre and margins. The cult site on Mount Lykaion was prominent in this changed religious landscape, and on Lykaion, as we have seen, Pan played a particularly important rôle. This importance was without doubt fuelled by (and at the same time contributed to) the perception that Pan was uniquely Arkadian, and expressed some significant component of the Arkadian character that was striving for expression.

What that component was has been explored at length by Borgeaud and others, but aspects which were once thought to be fundamental to it have been called into question. For example, it was in the past believed that Pan was a direct reflection – a representation, almost – of his Arkadian worshippers; that the cult of the god of flocks was tended almost solely by human shepherds whose worship was founded on the intimate affinity between themselves and

---

[107] See Borgeaud (1988), 5: 'Arcadia is the result of a dialectic where the rôle of one party is incomprehensible without that of the others. Consequently, even though Pan actually originates in Arcadia, this origin has from the outset the standing of a representation accompanied by a point of view always exterior to it.' In other words, presentation and self-presentation are impossible to separate.

[108] An interesting exception may well be found in the cult of the quintessentially Thessalian goddess Ennodia, whose worship – previously highly localised around Pherai – came to have a pan-Thessalian, if not a pan-Hellenic, basis, at least from the fourth century. See Morgan (1997), 170-75; the main work on this goddess and her cult is that of Chrysostomou (1998).

the divine recipient. The reality of the situation has been shown, inevitably, to be more complex. Pan may still be seen as the embodiment of a certain way of life, characterised by herding and hunting; that is clear. It is the nature of his worshippers, and their requirements of him, that have had to be reappraised.[109] As Borgeaud has made clear, Pan's nature was part of the *idea* of Arkadia and the Arkadian life, forged from within and from without, and it was this *idea,* rather than a straightforward affinity, which came into play when worshipper and god related. None the less, the pursuits which characterise him, herding and hunting, were important in the actuality of Arkadian society. Even by Greek standards Arkadia is mountainous, with nothing like the broad plains of its western neighbour Achaia, let alone Thessaly. Hunting and mountains went together in the reality as well as in the thought of ancient Greece. In the parts of Arkadia which were suitable for the cultivation of crops, conditions were temperamental, with a tendency to both flooding and drought. With agriculture rendered thus difficult and uncertain, hunting and herding were both required as supplementary food-providers of some importance. So in this respect, the characterisation of Pan as both hunter and herdsman fitted in with the reality of an Arkadian existence, as well as with the myth of one.

The concept of Pan as a divine expression of the idea of Arkadia is founded on the vital principle of his autochthony, an autochthony which went unchallenged: however enthusiastically other parts of Greece adopted the god into their own religious structures and landscapes, this adoption never involved claiming him as a product; his Arkadian origin was, if anything, stressed, not denied. The autochthony of Pan[110] went hand in hand with the autochthony of the Arkadians. As we have seen, he appears to parallel, rather than pre-date, human origins in the land, functioning alongside primary human founder-figures.

It has been described how Cheiron's connections with his Thessalian homeland are very largely founded upon his participation in a number of interlocking myths describing the Thessalian past. Like him, Pan crops us repeatedly in the myths of Arkadia's past, though the way in which he does so, and the nature of his contribution, reveal interesting divergences from the patterns in Cheiron's case. Cheiron's functions can be seen as being twofold: first, as a helper to humans, especially against the antithetical forces of the group-centaurs; secondly, for infant heroes, as a source of passage into the adult world and of *paideia* in a number of largely aristocratic virtues. In other words, Cheiron in the Thessaly of the remote, heroic age is a powerful agent of civilisation, of maturation, often ranged in opposition to representatives of the primitive and the destructive. Though half-animal himself, he counteracts what can for the most part be seen as animal qualities. How does Pan's rôle in the myths of Arkadia compare with this?

---

[109] See e.g. Hübinger (1990), 203-4.

[110] *Autochthôn/gêgenês*: schol. Theok. *Id.* 1.3-4; Apollodoros *FGrHist* 244 F 134a; Ant. Lib. *Met.* 23.

In fact, the situation with Pan is more complex and ambiguous. A wealth of myths describe his birth and career, of which two are especially revealing in this matter. The first is the story that when Demeter Melaina, in her anger, hid herself in the cave at Phigalia, causing famine and death, she was finally found there by Pan. This discovery by Pan led to her being brought back into the agricultural domain and induced to exercise her beneficent powers once more. As has been described, the famine carried with it the threat not just of human suffering but also of an accompanying slide back into a barbarous past state characterised by cannibalism. Therefore, in this story, Pan is responsible for preventing a fundamental regression away from civilisation and towards the primitive. He is not the agent of civilisation, but he does something to secure it. To move away from a purely Arkadian view, this myth is highly reminiscent of the function of Panes (usually in flanking pairs) painted on some Attic vases: with dancing and, to judge from their open mouths, cries, they attend the return of Persephone from the underworld. The difference between such scenes and the Phigalian story is that whereas the vase Panes assist, or perhaps merely spectate, at the prevention of famine, Arkadian Pan also staves off a far worse human crisis than not eating at all: that is, eating wrongly, eating transgressively, eating savagely. Again, though half-animal, he works to ward off the worst excesses of the animal nature.

As *didymos* of Arkas, however, Pan appears rather differently. He is the product of the animal-form union of Kallisto and Zeus, a union which is one of the founding moments of the mythical Arkadia. Metamorphoses of humans (and gods) into animals abound in Arkadia, and it is significant that one lies at the very basis of the land's imagined history. As does Pan. A metamorphosis and a mixanthrope: both underpin Arkadia's character. And whereas in the Phigalian episode Pan assists in preventing a dangerous loss of the distance between human beings and animal savagery, his genesis is testament to the possibility of the two states becoming very close indeed, a closeness which is more prevalent in the myths of Arkadia than in any other part of Greece. A mixanthropic being, besides, always represents the juxtaposition of the two states in graphic form. But whereas with Cheiron the animal seems to be much in abeyance to the human and the humanizing, Pan continues to reflect both possibilities: the animal as past, distant, progressed beyond; and the animal as ever-present, either as actuality or as threat. Of course, Cheiron character seems designed always to be viewed in the light of the other centaurs, his personality shaped by contrast with theirs. They are the vehicles for so much that is negative in the characterisation of the mixanthrope and of the animal. Pan, on the other hand must alone contain both positive and negative aspects, the benign and the destructive.

Indeed, in many ways the relationship between Pan and Arkadia seems to resemble the relationship between the group-centaurs (not Cheiron) and Thessaly. Like the centaurs on Pelion, for example, Pan can sometimes be a dangerous and threatening presence in the countryside, and this quality is an extension of some quality of the rural landscape itself. To Pan are attributed many of the landscape's baffling, unexplained, supernatural qualities: its unexplained sounds,[111] its confusing effect on the human mind, especially at noon.[112] Interestingly, whereas the centaurs wreak their destruction in person, appearing suddenly, Pan's presence is sometimes felt without the god being seen or directly encountered: it is a matter not just of violence but of mystery, uncertainty and ambiguity. One feature remains in common between the centaurs and Pan: that in their respective landscapes they had the potential suddenly to become present in some form. In the case of the centaurs, this is expressed in mythological terms, relating to the distant past, in stories of Peleus and the Lapiths; with Pan, on the other hand, it is made very clear that he *continues* to inhabit the Arkadian landscape, and that any traveller or shepherd (not just a famous hero) might possibly encounter him. In both cases, however, the region is imagined as one haunted by half-human figures, not necessarily benign.

A word must be said to qualify the observations already made about the place-specificity of Pan and the huge mutual importance between him and the imagined Arkadia. Unlike the centaurs, Pan is not always described as being in Arkadia. In fact, the *Homeric Hymn* to the god, for example, gives him a strikingly universal quality:

> He had as his portion every snowy summit,
> The ridges of mountains and their rocky peaks.[113]

The word *lelonche* is striking. Pan has attained as his portion (his natural preserve, one might say) every mountain peak. This might be argued to dissolve entirely the idea of an intimate and lasting association in Greek thought between Pan and his homeland. But in fact something rather different is at work. Arkadia itself is exportable. Reflections of it may be found wherever there is a certain kind of terrain, an 'Arkadian-style' terrain of mountain peaks and grottoes. Borgeaud has shown that when the Athenians, for example, installed the cult of Pan in a cave, they were surrounding the god with a little patch of his perceived natural environment, so that even when far from Arkadia, Pan carried a portion of that region with him always. This observation holds true on a wider basis. Wherever Pan roams, the land is in a way an Arkadian one. We may see this as part of the process of 'Arkadian' taking on something of an adjectival force, conveying not

---

[111] Most frequently referred to is the music of Pan's pipes being heard unexpectedly in the countryside and causing alarm; see e.g. Lucr. *de Rer. Nat.* 4.580-94. The piping is not always presented as purely fear-inspiring; sometimes it is lauded as sweet, as in *Hom. Hym.* 19.14-18.

[112] For Pan-induced delirium and for noon as the time when the god's power is especially strong, see e.g. Plato *Phaidr.* 230b-c, 241e-242a, 279b. For fear of the god at noon, Theok. *Id.* 1.15-20. Borgeaud (1988), esp. 88-116 on Pan-inspired fear and possession.

[113] *Hom. Hym.* 19.6-7: ... πάντα λόφον νιφόεντα λέλογχε | καὶ κορυφὰς ὀρέων καὶ πετρήεντα κάρηνα.

merely ethnicity but also a quality, which can be found and created anywhere. Thessaly is not exportable. It is always the land in the north, reachable but distant, often more or less explicitly contrasted by Athenians with their own culture. Thessaly is allowed to stay put, and her mixanthropic inhabitants with her.

To sum up: mixanthropic deities have a strong tendency to have and maintain a particularly significant connection with certain regions of Greece, both practically, in the form of cult, and on the level of thought and imagination. The place-god relationship is always mutually effective in terms of identity, deities being regarded as products of a particular place and sharing in that place's character, actual and perceived, while at the same time places exploited the potential of their local mixanthropes to reinforce their own local identity. While examples of this relationship are to be found all over the Greek world, in Thessaly and Arkadia it found especially strong expression. Arkadia was the land of Pan; Thessaly, while the connection was not made so explicitly, was the land of Cheiron and the centaurs. They were places thought to be inhabited not just by the cults of these beings but also by their presence, mythical, potential, sometimes actual. Mixanthropes were among their most famous products and defined the attitudes of other Greeks towards them.

3.2. Outside the Greek world

In general terms, mixanthropes have their place among the marvels thought by the Greeks to inhabit distant lands. Phlegon's centaurs were Arabian. A more intricate example is the community of the Kunokephaloi, dog-headed beings described by (among others) the late-fifth-century BC author Ktesias of Knidos in his *Indika* (chs. 20-23). Romm demonstrates that these people are treated with the same ambivalence regarding the primitive which has been discussed above in connection with Cheiron, Kronos and Pan – an example of the persistent equation of distant place with distant time in Greek thought.[114] Their primordial way of life (as well as their mixanthropy) makes them like animals: they mate *a tergo* and publicly; they do not cook their food except by letting it broil in the sun; they are without human speech. All this sets them at variance from human identity. At the same time, they are described as 'just' (reminiscent of the Arkadians' legendary piety), and their *modus vivendi* has a certain savage nobility. They are mixed both in anatomy and in nature. They reflect the mixanthrope's inclusion in the 'canon of the strange', a class of beings often placed in exotic regions of the imagined world. But what of mixanthropic gods? Do they share in this geographical identification?

The answer is, not consistently. As was shown in the Introduction, the Greeks were not keen to exploit Egypt as a way of explaining the origins of their mixanthropic deities. The post-Classical age saw a growing interest in, and

---

[114] Romm (1992), 77-81.

hostility towards, Egyptian animal-worship and – occasionally – mixanthrope-worship, but this did not affect the fact that Greece's mixanthropic gods were regarded as Greek, with no systematic attempt at 'disowning' them into another culture.

There are some elements of self-reflection in narratives concerning Egyptian theriomorphic/mixanthropic gods, one of the most intriguing being the myth, recorded by several authors, of the gods' flight from Typhon (or, in Lucian's version, the Giants). In this story, the Olympian deities, fleeing the attack, escape into Egypt and there disguise themselves by taking on animal forms.[115] Deities which are assumed in the myth to be wholly anthropomorphic in Greece adopt theriomorphic qualities when they enter Egypt, the natural home of the animal-form god. Egypt is for the first time a *contributor* of theriomorphism rather than simply reflecting back existing Greek phenomena. It is a place where such a metamorphosis is possible. Changing into animal (or indeed plant) form is in Greek myth a common way of eluding an attacker (one has only to think of Demeter becoming a mare in an attempt to shake off the amorous Poseidon). However, the Egyptian location is highly significant in this case. This is reflected in the animals whose forms are used. Though the several accounts differ on the details, the ibis and the hawk are repeated motifs, birds surely charged with Egyptian cult associations (mainly with Thoth and Horus respectively).

Of course, the myth has an allegorical function, though not all the sources make this explicit. Indeed, only Lucian, Diodoros and Ovid enter into any discussion of the symbolism. Lucian tells the reader, in tones of contempt, that in Egypt he may see various gods – given their Greek names – in animal/animal-headed form. If the reader wants to know why, learned persons will tell him (and here it seems likely that he means learned Greek persons) the story that after the war against the Giants (Typhon is not here mentioned) the gods fled to Egypt and took on animal disguises. He then says, 'And so the shapes adopted by the gods then are preserved even now.'[116] In other words, the mixanthropic/theriomorphic deities visible in Egyptian iconography at the time of composition are left over from the mythical event. The story, then is an *aition* which explains how the Egyptian gods first obtained their special characteristics. This use of the myth is found also in Ovid. It is an interesting motif, for it makes Greece, in a way, the source of Egypt's deities – Greece provides the gods, so to speak.[117] But

---

[115] The frequency and consistency of the story's appearance are striking: see Lucian, *de Sacr.* 14; Apollod. *Bibl.* 1.6.3; Ant. Lib. *Met.* 28; Plut. *de Isid. et Osir.* 72; Ovid, *Met.* 5.319-331.

[116] Lucian, *de Sacr.* 14: διὸ δὴ εἰσέτι καὶ νῦν φυλάττεσθαι τὰς τότε μορφὰς τοῖς θεοῖς.

[117] Diodoros (1.86.3) gives a clearly related but different version in which the identity of the gods is left unspecified (from the context we are to assume that they are not Greek but Egyptian). Typhon is not mentioned; the gods' adversaries are 'earth-born men', that is, the Giants. The myth is presented as an Egyptian one, though as has been said this is highly unlikely. The author gives it as one of the reasons (the least plausible, in his opinion) for the Egyptians'

their animal forms are not Greek. They are a product of the situation, being assumed either on the run or once the gods have arrived at their destination.[118] In any case, however, it is interesting that the story is *not* used to explain away any mixanthropic features of *Greek* deities, though that might seem a very likely impulse. The animals into which the gods change reflect Egyptian rather than Hellenic cult associations.

A rather different way of associating mixanthropic god with Egypt is found in the motif of the mixanthrope as foreign ruler, the clearest examples of which are Proteus and Midas. Midas takes us from Egypt to Phrygia; he is also not a cult-receiving deity in his own right, though with significant cultic status. However, he is worth mentioning for the further insight he provides into this *topos*, which in any case represents a deliberate straddling of the god/mortal divide.

Proteus had, as we have seen, links to various places, chiefly Pharos, Karpathos, Chalkidike and Thrace. In addition, however, there emerges a rather different connection with Egypt. This is fully articulated first by Herodotos:

> They said that a man of Memphis succeeded him to the throne, whose name in the Greek tongue was Proteus. There is even now a *temenos* of him in Memphis, very beautiful and well-appointed, which lies to the south of the Hephaisteion.[119]

Here we find someone called Proteus ruling as a mortal king at Memphis and integrated into the succession there. What follows is a version of the story that Helen never went to Troy but stayed for the duration of the war in Egypt – in, we are told, the court of this Proteus. This detail appears not to have been an invention of Herodotos. There is an apparent mention in a fragment of Hesiod's *Catalogue of Women*.[120] Stesichoros in his Palinode may also have made the real (non-*eidôlon*) Helen stay with Proteus, though the contents of this lost work have been called into question, cogently, by Wright. The antecedents to the story are shady.[121]

The mention of a 'sacred precinct' could be thought to give a slight suggestion that this Proteus is more than a mortal ruler, though given the divinity of Pharaohs this detail is perhaps less meaningful than that. Overall, Herodotos' Proteus seems to have no overt connection with the shape-changing sea god familiar from other sources. It has been suggested that the name Proteus may

---

religious reverence of animals: the gods are so grateful to the animals whose forms they borrowed that they confer on them special sanctity.

[118] The former: Apollodoros, Antoninus Liberalis; the latter: Lucian, Ovid. Some authors leave it vague.

[119] Hdt. 2.112.1: τούτου δὲ ἐκδέξασθαι τὴν βασιληίην ἔλεγον ἄνδρα Μεμφίτην, τῷ κατὰ τὴν Ἑλλήνων γλῶσσαν οὔνομα Πρωτέα εἶναι· τοῦ νῦν τέμενός ἐστι ἐν Μέμφι κάρτα καλόν τε καὶ εὖ ἐσκευασμένον, τοῦ Ἡφαιστείου πρὸς νότον ἄνεμον κείμενον.

[120] Hes. fr. 23a.17-24 MW.

[121] For all the certain and possible versions, and for the Stesichoros-controversy, see Wright (2005), 83-113.

have been brought in by the author because he confused it with Prouti, an Egyptian title.[122] In any case, the appearance of the name seems fairly arbitrary in this text.

Other authors take up the idea of Proteus as Egyptian king, the first being Euripides in his *Helen*; and once more the context is the stay in that land of the real Helen during the Trojan War. Though Proteus is still a mortal ruler, the strong air of historicism pervading Herodotos' account has vanished, to be replaced by a far more mythical, even magical atmosphere.[123] Proteus is the son of Nereus (thus he is equipped with some of his Greek mythological context); his wife is Psamathe, a sea-nymph.[124] He rules not in Memphis but in Pharos, though his dominion extends over the whole of Egypt. He is not a god in the Olympian sense; indeed, he is dead, and his tomb, functioning perhaps like that of a cult-receiving hero, is an important piece of scenery in the play.

The third author to take up the theme is Diodoros.[125] He is not concerned to mention the story of Helen. His account is framed, like that of Herodotos, in terms of monarchic succession, but within these parameters we find some material unlike anything in the first two versions. He tells how an Egyptian king called Mendes is succeeded by one Ketes, thought of as Proteus by the Greeks. Ketes/Proteus knows the secrets of the winds, and of shape-changing; this, says Diodoros, is corroborated by 'the priests', who say that Ketes/Proteus learned his special knowledge from astrologers with whom he constantly consorted. But, says Diodoros, the Greeks believe that the shape-changing story derived from the Egyptian rulers' practice of wearing animal (or sometimes plant) head-dresses.

Now in the latter half of this passage, Diodoros is clearly indulging in a bout of the clumsy pseudo-historicist interpretation for which he had a distinct taste. Before that, however, we find a crucial element: the introduction of Proteus' familiar mythical persona as a shape-changing being, peculiarly fused with the rôle as a mortal king. The uneasy join is smoothed over by the remark about the king learning his magic abilities from astrologers. The contrived welding is

---

[122] See How and Wells (1912), 223.

[123] On the relationship between this atmosphere and the Egyptian setting, see Segal (1971). Wright, however, (2005, 165-6) makes two important modifying observations: first, that in Euripides' day many Greeks would have detailed knowledge of Egypt either from report or from their own travels; and second, that, given this fact, it is striking how *few* Egyptian paraphernalia of setting Euripides inserts into the *Helen*. There are no animal-headed gods or exotic monuments. Rather, the setting is one of *generic otherworldliness*. On Egypt as standing for 'beyond', 'other' and the merging of reality and unreality, see also Dowden (1992), 129-33.

[124] Undoubtedly a *nom parlant*. It has both general and specific marine associations, since *psamathos* is 'sand', and Psamathe is also the name of a Nereid raped by Aiakos, the father of Peleus, and by him the mother of Phokos ('Seal'). See Apollod. *Bibl.* 3.12.6; Larson (2001), 71-2. Wright (2005, 203-12) has argued convincingly that Proteus' nature (in Greek thought, that is) contributes to an important rôle played by the sea in the *Helen*: his shape-changing accords with its fluid, unstable quality and is thus a component of the play's *mise en scène*.

[125] Diod. 1.62.

necessary, for Diodoros has brought together what appear to be two completely separate Proteuses. Surely, one might think, this is simply a mistaken conflation. The Proteus ruling in Egypt – the corruption, perhaps, of *Prouti* – is a Greek invention quite removed from the shape-changing god of the sea. And yet, the distinction is perhaps not as complete as it might seem.

For a start, as has been suggested, the version of Euripides itself edged towards Proteus the god in acknowledging the divinity of his father and wife, and perhaps in giving his tomb the quality of a religious monument. More significantly, the divine Proteus does seem to have had a strong and important cultic presence in Egypt (more precisely on Pharos), both in the Greek imagination and in reality. Herodotos took his Proteus away from this when he placed him in Memphis; Euripides allows him to slide back towards his cult site, while retaining his rôle as king of Egypt. Diodoros goes furthest, for while he does not mention Pharos, and while he couches things in realistic terms, he accords to Proteus the king the powers of Proteus the god. Moreover, the alternative name accorded him, Ketes, certainly contains an echo of κῆτος, 'sea-monster', the clearest possible indication that Proteus' sea god identity has slipped in through the net of historicity.

To sum up, even if Herodotos was merely using the name mistakenly to denote an Egyptian ruler, he chose a name laden with mythical and cult significance in the area. Subsequent treatments, while keeping assiduously to the idea of the mortal king, elide king and god more and more, slipping into a divine persona already strongly associated with the region. We cannot of course disentangle 'real' and 'imagined' figures here. What is interesting is that, against the odds, the divine nature of Proteus does crop up in the persona of the Egyptian monarch. At the same time, the persona of the monarch, established by Herodotos, is not abandoned. It seems to have become an important way of expressing the rôle and the power of Proteus in the region. Proteus' godhead is uncertain and hard to maintain, and thus is transformed into mortal royalty; but at the same time, key aspects of his divinity continue to appear in some sources. He is a king, but a distinctly magical one.

In this character, the idea of Egypt is influential. It is particularly interesting to examine the rôle of that land within Diodoros' rationalising account (quoted above). The author gives two separate explanations of king Proteus' supernatural powers. The first is attributed to Egyptian priests, and tells that Proteus learned his abilities from astrologers with whom he consorted. The second explanation is designated the Greek one, and explains the king's shape-changing by reference to the old custom of Egyptian rulers of wearing emblems of animal, tree or fire on their heads. Now these two explanations work in different ways, and from different points of reference. The second, the Greek, is rationalising. It points to old Egyptian customs in the manner of the anthropologist with his all-seeing eye, cutting through superstition. The first appears to have, by contrast, a wholly Egyptian perspective. The Egyptian priests credit Proteus with real powers, learned from contact with astrologers. But in a way, the apparently purely Egyptian viewpoint of this latter is an illusion. We are still viewing the whole situation through Greek eyes. The Egyptian priests believe in the magical powers – well, they would! How very Egyptian. They put it down to the influence of astrologers – again, how typical of that culture! The Egyptian explanation is, I suggest, another Greek interpretation, packaged and dressed by its use of a foreign focaliser. Diodoros has effectively *created* two opposing standpoints, labelling one Egyptian and the other Greek.

Egyptians as believing in magic, Greeks as rationalising and explaining away: the two different reactions to the figure of Proteus point up the character of Egypt in the matter. It is worth pointing out that Diodoros could so easily have avoided the whole question by choosing to adhere to Herodotos' view, in which Proteus is purely human. This he does not do. Instead, he raises the question of what Proteus really is: and the answer to that questions depends on whether his audience sides with the Egyptians or with the Greeks. The character of Egypt is thus the key to the character of Proteus.

Proteus is not the only mixanthrope to be presented as a mortal ruler in an exotic land. Closely parallel is the case of Midas, the mythical Phrygian ruler whose scandalous ears and the circumstances of their acquisition are the subject of a long treatment by Ovid.[126] Midas is not himself a divinity,[127] and thus cannot be accorded detailed discussion in this book. But it is interesting to note that in his case also the identity of a foreign ruler and the identity of a mixanthrope are brought together. In Ovid's account, Midas hides his monstrous ears with a purple turban, the ultimate accessory of the Eastern king.[128] As with Proteus, Midas' mixanthropy is exceptional, extraordinary, shocking, and yet not out of

---

[126] Ovid, *Met.* 11.174-93. Ovid did not invent the story of Midas' ears entirely, though we cannot say precisely which details he contributed as reteller; for an earlier mention, see Aristoph. *Plout.* 286-7.

[127] He is, however, a close associate of Kybele. According to Hyginus (*Fab.* 191.1) he is her son; and in Diodoros' narrative (3.59.8) he is the chief promoter of her cult. This latter rôle appears to relate, intriguingly, to the *historical* figure of Midas, a Phrygian dynast mentioned in eighth-century Assyrian records. The name Midas also appears on the so-called Midas Monument, the inscribed cult monument dedicated to Kybele (Brixhe and Lejeune [1984], M – 01a; Roller [1999], 69-70). The precise relationship between reality and myth is of course lost to us: for further discussion, see Roller (1983) and Bömer (1980), 259-63. On the Greek cult of Kybele down to the time of her introduction into Rome, see the very detailed iconographic treatment by Naumann (1983). At 17-36 he discusses the relationship between the Greek-conceived goddess and her genuinely Phrygian counterparts.

[128] 11.180-1: '… *turpique pudore | tempora purpureis temptat velare tiaris.*'

keeping, on one level, with the exotic Phrygian setting and with the figure of the foreign ruler.[129]

The conferral of monarchic status on a mixanthrope obviates a persistent issue dogging many mixanthropic figures in Greek culture. They are divine, but not Olympian; their worship is highly limited, often slight; their godhead is of an uncertain kind, liminal, confused by their contact with the canon of monsters, by their frequent rôle as adversaries of heroes. Making them foreign kings clarifies their position, establishes them in a power which is mortal but at the same time allows for expression of their superhuman traits and abilities. The entity which in Greece must be a god or *daimôn*, may, in a remote eastern land, be a mortal. Mythical eastern kings have something of the status, in Greek thought, of a *daimôn*; they are long dead, belonging to a remote past, and are quite able to possess inhuman and magical qualities without contradiction, because they belong to a fantastical place. In the case of Proteus, this identity sat alongside that of cult-recipient; Midas, on the other hand, was the satellite of a deity rather than receiving worship in his own right. In both cases, monarchic identity gave the Greek a way of defining the mixanthropes' nature, their power, and their relation to his own culture and his own land.

An interesting case to add to this discussion is that of Kekrops. As was said in Chapter 2, Kekrops is almost always designated a native of Attica in the most extreme sense, as a being who emerged from its very soil, thus spearheading in myth the Athenians' own historical claims to autochthony. However, one cannot simply ignore the existence of an alternative tradition, whereby Kekrops settled and ruled Attica only after having arrived there from his native *Egypt*.[130] Here the foreign ruler motif familiar from Proteus seems to be being incorporated within the discourse of Kekrops' autochthony: exotic mixanthrope and home-grown mixanthrope collide. Why? One reason is suggested by Fourgous: that Kekrops is used as a means of testing and debating the idea of Greek identity and in what it truly consists. She identifies different groups in different contexts who were interested in developing particular aspects of this debate with Kekrops as its symbolic core and whose preoccupations lie behind the major narratives.[131] This is a cogent interpretation, since mythological constructs in antiquity are seldom allowed to remain unilateral, but rather take on new facets with every fresh exploitation as they are incorporated within key ideological testing-grounds. Kekrops as *autochthôn* is swiftly presented with his opposite, the in-coming Egyptian. The autochthonous Kekrops appears in our sources earlier, but the

---

[129] For an interesting treatment of the Midas story with reference to comparative folklore motifs, see Crooke (1911).

[130] See Philochoros, *FGrHist* 328 F 93; Diod. 1.28; schol. Ar. *Plout.* 773; *Suda s.v.* 'Kekrops'; Fourgous (1993), 233-46.

[131] Fourgous (1993), esp. 239-42.

debate in which he plays his part is no late development: the idea of tracing Greek communities back to barbarian origins is found for example in Herodotos.

Although Fourgous is right to identify the specific themes manipulating Kekrops' presentation, at the same time the co-existence of the two traditions (autochthony and ingress) does reflect the significant and more widespread concurrence of the two themes with regard to mixanthropic deities. Do their animal parts tie them to the heart of Greece or render them strange and foreign? As has been shown, individual mixanthropes incline to one side or the other of this dichotomy; Kekrops is striking in that he combines the two within the range of his mythology.

Time and place: conclusion

It is not surprising to find that mixanthropic gods are strongly associated with both temporal and spatial distance, with ages and places remote from everyday experience. After all, there is an abiding connection between far-flung locations and the primitive, the primordial, the original. This is made clear by Romm in his analysis of Greek attitudes towards exotic peoples such as the Hyperboreans and the Ethiopians.[132] His work shows that such remote communities were consistently thought of as occupying a remotely early phase of human social development. As such they tended to be characterised as both savage and utopic, preserving the worst and the best aspects of man's primordial nature. This is strikingly reminiscent of the observations made in this chapter about the Greek ambivalence to the past and to the mixanthropes which inhabited it: were they products of a Golden Age or of a time of lawlessness and chaotic violence?

But exotic mixanthropes such as Proteus and Midas are only half the story. Figures like Cheiron and Pan are not only Greek but *über*-Greek, rooted as they are in the two areas – Thessaly and Arkadia respectively – most strongly characterised as primitive and untouched and representative of the Greek past. We have here an apparent schism between the urge to place mixanthropes at the end of the world, and the urge to tie them to the very heart of Greece and its history. The choice seems to be one, partly, of owning or disowning, and must surely reflect the uncertainty with which mixanthropic deities were regarded, the question-marks appended to their benignity and desirability explored in Chapter 4. Keeping them tethered to the remote past, however, could be thought to ensure that, even when they are there in the Greek heartland, the presence is tempered by constant references to their obsolescence.

It is interesting to compare the ways in which modern scholars have used the idea of a mixanthrope's spatial and temporal associations. Occasionally, it has been claimed that a mixanthropic god was imported into Greece from

---

[132] Romm (1992), 45-81.

another, usually Eastern, culture. The motivation for taking this line is sometimes striking, as is illustrated by the words of Farnell concerning the depiction of Zeus Ammon with the horns of a ram: 'The type of the god with ram's horns would never have appeared in Greek art of the fifth century, as it did, except through the influence of Egypt; *the Hellenic sculptors of this age could never have represented their own native supreme god with any touch of theriomorphic character* [my italics].'[133] In other words, a foreign origin is drafted in when Hellenic identity seems inappropriate.[134] Farnell's reaction to the mixanthropic Zeus may be contrasted with that of Cook, who is eager to discover the animal-form Zeus wherever possible, whatever contortions of the evidence may be required. Cook regards the animal-form Zeus as an essential and primal component of the god's development, Farnell as a mere import, a superficial add-on from another very different culture. Claiming or disowning the mixanthropic/theriomorphic god on behalf of the Greeks: this choice is not dissimilar from that apparent in ancient attitudes. In modern scholarship, however, claims of non-Greek identity are comparatively rare, compared with the far stronger desire to place mixanthropic gods at the heart and the source of Greek religion, to make them both proto-Greek and *über*-Greek.[135]

The most consistent and crucial single instance of this duality in modern thought has always been – and continues to be – Arkadia, whose importance to the scholarly picture of divine mixanthropy is so great as to merit a separate chapter to itself.

---

[133] Farnell, vol. 1 (1896), 95. Farnell here has both fact and fiction. Zeus Ammon is a clear case of non-Greek borrowing; and yet the statement that follows, to the effect that theriomorphic traits were quite incompatible with the Greeks' treatment of, and attitude towards, their chief deity, takes us into much more dubious territory, making no allowance, for example, for the numerous depictions of Zeus in snake-form.

[134] An especially interesting example of this for the current study is Bérard's contention (1894) that substantial elements of Arkadian cult originated in Phoenicia, a claim which now has no adherents. It is very interesting, however, to note the terms in which it is made. A lengthy discussion is given (104-8) of the problematic form of Demeter Melaina's *xoanon*, its mare-head which sits so ill with the tenets of Greek religious iconography and which Bérard calls an embarrassment to certain scholars (106). This embarrassment is done away with, however, by the claim of non-Greek origins, in a manoeuvre strikingly reminiscent of Farnell's denial of the Greek mixanthropic Zeus.

[135] An example is Herbig's strenuous argument that Pan was a completely indigenous Greek god, and his determination to deny any Eastern influence (correct, surely, but significant) – see Herbig (1949), 15-18.

Chapter VI

The fallacy of Arcadia

Introduction

The general premise which this chapter examines has already been described from various angles. With regard to the ancient material, it consists of an important general association between mixanthropic deities and Arkadia, expressed most of all through the figure of Pan; at the same time, both Arkadia and its mixanthropic denizens were perceived generally as belonging to the remote past. The modern counterpart to these ideas is the theory, discussed in the previous chapter, that mixanthropic gods are the victims of a growing scarcity. Arkadia's allure to the exponents of such a theory lies in the fact that it appears to be the exception to this rule. Arkadia has acquired a reputation for having had more than the usual concentration of theriomorphic gods in general, and mixanthropic representations of gods specifically. This perception runs, for example, through Madeleine Jost's monumental work on Arkadian cults,[1] and is to be found in several less extensive discussions of the matter, such as that of Nilsson,[2] Adshead[3] and Nielsen.[4] This relative abundance is interpreted as a case of *survival* and *preservation*; Arkadia is remote and conservative, and is therefore less prone to the kinds of religious changes which caused mixanthropic gods to become less widespread.[5] This is the argument, summed up by Nilsson's statement that such figures as Demeter Melaina preserve a 'primitiven Wildheit'.[6] Arkadia would therefore appear to offer instant corroboration for the notion that mixanthropic gods were once more common, because it acts as a kind of

---

[1] Jost (1985). See also her most recent treatment of Arkadian religion (Jost, 2007), in which she says of Pan that he 'presented the hybrid form *typical of Arcadia* [my italics].'

[2] Nilsson, vol. 1 (1941), 214.

[3] Adshead (1986), 21-2.

[4] Nielsen (1999), 40.

[5] For example, Jost (1985), 558, says that the prevalence of various forms of religious theriomorphism in Arkadia reveals 'une mentalité religieuse étonnament conservatrice.' Similar is the claim by Loukas and Loukas (1988, 31), with regard to Lykosoura, its rites and iconography, that divine theriomorphism is 'the most primitive substratum of Greek religious ideas and beliefs.'

[6] Nilsson, vol. 1 (1941), 214.

reservation or museum from which we may have a glimpse of what the rest of Greece, too, was once like. If this were so, we would expect to find an abundance of mixanthropic depictions of gods in Arkadian religious sites; and one would expect to find them occupying positions of importance. Is this the case? Does Arkadia live up to our expectations?

This chapter falls into two related parts. The first examines the evidence for mixanthropic imagery in Arkadian cult, starting with the eighth book of Pausanias's *Periegesis*,[7] and going on to the archaeological material. The second examines the more general question of Arkadia as isolated repository of strange religious survivals. Should it really be given that persona and rôle?[8]

1. Mixanthropic imagery in Arkadian cult

In Chapter 4 it was described how Demeter Melaina's mare-headed *xoanon* is at the centre of a mythical *topos* concerning the goddess's withdrawal and absence. It is clear that we cannot rely on this image, which appears a thing more of legend than of fact, in any search for mixanthropic representations of deities in Arkadia. Does Pausanias provide any more instances which might be more reliable?

There are indeed other mixanthropic images in Book Eight, and these tend to be less weighted with myth than the Phigalian example, and in this respect less suspect. For example, not far from the cave of Demeter Melaina, where the Lymax and Neda rivers meet, Pausanias visited, he tells us, a sanctuary of Eurynome, regarded by local people either as a form of Artemis or a daughter of Okeanos akin to Thetis. About the cult statue of this goddess the Phigalians tell Pausanias:

---

[7] Pausanias, his attitudes and his context have already been discussed in Chapter 4. The extensive use of his work in this chapter, however, necessitates further brief comment on its value and limitations. To simplify extremely, the Arkadian book undeniably conveys both Arkadian mythology and the details of material structures, such as temples and effigies, which existed there at the time of Pausanias' visit. This element of reportage is, however, combined with an equally undeniable tendency to order and employ material according to certain authorial aims. This latter characteristic is of course the subject of numerous scholarly discussions, particularly pronounced in Elsner (2001). Pritchett's (1999) work is distinguished by its full appraisal of religious issues; see also Ellinger (2005) for a recent treatment of certain complex themes in Pausanias' narrative which focus significantly on the Phigalian section of Book 8. For the purposes of the current discussion, reliance on Pausanias is a matter of necessity more than of choice, given the paucity of alternative evidence; but it is felt that such use is on the whole justifiable as well as unavoidable (this basic belief in the accuracy of Pausanias' narrative underpins the still-important work of Habicht [1985]). In any case, Pausanias is not simply functioning as a source of information but also as the possessor of a point of view, and as the vehicle of more widely held attitudes; and archaeological evidence will be brought in to highlight this rôle and restore the balance of our judgment.

[8] The ensuing discussion partly reproduces material included in Aston (2009).

Gold chains bind the *xoanon*, and it is in the likeness of a woman down to the buttocks, but below that is a fish.[9]

This time the mixanthropic cult statue is in mermaid form. Far from being flagged up in myth, this effigy is treated with a certain reticence by the Periegete, especially when it comes to ascribing such an outlandish form to Artemis.[10] It is hard to see how it would fit Pausanias' authorial aims to invent an image like this if one did not exist, or to exaggerate its mixanthropic qualities. Again, we may assume that he is reporting what he was told at the scene.

But here we come up against a now-familiar stumbling block. As at Phigalia, Pausanias does not himself see the statue, this time because the sanctuary is only open to the public one day a year and is shut when he visits. As at Phigalia, he merely tells us what he was told about the image and its form. Unlike before, the description is not couched in unrealistic and supernatural terms, and there is no good reason for arguing that a mermaid-form statue was *not* housed in the sanctuary. All the same, it is important to bear in mind that both the mixanthropic images so far discussed have been unseen, for one reason or another. They have been rendered invisible, one by mythical loss, the other by religious restrictions. So far we have the rumours of mixanthropic representations and no real sightings.

At the time of Pausanias' visit, images of Pan in his mixanthropic form were in evidence in his several cult sites in Arkadia. These receive mention[11] but not description; probably the form was simply too well-known by then to be thought to require it. Besides Pan, only one actual mixanthropic statue is to be found in Book Eight: in Megalopolis we are told of a house that was built for Alexander the Great, besides which stood an image of Ammon, with rams' horns on its head.[12] It would be hard, however, to take this as an instance of native Arkadian cult. Ammon's non-Greek associations are indisputable,[13] and it is also probable that his presence here owes something to the connection with Alexander, who had a special relationship with the god.

So much for mixanthropic cult statues. There remains, before we leave the narrative of Pausanias, one further and rather different case of mixanthropic representation in a cult context. It occurs in the description of Stymphalos and the sanctuary there of Stymphalian Artemis. We are told that the temple is old;

---

[9] Paus. 8.41.6: χρυσαῖ τε τὸ ξόανον συνδέουσιν ἀλύσεις καὶ εἰκὼν γυναικὸς τὰ ἄχρι τῶν γλουτῶν, τὸ ἀπὸ τούτου δέ ἐστιν ἰχθύς.

[10] Paus. 8.41.6. The sense of the image's strangeness is, I believe, conveyed implicitly in Pausanias' remark that Artemis could not reasonable be connected with *toioutou schêmatos*, 'a form of that kind'.

[11] Paus. 8.37.11

[12] Paus. 8.32.1.

[13] Parke (1967), 194-6.

that the effigy in it is a *xoanon*; that images of the Stymphalian Birds decorate the temple near the roof. Pausanias then adds, rather cursorily:

> There are also, here, maidens of white stone; they have the legs of birds, and they stand behind the temple.[14]

So here the situation has shifted: the cult statue itself is, we may be certain, completely devoid of mixanthropic features. A motif of birds decorates the temple; and behind the temple we find a rank of anonymous bird-legged girls. The identity of the former is made clear: they are the man-eating Stymphalian birds which the hero Herakles either killed or chased from the local lake, and Pausanias recounts this myth to leave us in no doubt (just prior to the passage cited). The relationship between Artemis and the Stymphalian Birds is illuminated by Borgeaud,[15] who argues that the latter represent the destructive waters of Lake Stymphalos, which was extremely prone to flooding. Flooding threatens agriculture and thus works against the mainstay of human development and civilisation. The birds, because they are man-slaying, represent a world both distorted and regressive, where animals hunt man rather than the other way round.[16] They, together with the waters of the lake, stand for the forces that work against human progress and civilisation; Artemis, if properly treated, will keep such malign natural agencies at bay. The fact that the birds decorate her temple show that they are under her control. The bird-legged girls express through their mixanthropy the uneasy truce between man and destructive nature over which Stymphalian Artemis presided. For the purpose of the current discussion, however, perhaps the most important observation to make is that the mixanthropic beings are strongly connected with the central deity of the cult but are separate from her, forming a decorative element within her sanctuary.

So, to sum up, Pausanias tells us of a number of mixanthropic cult statues. Those of Demeter and Eurynome are described but not seen. Those of Pan were seen but are not described. Ammon he both saw and described but sadly this example is less valuable because imported. Then there is the case of the mixanthropes who play some part in a sanctuary alongside a non-mixanthropic cult statue, and who are not themselves the object of worship. The mixanthropic being in one form or another pervades the book, most often through rumour and report; none the less, Arkadia does not emerge from the account of Pausanias as the clear and abundant source of mixanthropic deities that its reputation might have led us to expect.

---

[14] Paus. 8.22.7: εἰσὶ δὲ αὐτόθι καὶ παρθένοι λίθου λευκοῦ, σκέλη δέ σφισίν ἐστιν ὀρνίθων, ἑστᾶσι δὲ ὄπισθε τοῦ ναοῦ.

[15] Borgeaud (1988), 17-9; this *contra* the rather rationalist view of Pollard (1977), 98-99.

[16] Also, according to Diodoros (3.30) they directly damage crops, highlighting their opposition to the agrarian world.

Archaeology supplies some interesting cases. At Lykosoura, around eighteen kilometres from Phigalia, there was a large and important sanctuary in which a number of deities were represented but primarily Despoina, and in which Mystery rites were conducted.[17] In the temple of Despoina there stood an ambitious statue group by Damophon of Messene,[18] depicting Despoina herself, Demeter, Artemis and the Titan Anytos who brought up the infant Despoina.[19] Phigalian echoes will immediately be felt, as Despoina was the daughter whom, according to myth, Demeter bore to Poseidon while both were in equine form. This myth is part of the Phigalian cult *aitia*. Given both geographical and religious proximity, we may assume some form of practical connection, at some stage, between the two sites. (The functional relationship which probably existed between the Phigalian cave and Lykosoura has been discussed in Section One.)

Something must be said, however, on the subject of relative dating. This is a vital preliminary to any detailed discussion of the relationship between the Lykosoura sanctuary and Demeter's Phigalian cult. The dating of the sanctuary, and especially the statue-group, has been a fraught issue; even knowing from Pausanias the name of the sculptor, Damophon of Messene, does not provide certainty. To summarise an extremely complex debate,[20] three periods are possible: fourth to earlier third century BC, early second century BC, and second century AD, with the first two the strongest candidates. The key point is that whatever view one takes, it is safe to say that the statue-group was of far later date than either the *xoanon* of Demeter Melaina – if it existed – or the mermaid Eurynome. When Pausanias visited Arkadia, Damophon's work was there to see; Demeter's Phigalian *xoanon* was not. We are not dealing with two sets of imagery that existed at the same time. That said, it is clear that the memory of the *xoanon*, and the concept of mixanthropy generally, were very much 'alive' in Phigalian mythology. It is therefore licit to assume that a connection would have continued to be felt between the two sites and their different depictions of mixanthropy. But it must be born in mind that the Phigalian sculptures are the products of a later and very different age from that of the Archaic *xoana*. This very fact has led to some revealing assumptions, to which we shall return.

---

[17] On the cult, especially the Mysteries associated with Despoina, see Loukas and Loukas (1988); Jost (2003); Pirenne-Delforge (2008a), 312-5; Guimier-Sorbets, Jost and Morizot edd. (2008).

[18] The fullest and most recent discussion of this artist, his work and context is that of Themelis (1996).

[19] Reports of the excavation of the site and of the finds: see Kavvadias (1893), Kouroniotis (1911 and 1912), and Leonardos (1896). For the style and characteristics of the Damophon group as a whole, see Pollitt (1986), 165-7; Stewart (1990), 94-6.

[20] See Wace (1934), Thallon (1906) and Lévy (1967); Pollitt (1986), 312 ch. 8 n. 2; Ridgway, vol. 2 (2000), 237 and 258 n. 19; Macardé (2008); Sève (2008).

Fig. 30

Of the statue-group we have a description in Pausanias, but this is one occasion when we may corroborate his testimony with material evidence, since sizeable fragments of the group have been discovered.[21] On the whole, the overlap between the two is heartening. There is one detail of the statues that Pausanias does not, however, mention, but which is to the scholar one of their most interesting characteristics.

The detail in question is a veil which, it is generally agreed,[22] formed part of the drapery of the figure of Despoina in the group (fig. 30).[23] It is closely carved with bands of figures, separated by repeat-patterning. On the top-most level are eagles, their wings extended. Below them is a parade of fabulous marine beings, Nereids and hippocamps and Tritons. The level below that bears winged female figures holding elaborate torches. Finally, on the lowest frieze, is a series of dancing people with the heads of animals, including a number of species: horse, ass, sheep, fox, and one or two others which defy certain identification.

Though the veil was attached to Despoina, rather than Demeter, it is generally realised that the figures of the animal-headed dancers in particular must have some connection with Demeter's (rumoured) mare-headed *xoanon* at Phigalia and about her metamorphosis. Human figures with the heads of animals, especially in such a profusion of species, are not the norm when it comes to the anonymous mixanthropes common in Greek art: these latter tend to be the human-faced monsters of the orientalizing canon. And given the religious connections between Phigalia and Lykosoura one cannot dismiss the mixanthropes on the vestment as mere decorative motifs without any link to the goddess's own animal-

---

[21] Paus. 8.37.3-4. In addition to the surviving sculptural fragments, a coin was discovered depicting the group. This coin ratifies to a striking degree the reconstruction of the group created by Dickins on the basis of the fragments, and reassures us that we are not working on the basis of a fiction. See Dickins (1906-7 and 1910-11); Jost (1985), 327 and pl. 44, fig. 2. A useful reconstruction of the statue-group is given in Stewart, vol. 2 (1990), 788.

[22] An alternative interpretation of the carved drapery as coming from Despoina's tunic and himation is laid out by Morizot (2008).

[23] See Jost (1985), 328-9.

associations. Besides, other echoes of Phigalian Demeter can be detected in the design. The marine creatures, for example, remind us of the dolphin which her *xoanon* is described as having held, and of her connection with Poseidon.[24] The winged figures, which have been vaguely branded Victories, may in fact have the closest ties of all to Demeter, who on Phigalian coins was herself represented with wings.[25] But what was the relationship between the myth of the mixanthropic cult-statue and these multiple, anonymous figures on the robe of a *different* goddess,[26] among which are represented many species of animals not discernible in the Phigalian cult at all? This question many have chosen to skate over, and one can see why. It is, however, one to which I shall return, for I would argue that it is central to our understanding of the rôle and position of the mixanthropic form in Greek cult.

The sanctuary of Despoina at Lykosoura has also yielded numerous (one hundred and forty, in fact) terracottas in the form of women with the heads of cows or sheep (fig. 31).[27] The same questions of identity hang over them as over the figures on the veil. Are they masked humans,[28] or some form of divinity?[29] There is no way of knowing. Here, it is important merely to note that the animal element of the figurines does not directly match that of any of the goddesses worshipped on the site, and therefore it would be hard to label them as direct representations of these.

The effigies are striking and unambiguously mixanthropic, and their discovery was remarked by Perdrizet[30] with great excitement and with the claim that

---

[24] For a discussion of the various levels of decoration on the veil and their significance with regard to the persona and powers of Despoina, see Ridgway, vol. 2 (2000), 236-7 and 258, n. 17.

[25] See Jost (1985), 90 and pl. 23, fig. 5.

[26] Why, given the clear echoes of Phigalian Demeter in Lykosoura, was the mixanthropic imagery conferred not on her but on her daughter? This question seems unanswerable, though some observations may be made. The first is that, according to Dickins' (1906-7) reconstruction of the statue-group, the sculpted veil, though part of Despoina's raiment, is not actually placed on the person of the goddess herself, but is draped at some distance from her over the back of the throne on which she and Demeter sit; this renders less exclusive its connection with Despoina. The reconstruction given by Stewart, however, places the drapery rather differently, descending sideways from Despoina's lap. We must admit the uncertainty. The second important point to make, however, is that in Lykosoura, Despoina has gained undoubted precedence over her mother as cult figure (see Jost [2003], 145; Stewart [1990], 95), and therefore may have attracted to herself significant attributes which were once the preserve of Demeter. Thirdly and most basically, however, Demeter and Despoina share almost equally the animal associations which pervade the Phigalian *aitia*, and we should not be surprised when those attributes move from one goddess to another.

[27] For these objects, see Kavvadias (1893), 28; Kourouniotis (1912), 155-9.

[28] This is the firm contention of Jost, who tries to reconstruct mystery rites using the figurines and the veil: see esp. Jost (2003). They are interpreted as masked human worshippers by Loukas and Loukas (1988).

[29] This line is taken by Perdrizet (1899).

[30] Perdrizet (1899).

they shed new light on Arkadian cult's most primitive and fundamental aspects. Only very cursorily is it acknowledged that the great majority of the terracottas date from the Roman era, centuries after Archaic *xoana* and infused with a completely different religious milieu from that of the Archaic and Classical periods.[31] The general determination to see them as early is significant. Hejnic exclaims wistfully in his monograph on the Arkadian book of Pausanias that the terracottas are 'so highly archaic-looking.'[32] Somehow, early mixanthropes seem much more satisfactory than late ones. They accord with the Pausanian impression that mixanthropy is largely a feature of the oldest and most primitive religious sites and practices.

Also found in the temple of Despoina at Lykosoura was a small number of small sculpted marble figures with fish tails in place of legs.[33] Like the carved drapery, these objects clearly had some kind of rôle as decoration on a larger object: they have been conjectured to have been ornaments on the throne on which the statues of Demeter and Despoina were seated. They also seem to echo other iconographical elements in their vicinity, especially the parade of marine creatures on the drapery, but are even further detached from the central figures of the deities. They are literally part of the furniture.

There are many things to be noted in the archaeological material described. First, and most basically, it is all from Lykosoura. Of course, Lykosoura, unlike many other parts of Arkadia, has been excavated thoroughly; we cannot say what investigation elsewhere would turn up. But this factor would not account entirely for the concentration of mixanthropic imagery at Lykosoura. Plainly the cult of Despoina required, or perhaps facilitated, a certain kind of representation, as did the cult of Pan, that did not occur so much, for whatever reasons, elsewhere.

Secondly, few as they are, we may make some tentative observations about the nature of the finds. With the possible exception of the late terracotta votives, the

Fig. 31

mixanthropic figures are not themselves the divinities to whom the sanctuary was dedicated. The identity of the figures on the robe in particular (and to a lesser

---

[31] Perdrizet (1899), 635. Attempts have, however, been made to connect the effigies with a Hellenistic context of dedication by suggesting that they are the *agalma[ta]* stipulated in the third-century sacred law, *IG* V² 514. For discussion of this possibility, see Jost (2008), 100-101.

[32] Hejnic (1961), 28.

[33] The position of the figures within the goddess's throne can be clearly seen from the reconstruction in Stewart, vol. 2 (1990), 788.

extent that of the terracottas) has been the subject of much disagreement, with theories polarized between those who see them as humans wearing animal masks[34] and those who call them divinities,[35] without saying which divinities or why they are so many and varied. Either way, we do not have any representation of Despoina or Demeter with integral animal characteristics. We find nothing at Lykosoura like the archaic mixanthropic *xoana* which Pausanias describes but did not see.

Thirdly, both the figures on the drapery and the mermaid throne attachments were used as decoration,[36] however much they seem to echo vital religious themes, and their position has a certain marginality. They would have been visible, but easy to ignore; Pausanias ignored them, as must others have done. The eye of the visitor went straight for the central figures of Damophon's creation; only a careful observer would have taken in the patterns on a goddess's robe, let alone the mixanthropic figures adorning the edges of sacred furniture. The mixanthropic motifs are obscure compared with other features of the statue-group, for example the torch and the *kiste*, both common components of Eleusinian iconography and imagery.

This accords with the impression we have already begun to receive: that the mixanthropic form in Arkadian cult was by no means clearly visible. The cult statues mentioned by Pausanias tend to be unseen, consigned either to the cult's past or to deep religious secrecy; whether or not we think they existed, they did not do so under the eyes of all. It is worth recalling the observation made about horned gods of the Peloponnese; Arkadia worships an Apollo Kereatas, according to one mention by Pausanias,[37] and Clement claims the Arkadians have an Apollo Nomios whose father is Silenos.[38] This connects Arkadia with a wider Peloponnesian phenomenon of the pastoral horned Apollo, which of course accords well with Pan, but it does not provide any clear mixanthropic depictions;

---

[34] Predictably, this is the view of Cook (1894, esp. 162); but it has also found favour in more recent scholarship which has sought to find in the veil's figures a reflection of a ritual involving animal masks which was actually performed in the sanctuary at Lykosoura. (E.g. Jost [1985], 332-3; [2003], 157-61; Loucas [1989], 101). While it seems extremely likely that such a ritual did take place, the attempt to use the veil as evidence for it has led to some clumsy interpretation of the dancing figures. For example, Jost [2003], 160 argues that 'their arms and their legs are covered or prolonged by animal limb additions.' I can see no sign of such 'accessorizing' in the carvings themselves. If they do represent masked humans, it is interesting how little the artist has tried to make this apparent.

[35] Perdrizet (1899), 636.

[36] Marine mixanthropes were popular in antiquity as decorative elements in furniture. Mermen occur on, for example, a throne carved in relief on the Harpy Tomb in Lycia (clearly among other mixanthropic forms) – see Shepard (1940), 22-3; also on the throne of Apollo Hyakinthos at Amyklai (see Paus. 3.18.9). It would be interesting, in another context, to investigate this relationship between mermen/-maids and seating.

[37] 8.34.5.

[38] *Pr.* 2.28.3.

rather, we have a horns-related *epiklesis* and a mixanthropic parent, both indirect manifestations of mixanthropy. The mixanthropic images brought to light by archaeology are not cult statues at all but either small votives (and these mainly from the Roman period) or decorative marginalia. Mixanthropic images, and even more than that the rumoured presence of hybrid images, certainly cluster in Arkadia; but if we expected the area to give us large, central and manifest hybrid images, our expectation has not been fulfilled. If one is looking for evidence of an earlier stage in Greek religious life at which deities were worshipped and represented in overtly mixanthropic forms, we do not find it in Arkadia. In fact, the material from Arkadia accords strongly with some wider – and older – patterns of mixanthropic imagery, which will be discussed in Chapter 9. It is by no means as exceptional as it has sometimes been imagined to be. But then, the expectation that it, of all regions, should provide something unique in this regard is founded on a broader misconception of the nature of the region, which I shall now proceed to discuss.

2. Arkadia: a place of uncontaminated survivals?

Of course, no part of Greece could be argued to preserve entirely unaltered religious beliefs and practices from an earlier age; even for Arkadia that claim has never been made. However, as has been noted, it is a common assumption that the isolated quality of Arkadia makes it religiously conservative to a high degree, and that divine theriomorphism in all its aspects is the single most notable result of this preserving tendency. This sub-chapter will question, first, the extent to which Arkadia was isolated from external influences, and second, the extent to which mixanthropy in cult is a product of isolation, simply a survival intact of earlier practices.

The chief cause of Arkadia's isolation typically cited is geography: the region is mountainous[39] and land-locked and the lives of its inhabitants are seen as having matched the requirements of such a terrain: they were small-time herdsmen and hunters, whose concerns extended only as far as their own pasturage. But it could also be argued that geographical factors were instrumental in the one discernible social phenomenon which serves to challenge most strongly the notion of Arkadia as uniformly isolated: what one might term the Arkadian mercenary-habit.[40]

In ancient treatments of any form of mercenary warfare, the frequency with which Arkadians feature in the roll-call of hired troops is striking. A telling

---

[39] Cf. Jost (1992b, 67): 'La montagne a été en Arcadie un refuge de vieilles pratiques et de vieilles croyances.'

[40] On this, see esp. Roy (1999), 346-7: he ties in mercenary service with other factors at work in the Arkadian economy, and argues cogently for its huge economic significance.

passage on the subject occurs in Xenophon's *Hellenika*, during a description of the activities of Lykomedes of Mantineia, the man who founded the Arkadian League in around 370/69 BC.[41]

> This man filled the Arkadians with high spirits, saying that they alone could claim the Peloponnese as their homeland, for they alone were autochthonous inhabitants; and the Arkadian race was the greatest of the Greek races, and had the strongest bodies. He declared them also to be the bravest, presenting as proof the fact that whenever people needed mercenaries, there was no-one they would rather ask than the Arkadians.[42]

The context of this passage is of course important: Lykomedes is trying to give his Arkadian hearers a sense of regional pride. But the terms in which he does so are interesting and revealing. Autochthony is teamed with courage; the Arkadians' special close relationship with their own land gives them extraordinary qualities. But it does not restrict them to that land, or keep them within its boundaries. Rather, the qualities which it confers lead to them having a wider range of operation, employed by countless other states and groups and individuals.

A great deal of our evidence about Arkadian mercenaries is fourth-century in date, and can therefore be tied to a rise in confidence and ebullience which accompanied the burgeoning expression of Arkadian identity at that time. Before the foundation of the Arkadian League, it must be remembered, there was no such thing as Arkadia in any sense of political or functional unity. But there are also sources which reveal that, at much earlier dates also, Arkadians were being employed in wars beyond their own state. Gelon of Syracuse at the start of the fifth century forges ties with Arkadian nobles so as to facilitate a supply of hired fighters for his campaigns;[43] Arkadians also fight for Xerxes after the battle of Thermopylai.[44] Mercenary service is clearly not dependent on a sense of regional unity. Rather the opposite: Trundle argues convincingly that the suppression of local identity, such as Arkadia traditionally suffered at the hands of the Spartan super-power, is actually a factor behind high rates of mercenary service in a given community.[45] So is geography: Arkadia is a

---

[41] For the event, its date (disputed) and its context of growing Arkadian self-assertion, see Rhodes (2006), 217-8.

[42] Xen. *Hell.* 7.1.23: οὗτος ἐνέπλησε φρονήματος τοὺς Ἀρκάδας, λέγων ὡς μόνοις μὲν αὐτοῖς πατρὶς Πελοπόννησος εἴη, μόνοι γὰρ αὐτόχθονες ἐν αὐτῇ οἰκοῖεν, πλεῖστον δὲ τῶν Ἑλληνικῶν φύλων τὸ Ἀρκαδικὸν εἴη καὶ σώματα ἐγκρατέστατα ἔχοι. καὶ ἀλκιμωτάτους δὲ αὐτοὺς ἀπεδείκνυε, τεκμήρια παρεχόμενος ὡς ἐπικούρων ὁπότε δεηθεῖέν τινες, οὐδένας ᾑροῦντο ἀντ' Ἀρκάδων.

[43] See Pind. *Ol.* 6.7, 74, 101-5; Paus. 5.27.1.

[44] Hdt. 8.26.1. As Griffith (1935, 237) puts it, in the fifth century the Arkadian hoplite 'began to come into his own.' (Which was, largely, to fight for other people!)

[45] Trundle (2004), 75: 'Spartan hegemony in the Peloponnese denied to most Peloponnesians the option to fight for their own states' causes.' He goes on, moreover, to note that once the Arkadian League is formed, there is a sharp drop in Arkadian mercenary activity as represented in

relatively poor land, given to both flood and drought at different times, and too mountainous to have great crop-growing potential; this poverty, when combined with Greek patterns of inheritance, may well have encouraged many to seek a livelihood abroad.[46] Mercenary service is a means of doing so for which we have a lot of evidence; plunder was an especially lucrative source of wealth. One can also imagine Arkadians leaving their home state to take part in other commercial activities, though, if this is so, these are not as clearly represented in our available evidence.[47] So mercenary service is an especially valuable source of insight into Arkadians abroad.

Even by itself, the prevalence of Arkadians among known mercenaries immediately threatens our picture of an exceptionally isolated region, though it does require more scrutiny. Can we be sure that Arkadian mercenaries typically came home again after their wars abroad? Only if they did may we see them as an important means by which two-way cultural traffic was sustained between Arkadia and other regions, Greek and non-Greek. Otherwise, one might argue for the diffusion of Arkadian culture outside the region, but not that Arkadia itself was open to influence in return. Trundle argues on this point that mercenaries did tend to return to their native states after service, citing two pieces of evidence: first, the fact that we know of many occasions on which mercenaries could settle abroad and positively declined to; and second, the possible interpretation of the cult and the title of Apollo Epikourios at Bassai. The latter has especially interesting implications for the Arkadian situation, particularly as it is very close to the sacred cave of Demeter Melaina.

It is the argument of Cooper that Arkadian mercenaries returned from fighting on the Athenian side during the earlier stages of the Peloponnesian War, and dedicated the Classical (the so-called 'Iktinian') temple to give thanks to Apollo for ensuring their survival of the Great Plague which afflicted Attica in 429 BC. Apollo Epikourios, however, was already a 'god of mercenaries' (*epikouroi*);[48] this association was formed when Arkadian fighters were aiding the Messenians in the first and second Messenian wars between Messenia and Sparta. This would make the Bassai site consistently associated with relations

---

the sources; this certainly lends support to his theory. At 59 he makes the more general assertion that a tribal society allows for fighting abroad by its members because it weakens their identification with the wider *ethnos* as a whole: small groups of men follow petty local leaders on campaign, and serve these leaders' interests and their own, rather than those of a unified state.

[46] The poverty-factor behind the Arkadian mercenary-habit is cited explicitly by Herodotos, 8.26.2. For domestic pressures in the motivation of mercenaries, see Miller (1984); Trundle (2004), 54-63 on the factors behind, especially, the so-called 'mercenary explosion' of the fifth century.

[47] This point is made by Roy (1999), 346.

[48] For the changing meaning of the word (from 'ally' to 'mercenary') see Cooper, vol. 1 (1996), 75-9. On the ancient terminology involved, and what constituted a mercenary, see Trundle (2004), 12-24.

between Arkadian soldiers and other states, sometimes beyond the Peloponnese. Cooper's theory about the chief meaning of Epikourios as referring to mercenary service is not unassailable; opposition has come from Jost,[49] for example, who argues that the specific word *epikouroi* is not used of Arkadian mercenaries as early as the Messenian wars (the first reference appears to be in Thucydides[50]). However, it remains attractive to suppose that wealth gained in foreign wars contributed to the building of the 'Iktinian' temple, even if more caution should be applied to the meaning of the god's title. The lavish structure, far larger and more expensive than other sanctuaries in the region, has always been regarded as an anomaly among the crags of upland Phigalia.[51] It may be taken as possible evidence that even the Phigalian *chôra* saw influxes of people, money and perhaps ideas from outside Arkadia. This would accord with the wider indisputable truth that Arkadian soldiers were leaving the region, spending time in far-flung lands, and returning home with plunder.

So we are starting to build up a picture of Arkadia as considerably less isolated than has often been supposed, and this is reinforced if one looks at its important participation in the struggles between Sparta and Messenia.[52] Sporadic bids to assist or ally with Messenia[53] accompany a series of Spartan attacks on Arkadia[54] which only came to a firm end with the battle of Leuktra in 371 BC. To regard Arkadia as especially remote, always left to its own political and social – and religious – devices, overlooks its strategic position and rôle within a conflict-ridden Peloponnese. This can also be said of Phigalia in particular, despite the fact that it tends to be regarded as especially remote within Arkadia, and cut off from trends and events.

Phigalia is not the only site that should not be mistaken for a place of obscurity. In fact, if one looks at the places from which come significant quotas of

---

[49] Jost (1985), 486-8.

[50] The following are instances of the word *epikouroi* used of Arkadian soldiers in Classical sources: Thuc. 3.34.2, 6.43.1, 7.57.9, 7.19.4, 7.58.3; Xen. *Anab.* 1.1.2, 6.2.10.

[51] A thought expressed by Cooper, vol. 1 (1996), 1: 'The very presence of one of the most famous monuments in the ancient world at such a remote site prompts the visitor to ask "Why here?".'

[52] For discussion and ancient sources regarding the Arkadia-Messenia relationship, especially mercenary assistance from one to the other, see Cooper, vol. 1 (1996), 46-59.

[53] In addition to military support, one might cite the marriage between Aristomenes the famous Messenian freedom-fighter and the sister of a Phigalian ruler: see Paus. 4.24.1. Phigalia itself appears to have had a not inconsiderable rôle in the conflicts, even if we do not go so far as to believe Cooper's claim (vol. 1 [1996], 58-9) that the Apollo sanctuary at Bassai was attended by and sacred to both Arkadians and Messenians, a sort of religious interface between the two cultures which expressed their shared opposition to Sparta. That Arkadians and Messenians actually met in the sanctuary is perhaps hard to prove; but it is certainly the case that many Messenians, under Spartan oppression, settled in Arkadia; and the Bassai sanctuary was right on the border between the two states.

[54] See e.g. Polyain. 6.27.2 (Spartan aggression against Arkadia around 418 BC).

either mixanthropic or theriomorphic cult imagery (both visual and *via* mytho-logical narratives) the opposite picture emerges. Phigalia and Lykosoura are both near to the borders with Messenia and Lakonia and, as we have seen, by no means cut off from inter-state relations. Megalopolis was in part a gestural creation with the Spartan adversary in mind, and as will be discussed below, mixanthropy and theriomorphism were important elements in the cults of that city. Mantineia, the centre of the worship of Poseidon Hippios,[55] is fairly near the border with the Argolid; more importantly, in the period of maximum Arkadian political self-aggrandizement, it, like Phigalia, had definite ambitions. In 370, at roughly the time of the synoecism of Megalopolis, it too synoecised (undoing the fragmentation of its polis by the Spartans in 385), after which it joined the burgeoning Arkadian federation.[56] Were space available, a very interesting study could be made of the relationship between such developments and the promotion of unusual (especially theriomorphic and mixanthropic) local deities: did the two go hand in hand? Did places like Mantineia after its synoecism flag up such deities as part of their self-definition, as Megalopolis certainly did (see below)? A study of this kind regarding a specific instance – Tegea and its mythology – has suggested an answer in the affirmative.[57]

For my purposes here, however, it is important just to note two more general points. First, the sites in Arkadia which give us our main evidence for mixan-thropic deities are by no means backwaters; and second, the nature of their external contacts might suggest that they were considering their image in the eyes of other Greeks, and cults would surely have contributed greatly to that image.

So their position places many of the cults examined in this book within the range of contact with other, sometimes hostile, states. Also, while in many Greek states a position on the edge of the territory is also one in particularly rugged and impassable terrain, this is not really the case in Arkadia. Arkadia does not consist of a plain fringed by mountains, as do several central Greek states in particular, such as Attica, Boiotia and Megara. Rather, in Arkadia, the highest mountains are in the centre (Mount Mainalon) and in the very north-east corner (Mounts Kyllene and Aroania). Phigalia, Thelpousa and Lykosoura

---

[55] On the cult, see Mylonopoulos (2003), 107-11.

[56] Xen. *Hell.* 6.5.2-5.

[57] This is the study by Pretzler (1999) in which (in addition to making some very valuable general points about the creation of group identity: see esp. 99-105) she plots the relationship between aggression from, and defiance of, Sparta, and the Tegeans' use of local religious and mythological institutions to emphasise their identity and worth. Here neither mixanthropy nor theriomorphism really feature. These elements are not the only harnessable source of local uniqueness. Some places made use of them (Lykaion, Lykosoura, Phigalia, Megalopolis and Mantineia); others found a formula of their own. It should be said that archaeology has yielded one curious mixanthropic figure from Tegea (see Jost [1985], 374; Voyatzis [1990], pl. 58; Dugas [1924], 354-5 and pl. 17). But this element does not feature in mythology and certainly contributes nothing to the self-definition of the place.

are in mountains of moderate height on the western side, as is Mantineia (home of the cult of theriomorphic Poseidon Hippios) on the east. Megalopolis, the new town-foundation of the fourth century BC, is down on relatively low land in the south-west. Overall, the sites in which we find mixanthropic and theriomorphic deities and imagery are by no means in the most inaccessible, or the wildest, parts of Arkadia.[58]

A significant number of sites associated with divine mixanthropy and/or metamorphosis are located within the sphere of Megalopolis founded around 369 BC. As Jost has shown, the selection and distribution of deities and cults in the new settlement is by no means chaotic: rather, it shows us which aspects of their own religion the Arkadians (at that critical moment in their history) wanted to present to the view of other states. In effect, Megalopolis was a massive work of self-definition and the encapsulation of Arkadian identity.[59] In particular, Jost has shown[60] that doublets of rural sanctuaries were created in Megalopolis itself, to form functional connections between town and *chôra*, and to emphasise the unity of both. Most prominent in this technique was the Megalopolitan sanctuary of Zeus Lykaios and Pan Sinoeis, which explicitly re-creates the Zeus-Pan relation-ship on Mount Lykaion. So at the heart of the new settlement was a cult comprising elements of both mixanthropy and metamorphosis.[61]

---

[58] That said, it has to be borne in mind that the significance of topography depends very much on one's perspective. To take the case of Phigalia again, we – with the broad perspective offered by an accurate map – may say, rightly, that the sanctuary of Demeter Melaina is not in the wildest or remote part of Arkadia. However, this is not the perspective of an inhabitant of the town of Phigalia. For him, the sacred cave would have been outside the centre of settlement, up in the hills which span the northern and eastern sides of the Phigalian *chôra*. Processions from the town to Demeter's shrine would have taken him out of the lowland zone and into the domain of shepherds and hunters; this aspect of the cave's location has already been touched on, and remains valid. We have to imagine two simultaneous perspectives, the local – in which Demeter's shrine is remote, away from the main area of habitation – and the pan-Arkadian, in which Phigalia as a whole, and the shrine within it, is in fact close to the border of the state and certainly not out of all contact with the rest of the Peloponnese. Doubtless much of the time it was the local perspective which was dominant in the lives and minds of those concerned with Demeter's worship. But from the fourth century BC in particular, the pan-Arkadian dimension does enter the frame, and must be taken into account.

[59] Jost (1985), 184. Megalopolis is not of course the only Greek city to use cult doublets in this way; Richer (2007, 243-6) shows, for example, that Sparta had within the city itself versions of the extraurban shrines of Orthia and Poseidon of Tainaron. Megalopolis is unusual in the sheer concentration and complexity of the refences made, in the city, to the surrounding countryside and its shrines. But what is really important is the *contrast* between what Megalopolis reveals and what we expect from Arkadian religious practice – the primitive, the 'natural', even the chaotic. All this Megalopolis helps to refute. Other regions do not carry quite such expectations.

[60] See esp. Jost (1994), 225-30.

[61] The latter will have remained in the background; as Jost observes, there was no question of the peculiar werewolf-rite which seems to have taken place on Lykaion being staged within the urban setting of the Megalopolitan sanctuary. But that and the mythical figure would have been implicitly echoed in the new cult. On the importance of Zeus Lykaios as a peculiarly Arkadian figure – and used as such – see Adshead (1986), 21-2. Perhaps the clearest indication that Zeus

What is striking about mixanthropy and theriomorphism in Arkadian religion is how coherent it is. The sites with which it is chiefly connected are all in some form of relationship with each other, either of mythology or of cult practice. Phigalia has its most obvious ties with Lykosoura; but the theme of cannibalism at the heart of Demeter's cult there also recalls the sanctuary of Lykaion and Lykaon's crime. Lykaion too is connected with Lykosoura, which according to myth was founded by Lykaon himself.[62] Both cults – those of Zeus and of Demeter Melaina – are echoed in the religious arrangements in Megalopolis. Pan is a hugely important linking factor, appearing, in myth and/or cult, at all three key sites. There is a level of interrelation not found in any other part of Greece.[63] I believe that it is the consistency of the religious theme that has drawn scholars' attention to Arkadia, but not perhaps to its full complexity.

The fallacy of Arkadia: conclusion

So we need drastically to re-consider what it is that Arkadia gives us. On the one hand, mixanthropic images from the region were sometimes of great antiquity. Although Pausanias places undue emphasis on the *xoanon* as mixanthropic artefact *par excellence*, this does not detract from the fact that mixanthropic *xoana* did actually exist. More significantly, perhaps, it will be argued in the next section that even when the form of Arkadian mixanthropic effigies is not that of the *xoanon* – even when it is rather an object like the veil of Despoina at Lykosoura – some important long-standing trends of representation are to be discerned. So it is not the case that Arkadia is a place purely of innovation.

On the other hand, the mixanthropes of Arkadia are not preserved in a cultural vacuum as has often been supposed. This is revealed by the cases of Lykosoura and Megalopolis. In these sites we find cults of great antiquity echoed in a newer setting: re-presented and re-framed in a way which reflects the changing concerns of the times. The prevalence of mixanthropic imagery in these contexts is interesting. Why *are* mixanthropes so useful for self-definition? Their very peculiarity makes them suitable for a process of setting-apart, of one state distinguishing itself from others; after all, it is the mare-metamorphosis of Demeter and her mixanthropic statue which, above all else, really set her Phigalian manifestation apart from the Eleusinian persona which dominated on a pan-Hellenic scale. Adshead takes the matter further: taking a particular

---

and Pan emerge as the key figures of Arkadian religious self-definition is their appearance together on the coinage of the Arkadian League. A very clear example is to be found in Jost (1985), pl. 63, no. 4. See also Caspari (1917), 170-71.

[62] Paus. 8.2.3.

[63] On the particularly pan-Arkadian quality of Despoina, Pan and Zeus Lykaios, see Jost (2007), 264-9.

animal species as emblematic within its religion allows a state to use it as a quasi-totemistic figurehead. 'For this is the *fons et origo* of theriomorphism, to mark off who do and who do not belong in a given society.'[64] But there is more, I think. Mixanthropes allow for a negotiation between past and present, between old and new. Their association with the remote past of Arkadia and with its founder-figures (discussed above) makes them the perfect bridging device between primordial mythology and new aims. And yet at the same time they are not so mired in the past that they lose their symbolic valency. Rather they are flexible, adaptable, constantly available for re-invention. The complexity of their continued rôle is belied by any attempt by scholars to fit them neatly into an obsolete bracket of time; and Arkadia is similarly Protean.

---

[64] Adshead (1986), 22.

Section Three:
Mixanthropy and representation

Introduction

In the final four chapters of the book, I shall explore the relationship which existed between mixanthropic beings and the idea and the process of artistic representation. This will present an explanatory background to the observation which dominated Chapters 4 to 6: the importance in the depiction of mixanthropic deities of themes of movement, absence and loss. It will be argued that much light may be shed on these themes and their importance by examining the rôle of visual representation of mixanthropic deities. This will lead the discussion at times into quite general territory. As has been noted, a great proportion of the mixanthropic imagery which survives from the ancient world has no explicit link with cult, depicting not deities but monsters and fabulous beings, sometimes named, sometimes anonymous. However, it is the contention of this section that the decorative and representational aspect of mixanthropy generally has great bearing on the nature and function of mixanthropic deities.

By its very nature, a mixanthrope of any kind places particular emphasis on visual representation. After all, mixanthropes do not exist in everyday life. The Greeks – some Greeks – may have believed that centaurs roamed the hills of Thessaly and that Pan haunted Arkadia's wilder parts. Phlegon of Tralles[1] may have had no difficulty in imagining centaurs in distant Arabian Saune. But the ancients were well aware that such beings did not come within the scope of normal existence. The placing of mixanthropes in remote places and times is a way of rendering them both possible and invisible: there was a need to imagine them in existence somewhere, but rarely could they be brought into line with the common experience of reality.

So the depiction of a mixanthrope is not straightforward representation of something which the artist actually saw. Rather, it has a strong component of creation, of invention, even if one takes into account artistic copying and the following of convention. A mixanthrope does not indubitably exist until it has been depicted; depiction is a bringing into existence rather than a simple reflection of something that already exists. The mixanthrope is the product of this creative process; thus, in this area, depiction is of more than usual importance.

Moreover, as will be discussed, it is not always even the case that in depicting a mixanthrope an artist is necessarily depicting a being which is imagined to exist in that form. Sometimes the gulf between representation and imagined reality is even wider, with the mixanthropic form having a symbolic rather than a mimetic purpose. What the symbolic purpose of a mixanthrope might be will be explored in the ensuing chapter.

---

[1] Phleg. *peri Thaum.* 35.

The functional importance of the act of representation is illustrated by returning to the observations which arose from the earlier examination of mixanthropic imagery to be found in Arkadian cults. Above all, it was argued that Arkadian mixanthropic deities were:

- Rare
- Obscure and/or marginal
- Unique images, 'one-offs'

This last point is particularly striking. What Arkadia offers is some unique mixanthropic depictions of deities who – for all their animal associations – are not elsewhere shown in such a form. Of this type are Demeter Melaina[2] and the fish-tailed Eurynome, both of them mired in rumour and invisibility. By contrast, the mixanthropes brought to light by archaeology, which can be seen and admired as real, are typically not deities at all but decorative adjuncts like the animal-headed figures on the Lykosoura veil. As has been said, this does not marry easily with the common belief that Arkadia was a *cache* of mixanthropic deities.

However, there were other places in which images of mixanthropic gods did not have this unique, this 'one-off' quality. Attic cults, for example, fulfil much more closely what we imagine Arkadia will provide. In numerous rural shrines have been found cult-images of gods with unabashed mixanthropy, Pan and Acheloos being the most prominent examples, though Kekrops also deserves mention; his image was incorporated into the cult setting of the acropolis, central to Athenian religious life. In contrast to the Arkadian evidence, we may see that in Attica there was no reticence about depicting certain deities as mixanthropes, about depicting them *repeatedly* as such, or about locating their images prominently in sacred spaces (though it is noteworthy that they tend to be portrayed in relief-form rather than in the round; this will be discussed later). If we are looking for manifest, overtly mixanthropic deities, Attica provides them far more satisfactorily than does Arkadia.

There is also another region within the Greek world where mixanthropic deities cluster: Magna Graecia. In this area we find the densest concentration of river-god depictions, a good proportion of them identifiable as Acheloos. Cults of the Sirens were focused on this region (see above in Chapter 1), though unfortunately we have no cult image from their shrines, and cannot be sure whether any existed. We also, in this area, find a general abundance of mixanthropic and fantastical imagery, on coins, on vases, and in architecture (for example the many antefixes in the form of Acheloos-masks, satyr-masks and gorgoneia). In this region, as in Attica, there are strong and consistent conven-

---

[2] Even if we regard her mare-headed *xoanon* as more idea than reality, the potency of the idea within her cult entitles it to rank among actual images in terms of symbolic significance, as has been argued.

tions of depiction. There are clear river-god types (chiefly either man-faced bull or man with horns and bull-ears) and repetitive depiction. Once again, this is quite different from the situation in Arkadia and that region's unique and aberrational divine forms.

If we isolate the fundamental difference between the situation in Arkadia and that prevailing in these other regions with regard to mixanthropy, we learn much about how mixanthropy should be interpreted and read. Essentially, what distinguishes the Arkadian mixanthropic deities from those of the other regions mentioned is that their visual representation is so limited. Those deities who have an established mixanthropic form all have one thing in common: some process has been in place in their development by which their form has been established, canonised and fixed. There are three factors which can contribute, singly or in combination, to such a process.

One is the adoption into Greek usage of a mixanthropic image already formed in another, usually Eastern, culture. It is generally accepted that this factor was in place in the case of Acheloos: his physical composition was clearly at some stage, and by some route, derived from such images as the great man-faced bulls that guarded Neo-Assyrian palaces in Mesopotamia.[3] Once in use in Greek contexts his image is adapted, of course; but the great prevalence of the Mannstier type in his representation clearly owes much to its pre-formation in the East.[4] This is also the case to some extent with horned Ammon, though that god was much more explicitly an Eastern import whose chief cult centre remained the Libyan oracle at Siwah.[5] As has been shown in the previous chapter, it is not that the Arkadians were simply cut off from the rest of the world. But the chief factor behind mobility, mercenary work, only really took off in the fifth century, by which time one of the significant periods of Oriental influence on Greek culture was already over.[6] Early and consistent sea-trade can certainly not be imagined as having happened to and from Arkadia. In any case – and this is the most cogent point – Arkadia appears to have been uninterested in adopting mixanthropes from abroad. It is the indigenous quality of figures like Pan that gives them their symbolic power for the Arkadians of the fourth century especially.

---

[3] D'Alessio (2004), 25-7; Isler 1970, 76.

[4] Childs (2003), 54: he rightly questions the existence of any substantial connection between Acheloos and his Near Eastern models on the level of character and mythological significance.

[5] For discussion of the continued expression of Greek-Libyan territorial connections, and the rôle therein of Ammon's oracle, see Malkin (1994), esp. 158: '… the Greeks interested in Libya saw Zeus Ammon as its tutelary deity. Both Sparta and Cyrene viewed colonisation there as arrival in the precinct (temenos) of Zeus Ammon, and in time Cyrenaica was in fact delineated by his sanctuaries.'

[6] For the dates and context of the so-called 'Orientalizing revolution' in Greek culture (taking place c. 750-650 BC), see Burkert (1992), 9-25.

The second factor which contributed to the establishment of a mixanthropic type was its repeated depiction in art, especially in painted pottery, which delighted in Mischwesen and which can be seen as normally at some remove from cult practices. One can discern the Athenian Pan-form being re-used, refined and perfected on the vases of the Athenian painters, and this process probably fed back into cult imagery.[7] Of course art exercised greater flexibility than did cult representation, which tended far more to take a developed image and stick with it (witness for example the striking preservation of a certain physical type in the Attic cults of Acheloos), but for that image to be developed in the first place a process of repetition outside cult is very important. This is not to say that such repetition guarantees or even encourages the conferral of divine honours: the huge majority of the mixanthropes on Korinthian and Athenian pottery did not have cults of their own, and were instead considered members of the canon of monsters. The centaur Cheiron receives considerable attention from vase-painters, but in his various cult sites not a single statue or other religious image has been discovered. But for the mixanthropes whose cult representation was frequent, as I have said, the process of artistic repetition clearly tended to play an important rôle. And this process, this mechanism, was not in place in Arkadia to anything like the extent it was in Athens.

It must be said that even if Arkadia had had a flourishing pottery-industry on a par with Athens, it is very unlikely that such figures as Demeter Melaina would have featured much on the resulting wares. Certain mixanthropic forms achieved artistic repetition because they had some appealing quality. Pan, for example, lends himself to imaginative and playful depictions, and his goat element is intimately connected with his light-heartedness.[8] Since it is hard to visualise a mixanthrope as inherently beautiful, scholars have tended to regard those frequently depicted as 'good to think with.'[9] This leads me to the third factor that seems significant in fixing a mixanthropic image.

In the cases where the image is established and canonised, one can discern, without any fanciful interpretation, a clear association between the animal components of the form and a prominent aspect of the god's divine personality.

---

[7] See Boardman (1997) for the major trends in Pan's depiction. In his 1992 study of Pan's early Arkadian iconography, Hübinger argues not merely that the Athenian treatment of Pan's image was influential on his Arkadian visual persona, but that it was in Athens, not Arkadia, that the canonical mixanthropic Pan was created; Arkadia, along with countless other regions, then took it on. This is of the greatest possible significance to the present discussion. Arkadia provided the deity, but Athens provided a consistent means of representing him.

[8] See e.g. the red-figured Attic krater on which a small, plump Pan dances before a piping satyr (dated c. 400 BC; Lecce, Museo Provinciale 773). Ancient humour is of course hard to judge securely, but here Pan's wild flinging out of legs can hardly have been viewed without a smile. See Boardman (1997), 28-9.

[9] I borrow Lévi-Strauss's famous phrase. For a discussion of its repeated use, see Lloyd (1983), 8, n.7.

This is undeniably the case with Pan. Though more recent scholarship has destroyed the notion that he was the patron god of shepherds, worshipped only by simple herdsmen who saw in him a paradigm for their way of life and their concerns, he certainly continued to be associated in thought at least with animal herding and the rural *chôra*. As importantly, perhaps, his character tallied significantly with the perceived character of the animal whose parts he incorporated, the goat. Both things ensured that his mixanthropy remained relevant to his persona and important for its expression. Similarly, in the case of Acheloos, horns, bulls, water and natural abundance form a cluster of meaning which makes their combination expressive and valuable. The snake-mixanthropy of Athenian Kekrops was argued to be a visual expression of his vital symbolic rôles as *autochthôn* and mediator. In such cases the contribution of the animal part is clearly discernible and important. That in all three instances Athens and Attica supply the bulk of the surviving imagery is by no means coincidental. Not only was Athens simply producing more art than other regions, she also seems to have given mixanthropes – Pan and Kekrops especially – positions of great significance within the processes of mythological self-definition.

No such clear connection between divine persona and animal persona is in evidence in most of the Arkadian cases discussed. Eurynome's fish tail and Oceanid identity suggest sea-associations which seem anomalous in a part of Greece so thoroughly embedded in the interior, far from any coast. Demeter Melaina's horse element is clearly key to her nature and various theories may be – and have been – advanced as to its significance (see Chapter 2), but it fails to provide a clear opportunity for characterisation. It is easy to see why such cases did not appeal to the desire to unite form and personality which undoubtedly existed in Greek religion. Moreover, special problems are presented when a deity familiar by name at least on a pan-Hellenic level, such as Demeter or Artemis, crops up in a form so out of keeping with the usual iconographic trends. No wonder Pausanias was unwilling to allow Artemis, the fair maiden huntress, to be conflated with the mermaid of Arkadia. Conversely, in the culture of Athens, both Pan and Acheloos easily found places among cave-dwelling nature deities, in company with the nymphs, and in this divine company their animal elements, and the associations with the forces of the natural world which those elements conveyed, were quite unproblematic.

So the deities whose mixanthropic form we tend to take for granted have for the most part been subject to at least one of these three factors (the adoption of a ready-made non-Greek form; repeated depiction of the image in art, especially vase-painting; the presence of a functional and sustained connection between the mixanthropy of the entity and its character); and this has worked to establish their mixanthropic form as a permanent part of their representation. By contrast, most of the Arkadian examples of mixanthropic imagery are not Eastern imports; they are 'one-offs', peculiarities never taken up in a wider artistic context; the link between animal component and character is not clearly defined. The great exception to much of this is of course Pan, Arkadia's most successful export, and he acts as a valuable contrast with cases such as Demeter Melaina and Eurynome; but in any case, just how Arkadian his mythical characterisation really is is of course debatable.

These observations should lead us, I believe, to ask questions about what, in its earlier forms, the representation of a deity as mixanthrope really signified. In past scholarship, there has been a tendency to regard animal features in deities as fixed and immutable, and, as a reflection of this, these elements have often been turned into pseudo-*epikleseis* with no ancient linguistic basis. For example, in discussing the taurine features which occasionally appear in the iconography of Dionysos, Jane Harrison talks without reservation about 'Dionysos the Bull-god and Pan the Goat-god' as if at an earlier stage this was the *true*, the *definite*, form (later lost) of each god. We can see from our observations thus far, however, that to perceive a deity's animal form as an inherently fixed thing is mistaken. Without doubt, certain gods were portrayed with certain animal attributes at certain times and in certain circumstances, but the resulting objects should not lead us to suppose that they were viewed as always possessing those features. Even if at one stage Demeter Melaina was depicted as having the head of a mare, this does not entitle us to refer to the goddess of Phigalia as Demeter the Mare-goddess, or even mare-headed Demeter. Her mare-headed form, the fish-tail of Eurynome, must have expressed an aspect of the deity's nature relevant to the context of the local cult; that is really the most we can say. As Forbes Irving has remarked, the relationship between a deity and an associated animal 'is a complex one, somewhere between metaphor or symbol and identification.'[10] This is the case when a mixanthropic depiction is created. Then, as we have seen, other processes, most importantly artistic re-use and repetition, can turn the highly specific into the more general, the highly local into the more universal. A single symbolic representation can become a set type, Pan the goat-faced, goat-legged god, or Cheiron the divine centaur of Thessaly.

However, I would argue that that is not the end of the matter. The importance of artistic repetition derives from more than the fact that a mixanthropic cult image originally depicts highly specific and fleeting animal associations. It is the contention of this book that mixanthropic forms are by their essential nature highly impermanent and fluid. This is, as has been said, largely because in their earliest states they are not simply mimetic; they are an attempt to capture an idea or phenomenon which is itself highly elusive and fluctuating. As will now be argued, the fundamental purpose of a mixanthropic image is to represent *metamorphosis*.

---

[10] Forbes Irving (1990), 41.

Chapter VII

Mixanthropy and metamorphosis

1. Representing the unrepresentable

Greek myth abounds with stories in which a human being turns into an animal, and a significant number of ancient vase-painters chose to borrow famous mythical metamorphoses to decorate their pots. This presents a unique artistic challenge: that of representing a dynamic process in a static and two-dimensional design. In resolving this dilemma, a number of striking depictions were produced.[1]

Needless to say, the relationship between the idea and the image of metamorphosis is not always a simple one in which art responds to myth or to literature. There are cases in which the process may have worked the other way round, with myths being formed in response to material images. An example of this not directly concerned with mixanthropy is the case of Medusa. Her disembodied face may well have existed as a decorative motif before the first appearance of the myth in which she is decapitated by Perseus; the *gorgoneion* as decoration is mentioned in Homer,[2] whereas the story of Medusa's decapitation by Perseus first occurs in Hesiod's *Theogony*,[3] whose composition is generally thought to have been a little later in date. The situation is extremely unclear, but we have to entertain the possibility that the story of Perseus cutting off and using her head was at least in part shaped by the existing phenomenon of the apotropaic *gorgoneion* as visual emblem. In the case of the vase-paintings discussed here, however, we can discern a known myth to which the artist had access, often through a particular literary version, and which he adopts as a subject: therefore, in this, visual art responds to the process of metamorphosis already on the scene, so to speak.

---

[1] A number of brief treatments of the representation of metamorphosis in Greek art exist, for example those of Sharrock (1996) and Woodford (2003). By far the most detailed and important discussions, however, are those of Frontisi-Ducroux (2003) – which is significant for the current study because it makes the connection between artistic conventions and divine iconography – and Buxton (2009), 76-109.

[2] Hom. *Il.* 11.36-7.

[3] Hes. *Theog.* 270-83.

Fig. 32

One of the earliest and most popular themes is the scene from Homer's *Odyssey*[4] in which Odysseus' men are transformed into swine by the sorceress Circe. Vase-painters tackle this episode in a number of ways,[5] but there are some consistent patterns. Typically, they show the companions of Odysseus as humans with animal heads; frequently, feet and hands are also those of animals.[6] Does this composite form indicate metamorphosis still in progress, or complete? For Davies,[7] the mixanthropic form shows metamorphosis complete, and is used by the artist to show that the beings are not simple animals but retain human faculties; thus inner state is given an external manifestation. For Snodgrass, on the other hand,[8] the artist has frozen the being mid-way through transformation in order to capture the sense of ongoing change. In fact there appears to be a great deal of variety from image to image. Metamorphosis still in progress seems to be depicted on a Nolan amphora in which Circe is still in the act of waving her wand over one victim, who reels away, clutching his animal head with one hand, while the fingers of the other appear to be clumping into trotters.[9] One could perhaps read a panic-reaction into the open-mouthed prancing of the Daybreak

---

[4] *Od.* 10.133-399. For a discussion of Homer's treatment of Circe and the transformations she inflicts, see Buxton (2009), 37-47.

[5] Buxton (2009), 88-95.

[6] It is very interesting and significant that in vase-paintings Circe's victims are turned into a wide variety of animals, not just pigs. On the importance of this, see below, Chapter 9.

[7] Davies (1986), 182.

[8] Snodgrass (1982), 7.

[9] Berlin, Staatl. Mus. F2342.

Painter's figures on a Tarentine lekythos from the end of the sixth century,[10] and into the gestures of those on the Persephone Painter's mid-fifth-century kalyx krater, also from Tarentum.[11] The pig-headed figure on a Boiotian skyphos, however, (fig. 32) seems undeniably fixed in form: he lounges with an animal's squatting posture and watches quite calmly while Circe tries her wiles on his captain. Even less ambiguous are the animal-headed forms by the Painter of the Boston Polyphemus (fig. 33). The foremost figure is receiving the potion which will restore them to wholly human form; so their metamorphosis must be finished. They have not yet, it seems, taken the potion and applied it; therefore it seems unlikely that they could be undergoing change in the reverse direction, back into human form. This animal to human process is, besides, a strikingly rare one in ancient sources, with much more interest and attention accorded to the loss of humanity than to its recovery, even when such a recovery does take place in a story. The anatomical forms achieved by Odysseus' men on these vases can typically be taken as their final ones – the final product of metamorphosis.[12]

Fig. 33

Other metamorphosists in art share the compositional patterns of Circe's victims. One of the most striking is found on an Apulian red-figure jug dated to 360 BC which shows the early stages of Kallisto's transformation into a bear (fig. 34).[13] The signs of the process's working are so subtle that they may not immediately be spotted. It is by following Kallisto's anguished gaze that we notice that her hands are becoming paws. Her moment of realisation becomes ours; we share a portion of her shock.[14] Thence the eye of the viewer moves on to notice

---

[10] Taranto Museum 9125.

[11] New York Metropolitan Museum of Art 41.83.

[12] A very full collection of images – though with little discussion of their iconographic significance – is provided by Brommer (1983), 70-78.

[13] See Lefkowitz (2003), 216-18; Frontisi-Ducroux (2003), 151-3.

[14] In reading this Kallisto as a figure still in change, I concur with Trendall (1977). It is true that a little way to her right on the vase Hermes is picking up her child Arkas, a scene which in the myth takes place well after her metamorphosis. There is, however, no barrier to reading this

other details: the ear that is visible does not look like a human ear, the hair has the texture of pelt, and a touch of the hirsute invades the arms and shoulders. This depiction is sophisticated and highly individual. Yet it shares a few important features with other representations of metamorphosis in vase paintings. Extremities are affected first: the head and thus the face are in some way altered.

Aktaion, another favoured subject in both pottery and sculpture,[15] sprouts the antlers of the stag he is becoming, and on several vases this is accompanied by the development of a long, pointed ear.[16] In at least one representation he is deer-headed.[17] Similarly, in fig. 35, the hunter is horned while still attacking the deer; a case of synoptic composition, but one which significantly casts him in mixanthropic form outside the basic context of narrative chronology.

Not every artist chose to use such mixanthropic forms to suggest the metamorphosis. Another fairly

Fig. 34

popular expedient is to depict him wearing a kind of stag-costume – enough to mislead his hounds – though this can suggestively alter his outline, the face of the deer crowning his own and its feet protruding from his human body in a way

---

as a typical case of conflation of mythic elements into one vase-painting. A scene in a vase painting may contain a narrative, not simply a single episode, and it is possible that the viewer is meant to 'read' the oinochoe's decoration from left to right, taking in one stage of the story after another. On this synoptic technique in vase paintings in connection with the depiction of metamorphosis, see Snodgrass (1982), 5-7.

[15] Buxton (2009), 98-107.

[16] See e.g. the scene on a later red figure skyphos from Paestum in which the pointed ear is combined with rough locks somewhat reminiscent of the Kallisto depictions described above. (*LIMC s.v.* 'Aktaion', cat. no. 49; Karlsruhe Bad. Landesmus. 76/106.)

[17] It should be noted that the fully animal-headed form takes us into a different medium: a Lokrian clay relief of c. 450 BC in which the deer-headed hunter slumps as the dogs attack him. (*LIMC s.v.* 'Aktaion, cat. no. 76; Reggio Calabria Mus. Naz. 4337.)

which almost creates the illusion of changed form.[18] Thus the slight difficulty of representing actual metamorphosis is avoided altogether.[19]

The depiction of a meta-morphosist as a mixanthrope must be largely due to artistic necessity. The viewer could not be trusted, familiar as the origi-nal myths were, to recognise the story and realise that what they were seeing was not a normal animal but an animal that had once been human and that still had a human mind. A metamorphosed human-as-animal is an extremely complex entity; Homer[20] tells us that Circe's victims retain their human minds, and also the ability to weep, and Ovid, much later, makes full play of the uncertainty as to which faculties (mind, speech, emotion) remain human, and how they relate to the animal

Fig. 35

exterior. It is likely that the mixanthropic form used in art serves to capture two essential things: chiefly transformation, depicted as if arrested while in progress, but at the same time this complexity of the finished product, the fact that even when metamorphosis is complete animal and human elements co-exist uneasily in a single entity.

Artistic convention, however, cannot wholly explain the persistent tendency for the animal parts to be the head, face, hands and feet. This physical distribu-tion is not random. It follows a pattern. And that pattern is familiar from elsewhere. It is the pattern of the animal-headed mixanthrope. As Woodford says of the Persephone Painter's kalyx-krater: 'There is no clue, therefore, that these men are in the process of turning into beasts: to look at them, they might just as well be complete and immutable monsters, rather like the minotaur.'[21] Artistic necessity makes of the metamorphosis-victim a mixanthrope; but something

---

[18] This form of depiction is seen on the neck of an Attic red-figure amphora of c. 490 BC: *LIMC s.v.* 'Aktaion', cat. no. 27; Hamburg Mus. für Kunst und Gewerbe 1966.34.

[19] On the representation of Aktaion wearing a deer-skin, see Frontisi-Ducroux (2003), 108-10

[20] Hom. *Od.* 10.240-41.

[21] Woodford (2003), 170.

more makes it follow so closely the model of Pan, satyrs, Silenoi – an undeniable mixanthropic *type*.[22] Sometimes the painter makes it clear that we are *not* looking at a mixanthrope but at a metamorphosist; thus Kallisto's pose of horror. But in most cases we could, as Woodford says, be looking at a static and unchanging mixanthropic form.

Rare exceptions inevitably exist. On one vase, one of Circe's victims is shown not as an animal-headed human but as a man-faced pig standing on its hind legs (fig. 36). Here, clearly, the artist experiments with convention and form. Another interesting example is the Etruscan black figure hydria attributed to the Micali painter (fig. 37) which shows the Tyrrhenian pirates who in myth were turned into dolphins by Dionysos.[23] All but one of the figures follow – roughly – the typical pattern of metamorphosis-depiction in that their bodies are still human but their heads have been replaced by those of dolphins, and their arms have become flippers. The far left-hand pirate, however, is in Triton-form, with human head, torso and arms and a fish-tail in lieu of legs. This variation, along with the fact that they are shown just plunging into the waves, suggests that we are meant to imagine their transformation as still going on. As Frontisi-Ducroux says, this image shows the artist's interest in showing temporality and narrative within a single image; metamorphosis issues this challenge more stridently than any other subject.[24]

Fig. 36

Into this equation must be written the ever-present power of artistic convention. It is the case in all forms of Greek visual art that a formula, once used successfully, tends to be repeated by different practitioners over quite long stretches of time, and undoubtedly that is one factor in the constant reiteration of the Pan-type mixanthropic form in the rendering of metamorphosis. Various

---

[22] On this type and its importance in ancient thought and iconography, see Dowden (1998), 125.

[23] See *Hom. Hym.* 7.6-53.

[24] Frontisi-Ducroux (2003), 83-4; on the context of this image, see Bonfante (1993), 225-8.

things militate against convention being the only motive behind selection. Most importantly, the type was chosen in the first place, and at that initial stage the congruence with the mixanthropic form is striking. Striking too is how little deviation from the type occurs over a span of centuries and a considerable geographical spread. Rather than denying the rôle of convention, I would argue that we have here a convention of unusual and significant vigour, and that the factors which influenced its birth continued to fuel it through its long and well-developed life, making divergence especially unattractive. All variants, the tricks and innovations of individual artists taking a fresh look at the metamorphosis theme, nevertheless make no attempt actually to shed the type, which after all may be thought to have had disadvantages, from an artist's point of view: surely it risked confusion with mixanthropy, which could undermine the narrative impact? Conventions only survive if they continue to fulfil a need or tally with a significant aspect of the creator's cultural climate.

The artistic application of mixanthropy in depictions of metamorphosis has immediate implications for our approach to the phenomenon of the animal-headed divine image. It is the first real clue which suggests that such images represent not necessarily permanently half-animal deities but rather deities subject to metamorphosis, to movement between the two states of human and

Fig. 37

animal. Mixanthropy in essence is dynamic rather than static. The animal-headed type lends itself particularly strongly to this association. Changes to the face recall masks, which are the most potent means of transforming identity; masks are important in the iconography of several mixanthropic deities, as is discussed in Chapter 8, below. However, the animal-headed type is not the only mixanthropic type used to depict metamorphosis. Aquatic shape-changers tend rather to be given a non-human lower half, a fish tail. This is the second type with strong connections to metamorphosis and its depiction.[25]

---

[25] An unusual alternative to the fish-tailed form as a means of depicting marine metamorphosis occurs in a depiction of the pirates who affronted Dionysos being turned into dolphins as punishment (see above, pp. 266). One of the pirates is shown with fish-tail; the others have

Frontisi-Ducroux has argued, in her work on the depiction of metamorphosis in Greek art, that the fish-tailed form of sea-deities such as Nereus and Proteus may be interpreted as an expression of their metamorphic quality, and even, in some cases, as the representation of transformation actually taking place.[26] She makes the vital point that metamorphosis and mixanthropy are not mutually exclusive alternatives for the interpretation of an image; mixanthropic deities are *both* composite forms *and* forms undergoing change; both are important aspects of their character.[27] This is true, and is certainly not restricted to marine deities, though they are of course hyper-metamorphic. In fact, few mixanthropic deities are without some connection to metamorphosis, even if it is not immediately apparent.

To demonstrate this, something more than vase-paintings is needed. Their connection to cult and cult practice is hard to establish and by themselves they provide unbalanced evidence. Moreover, proof is required that one is seeing more than repetitious artistic convention. In the next part of this sub-chapter, therefore, the connection between mixanthropy and metamorphosis in the myths and cults of mixanthropic deities will be discussed, and it will be argued that the relationship is both important and causal.

2. The rôle of metamorphosis in the mythology of mixanthropic deities

All gods have the ability to change their form; that is what makes them especially baffling and awe-inspiring to humans. Brief animal-form epiphanies are frequent in myth; Zeus' many love-affairs, for example, often make use of them. And while Zeus' metamorphosis-matings, to continue the example, were common currency in Greek story-telling, his mixanthropy was limited to very particular forms and contexts. So it would be wrong to claim that only gods with strongly mixanthropic iconography are prone to metamorphosis. What *can* be said is twofold: first, that while not all divine metamorphosists are mixan-

---

human hind-parts but the heads of dolphins. These follow the animal-headed type, and suggest that when an artist wants to show a particular instance of transformation, changing the identity of the *face* is after all important and useful. In fact, the fish-tailed form on which Frontisi-Ducroux bases her statement of the relationship between mixanthropic deities and metamorphosis is perhaps not the most useful type: the animal-headed variant shows up the iconographic convergence far more convincingly.

[26] Frontisi-Ducroux (2003), 38-45.

[27] Frontisi-Ducroux (2003), 40: 'L'hybridité est inhérente au monde des divinités marines au même titre que la polymorphie. Ces deux notions sont en fait deux modalités, l'une spatiale, l'autre temporelle, d'une même réalité : la nature polyvalente et mouvante des créatures marines, fluides comme l'eau, changeantes comme la mer, se renouvellent sans cesse comme les vagues.' This is an extremely valuable encapsulation of the relationship between mixanthropy and metamorphosis, spatial and temporal, and the impossibility of keeping them apart.

thropic, one is hard put to find a mixanthrope who is not in some way a metamorphosist; second, that mixanthropes have a particular relationship with metamorphosis, in which there is an unusual emphasis on questions of genealogy and lineage. What often sets mixanthropic deities apart is the extent to which episodes of metamorphosis are *embedded* in the myths of how they came to be born, and the nature of the offspring they themselves produce. Metamorphosis above all shows up the *mélange* of animal and human of which the mixanthropic deity is composed. It plays with combinations and with separations of human and animal.

The shape-changers will also be discussed; but, for them, metamorphosis takes a very different form. Their transformational natures are overt. Frontisi-Ducroux has already laid out the relationship between their shape-changing and the mixanthropy of their iconography.[28] Important though this is, it neglects the extent of *latent* metamorphosis at work in the stories about the parentage and the offspring of mixanthropes who at first give very little indication of harbouring such qualities. This is therefore the first aspect discussed. Few mixanthropes are without some connections with metamorphosis (the only discernible case is in fact Kekrops); concentration here is, however, on the most important and well-documented cases.

2.1. Demeter Melaina and Demeter Erinys[29]

At first sight, Arkadian Demeter's mare-transformation seems to fall into the well-stocked category of the erotic metamorphosis.[30] As the female half of the pair she is, typically, avoiding a god's advances, and using an animal form in her attempt to shake him off, an attempt which, predictably, fails. The god is Poseidon; he and Demeter mate in equine form. This episode clearly bears the strongest possible relationship with Demeter's mare-headed depiction, whether one regards that as historical or mythological.

That metamorphosis is not a superficial conceit in this story will only become fully apparent when other cases are compared; but its deep importance to the religious system of Arkadia is clear. It was argued in Chapter 2 that the horse and

---

[28] Frontisi-Ducroux (2003), 38-59.

[29] For the details of the cults and myths involved, see Chapter 2. As will become apparent when the details are discussed, both forms of the goddess, worshipped in Phigalia and Thelpousa respectively but very closely related, are relevant. Only Demeter Melaina was associated with mixanthropic depiction. Pausanias describes the cult statue at Thelpousa (8.25.6-7), and it contains no animal element. Whether or not one agrees with Jost's suggestion that Thelpousa would once have had a mixanthropic image (see Jost [1985], 302), there is already quite enough to suggest a significant juxtaposition of mixanthropy and metamorphosis in that case also. It has been shown that equine mixanthropy attends the figure of Medusa, intimately linked with Demeter Erinys and with the myth of her mating with Poseidon.

[30] For detailed discussion and tabulation of rapes by gods in animal form, see Robson (1997), 74-5.

its associations contribute greatly to Arkadian Demeter's divine character. And they are not limited to her, as we see if we examine the result of Demeter's mating with Poseidon. The resulting offspring are the *Überpferd* Areion, and an anthropomorphic daughter, sometimes called Despoina. The latter was paramount deity at Lykosoura.[31]

What was the relationship between mixanthropic statue and myth of metamorphosis? Past scholarship has favoured an aetiological approach whereby the statue is the primary component and the myths then arise to comment on it. This rests on the automatic assumption that the mare-headed *xoanon* can be taken as historical fact, on which the myths are a consequent explanatory accretion.[32] At the time of its creation, the statue represents the perceived nature of the goddess. The mare's head expresses some association with the horse which is compelling at the time. The statue, as a cult artefact, is preserved as the centre of worship for generations, and during this span of time a gradual change in the social and religious climate takes place. Eventually a point is reached at which the mare-headed image does not 'make sense' any more, because the original belief which fuelled its creation has been lost or rejected. The image has become an anomaly, conspicuously strange, out of keeping with the new – probably Eleusis-dominated – idea of Demeter which has crept in. Its incongruous and – it now seems – grotesque form needs explanation and apology. And so the myth of metamorphosis is developed to give context and background to the human-animal combination of the effigy.

This view of myths, as reacting to something inherited from a previous generation, minus its original context, is sometimes of value. In this case, however, this approach raises various objections. The most obvious is that when an *aition* is being employed to explain and justify it tends to be presented in this light, rather as one of Kipling's *Just So Stories*. Pausanias' narration itself is full of such explicit remarks of causation. The metamorphosis-story, however, is not flagged up in this way, and thus does not serve the aetiological function at all in Pausanias' rendition (though that does not by itself mean that it was not designed to do so). Indeed, Pausanias feels that the earlier mixanthropic statue at Phigalia still needs explaining, though his attempt to supply an explanation is cryptic.[33] The second objection is broader. The metamorphosis-myth is one of a huge body of such

---

[31] At the start of his description of Phigalia (8.42.1), Pausanias tells us that 'the Phigalians believe all that those in Thelpousa say about the mating of Poseidon and Demeter, but they say that Demeter gave birth not to a horse but to Despoina, as she is called by the Arkadians' (for the Greek text, see the Appendix below). This is one of a number of slight divergences between the Phigalian and Thelpousan versions, which none the less agree on the salient points.

[32] See e.g. Nilsson (1925), 65; Guthrie (1950), 95.

[33] Paus. 8.42.4. Here Pausanias remarks: 'Why the Phigalians had the *xoanon* made in this manner is clear to any man who is not without understanding and who has a good knowledge of traditions.' What he seems to be suggesting is that the form of the *xoanon* reflects the myth of metamorphosis.

stories widespread in Greece, and it is likely that this *topos* was older than the oldest *xoanon*. The Homeric poems give us the earliest (roughly) dateable instances of divine metamorphosis (an example is Athene's swallow-epiphany at *Od.* 22.239-40); but it is certain that many of the myths of metamorphosis recounted by later authors have roots that go back even further. It seems far more plausible therefore that both the image and the myth were responding to an aspect of the goddess's nature which was about transformation, about a position on the shifting borderline between animal and human. Mixanthropic representation is one way of capturing a deity's potential for fluidity and change.

It is possible to represent the story of Demeter's metamorphosis and its result in a simple family tree:

Sometime mixanthrope (Demeter) + Poseidon Hippios

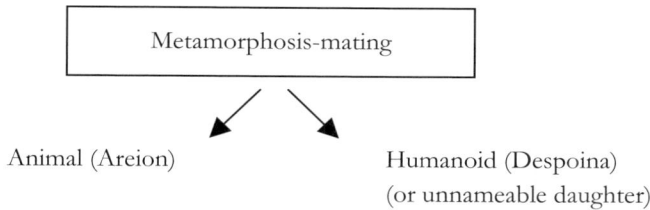

┌─────────────────────────────────────┐
│   Metamorphosis-mating   │
└─────────────────────────────────────┘

Animal (Areion)   Humanoid (Despoina)
                               (or unnameable daughter)

In this case, therefore, the animal traits which are *combined* in both parents (in the mixanthropy of Demeter and the metamorphosis of both) are *separated* in the offspring, one of whom is wholly animal, the other wholly humanoid.

2.2. Cheiron

With Cheiron, we have a greater genealogical range: he is both offspring and parent. He is the product of a metamorphosis-mating not unlike that of Demeter and Poseidon, this time between Kronos and the nymph Philyra (or Phillyra). In an interesting variation on the familiar motif in which a nymph or goddess (such, indeed, as Demeter) undergoes metamorphosis to escape a god's advances, Philyra is turned into a mare by Kronos when Rhea surprises them already busy making love. Kronos assumes horse form himself at the same instant, and the product of their encounter is Cheiron, half-horse, half-man.[34]

---

[34] Verg. *Georg.* 3.92-4; Serv. Verg. *Georg.* 3.93; Hyg. *Fab.* 138; Ap. Rhod. *Arg.* 2.1232-42. See Guillaume-Coirier (1995), esp. 115; Robson (1997), 87-8. There are other examples in Greek thought of the *circumstances* of a mating having an effect on the nature or state of the resulting offspring. One partly analogous case is the idea of porphyrogenesis, important in the Spartan monarchy. It was essential for a king to have been conceived while his father was in possession of the kingship; that is, his condition was determined by that of his father at the time of conception. See Ogden (1996), 252-5. It is also interesting to note Philyra's second metamorphosis into the lime-tree which bears her name. This transformation she herself chose as a way of escaping the horrid issue of her mating with Kronos (Ovid, *Met.* 7.350-93).

Cheiron's case is of especial interest, however, because of the way in which the metamorphosis motif is handed on, missing a generation. Horse-metamorphosis produces the horse-mixanthrope Cheiron; in addition to some anthropomorphic nymphs, the *kourai hagnai* mentioned by Pindar,[35] Cheiron produces Hippo (or Hippe), who, in Euripides' *Melanippe Sophe,* transforms into a horse. This is a striking example of the same animal cropping up repeatedly within a family, and of the sequential alternation between metamorphosis and mixanthropy. The family tree is as follows:

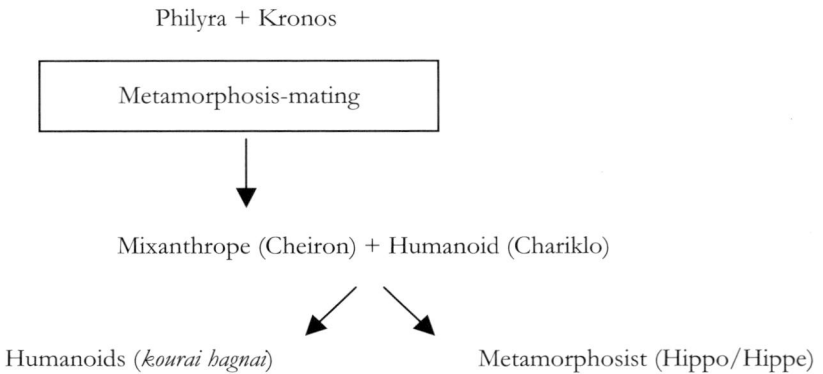

Philyra + Kronos

```
┌─────────────────────────────────┐
│   Metamorphosis-mating          │
└─────────────────────────────────┘
                │
                ▼
```

Mixanthrope (Cheiron) + Humanoid (Chariklo)

```
           ↙          ↘
```

Humanoids (*kourai hagnai*)   Metamorphosist (Hippo/Hippe)

In the first stage, metamorphosis produces not separate animal and human beings, as with Demeter, but a combination of the two states, a mixanthrope. The next stage, however, reverts: Cheiron begets another metamorphosist. Metamorphosis skips a generation.

2.3. Pan

In the case of Pan, mixanthropy is very much to the fore of his representation, in contrast with its vestigial nature in the cults of Demeter Melaina and Erinys. Whereas Demeter Melaina's mixanthropy was something that had to be brought to light by the touristic detective-work of Pausanias, Pan's was very much in evidence and indeed can be seen as one of his chief characteristics in belief and representation. Its cultic presence was strongly reinforced and augmented by the repetition of his image on vase-paintings, which rarely fail to make use of the striking goat-headed formula.

On the other hand, myths of metamorphosis seem on first inspection to be far less in evidence in Pan's cult. Little significance can be thought to lie in the metamorphoses of various nymphs while trying to evade his advances. Their transformations do not connect with Pan's state, and at times have the feel of

---

[35] Pind. *Pyth.* 4.103.

poetic elaborations rather than myths of real antiquity.[36] For religiously significant metamorphosis one must look to Pan's genealogy. Confusion, however, results from the great number of different accounts of Pan's parentage.

A combination found in a number of sources is that of Zeus as father, Kallisto as mother. Scholiasts on Euripides and Theokritos preserve Epimenides' belief in this parentage,[37] which also occurs in a fragment of Aischylos.[38] These sources also, crucially, call Pan the *didumos* of Arkas: that is, he and Arkas are both products of Kallisto's seduction by Zeus, an episode in which the motif of metamorphosis is central. Exactly what position the bear-metamorphosis of Kallisto occupies in the birth of Arkas and Pan depends on the account. Sometimes she is already in bear form when she has her sexual encounter with Zeus;[39] sometimes the transformation occurs after mating but in time for the birth of Arkas (and therefore of Pan).[40] In either situation, Pan as son of Kallisto clearly springs, like Cheiron, from Kallisto in her animal form. His mixanthropy derives from her metamorphosis.

One might wonder about this genealogy, and about the production of goat-Pan from bear-Kallisto, which seems to transgress a strong divide between the wild carnivore and the animal of the herd. It is worth asking whether perhaps Arkas – whose name means 'bear', after all – was not the original child of Zeus and Kallisto, with Pan being grafted on at a later stage. There is, after all, a possible reason for this development. In the cult-complex of mount Lykaion, Pan was strongly connected both with Zeus and with Arkas. (For instance, the first prophetess in Pan's oracle on Mt. Lykaion was said to be Erato, Arkas' wife.)[41] This cultic association may have prompted the development of a genealogical association in local myth. One could, however, read the situation rather differently and argue that Pan's cult connections with Zeus and Arkas on the Lykaion site reflect a pre-existing link between the three which resulted in their sharing a site of worship. The fact remains, however, that Pan's goat

---

[36] For example, the story of Syrinx, transformed into a reed, and plainly a late *aition* for Pan's famous pipes: see Forbes Irving (1990), 277-8, for the story's literary quality and associations.

[37] Epimenides fr. 16 DK.

[38] For which we are once more indebted to the scholia on Euripides' *Rhesos* 36: see Aisch. fr. 65 b-c Mette. Pan the son of Zeus was only one of the two Pans Aischylos is said by the scholiast to have believed in; discussion of the second Pan occurs below.

[39] Eur. *Hel.* 375ff. In this, Kallisto is also described as having the σχῆμα λεαίνης, but Forbes Irving (1990, 203) is surely right to observe that Euripides' alterations may owe as much to poetic requirements as to a separate mythic version.

[40] In Apollodoros' account, for instance (*Bibl.* 3.8.2), Zeus turns her into a bear to keep her from the wrath of Hera; the implication is that this occurs after their intercourse. See also Hyg. *Astr.* 2.2. Otherwise, Hera is the one to transform her, out of anger, then arranging for her to be shot by Artemis (Hyg. *Fab.* 177; Paus. 8.3.6). A third variant has Artemis, angry at Kallisto's failure to preserve her virginity, turning her into a bear herself (Hesiod, preserved in Ps.-Eratosthenes *Katast.* fr. 1; Hyg. *Astr.* 2.1; Ovid, *Met.* 2.409 ff.; schol. Arat. 27).

[41] Paus. 8.37.11.

persona, so strong a feature of his divinity, sits puzzlingly alongside the bear and wolf combination of Zeus and Kallisto, in a way which the name and associations of Arkas do not.

A number of stories make Penelope Pan's mother, though the identity of the father remains variable: Hermes,[42] Odysseus[43] or, in one extreme version, all the suitors. In one of these versions at least, that which makes Pan the child of Penelope and Odysseus, metamorphosis surfaces again, and with interesting results. Traces are visible of a mythic tradition in which Odysseus transformed into a horse. Unfortunately this story is preserved only in late sources, and in cursory, cryptic form. Most detailed is the version given by Servius,[44] who says that when Odysseus discovered that Penelope in his absence has given birth to Pan, he fled in horror, finally being transformed into a horse by Minerva.

The inadequacies of this for our present discussion are manifest. In no account is Odysseus in horse form when he conceives Pan; it occurs when he is wandering, in shock at his offspring's monstrous form, and may be thought to belong to the canon of metamorphoses which come about when the subject wishes to distance him or herself from a trauma already suffered.[45] There is, however, a particle of Arkadian material which places a slightly different complexion on the matter. Pausanias tells us[46] that at Pheneos was a statue of Poseidon Hippios which had been set up by Odysseus. This has been taken by some scholars as the vestige, shrouded in local legend, of a much earlier cult connection, or even equivalence, between Odysseus and Poseidon Hippios.[47] If so, this would put a different complexion on the myth of Odysseus' transformation, and suggest that this metamorphosis may have been part of Pan's begetting in the original version of the myth. In other words, this would be reminiscent of the mating of Poseidon and Demeter in horse form. There is, however, no firm and unequivocal evidence with which to support what is, as it stands, a fragile theory. The Odysseus-Poseidon Hippios connection must remain nebulous, another possible strand of metamorphosis in Pan's production.[48]

---

[42] Hdt. 2.145; Hyg. *Fab.* 224; Luc. *Dial. Deor.* 2; schol. Theok. *Id.* 7.109. These sources explicitly say that the mating of Hermes and Penelope involved metamorphosis into goat form.

[43] Schol. Theok. *Id.* 1.121; schol. Lucan 3.402.

[44] Serv. Verg. *Aen.* 2.44.

[45] In the *Homeric Hymn to Pan* (36-9), Pan's unnamed nurse runs away at the sight of the monstrous newborn, though she does not go so far as to transform to escape the sight. Even more similar is the metamorphosis of Philyra into a lime tree – voluntary, and motivated by disgust at her offspring Cheiron's half-equine form (see Hyg. *Fab.* 138).

[46] Paus. 8.14.5 ff.

[47] The chief exponent has been Fougères (1898): see esp. pp. 240-49.

[48] Some slight support for the idea of Odysseus (his nature clearly diverging wildly from the Homeric one) as horse-father in this myth, equivalent to Poseidon in the myth of Demeter's mating, is supplied by the rôle of Kronos as father in some accounts of Pan's birth (e.g. Aisch. fr. 65 b-c

Another version of Pan's origins relates that his mother was Aix, the goat extraordinaire which nursed Zeus in Cretan tradition. This seems logical, but our chief source for the tradition presents us with a slight problem of interpretation.[49] The source is once more the fragmentary *Kretika* of Epimenides, preserved by Pseudo-Eratosthenes, who, though he describes a being who is honoured as the *suntrophos* of Zeus and the son of Aix (lines 9 and 14 respectively), does not call him Pan, but Aigokerôs, and says of him: 'This being is the same as Aigipan in appearance; for he is sprung from him.'[50] So Aigokerôs is like Goat-Pan in appearance,[51] and is sprung from him; but the two are not quite one and the same. This said, it seems very likely that the account of Epimenides which follows, about the being's rôle in the war against the Titans, is a myth which, at least originally, related to Pan.[52] In this version, then, we have a mother who is not a metamorphosist but wholly and permanently animal. The implications of this will be looked at below.

We therefore have, for Pan, three main possible family trees.[53]

I.

Zeus + Kallisto

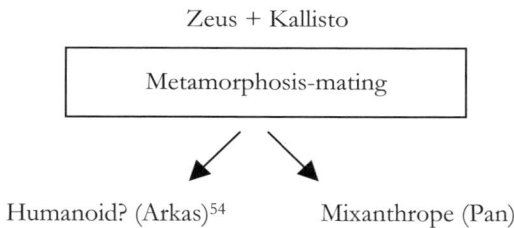

Humanoid? (Arkas)[54]   Mixanthrope (Pan)

Mette). Though horse form is not stated, the appearance of Kronos must surely recall the conception of Cheiron and the rôle that equine metamorphosis plays in that myth. Goat form and horse form are often closely allied in Greek thought (satyrs, for instance, occur on vases with the hooves and other attributes of either animal, depending on the date and the artist's predilections). Combined, the appearance of Kronos and the tale of Odysseus' transformation support the suggestion that horse-metamorphosis was an ingredient in one early account of Pan's begetting.

[49] A problem which Borgeaud (1988, 42-4) fails even to acknowledge, citing the Epimenides fragment in question as his sole authority for the Aix version, a reliance surely misplaced.

[50] Lines 7-8: οὗτός ἐστι τῶι εἴδει ὁμοῖος τῶι Ἀιγίπανι· ἐξ ἐκείνου γὰρ γέγονεν·

[51] The fragment further relates (lines 8-9) that Aigokerôs has a beast's nether limbs and horns – exactly Pan's usual form. Moreover, the horn which Aigokerôs is said to have found and used to rout the Titans is called '*panikon*' (line 13). When Aigokerôs is made a constellation, we are told, he is given a fish-tail (in the style of Aigipan) because he found the horn in the sea (lines 15-16).

[52] There is an alternative tradition which has Pan himself routing the Titans: see Diod. 3.57.66; Nonn. *Dion.* 27.290.

[53] I am not including the one which makes Pan the son of Odysseus *qua* Poseidon; it is too shaky to merit a diagram, but may be seen to relate quite closely to the Zeus and Kallisto version: metamorphosis-mating produces mixanthrope.

[54] The question-mark relates to a single vase-painting, especially mysterious because of its fragmentary form, in which bear-headed Kallisto is accompanied by a bear-headed male, thought to be Arkas (see Reeder ed. [1995], cat. no. 100, pp. 327-8). This would suggest the existence of a belief that the result of Kallisto's metamorphosis-mating was a mixanthrope. This is extremely interesting, but without corroboration from other sources must be considered atypical.

II.

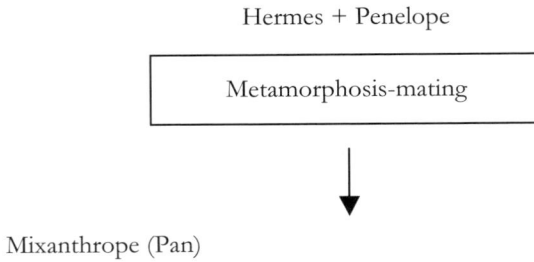

Hermes + Penelope

Mixanthrope (Pan)

III.

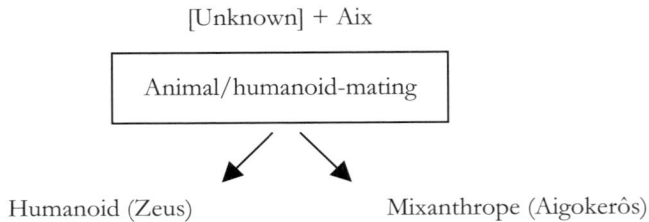

[Unknown] + Aix

Humanoid (Zeus)   Mixanthrope (Aigokerôs)

It will by now be clear that the first two diagrams represent a typical parent-age-situation; the third, with one wholly animal parent, is very unusual.[55]

And in Pan's case we have what in others we lack: in one version at least, a straightforward 'recipe' consisting of one animal parent (Aix) and one human. It is very striking how rarely this seemingly logical combination appears in the genealogies of mixanthropes; metamorphosis is a much more consistent theme. This is not so much the case for Pan. One might claim that a straightforward combination-parentage – god with goat – emerged because it seemed more suitable for a god whose human-goat mixanthropy had become such a fixed and immutable artistic phenomenon. But Epimenides might, depending on his date, be thought to predate by a good margin the development of a consistent Pan-form in art.[56] In this case, another explanation must be sought. Most suggestive on this

---

[55] It remains an undeniable and crucially important fact that, in stark contrast to the case of Demeter Erinys/Melaina, where the goddess's transformation is firmly connected with the birth of her horse offspring, the myth-structure around Pan does not preserve a strong central account of parental metamorphosis at his conception or birth. What we seem to have are faint traces of such an event in disparate local traditions; but the key point is that no concerted effort was made to maintain the metamorphosis element as a central part of Pan's birth. Perhaps it was simply ousted by more important concerns, such as – in certain areas – bringing Hermes to the fore, or achieving an etymological pun (hence the story about all – *pan* – the suitors). In any case, metamorphosis clearly was not an important aspect of the god's career.

[56] Epimenides and his career are so heavily mythologized in the ancient sources as to make dating all but impossible. Diels treats him as a historical figure of the seventh century BC, while acknowledging the questionable authorship of the surviving fragments (Diels [1891], 387 ff); Wilamowitz (1891) is more sceptical. For a treatment of the controversy, see Dodds (1951), 141-

score are the early representations, in Arkadia and elsewhere, of upright goats, thought by some to be the precursors to Pan; if the god himself had his roots in a wholly animal form, it is not surprising to find him appearing as the offspring of one.

2.4. Dionysos

In Chapter 2, metamorphosis was shown up as important in the parentage of the Orphic Dionysos, problematic as the sources tend to be.[57] This instance, however, largely accords with the patterns already identified: Zeus and Persephone mate in snake form, and produce a child with mixanthropic features.

Zeus + Persephone

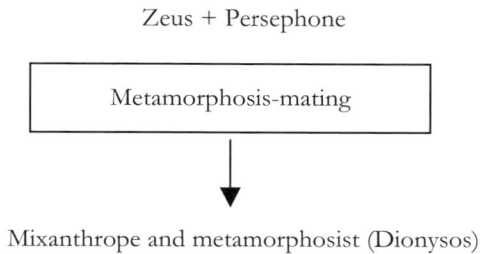

Mixanthrope and metamorphosist (Dionysos)

This case is distinguished by the tangle of mixanthropy and metamorphosis which results (Dionysos displays both, as has been shown); also by the combination of species, whereby a snake-form mating produces a bull-horned child. Such mixtures are not, however, unknown; the bear/goat confusion in the parentage of Pan has already been discussed in this chapter, above.

2.5. The shape-changers

Finally, there are the shape-changers, chiefly Proteus, Thetis and Acheloos.[58] In these cases, we do not have to search for traces of metamorphosis in their mythological backgrounds; it is their defining feature, and takes an extreme form: numerous, rapid transformations. Patent in their integral natures, metamorphosis is strikingly absent from their genealogy.[59] Genealogy, after all, brings out metamorphic elements which are latent; shape-changers have no need of this.

2; he argues that the particular shamanistic character of Epimenides in Greek sources derives from the seventh century, even if the fragments do not.

[57] The main sources are *Orphic Hymn to D.* 30; Nonn. *Dion.* 5.562 ff. and 6.155 ff. On these texts and their problems, see Chapter 2.

[58] These three are the figures who are included in this study because they receive cult, but myth supplies others, such as Nereus and Periklymenos. For a recent discussion of the group, see Buxton (2009), 168-77.

[59] Mixanthropy does not much feature in their parentage or their offspring, either. A rare exception is Acheloos' parentage of the Sirens. For the most part, both metamorphosis and

They are interesting, however, in that they show up especially clearly the difference between textual sources, which are able to, and do, describe metamorphosis in all its fluidity, and visual ones, which make use of the convention of mixanthropy. Proteus is fish-tailed, in accordance with Triton and Nereus also; Acheloos in a single depiction shares this form, but is more usually half-bull, half man. There is no doubt that these mixanthropic forms achieve orthodoxy in how the shape-changers were imagined and portrayed; at the same time, metamorphosis continues to dominate their literary depictions. Sometimes the latter make no mention of mixanthropy; all that we learn about Proteus from Homer's description in *Odyssey* 4 of his encounter with Menelaos, for example, is that he is an old man, the Halios Gerôn. It is quite possible, indeed probable, that at this time mixanthropy was not to the fore in his physical conception, and that it had not yet been adopted as the standard artistic formula for the shape-changer. The Proteus type first appears in the seventh century,[60] rather later than the supposed date of the composition of the Homeric poems.

This is surely a case of an existing mythological figure being depicted using a form generically associated with sea-divinities, a form which was felt adequately to capture Proteus' nature and deeds, and especially his metamorphic quality. A similar process may be seen at work with the shape-changing river-god Acheloos, though there the image applied to the myth is not wholly Greek in origin, a fact which brings its own implications. The forms which later become so firmly associated with Acheloos, especially the man-faced bull type, appear on the Greek scene very early (from the mid seventh century BC) in East Greek art especially, though they have a far earlier manifestation in the monumental stone man-faced bulls which guarded neo-Assyrian palaces. Discussing the early Greek Mannstier images in his monograph on Acheloos, Isler tends to designate them as depictions of Acheloos; but in reality it is only later that we get clearly identifiable images of the god. Attic vase-paintings and inscribed votive reliefs from the Classical period and later are our chief sources of named Acheloos-images. The earlier man-bull mixanthropes are more mysterious, and in many cases may refer to another local river-god or to an entity with which we are not familiar. So we may see that forms which exist independently of Acheloos, and which owe much to non-Greek artistic traditions, come to be used for his depiction.

Meanwhile, in the literary tradition, shape-changing is uppermost, though not untouched by mixanthropic elements. The earliest literary treatment of Acheloos' form occurs in Sophokles' *Trachiniai*. In this text, Deianeira describes the approach of the river-god, who comes to ask her father for her hand in marriage,

---

mixanthropy remain vested in the deities themselves and are not manifested in their surrounding family relationships.

[60] The earliest example I have been able to discover is a seventh-century island gem showing a human (Herakles?) wrestling a fish-tailed person (London BM 212).

to her horror. The description given of his shape-changing is extremely significant:

> For a river was my suitor, Acheloos I mean,
> who, in threefold shapes, asked my father for my hand,
> visiting in the form of a bull, then as a coiling,
> glittering snake, then bull-fronted but with human body…[61]

As Isler notes, what is striking here is that the forms taken by the god as he transforms include not only whole animals – snake and bull – but also a mixanthropic form. The animal forms are perfectly familiar to us from the shape-changing of Proteus, Thetis and Dionysos; they are inherent in the shape-changing motif. The mixanthropic element, on the other hand, appears to be a borrowing into myth of an element of the god's iconography. Interestingly, it is not the one most often found in his cult-imagery: rather, the adjective *bouprôros* seems to denote a human with a bull's head, like a minotaur. This is a form not unknown in Acheloos' representation (and that of other river-gods), though it is not much used in cult contexts. So two separate realms of representation seem to be coming together. Acheloos' mythical persona is defined not by mixanthropy so much as by metamorphosis. (Sophokles' text is our earliest source; but I think we may be fairly certain that this aspect of Acheloos was an early one, given his strong connection with marine deities, whose shape-changing goes back as early as Homer.) His visual depiction, when we find one, makes use of existing conventions of mixanthropic imagery in order to express the metamorphic quality. There is some overlap, but on the whole, metamorphosis is found in the textual and mixanthropy in the visual sources.

Conclusion

1. Recipes for mixanthropy

The above examination of genealogy and mixanthropic origins has revealed some vital points. First, it has perhaps confounded expectations. It has been shown that a Greek mixanthrope is in no way a *hybrid* in the biological sense (further justification for shunning the term): that is, one did not make a mixanthrope by breeding an animal with a human. A mixanthrope is rarely just a genealogical combination of two elements. There is no single recipe, and the

---

[61] Soph. *Trach.* 9-13 (cf. 508-19): μνηστὴρ γὰρ ἦν μοι ποταμός, Ἀχελῷον λέγω, | ὅς μ' ἐν τρισὶν μορφαῖσιν ἐξῄτει πατρός, | φοιτῶν ἐναργὴς ταῦρος, ἄλλοτ' αἰόλος | δράκων ἑλικτός, ἄλλοτ' ἀνδρείῳ κύτει | βούπρῳρος…

many possibilities one finds defy scientific logic.[62] The one consistent ingredient in almost all the recipes involved in mixanthropes' creation is *metamorphosis*. Metamorphosis is present in the past, the present and the posterity of mixanthropes. They come out of metamorphosis, out of transformational matings; they themselves are frequently given to metamorphosis; they can produce offspring with the same trait.[63] What does all this mean?

The single most revealing fact is that while art gives us mixanthropes, in literary retellings of myth we find metamorphosis (see table below). Demeter's *xoanon* corresponds to her mythical transformation; the shape-changers likewise are hyper-metamorphic in literature, in art consistently mixanthropic. This discrepancy between image and text brings us back to our earlier observations about the representation of metamorphosis on vase-paintings. An artist cannot depict a process of change; mixanthropy is the favoured way of getting round this. Tendentious as an argument about origins always is, I would claim that the essential, initial nature of the mixanthrope is as an expression of metamorphosis. This does not continue in the conscious domain. No artist depicting Cheiron thought of his form as an expression of anything except what Cheiron was actually imagined to look like. The shape-changers stay closer to their roots because transformation remains the essential feature of their natures, but even there mixanthropic anatomy becomes fixed and constant. For the huge majority of mixanthropes, however, genealogy preserves their original associations with change. Myths, especially, in which mixanthropes are born from a metamorphic mating reflect their origins. The family background of a mixanthrope is used as a sphere in which their earliest nature is allowed to lurk, without destabilizing or undermining the constancy of their form. (Except, again, in the case of the shape-changers, in whom flux is desirable.)

Moreover – and this is the final vital point – *metamorphosis is far more important to the god than to the monster.* The table below reveals the basic point that monsters, the beings in the third grouping, are far less frequently metamorphosists themselves than are gods; and the same goes for their genealogy. The difference between the 'recipes' for mixanthropic gods and for mixanthropic monsters is illustrated perfectly by the divergence between Cheiron and the group-centaurs, touched on already in the section of Cheiron's composition. It will be recalled that while Cheiron is the product of a metamorphic mating between god and nymph, the group-centaurs are, in the dominant tradition, created in a wholly different way: their grandparents are Ixion and the woman-shaped cloud, the vain *eidôlon,*

---

[62] Robson (1997, 74-5) remarks, though without reference to their religious significance, on the variety of possible offspring (mixanthrope, animal, human with latent animal features) which may result from a metamorphosis-mating.

[63] There are of course exceptions to this pattern. Kekrops is born from the earth, and his snake tail is a reflection of this. Glaukos acquires his mixanthropy abruptly when he leaps into the sea. Great variety attends individual contexts. But the pattern here described is the only one which holds firm across several instances.

Nephele, whom, in his impiety, Ixion believes to be Hera. This latter is a typical monster origin: a futile, unnatural and transgressive mating. Ogden has shown that monsters are typically produced from such circumstances: unnatural or lopsided parentage, and a breaking of both natural and god-given ordinances.[64] Metamorphosis is unimportant. But for the *divine* mixanthrope, it is crucial. Thus we may conclude that metamorphosis is not just an ingredient of the strange, the abnormal; rather, it characterises the numinous, and sets mixanthropic deities apart from the monsters they so closely resemble.

2. Mixanthropy, metamorphosis and divinity

The table below collates basic information on the representation of key mixanthropes both in art and in myth. It will hopefully show at a glance that some interesting patterns and variations are afoot. The second column indicates the form in which the mixanthrope is shown in cult representation; that is, in depictions which clearly functioned within the site and practices of a cult, such as cult images and votives. The third column indicates the form in which the mixanthrope is shown in art-forms not closely associated with cult, those that would have been used not exclusively within a religious context, most often painted pottery, whose use was normally domestic. The third column indicates the form taken by the mixanthrope in textual retellings of myth; these, it may be seen, are often strikingly at variance from the first two forms of representation. For interest and comparison, some prominent mixanthropes who have no firmly attested cult, and who have consequently not had a significant place in this study, are included here. For the sake of diagrammatic clarity, ancient citations are not included in the table; they may be found in the relevant parts of Section One.

---

[64] Ogden (1997), 9-14.

	DEITY	FORM IN CULTIC REPRESENTATION	FORM IN NON-CULTIC REPRE-SENTATION	FORM IN TEXTUAL RETELLING OF MYTH
DEITIES WITH MAINLY CULTIC REPRESENTATION	Demeter Melaina	mixanthropic (alleged)		metamorphosist
	Dionysos	wholly anthropomor-phic, wholly animal, mixanthropic	anthropomorphic	anthropomorphic with mixanthropic attendants, meta-morphosist, mixanthropic
	Eurynome	mixanthropic	anthropomorphic	anthropomorphic
	Horned Gods: Apollo Karneios	mixanthropic	one instance only: wholly anthropo-morphic	anthropomorphic, metamorphosist, mixanthropic
	Horned Gods: Zeus Ammon	mixanthropic		anthropomorphic
	Pan	mixanthropic, wholly animal (questionable identification)	mixanthropic	mixanthropic and · metamorphosist
	Thetis	wholly anthropomor-phic; unseen image, probably mixanthropic	wholly anthropo-morphic, shape-changing	anthropomorphic, shape-changing

	Acheloos	mixanthropic	mixanthrope / wholly human (rare)	metamorphosist and mixanthropic
DEITIES WITH WIDESPREAD NON-CULTIC REPRESENTATION	Cheiron	(no known cult image)	mixanthropic	mixanthropic
	Kekrops	mixanthropic, anthropomorphic with attendant snake (questionable identification)	mixanthropic	mixanthropic
	Pan	mixanthropic, wholly animal (questionable identification)	mixanthropic	mixanthropic and metamorphosist
	Proteus	(no known cult image)	mixanthropic	mixanthropic and shape-changing
	Sirens	(no known cult image)	mixanthropic	metamorphosist, and as a result mixan-thropic

MIXANTHROPES WITHOUT KNOWN CULT	Medusa		mixanthropic	metamorphosist, mixanthropic
	Satyrs and silenoi		mixanthropic	mixanthropic
	Skylla		mixanthropic	metamorphosist, and as a result mixanthropic
	Sphinx		mixanthropic	mixanthropic
	Triton/Nereus		mixanthropic	mixanthropic
	Typhon		mixanthropic	mixanthropic

It will be seen that the mixanthropes have been divided into three groups, suggested by the table's contents themselves (of course, the divisions thus created, while useful in such a general summary, are somewhat artificial and in practice are often blurred). The first is of deities whose representation is limited to cult contexts and does not feature in the 'secular' domain; these figures tend to have an established and unquestioned divinity. By contrast, the second group comprises lesser deities and *daimones*; their images are used – in some cases extensively – in contexts which are not specifically religious. Some items jump out: Pan, for example, has been placed in both groups to reflect an interesting dichotomy: on the one hand, ancient authors take pains to include him in the Olympian canon;[65] on the other, several features of his birth and nature suggest a closer association with the category of nature-*daimones*. In any case, it may be seen that the trends of his representation suit the second group in the table more closely than the first. Pan is often apparently anomalous, and this will form an important part of later discussion. Another striking case is that of Cheiron, whose cult is attested, as will be shown, but is completely void of representation in any form; at the same time, the centaur is a popular subject of non-cultic art, particularly vase-painting.

Apart from these two instances, however, the table illustrates some of the very strong patterns at work in mixanthropic imagery. They include the following observations:

---

[65] See for example the *Homeric Hymn to Pan*, which has Hermes bringing his young son Pan to join the company of the Olympian gods, who receive him gladly (lines 40-47). The very nature of the story, however, reinforces Pan's initial outsider status as he is brought into the community from his Arkadian home, and his parentage (a god and a nymph) would seem to equip him for demigod or divine hero status rather than full godhead.

–   In the first category, most of the entries are unusual local forms of deities who also have a wider, pan-Hellenic identity, and who are not predominately known as mixanthropes. Their representations are generally limited to one or two particular cult sites, and are often very few.

–   Within this category, mixanthropy is sometimes only one of a range of animal-related representational types, existing alongside attendant animals, animal metamorphosis and wholly animal form in both mythical and artistic depictions.

–   By contrast, the beings in the second category are mixanthropes first and foremost; other types of depiction are secondary, rare, and often doubtful. That said, animal metamorphosis is a significant component of their myths.

–   The table clearly illustrates the fact that mixanthropy is generally a product of visual imagery, whereas metamorphosis dominates in the textual sources. This is about the difference in what the image and the text can achieve. For the writer, all the contortions of transformation are available for expression and description. For the artist, things are not so flexible; and mixanthropy is the favoured means of representing the unrepresentable.

–   Though members of the table's second category all received cult, a significant number have no attested cult image. This must in some instances be due to accidents of preservation – texts failing to mention an image which did exist, archaeological material being unavailable – but it is also probably the case that it reflects a genuine tendency of the group not to receive straightforward cult representation. Though religiously significant, their mixanthropy is established and canonised by non-cultic representation, and draws its permanence and consistency from the fixative process of artistic repetition.

–   In a sense, the members of the second category can be seen as occupying a middle ground between those of the first and those of the third. This is the case on the level of character, persona and rôle in myth, as well as in the trends of depiction. The members of the second group have the cult-recipient status which characterises the first. But they also, in most cases, have a share of, or are associated with, the monstrous and adversarial quality which characterises the third. For example, Acheloos, Proteus and the Sirens are all pitted against heroes in various myths; Cheiron as a centaur cannot but be associated with that species' struggles against various human opponents.

–   The members of the third category, the monsters, are overwhelmingly mixanthropic, and metamorphosis is largely absent from the way in which they were imagined, even from the literary treatments.[66]

---

[66] One of the two exceptions, Medusa, is partly explained by her very close similarity with Demeter Melaina.

This is perhaps the most striking feature of the table for the topic of this chapter: it reveals an abiding connection between divinity and metamorphosis. Although monsters occasionally display an association with metamorphosis, it is not so important to their character as a class. For deities, on the other hand, it is vital. For monsters, mixanthropy is a matter of unnatural combination, anatomical transgression, the uncanny and the unnerving. For deities, it has another – though related – dimension: that of fluidity, impermanence and change. Just as in myth metamorphosis is so often used for the purposes of evasion – like Thetis, deflecting with her rapid animal and elemental changes the attempt by Peleus to catch and hold her – so across the range of their characterisation, it is the association of mixanthropic deities with metamorphosis which lies at the heart of their elusiveness, and their tendency towards departure and absence.

Chapter VIII

Mixanthropy and masks – the iconography of Acheloos

Introduction

The previous chapter ended with the importance of the relationship between the fluidity of metamorphosis and the immobility of the visual image. In the current chapter this relationship continues to be scrutinised with regard to a very particular element in the iconography of mixanthropic deities: the mask. Two aspects will be considered. First I shall explore the paradoxical quality of the mask as both facilitating transformation and being itself exceptionally inanimate. Second, it will be argued that this paradox may be resolved by seeing both mask and metamorphosis as two sides of a coin: the coin of questionable presence. This will be tied into the cult persona of mask-associated mixanthropes and into the observations already made concerning their extreme tendency towards mobility and absence.

A particularly clear example of the rôle of the mask in mixanthropic cult imagery is provided by the river-god Acheloos. Moreover, it is an aspect of his iconography which has received almost no attention in previous scholarship. Acheloos, therefore, will provide the main model for the argument, but other examples will be brought in where relevant.

Our most copious and consistent material regarding Acheloos and the mask is in the form of votive reliefs dedicated to Acheloos and a number of other deities (most often the nymphs, Hermes and Pan), most of which came from sites in central Greece, especially Attica.[1] These reliefs are numerous enough to allow analysis of the representational trends at work, some of which emerge very strongly. The god is depicted either as a human-faced bull, or as a mask looking out at the viewer from somewhere in the scene depicted (fig. 17, above p. 86). Interestingly, even when he has a body, his face tends to be mask-like: pronounced and sometimes disproportionately large. So both mask and mask-like face are possible.

---

[1] Examples are given at figs. 13 and 15-17.

The scene shown in the reliefs tends to be the interior of a cave, and as such mirrors the typical setting, in real life, of the cult itself; the sanctuaries we are dealing with here are almost all extraurban, and many sited in caves. So – although the deities themselves are of course supernatural beings – the reliefs depict what is in effect a realistic setting, and the Acheloos-masks are part of this: such masks as objects, in the round, have been found, and appear to have been designed to rest upon cult tables or to hang from a wall. All of which must prompt one to ask whether in the reliefs the masks are a manifestation of Acheloos' presence at all, or simply of a piece of cult 'furniture' which typically adorned rural shrines in actuality. However, this question is far deeper in its significance than one might think, and it will be argued below that one is not meant to be able to answer it. The masks themselves constitute a question.

Several other mixanthropes, both cult-receiving and not, share Acheloos' association with the mask. The *sine qua non* of divine mask-iconography is of course Dionysos, whose cult image in several places was a mask, and whose depiction, especially in vase-paintings, extends this association.[2] However, it could be argued that satyrs – figures in the surroundings of a god rather than gods themselves – provide the closest analogy to Acheloos. And they, like Acheloos, have the following aspects of the mask-association:

–   Actual satyr-masks were used in drama[3] and also appear in other ritual contexts,[4] though not necessarily in a form designed for wearing.

–   Satyr-faces without bodies are a frequent decorative motif in Greek art and architecture (see fig. 38).[5]

–   Even when satyrs are depicted with bodies and within narrative settings, their faces often have mask-like qualities,[6] for example staring eyes and – occasionally – full frontality.[7]

---

[2] For an example of Dionysos' cult image as a mask, see Paus. 10.19.3 on the god's worship at Methymna; the same phenomenon was known at Naxos (Athen. *Deipn.* 3.78c). See Otto (1965), 86-91; for the artistic treatment of Dionysos-as-mask, see Frontisi-Ducroux (1989).

[3] One striking form of evidence is the number of vase-paintings which show actors holding or wearing satyr-masks. A clear example is to be found at Bérard and Bron (1989), 143, fig. 195.

[4] For example, of all the mask-types represented in the finds from the sanctuary of Orthia in Sparta, a significant number are of the 'satyric' type, bearded and with animal ears. See Carter (1987), 355-60. Another interesting example is the masks found at Tiryns, which appear wearable rather than purely votive; on the rituals which may have included both the Spartan and the Tirynthian masks, see Jameson (1990).

[5] For example, they are fairly common among the motifs on terracotta antefixes: an example may be found in Padgett ed. (2003), cat. no. 59, pp. 251-3. On the mask-like faces of satyrs, see Frontisi-Ducroux (1995), 106-12: she makes the point that in such iconography there is no distinction made between the mask and the full-frontal face; this is interesting when compared with the rôle of both in the representation of Acheloos.

[6] In fact, there is often (deliberate) confusion in vase-paintings between men wearing satyr-masks and satyrs with their mask-like faces: see Bérard and Bron (1989), 143-5. Satyrs' faces would always have been reminiscent of the masks used to impersonate them.

So the satyric face with snub nose, beard and pointed ears would have been familiar as a face, and as a functional/ritual mask. The same style of face is shared also by centaurs, including Cheiron. It is the type which Acheloos also has.

Fig. 38

Thus one can discern what one might term a 'Dionysiac cluster' with regard to the mask or mask-like face. Another type is that of the gorgon, which has very similar manifestations as either the gorgoneion, a disembodied face with a decorative function (the decorative sphere accounts for the huge majority of gorgon-faces),[8] or as a mask-like face attached to a body, with the mythical identity of Medusa or one of her sisters. In this case, even more than the satyric, great emphasis is placed on the grotesque quality of the face and on its glaring eyes. The focus of the viewer is intended to rest almost entirely on this element, whereas mixanthropes like Acheloos and the satyrs have a more complex visual identity in which other anatomical parts, especially animal ones, are also of great importance.

1. Masks, costumes and transformation

In the last chapter it emerged how consistently mixanthropic deities were associated with metamorphosis, with changes in state. In light of this, it is on one level unsurprising to find them – and Acheloos in particular – associated with masks. Masks facilitate rôle-playing in many areas of ancient ritual. In the theatre they allow an actor to take on the being of the character he plays.[9] The theatre of

---

[7] See for example Bérard and Bron (1989), 156, fig. 215. Dionysos also is often shown on vases with the intense, full frontal face, as for example on the François vase, where, as Otto remarks (1965, 90), he is distinguished from all the other figures by his direct outward gaze. On mask and face imagery in vase-paintings of Dionysos and the satyrs, see Hedreen (1992), 169-70, with discussion of the ambiguous juxtaposition between fantasy and ritual reality in such scenes.

[8] On this, see Karagiorga (1970), 8-22 for the vexed, and still unanswered, question of primacy between the gorgoneion and the gorgon with body. For examples of gorgoneion-antefixes, see Padgett ed. (2003), cat. nos. 88 and 89, pp. 324-7.

[9] The importance in theatre of the transformational property of masks is emphasised by Lesky (1966), 223; see also Wiles (2004). At 245-6 Wiles remarks: 'The western and Islamic worlds are unusual in regarding the mask as a mode of concealment, not a mode of revelation and transformation.' I think there is room for both qualities; indeed, that they are in a functional interrelationship of some sort. As Napier says (1986, 3): 'The *potential* for ambiguity … remains fundamental to change despite any claims we might make about an inferred, innate or even empirically perceived identity, and disguise is, in our ontological experience, the primary way of

course comes within the sphere of Dionysos, and Dionysos is both a mask-associated god and a god of transformation, both his own and others'. More widely, in religious practice, masks are important for assuming a new identity in rituals that are as much transformational as mimetic.[10]

With regard more specifically to mixanthropes, we may see them as part of a broader connection between mixanthropy, metamorphosis and costume. There are two chief ways in which this connection is manifested. The first is more general, less specific to divinity: that costume is another (though less popular) way in which artists may choose to depict metamorphosis in a mythological scene. An example has already been mentioned above, in the previous chapter: the vase which shows Aktaion, as he transforms into a deer, not with any integral animal parts but rather as a human draped with a deer's skin. So, like mixanthropy, a costume may be used to suggest movement between human and animal.[11]

Second, costume is sometimes used as a way of explaining divine mixan-thropy, as when Herodotos tells us that Egyptian Zeus obtained his animal parts from an occasion in which he dressed in a ram's skin and head for the benefit of Herakles;[12] or as when Silius Italicus says that Zeus Ammon used to be a king with a horned helmet.[13] Particularly with the almighty Zeus, the peculiarity of a mixanthropic form is explained using costume and accessory, and the choice of this explanation is further indication of the underlying connection which existed between coverings and mixanthropy.

Mention of the horned helmet of Zeus Ammon raises the particular connec-tion of horns with the realm of costume and accessories, doubly worth noting here because masks and mask-like faces, in connection with Acheloos and with satyrs, are so frequently accompanied by horns. It was pointed out in Chapter 3 that horns constitute a form of superficial, non-integral mixanthropy; in addition, however, the way in which they are depicted often deliberately casts them as an attachment rather than a body-part. The so-called Ingot God of Cyprus, for

---

expressing this ambiguity. The use of disguise is thus conducive both to make-believe and to changes of state that are imputed to be real.' At the same time, it is certainly true that to regard the mask solely as a means of deception is to neglect the fact that for a Greek its effect was as much to transform as to disguise identity or state.

[10] An example comes from Arkadia: Pausanias tells us (8.15.3-4) that in the rites of Demeter Kidaria at Pheneos, the priest would don a mask of the goddess and then beat with a rod 'the *hypochthonioi*'. Jost argues, plausibly, that the masks allow the priest to become the goddess; she cites other examples of religious officials temporarily taking on the deity's identity. See Jost (1985), 319-22. On the power of the mask to cause a complete change of identity, and on the relationship between masks and identity in Greek thought, see Frontisi-Ducroux (1995), 39-44.

[11] A comparable case is a haunting described by Pausanias (6.6.7-11) in which the ghost, Lykas, who hovers dubiously on the animal/human divide, wears a wolf-skin as – I think – further expression of his uncertain identity. See Winkler (1980).

[12] Hdt. 2.42.

[13] Sil. 1.415.

example, wears a horned helmet,[14] and Near Eastern mixanthropes sometimes wear a crown of horns as a symbol of power and divinity.[15] The example of the Successors of Alexander and their royal iconography shows that horns may readily be assumed, put on, to make a particular claim of state and status; sometimes, Hellenistic monarchs are shown with horns growing organically from the skull, but in other cases what we see is a helmet or head-dress which might be donned and removed along with other regalia.[16] On the whole, Greek horned gods, unlike their Cypriot or Near Eastern counterparts, appear to have horns that are anatomically rooted; however, horns retain something of the detachable quality of an accessory. Removable faces are perhaps more striking than removable horns, but both fall under the same basic heading: expressions of the mixanthrope's ability to transform, and particularly to move from one side to the other on the animal-human scale.

There is another connection between metamorphosis and costume which should be noted: the (almost certain) existence of dances in which the practitioners used masks and costumes to 'become' certain birds and animals. Mute images themselves, such as the Lykosoura veil, can never give us reliable evidence for such rituals. But Lawler in particular, in numerous articles,[17] has assembled literary references which, though themselves not unproblematic, suggest that animal dances in costume did exist.[18] Given their rôle in theatrical contexts, we may be fairly certain she is right. And there is an undoubted relationship between such rituals and mixanthropy. The masked and costumed humans of comic choruses are in a sense the real-life counterpart of the mythical mixanthropes of the Dionysiac retinue, the satyrs and the Silenoi. All in all, it is no surprise that mixanthropes such as Acheloos should have this connection with masks and costume, given their abiding association with transformation, which masks and costume make possible both in the imagination and in real life.

So surely a mask-face, whether disembodied or with body attached, is an unproblematic item to find in the iconography of a god like Acheloos who is so consistently represented in literature as given to changes of form. After all, the function of the mask is reinforced in Acheloos' imagery by the depiction which

---

[14] This is the modern moniker of a mysterious figure seemingly accorded worship at Enkomi on Cyprus, depicted with a horned helmet; see Schaeffer (1965). Cyprus also provides the one unambiguous example of the depiction of horns being donned or removed: a number of clumsily-made terracottas showing humanoid figures holding horned masks before their faces. See Karageorghis (1971) figs. 1-5, pp. 265-8; id. (1996), ch. 1; Sophokleous (1985), 17; Burkert (1985), 65.

[15] An example is to be found in Athanassopoulou ed. (2003), cat. no. 24: Louvre AO 2752.

[16] Smith (1988), 39-45.

[17] Lawler's approach is best summed up in her 1952 article. For more species-specific studies, see Lawler (1941) and (1954).

[18] This is in addition to their undoubted rôle in Old Comedy.

apparently shows him wearing a human mask over an animal face.[19] What clearer expression could one have of the mask's rôle as facilitating a change of both appearance and state? And yet, it will be argued in the next sub-chapter that there is another side to the matter.

2. The mask as inanimate object

Masks may be heavily involved in the theme of transformation, but they are themselves strikingly inanimate. Masks of Acheloos and satyrs, like gorgoneia,

Fig. 39

are extremely common elements in decorative art and architecture, featuring frequently in jewellery and other small wares,[20] as well as on the decorative members of temples, for example terracotta antefixes (fig. 39). All over the Greek world, they would have been familiar in this aspect, as decoration. They were certainly part of the world of objects, things, furniture. Despite their connection with metamorphosis, therefore, it is striking to find them used to depict deities whose chief qualities are fluidity and changeability.

This relationship between static representation and dynamic metamorphosis becomes more pointed when we examine another aspect of Acheloos' iconography. In the reliefs here discussed, even when Acheloos is depicted not as a mask but as a three-dimensional anatomical entity, a man-faced bull, he tends to be shown as preternaturally, monumentally still. This is especially clear in figs. 13 and 16. The forms around him are clearly in motion, in fig. 16 dancing; he stands fore-square. If motion and flux are the essence of the hybrid, why is Acheloos typically so motionless?

---

[19] Isler (1970), cat. no. 170.

[20] An example is a small metal pendant in the form of Acheloos' head, from S. Italy and dating to c. 480 BC: *LIMC s.v.* 'Acheloos', cat. no. 136; see also Isler (1970), cat. no. 283; Paris Louvre Bj. 498.

This question becomes more interesting when we add in the fact that artists working from the Classical period onwards had a number of existing Acheloos-forms to choose from. One shows the god with a human neck as well as head (especially apparent in fig. 13); the other with bull's neck to accord with the animal body (fig. 15). Both these types are represented in the reliefs here discussed; but the reliefs preserve and favour the human-necked type long after it has been abandoned in other contexts. Whereas the bull-necked Acheloos tends to be depicted in smaller media, on coins, seals and small ornaments, the human-necked version almost certainly had its genesis in monumental forms, huge gate-guardians of the Assyrian palaces.

The artists of the reliefs could also have chosen another common river-god form, that composed of a human body, limbs and head, with animal horns and ears.[21] This form could be considered more anatomically convincing; but they declined to use it. It strikes me as extremely interesting that in cult imagery, Acheloos, explicitly the god of flowing waters and a fluid form, is represented using a form associated with, if anything, the massive and the immobile. This is chosen instead of types that are far more often used in scenes of movement and activity. The bull-necked version, for example, is very often shown in the position known as Knielauf, with front leg bent to indicate running.[22] There seems, however, to be a desire to keep the god as still and sculptural as possible: a stark contrast is created between his widely acknowledged associations with fluidity and change, and the immobility of his form in the reliefs.

Acheloos is not the only mixanthrope in whose case decorative depiction influences representation in other contexts. One of the most striking examples of this trend is the Sphinx. Several vase-paintings depict Oedipus and the Sphinx face to face, in the mythical context made famous by Sophokles. In textual sources, she is portrayed sitting on a crag, in line with the consistent monster/mountain connection; from this peak she flings herself when her riddle is solved.[23] Several vase-paintings, however, place her on a column. This and her stiff posture[24] show clearly that they are copying the Sphinxes of decoration, who are really quite different entities from the individual monster of that name in the *Oedipus Tyrannos*.[25] The rigid conventions of a decorative member have invaded the depiction of mythical narrative.

---

[21] This form is used of Acheloos on a coin of Metapontum, discussed in Chapter 1.

[22] This posture is also typically used for the gorgon Medusa, running from Perseus, and seems to have Eastern antecedents. See Burkert (1994), 82-7.

[23] See Paus. 9.26.2; Diod. 4.64.4. Apollodoros varies the motif by having her leap from the acropolis: *Bibl.* 3.5.8.

[24] A clear example of the rigid Sphinx facing Oedipus from her column is to be found on an Attic red figure amphora attributed to the Achilles Painter, mid fifth century BC. (*LIMC s.v.* 'Oidipous', cat. no. 14; Boston MFA 06.2447.)

[25] A famous example is the Sphinx dedicated at Delphi by the Naxians in c. 570-60 BC, which shows clearly the type being copied (*LIMC s.v.* 'Sphinx', cat. no. 31; Delphi Archaeological Mus.).

This example might almost be dismissed as a matter of artistic habit, its influences and stages of development. But in Acheloos' case there is more going on than a simple transference of architectural styles into other media. It is the contrast between mobility and immobility which sets his case apart, and on this the mask and the Mannstier (especially the human-necked form) work in concert. Both have dominant existing associations with objects and artefacts, with decoration and with material art. Depicting the god either as mask or as human-necked Mannstier is depicting him as an object, a piece of furniture almost. Constantly in these reliefs, then, we find depictions not of a living, moving deity, but of objects, inanimate representations. The Mannstier Acheloos has bulk and majesty but not life; he is an onlooker in the scene but not a dynamic presence. It is a particularly striking way of rendering a being who was so often associated with violent movement and change – with not only animation, but hyper-animation.

Fig. 40

The other deity who reveals this combination of the inanimate and the hyper-animate is Dionysos, who is, as was described in Chapter 2, a metamorphosist and even, in some contexts, a shape-changer, akin to Acheloos, and who also carries intense object-associations. The mask-properties of Dionysos have been noted; in addition, vase painting in particular engages in a sort of visual interrogation strikingly similar to that performed by the Acheloos-reliefs: that is, they question the relationship between living god and lifeless image. There are many different gradations of this theme. In its weakest form, it may be observed in a general tendency to depict Dionysos as physically still while the figures around him move more dynamically (for example in fig. 40). This tendency will be discussed in more detail in the next chapter. More extreme, however, is the frequency with which Dionysos is depicted in such a way as to make the viewer uncertain as to whether he or she is looking at a representation of the god, or at a representation of a representation of the god: that is, a painting of a statue. Depictions of the worship of Dionysos-masks make clear that an object is shown, and fig. 41 for example seems to represent a cult statue; but there are plenty of examples where such certainty is deliberately withheld and a stiffly positioned figure might be either god or image.[26] The confusion is deepened by the fact that, even where a ritual scenario appears to be shown (suggesting that one might reasonably expect the god to be in statue form), the attendant figures often have an element of the mythical – for example the inclusion of satyrs – which prevents a simple reading of the image as real-life cultic activity around a statue. Thus the iconography of Dionysos on vases, like that of Acheloos in the reliefs, deliberately poses a challenge to our understanding of what we see.

Fig. 41

So we appear to have a paradox at the heart of Acheloos' iconography. The significance of the mask as instrument of change and mobility seems to be undermined or even negated by its own status as an inanimate object, which is picked up on by other aspects of the reliefs. One could say that the very contrast is deliberate: that the highly static form works to counteract the fluidity of the being depicted. In the previous section it was shown that statues and other

[26] For example, a red-figure krater shows women adorning a seated statue of Dionysos; at least, we suppose it to be a statue because of their actions, but in itself it differs not at all from other depictions of the god sitting in which a statue does not seem to be meant (see Bérard and Bron [1989],183 and 201).

physical depictions of mixanthropes play an important rôle in the presence/absence discourse. The withdrawal or disappearance of a mixanthrope is sometimes expressed in terms of the loss or destruction of its cult image; likewise, bound mixanthropic statues show the importance of the image as a means of keeping the deity's destructive powers in check. (That said, the binding also suggests that sometimes a statue by itself is not enough; a further measure is required to ensure its immobility.) The cultic use of images as a means of containing, harnessing and manipulating dangerous divine forces is well-documented in the ancient material.[27] No doubt the extreme immobility of images such as Acheloos' reflects and counters, inversely, the extreme mobility of the deity himself. The final sub-chapter, however, suggests that rather than working in opposition, mobility and immobility actually converge on an important point, one of great importance to the mixanthropic deity.

3. Acheloos as 'not all there'

Mixanthropic gods are given to extreme mobility. They are metamorphosists; but they are prone to spatial movement as well as – or rather as a counterpart to – movement between states; this was shown in Chapter 4. The extreme form of spatial movement is disappearance: from a cult site, from the agricultural sphere, from the realm of the living. So the mobility of mixanthropes makes them beings of uncertain presence. Shape-changers are particularly prone to escaping mortal grasp and becoming absent. But if hyper-animation can cause (potential) absence, so can a lack of animation.

The god-as-object – as either mask or man-headed bull – questions his own presence. Are we looking at the god, among his fellow-gods, or are we looking at a thing? Is the god actually there in the scene, or just a simulacrum? We know that the mask may ask such questions because we have other material in which that appears to be its rôle. In a fragment of a satyr-play by Aischylos, the full story of which is not known, the satyrs of the chorus wonder at images of themselves, most probably masks or protomes, and the chorus-leader says of his likeness:

> It would give my mother a bad time! If she could see it, she would certainly run shrieking off, thinking it was the son she brought up, so like me is this fellow.[28]

---

[27] The most detailed discussion of the use of potent effigies in Greek religion is that of Faraone (1992).

[28] *P.Oxy*, 2162 fr. 1a, ll. 13-16: τῆι μητρὶ τἠμῆι πράγματ᾽ ἂν παρασχέθοι· | ἰδοῦσα γάρ νιν ἂν σαφῶς | τρέποιτ᾽ ἂν ἄξιαζοιτό θ᾽ ὡς | δοκοῦσ᾽ ἔμ᾽ εἶναι τὸν ἐξ-|έθρεψεν· For this text I use the translation by Lloyd-Jones given in Faraone (1992), 37. The fragment almost certainly comes from Aischylos' *Isthmiastai* or *Theoroi*, and is F 78a in Krumeich, Pechstein and Seidensticker edd. (1999); discussion at pp. 131-48.

There is a great deal of significance in this fragment, but for our purposes here, what it chiefly reflects is the fact that a mask holds out the appearance and the promise of a living presence, but in fact is no such thing; it is just an uncanny mimesis. Likewise, the Acheloos masks in the relief are emblems of the god, but not necessarily the god himself; we have already seen that they echo actual objects known to have been involved in the worship of Acheloos, and found more widely in cult and in general artistic representation. Implicitly, the Mannstier-type in its most monumental form carries the same uncertainty. Not only does it carry associations with inanimate objects; depicted in this form, Acheloos strikingly fails to interact with the other figures in the scene. Typically, the other deities shown – most often the nymphs and Hermes – hold hands in a kind of processional dance; their participation in group activity is physical and explicit. Acheloos is more detached. Whether his neck is human or taurine, he stands like a motionless adjunct. Interestingly, something of this quality is shared by his fellow-mixanthrope Pan when the latter also features in the reliefs. On the face of it, Pan looks far more dynamic; he is sometimes playing his pipes, presumably accompanying the dance and therefore participating. But he never holds hands with the others; he tends to be shown on a smaller scale and not as one of the choreographic rank. Moreover, when playing the pipes he looks out at the viewer[29] like the Acheloos-mask, and as with Acheloos this partly lifts him out of the company in the relief into the realm of the viewer whose gaze he returns.

So the stillness of the god as mask or as man-headed bull in fact accords with the mixanthrope's wider tendency towards questionable presence. There is more: another aspect of the imagery in the reliefs has the same import. When Acheloos is shown as a man-headed bull, his form is remarkably consistent, but there is one vital variable: the extent to which he intrudes into the scene. Sometimes his whole front half is within the 'frame'; sometimes his foreparts up to and including the shoulder; sometimes he is just a huge face in profile. Never is the whole god shown. To some extent, this must depend on how much space in the scene the artist wants to allow a bulky mixanthrope, but there is something else at work. Most interesting is the disproportionate face: it is essentially a mask in profile, and shows that the full-frontal mask is just the extreme point of a graded scale of absence and presence. The face itself is required to indicate identity;[30] but everything else may be made invisible, out of the picture. This allows the artist to depict the god as 'not all there', and for the reliefs as a group of artefacts to play with his variable presence/absence.

---

[29] On the significance in Greek thought of the pipe-player's full frontal face, see Vernant (1991), 125-9.

[30] For the face as essential for identity, see Plat. *Gorg.* 505d; *Tim.* 69a.

Mixanthropy and masks: conclusion

Thus mobility and immobility are two sides of the coin of potential absence. This convergence sheds light, I believe, on the quite wide-ranging connection between mixanthropes and masks. The connection is probably a 'spin-off' of the Dionysiac sphere, since it chiefly concerns figures who operate within that milieu. In Greek art, Dionysos himself is the mask-god *par excellence*, being depicted on vase-paintings especially as a full frontal face, or (with a little more context) as a mask on a pillar, or as a whole figure whose face has striking mask-like qualities. As with Acheloos, the mask's rôle in his iconography cannot be considered unrelated to the importance of metamorphosis and shape-changing in his persona, discussed above in the section on his composition.

Dionysos is also, as has been argued above, a god of sudden appearances and disappearances, and the trends of his representation – the depiction of the god not only as mask but also as quasi-effigy – build on the viewer's uncertainty as to whether the god is depicted as present, or simply a lifeless object. That other mixanthropic deities should take on this association reinforces a very important point: that we are right to see the absence/presence question as continuing to dominate their character and their iconography. Acheloos' case gives us a particularly valuable view of this theme at work in the imagery of cults active, in some cases, throughout the Classical period and into the Hellenistic. The theme is not just a feature of myth and literature: it is influential in the realities of worship and its settings.

Chapter IX

Mixanthropy and plurality

Introduction

The topic of this book is the mixanthropic deity as a named individual and recipient of cult. However, groups have been surfacing regularly; most recently it was seen that Acheloos overwhelmingly receives worship, and is depicted, as part of a group of divinities: the 'kourotrophic collective' in which Pan, and sometimes Cheiron, are also included. The religious functionality of this group, drafting in several deities to humanity's aid, is part of the story, but there is a representational dimension which also requires discussion. Plurality has a special relationship with mixanthropy. In the reliefs, Acheloos is named and identifiable, but there are cases in which the plurality of mixanthropes overrides individual identity and establishes instead a quality of the generic that is vital to the mixanthropic nature. Acheloos is a cult-receiving god, but mixanthropic plurality will take us away from the figure of the deity himself into his surroundings, his environs, a domain which cannot afford to be ignored since it illustrates some essential aspects of the meaning of mixanthropy in religious contexts.

1. The Lykosoura veil again

In Chapter 6, it was shown that Arkadia was not the repository of unambiguously depicted mixanthropic deities that its reputation would have one believe. Further, it was shown that mixanthropy, so far from being essentially primitive, tends in its established forms to be the process of an artistically dynamic society and of a corroborating process of visual repetition which fixes and canonises a form that is fundamentally fluid. For this reason, Attica gives us a larger number of actual mixanthropic depictions of gods than does Arkadia. However, Arkadia should not merely be dismissed as backward and inadequate. Though it does not give us clear representations of mixanthropic gods, yet it does provide the most valuable example of mixanthropic imagery in the environs of a deity: the carved drapery worn by the figure of Despoina in Damophon's statue-group in the sanctuary of Demeter and Despoina at Lykosoura.

Many temples and sanctuaries in the Greek world contained mixanthropic imagery. Famous examples such as the centauromachies at Athens, Olympia and Bassai were discussed in the Introduction; countless less patent instances abound in the archaeological record, reflecting the popularity of fabulous beings as decorative elements. However, what is typically lacking is any possibility of assessing the symbolic relationship between the mixanthropes and the deity. Even in the well-documented context of the Parthenon, it is debatable how centaurs related to Athene, the temple's chief occupant. There is certainly room for a systematic study of mixanthropic imagery within sanctuaries; such a study would probably reveal meaningful trends. But without this comprehensive treatment, few individual instances allow for a satisfactory analysis of meaning. However, Lykosoura is different. We know, thanks to Pausanias, the main myths surrounding Demeter and Despoina, myths which linked the sites of Phigalia, Thelpousa and Lykosoura, myths full of metamorphosis and mixanthropy; we also have some awareness of the cult at Lykosoura. We can examine the mixanthropic imagery there in the light of this background knowledge.

The carved veil has already been described in Chapter 6, and can be seen at fig. 30. The marine thiasos in the upper half is a favourite decorative theme from the fourth century BC onwards, but the figures in the lowest register are more unusual, dancers and musicians with animal heads among which various species are represented. So unique are these forms that they deserve to be regarded as having some special connection with the cult and its deities: but what connection? Who or what are the dancing people? Most scholars have been convinced that they depict masked participants in an orgiastic ritual such as was performed in the worship of Demeter and Despoina. The performance of such a ritual is plausible, though hard to prove, but nothing in the figures themselves suggests the presence of masks and costumes,[1] and they are just as likely to be fabulous beings as humans wearing fabulous disguises. The tone of the veil's carving as a whole is certainly more mythical than historical, given the marine creatures on the upper half, and the winged beings in the central register. Visual precedent in

---

[1] *Pace* Jost, who claims, 'les gestes sont humains, les pattes, lorsqu'elles apparaissent, sont figurées de telle sorte qu'elles peuvent fort bien recouvrir ou prolonger des membres humains.' Jost (1985), 329; cf. Jost (2003) and Jost (2008). She is not the only exponent, although she is an especially influential one. Once more using the mixanthropic artefacts from the site as the chief evidence, Loukas (1989) argues that animal masks were used in the Mysteries at Lykosoura to inspire ritual terror. The accompanying discussion of the use of masks to arouse strong emotion in ritual contexts is extremely valuable (cf. Lada-Richards [1998], 48, on the use of similar devices at Eleusis); but as usual the claims concerning actual rites performed at Lykosoura rest on a shaky basis – the enigmatic mixanthropic forms themselves. The same objection may be made to Loucas-Durie's discussion (1992) of orgiastic rites at Lykosoura, where it is claimed that 'Au *mégaron* de la déesse, les fidèles déguisés en animaux se livraient à un *drômenon* orgiastique' (page 87; similarly, Jost (2008, 105-6) interprets the terracottas as masked initiates. The layout of the megaron's remains contributes to the reconstruction of ritual, but most weight rests on the carved drapery and on the mixanthropic terracottas.

Greek art as a whole favours reading the dancing figures as a variation on the *thiasos* motif: imaginary beings dancing in honour of the goddesses, not deities themselves but closely allied to them.

What is important here is the abnegation of a mixanthropic deity *per se*. For all the rumours of a mixanthropic image of Demeter at Phigalia, Damophon was not interested in depicting either Demeter or her daughter as mixanthropic. Instead, mixanthropic imagery was included in a more marginal position, as ornament. Instead of a single, central mixanthropic image we have a series of small, anonymous figures, literally on the fringes. In addition to the veil, there were fish-tailed figures as decorative attachments on the goddesses' throne; also those mysterious terracottas showing ram-headed entities: in other words, no mixanthropic cult statue, but a profusion of surrounding mixanthropic figures, plural and anonymous. It is all too easy to assume that this manifestation of mixanthropy on the margins is the result of religious squeamishness, a reluctance to depict either Demeter or Despoina herself as a mixanthrope; and such depiction would indeed have been an iconographically drastic choice. But the peripheral mixanthropes should not be seen merely as the furtive inclusion of characteristics nervously displaced from the central position. On the contrary, the placing of mixanthropy in the surroundings of a deity has some early and important precedents, as does the plurality of the Lykosouran mixanthropes.

2. The Dionysiac thiasos and the Mistress of Animals

The animal-headed figures on the Lykosoura veil seem to be a variation on the groups of beings, generally dancing, which accompany the god Dionysos in visual representations from the early sixth century. These groups typically include various mixanthropes: most prominently the satyrs, but also Silenoi and Panes, and – less frequently and in different contexts – Acheloos. The *thiasos* is a matter both of artistic convention (the depiction of the god in the midst of a frieze of dancing forms) and of imagined 'life': when Dionysos is described in textual narrative it is often as with his *thiasos* around him, and this accords with his depiction in art. As an artistic motif, the *thiasos* is a particular favourite of vase-painters, and examples abound; an example is given at fig. 42.[2]

The mixanthropes of the *thiasos* are not the god; they are often divine or semi-divine, but the central figure and recipient of worship is Dionysos, and he is anthropomorphic. In Chapter 2, it was shown that mixanthropic depictions of Dionysos were not unknown in antiquity; yet they are few, and tend to be late, far later than the depiction of an anthropomorphic Dionysos surrounded by a mixanthropic retinue. The latter is clearly the earlier and more important type.

---

[2] On the treatment of the *thiasos* on vases, see Bérard and Bron (1989).

Fig. 42

That said, there is no doubt that the mixanthropes around Dionysos reflect aspects of the god. Though shown almost always as anthropomorphic, Dionysos was a shape-shifter in myth, particularly given to the adoption of animal forms. This manifestation of divine attributes in the immediate surroundings of the god rather than in his actual person is not limited to mixanthropy; another example is one of behaviour. As was observed in the previous chapter, Dionysos tends often to be shown relatively still and composed while his *thiasos* cavort around him; and yet we know from the textual evidence that he was considered himself as a being with the potential for violent movement and for loss of self-control. In the words of the Elean hymn, he is implored to come θύων – 'rushing' – and in Euripides' *Bacchai* he is described as dancing[3] and as accompanying his frantic celebrants.[4] However, even in that play the frenzied actions are more often performed by those around and affected by the god than by the god himself, who generally gives an impression of poise and calm. In myth too (for example that of the Minyades' punishment) chief emphasis is placed not on the god's own persona as wild and uncontrolled, but on his inflicting such a persona on others. In the same way, mixanthropy and animal metamorphosis are part of the god's nature, but far more obviously are inflicted on, and manifested in, people and beings in his vicinity. This is the case with the satyrs and other mixanthropes of his train, in whom animality and violent motion combine. So the case of Dionysos reveals a situation in which the mixanthrope is not the god, but reflects the god. Though

---

[3] Line 21, spoken by the god himself.

[4] See e.g. line 115 – Dionysos leading the *thiasos*.

the Lykosoura veil is a very different case, a piece of decoration on the edge of a statue-group, we can see how mixanthropy in the vicinity of a deity is used to reflect aspects of mythological significance while the anthropomorphism of the main image is maintained.

In the *thiasos*, plurality has implications for identity. Individual identity is subordinated to the identity of groups – satyrs, Silenoi, Panes, or, even more broadly, the *thiasos*. This is in striking contrast with the singularity of Dionysos, just as their marginality was in contrast to his centrality.[5] Plurality, marginality and a certain individual anonymity: these characteristics are naturally concomitant when mixanthropy occupies a deity's surrounds.

An illuminating counter-example of a rather different nature is the case of Circe and her treatment of Odysseus' shipmates. In Homer's narrative, the dangerous sorceress changes her victims into swine. Renderings of the story on painted pottery make some significant changes: first, the transformed men are shown as mixanthropes rather than as whole animals (this has been discussed in Chapter 7); and second, their animal parts include several species even within the same scene, not just pigs.[6] Though a desire for visual variety probably fuelled this, an additional aspect is that the abundance of species results in an arrangement far more analogous to the *thiasos* in terms of the features described above. Circe is shown surrounded by a frieze of largely animal-headed forms. She is not herself a mixanthrope or a metamorphosist, but she has the ability to inflict both these states on those in her vicinity. The mixanthropes around her are numerous and have no individual identity, at least as conveyed visually. The profusion of species is interesting. It recalls Lykosoura and the veil, because there too myth presents a single species (in that case the horse), whereas art opts for the maximum variety: horse, ass, fox, hare, and so on. Variety of forms within a *thiasos*-type scene seems a consistent artistic convention.

The resemblance of the Circe-scene on vases to the *thiasos* has been noted by Alexandridis.[7] It also, however, has another association, which is emphasised by Lawler in an article on animal dances in Greek culture: the figure of the *potnia thêrôn* or Mistress of Animals. 'There can be no doubt that Circe was at one time a lesser deity of the "Mistress of Animals" type.'[8] Doubt is in fact a reasonable reaction to such a blunt claim of hypostasis; and yet it remains true that aspects of

---

[5] Sometimes there is another singular figure within the hurly-burly of the *thiasos*: the god Hephaistos, returning to Olympos after his expulsion, escorted by the mixanthropes of Dionysos' train. For the Dionysiac imagery of this scene, see Carpenter (1986), 13-29.

[6] Homer does mention other animals bewitched by the sorceress (*Od.* 10.212-19), but Odysseus' transformed men are uniformly porcine. In Apollodoros (*Epit.* 7.14) their species are various (wolves, pigs, asses and lions); but it seems likely that he was influenced by the widespread artistic practice of showing them with such a variety.

[7] In a paper – unpublished – given at the Celtic Conference at the University of Lampeter (Aug. 30-Sept. 2).

[8] Lawler (1952), 317.

the Mistress of Animals type do tie in with some of the features of mixanthropic depiction which have been dealt with here. On the Minoan and Mycenaean gemstones, for example, animals and animal-*daimones* are interchangeable in the rôle of flanking attendants to female divinities. More generally, animals and mixanthropes rub shoulders in decoration, both cultic[9] and non-cultic.[10] So it could be said that in the case of a female deity or divine figure, mixanthropes in attendance indicate *potnia thêrôn* status. This would be an interesting (though by no means as clear-cut) counterpart to the Dionysiac *thiasos*: one a male context, the other female, both indicating the deity's dominance over the animal kingdom and nature more generally. Certainly this is the view of Lawler, who includes Lykosouran Despoina in her theory. Having described the animal-headed dancers on the carved veil of the goddess, Lawler concludes, 'Despoina is of course a Mistress of Animals, having close connections with Artemis.'[11]

However, such claims inexcusably elide the difference between attendant animals and attendant mixanthropes; surely the latter raise quite separate issues and have a quite distinct significance? Lawler (1952) deals with this question by arguing that attendant mixanthropes represent – or were once intended to represent – masked humans engaged in mimetic animal dances. In other words, depictions of a Mistress of Animals figure with attendant mixanthropes are the depiction of ritual. However, it is certain that the beings around Dionysos and around Circe (and probably those on the veil of Despoina) were conceived as supernatural beings. And there is a very simple element which distinguishes attendant mixanthropes from their wholly animal counterparts. That is, the strong theme of metamorphosis. Whereas the animals flanking a *potnia thêrôn* figure may be seen as chiefly subordinate to her divine power, a more complex relationship exists between beings like Dionysos and Circe and the mixanthropes around them.[12] As has been said, the mixanthropes reflect aspects of the central figure, and chief among such aspects is the property of transformation, of fluidity of form. Circe causes metamorphosis; Dionysos both causes and undergoes. In either case, given the functional connection, outlined in Chapter 7, between mixanthropy and metamorphosis, there is no doubt that that is what the mixanthropes around Dionysos and Circe chiefly represent. Wholly animal attendants

---

[9] For example, the carved decoration on and around the *polos* of the caryatid on the Siphnian treasury at Delphi incorporated both mixanthropes (satyrs) and animals (lions attacking a stag on the crowning capital). See Themelis (1992), 53.

[10] For example on Corinthian black-figure vases, on which the decorative friezes of forms include both real and fabulous (including mixanthropic) animals.

[11] Lawler (1952), 320.

[12] The servile nature of the animals in Circe's power is clear from Homer's description: lions and wolves that she has bewitched fawn on passing humans in an unnatural manner Hom. *Od.* 10.212-19). Perhaps we are to imagine them fawning on Circe, an image which certainly increases her resemblance to the figure of the *potnia thêrôn*. The mixanthropes ranged about her in art, however, present a rather different relationship.

would not carry this significance, and would not suit the thematic needs of such divinities. In the case of Despoina also, given the myth of metamorphosis in which her birth is framed, the transformational aspect of mixanthropic imagery adorning and surrounding her statue is quite appropriate. No ritualist theories are required to explain it.

So I would argue that while the figure of the *potnia thêrôn* bears some similarities with that of the divinity attended by mixanthropes, the latter has far more to do with the transformational milieu of Dionysos. After all, the cult of Despoina, like that of Dionysos, was one of mystery and revelation, and in both these, movement between states is a central theme.

It should be noted that mixanthropic retinues or attendants of deities have a long, though not straightforward, pedigree. Especially hard to interpret is the material from the Mycenaean and Minoan cultures; the seals and sealings, which form the bulk of the evidence,[13] are extremely problematic, not only because of the highly mysterious imagery they contain, but also because it is hard to be certain whether in general the unusual forms which appear on them so frequently – typically referred to as demons or genii – are indeed mixanthropes in the true sense.[14] Most look more like animals standing on their hind legs, normally with some form of clothing or covering to complicate the issue.[15] They certainly present a blurring of the animal-human divide by placing animals in human postures, but seldom do so by showing actual anatomical combination. None the less, some patterns are noteworthy. Animal characteristics are almost never invested in a single, central figure. Centrality is almost always the preserve of a single humanoid figure, around which monstrous, mixanthropic or animal forms are grouped.[16] They appear to hold an auxiliary function, rather

---

[13] On the nature of these artefacts and their imagery, see Higgins (1981), 180-88. A brief discussion of the fantastical imagery is to be found in Vermeule (1964), 284-9.

[14] There are a few cases where an animal head and torso appear to be attached to human legs and feet; an example may be seen in Kenna (1960), 56, fig. 117 (LM II basalt lentoid, Oxford Ashmol. Mus. 1938.1071). However, as Kenna himself observes with regard to such a type, it appears in part to result from the 'torsional tendency' of the art of the time, a trend which increasingly divides the body of the subject into upper and lower half, encouraging experiments in hybridism quite different from the genii in whose depiction animal and human parts are by no means graphically partitioned.

[15] For discussion of these figures and the questions surrounding their identity, see Nilsson (1971), 376-81; Hooker (1976), 199-201; Marinatos (1993), 196-7. Ultimately their identity and rôle remain almost entirely mysterious. The most common, and most sensible, expedient has been to refer to them as daimones or genii, which acknowledges both their supernatural quality and the fact that they appear, from their often servile positions in the imagery involved, not to be deities of the highest status.

[16] Prent makes the important observation (2005, 185) that mixanthropes on their own (rather than flanking a deity or in a group) appear *relatively late* in Minoan art. Their participation in group-scenes is their earlier manifestation rather than a consecutive development.

than being the chief recipients of worship in their own right.[17] The monstrous forms on the gems often perform tasks such as bearing vessels and other objects before a (presumably) deity. This trend accords with Near Eastern imagery, in which monstrous and mixanthropic forms are very often in subordinate positions; they are also typically plural. It is impossible to establish the connections and influences between these cases and the Classical imagery of Dionysos and Circe, but one can be certain that mixanthropic retinues and attendants are no fifth-century innovation, and are historically not limited to Greek culture either.

3. Pan, or Panes?

Within the *thiasos*, as within the nymph-reliefs containing Acheloos, one can discern named individuals. However, many beings included have a group rather than individual identity, such as the nymphs and the satyrs. Moreover, mixanthropes who have an individual identity often carry a generic one in addition, and the interplay of individual with generic is of the greatest significance. The most striking example of this interplay is Pan.

Pan is a figure whose Classical and post-Classical manifestations in iconography are dominated by the interchangeability between, on the one hand, a single figure with individual identity and, on the other, a being whose identity is generic rather than personal. Like Acheloos, Pan is often represented in company, either with Dionysos and his retinue, or (in cult imagery) with the nymphs, Hermes and Acheloos. Unlike Acheloos, his collective identity has another strand: he can appear in plural, as several, or pairs of, Panes. Panes appear on vases and other popular media from the Classical period onwards,[18] and the first literary reference to the plural is in Aristophanes.[19] On the whole the plural form appears more in non-cultic imagery, though there are exceptions.[20] So the appearance of Panes in non-cultic art, especially Attic pottery, is roughly contemporary with the flowering in popularity of the single form, and also with his arrival into Athens as a cult-receiving deity. However, it is tempting to ask whether there are in fact

---

[17] Marinatos (1993, 196-7) argues that in Minoan artefacts one may discern a hierarchy among the figures whereby quasi-animal 'demons' are subordinate to anthropomorphic deities but rank higher than simple animals, which they often hunt and kill. The various interrelationships are clearly illustrated by the images he gives on pp. 198-200.

[18] For multiple Panes, see *LIMC s.v.* 'Pan', cat. nos. 133-5; attending other gods, *ibid.* cat. nos. 190-243.

[19] Aristoph. *Ekkl.* 1069.

[20] Paus. 8.37.2 tells us of a relief showing nymphs and Panes on the portico of Despoina's temple at Lykosoura. Iconographically, the link between nymphs and Pan is of course a consistently strong one (see Larson [2001], 96-8 on their cultic relationship), although in votive reliefs with the nymphs (and Acheloos) Pan tends to be singular rather than plural; multiple Panes are more frequently found in non-cultic depictions.

early variants of the plural Pan form among the anonymous mixanthropes of the archaeological record. A particularly attractive possibility is presented by the small bronze group from Methydrion in Arkadia (fig. 22) showing a circle of animal-headed forms, perhaps dancing, humanoid in body or at the very least of humanoid upright posture. As was said in Chapter 2, these have been regarded by some as antecedents of the 'upright goat' Pan-type seen on a few Attic black figure pots. Their date is not precisely known (they are either seventh or sixth century), but they seem to predate any named individual Pan: should they therefore encourage the idea that Pan's earliest form was a plural rather than singular one, and that the specific grew out of the generic?

This is problematic and proof is not forthcoming. The Methydrion figures are mysterious, and to label them as Panes is highly conjectural; in any case, a focus on the original form of a deity is rarely sustainable.[21] It is in fact more fruitful to remark on the coincidence of singular and plural, the fact that at the same time and within the same media Pan could be both an individual and a type. This duality raises a question over every Pan image: is it Pan, or *a* Pan? Even when he is represented singly, the generic identity is bound to have been in the back-ground. A modern counter-example might be a stuffed toy in the form of a cartoon cat. Such an object is both Garfield and *a* Garfield, and the two identities are not really in conflict.

The tendency of mixanthropes to have a plural and/or generic dimension of this kind is intriguingly strong. The satyrs always have this identity, and know no other. On the other hand, there are Silenoi, but there is also Silenos, who is a personality in his own right. The centaurs have in their past the shadowy character Kentauros, though in a sense an eponymous ancestor-figure has a rather separate *raison d'être*. Even Cheiron, that most singular centaur, has a little flicker of plurality: Kratinos wrote a comedy called *Cheirones*, 'the Cheirons';[22] the group-centaurs may also be viewed as his plural equivalent. The Sirens operate collectively in myth, but cult does something to distinguish individuals, especially

---

[21] Nilsson certainly oversimplified the situation when he declared that plurality of divine figures was always a sign of the very earliest forms of deity and cult. His theory was that groups of deities were largely a feature of the earliest forms of nature-worship, since an awareness of the numinous character of landscape – the sacrosanctity of all groves, springs etc. – naturally lends itself to plural rather than singular divinity. There is a great deal of truth in this; but in focusing on origins, Nilsson's observation neglects the tendency for retrogressive, archaising developments such as we find in the Attic treatment of Pan and Acheloos. The sacred cave in Attica from the Classical period onwards may be seen as recreating, in a new context, what were felt to be essential and primordial features of the deities involved. Mannhardt takes a similar line to that of Nilsson, suggesting that, at the earliest stage of Greek religious development, the countryside was felt to be haunted by various nature-daemons, the fore-runners of Silenoi and satyrs. See Mannhardt (1877), 132-48; see also Nilsson (1972), 10-14.

[22] See Heath (1990), 148. Heath translates the title of the play as 'Cheiron and his Companions', but this does not remove the peculiarity of the plural; surely Kentauroi would be the expected group term.

Parthenope. On the whole, it is generally non-cult-receiving mixanthropes who have a strongly plural dimension. Sometimes, the same physical form is shared by, on the one hand, a singular being who receives cult, and plural ones who do not: this is the case with Proteus and Triton, the latter a being whose plural dimension is strongly represented in visual media, especially in the context of the marine *thiasos*. On the whole there appears to be a correlation between singularity and status. Qualities of wisdom and power, especially prophetic, attach more strongly to single mixanthropes than to pluralities. Qualities of the ludicrous, the violent, the wild, are slightly more strongly attached to groups, though a singular figure like Pan certainly has his share.

There are many divine pluralities at work in the Greek pantheon, some of them recipients of cult. The nymphs are the most famous plural constituents of the kourotrophic collective; there are also vengeance-related pluralities called variously the Semnai Theai, Eumenides and Erinyes; and there are masculine pluralities such as the Daktyloi, the Telchines and the Kabeiroi. Sometimes an individual name is known, or more often a list of names, but this is not always required by either religious or narrative context. On the one hand, several mixanthropic gods clearly belong to this religious sphere where generic identity is important; on the other, individual identities emerge more strongly among divine mixanthropes than among the above pluralities, and the result is an abiding relationship between the named and the anonymous, the individual and the generic, which is never fully dissolved.

Conclusion

Plurality and anonymity attend the mixanthropic form in its decorative manifestation, ubiquitous in Greek art from the frieze-patterns of Korinthian pots to the hybrid forms in jewellery and other small wares. Sometimes one suspects that a specific identity lurks behind an image; at other times it is probable that the ancient viewer would have had none such in mind. For mixanthropes to appear together, in nameless pairs, sequences and clusters, would have been a visual cliché in the ancient world, too prevalent to excite notice.

Yet this is plainly more than just a case of artistic convention, the aesthetic and technical desirability of repeat-patterns. It has been shown that the plurality and anonymity of mixanthropes are of considerable religious significance as well. In certain contexts, it suits an artist or a narrator to turn away from the single named form, and this abnegation is not just a matter of trend-following. In fact, plurality and anonymity are in some ways particularly suited to what a mixanthrope stands for. In terms of symbolic expression, there are some things which the group can achieve that the individual cannot.

Looking back over the last four chapters, we may see that plurality of forms in particular is inherently suitable for mixanthropes given their nature as embodiments of metamorphosis. Their frequent depiction in votive reliefs and friezes, rather than as separate figures in the round, is significant here. More than a single effigy, a frieze allows for a certain amount of (implicit) narrative, movement and change. The eye travels over its surface taking in a sequence of forms. Whereas a single effigy freezes its subject absolutely in the moment, the frieze – somewhat like a cartoon-strip – gives him space within a little story, in which movement and change are not wholly eradicated. We have seen that the mixanthrope bows to, and compensates for, the impossibility of depicting transformation in art. But perhaps the frieze does something more to counteract the static nature of the visual image. The figures on the Lykosoura vestment certainly make the most of this possibility: the variety of species represented, like the analogous variety among the victims of Circe, increases the sense of transformation within the line; and the figures are engaged in the lively movement of the dance. The ways in which the medium of the frieze manipulates the conjoined ideas of mobility and immobility were explored in the previous chapter, in relation to Acheloos. Dionysiac imagery is dominated by the same basic duality in the relationship between the still god and the moving forms around him; and the plurality of the *thiasos*, the way in which its proportions make the viewer's eye travel along its length, taking in variation and sequence, certainly enhances its dynamism.

Away from purely visual terms, what plurality allows is the transcendance of individual identity. Mixanthropes are boundary-crossers, always potentially metamorphic, not restricted to a single shape, and it seems that they are also unwilling to be confined within a single identity as imposed by the rigid limits of the singular. By being part of a group and by being many, mixanthropes have a flexibility and a divisibility which accords well with their general fluidity of form and character. Essentially, plurality expresses the same qualities as do the processes of metamorphosis and shape-changing, and though plurality is by no means limited to metamorphosists it and the ability to transform make a powerful semantic combination.

It has also been shown that mixanthropy in its plural form sometimes occupies not the person of the god but his surroundings. This has implications for our modern understanding and approach. The mixanthropic god has great symbolic power, but it is wrong to expect the qualities of any deity always to be coterminous with his anatomy. Some deities are depicted without mixanthropy of their own but rather radiate mixanthropy, projecting their properties of metamorphosis and combination onto their immediate environs. Why not? Gods are not, as humans are, discrete bodies with more or less solid limits and boundaries. They are complex clusters of meaning and association, whose semantic force forms an aura around them. This is the case with all deities, but some in particular seem especially ill-suited to the restriction of fixed, single identity. Mixanthropy is one way of circumventing this restriction, another is metamorphosis, a third is plurality; all three are used, often in combination, to depict beings for whom the single, stable and united anatomic form is just too simple. For deities, physicality is always a potential source of limitation; it struggles to accommodate the divine, and so does representation. This struggle is the subject of the final chapter of this book.

Chapter X

Gods, monsters and imagery

Introduction

During Section Three of this book, it has been established that mixanthropic deities had a special relationship with the theme and the process of representation. Mixanthropes do not – cannot – exist in nature, and so to depict them is not just an act of mimesis but the conception of something extraordinary; it is, in a sense, a type of creation, of giving form and substance to the impossible. It is more than depiction. In addition, it has been shown that the representation of a mixanthrope was in essence the representation not just of a thing but of a process: the process of metamorphosis. So as well as showing what cannot exist, a mixanthropic image shows what cannot be shown, movement and change. It does not just depict, it also fixes, captures, holds. This is art working as hard as it can be made to work.

It has also emerged that themes of representation played a significant rôle in the characterisation of certain mixanthropic deities, chief among them Acheloos. By highlighting their identity as objects, by using art to depict art rather than an unambiguously animate subject, the Greeks were able to find in the visual dimension an extension of a theme strongly represented in literature: the theme of questionable presence. Is that a god, or the lifeless image of a god? Is the god here? Such questions are posed by the iconography of Acheloos and, closely linked, that of Dionysos.

Modes of representation are more than just artistic convention or convenience; the Greeks were quite capable of manipulating their own conventions for expressive purposes, and in any case conventions do not emerge from a vacuum but from a communicational need. So with the iconography of Acheloos; so also with the predominance of mixanthropic plurality and marginality discussed in Chapter 9. Time and again, the most technical aspects of representation have been shown to be in a symbolic relationship with the personae of mixanthropic deities, and would be ignored at our peril. Their thematic correspondence with the themes identified in the literary record is striking.

And yet: it should not be overlooked that the representation of gods generally carries its own ancient discourse. It has been said that the representation of metamorphosis poses a challenge; but representing the numinous, representing divinity, is surely inherently challenging as well. Divinity is a property as subtle as the mobility of the mixanthrope; it is far more than the deathlessness which is its fundamental basis. Moreover, gods, like mixanthropes, are beings which do not appear in the daily lives of mortals on a regular basis (though their effects are of course perceived, and communication is possible), so that their depiction, like that of mixanthropes, has an element of creation in it; it certainly does not simply depict what is patent and visible to human eyes. This chapter contextualises the relationship between mixanthropy and depiction by discussing the wider questions and tensions which, in ancient thought, surround the physicality of gods and their visual representation.

1. Depicting the divine

In one sense, representing gods and goddesses in Greek culture is extremely straightforward. The anthropomorphic form which dominates Greek iconography presents an unambiguous convention by which the 'base' of any divine portrait is an idealised humanoid form which fits into one of the universal sculptural types: bearded older man, beardless youth, beautiful woman. Onto this generic template are added 'accessories', items of clothing or equipment, attendant objects or animals, which give the deity individual identity and also symbolise his or her particular powers and functions. This convention of the symbolically supplemented anthropomorphic form would have been quite easy to 'read' as well as to create.[1] A Greek would be able to look at a depiction of Artemis with hound at heel, or one of Apollo crowned with laurel, and understand at once how these iconographic elements fitted in with the characterisation of the deity and his or her divine function. Certainly there were depictions whose symbolism was more puzzling, such as an armed Aphrodite, and such peculiarities excited comment and explanation. Still, it is not in doubt what such representations were, namely a combination of the mimetic and the symbolic. It is odd to speak of mimetic (or veristic) art in the case of beings who were not commonly seen. Art did not simply capture how the gods were, but how they were imagined to be: a kind of mimesis of the imaginary. But there was a strong convention about the gods' appearances, reinforced in both the visual and the literary domains, a convention with, for the most part, pan-Hellenic currency. At first glance, this iconographic system seems uncomplicated, and an example of the famous rationalism which used to be attributed to the Greeks before

---

[1] Mylonopoulos (2010b) discusses the semantic use of attributes, and points out that their 'readability' in antiquity would have derived in part from their combination with other elements, such as *epikleseis* and setting.

Dodds valuably muddied the waters. The gods look like us, and act rather like us, so imagining and depicting them are unproblematic.

There is, however, more to the matter than that. It is important to distinguish between two basic types of religious imagery. On the one hand are depictions and descriptions of the gods in the godly sphere pursuing their divine 'lives'; examples would be gods featuring in mythical scenes on vases, or Homer's accounts of quarrels on Olympos. On the other are depictions and descriptions which involve some contact and interaction between gods and humans. On an imaginary level, this might take the form of a mythical encounter between god and human; in real life, images of the gods were of course heavily involved in ritual. It is in these contexts where the god has to be depicted in such a way as to effect interaction with humanity that the tensions and the complications seem to reside. To depict the appearance of a god is relatively straightforward; to depict the meeting of human and god is far less so. For all the apparent simplicity of anthropomorphism, its limits are revealed once interaction is in the frame.

In Herodotos 1.60.4, the exiled tyrant Peisistratos engineers his return to Athens by making it seem that Athene favours his recall. In order to do this, he turns up with a fake Athene, a mortal woman of unusual height and beauty (she is *eueides*); he arrays her in the armour which the people would expect Athene to wear, and generally makes the spectacle of her appearance on the scene as impressive as possible. The success of his ploy suggests that the people of Athens have a basic idea of the goddess's appearance which a tall and attractive mortal, suitably decked, can easily fulfil. The historicity of the episode is irrelevant here; its import is the suggestion that, apparently, epiphanies are so straightforward that they can easily be staged by a wily statesman. And yet, even a brief inspection of the *genuine* epiphany in literature reveals other aspects.[2] The most telling is the prevalence of disguise. Some disguises involve a drastic transformation, for example into the form of an animal as in the many couplings of Zeus with mortal women. In other cases, however, the situation is subtler: the form of the deity is not unlike that which all the evidence encourages us to think of as their 'normal' one, and yet some word or phrase – such as *eoikôs*, resembling[3] – suggests that once again the adoption of a temporary guise is what is being described.[4] Nowhere in the ancient literary corpus – outside the atypical ranks of philosophers – is it suggested that the *true* form of god lies entirely outside the physical, is entirely ineffable or impossible to depict; basic physicality, normally anthropomorphic, is routinely assumed. Epiphany narratives and the prevalence of disguise suggest, rather, that some alteration or concealment of form is a prerequisite of mortal/immortal communication.

---

[2] On the imagery of epiphanies, see Versnel (1987).

[3] See e.g. *Hom. Hymn* 7 (to Dionysos), line 3: the god appears 'like a young man'.

[4] Versnel (1987), 45.

An especially telling example is the account in the *Homeric Hymn to Aphrodite* (5) of how the goddess, having fallen in love with the young mortal Anchises, contrives to encounter him on Ida. Aphrodite chooses to appear 'like a pure maiden in height and mien' so as to avoid frightening Anchises;[5] intriguingly, he is not at first taken in by this, and continues to appeal to her as to a deity, until she manages to persuade him of her humanity with cunning words; the disguise by itself was not enough to conceal the signs of divinity.[6] These signs are revealed in full when, her erotic mission accomplished, Aphrodite resumes her undisguised form, which is typical in its details: unearthly beauty, superhuman stature, and a kind of radiance or luminescence.[7]

As Buxton emphasises, when gods reveal their true form to mortals in situations like this, the response is astonishment and awe.[8] There are extreme forms which suggest that undisguised divinity is not only frightening but actually dangerous; the most famous such case is the fate of Semele, burned up by a direct, unshrouded epiphany by Zeus.[9] Such a contingency, however, is rare; more often the impression received is simply that for human and god to interact some mitigation or alteration of divine form is required. Contact is by no means as direct or simple as anthropomorphism might lead one to expect; a mediating mechanism is required. Sometimes, intriguingly, this takes the deity further away from the very anthropomorphic form which might at first seem such a promising and easy one for purposes of communication and interaction; the majority of Zeus' erotic conquests are the perfect example of this. Rather than exploiting the basic compatibility of form that anthropomorphism provides, authors frequently have the god shroud his divinity in animal (or other non-anthropomorphic) form, which of course offers greater concealment but shows that we cannot take anthropomorphism as a guarantee of uncomplicated interaction, even in the mythological sphere.

Such mechanisms for interaction remain pertinent when one turns to the visual domain and to the realm of ritual, away from the heroic territory of literature in which gods and heroes regularly interact. It has been argued in this

---

[5] *Hom. Hymn* 5.82-3.

[6] This is not the only case of unsuccessful divine disguise in ancient literature: a famous example occurs at Hom. *Od.* 22.203-214. Athene chooses the guise of an established comrade of Odysseus in order to advise the hero, but interestingly Odysseus sees through her disguise, though he chooses not to make this fact obvious, 'playing along with' the deception. This subtle play emphasises the closeness of hero and deity; disguise facilitates contact, but does not then circumscribe it. On epiphanies in the *Odyssey*, see Buxton (2009), 29-48.

[7] Beauty-designating adjectives and epithets of goddesses fill, for example, the *Theogony* of Hesiod, such as *liparos*, which also implies shining (see e.g. line 901 where the word is used of Themis), *kallikomos* and *kallipareios* (e.g. lines 915 and 270 respectively), *thaleros*, which suggests bloom and abundance (used e.g. of Hera at line 921), and many more. On these qualities of divine physicality, see Gladigow (1990), 98-9.

[8] Buxton (2009), 157-90.

[9] Apollod. *Bibl.* 3.4.3.

book that the presence of mixanthropic deities was essentially unreliable, but it will now be shown that this unreliability must be viewed against the wider tensions surrounding divine presence more generally. These tensions are clearly illustrated by examining the rôle in ritual of the cult image. Did images in Greek cult allow deities to be present and involved in ritual in an unproblematic way?

A great deal of recent debate has focused on the precise meaning of 'cult image', and whether the concept is in fact sound when held up against ancient attitudes and practices. In particular, it has been argued, not without good reason, that it is mistaken to draw a clear distinction between cult images and votives, and especially to claim that only cult images could represent or facilitate divine presence.[10] This argument is a sound one, and yet for the purposes of the current chapter its implications are not as vital as they might seem. The ensuing discussion focuses on images which are the direct recipients of ritual attention and which would traditionally be designated as cult images rather than votives, but it is not my intention to suggest that the epiphanic properties they will be shown to possess are not shared, in varying ways and degrees, by other forms of divine representation in cultic contexts.

The Greeks did not think that cult images *were* deities in a permanent and coterminous sense. The fact that ancient authors frequently use a god's name to refer to his image is interesting, but does not indicate a failure to recognise the difference between god and image; rather, it reflects the existence of a common verbal shorthand not unknown today.[11] (If I say that I have two dogs on my mantelpiece, the reader understands that these are dogs of china, not of flesh: context is everything.) The Homeric depiction of the Olympian gods living on Mount Olympos surely reflects popular imagination down through the Classical period and beyond, and other deities dwelt elsewhere, Pan in the wooded glens of Arkadia, Thetis in the depths of the sea, and so on. They were not fixed in their sanctuaries; rather their mobility was extreme and superhuman, allowing for lighting-swift passage over land and sea, and sudden appearances in the world of men.

And yet at times their presence and participation are essential. Ritual hinges on acts of communication, chiefly the speaking of prayers and the giving of gifts, both of which hope for some response, some return. Gods are partners in a system of reciprocity, and for this to function properly, some form of ritual interaction is required. How can this be managed, when gods are both mobile and (if they choose to be) distant?

Images do seem to provide the chief answer to this conundrum. Scholars have shown that certain symbolic acts had the purpose and function of 'activating' a cult image so that it could be a participant in worship and allow for com-

---

[10] See e.g. Scheer (2000), esp. 130-43; Mylonopoulos (2010a), 3-6.

[11] On this tendency in ancient literature and inscriptions, see Scheer (2000), 50-53.

munication between humans and deity. In particular, Pirenne-Delforge has demonstrated that some form of ritual *hidrysis*, or setting up, tends to be involved as a way of 'switching on' an image; thereafter, regular ritual tendance maintains its activation.[12] The forms which such tendance took could often be strongly suggestive of the identification of statue with deity: rituals of washing, feeding, dressing and even beating of statues[13] are the most striking examples of such an identification, but there are more subtle manifestations, such as the frequent emphasis on the statue in a temple being allowed to see and hear ceremonial approaches.[14]

Such direct approaches and forms of tendance are one illustration of the fact that, for the Greeks, the gods were capable of being their images, not permanently, not indistinguishably, but in certain specific situations. Perhaps 'inhabiting' is a better word than 'being': Scheer has shown that the word *hedos* was frequently used to describe a cult statue, and that this term, meaning 'seat' or 'base', reflects how the statue was thought to function as a facilitator of divine presence: "Εδος wäre dann etwas, auf dem oder in dem die Gottheit Platz nimmt, wo sie sich gerne aufhält, ohne aber zwanghaft dort festbunden zu sein.'[15] Ritual might provoke the deity into residing within an image, but the image should not be seen as the permanent embodiment of the god.

Something of this subtlety may be seen in book 6 of Herodotos, in a story about the family of the Spartan king Ariston. Ariston's baby daughter is ugly, and her nurse, in order to enlist divine remedy, takes the baby daily to the sanctuary of the cult-heroine Helen.

> Every time the nurse carried the child there, she set her beside the image and beseeched the goddess to release the child from her ugliness. Once as she was

---

[12] See Pirenne-Delforge (2008b) and (2010), esp. 126-9.

[13] Sacred laws, for example, provide plenty of examples of such treatment of statues. Washing is prescribed in *IG* II² 659 (line 26), an early-third-century BC decree concerning the sanctuary of Aphrodite Pandemos at Athens; the robing of a statue in a peplos is to be found in *IG* I² 80, an inscription about the ritual rôle of the Praxiergidai at Athens (line 11). For discussion of such rites, see Gladigow (1985-6), 115-6; Scheer (2000), 57-65; Bettinetti (2001), 137-60. When it comes to the ritual mistreatment of statues, the most graphic example is the Theokritos passage discussed in an earlier chapter (*Idylls* 7.106-10) in which Pan is threatened with whipping and other torments if he does not provide the Arkadian hunters with game. Because of the scholion on this text we know with reasonable certainty that it is the god's *statue* that would receive the whipping, but there is no mention of this in the poem ('if you do this, dear Pan, may the boys| of Arkadia not whip you with squills…'). Of course, this makes the address to the god more vivid and direct, but it goes beyond poetic effect to ritual sense: to whip Pan's statue was in a sense to whip Pan. This is reminiscent of the ritual use and abuse of amulets which was extremely prevalent in magical practice. (Ancient 'voodoo-dolls' – *kolossoi* – and the texts connected with them are collected and discussed in Ogden [2002], 245-74.)

[14] For example, during a large public sacrifice at the altar outside a temple the temple's doors were very often opened so that the offering was within the line of 'sight' of the statue within, as well as the statue being visible to the worshippers outside. See Scheer (2000), 61-5.

[15] Scheer (2000), 121; on cult images as vessels, see also Steiner (2001), 79-95.

leaving the sacred precinct, it is said that a woman appeared to her and asked her what she was carrying in her arms. The nurse said she was carrying a child and the woman bade her show it to her, but she refused, saying that the parents had forbidden her to show it to anyone. But the woman strongly bade her show it to her, and when the nurse saw how important it was to her, she showed her the child. The woman stroked the child's head and said that she would be the most beautiful woman in all Sparta. From that day her looks changed.[16]

In this story, the anxious nurse uses the cult statue as if it is the divine Helen – or at least as if it contains and may channel her powers. However, when help does come, it is not directly effected by the statue, but by a mysterious woman, whom we may take to be the heroine in disguise,[17] who is able to reverse the baby's ugliness just by stroking her head (physical contact is plainly crucial here). Here, then, epiphany and statue go together, and the nurse in effect provokes the manifestation by her appeal to the statue. The statue, then, is a point of communication, a proxy for the heroine's presence, a vessel of divine agency activated by prayer. A very similar character attaches to temples. *Naos* is linked to *naomai*, 'I dwell', yet permanent residence is not to be envisaged; as has been said, most of the gods were widely imagined to reside on Mount Olympos, far from their shrines and from mortal affairs. Temples could be visited by gods, temporarily inhabited,[18] just as cult statues could temporarily and partially constitute the divinity's presence in a kind of material epiphany.[19]

So cult images and – crucially – the ritual surrounding them were mechanisms for achieving and regulating divine presence. Their limits in this regard (the fact that they were not permanent or total containers of the god), and indeed the very fact that such mechanisms were necessary, reveals the extent to which attaining a

---

[16] Hdt. 6.61.3-5: ὅκως δὲ ἐνείκειε ἡ τροφός, πρός τε τὤγαλμα ἵστα καὶ ἐλίσσετο τὴν θεὸν ἀπαλλάξαι τῆς δυσμορφίης τὸ παιδίον. καὶ δή κοτε ἀπιούσῃ ἐκ τοῦ ἱροῦ τῇ τροφῷ γυναῖκα λέγεται ἐπιφανῆναι, ἐπιφανεῖσαν δὲ ἐπειρέσθαι μιν ὅ τι φέρει ἐν τῇ ἀγκάλῃ, καὶ τὴν φράσαι ὡς παιδίον φορέει, τὴν δὲ κελεῦσαί οἱ δέξαι, τὴν δὲ οὐ φάναι· ἀπειρῆσθαι γάρ οἱ ἐκ τῶν γειναμένων μηδενὶ ἐπιδεικνύναι· τὴν δὲ πάντως ἑωυτῇ κελεύειν ἐπιδέξαι. ὁρῶσαν δὲ τὴν γυναῖκα περὶ πολλοῦ ποιευμένην ἰδέσθαι, οὕτω δὴ τὴν τροφὸν δέξαι τὸ παιδίον· τὴν δὲ καταψῶσαν τοῦ παιδίου τὴν κεφαλὴν εἶπαι ὡς καλλιστεύσει πασέων τῶν ἐν Σπάρτῃ γυναικῶν. ἀπὸ μὲν δὴ ταύτης τῆς ἡμέρης μεταπεσεῖν τὸ εἶδος.

[17] Helen's rôle here is somewhat similar to that of Demeter in the *Homeric Hymn* and her treatment of the baby Demophon: an unrecognised goddess intervening to improve or elevate a mortal infant.

[18] Greek deities visit their temples rather as a medieval baron visited his hunting-lodges: for convenience and pleasure, and to receive fealty. A picturesque example occurs – again – in the *Homeric Hymn to Aphrodite* (5), in which the goddess uses her temple as a boudoir, a place to prepare herself for her seduction of Anchises. (See lines 59-64.)

[19] Some aspects of ritual highlight the epiphanic qualities of the cult image: see e.g. Broder (2008), 133, on types of 'theatre of revelation' whereby the image is suddenly displayed to watching worshippers, a practice especially associated with Dionysos (for an example, see Paus. 2.7). As Broder here points out, Dionysos is also the deity most often associated with processions which carry the deity from one ritual space to another, a reflection of his character as 'god of arrivals'. See also Gladigow (1985-6), 116-7.

god's presence is a difficult business and only ever successful in part.[20] It is important to acknowledge this as a wider backdrop to the tensions and uncertainties surrounding the presence of mixanthropic deities. But what is really striking in the case of the latter is the extent to which the power of the cult statue to achieve at least limited presence and facilitate at least limited interaction actually appears to have been abnegated.

The first aspect to note is the complete absence of a single unquestionably proven mixanthropic cult statue. In the discussion of divine representation above, I have preferred the phrase 'cult image' to 'cult statue', to allow for varieties of medium, but in fact statues appear to have been favoured, almost without exception, as components within direct acts of worship. Mixanthropes, divine and otherwise, were favoured subjects in art, but one searches in vain for a case of a mixanthropic statue unambiguously present within a ritual context, receiving ceremony in the way described above. There is an obvious problem with an *argumentum ex silentio* of this nature: archaeological discovery and publication are patchy, and it is possible that a mixanthropic cult statue existed which has simply not been discovered. However, the shortage of ancient literary references to such statues is telling, especially given the probability that their iconographic peculiarity would have made them worthy of mention in the eyes of ancient narrators such as Pausanias. The one mixanthropic statue of which we have detailed mention is that of Demeter Melaina, and it has been shown that this object is shrouded in legend and cannot be asserted beyond doubt ever to have existed in actuality. Moreover, it was shown that Demeter Melaina's statue was a component within a well-developed *topos* of absence, and was more significant for this than for confirmed existence.

Even more significant than the scarcity of cult statues is the prevalence of an alternative mode of representation: the relief. Reliefs account for all the known representations of Acheloos in cult sites, and the great majority of Pan's also. They form the bulk of mixanthropic cult imagery across the board. It was demonstrated in the previous chapter that the relief accords with mixanthropes' tendency to be depicted as part of a plurality of beings, and also that it was powerful in its ability to convey narrative, movement and change, the essence of the metamorphic mixanthrope. At this stage, we may add another strand of significance: plurality is not the only feature of the reliefs worth noting here. After all, we hear of statue-*groups* in the key ceremonial position. Mylonopoulos has argued that a distinguishing feature of the cult statue or statue-group was that it depicted the deity or deities without a narrative setting.[21] Rather than being

---

[20] Interestingly, several ancient authors dealt playfully with the fantasy of statue and god being one, by having the statue speak as if this was so: a particularly full (and funny) example is Kallimachos' seventh *Iambos* in which a statue of Hermes narrates the vicissitudes which have befallen it. For discussion of the poem and of comparable examples, see Petrovic (2010).

[21] Mylonopoulos (2010a), 11-12.

shown immersed in their mythological deeds, deities in cult statue form are generally simply standing or sitting. Moreover, they relate chiefly with the viewer rather than with the other *dramatis personae* of a mythological episode. This is vital, as it allows for the sort of direct communication between worshipper and epiphanic cult statue that was described above.

So, not only was the function of reliefs in which Acheloos and other appeared chiefly votive, but their very form has implications for whether we read such images as an attempt to engineer divine presence. In the reliefs, Acheloos and Pan are part of interaction between divinities, in which the human viewer is not involved but is rather a bystander or observer. So reliefs do not appear to be evocative of presence in the way that a statue in the round, without narrative framework, may be. The persistent selection of the relief medium for Acheloos and others may be read as a disinclination to exploit the potential of visual depiction as a means of ensuring and regulating and harnessing at least temporary presence. And yet: as has been observed, Acheloos often appears to divide his interaction between his divine companions and the human viewer, by presenting outwards a full frontal face, by occupying a marginal position on the edge of the dancing band, and by declining to participate fully in its actions. Pan partly follows this ambiguous tendency. Thus the mixanthropic deities in the reliefs tantalise the viewer with uncertain communication, and once again, the deity's presence before mortals is profoundly questioned rather than in any way guaranteed: always possible, never certain.

Acheloos and Dionysos were also argued, in Chapter 8, to be subject to another representational trend: depicting them in such a way as to suggest that they are inanimate objects rather than 'living' gods. In a sense, this makes play of the cult image's potential to facilitate divine presence. Acheloos and Dionysos are depicted, sometimes, as 'mere' images, whose divine habitation is insecure. Is the image functioning as a *hedos*, is the god within it, or is it just an empty shell? Such questions seem teasingly to be posed. A cult statue itself, the real thing, may be a container for divinity, but the *depiction* of a cult statue, in a relief or a painted vase, is far more ambiguous, especially when its immobility is contrasted with lively, living forms shown moving around it.

It is interesting at this point to remind ourselves of some observations made in the Introduction to this book about the representation of monsters in ancient art. It was there asserted that in both Greek and – to an even greater extent – Near Eastern culture, depicting a monster was seen as capturing and harnessing its dangerous potential. Monstrous images are amuletic: they contain and channel the monster's powers. Not so the image of the mixanthropic deity. To depict a mixanthropic deity is to show its fluidity in a stable form, but the limitations of representation, its inability to contain and to control, remain to the fore. Likewise, no god may be reduced to an image, or fully controlled through representation, but mixanthropic deities seem to constitute an extreme form of this basic truth.

Or, to put it another way, mixanthropy is used as a way of conceiving and imagining deities who are especially resistant to confinement within the parameters of a single physical form, and for whom such resistance is a major element of their divine character.

The discussion of non-mixanthropic divine representation above, however, is not quite complete without acknowledgment of a slightly different class of cult images which in one sense do appear to bring mixanthropic and non-mixanthropic deities somewhat closer together. These are aniconic images, ones which do not follow the 'mimesis of the imaginary' which generally prevailed. Traditionally, aniconic images in Greek religion have been thought by scholars to consist of such objects as unworked stones, pillars, and wooden planks,[22] but the important recent study by Gaifman has established the importance also of what is termed 'empty space aniconism', that is cases where the deity is indicated by a pointedly framed space such as an empty niche or (most graphically) throne.[23] Empty space aniconism clearly functions differently from the anthropomorphic cult image; although something like a throne can serve as a *hedos* for divinity as an image can, the abnegation of visualisation is striking and acknowledges far more directly the impossibility of anchoring a deity permanently within a material container.

It is also possible to see aniconic images such as unworked stones as an expression of divine *absence*. Vernant has explained the religious potency of non-mimetic cult images in precisely these terms. He argues for a progression in Greek religious art from aniconic and very simple cult images towards the fully mimetic, a progression which is in part a modern variant on ancient theorising by such as Pausanias.[24] This evolution is not without problems; it does not really take into account Donohue's effective deconstruction of the evolutionary development of the cult image, for one thing. But even though the teleological aspect of his approach may be open to challenge, Vernant's remarks about what certain kinds of cult object were intended to accomplish are illuminating. His claims are made for the nebulous concept of the *xoanon*, and though this is a concept which does not really survive Donohue's work with any absolute meaning intact, his observations are still pertinent here. For Vernant, the crude *xoanon* is not an inadequate early attempt at verism, but powerful because it does

---

[22] Scholarly interest in such objects largely derived from their relative prominence within the work of Pausanias, who was plainly preoccupied by them and intrigued by their deviation from the anthropomorphic norm. See Pritchett (vol. 1, 1998), 97-170.

[23] Gaifman (2005), 170-95.

[24] Vernant (1991), 151-63. It is the major achievement of Donohue (1988) to have revealed the ancient discourse in all its complexity, and in so doing to have rendered unsupportable all evolutionary readings of Greek religious art from aniconic to figural. On the formative rôle of the evolutionary schema within modern discussions, see also Donohue (2005), esp. 56-9. For criticism of the assumption that aniconism predates mimetic cult art, see also Gaifman (2005), *passim* but esp. 29-57.

not accurately and in detail reproduce the anthropomorphic form. Its function is not to represent divinity in full, but rather to suggest what is absent, what is above and beyond:

> However the sacred power is represented, the aim is to establish a true communication, an authentic contact, with it. The ambition is to make this power present *hic et nunc*, to make it available to human beings in the ritually required forms. But in its attempt to construct a bridge, as it were, that will reach toward the divine, the idol must also and at the same time and in the same figure mark its distance from that domain in relation to the human world. ... it must also emphasize what is inaccessible and mysterious in divinity, its alien quality, its otherness.[25]

A work such as Pheidias' Athene in the Parthenon uses form and material to capture presence, to be epiphanic, to give the impression that the god (huge and shining) is there in the worshippers' midst.[26] This has its own visual power which the ancients recognised and respected. But other types of divine object work to capture absence, and therefore *potential*. The aniconic image, and the very crude and simple anthropomorphic statue, do so through omission, omission of features and of elements of mimesis. Their transcendental quality is strongly conveyed in ancient narratives through stories of the miraculous and supernatural ways in which they arrive among their worshippers and become objects of cult. Many such accounts describe a sacred stone descending from heaven, like a meteorite; a historically significant example is that connected with the Athenian disaster at Aigospotamoi, mentioned by Plutarch. Having descended, the stone is worshipped in the Chersonese.[27]

The motif of the miraculous arrival has two effects: first, it endows the object with its own limited magical agency; and second, it removes altogether the element of human manufacture. The object is sometimes found, but it is never made, and this allows it to derive from the sphere of the divine, the otherworldly, with a minimum of mortal mediation. Thus the aniconic cult object in myth does far more than just looking like a god: it comes from a god, and its very unworked state is the key to and the indication of its divine origins. A worked image by contrast displays by its very mimetic artifice that it owes its existence to mortal labour rather than divine agency. It is therefore not hard to see why the non-mimetic aniconic type should have been accorded its own aura of potency in the Greek religious imagination. A similar kind of power occasionally also attaches to

---

[25] Vernant (1991), 153.

[26] Spivey (1996), 170, cites, in relation to Pheidias' other famous creation, the chryselephantine cult statue of Zeus at Olympia, Livy's awestruck comment that 'Iovem velut praesentem intuens motus animo est,' (Livy, *Hist.* 45.28), and remarks that this was exactly the response Pheidias would have wanted. On the emphasis on luminescence in Pheidias' works and the echo between this and divine epiphanies, see Steiner (2001), 95-102.

[27] Plut. *Lys.* 12. Sacred stones can also refer to important mythological events, as does that reported to have stood at Delphi, which was, in ancient eyes, the stone which Kronos swallowed in place of Zeus: see Paus. 10.24.6.

certain kinds of worked images. For example, Pausanias tells us that the image of Athene at Athens considered most holy was an *agalma* whose veneration predated the union of the demes: the legend, he says, is that it fell from heaven.[28] So a simple figural image may arrive miraculously, in which case its workmanship is divine, not human, and it carries the same numinosity as the unworked object, and the same sense of extreme age.[29]

Such objects and images are potent because of, not despite, their unlifelikeness. They harness the power of the *thing*, and in their very inanimation manage, in ancient eyes, to be especially *entheos*. They are talismanic, tools for imagining the elusiveness of the divine as well as the potential for intense presence.[30] There and not there: this is the special formula of the divine. The fully mimetic statue by contrast imposes limits through its artifice, and divinity must sometimes be allowed to transcend such limits, just as mixanthropic deities always seem to do. Mixanthropy and aniconism may be seen as semantic systems used to express similar things: chiefly the inadequacy of mimetic anthropomorphism for the depiction of the divine. This inadequacy only rarely finds explicit expression, in the works of philosophers[31] who cannot be taken as typical of conscious thought at the time;[32] however, its implicit manifestations, far subtler than an actual rejection of divine representation such as occasional philosophers undertake, are indeed there to see, under the surface.

---

[28] Paus. 1.26.6. As well as falling from the sky, images can emerge from the sea, e.g. in Paus. 10.19, which describes Methymnean fishermen drawing up in their nets an outlandish mask-effigy of Dionysos, whose worship at Methymna is then prescribed by the Delphic oracle.

[29] For full discussion of the miraculous arrival of cult images in Greek myth, see Bettinetti (2001), 89-105.

[30] For Steiner (2001, 81) they are also to be regarded as one of a range of disguises in which divinity cloaks itself, being unwilling to reveal its true or full form to the human viewer.

[31] A famous instance is the remark by the mid-sixth-century Ionian philosopher Xenophanes that man simply depicts gods in his own image: 'But if cattle or lions had hands, so as to paint with their hands and produce works of art as men do, they would paint their gods and give them bodies in form like their own – horses like horses, cattle like cattle.' (B15 DK) Xenophanes seems to have posited a transcendental divinity beyond the reach of representation, but unfortunately the fragmentary nature of Xenophanes' work prohibits gaining an entirely coherent picture of his views. Another example of Ionian statue-criticism is to be found in Herakleitos (B5 DK), who compares those who pray to statues to people conversing with houses, 'not recognising what the gods or even heroes are like'. This conveys the idea that the statue does not show true divine form; rather, it is a vessel or container. This is intriguingly close to what we have argued to be the symbolic purpose of a cult image, but for Herakleitos the *hedos*-function is insupportable because of its complete failure to reflect or allow knowledge of actual divinity. See Steiner (2001), 79-80 and 121-4.

[32] This point is argued cogently be Scheer (2000), 35-43.

2. Gods, monsters, manufacture

So the unworked or simply worked cult image had a significant rôle to play in ancient reflection on the depiction of divinity. At the same time, however, it is possible to discern an antithetical yet related theme, that of craftsmanship, of the very process of manufacture, which may reveal another facet of the position held by mixanthropes within ancient attitudes towards representation. The ensuing sub-chapter will explore how both gods and monsters (mixanthropic and otherwise) are brought into significant convergence by being cast as the products of miraculous craftsmanship. Such a portrayal places emphasis once more upon their rôle as objects, a rôle which we have seen attributed to Acheloos and Dionysos in particular, but which, it will be argued, should be viewed against the wider backdrop of ancient narratives about legendary acts of manufacture. The densest cluster of such narratives surrounds the figure of the Cretan Daidalos and his various creations and inventions at the court of King Minos; other examples will be brought in for purposes of comparison to demonstrate that the theme extends more widely into ancient myth.

2.1. Daidalos and the animation of objects

The Greeks knew Daidalos as the inventor and creator of various devices, structures, and creative methods, most of which discoveries took place either on Crete or on Sicily.[33] In this context, however, what concerns us is his association with statues, and with statues of gods in particular. In modern art history, Daidalos has given his name to the so-called 'Daedalic' or 'Daedalian' style, terms which are used to denote the archaic sculpture of the seventh century BC. This derives from the ancient attribution to Daidalos of a certain type of sculpture.[34] The modern term 'Daedalic' and its forms indicate above all an early and primitive type of statue, simple and relatively crude, lacking the detailed verism of Classical counterparts. Some ancient remarks foreshadow this association. For example, Pausanias comments that the statues made by Daidalos would seem foolish to modern (that is, second-century) eyes. But such comments overlay a much deeper perception of Daidalos as *innovator*, as creator of a sculptural form that is new and daring rather than crude and archaic. At 4.76.2-3 Diodoros says:

> In the carving of statues he was so much better than all other men that later ge-
> nerations invented the story about him that the statues made by him were very like
> living beings; they could see, they said, and walk and, overall, preserved so well the
> appearance of the entire body that an image made by him seemed to be a being

---

[33] Spivey (1996), 56-9.

[34] Morris (1992), 238-56. Pp. 251-6 for the modern concept, on which see also Donohue (1988), 179-88.

endowed with life. And since he was the first to represent the eye open, the legs separated in a stride and the arms and hands extended, he was quite naturally admired by mankind; for the craftsmen before his time had carved their statues with the eyes closed and the arms and hands hanging and attached to the sides.[35]

Moreover, Morris demonstrates that words with the *daidal-* root are used in ancient texts from Homer onwards not to denote archaic simplicity but rather objects of especial elaborateness, of particular cunning of detail and design, the results of ingenious work and craftsmanship.[36] We seem to have two themes which somewhat contradict each other: one sees Daidalos as articulating, elaborating, applying unheard-of *technê* to raw materials; the other, far less strongly represented in the sources, sees him as primitive rather than innovative (or rather innovative in a way which has come to be seen as primitive) and therefore the creator of crude, simple objects.

The former portrayal is the earlier, and in fact rests upon one of the fundamental aspects of Daidalos' art. In his creation of statues, Daidalos brings new elaboration and articulation. He gives his images differentiated limbs and open eyes. In the quotation above, Diodoros the Sensible says that this new articulation gave rise to the (credulous and mistaken) idea that the statues were endowed with life, but this is an accretion of rationalization over a deep mythical stratum in which lies the magical ability of the craftsman to animate lifeless materials and create living, moving things out of metal and stone.[37] Daidalos does not just make lifelike things; he makes things that are (unexpectedly and miraculously) alive.

This ability finds other exponents. One is the god Hephaistos, famous as the divine smith, and also a creator of objects which move, which display all the signs of life within their hard exteriors. Automotive tripods and robotic handmaidens[38] give the god a bizarre glamour in the *Iliad*, quite at odds with his rôle as a source of malicious laughter. When Hephaistos appears among the company of the other gods, he may be a figure of fun, with his ungainly and deformed body,[39] but in his own territory he is a mighty worker of miracles.

---

[35] κατὰ δὲ τὴν τῶν ἀγαλμάτων κατασκευὴν τοσοῦτο τῶν ἁπάντων ἀνθρώπων διήνεγκεν ὥστε τοὺς μεταγενεστέρους μυθολογῆσαι περὶ αὐτοῦ διότι τὰ κατασκευαζόμενα τῶν ἀγαλμάτων ὁμοιότατα τοῖς ἐμψύχοις ὑπάρχει· βλέπειν τε γὰρ αὐτὰ καὶ περιπατεῖν, καὶ καθόλου τηρεῖν τὴν τοῦ ὅλου σώματος διάθεσιν, ὥστε δοκεῖν εἶναι τὸ κατασκευασθὲν ἔμψυχον ζῷον. πρῶτος δ' ὀμματώσας καὶ διαβεβηκότα τὰ σκέλη ποιήσας, ἔτι δὲ τὰς χεῖρας διατεταμένας ποιῶν, εἰκότως ἐθαυμάζετο παρὰ τοῖς ἀνθρώποις· οἱ γὰρ πρὸ τούτου τεχνῖται κατεσκεύαζον τὰ ἀγάλματα τοῖς μὲν ὄμμασι μεμυκότα, τὰς δὲ χεῖρας ἔχοντα καθειμένας καὶ ταῖς πλευραῖς κεκολλημένας.

[36] Morris (1992), 3-35.

[37] Spivey (1995), 447; Steiner (2001), 143-4.

[38] Several of Hephaistos' other automata are in animal form, significantly; a famous example is the set of animated gold and silver dogs which he makes for the Phaiakians (Hom. *Od.* 7.91-4). See Faraone (1992), 18-21.

[39] On the lameness of Hephaistos and Hera's desire to discard and conceal him, see Hom. *Il.* 18.395-405; *Hom. Hymn* 3.316-21. The gods on Olympos laugh at Hephaistos' ungainly movement:

Daidalos' Cretan associations and his employment by Minos link him with Hephaistos further: Hephaistos in some accounts is designated as the creator of Talos, the animated bronze giant who guards Crete for its ruler.[40] Another oblique association between Talos and Daidalos may lurk in the figure of the craftsman's apprentice, another Talos, whose murder necessitates Daidalos' flight to Crete from Athens, in Apollodoros' account.[41] All automata are by definition monsters in that they are unnatural in their creation, composition and nature, but Talos adds other monster features: extraordinary size and a guardian function. Like that of Kerberos at the gate of Hades, Talos' unnatural might is harnessed for the preservation of a realm; thrice every day he stalks around the perimeter of Crete, throwing rocks at all who approach.[42] The manner of his defeat is significant: according to Apollonios, when Medea arrives on Crete with Jason, she casts a spell on Talos so that he is rendered vulnerable and, scraping his ankle on a rock, suffers a wound through which the animation-giving fluid within him escapes, leaving him a drained and lifeless shell.

Daidalos' manufacture of animated objects extends into the representation of the divine.[43] An example where the animated statue is explicitly that of a deity is to be found in a metaphor used by Aristotle. Describing how, according to Democritus, the movement of the body is caused by the soul within it, he compares this with a dramatic conceit:

> In saying this he is like Philippos the writer of comic plays. For Philippos says that Daidalos made the wooden Aphrodite move, by pouring in quicksilver.[44]

Walking, talking statues of gods seem to have been remarkably popular in comedy and satyr plays, and Daidalos is an important figure in the scant

---

Hom. *Il.* 1.595-600. It is possible to ask whether the anatomy of Hephaistos has mixanthropic qualities, since his twisted or hook-shaped lower limbs in vase-paintings do echo the mixanthropic features of anguipedes, but on the whole he belongs more strongly to the discourse of the deformed, rather than being characterised by a definitely animal element. (See Ogden [1997], 35-7; Faraone [1992, 133-5] argues rather differently, that the twisted feet of Hephaistos signal the confinement of a dangerous power.) None the less, mixanthropy can never be wholly divorced from other types of unnatural anatomy, a point raised in the Introduction to this book. On the iconography of Hephaistos, see further Delcourt (1957), 110-36; Carpenter (1986), 16-17.

[40] For example this seems to have been described in the work of Simonides and in the *Daidalos* of Sophokles: see Simon. fr. 202a Bergk, Soph. frr. 163-4 Nauck. Apollodoros (*Bibl.* 1.9.26) records some fascinating variations: the version which makes Talos a bronze giant given to Minos by Hephaistos is cited, but so is another in which he is not a humanoid but a bronze bull. Finally, the author records the rare alternative, that rather than being the product of manufacture he is one of the 'race of bronze', primordial men.

[41] Apollod. *Bibl.* 3.15.9; Morris (1992), 226-7.

[42] Ap. Rhod. *Arg.* 4.1639-93. On the prevalence of the guardian function in the characterisation of ancient monsters, see Faraone (1992), 18-35.

[43] On Daidalos and the creation of divine images, see Donohue (1988), 179-83; Pritchett, vol. 1 (1998), 170-204.

[44] Aristotle, *de An.* 406b 9: παραπλησίως λέγων Φιλίππῳ τῷ κωμῳδοδιδασκάλῳ· φῆσι γὰρ τὸν Δαίδαλον κινουμένην ποιῆσαι τὴν ξυλίνην Ἀφροδίτην, ἐγχέαντ' ἄργυρον χυτόν.

references that have come down to us. Several fragments of comic drama reinforce the suggestion that in Athens there was a running joke about the elusive and slippery properties of Daidalos' works.[45] An excerpt from Plato's *Meno* is also illuminating and proved the motif to have currency in other genres. Sokrates is gently teasing his Thessalian interlocutor for failing to understand the value of 'true opinion'; this failure, he says, might be because, being Thessalian, Menon has never seen the statues of Daidalos, whose properties he goes on the describe, saying that 'if they are not fastened up they play truant and run away; but, if fastened, they stay where they are.'[46] In Greek religion, the process of manufacture can provide a container for transcendent divinity: we have seen above that this is how cult images functioned in much of ritual life. The statues made by Daidalos, however, turn this function on its head, by overturning our expectations of objects. Material is no longer safely immobile and lifeless; it is endowed with all the instability of the divinity it represents. Both monsters and gods take a share of this dangerous animation.

2.2. Pasiphae's cow

So Daidalos is able, through magical *technê*, to break down the boundary between the living and the lifeless, the animated and the inanimate, and in so doing to interrogate the properties and the limitations of images and image-making. There is, however, another important divide which his craftsmanship oversteps: that between human and animal. He is, in fact, intimately associated with mixanthropy, non-divine mixanthropy, the mixanthropy of the monster.

Ancient authors tell the story of Pasiphae, the wife of Minos, who becomes a channel for divine retribution when he offends Poseidon by failing to sacrifice to the god an especially fine (in some versions supernatural) bull.[47] Cursed with a terrible passion for this very bull, Pasiphae commissions Daidalos to make for her an ingenious hollow cow in which she hides and so manages to mate with the animal. The offspring resulting from this unnatural conjunction is the

---

[45] See Spivey (1995), 446-7 and Morris (1992), 215-226, for the dramatic references. Morris argues that Daidalos was claimed as an Attic hero in the Classical period, a process which involved the increasing characterisation of Minos as antagonist. Daidalos was in fact worshipped at Alopeke: there is a reference to a Daidaleion, a sanctuary of Daidalos, in a fourth-century inscription: *SEG* XII, 100.

[46] Plato, *Meno* 97d-e.

[47] The story of Pasiphae goes back to the *Ehoiai* (Hes. fr. 145 MW), and finds another early exposition in an Ode of Bacchylides (26). In some accounts, the bull has originally been sent from the sea by Poseidon himself (see e.g. Apollod. *Bibl.* 3.1.3-4), in others it is just an especially fine specimen in Minos' herds, which he should sacrifice but which he impiously chooses to keep (e.g. Diod. 4.77.1-4). An alternative variant makes the anger that of Aphrodite, aimed against Pasiphae, who fails to honour her (e.g. Hyg. *Fab.* 40); however, this feels rather like a literary conflation of Pasiphae's story with that of the transgressive love of her daughter Phaidra for Hippolytos, in which the anger of Aphrodite is the cause.

minotaur, who provides us with a very rare example of a mixanthrope being the product of sex between human and animal.

In this story, the rôle of Daidalos is as someone who is able to fit together animal and human, elements incompatible in nature, and allow for their combination. The first such combination is that of Pasiphae and the artificial cow; the second is that of Pasiphae and the bull she is thus able to mate with. The third combination is the result of this mating: the minotaur, bull-headed, human-bodied, a monstrous mixanthrope. Daidalos does not manufacture the minotaur; this being is produced by a travesty of the natural processes of reproduction. It is interesting to observe the varieties of animal/human juxtaposition in this sequence. Its end product is a mixanthrope, in which both ingredients are externally displayed and anatomically conjoined, but what Daidalos produces is rather different. The Pasiphae/cow confection is a case of combination in layers, cow without, woman within. This outside/inside discrepancy is reminiscent of the physical manifestation of the automaton, that combines a lifeless exterior, the shell of an object, with a core of life and animation, represented as a magical fluid like quicksilver. In the case of the minotaur and the animal/human dichotomy, mixanthropy is then the way in which the two elements are resolved, brought into simultaneous view, in the final product or consequence of the layering operation. The creation of divergent layers as a way of fusing antithetical ingredients appears to be at the heart of the theme of manufacture in ancient thought, as may be seen by examining a comparable, though very different, example.

2.3. Manufactured women

According to Plutarch, the *aition* of the Boiotian festival of the Daidala was as follows:[48] annoyed at Zeus' infidelities, Hera hides from him, and Zeus determines to win her back by pretending to marry another. He undergoes a wedding ceremony with a statue carved of wood, decked in women's garb and ornament and given the female name Daidale, a ruse which takes Hera in so that she rushes up in a jealous passion; the revelation of the trick played effects a reconciliation, and the effigy of 'Daidale' becomes a cult image with its own festival, named after it. This story is on the one hand one of those reflecting the persona of Daidalos as someone who can use his *technê* to make a mere object seem a being of flesh and blood. The decking of a female effigy, however, and its use for purposes of deception, is a theme which extends beyond Daidalos, and reveals another vital angle on ancient myth-making on the subject of images and their power.

---

[48] Plut. *de Daed. Plat.* 6 (= Euseb. *Praep. Ev.* 3.1.85c – 86b); on the attendant rituals, see Burkert (1979), 129-38.

The most famous manufactured human in ancient myth (and arguably in modern thought also) was Pandora. Occasional vase paintings depict the scene in which Pandora is constructed by the gods, and their representation of a stark, statue-like form is very striking. On a kalyx krater by the Niobid Painter,[49] for example, Pandora, complete but for a wreath which Athene holds out towards her (the finishing touch), stands facing the viewer with full-frontal face and a rigid stance. We know from Hesiod's bitter tale that, once made and animated, she was in fact all too capable of movement and independent action, though driven by the will of Zeus and the instrument of his punitive intentions: she it is who notoriously released the world's ills from their resting-place within a jar, and thus ushered mankind through one of the stages of degradation which are so dominant within the *Works and Days*. So Pandora was no mere automaton (though her chief fabric was moulded by the automaton-making Hephaistos), but the process of her creation makes her part of the *topos* of the animated statue, and in this regard, we find once again the motif of layers, layers whose discrepancy is a source of peril.

> At once the glorious Lame God moulded from clay
> the likeness of a modest girl, in accordance with the plans of Kronides.
> Grey-eyed Athene put upon her girdle and ornaments,
> and the divine Charites and lady Peitho
> placed golden necklaces upon her skin, and the Horai
> with the lovely hair crowned her with spring flowers.
> All these things Pallas Athene attached to her skin, as ornament.
> And in her breast, the Guide, Argeïphontes,
> forged lies and crafty words and a deceitful nature,
> according to the plans of deep-thundering Zeus.[50]

Much of this passage is concerned with *kosmos*, adornment, the kind of adornment on which female attraction so often rests in Greek literature. Most of the elaboration of Pandora's manufacture happens on the outside, in the painstaking creation of a pleasing exterior. Only at the end of the passage are we told about the composition of what is inside, and this is the contribution of the trickster Hermes, who, appropriately, gives her a deceitful nature and (on line 67) what is generally translated into English as a 'shameless mind'. The Greek phrase, however, is *kuneos noos*, a bitch-like mind, the mind of a bitch.

---

[49] Attic red-figure kalyx krater by the Niobid Painter; c. 460 BC. (London BM 1856,12-13.1.) See Reeder ed. (1995), cat. no. 80, pp. 282-4.

[50] Hes. *W&D* 70-79: αὐτίκα δ᾽ ἐκ γαίης πλάσσεν κλυτὸς Ἀμφιγυήεις | παρθένῳ αἰδοίῃ ἴκελον Κρονίδεω διὰ βουλάς· | ζῶσε δὲ καὶ κόσμησε θεὰ γλαυκῶπις Ἀθήνη | ἀμφὶ δέ οἱ Χάριτές τε θεαὶ καὶ πότνια Πειθὼ | ὅρμους χρυσείους ἔθεσαν χροΐ· ἀμφὶ δὲ τήν γε | Ὧραι καλλίκομοι στέφον ἄνθεσιν εἰαρινοῖσιν | πάντα δέ οἱ χροΐ κόσμον ἐφήρμοσε Παλλὰς Ἀθήνη. | ἐν δ᾽ ἄρα οἱ στήθεσσι διάκτορος Ἀργεϊφόντης | ψεύδεά θ᾽ αἱμυλίους τε λόγους καὶ ἐπίκλοπον ἦθος | τεῦξε Διὸς βουλῇσι βαρυκτύπου...

Pandora is herself like the pithos of ills,[51] packed with destructive potential, but in this context the animal component is especially interesting. Like Pasiphae in her cow-shell, she comprises woman and animal parts, but her composition is the reverse of her Cretan counterpart's. Pasiphae was aiming to seduce a bull, so she concealed her humanity within the form of an animal; Pandora is designed to seduce men, so her exterior is human, and beautiful; within, however, lurks the dangerous character of the animal. Pandora's quality as a *pêma*, a bane to men, hinges on the discrepancy of her layers and of the successful concealment of the animal within the human; this is the essence of her trickery. There is a tiny hint of her nature on the outside: in the subtly different account in the *Theogony*, Pandora is equipped with a head-dress made by Hephaistos, ornamented with many *daidala* (elaborate, curious, tricky designs): these *daidala* are depictions of 'all the *knôdala* which the earth and the sea nurture', and they are described as miraculous (*thaumasia*) and 'like living creatures with voices'.[52] Not only is Pandora herself a miraculously animated work of manufacture, but the beasts on her crown come close to having the same magic property. They also, perhaps, refer to beastliness within, though poor Epimetheus does not recognise the warning.

This characterisation of Pandora finds striking echoes in that of Helen. Helen, too, is a bane to men, another cause of lengthy human suffering. Once again, beauty baits the trap; once again, beauty is not to be relied on as an indicator of harmlessness.[53] Bitch-imagery crops up again, significantly: repeatedly Helen calls herself both bitch-faced, *kunôps*, and simply *kuôn*, 'bitch'.[54] Though dog-imagery ties Helen in with the Pandora motif, the word *kunôps* is itself surprising, since literally it seems to refer to external appearance. We *know* that Helen's face is not dog-like in the physical sense; she is a paradigmatic beauty. There are two ways of interpreting this peculiarity. One is that it is the dog's notorious shamelessness that is being applied to Helen's countenance: her beauty is brazen and wanton, inhumanly so. The other is that the bitch mind is being extruded, so to speak, onto the visible plane from the invisible, and that Helen does so to shock, by revealing what lies within her perfect form. Either way, it is a remarkable display of self-excoriation, one which actually confuses the Pandoran inside/outside dichotomy to which Helen, as snare of men, is inherently prone.[55]

---

[51] For further discussion of container-imagery in this context, see Lissarrague (1995).

[52] Hes. *Theog.* 570-89, esp. 578-84.

[53] For Helen as ambiguous sorceress, skilled in both healing and baneful herbs, see Hom. *Od.* 4.219-232.

[54] E.g. at *Il.* 3.180 (*kunôps*) and 6.344 & 356 (both *kuôn* in the genitive, *kunos*).

[55] Animal imagery does not always occur in the form of this delicate opposition of latent and patent. In the verse of Semonides, the outward appearance of the various female types lampooned is, like their characters and behaviour, unflatteringly compared with that of various animal species: the monkey-women has a scrawny rump, for example. (See Lloyd-Jones [1975].) However, the animal characteristics employed by Semonides in this way are indicative of ridicule and dismissal rather than deep anxiety; the latter is attached chiefly to *hidden* bestiality.

Helen, too, has an element of the artificial, if one takes into account the curious story of the fabrication of a Helen-*eidôlon*, a story given fullest elaboration in the *Helen* of Euripides, though possibly discernible as early as Stesichoros.[56] The motivation behind this act of manufacture is not dissimilar from that which provoked the creation of Pandora, that is, a direct desire on the part of Zeus to oppose mankind and to use a deceptively beautiful female as the means.[57] In the extant summary of the *Kypria* we hear of Zeus and Themis plotting to engineer the Trojan War, and more detail is provided by a scholion on the *Iliad* which describes how the births of both Achilles and Helen are the twin mechanisms behind the catastrophic conflict.[58] Once again, we have the manufactured woman, beautiful yet monstrous in her combination of human and animal, being used to trick mankind into loss and suffering.

Helen and Pandora are both vital instruments of the gods' manipulation of mankind, and as such have drastic implications for the very fabric of humanity's mythical past. One further example of the manufactured woman, another *eidôlon* in fact, is far less powerful in scope, but should be recognised as a telling further example of the connections between manufacture, monstrosity and mixanthropy. This character is Nephele, 'Cloud', the woman created in the likeness of Hera to deflect from the goddess the erotic aggression of Ixion. Ixion rapes the cloud-woman in the belief that she is Hera, and though Nephele herself has no explicit animal elements, the result (immediate or eventual) of their unnatural union is the centaurs, horse-mixanthropes.[59] Most authors make Ixion and Nephele not the parents but the grandparents of the centaurs; the horse element is provided by the mares of Pelion, their mothers. This dilutes the connection between manufacture and mixanthropy significantly, but the connection is there, faintly, none the less.

---

[56] See Wright (2005), 83-113.

[57] On the ancient motif of the aggressive use of deceptive containers like Pandora, see Faraone (1992), 94-112.

[58] Schol. Hom. *Il.* 1.5-6; see Gantz (1993), 567-8 for analysis of this and other sources. The underlying divine motivation is a desire to reduce the numbers of mankind, as they weight heavy on Earth and have besides become impious. This is different from the divine agenda in Hesiod, which revolves around conflict between Zeus and Prometheus, the latter in the rôle of mankind's chief helper. But the overall thrust, the use of the dangerous female against mankind, is the same in both cases.

[59] In Hyg. *Fab.* 62, the mating of Ixion and Nephele produces the Kentauroi, but most other, and earlier, accounts have an intermediate genealogical stage: for example, in Pind. *Pyth.* 2, the offspring is the human-formed Kentauros, who mates with the mares of Pelion to produce the Kentauroi; in the unusually elaborate account of Diod. 4.69-70, Ixion and Nephele produce the *Kentauroi anthrôpophyeis*, who mate with Pelian mares to produce the *Hippokentauroi*.

2.4. Thetis

To return to the theme of layers, and the discrepancy between outside and inside, perhaps the most notable example of this characteristic is in fact Thetis. As was shown in Chapter 1, Thetis was sometimes characterised using the imagery of the *sepia*, a creature that is white externally but full of black ink which it employs as a *dolos*, a trick (a word with Pandoran echoes). By no means coincidentally, Thetis is also strongly associated with the theme of manufacture, though she has no manufactured quality herself. It was seen above that Thetis was closely linked with Hephaistos, and that in fact *technê* forms the basis of their association, through the episode of Achilles' shield, its commissioning and collection by Thetis when she visits Hephaistos in his miraculous domain, an occasion which prompts, in the *Iliad*, a remarkable digression on the origins of their intimacy, the help and shelter which Thetis afforded the smith-god when he had been cast out by his mother Hera. However, the Thetis/manufacture association goes further than this.

In a tradition which cannot be taken as widespread in ancient belief, but which none the less finds echoes elsewhere, the seventh-century poet Alkman includes Thetis in a cosmogonic poem, of which only a summary survives today.[60] From this summary it appears that the kosmos originates in a condition of formlessness; Thetis, however, exercises a demiurgic function and distinguishes matter from matter in a way which the commentator compares to the actions of a *technités* manipulating metal. This is a rare rôle for the goddess, and curiously divergent from her more famous position as the mother of Achilles, and yet, as Detienne and Vernant observe, it comes to mind when one considers her Iliadic interaction with the arch-*technités* Hephaistos. In the *Iliad*, it will be recalled, Hephaistos and Thetis enjoy a striking intimacy, and the scene in which she stands at his side in his forge while he crafts the miraculous arms of Achilles surely carries resonances with the demiurgic Thetis of Alkman, though without the cosmogonic function.

Though not herself characterised as the result of manufacture, Thetis does share with Pandora and Helen one further significant aspect: a link, faintly causal, with the Trojan war. According to some ancient accounts, it is at the wedding of Peleus and Thetis that the conflict is made inevitable, through the action of Eris, Strife, who introduces the Apple of Discord which will set goddess against goddess in the beauty contest judged by Paris. Paris' judgment will then lead on to the abduction of Helen, the direct and immediate cause of the war. This is not to mention the fact that Thetis' son, Achilles, is destined to be the most famous hero involved in the conflict. In her association with the Trojan war, Thetis

---

[60] For the commentary, see Page, *PMG* fr. 5, pp. 23-4; for analysis and discussion see West (1963 and 1967), and Detienne and Vernant (1978), 133-74, in which the Alkmanic Thetis is also compared with the Orphic figure of Metis, another world-shaper.

displays a curious mixture of potency and helplessness, which Slatkin has studied at length. Though herself a demiurgic figure of cosmic scope, in the setting of the war and its inception her power is wholly subordinated to the dual agencies of Zeus and Fate.

2.5. Manufacture and metamorphosis

The wooden cow made by Daidalos for Pasiphae effects a kind of *dolos* which relies on concealing one nature within another, and the theme of concealment is indeed strong, being continued in the story of Daidalos' construction of the labyrinth as a place of concealment and confinement for the monstrous minotaur, the result of his facilitation of Pasiphae's bestial union. However, the hollow cow is also an example of the legendary craftsman's ability to bring about changes of shape. We know that Pasiphae does not actually transform, she merely dons a disguise; and yet it was shown in Chapter 8 that the imagery of disguises, of costumes, masks and coverings, is intimately connected with that of actual metamorphosis. Others of the deeds of Daidalos too display this use of coverings of some kind to bring about a dramatic change of state, the most famous being his invention of artificial wings which allow him and his son Ikaros to fly from Crete when the circumstances of the minotaur's conception, and Daidalos' hand in them, have become known, arousing the murderous rage of Minos.[61] In the production of the wings, Daidalos' miraculous *technê* creates a way for him and his son to leave behind terrestrial identity and enter the alien element of the air, even though for Ikaros the experience is a fatal one. Thus Daidalos is, in a sense, himself a metamorphosist.

This property of the mythical craftsman may be seen very strongly in the case of the Telchines, fellow-islanders, though Rhodian rather than Cretan, and also exponents of *technê*. The technological inventions of the Telchines are very closely related to those of both Hephaistos and Daidalos. They make arms (the sickle of Kronos);[62] they make images of the gods.[63] Of course, it is important not to lump all these mythical personalities together without distinction; the Telchines are not just craftsmen but are particularly associated with the development of metalworking, belonging to a group of beings (containing also the Daktyls) whom Morris aptly calls 'mischievous and mobile spirits of metal'.[64] The range of their achievements, however, takes them out of this narrow sphere and places them firmly within the *topos* of the magical creator of potent and talismanic things.

---

[61] Apollod. *Epit.* 1.12-13.

[62] Strab. 14.2.7.

[63] Diod. 5.55.2.

[64] Morris (1992), 88. See also pp. 164-70. She stresses the geographical dimension, seeing characters like the Telchines as reflecting movements and migrations of craftsmen and their skills through the Aegean and beyond. On the metallurgical *daimones* as a strongly interrelated group in Greek mythology, see Blakely (2006), 13-31.

What is especially striking, in combination with this, is their ability to inflict the process of metamorphosis on their surroundings. This ability is described in most detail by Diodoros,[65] who tells us:

> The Telchines are also said to have been wizards, and to have been able to summon clouds and rain and hail when they wished, and likewise even to bring on snow. The stories say that they did these things just as the Magoi do. They could also change their own shapes, and they were jealous [*phthoneroi*] about teaching their skills.[66]

This passage brings out a consistent trait of the Telchines in ancient narratives: their jealousy, which fits in with their frequent representation as the displaced early inhabitants of Rhodes.[67] It also reflects the extent to which such legendary craftsmen, rather than being limited to transformations of beings and objects from one form to another, were believed to be able to distort the very systems and processes of nature. In such cases, metamorphosis in the 'traditional' sense (such as human to animal) is part of a far more general ability to manipulate the natural environment and flout its normal laws. Daidalos' ability to transgress the boundaries of living and inanimate, human and animal, terrestrial and winged, though perhaps narrower in scope, should be viewed against the backdrop of this broader motif. The Telchines also show themselves to be metamorphic; as has so often been shown in this book, it is a quality of the metamorphosist that he is able to impose his fluctuations on the environment around him.

The connection between the transgression of the two key boundaries, animated/inanimate and animal/human, is also one with wide currency in ancient thought. Steiner argues that the contrasting relationship between immobility and mobility was one which countless ancient authors found piquant and productive.[68] Statues and other images were used as expressions of the essence of immobility, but this also had the effect of making their immobility ripe for transcendence and negation, though various means. The automata of Daidalos and Hephaistos are one way in which this is achieved; the link with metamorphosis provides another; and it is highly significant that tales of non-animal metamorphosis tend to end in immobility, in the transformation of the victim from living, breathing being into rigid rock or tree. Animal metamorphosis tests the border between the human and the non-human state; object-metamorphosis

---

[65] Several ancient texts seem to have dwelt at length on the Telchines, but do not now survive, for example Epimenides, who wrote a Telchinic History (see Blakely [2006], 15). For an early mention, see Bacchyl. 1.1-9.

[66] Diod. 5.55.3: λέγονται δ᾽ οὗτοι καὶ γόητες γεγονέναι καὶ παράγειν ὅτε βούλοιντο νέφη τε καὶ ὄμβρους καὶ χαλάζας, ὁμοίως δὲ καὶ χιόνα ἐφέλκεσθαι· ταῦτα δὲ καθάπερ καὶ τοὺς μάγους ποιεῖν ἱστοροῦσιν. ἀλλάττεσθαι δὲ καὶ τὰς ἰδίας μορφάς, καὶ εἶναι φθονεροὺς ἐν τῇ διδασκαλίᾳ τῶν τεχνῶν.

[67] Cf. Strab. 14.2.7-8.

[68] Steiner (2001), 135-84.

suggests that animated/inanimate is another vital dichotomy in the ancient world view.

Gods, monsters and images: conclusion

This chapter has taken in a great deal of diverse material; it is time to recap, and in particular to reassert the application of this material to the topic of this book: mixanthropic deities. First, however, the findings of the chapter may be summarised as follows.

In the first sub-chapter, it was shown that the tense and complicated relationship between mixanthropic deities and the processes of representation should not be allowed to obscure the challenges inherent in the depiction of the divine; despite the superficially simple system of divine anthropomorphism, great inherent difficultly lay, not so much in depicting the divine, as in doing so in such a way that deity and mortal could interact, whether in the fictional setting of an epiphany or in the real-life setting of ritual. Both settings require mechanisms to effect contact and communication; yet an exploration of cult statues and the beliefs surrounding them showed that even though they, and attendant ceremonial, did function as ways of ensuring divine participation in the dialogue of worship, they did not in the least suggest permanent divine presence. It was, however, argued that mixanthropic deities represent an extreme end in the spectrum of such impermanence. By the abnegation of the mechanism of the cult statue in particular, mixanthropic deities were kept as free from material confinement as was possible within the parameters of cult. The necessity was reasserted of seeing mixanthropy as a symbolic mode chosen for the envisaging of deities with certain properties, properties not limited exclusively to those with mixanthropic representation, but found with special intensity among their ranks.

In the second sub-chapter, the figure of Daidalos was used to show that, although the representation of gods posed special challenges in the ancient mind, this theme may once again be illuminated from outside, by considering the manifestation in Greek mythology of themes of manufacture more widely. Not only does the creation of the divine image rest within this discourse, but there it reveals significant proximity with the creation of monsters, mixanthropes among them. In myth, the creation of images of gods is the preserve of magical craftsmen such as Daidalos, Hephaistos and the Telchines, and the creation of other miraculous beings (monsters, automata) is another speciality of such figures.

The figure of the manufactured woman may be especially revealing when held up against the visualisation of the divine. In particular, the rôle of *kosmos* in the creation of Pandora is reminiscent of its rôle in the *Homeric Hymn to Aphrodite*, as part of the goddess's preparations to meet and seduce Anchises. Of course, one significance of *kosmos* is as a mechanism of seduction, and this is how it may work in deity/deity interaction too, most famously in Hera's preparations for the seduction of Zeus in the *Iliad*, an episode in which *kosmos* has the element of deception that so often accompanies it.[69] Ornament is the machinery of seduction, and has been shown to bear striking parallels to the male equivalent of the donning of armour.[70] Another potential strand of meaning can, however, be suggested: that the adornment of a goddess gives her a faintly manufactured character. In the *Homeric Hymn*, Aphrodite goes through the *kosmos*-process in her temple; would we be wrong to suggest that this brings her into close relationship with the idea of the statue? That when she dons the material accessories that form such an important part of her ability to enchant, the process is not just one of decoration but of physical embodiment? Thus even a face-to-face epiphany may involve the deity taking on some of the properties of a statue, a (self-) manufactured object.

Are gods and monsters born, or are they made? Born of course, in that genealogical myth-making lavished parentage and the circumstances of conception and birth on individuals of both classes. And yet the intrusion of both gods and monsters into real life was almost exclusively through objects and images, things subjected to processes of manufacture. With regard to divine images, two mythological contingencies could address this basic reality: stories of cult objects arriving mysteriously ready-made, and stories which place the process of creation in the hands of a miracle-worker such as Daidalos. Both types take the responsibility for creation out of normal mortal hands, out of banal reality, into the fantastical sphere in which monsters also dwell, beings whose birth, though possible in the imagination, cannot find a place among the biological realities of daily life. And for both gods and monsters, images were more than just means of depiction; they were powerfully talismanic.

Perhaps the strongest uniting theme, however, is that of the relationship between outside and inside, surface and contents. With regard to images of gods, this theme hinges on an implicit question: does this image (most often a statue) contain divinity? Ritual engineers an answer in the affirmative, on a temporary basis, through the characterisation of the cult image as a container or seat in which a deity may take up brief residence. On the side of myth, Daidalos contrives a miraculous 'yes' through artifice, through his creation of divine images that defy the parameters of their external lifelessness, either through a magical core of fluid or through special articulation. Perhaps the bridge between real-life ritual and the unattainable world of Daidalos is the cult image to which attaches

---

[69] Hom. *Il.* 14.153-86. In fact, the adornment of Hera is strongly comparable to that of Aphrodite. Rich and luminescent objects and materials are emphasised: shining hair (176), jewellery from which *charis* shines (183), a veil like the sun (185). The familiar motif of unearthly fragrance also appears (170-74).

[70] Morris (1992), 4-21.

stories of miraculous arrival or miraculous agency, since such objects have their own numinosity.

The inside/outside relationship goes further. With mythical automata the implicit question is whether something which appears to be an object is indeed an object all the way through, and the answer is in the negative. Rather, the lifeless exterior belies the truth of such beings as Talos or the handmaidens of Hephaistos, because within the manufactured shell life has miraculously been implanted. Automata can be alarming, but they, like the *topos* of the animated cult statue, also reveal a fantasy of sorts, about the creation of life in the most unexpected way, and about the transcension of the purely material into divinity and magic.

It is, however, with the rôle of animal ingredients in the inside/outside theme that we are perhaps most concerned, for it was shown that animal elements were powerfully placed within the discourse. The question posed by beings such as Pandora is: the outside of this creature is human, and indeed beautiful, but is this matched by what lies within? The basis of this question is a fundamental doubt as to whether external appearances can be trusted, and of course in the cases of Pandora and Helen they cannot. The animal element is used as a component of the *inside* condition, which belies the human exterior, though Pasiphae's cow turns this schema on its head: since it is a bull whose tastes must be appealed to, it is a bovine form which forms the shell, with a human lurking within. Two aspects of such animal/human combinations are especially important. The first is that they are arranged in layers, one on the outside and one on the inside. The second is that the primary purpose of this configuration is deception. The concealment of animal within human (or *vice versa*) is part of some *dolos*. The untrustworthiness of the external appearance is not coincidental: it is a major element of motivation. This element of deliberate deception may be the key distinction between the motif of the manufactured woman and one closely related instance of a *male* figure harbouring dangerous concealed animality. In a story bizarre even by the standards of ancient mythology, it is told that Minos, king of Crete, was cursed with a condition whereby, *in coitu*, he would ejaculate snakes and scorpions into the body of his female partner, killing her. Thus Minos too harbours hidden and damaging animal forces; but this is not woven into an explicit narrative of duplicity.[71]

Overall, animal/human combinations are an important component within the theme of the inside/outside relationship, and indeed elements of mixanthropy and metamorphosis surface, such as in the flippers of the Telchines and Daidalos' wings, expressive of the boundary-crossing abilities of such figures. But the really striking discovery is that legendary craftsmen, though makers of monsters as well as gods, are not responsible for the direct manufacture of mixanthropes as we

---

[71] Apollod. *Bibl.* 3.15.1; Ant. Lib. *Met.* 41. The condition is inflicted on Minos by the spell-casting Pasiphae, in revenge for his adulteries, and according to Hyginus the creatures ejaculated by the king are snakes, scorpions and millipedes.

know them in this study, that is, animal/human combinations in which both ingredients are physically and externally apparent. Mixanthropes are not possible in nature, and it is easy to imagine figures like Daidalos and Hephaistos slotting one together, beast-part onto man-part, as part of their unnatural manipulation of nature, joining, say, an animal head to a human trunk to create a monster of a type recognised in the ancient canon of the strange. And yet, this does not happen. Instead, mythical craftsmen are far more strongly associated with the creation of layers, with the concealment of one nature within another. This fact is highly significant. The fact that ancient mythical narratives decline to show 'true' mixanthropes as the direct product of manufacture but do ascribe the 'layered' configuration to such processes is by no means meaningless, but rather, leads on to one of the concluding observations of this book. The discourse of manufactured layers is essentially a *negative* one, especially dominated by dysfunctional interaction between humanity and the gods, exemplified by Zeus' use of Pandora as a weapon against men. The fact that mixanthropy does not participate fully in this discourse reflects, as will be argued, the *value* of mixanthropy as an alternative to other arrangements of human and animal, and its rôle as a solution to problems of communication and interaction.

Conclusion

1. Monstrous gods?

By depicting certain of their deities as mixanthropes, the Greeks were selecting a form that was overwhelmingly associated with the monstrous adversaries of myth. Occasionally, gods were also monsters, as in the case of the Sirens. The Greeks almost never remarked on this convergence. But this book has shown, among other things, that it is consistently significant.

Monsters are foes, to be defeated. They are destructive, and work against the lives and the achievements of man. They belong either to the remote past of myth, or to distant lands, or, since space and time work hand in hand in the Greek imagination, to both. As symbols, they are evergreen; as beings, they are typically absent.

So many of these characteristics have been shown to dominate the personalities of mixanthropic gods also. Destructive potential such as they exhibit is a feature of all gods, as of all monsters; but the theme of absence occurs with special strength among the mixanthropes. As with monsters, this can be expressed spatially, through themes of movement and departure, or temporally, through the relegation of mixanthropic gods to a distant and obsolete time. So far it would seem that the Greeks simply had certain monsters who were also gods, certain gods who also happened to be monsters, so much similarity is there in the respective personalities of the two groups.

However, this is very far from true. It has also been shown that mixanthropic gods are illuminated by their *difference* from the pattern of the defeated monster. Whereas the monster's expulsion is wholeheartedly desired and applauded, and benefits mankind, the absence of mixanthropic deities is typically couched in terms of anxiety and regret. Moreover, whereas absence is something which monsters always have inflicted on them, mixanthropic deities are not always so passive; they can sometimes, as in the cases of Demeter Melaina and Thetis, use absence as a weapon, punitively withdrawing their powers.

So mixanthropy is used to depict deities who are surrounded by a condition of tense ambivalence. Moreover, it has been shown that there is more to mixanthropy than its monstrosity. There is also its connection with metamorphosis, a connection far more in evidence in the case of cult-receiving than non-cult-receiving mixanthropes. The mixanthropy of deities, unlike that of monsters, is strongly connected with their ability to transform, to slide between states, to abnegate permanence.

2. Why have mixanthropic deities?

So it is clear that mixanthropy offered a powerful tool for expression which could capture and heighten the perilous relationship between humanity and divinity. But the picture created is full of discomfort, and the deities described in this book can come to seem almost intolerable: dangerous and unreliable beyond the usual run of the divine. In other words, they seem to raise and to embody all that is problematic about gods. This is not to say that their characteristics are wholly negative – far from it. We have seen mixanthropes offering prophecy, divine kourotrophy, civic identity, and numerous other advantageous things which a deity in general may be thought to provide. Here, however, it will be suggested that by its very nature as a composite being, a mixanthrope may also offer something very particular not obtainable from purely anthropomorphic gods. It is also the case that mixanthropic gods do not simply pose problems – they also provide solutions.

By itself, the mixanthrope's animal part confers some positive associations. Connected with the animal element are the mixanthrope's special (often mantic) knowledge, its frequent magical musicality, its participation in the benefits of the Dionysiac sphere. Pan especially – lively, humorous, fertility-bringing – embodies the good as well as the frightening sides of animality. The Sirens' bird-parts clearly contribute an association with melodious song. But recognising this brings us no closer to what makes a mixanthrope, a composite of animal and human, particularly valuable as symbol and god.

In addition to containing animal traits, many mixanthropes display a surprising capacity for humanity. Those who herd and/or hunt animals do so from a standpoint which is, of course, human. They themselves, as half-animal and half-human, encapsulate the key aspects of man's day-to-day interaction with the animal world, and they do so from man's own perspective. Pan clearly shows the humorous potential of this possibility: one moment he is butting, or mating with, goats, in goat mode; the next he is herding, managing and ordering the same animals. He can be either quasi-human or quasi-animal, depending on the whim of the artist; but he is never wholly one or the other.

Some mixanthropes, however, achieve what might be termed *super-humanity*, which is striking and even surprising given that their humanity appears anatomically compromised. Rather than being less than human, as one might expect, they are, on one level, more human than humans. The outstanding examples of this are Cheiron and Kekrops. The former in myth is an agent of *paideia*, of education. He initiates young heroes into aristocratic adulthood, leading them away from the finite savagery that is childhood. Kekrops is a founder of human institutions, most notably monarchy – he is the first king of Athens – and monogamous marriage, customs which Greeks considered crucial in distinguishing man from beast, especially marriage. Thus both Cheiron and Kekrops are directly responsible for two major pillars of human – as opposed to animal – life. This is a startling rôle for a mixanthrope, half-animal, to hold.

The ways in which they fulfil it are also illuminating. They themselves present antitheses to the human institutions for which they stand. Cheiron may be wise, but he is also firmly outside the human society into which he leads young heroes. While they are with him, they experience a way of life at least partially in contrast with that for which they are being prepared: they live in a cave beyond the normal zone of habitation of men; they eat the marrow of bears and similar unorthodox foodstuffs. They share the centaur's *modus vivendi* for a brief, transitional period, before leaving it forever.[1] This has all the hallmarks of a rite of passage, essential to individual progress.

Kekrops invents monogamous marriage and therefore the birth of legitimate children; and yet his own birth is quite different. He has a single, elemental and primordial parent, the Earth. The genesis of Kekrops himself is at complete variance with the human institutions which he creates and represents. Mixanthropic deities like Cheiron and Kekrops stand at junctions, chiefly temporal. They themselves embody a primitive state, whether it is the childhood of an individual or the early stages of an entire human society. They embody the old, but they usher in the new. They themselves cannot fully occupy the new order which they facilitate; they are rooted in the *ancien régime*. But they make transition possible; and their dual nature must be a visual expression of this. (That they are both repeatedly called *diphuês*, emphasising the balance of the animal and the human in their composition, is surely significant here.)

But mixanthropy does more than expressing transition. To uncover the true depth of its value, it is illuminating to compare mixanthropes with other mythical combinations of animal and human. If one does this, mixanthropy appears not so much as a problematic state – liminal, unstable – as a resolution of problems. There are two things which the mixanthrope avoids:

–   Complete fluidity of state
–   Concealed animal elements

It was argued in Chapter 7 that mixanthropy is a way of both depicting and fixing a being undergoing the complete fluidity of metamorphosis. Metamorphosists who do not have mixanthropic representation are overwhelmingly accorded negative associations. Grief-stricken or assaulted women undergo

---

[1] Though *paideia* is one of the hallmarks of human civilisation, von Blanckenhagen is surely right to remark (1987, 87) that 'Cheiron teaches natural wisdom which is close to animal instinct.' While with him, young heroes receive a portion of some qualities which are absent (lost?) from mankind itself.

metamorphosis as part of their status as victims; but other characters are actively malign. Lykaon is the chief human example of this. His metamorphosis is contingent on his savage and transgressive human sacrifice. He is by nature a breaker of codes, both human and divine; his boundary-crossing transformation is the culmination of a life characterised by the disastrous blurring of the human and the animal. His adoption of wolf-form merely makes manifest the wolfishness which has always been inside him.

Pausanias explicitly contrasts the benevolent Kekrops and the impious Lykaon,[2] and indeed, there is an underlying discrepancy between them in this regard also. Kekrops' invention of monogamous marriage puts an end to a chaotic scrambling, not of animal and human but of male and female: a primordial situation in which man and women mate promiscuously and in which children are ignorant of the identity of their fathers, and vice versa.[3] This rôle finds a rare visual echo in descriptions of Kekrops not as a mixanthrope proper but as a combination of male and female parts:[4] once again, the hybrid with its distinct division of components can express a resolution of elements which have been, or which risk being, mingled together in a worrying state of confusion. As with the transgression of Lykaon, this chaos is a condition of the primordial past, which the hybrid helps to usher out. As Parker has observed, the reign of Kekrops in Athens is characterised in such a way that it resembles the Golden Age of Kronos,[5] and yet Kekrops' rôle is not to ensure the continuation of a time of bliss but to facilitate progress and development.

With such examples of the resolving power of mixanthropy may be compared figures like Dionysos and Demeter Melaina. In these two cases, mixanthropic representation – while it is conceptually important – is iconographically slight. Is it merely coincidental that these two deities, of all the mixanthropes studied, are most strongly associated with destructive deconstruction of boundaries? Demeter when angry forces men to re-enact the wolfish crime of Lykaon and eat their own offspring; she pushes man back into the animal state which it has left behind. Dionysos too causes humans to cross the human/animal line, either by reducing them to madness and savagery, or by actually turning them into animals. He also famously leads Pentheus to move across the male/female divide. So while figures like Cheiron and Kekrops preside over and preserve vital boundaries in human life, most significantly that between mankind and the wild, the animal, Demeter Melaina and Dionysos threaten the security of those boundaries. Protective mixanthropes appear to have far more widespread and canonised mixanthropic

---

[2] Paus. 8.2.2-3. Ancient narrators did from time to time disturb the dichotomy between Lykaon and Kekrops, eliding their deeds and their ethics; for a discussion of these trends, see Fourgous (1993).

[3] Klearchos in Athen. *Deipn.* 13.555d.

[4] *Suda s.v.* 'Kekrops'; Fourgous (1993), 234.

[5] Parker (1987), 197-8.

depiction; destructive ones are far less secure in their form. Their animal component is often a matter of uncertainty; it is not fixed or stable; and it is not always apparent.

This brings me to the question of latent or concealed animal nature. The anxiety attendant on this in Greek thought is exemplified by the characters of Pandora and Helen, described in the previous chapter. In Hesiod's admittedly extreme treatment,[6] Pandora is both the epitome of the feminine and the source of all man's travails. She also carries a special form of latent animality, which is the basis of her rôle as a *dolos*, or trick, designed to entrap Prometheus and so mankind. When she is created, various gods lavish on her exterior the graces that characterise feminine allure; Hermes, however, places within her a *kuneos noos*, the mind of a bitch.[7] Pandora displays, and is fatal because of, an extreme and significant form of the inside/outside discrepancy. Her perfect beauty conceals its antithesis: an element not only of the animal, but of an animal proverbially connected with shamelessness and vice.[8] Helen reveals a variant on this characterisation with her *kuôn/kunôps* imagery.

Pandora and Helen represent a particular female element of the inside/outside discourse, but it is not limited to femininity; the figure of Lykaon, who is at his most transgressive and despicable when his wolf-nature lies hidden beneath a human exterior, shows that. Mixanthropes, however, resolve the situation by externalising and making manifest the animal/human combination. Their composite and contradictory aspect is displayed in plain view, whereas with a figure like Pandora it is part-hidden and therefore more dangerous. Thetis, whose mixanthropic depiction is slight, has some of Pandora's frightening inner/outer discrepancy, expressed in images of outer whiteness and inner blackness (see Chapter 1).

In Chapter 7 it was remarked that Snodgrass and Davies put forward opposing views of the use of mixanthropic forms to show metamorphosists in art. Snodgrass argues that the mixanthropic form shows change by capturing a being mid-way between two states. Davies counters by claiming that what the mixanthropic form shows is the divergence between inner (still human) and outer (animal). I would argue that with regard to deities especially, mixanthropy achieves both things. It captures change, and it makes manifest the inside/outside discrepancy. There is really no conflict between the two. Mixanthropy

---

[6] *Theog.* 570-616; *W&D* 57-105.

[7] *W&D* 67.

[8] It is interesting to note that, as has been observed above, one aspect of Pandora's divinely-created appearance gives, perhaps, a subtle warning of what lies within, at *Theog.* 582: her crown or chaplet is decorated with all kinds of *knôdala*, beasts, a word which carries strongly negative associations. On the one hand, animal imagery was a fairly staple element of decoration in Greek material culture; on the other, in Pandora's case the *knôdala* motif may reasonably be thought to pick up on an element of her inner nature.

and disguise sometimes go together. For instance, Pasiphae concealed in her wooden bull, a strange combination of inner and outer identities, produces the Minotaur, in whom the combination is worn on the surface. Both are monstrous, but it is Pasiphae, mistress of deception, who is the active transgressor in the story.[9]

Even repeated mixanthropy does not obviate the possibility that the deity's destructive animal side will be manifested punitively to the detriment of mortals. But this possibility is kept firmly in view by the composite form. Mixanthropy is a visible reminder of possible divine aggression, but its very visibility appears to diffuse some of its fear-inspiring power. It is both a warning and a reassurance. So a mixanthropic deity whose representation achieves a certain stability seems able to protect man from the baneful aspects of the animal elements the dual form contains. By counteracting the fluidity and chaos of metamorphosis and by making manifest the juxtaposition of animal and human, the deity can offer a resolution to the two abiding uncertainties of human identity. The first is, 'Is human identity secure or will it succumb to retrogressive transformation?' The second is, 'Is the humanity of the outside form matched by the nature residing within?' In the face of these questions, the mixanthropic deity appears to offer some comfort.

Mixanthropy, then, is less problematic than the alternatives: on the one hand metamorphosis, on the other a deceptive human form. It also has its own positive value. This explains at least in part its endurance, in some cases its abiding popularity, despite all the negative aspects on which this book has dwelt at length. It explains why a mixanthrope can be a god, as well as a monster, because it places them at the heart of human needs and concerns. Monstrous forms are often seen as an expression of the Other, and this is one aspect of them; but the deities here studied are not simply a straightforward antithesis to humanity. They cannot be dismissed as curiosities or whimsies of art. Nor are they the obsolete products of an age before texts. So far from being simply primitive relics, they are a reflection of the ancient sense of human progress away from the primitive. Their persistent relevance in ancient cult makes them worth detailed study, and their great attraction lies in the fact that they are at once highly unusual and, in many regions, essential to the themes and needs of Greek religious life.

---

[9] Frontisi-Ducroux (1975), 137-41.

Appendix

Text and translation of Pausanias 8.42[1]

τὸ δὲ ἕτερον τῶν ὁρῶν τὸ Ἐλάιον ἀπωτέρω μὲν Φιγαλίας ὅσον τε σταδίοις τριάκοντά ἐστι, Δήμητρος δὲ ἄντρον αὐτόθι ἱερὸν ἐπίκλησιν Μελαίνης. ὅσα μὲν δὴ οἱ ἐν Θελπούσῃ λέγουσιν ἐς μῖξιν τὴν Ποσειδῶνός τε καὶ Δήμητρος, κατὰ ταὐτά σφισιν οἱ Φιγαλεῖς νομίζουσι, τεχθῆναι δὲ ὑπὸ τῆς Δήμητρος οἱ Φιγαλεῖς φασιν οὐχ ἵππον ἀλλὰ τὴν Δέσποιναν ἐπονομαζομένην ὑπὸ Ἀρκάδων· τὸ δὲ ἀπὸ τούτου λέγουσι θυμῷ τε ἅμα ἐς τὸν Ποσειδῶνα αὐτὴν καὶ ἐπὶ τῆς Περσεφόνης τῇ ἁρπαγῇ πένθει χρωμένην μέλαιναν ἐσθῆτα ἐνδῦναι καὶ ἐς τὸ σπήλαιον τοῦτο ἐλθοῦσαν ἐπὶ χρόνον ἀπεῖναι πολύν. ὡς δὲ ἐφθείρετο μὲν πάντα ὅσα ἡ γῆ τρέφει, τὸ δὲ ἀνθρώπων γένος καὶ ἐς πλέον ἀπώλλυτο ὑπὸ τοῦ λιμοῦ, θεῶν μὲν ἄλλων ἠπίστατο ἄρα οὐδεὶς ἔνθα ἀπεκέκρυπτο ἡ Δημήτηρ, τὸν δὲ Πᾶνα ἐπιέναι μὲν τὴν Ἀρκαδίαν καὶ ἄλλοτε αὐτὸν ἐν ἄλλῳ θηρεύειν τῶν ὀρῶν, ἀφικόμενον δὲ καὶ πρὸς τὸ Ἐλάιον κατοπτεῦσαι τὴν Δήμητρα σχήματός τε ὡς εἶχε καὶ ἐσθῆτα ἐνεδέδυτο ποίαν· πυθέσθαι δὴ τὸν Δία ταῦτα παρὰ τοῦ Πανὸς καὶ οὕτως ὑπ' αὐτοῦ πεμφθῆναι τὰς Μοίρας παρὰ τὴν Δήμητρα, τὴν δὲ πεισθῆναί τε ταῖς Μοίραις καὶ ἀποθέσθαι μὲν τὴν ὀργήν, ὑφεῖναι δὲ καὶ τῆς λύπης. σφᾶς δὲ ἀντὶ τούτων φασὶν οἱ Φιγαλεῖς τό τε σπήλαιον νομίσαι τοῦτο ἱερὸν Δήμητρος καὶ ἐς αὐτὸ ἄγαλμα ἀναθεῖναι ξύλου. πεποιῆσθαι δὲ οὕτω σφίσι τὸ ἄγαλμα· καθέζεσθαι μὲν ἐπὶ πέτρᾳ, γυναικὶ δὲ ἐοικέναι τἆλλα πλὴν κεφαλήν· κεφαλὴν δὲ καὶ κόμην εἶχεν ἵππου, καὶ δρακόντων τε καὶ ἄλλων θηρίων εἰκόνες προσεπεφύκεσαν τῇ κεφαλῇ· χιτῶνα δὲ ἐνεδέδυτο καὶ <ἐς> ἄκρους τοὺς πόδας· δελφὶς δὲ ἐπὶ τῆς χειρὸς ἦν αὐτῇ, περιστερὰ δὲ ἡ ὄρνις ἐπὶ τῇ ἑτέρᾳ. ἐφ' ὅτῳ μὲν δὴ τὸ ξόανον ἐποιήσαντο οὕτως, ἀνδρὶ οὐκ ἀσυνέτῳ γνώμην ἀγαθῷ δὲ καὶ τὰ ἐς μνήμην δῆλά ἐστι· Μέλαιναν δὲ ἐπονομάσαι φασὶν αὐτήν, ὅτι καὶ ἡ θεὸς μέλαιναν τὴν ἐσθῆτα εἶχε. τοῦτο μὲν δὴ τὸ ξόανον οὔτε ὅτου ποίημα ἦν οὔτε ἡ φλὸξ τρόπον ὅντινα ἐπέλαβεν αὐτό, μνημονεύουσιν· ἀφανισθέντος δὲ τοῦ ἀρχαίου Φιγαλεῖς οὔτε ἄγαλμα ἄλλο ἀπεδίδοσαν τῇ θεῷ καὶ ὁπόσα ἐς ἑορτὰς καὶ θυσίας τὰ πολλὰ δὴ παρῶπτό σφισιν, ἐς ὃ ἡ ἀκαρπία ἐπιλαμβάνει τὴν γῆν· καὶ ἱκετεύσασιν αὐτοῖς χρᾷ τάδε ἡ Πυθία·

Ἀρκάδες Ἀζᾶνες βαλανηφάγοι, οἳ Φιγάλειαν
νάσσασθ', ἱππολεχοῦς Δηοῦς κρυπτήριον ἄντρον,
ἥκετε πευσόμενοι λιμοῦ λύσιν ἀλγινόεντος,
μοῦνοι δὶς νομάδες, μοῦνοι πάλιν ἀγριοδαῖται.
Δηὼ μέν σε ἔπαυσε νομῆς, Δηὼ δὲ νομῆας
ἐκ δησισταχύων καὶ ἀναστοφάγων πάλι θῆκε,
νοσφισθεῖσα γέρα προτέρων τιμάς τε παλαιάς.
καί σ' ἀλληλοφάγον θήσει τάχα καὶ τεκνοδαίτην,
εἰ μὴ πανδήμοις λοιβαῖς χόλον ἱλάσσεσθε
σήραγγός τε μυχὸν θείαις κοσμήσετε τιμαῖς.

ὡς δὲ οἱ Φιγαλεῖς ἀνακομισθὲν τὸ μάντευμα ἤκουσαν, τά τε ἄλλα ἐς πλέον τιμῆς ἢ τὰ πρότερα τὴν Δήμητρα ἦγον καὶ Ὀνάταν τὸν Μίκωνος Αἰγινήτην πείθουσιν ἐφ' ὅσῳ δὴ

---

[1] For convenience and consistency I use here the text and translation of W.H.S. Jones in the Loeb edition.

μισθῷ ποιῆσαί σφισιν ἄγαλμα Δήμητρος· τοῦ δὲ Ὀνάτα τούτου Περγαμηνοῖς ἐστιν
Ἀπόλλων χαλκοῦς, θαῦμα ἐν τοῖς μάλιστα μεγέθους τε ἕνεκα καὶ ἐπὶ τῇ τέχνῃ. τότε δὴ ὁ
ἀνὴρ οὗτος ἀνευρὼν γραφὴν ἢ μίμημα τοῦ ἀρχαίου ξοάνου – τὰ πλείω δέ, ὡς λέγεται, καὶ
κατὰ ὀνειράτων ὄψιν – ἐποίησε χαλκοῦν Φιγαλεῦσιν ἄγαλμα, γενεαῖς μάλιστα <δυσὶν>
ὕστερον τῆς ἐπὶ τὴν Ἑλλάδα ἐπιστρατείας τοῦ Μήδου. μαρτυρεῖ δέ μοι τῷ λόγῳ· κατὰ γὰρ
τὴν Ξέρξου διάβασιν ἐς τὴν Εὐρώπην Συρακουσῶν τε ἐτυράννει καὶ Σικελίας τῆς ἄλλης
Γέλων ὁ Δεινομένους· ἐπεὶ δὲ ἐτελεύτησε Γέλων, ἐς Ἱέρωνα ἀδελφὸν Γέλωνος περιῆλθεν ἡ
ἀρχή· Ἱέρωνος δὲ ἀποθανόντος πρότερον πρὶν ἢ τῷ Ὀλυμπίῳ Διὶ ἀναθεῖναι τὰ ἀναθήματα
ἃ εὔξατο ἐπὶ τῶν ἵππων ταῖς νίκαις, οὕτω Δεινομένης ὁ Ἱέρωνος ἀπέδωκεν ὑπὲρ τοῦ
πατρός. Ὀνάτα καὶ ταῦτα ποιήματα, καὶ ἐπιγράμματα ἐν Ὀλυμπίᾳ, τὸ μὲν ὑπὲρ τοῦ
ἀναθήματός ἐστιν αὐτῶν,

> σόν ποτε νικήσας, Ζεῦ Ὀλύμπιε, σεμνὸν ἀγῶνα
> τεθρίππῳ μὲν ἅπαξ, μουνοκέλητι δὲ δίς,
> δῶρα Ἱέρων τάδε σοι ἐχαρίσσατο· παῖς δ' ἀνέθηκε
> Δεινομένης πατρὸς μνῆμα Συρακοσίου·
> τὸ δὲ ἕτερον λέγει τῶν ἐπιγραμμάτων·
> υἱὸς <μέν> με Μίκωνος Ὀνάτας ἐξετέλεσσεν,
> νάσῳ ἐν Αἰγίνᾳ δώματα ναιετάων.

ἡ δὲ ἡλικία τοῦ Ὀνάτα κατὰ τὸν Ἀθηναῖον Ἡγίαν καὶ Ἀγελάδαν συμβαίνει τὸν Ἀργεῖον.
ταύτης μάλιστα ἐγὼ τῆς Δήμητρος ἕνεκα ἐς Φιγαλίαν ἀφικόμην. καὶ ἔθυσα τῇ θεῷ, καθὰ
καὶ οἱ ἐπιχώριοι νομίζουσιν, οὐδέν· τὰ δὲ ἀπὸ τῶν δένδρων τῶν ἡμέρων τά τε ἄλλα καὶ
ἀμπέλου καρπὸν καὶ μελισσῶν τε κηρία καὶ ἐρίων τὰ μὴ ἐς ἐργασίαν πω ἥκοντα ἀλλὰ ἔτι
ἀνάπλεα τοῦ οἰσύπου, ἃ τιθέασιν ἐπὶ τὸν βωμὸν <τὸν> ᾠκοδομημένον πρὸ τοῦ σπηλαίου,
θέντες δὲ καταχέουσιν αὐτῶν ἔλαιον, ταῦτα ἰδιώταις τε ἀνδράσι καὶ ἀνὰ πᾶν ἔτος Φιγαλέων
τῷ κοινῷ καθέστηκεν ἐς τὴν θυσίαν. ἱέρεια δέ σφισίν ἐστιν ἡ δρῶσα, σὺν δὲ αὐτῇ καὶ τῶν
ἱεροθυτῶν καλουμένων ὁ νεώτατος· οἱ δέ εἰσι τῶν ἀστῶν τρεῖς ἀριθμόν. ἔστι δὲ δρυῶν τε
ἄλσος περὶ τὸ σπήλαιον καὶ ὕδωρ ψυχρὸν ἄνεισιν ἐκ τῆς γῆς. τὸ δὲ ἄγαλμα τὸ ὑπὸ τοῦ
Ὀνάτα ποιηθὲν οὔτε ἦν κατ' ἐμὲ οὔτε εἰ ἐγένετο ἀρχὴν Φιγαλεῦσιν ἠπίσταντο οἱ πολλοί·
τῶν δὲ ἐντυχόντων ἡμῖν ἔλεγεν ὁ πρεσβύτατος γενεαῖς πρότερον τρισὶν ἢ κατ' αὐτὸν
ἐμπεσεῖν ἐς τὸ ἄγαλμα ἐκ τοῦ ὀρόφου πέτρας, ὑπὸ τούτων δὲ καταγῆναι καὶ ἐς ἅπαν
ἔφασκεν αὐτὸ ἀφανισθῆναι· καὶ ἕν γε τῷ ὀρόφῳ δῆλα καὶ ἡμῖν ἔτι ἦν, καθὰ ἀπερρώγεσαν αἱ
πέτραι.

The second mountain, Mount Elaius, is some thirty stades away from Phigalia, and
has a cave sacred to Demeter surnamed Black. The Phigalians accept the account of the
people of Thelpusa about the mating of Poseidon and Demeter, but they assert that
Demeter gave birth, not to a horse, but to the Mistress, as the Arcadians call her.
Afterwards, they say, angry with Poseidon and grieved at the rape of Persephone, she
put on black apparel and shut herself up in this cavern for a long time. But when all the
fruits of the earth were perishing, and the human race dying yet more through famine,
no god, it seemed, knew where Demeter was in hiding, until Pan, they say, visited
Arcadia. Roaming from mountain to mountain as he hunted, he came at last to Mount
Elaius and spied Demeter, the state she was in and the clothes she wore. So Zeus learnt
this from Pan, and sent the Fates to Demeter, who listened to the Fates and laid aside
her wrath, moderating her grief as well. For these reasons, the Phigalians say, they
concluded that this cavern was sacred to Demeter and set up in it a wooden image. The
image, they say, was made after this fashion. It was seated on a rock, like to a woman in
all respects save the head. She had the head and hair of a horse, and there grew out of
her head images of serpents and other beasts. Her tunic reached right to her feet; on

one of her hands was a dolphin, on the other a dove. Now why they had the image made after this fashion is plain to any intelligent man who is learned in traditions. They say that they named her Black because the goddess had black apparel. They cannot relate either who made this wooden image or how it caught fire. But the old image was destroyed, and the Phigalians gave the goddess no fresh image, while they neglected for the most part her festivals and sacrifices, until the barrenness fell on the land. Then they went as suppliants to the Pythian priestess and received this response:

> Azanian Arcadians, acorn-eaters, who dwell
> In Phigaleia, the cave that hid Deo, who bare a horse,
> You have come to learn a cure for grievous famine,
> Who alone have twice been nomads, alone have twice lived on wild fruits.
> It was Deo who made you cease from pasturing, Deo who made you pasture again
> After being binders of corn and eaters of cakes,
> Because she was deprived of privileges and ancient honours given by men of
> > former times.
> And soon will she make you eat each other and feed on your children,
> Unless you appease her anger with libations offered by all your people,
> And adorn with divine honors the nook of the cave.

When the Phigalians heard the oracle that was brought back, they held Demeter in greater honour than before, and particularly they persuaded Onatas of Aegina, son of Micon, to make them an image of Demeter at a price. The Pergamenes have a bronze Apollo made by this Onatas, a most wonderful marvel both for its size and workmanship. This man then, about two generations after the Persian invasion of Greece, made the Phigalians an image of bronze, guided partly by a picture or copy of the ancient wooden image which he discovered, but mostly (so goes the story) by a vision that he saw in dreams. As to the date, I have the following evidence to produce. At the time when Xerxes crossed over into Europe, Gelon the son of Deinomenes was despot of Syracuse and of the rest of Sicily besides. When Gelon died, the kingdom devolved on his brother Hieron. Hieron died before he could dedicate to Olympian Zeus the offerings he had vowed for his victories in the chariot-race, and so Deinomenes his son paid the debt for his father. These too are works of Onatas, and there are two inscriptions at Olympia. The one over the offering is this:

> Having won victories in thy grand games, Olympian Zeus,
> Once with the four-horse chariot, twice with the race-horse,
> Hieron bestowed on thee these gifts: his son dedicated them,
> Deinomenes, as a memorial to his Syracusan father.

The other inscription is:

> Onatas, son of Micon, fashioned me,
> Who had his home in the island of Aegina.

Onatas was contemporary with Hegias of Athens and Ageladas of Argos. It was mainly to see this Demeter that I came to Phigalia. I offered no burnt sacrifice to the goddess, that being a custom of the natives. But the rule for sacrifice by private persons, and at the annual sacrifice by the community of Phigalia, is to offer grapes and other cultivated fruits, with honeycombs and raw wool still full of its grease. These they place on the altar built before the cave, afterwards pouring oil over them. They have a priestess who performs the rites, and with her is the youngest of their 'sacrificers,' as they are called, who are citizens, three in number. There is a grove of oaks around the cave, and a cold spring rises from the earth. The image made by Onatas no longer existed in my time, and most of the Phigalians were ignorant that it had ever existed at all. The oldest, however, of the inhabitants I met said that three generations before his time some stones had fallen on the image out of the roof; these crushed the image, destroying it utterly. Indeed, in the roof I could still discern plainly where the stones had broken away.

Bibliography

Adshead, K. *Politics of the Archaic Peloponnese: The Transition from Archaic to Classical Politics.* Aldershot: Avebury, 1986.

Alcock, S.E. and R. Osborne edd., *Placing the Gods: Sanctuaries and Sacred Space in Ancient Greece.* Oxford: Clarendon, 1994.

Alcock, S.E., J.F. Cherry and J. Elsner edd., *Pausanias: Travel and Memory in Roman Greece.* Oxford University Press, 2001.

Aldhouse-Green, M. and S. *The Quest for the Shaman.* London: Thames and Hudson, 2005.

D'Alessio, G.B. 'Textual Fluctuations and Cosmic Streams: Ocean and Acheloios.' *JHS* 124 (2004), 16-37.

Alexandridis, A., M. Wild and L. Winkler-Horaçek edd., *Mensch und Tier in der Antike: Grenzziehung und Grenzüberschreitung.* Wiesbaden: Ludwig Reichert, 2008.

— 'Wenn Götter lieben, wenn Götter strafen: zur Ikonographie der Zoophilie im griechischen Mythos.' In Alexandridis, Wild and Winkler-Horaçek edd. (2008), 285-311.

Alroth, B. ed., *Opus Mixtum: Essays in Ancient Art and Society.* Jonsered: Aström, 1994.

Annus, A. *The God Ninurta in the Mythology and Royal Ideology of Ancient Mesopotamia.* State Archives of Assyria Studies, vol. XIV. Helsinki: Neo-Assyrian Text Corpus Project, 2002.

Aston, E.M.M. 'Asclepius and the Legacy of Thessaly.' *CQ* 54 (2004), 18-32.

— 'The Absence of Chiron.' *CQ* 56 (2006), 349-62.

— 'Hybrid Cult Images in Ancient Greece: Animal, Human, God.' In Alexandridis, Wild and Winkler-Horaçek edd. (2008), 481-502.

— 'Thetis and Cheiron in Thessaly.' *Kernos* 22 (2009), 83-107.

Athanassopoulou, S. ed., *The Bull in the Mediterranean World: Myths & Cults.* Athens: Hellenic Ministry of Culture, 2003.

Atherton, C. ed., *Monsters and Monstrosity in Greek and Roman Culture.* Bari: Levante, 1998.

Bachofen, J.J. *Der Bär in den Religionen des Altertums.* Basel: Schwabe, 1863.

Baur, P.V.C. *Centaurs in Ancient Art: The Archaic Period.* Berlin: K. Curtius, 1912.

Bérard, C. *Anodoi: Essai sur l'imagerie des passages chthoniens.* Neuchatel: Paul Attinger, 1974.

— et al. edd., *A City of Images: Iconography and Society in Ancient Greece.* Trans. D. Lyons. Princeton University Press, 1989.

— and C. Bron, 'Satyric Revels.' In Bérard et al. ed. (1989), 131-49.

Bérard, V. *De l'origine des cultes arcadiens: essai de méthode en mythologie grecque.* Paris: Thorin et Fils, 1894.

Bettinetti, S. *La statua di culto nella pratica rituale greca.* Bari: Levante, 2001.

— and L. Spina, *Il mito delle Sirene.* Torino: Einaudi, 2007.

Bevan, E. *Representations of Animals in Sanctuaries of Artemis and Other Olympian Deities.* Oxford: B.A.R., 1986.

Billault, A. *L'univers de Philostrate.* Latomus vol. 252. Brussels, 2000.

Bingen, J., C. Cambier and G. Nachtergael edd., *Le monde grec: pensée, littérature, histoire, documents. Hommages à Claire Préaux.* Brussels: Éditions de l'Université de Bruxelles, 1975.

Black, J. and A. Green, *Gods, Demons and Symbols of Ancient Mesopotamia. An Illustrated Dictionary*. London: British Museum Press, 1992.

Blakely, S. *Myth, Ritual and Metallurgy in Ancient Greece and Recent Africa*. Cambridge University Press, 2006.

von Blanckenhagen, P.H. 'Easy Monsters.' In Farkas, Harper and Harrison edd. (1987), 85-94.

Blundell, S. and M. Williamson edd., *The Sacred and the Feminine in Ancient Greece*. London: Routledge, 1998.

Boardman, J. 'Very Like a Whale.' In Farkas, Harper and Harrison edd. (1987), 73-84.

— *The Great God Pan: The Survival of an Image*. London: Thames and Hudson, 1997.

— *The Archaeology of Nostalgia: How the Greeks Re-created their Mythical Past*. London: Thames and Hudson, 2002.

Bober, P.F. 'Cernunnos: Origin and Transformation of a Celtic Divinity.' *AJA* 55 (1951), 13-51.

Boedeker, D. and K.A. Raaflaub edd., *Democracy, Empire and the Arts in Classical Athens*. Cambridge MA: Harvard University Press, 1998.

Bömer, F. *P.Ovidius Naso Metamorphosen: Kommentar*. Vol. 5: Books 10-11. Heidelberg: Carl Winter, 1980.

Bonfante, L. 'Fufluns Pacha: The Etruscan Dionysus.' In Carpenter and Faraone edd. (1993), 221-35.

Bonnet, C., C. Jourdain-Annequin and V. Pirenne-Delforge edd., *Le Bestiaire d'Héraclès. IIIᵉ Rencontre héracléenne. Kernos* Suppl. 7. Liège: Centre International d'Étude de la Religion Grecque Antique, 1998.

Boosen, M. *Etruskischer Meeresmischwesen. Untersuchungen zur Typologie und Bedeutung*. Rome: Bretschneider, 1986.

Borgeaud, Ph. 'The Death of the Great Pan: The Problem of Interpretation.' *History of Religions* 22 (1983), 254-83.

—, Y. Christe and I. Urio edd., *L'animal, l'homme, le dieu dans le Proche-Orient ancien. Actes du colloque de Cartigny, Centre d'Étude du Proche-Orient Ancien (CEPOA), Université de Genève, 1981*. Leuven: Peeters, 1984.

— 'L'animal comme opérateur symbolique.' In Borgeaud et al. edd. (1984), 13-19.

— *The Cult of Pan in Ancient Greece*. Trans. K. Atlass and J. Redfield. University of Chicago Press, 1988.

— 'Note sur le Sépias. Mythe et histoire.' *Kernos* 8 (1995), 23-9.

Bowie, E.L. 'Greeks and their Past in the Second Sophistic.' *Past & Present* 46 (1970), 3-41.

— 'Inspiration and Aspiration: Date, Genre and Readership.' In Alcock, Cherry and Elsner edd. (2001), 21-32.

Branham, R.B. *Unruly Eloquence: Lucian and the Comedy of Traditions*. Cambridge MA: Harvard University Press, 1989.

Bremmer, J. 'Scapegoat Rituals in Ancient Greece.' *HSCP* 87 (1983), 299-320.

— ed., *Interpretations of Greek Mythology*. Kent: Croom Helm, 1987.

Brewster, H. *River Gods of Greece: Myths and Mountain Waters in the Hellenic World*. London: Tauris, 1997.

Brixhe, C. and M. Lejeune, *Corpus des inscriptions paléophrygiennes*. Paris: Éditions Recherche sur les Civilisations, 1984.

Broder, Ph.-A. 'La manipulation des images dans les processions en Grèce ancienne.' In Estienne et al. edd. (2008), 122-35.

Brommer, F. *Satyroi*. Würzburg: K. Triltsch, 1937.

— 'Pan im 5. und 4. Jahrhundert v. Chr.' *Marburger Jahrbuch für Kunstwissenschaft* 15 (1949-50), 5-42.

— *Odysseus: Die Taten und Leiden des Helden in antiker Kunst und Literatur*. Darmstadt: Wissenschaftliche Buchgesellschaft, 1983.

Brown, E.L. 'The Divine Name "Pan".' *TAPA* 107 (1977), 57-61.

Bruit, L. 'Pausanias à Phigalie. Sacrifices non-sanglants et discours idéologique.' *Mètis* 1 (1986), 71-96.

Burkert, W. *Structure and History in Greek Mythology and Ritual.* Berkeley: University of California Press, 1979.

— *Homo Necans: The Anthropology of Ancient Greek Sacrificial Ritual and Myth.* Trans. P. Bing. Berkeley: University of California Press, 1983.

— *The Orientalizing Revolution: Near Eastern Influence on Greek Culture in the Early Archaic Age.* Trans. M. E. Pinder. Cambridge MA: Harvard University Press, 1992.

Buschor, E. 'Kentauren.' *AJA* 38 (1934), 128-32.

— *Die Musen der Jenseits.* Munich: F. Bruckmann, 1944.

Buxton, R. 'Wolves and Werewolves in Greek Thought.' In Bremmer ed. (1987), 60-79.

— 'Imaginary Greek Mountains.' *JHS* 112 (1992), 1-15.

— *Imaginary Greece: The Contexts of Mythology.* Cambridge University Press, 1994.

— ed., *Oxford Readings in Greek Religion.* Oxford University Press, 2000.

— *Forms of Astonishment: Greek Myths of Metamorphosis.* Oxford University Press, 2009.

Bynum, C.W. *Metamorphosis and Identity.* New York: Zone Books, 2005.

Campbell, D.A. *Greek Lyric Poetry. A Selection of Early Greek Lyric, Elegiac and Iambic Poetry.* London: Duckworth (Bristol Classical Press), 1967.

Carpenter, T.H. *Dionysian Imagery in Archaic Greek Art: Its Development in Black-figure Vase Painting.* Oxford: Clarendon Press, 1986.

— and C.A. Faraone edd., *Masks of Dionysus.* Ithaca NY: Cornell University Press, 1993.

Carter, J.B. 'The Masks of Ortheia.' *AJA* 91 (1987), 355-83.

Caspari, M.O.B. 'A Survey of Greek Federal Coinage.' *JHS* 37 (1917), 168-83.

Cassin, B., J.-L. Labarrière and G.R. Dherbey edd., *L'Animal dans l'Antiquité.* Paris: Vrin, 1997.

Castriota, D. *Myth, Ethos and Actuality: Official Art in Fifth-Century Athens.* Madison: University of Wisconsin Press, 1992.

Childs, W.A.P. 'The Human Animal: The Near East and Greece.' In Padgett ed. (2003), 49-70.

Chrysostomou, P. Ἡ Θεσσαλικὴ θεὰ Ἐννοδία ἢ φεραία θεά. Athens, Dêmosieumata tou Archaiologikou Deltiou, 1998.

Classen, C.J. 'The Libyan God Ammon in Greece Before 331 BC.' *Historia* 8 (1959), 349-55.

Clay, J.S. 'The Generation of Monsters in Hesiod.' *CP* 88 (1993), 105-16.

Chourmouziades, G. *Magnesia, a Story of a Civilisation.* Athens: M. and R. Kapon, 1982.

Cole, S.G. 'Domesticating Artemis.' In Blundell and Williamson edd. (1998), 27-43.

Colvin, S. 'On Representations of Centaurs in Greek Vase-Painting.' *JHS* 1 (1880), 107-67.

Comparetti, D. 'Inscritti dell' antro delle ninfe presso Farsalos (Tessaglia).' *ASAA* 4-5 (1921-2), 147-60.

Cook, A.B. 'Animal Worship in the Mycenaean Age.' *JHS* 14 (1894), 81-169.

— *Zeus: a Study in Ancient Religion.* Three vols. Cambridge University Press, 1914-40.

Cooper, F.A. *The Temple of Apollo Bassitas.* Four vols. Princeton: American School of Classical Studies at Athens, 1992-1996.

Cosmopoulos, M.B. ed., *Greek Mysteries: The Archaeology and Ritual of Ancient Greek Secret Cults.* London: Routledge, 2003.

Crooke, W. 'King Midas and his Ass's Ears.' *Folklore* 22 (1911), 183-202.

Dalley, S. *Myths from Mesopotamia: Creation, the Flood, Gilgamesh and Others. Translated with an Introduction and Notes.* Oxford University Press, 1989.

Daraki, M. *Dionysus.* Paris: Arthaud, 1985.

Davidson, J. 'Time and Greek Religion.' In Ogden ed. (2007), 204-18.

Davies, M. 'A Convention of Metamorphosis in Greek Art.' *JHS* 106 (1986), 182-183.

Deacy, S. and K.F. Pierce edd., *Rape in Antiquity.* London: Duckworth and Classical Press of Wales, 1997.

Decourt, J.-C., *Inscriptions de Thessalie I: les cités de la vallée de l'Énipeus.* Athens: École Française d'Athènes, 1995.

Degani, E. 'Problems in Greek Gastronomic Poetry: On Matro's *Attikon Deipnon.*' In Wilkins, Harvey and Dobson edd. (1995), 413-28.

Delcourt, M. *Stérilités mystérieuses et naissances maléfiques dans l'antiquité classique.* Liège: Faculté de Philosophie et Lettres, 1938.

— *Hephaistos ou la légende du magicien.* Paris: Belles Lettres, 1957.

Detienne, M. and A.B. Werth, 'Athena and the Mastery of the Horse.' *History of Religions* 11 (1971), 161-84.

Detienne, M. and J.-P. Vernant, *Cunning Intelligence in Greek Culture and Society.* Trans. J. Lloyd. Hassocks: Harvester Press, 1978. (Orig. French Publ. 1974.)

— *Dionysos Slain.* Trans. M. and L. Muellner. Baltimore: Johns Hopkins University Press, 1979. (Orig. French publ. 1977.)

— and J.-P. Vernant, *The Cuisine of Sacrifice Among the Greeks.* Trans. P. Wissing. Chicago University Press, 1989. (Orig. French publ. 1979.)

Deyts, S. *Images des dieux de la Gaule.* Paris: Errance, 1992.

Dickins, G. and K. Kourouniotis, 'Damophon of Messene II.' *ABSA* 13 (1906-7), 357-404 and pll. XII-XIV.

— 'Damophon of Messene III.' *ABSA* 17 (1910-11), 80-87.

— *Hellenistic Sculpture.* Oxford: Clarendon, 1920.

Diels, H. 'Über Epimenides von Kreta.' Berlin: Sitzungsberichte der Königlich preussischen Akademie der Wissenschaften (1891), 387-403.

Dietrich, B.C. 'Demeter, Erinys, Artemis.' *Hermes* 90 (1962), 129-48.

Dillon, M. *Girls and Women in Classical Greek Religion.* London: Routledge, 2002.

Dodds, E.R. *The Greeks and the Irrational.* Berkeley: University of California Press, 1951.

Donohue, A.A. *Xoana and the Origins of Greek Sculpture.* Atlanta GA: Scholars Press, 1988.

Dörig, J. *Onatas of Aegina.* Leiden: Brill, 1977.

Dowden, K. 'Man and Beast in the Religious Imagination of the Roman Empire.' In Atherton ed. (1998), 113-35.

Dugas, Ch., J. Berchmans and M. Clemmensen, *Le sanctuaire d'Aléa Athéna à Tégée au IVᵉ siècle.* Paris: P. Geuthner, 1924.

Dunand, F. and C. Zivie-Coche, *Gods and Men in Egypt: 3000 BCE to 395 CE.* Trans. D. Lorton. Ithaca NY: Cornell University Press, 2004.

Ekroth, G. *The Sacrificial Rituals of Greek Hero-Cults in the Archaic to the Early Hellenistic Periods. Kernos* Suppl. 12. Liège: Centre International d'Étude de la Religion Grecque Antique, 2002.

Elsner, J. ed., *Art and Text in Roman Culture.* Cambridge University Press, 1996.

— 'Structuring "Greece": Pausanias' *Periegesis* as a Literary Construct.' In Alcock, Cherry and Elsner edd. (2001), 3-20.

Estienne, S., D. Jaillard, N. Lubtchansky and C. Pouzadoux edd., *Image et religion dans l'antiquité gréco-romaine. Actes du colloque de Rome, 11-13 décembre 2003, organisé par l'École Française d'Athènes, L'ArScAn (UMR 7041: CNRS, Paris I, Paris X), l'équipe ESPRI et l'ACI jeunes chercheurs ICAR,* Naples, Centre Jean Bérard/École Française d'Athènes, 2008. (*Collection du Centre Jean Bérard,* 28.)

Fabre, G. *La montagne dans l'antiquité.* Univ. de Pau et des Pays de l'Adour, 1992.

Faraone, C. *Talismans and Trojan Horses: Guardian Statues in Ancient Greek Myth and Ritual.* Oxford University Press, 1992.

Farkas, A.E., P.O. Harper and E.B. Harrison edd., *Monsters and Demons in the Ancient and Medieval Worlds: Papers Presented in Honor of Edith Porada*. Mainz am Rhein: P. von Zabern, 1987.

Farnell, L.R. *The Cults of the Greek States*. Five vols. Oxford: Clarendon, 1896-1909.

Fontenrose, J. *Python: A Study of Delphic Myth and its Origins*. Berkeley: University of California Press, 1959.

Forbes Irving, P.M.C. *Metamorphosis in Greek Myths*. Oxford: Clarendon, 1990.

Fougères, G. *Mantinée et l'Arcadie orientale*. Paris: A. Fontemoing, 1898.

Fourgous, D. 'L'hybride et le mixte.' *Mètis* 8 (1993), 231-46.

Frankfurter, D. 'The Perils of Love: Magic and Countermagic in Coptic Egypt.' *Journal of the History of Sexuality* 10 (2001), 480-500.

Frazer, J.G. *Pausanias' Description of Greece*, vol. 4. London: Macmillan, 1898.

— *The Golden Bough: A Study in Magic and Religion*. Eight vols. London: Macmillan, 1911-1915.

Frontisi-Ducroux, F. *Dédale : mythologie de l'artisan en Grèce ancienne*. Paris: F. Maspero, 1975.

— 'In the Mirror of the Mask.' In Bérard ed. (1989), 151-65.

— *Du masque au visage : aspects de l'identité en Grèce ancienne*. Paris: Flammarion, 1995.

— *L'homme-cerf et la femme araignée*. Paris: Gallimard, 2003.

Fusillo, M., A. Hurst and G. Paduano, *Licofrone: Alessandra*. Milan: Guerini, 1991.

Gaifman, M. *Beyond Mimesis in Greek Religious Art: Aniconism in the Archaic and Classical Periods*. Unpubl. D.Phil. Diss., University of Princeton, 2006.

— 'Aniconism and the Notion of the "Primitive" in Greek Antiquity.' In Mylonopoulos ed. (2010), 63-86.

Gais, R.M. 'Some Problems of River-God Iconography.' *AJA* 82 (1978), 355-70.

Gantz, T. *Early Greek Myth: A Guide to Literary and Artistic Sources*. Baltimore: Johns Hopkins University Press, 1993.

Garland, R. *The Eye of the Beholder: Deformity and Disability in the Graeco-Roman World*. London: Duckworth, 1995.

— *The Piraeus*. London: Duckworth (Classical Press of Wales), 2001.

Giannopoulos, N. "Ἄντρον νυμφῶν καὶ Χίρωνος παρα τὴν Φάρσαλον.' *BCH* 36 (1912), 668-9.

— 'Φαρσάλου ἄντρον ἐπιγεγραμμένον.' *Arch.Eph.* 1919, 48-53.

Gilhus, I.S. *Animals, Gods and Humans: Changing Attitudes to Animals in Greek, Roman and Early Christian Ideas*. London: Routledge, 2006.

Gilmore, D.D. *Evil Beings, Mythical Beasts, and All Manner of Imaginary Terrors*. Philadelphia: University of Pennsylvania Press, 2003.

Gladigow, B. 'Präsenz der Bilder, Präsenz der Götter. Kultbilder und Bilder der Götter in der griechischen Religion.' *Visible Religion* 4-5 (1985-86), 114-33.

— 'Epiphanie, Statuette, Kultbild. Griechische Gottesvorstellungen im Wechsel von Kontext und Medium.' *Visible Religion* 7 (1990), 98-121.

Goldhill, S. and R. Osborne edd., *Art and Text in Ancient Greek Culture*. Cambridge University Press, 1994.

Gourmelen, L. *Kékrops, le roi-serpent: imaginaire athénien, représentations de l'humain et de l'animalité en Grèce ancienne*. Paris: Belles Lettres, 2004.

Graf, F. *Nordionische Kulte: religionsgeschichtliche und epigraphische Untersuchungen zu den Kulten von Chios, Erythrai, Klazomenai und Phokaia*. Rome: Schweizerisches Institut, 1985.

Grégoire, H., R. Goossens and M. Mathieu, *Asklèpios, Apollo Smintheus et Rudra: Études sur le dieu à la taupe et le dieu au rat dans la Grèce et dans l'Inde*. Brussels: Théonoé, 1950.

Green, M. *Animals in Celtic Life and Myth*. London: Routledge, 1992.

Griffith, G.T. *The Mercenaries of the Hellenistic World*. Cambridge University Press, 1935.

Griffiths, J.G. 'The Orders of Gods in Greece and Egypt (According to Herodotus).' *JHS* 75 (1955), 21-3.

Guarducci, M. 'Paestum. Cippo arcaico col nome di Chirone.' *NSA* 73 (1948), 185-92.

Guillaume-Coirier, G. 'Chiron Phillyride.' *Kernos* 8 (1995), 113-22.

Guimier-Sorbets, A.-M., M. Jost and Y. Morizot edd., 'Rites, cultes et religion: le site de Lycosoura.' *Ktema* 33 (2008), 89-209.

Guthrie, W.K.C. *The Greeks and their Gods.* London: Methuen, 1950.

— *Orpheus and Greek Religion: A Study of the Orphic Movement.* London: Methuen, 1952.

Habicht, C. *Pausanias' Guide to Ancient Greece.* Berkeley: University of California Press, 1985.

Hägg, R. and G.C. Nordquist edd., *Celebrations of Death and Divinity in the Bronze Age Argolid.* Stockholm: Svenska institutet i Athen, 1990.

Hägg, R. ed., *The Iconography of Greek Cult in the Archaic and Classical Periods:* Proceedings of the First International Seminar on Ancient Greek Cult, Delphi, 16-18 November 1990. Athens & Liège: Centre d'Étude de la Religion Grecque Antique, 1992.

— ed., *Ancient Greek Cult Practice from the Epigraphical Evidence.* Stockholm: Aström, 1994.

Hall, J.M. *Ethnic Identity in Greek Antiquity.* Cambridge University Press, 1997.

Halperin, D.M. *Before Pastoral: Theocritus and the Ancient Tradition of Bucolic Poetry.* New Haven: Yale University Press, 1983.

Hammond, N.G.L. and G.T. Griffith, *A History of Macedonia*, vol. 2. Oxford: Clarendon, 1979.

Hansen, W., *Phlegon of Tralles' Book of Marvels.* University of Exeter Press, 1996.

Harrison, J. *Prolegomena to the Study of Greek Religion.* 2nd ed. Cambridge University Press: 1908.

— *Themis: A Study of the Social Origins of Greek Religion.* Cambridge University Press, 1912 (repr. London: Merlin, 1963).

Harrison, E. 'PAN, PANEION, PANIKON.' *CR* 40 (1926), 6-8.

Head, B.V. *Historia Numorum: A Manual of Greek Numismatics.* Oxford: Clarendon, 1911.

Heath, M. 'Aristophanes and his Rivals.' *G&R* 37 (1990), 143-58.

Hedreen, G.M. 'The Cult of Achilles in the Euxine.' *Hesperia* 60 (1991), 313-30.

— *Silens in Attic Black-figure Vase-painting: Myth and Performance.* Ann Arbor: University of Michigan Press, 1992.

Hejnic, J. *Pausanias the Perieget and the Archaic History of Arcadia.* Prague: Nakladatelství Ceskoslovenské Akademie Ved, 1961.

Herbig, R. *Pan: der griechische Bocksgott.* Frankfurt: Klosterman, 1949.

Hernández, P.N. 'Back in the Cave of the Cyclops.' *AJP* 121 (2000), 345-66.

Higgins, R.A. *Minoan and Mycenaean Art.* London: Thames and Hudson, 1981.

Hirst, G.M. 'The Cults of Olbia: I.' *JHS* 22 (1902), 245-67.

— 'The Cults of Olbia: II.' *JHS* 23 (1903), 24-53.

Hodkinson, S. 'Animal Husbandry in the Greek Polis.' In Whittaker ed. (1988), 35-74.

Hommel, H. *Der Gott Achilleus.* Heidelberg: Carl Winter, 1980.

Hooker, J.T. *Mycenaean Greece.* London: Routledge and Kegan Paul, 1976.

Hornung, E. *Conceptions of God in Ancient Egypt: The One and the Many.* Trans. J. Baines. Ithaca NY: Cornell University Press, 1982. (Orig. German publ. 1971.)

Horstmanshoff, H.F.J., H.W. Singor, F.T. van Straten and J.H.M. Strubbe edd., *Kykeon: Studies in Honour of H.S. Versnel.* Leiden: Brill, 2002.

How, W.W. and J. Wells, *A Commentary on Herodotus in Two Volumes*, vol. 1: Books I-IV. Oxford University Press, 1912.

Howe, T. *Pastoral Politics: Animals, Agriculture and Society in Ancient Greece.* Publications of the Association of Ancient Historians 9. Claremont CA: Regina Books, 2008.

Hübinger, U. 'On Pan's Iconography and the Cult in the "Sanctuary of Pan" on the Slopes of Mount Lykaion.' In Hägg ed. (1992), 189-212.

— 'Überlegungen zu den Bronzestatuetten aus dem "Pan"-Heiligtum am Südabhang des Lykaion.' In Palagia and Coulson edd. (1993), 25-31.

Hughes, D.D. *Human Sacrifice in Ancient Greece.* London: Routledge, 1991.

Hutton, W. *Describing Greece: Landscape and Literature in the* Periegesis *of Pausanias.* Cambridge University Press, 2005.

Huys, M. '125 Years of Scholarship on Apollodorus the Mythographer: A Bibliographic Survey.' *AC* 66 (1997), 319-51.

— and D. Colomo, 'Bibliographical Survey on Apollodorus the Mythographer.' *AC* 73 (2004), 219-37.

Imhoof-Blumer, F. *Die Münzen Akarnaniens.* Vienna: Druck der k.-k. Hof-und Staatsdruckerei, 1878.

Immerwahr, W. *Die Kulte und Mythen Arkadiens.* Leipzig: B.G. Teubner, 1891.

Isler, H.P. *Acheloos: eine Monographie.* Bern: Francke, 1970.

Isler-Kerényi, C. *Nike: der Typus der laufenden Flügelfrau in archaischer Zeit.* Zürich and Stuttgart: Eugen Rentsch, 1969.

Jaccottet, J.-F. *Choisir Dionysos. Les associations dionysiaques ou la face cachée du dionysisme.* Zurich: Akanthus, 2003.

Jameson, M. 'Perseus, the Hero of Mykenai.' In Hägg and Nordquist edd. (1990), 213-22.

Jannoray, J. 'Nouvelles inscriptions de Lébadée.' *BCH* 64-5 (1940-41), 36-59.

Janssens, E. 'Le Pélion, le Centaure Chiron et la sagesse archaïque.' In Bingen, Cambier and Nachtergael edd. (1975), 325-37.

Jeanmaire, H. 'Chiron.' In *Mélanges Henri Grégoire*, vol. 1. Brussels: Secrétariat des éditions de l'Institut, 1949, 255-65.

Jenkins, K. *Coins of Greek Sicily.* London: British Museum Press, 1976.

Jost, M. *Sanctuaires et cultes d'Arcadie.* Paris: Vrin, 1985.

— 'Image de l'Arcadie au IIIᵉ s. av. J.-C.: Lycophron, Alexandra, V. 479-483.' In Mactoux and Évelyne edd. (1989), 285-93.

— a) 'Sanctuaires ruraux et sanctuaires urbains en Arcadie.' In Schachter ed. (1992), 205-45.

— b) 'La vie religieuse dans les montagnes d'Arcadie.' In Fabre ed. (1992), 55-68.

— 'The Distribution of Sanctuaries in Civic Space in Arcadia.' In Alcock and Osborne edd. (1994), 217-30.

— 'Les schémas de peuplement de l'Arcadie aux époques archaïque et classique.' In Nielsen and Roy edd. (1999), 192-247.

— 'Mystery Cults in Arcadia.' In Cosmopoulos ed. (2003), 143-68.

— 'The Religious System in Arcadia.' In Ogden ed. (2007), 264-80.

— 'La vie religieuse à Lykosoura.' In Guimier-Sorbets, Jost and Morizot edd. (2008), 94-110.

Karageorghis, V. 'Notes on Some Cypriote Priests Wearing Bull-Masks.' *HTR* 64 (1971), 261-70.

— *Two Cypriote Sanctuaries of the Cypro-Archaic Period.* Rome: Consiglio nazionale delle ricerche, 1977.

— *The Coroplastic Art of Ancient Cyprus.* Vol. VI: *The Cypro-Archaic Period: Monsters, Animals and Miscellanea.* Nikosia: Leventis, 1996.

Karagiorga, Th. *Γοργείη Κεφαλή.* Athens: Archaiologike Hetaireia, 1970.

Kavvadias, P. *Fouilles de Lycosoura.* Athens, 1893.

Kearns, E. *The Heroes of Attica.* London: Institute of Classical Studies, 1989.

Keller, O. *Die Antike Tierwelt.* 2 vols. Leipzig: Engelmann, 1909-13.

Kenna, V.E.G. *Cretan Seals: With a Catalogue of the Minoan Gems in the Ashmolean Museum.* Oxford: Clarendon, 1960.

Kenner, H. *Der Fries des Tempels von Bassai-Phigalia.* Vienna: Deuticke, 1946.

Kirk, G.S. *Myth: Its Meaning and Function in Ancient and Other Cultures.* Cambridge University Press, 1971.

Kourouniotis, K. Ἀνασκαφὴ ἱεροῦ Νομίου Πανός.' *Prakt.* 1902, 72-5.

a)— Ἀνασκαφὴ Λυκαίου.' *Prakt.* 1903, 51-2.

b)— Ἀνασκαφὴ ἐν Κωτίλῳ.' *Arch.Eph.* 1903, 153-87.

— Ἀνασκαφαὶ Λυκαίου.' *Arch. Eph.* 1904, 153-214.

— τὸ ἐν Λυκοσούρας μέγαρον τῆς Δεσποίνας.' *Arch. Eph.* 1912, 142-61.

Krumeich, R., N. Pechstein and B. Seidensticker edd., *Das griechische Satyrspiel.* Darmstadt: Wissenschaftliche Buchgesellschaft, 1999.

Lada-Richards, I. "Foul Monster or Good Saviour'? Reflections on Ritual Monsters.' In Atherton ed. (1998), 41-82.

Lamb, W. 'Arcadian Bronze Statuettes.' *ABSA* 27 (1925-6), 133-48.

Langerlöf, M.R. *The Sculptures of the Parthenon: Aesthetics and Interpretation.* New Haven: Yale University Press, 2000.

Larson, J. *Greek Nymphs: Myth, Cult, Lore.* Oxford University Press, 2001.

— 'A Land Full of Gods: Nature Deities in Greek Religion.' In Ogden ed. (2007), 56-70.

Lattimore, S., *The Marine Thiasos in Greek Sculpture.* Los Angeles: University of California Institute of Archaeology, 1976.

Lawler, L.B. ΊΧΘΥΕΣ ΧΟΡΕΥΤΑΙ.' *CP* 36 (1941), 142-55.

— 'Pindar and Some Animal Dances.' *CP* 41 (1946), 155-9.

— '"Dancing Herds of Animals."' *CJ* 47 (1952), 317-24.

Leonardos, B. Ἀνασκαφαὶ τοῦ ἐν Λυκοσούρᾳ ἱεροῦ τῆς Δεσποίνης.' *Prakt.* 1896, 93-126.

Lesky, A. *Gesammelte Schriften. Aufsätze und Reden zu antike und deutsche Dichtung und Kultur.* Ed. W. Kraus. Bern and Munich: Francke Verlag, 1966.

Lévêque, P. 'Sur quelques cultes d'Arcadie: princesse-ourse, hommes-loups et dieux-chevaux.' *IH* 23 (1961), 93-108.

Levi, D. 'L'antro delle ninfe e di Pan a Farsalo in Tessaglia: Topographia e scavi.' *ASAA* 6-7 (1923), 27-42.

Lévi-Strauss, C. *The Raw and the Cooked.* Trans. J. and D. Weightman. London: Jonathan Cape, 1970. (Orig. French publ. 1964.)

Lévy, E. 'Sondages à Lykosoura et date de Damophon.' *BCH* 91 (1967), 518-45.

Lindsay, J. *Leisure and Pleasure in Roman Egypt.* London: Muller, 1965.

Linforth, I.M. *The Arts of Orpheus.* New York: Arno, 1973.

Lipinski, E. 'Zeus Ammon and Baal Hammon.' *Studia Phoenicia* 4 (1986), 307-32.

Lissarrague, F. 'Why Satyrs Are Good to Represent.' In Winkler and Zeitlin edd. (1990), 228-36.

— 'On the Wildness of Satyrs.' In Carpenter and Faraone edd. (1993), 207-20.

— 'Women, Boxes, Containers: Some Signs and Metaphors.' In Reeder ed. (1995), 91-101.

Lloyd, G.E.R. *Science, Folklore and Ideology: Studies in the Life Sciences of Ancient Greece.* Cambridge University Press, 1983.

Lloyd-Jones, H. ed., *Females of the Species: Semonides on Women.* London: Duckworth, 1975.

Lonsdale, S.H. 'Attitudes towards Animals in Ancient Greece.' *G&R* 26 (1979), 146-59.

Loraux, N. *Born of the Earth: Myth and Politics in Athens.* Ithaca NY: Cornell University Press, 2000.

Loukas, I. and E. Loukas, 'The Megaron of Lykosoura and Some Prehistoric Telesteria.' *JPR* 1988 II: 25-34.

Loukas, I. 'Ritual Surprise and Terror in Ancient Greek Posession-Dromena.' *Kernos* 2 (1989), 97-104.

Loukas, I. and E. Loukas, 'The Sacred Laws of Lykosoura.' In Hägg ed. (1994), 97-99.

Loucas-Durie, É. 'L'élément orgiastique dans la religion arcadienne.' *Kernos* 5 (1992), 87-96.

Lupu, E. *Greek Sacred Law: A Collection of New Documents.* Leiden: Brill, 2005.

Macardé, J. 'À propos du groupe cultuel de Lykosoura.' In Guimier-Sorbets, Jost and Morizot edd. (2008), 111-6.

Mactoux, M.-M. *Pénélope: légende et mythe.* Paris: Belles Lettres, 1975.

— and G. Évelyne edd., *Mélanges Pierre Lévêque, II : Anthropologie et Société.* Paris: Belles Lettres, 1989.

Malkin, I. *Myth and Territory in the Spartan Mediterranean.* Cambridge University Press, 1994.

Mannhardt, W. *Antike Wald- und Feldkulte aus nordeuropäischer Überlieferung.* Berlin: Bornträger, 1877.

Marinatos, N. *Minoan Religion: Ritual, Image and Symbol.* Columbia S.C: University of South Carolina Press, 1993.

— and R. Hägg edd., *Greek Sanctuaries: New Approaches.* London and New York: Routledge, 1993.

Mayor, A. *The First Fossil-Hunters: Palaeontology in Greek and Roman Times.* Princeton University Press, 2000.

Mellink, M.J. 'Anatolian Libation-Pourers and the Minoan Genius.' In Farkas, Harper and Harrison edd. (1987), 65-72.

Merivale, P. *Pan the Goat-God: His Myth in Modern Times.* Cambridge MA: Harvard University Press, 1969.

Merkelbach, J. 'Gefesselte Götter.' *Antaios* 12 (1971), 549-65.

Miller, H.F. 'The Practical and Economic Background to the Greek Mercenary Explosion.' *G&R* 31 (1984), 153-60.

Mitchell, L. and P.J. Rhodes edd., *The Development of the Polis in Archaic Greece.* London: Routledge, 1997.

Mitropoulou, E. *Deities and Heroes in the Form of Snakes.* Athens: Pyli Editions, 1977.

Morand, A.-F. *Études sur les hymnes orphiques.* Leiden: Brill, 2001.

Moraw, S. 'Die Schöne und das Biest: weibliche Mischwesen in der Spätantike.' In Alexandridis, Wild and Winkler-Horaçek edd. (2008), 465-479.

Morgan, C. 'The Archaeology of Sanctuaries in Early Iron Age and Archaic *Ethne*: A Preliminary View.' In Mitchell and Rhodes edd. (1997), 168-98.

Mossman, J. *Wild Justice: A Study of Euripides' Hecuba.* Oxford: Clarendon, 1995.

Moustaka, A. *Kulte und Mythen auf thessalischen Münzen.* Würzburg: K. Triltsch, 1983.

Murray, G. *Four Stages of Greek Religion.* New York: Columbia University Press, 1912.

Mylonas, G.E. *Eleusis and the Eleusinian Mysteries.* Princeton University Press, 1961.

Mylonas Shear, I. 'Mycenaean Centaurs at Ugarit.' *JHS* 122 (2002), 147-53 and pll. 3-4.

Mylonopoulos, J. Πελοπόννησος οἰκτήριον Ποσειδῶνος. *Heiligtümer und Kulte des Poseidon auf der Peloponnes.* Kernos Suppl. 13. Liège: Centre International d'Étude de la Religion Grecque Antique, 2003.

a)— ed., *Divine Images and Human Imaginations in Ancient Greece and Rome.* Leiden: Brill, 2010.

b)— 'Divine images *versus* cult images. An endless story about theories, methods, and terminologies.' In Mylonopoulos ed. (2010), 1-19.

Nagy, G. and T.J. Figueira, *Theognis of Megara: Poetry and the Polis.* Baltimore: Johns Hopkins University Press, 1985.

Napier, A.D. *Masks, Transformation and Paradox.* University of Chicago Press, 1986.

Naumann, F. *Der Ikonographie der Kybele in der phrygischen und der griechischen Kunst.* Tübingen: Wasmuth, 1983.

Newmyer, S.T. *Animals, Rights and Reason in Plutarch and Modern Ethics.* Oxford and New York: Routledge, 2006.

Niels, J. *The Parthenon Frieze.* Cambridge University Press, 2001.

Nielsen, T.H. and J. Roy edd., *Defining Ancient Arkadia.* Acts of the Copenhagen Polis Centre, vol. 6. Copenhagen, 1999.

— 'The Concept of Arkadia – The People, their Land, and their Organisation.' In Nielsen and Roy edd. (1999), 16-79.

Nilsson, M.P. *A History of Greek Religion.* Oxford: Clarendon, 1925.

— *Geschichte der griechischen Religion.* Two vols. Munich: Beck, 1941-50.

— *The Minoan-Mycenaean Religion and its Survival in Greek Religion.* 2nd ed. New York: Biblo and Tannen, 1971.

— *Greek Folk Religion.* Philadelphia: University of Pennsylvania Press, 1972. (Orig. publ. as *Greek Popular Religion,* Columbia University Press, 1940.)

Noegel, S.B. 'Greek Religion and the Ancient Near East.' In Ogden ed. (2007), 21-37.

Obbink, D. 'Dionysus Poured Out.' In Carpenter and Faraone edd. (1993), 65-86.

Ogden, D. *Greek Bastardy in the Classical and Hellenistic Periods.* Oxford University Press, 1996.

— *The Crooked Kings of Ancient Greece.* London: Duckworth, 1997.

— *Greek and Roman Necromancy.* Princeton University Press, 2001.

— ed., *A Companion to Greek Religion.* Oxford: Blackwell, 2007.

Osborne, C. 'Aristotle and the Fantastic Abilities of Animals.' In Sedley ed. (2000), 253-85.

Osborne, R. 'Framing the Centaur. Reading 5th-century Architectural Sculpture.' In Goldhill and Osborne edd. (1994), 52-84.

— *Greece in the Making: 1200-479 BC.* London: Routledge, 1996.

— *Archaic and Classical Greek Art.* Oxford University Press, 1998.

Otto, W.F. *Dionysus: Myth and Cult.* Trans. R.B. Palmer. Bloomington and London: Indiana University Press, 1965.

Padgett, J.M. ed., *The Centaur's Smile: The Human Animal in Early Greek Art.* Princeton University Press, 2003.

— 'Horse Men: Centaurs and Satyrs in Early Greek Art.' In Padgett ed. (2003), 3-46.

Palagia, O. and Coulson, W. edd., *Sculpture from Arcadia and Laconia.* Oxford: Oxbow Books, 1993.

— and J.J. Pollitt edd., *Personal Styles in Greek Sculpture.* Cambridge University Press, 1996.

Parisinou, E. *The Light of the Gods: The Role of Light in Archaic and Classical Greek Cult.* London: Duckworth, 2000.

Parke, H.W. *The Oracles of Zeus: Dodona, Olympia, Ammon.* Oxford: Blackwell, 1967.

Parker, R. *Miasma: Pollution and Purification in Early Greek Religion.* Oxford: Clarendon, 1983.

— 'Myths of Early Athens.' In Bremmer ed. (1987), 187-214.

— *Athenian Religion: A History.* Oxford: Clarendon, 1996.

— *Polytheism and Society at Athens.* Oxford University Press, 2005.

Perdrizet, P. 'Terres-cuites de Lycosoura, et mythologie arcadienne.' *BCH* 23 (1899), 635-8.

Petrovic, I. 'The life story of a cult statue as an allegory: Kallimachos' Hermes Perpheraios.' In Mylonopoulos ed. (2010), 206-224.

Pfeiffer, S. 'Der ägyptischer "Tierkult" im Spiegel der griechisch-römischen Literatur.' In Alexandridis, Wild and Winkler-Horaçek edd. (2008), 373-393.

Pfister, F. *Die Reisebilder des Herakleides.* Vienna: Rohrer, 1951.

Philippson, P. *Thessalische Mythologie.* Zurich: Rhein-Verlag, 1944.

Picard, Ch. 'Le culte et la légende du centaure Chiron dans l'occident méditerranéen.' *REA* 53 (1951), 5-25.

Piccaluga, G. *Lykaon. Un tema mitico.* Rome: Ed. dell'Ateneo, 1968.

Pirenne-Delforge, V. *L'Aphrodite grecque. Kernos* Suppl. 4. Liège: Centre International d'Étude de la Religion Grecque Antique, 1994.

a)— *Retour à la source. Pausanias et la religion grecque. Kernos* Suppl. 20. Liège: Centre International d'Étude de la Religion Grecque Antique, 2008.

b)— 'Des marmites pour un méchant petit hermès ! ou comment consacrer une statue.' In Estienne et al. edd. (2008), 103-110.

— 'Greek priests and "cult statues": in how far are they unnecessary?' In Mylonopoulos ed. (2010), 121-41.

Polinskaya, I. 'Liminality as Metaphor: Initiation and the Frontiers of Ancient Athens.' In Dodd and Faraone edd. (2003), 85-106.

Pollard, J.R.T. 'Muses and Sirens.' *CR* 2 (1952), 60-63.

— *Seers, Shrines and Sirens: The Greek Religious Revolution in the Sixth Century BC.* London: Allen and Unwin, 1965.

— *Birds in Greek Life and Myth.* London: Thames and Hudson, 1977.

Pollitt, J.J. *Art in the Hellenistic Age.* Cambridge University Press, 1986.

Porada, E. *Man and Images in the Ancient Near East.* Wakefield RI: Moyer Bell, 1995.

Porter, J.I. 'Ideals and Ruins: Pausanias, Longinus, and the Second Sophistic.' In Adcock, Cherry and Elsner edd. (2001), 63-92.

Powell, A. ed., *The Greek World.* London: Routledge, 1995.

Prent, M. *Cretan Sanctuaries and Cults: Continuity and Change from Late Minoan IIIC to the Archaic Period.* Leiden: Brill, 2005.

Pretzler, M. 'Myth and History at Tegea – Local Tradition and Community Identity.' In Nielsen and Roy edd. (1999), 89-129.

Prieur, J. *Les animaux sacrés dans l'antiquité. Art et religion du monde méditerranéen.* Rennes: Ouest-France, 1988.

Pritchett, W.K. *Pausanias Perigetes.* Archaia Hellas 6. 2 vols. Amsterdam: Gieben, 1998.

Quandt, W. *Orphei Hymni.* Berlin: Wiedmann, 1962.

Queyrel, F. *L'autel de Pergame: images et pouvoir en Grèce d'Asie.* Paris: Picard, 2005.

Radt, W. *Pergamon: Geschichte und Bauten einer antiken Metropole.* Darmstadt: Wissenschaftliche Buchgesellschaft, 1999.

Raglan, F.R. Somerset, Fourth Baron. 'The Cult of Animals.' *Folklore* 46 (1935), 331-42.

Reeder, E.D. ed. *Pandora: Women in Classical Greece.* The Trustees of the Walters Art Gallery, in association with Princeton University Press, 1995.

Renehan, R. 'The Greek Anthropocentric View of Man.' *HSCP* 85 (1981), 239-59.

Renner, T. 'A Papyrus Dictionary of Metamorphoses.' *HSCP* 82 (1978), 277-93.

Rhodes, P.J. *A History of the Classical Greek World.* Oxford: Blackwell, 2006.

Rice, M. *The Power of the Bull.* London: Routledge, 1998.

Ricciardelli, G. *Inni Orfici.* Rome: Fondazione Lorenzo Valla, 2000.

Richardson, B.E. *Old Age Among the Ancient Greeks.* Baltimore: Johns Hopkins University Press, 1933.

Ridgway, B.S. *Hellenistic Sculpture.* 3 vols. Madison: University of Wisconsin Press, 1989-2002.

Robson, J.E. 'Bestiality and Bestial Rape in Greek Myth.' In Deacy and Pierce edd. (1997), 65-96.

Roller, L.E. 'The Legend of Midas.' *CA* 2 (1983), 299-313.

— *In Search of God the Mother: The Cult of Anatolian Cybele.* Berkeley: University of California Press, 1999.

Romm, J. *The Edges of the Earth in Ancient Thought.* Princeton University Press, 1992.

Rosivach, V.J. 'Autochthony and the Athenians.' *CQ* 37 (1987), 294-306.

Roy, J. 'The Economies of Arkadia.' In Nielsen and Roy edd. (1999), 320-81.

Rudhardt, J. *Opera inedita: Essai sur la religion grecque & Recherches sur les Hymnes orphiques.* Edited by Ph. Borgeaud and V. Pirenne-Delforge. *Kernos* Suppl. 19. Liège: Centre International d'Étude de la Religion Grecque Antique, 2008.

Rutter, N.K. ed. *Historia Numorum: Italy.* London: British Museum Press, 2001.

Scarpi, P. 'Héraclès entre animaux et monstres chez Apollodore.' In Bonnet, Jourdain-Annequin and Pirenne-Delforge edd. (1998), 231-40.

Schachter, A. *Cults of Boiotia.* Four vols. London: Institute of Classical Studies, 1981-1986.

— ed., *Le sanctuaire grec.* Entretiens Hardt 37. Geneva-Vandoeuvres: Fondation Hardt, 1992.

Schaeffer, C.F.A. 'An Ingot God from Cyprus.' *Antiquity* 39 (1965), 56-7.

Scheffer, C. 'Female Deities, Horses and Death (?) in Archaic Greek Religion.' In Alroth ed. (1994), 111-33.

Scheer, T. *Die Gottheit und ihr Bild. Untersuchungen zur Funktion griechischer Kultbilder in Religion und Politik.* Zetemata 105. München: Beck, 2000.

Schefold, K. *Gods and Heroes in Late Archaic Greek Art.* Trans. A. Griffiths. Cambridge University Press, 1992.

Schlesier, R. 'Der Fuss des Dionysos: zu PMG 871.' In Horstmanshoff et al. edd. (2002), 161-91.

Scobie, A. 'The Origins of 'Centaurs'.' *Folklore* 89 (1978), 142-7.

Seaford, R. *Dionysos.* London: Routledge, 2006.

Séchan, L. and P. Lévêque, *Les grandes divinités de la Grèce.* Paris: Boccard, 1966.

Sedley, D. ed., *Oxford Studies in Ancient Philosophy* 19. Oxford: Clarendon, 2000.

Segal, C. 'The Two Worlds of Euripides' *Helen.*' *TAPA* 102 (1971), 553-614.

— *Euripides and the Poetics of Sorrow: Art, Gender and Commemoration in* Alcestis, Hippolytus *and* Hecuba. Durham NC: Duke University Press.

Sève, M. 'Le dossier épigraphique du sculpteur Damophon de Messène.' In Guimier-Sorbets, Jost and Morizot edd. (2008), 117-28.

Shapiro, H.A. 'The Cult of Heroines: Kekrops' Daughters.' In Reeder ed. (1995), 39-48.

— 'Autochthony and the Visual Arts in Fifth-Century Athens.' In Boedeker and Raaflaub edd. (1998), 127-51.

Sharrock, A. 'Representing Metamorphosis.' In Elsner ed. (1996), 103-30.

Shepard, K. *The Fish-Tailed Monster in Greek and Etruscan Art.* New York: private printing, 1940.

Shewan, A. a) Review of Thomson (1914). *CR* 29, no. 1 (1915), 20-21.

b)— 'The Waterfowl Goddess Penelope and her Son Pan.' *CR* 29, no. 2 (1915), 37-40.

Slatkin, L.M., 'The Wrath of Thetis.' *TAPA* 106 (1986), 1-24.

— *The Power of Thetis: Allusion and Interpretation in the Iliad.* Berkeley: University of California Press, 1991.

Smelik, K.A.D and E.A. Hemelrijk, '"Who Knows Not What Monsters Demented Egypt Worship?" Opinions on Egyptian Animal Worship in Antiquity as Part of the Ancient Conception of Egypt.' *ANRW* II.17.4 (1984), 1852-2000 and 2337-235.

Smith, C. 'Four Archaic Vases from Rhodes.' *JHS* 5 (1884), 220-40 and pll. XL-XLIII.

Smith, R.R.R. *Hellenistic Royal Portraits.* Oxford University Press, 1988.

Smith, W. R., *Lectures on the Religion of the Semites. First Series: The Fundamental Institutions.* London: A. and C. Black, 1894.

Snodgrass, A.M. *Narration and Allusion in Archaic Greek Art.* London: Leopard's Press, 1982.

Sophokleous, S. *Atlas des représentations chypro-archaïques des divinités.* Göteborg: Aström, 1985.

Sorabji, R. *Animal Minds and Human Morals: The Origins of the Western Debate.* Ithaca NY: Cornell University Press, 1993.

— 'Esprits d'animaux.' In Cassin, Labarrière and Dherbey edd. (1997), 355-73.

Spickermann, W. 'Lukian von Samosata und die fremden Götter.' *ARG* 11 (2009), 229-61.

Spivey, N. 'Bionic Statues.' In Powell ed. (1995), 442-59.

Stählin, F. *Das hellenische Thessalien: landeskundliche und geschichtliche Beschreibung Thessaliens in der hellenischen und römischen Zeit* . Stuttgart: J. Engelhorns, 1924.

Stern, F. van K. 'Heroes and Monsters in Greek Art.' *AN* 7 (1978), 1-23.

Stewart, A.F. *Greek Sculpture: An Exploration.* New Haven: Yale University Press, 1990.

Taylor, J.H. *Death and the Afterlife in Ancient Egypt.* London: British Museum Press, 2001.

Thallon, I.C. 'The Date of Damophon of Messene.' *AJA* 10 (1906), 302-29.

Themelis, P. 'The Cult Scene on the Polos of the Siphnian Caryatid at Delphi.' In Hägg ed. (1992), 49-72.

— 'Damophon.' In Palagia and Pollitt edd. (1996), 154-85.

Thomson, J.A.K. *Studies in the* Odyssey. Oxford: Clarendon, 1914.

Tsiafakis, D. '"ΠΕΛΩΡΑ": Fabulous Creatures and/or Demons of Death?' In Padgett ed. (2003), 73-104.

Trundle, M. *Greek Mercenaries: From the Late Archaic Period to Alexander.* London: Routledge, 2004.

Ustinova, Y. '"Either a Daimon, or a Hero, or Perhaps a God:" Mythical Residents of Subterranean Chambers.' *Kernos* 15 (2002), 267-88.

— *Caves and the Ancient Greek Mind: Descending Underground in the Search for Ultimate Truth.* Oxford University Press, 2009.

Van der Plas, D. ed. *Effigies Dei.* Leiden: Brill, 1987.

Vermeule, C. 'The Ram Cults of Cyprus: Pastoral to Paphian at Morphou.' *RDAC* 1974, 151-6.

Vermeule, E. *Greece in the Bronze Age.* Chicago University Press, 1964.

— *Aspects of Death in Early Greek Art and Poetry.* Berkeley: University of California Press, 1979.

Vernant, J.-P. *Mortals and Immortals: Collected Essays Edited by Froma I. Zeitlin.* Princeton University Press, 1991.

Versnel, H. 'What Did Ancient Man See When He Saw a God? Some Reflexions on Greco-Roman Epiphany.' In Van der Plas ed. (1987), 42-55.

— *Inconsistencies in Greek and Roman Religion II: Transition and Reversal in Myth and Ritual.* Leiden: Brill, 1993.

— 'Kronos and the Kronia.' In Versnel ed. (1993), 89-135.

Vian, F. *Nonnos de Panopolis: les Dionysiaques,* vol. 1. Paris: Belles Lettres, 1976.

Vidal-Naquet, P. *The Black Hunter: Forms of Thought and Forms of Society in the Greek World.* Trans. A. Szegedy-Maszac. Baltimore: Johns Hopkins University Press, 1986. (Orig. French publ. 1981.)

de Visser, M.W. *Die nicht menschengestaltigen Götter der Griechen.* Leiden: Brill, 1903.

Vogel, M. *Chiron: der Kentaur mit der Kithara.* Bonn-Bad Godesberg: Verlag für Systematische Musikwissenschaft, 1978.

Voyatzis, M.E. *The Early Sanctuary of Athena Alea at Tegea and Other Archaic Sanctuaries in Arcadia.* Göteborg: Aström, 1990.

— 'The Role of Temple Building in Consolidating Arkadian Communities.' In Nielsen and Roy edd. (1999), 130-168.

Wace, A.J.B and J.B. Droop, 'Excavations at Theotokou, Thessaly.' *ABSA* 13 (1906-7), 309-27 and pll. X-XI.

Wace, A.J.B, 'The Veil of Despoina.' *AJA* 38 (1934), 107-11.

Walcot, P. *Hesiod and the Near East.* Cardiff: University of Wales Press, 1966.

Wasilewska, E. *Creation Stories of the Middle East.* London: Jessica Kingsley, 2000.

West, M.L. 'Three Presocratic Cosmogonies,' *CQ* 13 (1963), 154-7.

— *Hesiod:* Theogony. Oxford: Clarendon, 1966.

— 'Alcman and Pythagoras.' *CQ* 17 (1967), 1-15.

— *The Orphic Poems*. Oxford: Clarendon, 1983.

Westenholz, J.G. *Dragons, Monsters and Fabulous Beasts*. Jerusalem: Bible Lands Museum, 2004.

Westlake, H.D. *Thessaly in the Fourth Century BC*. London: Methuen, 1935.

Whitmarsh, T. *The Second Sophistic*. Greece & Rome New Surveys in the Classics, no. 35. Oxford University Press, 2005.

Whittaker, C.R. ed., *Pastoral Economies in Classical Antiquity*. Cambridge Philological Society Suppl. vol. 14. Cambridge, 1988.

Wiggermann, F.A.M. *Mesopotamian Protective Spirits: The Ritual Texts*. Groningen: Styx, 1992.

Wilamowitz-Moellendorf, Count U. von. *Euripides,* Hippolytos. Berlin, 1891.

— *Der Glaube der Hellenen*. Two vols. Berlin: Wiedmann, 1932.

Wiles, D. 'The Use of Masks in Modern Performances of Greek Drama.' In Hall ed. (2004), 245-63.

Wilk, S.R. *Medusa: Solving the Mystery of the Gorgon*. Oxford University Press, 2000.

Wilkins, J., D. Harvey and M. Dobson edd., *Food in Antiquity*. University of Exeter Press, 1995.

Winkler, J. 'Lollianos and the Desperadoes.' *JHS* 100 (1980), 155-81.

Winkler, J.J. and F. Zeitlin edd., *Nothing to Do with Dionysos? Athenian Drama in its Social Context*. Princeton University Press, 1990.

Winkler-Horaçek, L. 'Fiktionale Grenzräume im frühen Griechenland.' In Alexandridis, Wild and Winkler-Horaçek edd. (2008), 503-525.

Witt, R.E. *Isis in the Graeco-Roman World*. London: Thames and Hudson, 1971.

Woodford, S. *Images of Myths in Classical Antiquity*. Cambridge University Press, 2003.

Woodward, A.M. 'Athens and the Oracle of Ammon.' *ABSA* 57 (1962), 5-13.

Wright, M. *Euripides' Escape-Tragedies: A Study of* Helen, Andromeda, *and* Iphigenia among the Taurians. Oxford University Press, 2005.

Table of figures

Fig. 1: One of a series of gold plaques decorated with bee-women, from Rhodes; seventh century BC. Actual size 2.5 by 2.7 cm. (Berlin Staatl. Mus. Misc. 8946.) Drawing by R. Aston.

Fig. 2: Boiotian black-figure Lekanis; c. 550 BC. Sirens, birds and panthers. University of Reading Ure Mus. 80.7.1. © Ure Museum 2010

Fig. 3: East Greek bronze statuette of a centaur; late sixth century BC. (Collection of Shelby White and Leon Levy.) Drawing by R. Aston.

Fig. 4: Attic black-figure lekythos; c. 490-480 BC. Peleus wrestles with Thetis. (London BM 1904,0708.5.) © Trustees of the British Museum.

Fig. 5: Attic red-figure neck-amphora attributed to the Berlin Painter; c. 490-480 BC. 30.8x18 cm. A merman with dolphin and sceptre. (Harvard Art Museums, Arthur M. Sackler Museum, Gift of Edward P. Warren, Esq., 1927.150.) Photo: Junius Beebe © President and Fellows of Harvard College.

Fig. 6: Cycladic terracotta 'Melian relief'; c. 465-435 BC. Skylla with fish tail and dogs' heads. (London BM 1867,0508.673.) © Trustees of the British Museum.

Fig. 7: Detail of Attic black-figure dinos by Sophilos; c. 580 BC. Okeanos with fish-tail. (London BM 1971.1101.1.) © Trustees of the British Museum.

Fig. 8: Detail from Etruscan black-figure amphora attributed to the Ivy-Leaf Group; c. 530 BC. Siren with arms holds flower. (Virginia MFA 60.3.) Drawing by R. Aston.

Fig. 9: Detail from Korinthian black-figure pyxis attributed to the Chimaera Painter; c. 570 BC. Bearded Siren. (Malibu J. Paul Getty Mus. 88.AE.105.) Drawing by R. Aston.

Fig. 10: Attic red-figure stamnos, name-vase of the Siren Painter; c. 480-470 BC. Odysseus resists the Sirens' song. (London BM 1843,1103.31.) © Trustees of the British Museum.

Fig. 11: Panel of the Harpy Tomb at Xanthos, Lykia; c. 480-470 BC. A Siren bears away a soul of the dead. (London BM 1848,1020.1.) © Trustees of the British Museum

Fig. 12: Egyptian wooden model of a *Ba*-bird; Late Dynastic – Early Ptolemaic period, c. 525-305 BC. (Boston MFA 72.4182.) Drawing by R. Aston.

Fig. 13: Relief dedicated by Xenokrateia at Echelidai, Attica; early fourth century BC. Numerous gods shown, including Acheloos. (Athens NM 2356.) National Archaeological Museum, Athens. © Hellenic Ministry of Culture and Tourism/Archaeological Receipts Fund.

Index of ancient authors

Aelian *HA* 12.34: 129[182]; 15.25: 96[20]; *VH* 3.18: 146[8]; 3.42: 74[98]

Aischylos *Choe.* 1048-9: 135[8]; *Prom. Vinc.* 453: 202[32]; Fr. 65b-c Mette: 211[71], 273[38], 274[48]; Fr. 38a Krumeich, Pechstein and Seidensticker: 296[28]

Alkman Fr. 5 *PMG*: 331[60]

Ampelius *Lib. Memor.* 2.1: 141[55]

Antoninus Liberalis *Met.* 6: 122[145]; 7: 96[21], 107[70], 184[139]; 10: 74[98], 128[180], 182[134]; 12: 19[34]; 20: 96[21], 107[69]; 21: 20[37]; 23: 222[110]; 28: 226[115]; 41: 336[71]

Apollodoros *Bibl.* 1.1.6: 153[1]; 1.3.4: 85[146]; 1.4.2: 204[37]; 1.6.3: 226[115]; 1.7.2: 202[28]; 1.9.21: 75[103]; 1.9.26: 325[40]; 1.19: 59[28]; 2.5.1: 158[24]; 2.5.1-12: 35[79]; 2.5.4: 94[12], 145[4], 157[16], 157[19], 216[88]; 2.5.8: 96[20]; 2.5.10: 96[20]; 2.5.11: 157[19]; 2.5.12: 153[3]; 2.7.5: 88[156], 88[157]; 3.1.1: 87[152]; 3.1.3-4: 326[47]; 3.4.3: 164[54], 314[9]; 3.5.8: 293[23]; 3.7.5: 85[145]; 3.8.1: 102[50], 208[59], 212[76]; 3.8.1-2: 212[74]; 3.8.2: 273[40]; 3.8.2-9.1: 212[76]; 3.9.2: 188[156]; 3.12.6: 228[124]; 3.13.3: 97[28], 188[155], 219[97]; 3.13.5: 161[41], 219[98], 219[99]; 3.14: 187[151]; 3.14.1: 121[137]; 3.14.3: 136[10]; 3.14.6: 97[25], 123[147], 126[167]; 3.15.1: 336[71]; 3.15.9: 325[41]; *Ep.* 1.12-13: 332[61]; 7.14: 303[6]; 7.18: 71[84]

Apollodoros *FGrHist* 244 F 134a: 222[110]

Apollonios Rhodios *Arg.* 1.503: 66[68]; 2.456-89: 217[92]; 2.1232-42: 96[23], 271[34]; 4.893-6: 69,[75] 71[82]; 4.896-7: 73[90]; 4.1639-93: 325[42]

Aristophanes *Ekkl.* 1069: 306[19]; 126: 64[52]; *Peace* 767: 205[38]; 771: 205[38]; *Plout.* 286-7: 230[126]; 730 ff.: 125[156]; *Wasps* 438: 126[161]; Fr. 230: 118[127]

Aristotle *De An.* 406b9: 325[44]; *De Gen. An.* 784a31-785a6: 205[38]; 717a: 17[26]; 769b: 44[106]; *De Part. An.* 642-3: 17[25]; 645a: 17[26]; 687a-b: 18[27]; *HA* 8c15: 123[149]

ps.-Aristotle *Mir.* 103: 68[71]

Arnobius 6.12: 142[60]

Arrian *Disc. Epic.* 1.6.18-20: 18[31]

Athenaios *Deipn.* 3.78c: 288[2]; 4.134d-137c: 63[48]; 7.296f: 77[112]; 11.476: 130[188], 200[25]; 13.555d: 342[3]; 15.672a-673d: 174[96], 186[145]

Bacchylides 1.1-9: 333[65]; 26: 326[47]

Cicero *De Nat. Deor.* 2.64: 18[31]; *Leg.* 2.63: 127[173]

Clement of Alexandria *Pr.* 2.28.3: 139[31], 243[38]

Diodoros 1.28: 13[7], 123[146], 231[130]; 1.62: 228[125]; 1.86.3: 226[117]; 1.87.2: 45[113]; 1.90.2: 45[111]; 2.55: 176; 3.30: 75[103], 238[16]; 3.57.66: 275[52]; 3.59: 204[37]; 3.59.8: 230[127]; 3.68-74: 141[52]; 3.73.1-2: 140[45]; 4.11.3-4: 158[25]; 4.12.8: 157[20]; 4.15: 95[19]; 4.64.4: 293[23]; 4.69-70: 96[24], 330[59]; 4.76.2-3: 323; 4.77.1-4: 19[36], 326[47]; 5.55: 203[36]; 5.55.2: 332[63]; 5.55.3: 333[66]; 14.31.3: 153[3]; 17.41.7-8: 173[93]

Dionysius Byzantinus *De Nav.* 49: 57[8]

Ephoros *FGrHist* 70 F 20: 80[128]

Epimenides Fr. 16 DK: 119[131], 211[71], 273[37]; Fr. 16.7-8 DK: 275[50]; Fr. 16.8-9 DK: 275[51]; Fr. 16.9 DK: 275; Fr. 16.13 DK: 275[51]; Fr. 16.14 DK: 275; Fr. 16.15-16 DK: 275[51]

ps.-Eratosthenes *Katast.* 1: 273[40]; 40: 157[21]

Euripides *Andr.* 16-20: 58[21], 160[34]; 18-19: 162[49]; 19-20: 161[42]; 1229: 219[101]; 1265-6: 165[57]; *Bacch.* 21: 302[3]; 100: 132[200]; 115: 302[4]; 519-20: 85[145]; 918-22: 327[1]; 920-22: 130[187]; 921: 132[200]; 1018: 130; *Cyc.* 624: 34[78]; *Hel.* 168: 71[83]; 167: 68[70]; 168: 206[43]; 168-78: 73[90], 89[162]; 375 ff.: 273[39]; *HF* 153: 34[77]; *Hipp.* 141-50: 182[132]; *Ion* 21 ff.: 187[151]; 265: 187[151];

General Index

Imprimé en Belgique par Snel – 55270
Septembre 2011